AN EXEGETICAL SUMMARY OF
ROMANS 9–16

AN EXEGETICAL SUMMARY OF ROMANS 9–16

David Abernathy

SIL International

© 2009 by SIL International

Library of Congress Control Number: 2009926117
ISBN: 978-155671-233-3

Printed in the United States of America

All Rights Reserved
No part of this publication may be reproduced, stored in a retrieval system, or transmitted in any form or by any means without the express permission of SIL International. However, brief excerpts, generally understood to be within the limits of fair use, may be quoted without written permission.

Copies of this and other publications
of SIL International may be obtained from

International Academic Bookstore
SIL International
7500 West Camp Wisdom Road
Dallas, TX 75236-5699, USA

Voice: 972-708-7404
Fax: 972-708-7363
academic_books@sil.org
www.ethnologue.com

PREFACE

Exegesis is concerned with the interpretation of a text. Exegesis of the New Testament involves determining the meaning of the Greek text. Translators must be especially careful and thorough in their exegesis of the New Testament in order to accurately communicate its message in the vocabulary, grammar, and literary devices of another language. Questions occurring to translators as they study the Greek text are answered by summarizing how scholars have interpreted the text. This is information that should be considered by translators as they make their own exegetical decisions regarding the message they will communicate in their translations.

The Semi-Literal Translation

As a basis for discussion, a semi-literal translation of the Greek text is given so that the reasons for different interpretations can best be seen. When one Greek word is translated into English by several words, these words are joined by hyphens. There are a few times when clarity requires that a string of words joined by hyphens have a separate word, such as "not" (μή), inserted in their midst. In this case, the separate word is surrounded by spaces between the hyphens. When alternate translations of a Greek word are given, these are separated by slashes.

The Text

Variations in the Greek text are noted under the heading TEXT. The base text for the summary is the text of the fourth revised edition of *The Greek New Testament,* published by the United Bible Societies, which has the same text as the twenty-sixth edition of the *Novum Testamentum Graece* (Nestle-Aland). Dr. J. Harold Greenlee researched the variants and has written the notes for this part of the summary. The versions that follow different variations are listed without evaluating their choices.

The Lexicon

The meaning of a key word in context is the first question to be answered. Words marked with a raised letter in the semi-literal translation are treated separately under the heading LEXICON. First, the lexicon form of the Greek word is given. Within the parentheses following the Greek word is the location number where, in the author's judgment, this word is defined in the *Greek-English Lexicon of the New Testament Based on Semantic Domains* (Louw and Nida 1988). When a semantic domain includes a translation of the particular verse being treated, **LN** in bold type indicates that specific translation. If the specific reference for the verse is listed in *A Greek-English Lexicon of the New Testament and Other Early Christian Literature* (Bauer, Arndt, Gingrich, and Danker 1979), the outline location and page number is given. Then English equivalents of the Greek word are given to show how it is translated by commentators who offer their own translations of the whole text and, after a semicolon, all the versions in the list of abbreviations for translations. When reference is made to "all versions," it refers to only the versions in the list of translations. Sometimes further comments are made about the meaning of the word or the significance of a verb's tense, voice, or mood.

The Questions

Under the heading QUESTION, a question is asked that comes from examining the Greek text under consideration. Typical questions concern the identity of an implied actor or object of an event word, the antecedent of a pronominal reference, the connection indicated by a relational word, the meaning of a genitive construction, the meaning of figurative language, the function of a rhetorical question, the identification of an ambiguity, and the presence of implied information that is needed to understand the passage correctly. Background information is also considered for a proper understanding of a passage. Although not all implied information and background information is made explicit in a translation, it is important to consider it so that the translation will not be stated in such a way that prevents a reader from arriving at the proper interpretation. The question is answered with a summary of what commentators have said. If there are contrasting differences of opinion, the different interpretations are numbered and the commentaries that support each are listed. Differences that are not treated by many of the commentaries often are not numbered, but are introduced with a contrastive 'Or' at the beginning of the sentence. No attempt has been made to select which interpretation is best.

In listing support for various statements of interpretation, the author is often faced with the difficult task of matching the different terminologies used in commentaries with the terminology he has adopted. Sometimes he can only infer the position of a commentary from incidental remarks. This book, then, includes the author's interpretation of the views taken in the various commentaries. General statements are followed by specific statements, which indicate the author's understanding of the pertinent relationships, actors, events, and objects implied by that interpretation.

The Use of This Book

This book does not replace the commentaries that it summarizes. Commentaries contain much more information about the meaning of words and passages. They often contain arguments for the interpretations that are taken and they may have important discussions about the discourse features of the text. In addition, they have information about the historical, geographical, and cultural setting. Translators will want to refer to at least four commentaries as they exegete a passage. However, since no one commentary contains all the answers translators need, this book will be a valuable supplement. It makes more sources of exegetical help available than most translators have access to. Even if they had all the books available, few would have the time to search through all of them for the answers.

When many commentaries are studied, it soon becomes apparent that they frequently disagree in their interpretations. That is the reason why so many answers in this book are divided into two or more interpretations. The reader's initial reaction may be that all of these different interpretations complicate exegesis rather than help it. However, before translating a passage, a translator needs to know exactly where there is a problem of interpretation and what the exegetical options are.

Acknowledgments

Like many other works, this one was the result of a team effort. Jean Goddard, Johanna Fenton, and Paula Bostrom assisted with the lexicon in several chapters. I greatly appreciate their contributions, without which this volume would not be what it is.

Special thanks goes to Richard Blight, who edited all the chapters and made numerous helpful suggestions, and who has been an encouragement to me for all the years that I have worked with him.

ABBREVIATIONS

COMMENTARIES AND REFERENCE BOOKS

AB — Fitzmyer, Joseph A. *Romans*. The Anchor Bible, edited by W. F. Albright and D. N. Freedman. Garden City, N.Y.: Doubleday, 1993.

BAGD — Bauer, Walter. *A Greek–English Lexicon of the New Testament and Other Early Christian Literature*. Translated and adapted from the 5th ed., 1958 by William F. Arndt and F. Wilbur Gingrich. 2d English ed. revised and augmented by F. Wilbur Gingrich and Frederick W. Danker. Chicago: University of Chicago Press, 1979.

BECNT — Schreiner, Thomas. *Romans*. Baker Exegetical Commentary on the New Testament, edited by Moisés Silva. Grand Rapids, Baker, 1998.

Gdt — Godet, F. *Commentary on the Epistle to the Romans*. Tr. by A. Cusin, revised and edited by Talbot W. Chambers, 1883. Grand Rapids: Zondervan, 1969.

HNTC — Barrett, C. K. *A Commentary on the Epistle to the Romans*. Harper's New Testament Commentaries, edited by Henry Chadwick. New York: Harper & Row, 1957.

Ho — Hodge, Charles. *Commentary on the Epistle to the Romans*. 1886. Reprint. Grand Rapids: Eerdmans, 1953.

ICC1 — Sanday, William, and Arthur C. Headlam. *A Critical and Exegetical Commentary on the Epistle to the Romans*. The International Critical Commentary, edited by S. R. Driver, A. Plummer, and C. A. Briggs. 1902. Reprint. Edinburgh: T. & T. Clark, 1971.

ICC2 — Cranfield, C. E. B. *A Critical and Exegetical Commentary on the Epistle to the Romans*. Vol. 1. The International Critical Commentary, edited by J. A. Emerton and C. E. B. Cranfield. Edinburgh: T. & T. Clark, 1975.

LN — Louw, Johannes P., and Eugene A. Nida. *Greek–English Lexicon of the New Testament Based on Semantic Domains*. New York: United Bible Societies, 1988.

Mor — Morris, Leon. *The Epistle to the Romans*. Grand Rapids: William B. Eerdmans Publishing Company, 1988.

Mu — Murray, John. *The Epistle to the Romans. The English Text with Introduction, Exposition and Notes*. Grand Rapids: William B. Eerdmans Publishing Company, 1968.

NAC — Mounce, Robert H. *Romans*. New American Commentary, edited by E. Ray Clendenen. Nashville: Broadman and Holman, 2001.

NICNT — Moo, Douglas J. *The Epistle to the Romans*. The New International Commentary on the New Testament, edited by Gordon D. Fee. Grand Rapids: Eerdmans, 1996.

NTC	Hendricksen, William. *Exposition of Paul's Epistle to the Romans*, vol. 1, chapters 1-8. New Testament Commentary. Grand Rapids: Baker, 1980.
SSA	Deibler, Ellis W. Jr. *A Semantic and Structural Analysis of Romans*. Dallas: Summer Institute of Linguistics, 1998.
St	Stott, John. *Romans. God's Good News for the World*. Downers Grove: InterVarsity Press, 1994.
TH	Newman, Barclay M. and Eugene A. Nida. *A Translator's Handbook on Paul's Letter to the Romans*. Helps for Translators. London: United Bible Societies, 1973.
TNTC	Bruce F. F. *The Epistle of Paul to the Romans An Introduction and Commentary*. Revised edition. The Tyndale New Testament Commentaries. Grand Rapids: Eerdmans, 1985.
WBC	Dunn, James D. G. *Romans 1-8*. Word Biblical Commentary, Vol. 38a. Waco, Texas: Word, 1988.

Some of the commentaries that have been reviewed for this summary are very thorough and have dealt with the subject exhaustively. Moo's commentary (NICNT) is particularly useful, in that it not only gives a very comprehensive review of other scholarship, but is also structured and arranged in a very reader-friendly way. Moo and Schreiner (ECNT), who both write from the perspective of Reformed theology, are the most up to date and comprehensive of the ones I have used. They were also the ones I relied on the most to identify and address the various exegetical issues involved, especially Moo.

Much could be said about the two-volume *Word Biblical Commentary* (WBC) by James D. G. Dunn, who has, along with E. P. Sanders, charted a new trajectory in Pauline scholarship that raises a serious challenge to the way Protestants since the time of the Reformation have interpreted Paul's understanding of justification, and even to the basic premises of the Reformation itself. Whether or not one agrees with Sanders and Dunn, they cannot be ignored, particularly in studies of Galatians or Romans.

One of Dunn's main premises is that Paul's emphasis on faith was not so much a matter of combating works-righteousness, but that Paul is trying to free God's law and promises from the narrow constraints of Jewish ethnicity. Dunn holds that Paul's discussions of circumcision are principally about the law in its social function as a boundary marker distinguishing Jew from Gentile, not about salvation by merit. That is, Paul's concern has as much to do with how the Jews and Gentiles stand in relation to each other as with how one is made right with God. Dunn's writing and premises can be complex and at times ambiguous, and, in certain important instances, well outside the stream of conservative Protestant exegesis.

I also found the International Critical Commentary by Cranford (ICC2) to be very good. Others also have their merits, particularly the classic work by Murray (Mu). But the four by Moo, Schreiner, Dunn, and Cranford are the ones most likely to identify and discuss exegetical issues relevant to the translation task.

GREEK TEXT AND TRANSLATIONS

GNT The Greek New Testament. Edited by B. Aland, K Aland, J. Karavidopoulos, C. Martini, and B. Metzger. 4th ed. London, New York: United Bible Societies, 1993.
CEV The Holy Bible, Contemporary English Version. New York: American Bible Society, 1995.
GW   God's Word. World Publishing: Grand Rapids, 1995.
KJV The Holy Bible. Authorized (or King James) Version. 1611.
NASB The New American Standard Bible. Nashville, Tennessee: Holman, 1977.
NCV The Holy Bible, New Century Version. Word Publishing: Dallas, 1991.
NET The NET Bible, New English Translation. Version 6r,715. Biblical Studies Press, 2006.
NIV The Holy Bible, New International Version. Grand Rapids: Zondervan, 1984.
NLT The Holy Bible, New Living Translation. 2nd edition. Wheaton, Ill.: Tyndale House, 2004.
NRSV The Holy Bible, New Revised Standard Version. Nashville: Thomas Nelson Publishers, 1989.
REB The Revised English Bible. Oxford: Oxford University Press and Cambridge University Press, 1989.
TEV Good News Bible, Today's English Version. New York: American Bible Society, 1976.

GRAMMATICAL TERMS

act.   active
fut.   future
impera. imperative
imperf. imperfect
indic.   indicative
infin.   infinitive
mid.   middle
opt.   optative
pass.   passive
perf.   perfect
pres.   present
subj.   subjunctive

EXEGETICAL SUMMARY OF ROMANS 9–16

DISCOURSE UNIT—9:1–11:36 [AB, BECNT, Gdt, ICC1, ICC2, Mor, NAC, NICNT, St, TNTC, WBC; REB]. The topic is justification and salvation through faith do not contradict God's promises to Israel of old [AB], God's righteousness to Israel and the Gentiles [BECNT], the rejection of Israel [Gdt], the problem of Israel's unbelief: the gospel in history [ICC1], the unbelief of men and the faithfulness of God [ICC2], the place of Israel [Mor], God's righteousness vindicated [NAC], the defense of the gospel: the problem of Israel [NICNT], the plan of God for Jews and Gentiles [St], human unbelief and divine grace [TNTC], the outworking of the gospel in relation to Israel [WBC], Israel and the Gentiles in God's plan [REB].

DISCOURSE UNIT—9:1–10:21 [NCV]. The topic is God and the Jewish people.

DISCOURSE UNIT—9:1–33 [St]. The topic is Israel's fall: God's purpose of election.

DISCOURSE UNIT—9:1–29 [BECNT, Gdt, NAC; NET, NIV, NLT]. The topic is God's saving promise to Israel [BECNT], the freedom of God [Gdt], the justice of rejection [NAC], Israel's rejection considered [NET], God's sovereign choice [NIV], God's selection of Israel [NLT].

DISCOURSE UNIT—9:1–24 [GW]. The topic is God's concern for the Jewish people.

DISCOURSE UNIT—9:1–18 [CEV, NRSV, TEV]. The topic is God's choice of Israel [CEV], God's election of Israel [NRSV], God and his people [TEV].

DISCOURSE UNIT—9:1–5 [AB, HNTC, Ho, ICC1, ICC2, Mor, Mu, NICNT, TNTC, WBC]. The topic is Paul's lament about his former coreligionists [AB], the unbelief of Israel [HNTC], advantages as Jews; Paul's love for Jews [Ho], the apostle's sorrow over Israel's unbelief [ICC1], the subject of this main division of the epistle is introduced [ICC2], the tragedy of Israel [Mor], the unbelief of Israel [Mu], the tension between God's promises and Israel's plight [NICNT], the problem of Israel's unbelief [TNTC], What then of Israel? Paul's concern for his kinspeople [WBC].

9:1 **I-speak[a] the truth in[b] Christ, I- do-not -lie,[c] my conscience[d] bearing-witness[e] (with/to) me in (the) Holy Spirit**

LEXICON—a. pres. act. indic. of λέγω (LN 33.69) (BAGD I.1.a. p. 468): 'to speak' [AB, BECNT, HNTC, ICC2, LN, NICNT, NTC, WBC; NIV, NLT, NRSV, REB, TEV], 'to tell' [BAGD, LN; CEV, GW, NASB, NCV, NET], 'to say' [KJV].

b. ἐν with dative (LN 89.119) (BAGD I.5.d. p. 259): 'in' [AB, BECNT, HNTC, ICC2, LN, NICNT, NTC, WBC; KJV, NASB, NCV, NET, NIV, NRSV]. The phrase 'in Christ' is translated 'I belong to Christ' [TEV], 'with Christ as my witness' [NLT], 'as a Christian' [GW, REB], 'I am a follower of Christ' [CEV]. This preposition marks a close personal relation [BAGD, LN].

c. pres. act. indic. of ψεύδομαι (LN **33.253**) (BAGD 1. p. 891): 'to lie' [AB, BAGD, BECNT, ICC2, LN, NICNT, NTC, WBC; all versions except NLT], not explicit [NLT]. The phrase 'I do not lie' is translated 'it is no lie' [HNTC]. This verb means to say something that is false in order to mislead [LN].

d. συνείδησις (LN 26.13) (BAGD 2. p. 786): 'conscience' [AB, BAGD, BECNT, HNTC, ICC2, LN, NICNT, NTC, WBC; all versions except GW], 'thoughts' [GW]. This noun denotes the psychological faculty which can distinguish between right and wrong [LN].

e. pres. act. participle of συμμαρτυρέω (LN 33.266) (BAGD p. 778): 'to bear witness with' [BAGD], 'to bear witness along with' [NTC], 'to bear witness together with' [BECNT], 'to bear witness to' [AB, NICNT], 'to bear (me) witness' [HNTC, ICC2, WBC], 'to testify in support' [BAGD, LN], 'to support' [GW], 'to confirm' [BAGD]. The phrase συμμαρτυρούσης μοι τῆς συνειδήσεώς μου ἐν πνεύματι ἁγίῳ 'my conscience bearing witness with me in the Holy Spirit' is also translated 'my conscience, enlightened by the Holy Spirit' [REB], 'the Holy Spirit is a witness to my conscience' [CEV], 'the Holy Spirit, along with my own thoughts, supports me in this' [GW], 'my conscience is ruled by the Holy Spirit' [NCV], 'my conscience, ruled by the Holy Spirit' [TEV], 'my conscience and the Holy Spirit confirm it' [NLT]. This verb means to testify with confirming evidence [LN].

QUESTION—What is being signaled by the lack of a conjunction between the two assertions 'I speak the truth in Christ, I do not lie'?

It gives solemn emphasis to what Paul is saying [NICNT, WBC]. It simply indicates that a new subject is being introduced [Mor]. It shows the strong and lively emotion that Paul feels about the subject he is introducing, and which is related to what he has been discussing [Gdt].

QUESTION—What is being signaled by the fact that the word ἀλήθειαν 'truth' occurs first in the sentence?

It shows emphasis [Mor, NICNT].

QUESTION—What is signaled by the double assertion, one positive 'I speak the truth', and one negative, 'I do not lie'?

It marks an emphatic assertion [AB, Ho, ICC2, Mor, Mu, NICNT, WBC], underlining his truthfulness [BECNT].

QUESTION—What relationship is indicated by the preposition ἐν in the phrase 'in Christ'?

He is saying that what he speaks is in the very presence of Christ [Gdt, Mor, NAC], and as accountable to him [NAC], and before whom it would be unthinkable to lie [Gdt, Mor, Mu]. He speaks with Christ as his witness [TH; NLT]. He speaks as one united with Christ [Ho, ICC1, Mu, NICNT, SSA, TH]. It means that he belongs to Christ [TH; TEV], or is a follower of Christ

[CEV], that he is a Christian [Ho; GW, REB]. He is conscious of his relationship with Christ [Ho, SSA, St], who lives in him [St]. Because he has just affirmed in 8:1, 11 that union with Christ makes sin impossible, he now appeals to that union to give credence to what he is about to say [ICC1]. He does not lie because he belongs to Christ [TH]. His love for Christ, whom the Jews have rejected, is in part the source of his sadness [NTC]. Paul's emotions and motives spring from his union with Christ, and as such have no share in the lie [Mu]. Paul speaks in accordance with standards appropriate for one who is in Christ and with a sense of accountability to him for the truthfulness of what he says [ICC2]. It is local; that is, he is in Christ, meaning that he is acutely aware of his dependence on the living Christ, so whatever says must have Christ's authorization and meet with his approval [WBC]. He is speaking in a solemn and religious manner [Ho].

QUESTION—What relationship is indicated by the use of the dative case of μοι '(with/to) me' as used in relation to the prefix συμ-, normally translated 'with', in the participle συμμαρτυρούσης 'bearing witness'?

1. The dative μοι means 'with me'; Paul's conscience testifies along with or in addition to Paul himself [BECNT, Gdt, Ho, ICC1, ICC2, NTC, SSA; GW, NASB]. His conscience is personified as offering another separate witness to Paul's sincerity [ICC1].
2. The dative μοι means 'to me'; Paul's conscience testifies to him [AB, NAC, NICNT, WBC; CEV, NCV, NET, REB, TEV].

QUESTION—What relationship is indicated by the preposition ἐν in the phrase 'in (the) Holy Spirit'?

His conscience is informed and guided by the Holy Spirit [BECNT, Ho, NAC, WBC], or controlled and guided by the Holy Spirit [SSA], ruled by the Holy Spirit [NCV, TEV], enlightened by the Holy Spirit [REB], supported by the Holy Spirit [GW]. He is indwelt and led by the Holy Spirit [NTC]. He speaks with a good conscience, one that is illuminated by the Holy Spirit [ICC2, Mor, St]. It indicates the union of Paul's spirit with the Holy Spirit [ICC1]. It is instrumental; Paul speaks by means of the Holy Spirit [NICNT, WBC]. This expression is parallel to the previous one about being in Christ; that is, the Holy Spirit certifies the truthfulness of what Paul's conscience testifies [Mu].

9:2 that my sorrow[a] is great[b] and unceasing[c] (the) anguish[d] (to) my heart[e]

LEXICON—a. λύπη (LN 25.273) (BAGD p. 482): 'sorrow' [AB, LN, NTC; CEV, GW, NASB, NCV, NET, NIV, NRSV, TEV], 'bitter sorrow' [NLT], 'distress, sadness' [LN], 'grief' [BECNT, HNTC, ICC2, WBC; REB], 'pain' [NICNT], 'heaviness' [KJV]. The phrase λύπη μοί ἐστιν μεγάλη 'my sorrow is great' is also translated 'I am in great sorrow' [CEV]. The noun denotes the state of having mental pain and anxiety [LN].

b. μεγάλη (LN 78.2) (BAGD 2.a.γ. p. 498): 'great' [AB, BAGD, BECNT, HNTC, ICC2, LN, NICNT, NTC, WBC; all versions except GW, NLT], 'deep' [GW], 'intense' [LN], 'bitter' [NLT], 'profound' [BAGD]. This adjective describes the upper range of a scale of extent [LN].

c. ἀδιάλειπτος (LN 68.55) (BAGD p. 17): 'unceasing' [BAGD, BECNT, NTC, WBC; NET, NIV, NRSV, REB, TEV], 'not ceasing' [LN], 'ceaseless' [HNTC, NICNT], 'unrelenting' [AB], 'continual' [ICC2; KJV], 'endless' [GW], 'unending' [NLT], 'constant' [BAGD], 'always' [NCV], not explicit [CEV]. This adverb means not ceasing from a continuous activity [LN].

d. ὀδύνη (LN **25.235**) (BAGD p. 555): 'anguish' [AB, ICC2, NICNT, NTC, WBC; NET, NIV, NRSV], 'sorrow' [KJV, REB], 'pain' [BECNT, HNTC; TEV], 'heartache' [GW], 'grief' [NASB, NLT], 'sadness' [NCV], 'distress' [**LN**], 'great distress, intense anxiety' [LN]. The phrase ἀδιάλειπτος ὀδύνη τῇ καρδίᾳ μου 'unceasing the anguish of my heart' is also translated 'my heart is continually grieved' [BAGD], 'my heart is broken' [CEV], 'I…always feel much sadness' [NCV]. This noun denotes the state of being in severe emotional anxiety [LN].

e. καρδία (LN 26.3) (BAGD 1.b.ε. p. 404): 'heart' [AB, BAGD, BECNT, HNTC, ICC2, LN, NICNT, NTC, WBC; all versions except GW, NCV], 'inner self, mind' [LN]. The phrase ὀδύνη τῇ καρδίᾳ μου 'anguish (to) my heart' is also translated 'heartache' [GW], 'sadness' [NCV]. This noun denotes the source of one's psychological life, especially one's thoughts [LN].

QUESTION—Is there any difference between Paul's use of λύπη 'sorrow' and his use of ὀδύνη 'anguish'?
1. There is little distinction here [ICC2, Mor, SSA].
2. There are distinctions that are made. λύπη is inward sadness, and ὀδύνη is lamenting that sadness, whether openly or inwardly [Gdt]. λύπη is grief as a state of the mind or heart, whereas ὀδύνη usually has more of a physical focus, though here it is applied to anguish of the heart [ICC1].

QUESTION—In what sense does he use the word καρδία 'heart'?
Here it refers to his emotions [Mor], or the deepest spring of the emotions [Gdt]. His use of καρδία shows the depth of his sincerity [NAC, WBC] as he describes this pain to his mind or spirit [WBC]. He feels the sorrow deeply [SSA].

9:3 For I myself (could) wish/pray[a] to-be anathema[b] from[c] Christ for[d] my brothers[e] of-my race[f] according-to (the) flesh,[g]

LEXICON—a. imperf. mid. (deponent = act.) indic. of εὔχομαι (LN **25.6**, 33.178) (BAGD 2. p. 329): 'to wish' [AB, BAGD, BECNT, HNTC, **LN** (25.6), NTC; GW, KJV, NASB, NCV, NET, NIV, NRSV, TEV], 'to be willing' [NLT], 'to pray' [ICC2, LN (33.178), NICNT, WBC; REB], not explicit [CEV]. The phrase ηὐχόμην γάρ 'for I (could) pray/wish' is also translated 'I could wish' [BECNT, HNTC, NTC; KJV, NASB, NET, NIV, NRSV, TEV], 'for I could even wish' [AB], 'I could pray' [NICNT, WBC], 'I would pray' [ICC2], 'I would even pray' [REB], 'I would gladly be' [CEV], 'I wish I could help...I would even wish' [NCV]. This verb means to desire something as a pious wish [LN (25.6)], or to make requests to God [LN (33.178)]. The imperfect tense here serves more or less as an optative, indicating a wish that is unattainable or cannot be fulfilled [AB, BECNT, Gdt, HNTC, Ho, ICC2, Mor, NAC, SSA], or potential action that is not actually carried out [NICNT].

b. ἀνάθεμα (LN **33.474**) (BAGD 2.a. p. 54): 'anathema' [WBC], 'accursed' [BAGD, LN, NICNT], 'something accursed' [**LN**], 'accursed and cut off' [AB, ICC2, NTC], 'cursed' [BECNT], 'separated by a curse' [HNTC]. The phrase 'anathema from Christ' is translated 'under God's curse and...separated from Christ' [CEV]. This noun denotes that which has been cursed [LN].

c. ἀπό (LN **89.122**) (BAGD I.5. p. 86): 'from' [AB, BAGD, BECNT, HNTC, ICC2, **LN**, NICNT, NTC, WBC; all versions], 'separated from' [LN]. This preposition marks dissociation, implying a rupture from a former association [LN].

d. ὑπέρ with genitive (LN 90.36) (BAGD 1.c. p. 839): 'for' [LN; KJV], 'for the sake of' [AB, BAGD, BECNT, LN, NICNT, NTC, WBC; GW, NASB, NET, NIV, NRSV], 'for the good of' [CEV], 'on behalf of' [BAGD, ICC2, LN]. This word is also translated 'if that would benefit' [HNTC], 'if that would help' [NCV], 'if it would help' [REB], 'if that would save them' [NLT], 'for their sake I could wish that...' [TEV]. This preposition means 'in the place of' as well as 'for the sake of' [NICNT]. This preposition marks a participant who is benefited by an event or on whose behalf an event takes place [LN].

e. ἀδελφός (LN 11.25) (BAGD 3. p. 16): 'brother' [AB, LN, NTC, WBC; NIV, REB], 'fellow Jew' [LN]. The phrase ἀδελφῶν μου 'my brothers' is also translated 'my brethren' [HNTC, ICC2; KJV, NASB], 'my brothers and sisters' [BECNT], 'my people' [NET, NLT, TEV], 'my own people' [CEV, NRSV], 'my fellow countryman' [BAGD, LN], 'my fellow Jews' [NICNT], 'my Jewish brothers and sisters' [NCV]. The phrase τῶν ἀδελφῶν μου τῶν συγγενῶν μου 'my brothers of my race' is translated 'others who, like me, are Jewish by birth' [GW]. This noun can denote a person belonging to the same socio-religious entity [LN].

f. συγγενής (LN 11.57) (BAGD p. 772): 'fellow countryman' [BAGD, LN, NTC; NET]. This plural noun is translated 'kindred' [BECNT, NICNT; NRSV], 'kinsfolk' [ICC2], 'kinsmen' [WBC; KJV, NASB], 'human kinsmen' [HNTC], 'kinsmen by descent' [AB], 'kinsfolk by natural descent' [REB], 'my people' [NCV, NLT], 'those of my own race' [NIV], 'my own flesh and blood' [TEV]. This noun denotes a person who is a member of the same nation [LN].

g. σάρξ (LN 58.10) (BAGD 4. p. 743): 'the flesh' [BECNT, ICC2, NICNT, NTC, WBC; KJV, NASB, NRSV], 'human nature' [BAGD, LN], 'physical nature of people' [LN], 'earthly descent' [BAGD], not explicit [CEV, NCV, NET, NLT]. The phrase κατὰ σάρκα 'according to (the) flesh' is also translated 'by descent' [AB], 'by natural descent' [REB], 'by birth' [GW], 'of my own race' [NIV], 'human' [HNTC], 'my own flesh and blood' [TEV]. This noun denotes human nature, particularly in reference to the physical aspect of human life [LN].

QUESTION—What relationship is indicated by γάρ 'for'?
1. It indicates the reason for Paul's sorrow, which is the unbelief of the Jewish people [BECNT, ICC2, NICNT, NTC]. It explains the nature of Paul's sorrow [ICC2].
2. In the immediate context it introduces another expression of how he responds to the sorrow he feels over the unbelief of the Jews [SSA].
3. It indicates the proof of Paul's sincerity [ICC1].

QUESTION—Why does Paul make such a strong assertion?
Some may have thought that his emphasis on the gospel and not on the Law, and his defense of his mission to the Gentiles meant that he was anti-Jewish, but he wants to show that this idea is not true [NICNT]. This recalls the prayer of Moses in Exodus 32 [AB, BECNT, Mor, NICNT, NTC, St, TNTC, WBC]. It shows Paul's deep concern for his people, and that he is not just a bitter renegade [Mor]. Paul wants people to know that he really loves the Jews [Gdt, NTC], despite the critical things he has just said about them [NTC]. Paul is also concerned that the rejection of the gospel by so many Jewish people would cast doubts on its validity [Mor, WBC]. This statement is significant in light of his assertion just a few verses before in 8:38-39 about the impossibility of being separated from Christ [BECNT, Mu, NTC, St]. He is concerned for God's reputation for faithfulness, which is bound up with what happens with Israel [BECNT].

9:4 who are Israelites, whose (are) the adoption-as-sons/sonship[a] and the glory[b]

LEXICON—a. υἱοθεσία (LN 35.53) (BAGD 1. p. 833): 'adoption' [BAGD, BECNT, ICC2, LN, NICNT, NTC, WBC; KJV, NRSV], 'adoption as sons' [NASB, NET, NIV], 'sonship' [AB]. The phrase ὧν ἡ υἱοθεσία 'whose (are) the adoption as sons/sonship' is also translated 'they were made God's sons' [HNTC], 'they are...chosen to be God's sons' [REB], 'he made them his sons' [TEV], 'they are...God's adopted children' [GW], 'they are...chosen to be God's adopted children' [NLT], 'they are...God's chosen children' [NCV], 'they are also God's chosen people' [CEV]. This noun denotes the action whereby someone who is not one's own child is formally and legally declared to be such, and is henceforth to be treated and cared for as one's own child, including complete rights of inheritance [LN].

b. δόξα (LN 79.18) (BAGD 3. p. 204): 'glory, splendor' [LN], 'honor or glory with God' [BAGD]. This noun denotes the quality of splendid, remarkable appearance [LN]. The phrase ὧν...ἡ δόξα 'whose are...the glory' [NASB] is also translated 'to them belong the glory' [NET, NRSV], 'theirs (is) the divine glory' [NIV], 'to whom pertaineth the glory' [KJV], 'they have God's glory' [GW], 'they have seen the glory of God' [NCV], 'God showed them his glory' [CEV], 'God revealed his glory to them' [NLT, TEV], 'theirs is the glory of the divine presence' [REB]. This noun denotes the quality of splendid, remarkable appearance [LN].

QUESTION—What relationship is indicated by the pronoun οἵτινες 'who'?

It is causal; 'because' they are Israelites, etc. [BECNT, ICC1, NICNT, NTC, WBC]. It may indicate something of a quality: such as are Israelites [Mor]. It characterizes them as people for whom it would be worthwhile to suffer such separation from Christ [Gdt].

QUESTION—Why does Paul use the term 'Israelites' as opposed to 'Jews'?

It is a title of honor [AB, Gdt, NTC] and dignity [Mu]. 'Jew' refers more to a national, ethnic, or political status [AB, NICNT], whereas 'Israelite' is a title of religious significance and honor, referring to their special religious position [NICNT], to their special position as the people of God [BECNT, Ho, ICC1, ICC2], God's chosen people [SSA], and favored by him [Ho]. It is their covenantal name [NAC, WBC], whereas 'Jew' is their national name [NAC]. He is referring to his people in their capacity as God's covenant people [Mor], and as partakers of the promises, especially the hope of a coming Messiah [ICC1]. It is a title which includes all the privileges which follow in this passage [BECNT, Gdt, Ho]. It emphasizes the fact that they were specially chosen by God [TH; TEV]. It is the name whereby they understood themselves, as opposed to the term 'Jew', which is the name by which other people knew them [BECNT, WBC]. Paul uses the present tense verb εἰσιν 'are' to indicate that the title and special status are still current [AB], and have not been revoked [NICNT].

QUESTION—To what does υἱοθεσία 'adoption-as-sons/sonship' refer?

1. It refers to their adoption, God's act of bringing Israel into relationship with him as a 'son' [HNTC, ICC2, Mor, NICNT, NTC, TH, WBC]. Though they did not naturally belong in such a relation to God, he graciously admitted them into it [Mor]. God set them apart from all other peoples for the purpose of blessing and of service [NICNT].
2. It refers to Israel's relationship as a son to God, receiving God's favor and fatherly affection, and obligated to be obedient to him [AB].

QUESTION—To what does δόξα 'glory' refer?

It refers to God's presence among the people of Israel [AB, Ho, ICC1, ICC2, Mor, Mu, NAC, NICNT, NTC, SSA, TH, TNTC], particularly at the time of the exodus and the wilderness journey, and in the tabernacle and temple [AB, HNTC, Mu, TH, TNTC]. He is primarily referring to the manifestation of God's glory during the time that Israel was in the desert [SSA]. It is the manifestation of the invisible God through the fire and cloud in the wilderness and at Mt Sinai [NTC], and which filled the tabernacle and Solomon's temple [NTC, St]. It is what is referred to as the *shekina* [Ho, ICC1, ICC2, NAC, SSA, TNTC], which is the visible manifestation of the invisible God [Gdt, ICC2], the representation of God's presence among the people [BECNT, Ho, Mu, TNTC]. It refers to various theophanies in the OT, but also speaks of a glory in which man was intended to share [WBC].

and the covenants[a] and the giving-of-law[b] and the worship[c] and the promises,[d]

LEXICON—a. διαθήκη (LN 34.44) (BAGD 2. p. 183): 'covenant' [AB, BAGD, BECNT, HNTC, ICC2, LN, NICNT, NTC, WBC; KJV, NASB, NET, NIV, NLT, NRSV, REB, TEV], 'agreement' [CEV, NCV], 'pledge' [GW]. This noun denotes the verbal content of an agreement between two persons specifying reciprocal benefits and responsibilities [LN].
  b. νομοθεσία (LN **33.339**) (BAGD p. 541): 'law' [BAGD, WBC; REB], 'legislation' [BAGD, ICC2, NTC], 'Moses' Teachings' [GW]. This noun denotes the giving or establishing of a law [LN]. This noun is translated as a phrase: 'the giving of the law' [AB, BECNT, **LN**, NICNT; KJV, NASB, NET, NRSV], 'the receiving of the law' [NIV], 'he gave the law' [HNTC], 'he gave them the law' [TEV], 'he gave them his law' [CEV], 'he gave them his law' [NLT], 'God gave them the law of Moses' [NCV]. This noun denotes the giving or establishing of a law [LN]. It occurs only here in the NT.
  c. λατρεία (LN 53.14) (BAGD p. 467): 'worship' [BAGD, ICC2, LN, NICNT, NTC; NRSV], 'true worship' [GW, TEV], 'temple worship' [HNTC; NET, NIV, REB], 'service' [BECNT, WBC], 'service of God' [KJV], 'temple service' [NASB], 'right way of worship' [NCV], 'cult' [AB]. The phrase ἡ λατρεία 'the worship' is also translated 'the temple is theirs' [CEV], 'he gave them the privilege of worshiping him' [NLT]. This noun denotes the performance of religious rites as a part of worship [LN].
  d. ἐπαγγελία (LN 33.288) (BAGD 2.a. p. 280): 'promise' [AB, BAGD, BECNT, HNTC, ICC2, LN, NICNT, NTC, WBC; all versions except TEV], 'God's promises' [TEV]. This noun denotes the content of what is promised [LN].

QUESTION—Which covenants is Paul referring to?
  1. He is referring to various covenants mentioned throughout the OT, including those with Abraham and with Israel at Sinai [Mor, Mu, NAC, NICNT, St], as well as with David [Mor, Mu, NICNT, St]. It is the numerous covenants God made with the patriarchs [Gdt]. It includes the covenant with Noah [Mor, NICNT, TNTC] and with Joshua [Mor], and the new covenant promised by Jeremiah [TNTC]. It refers to the covenants with the patriarchs and with David [AB]. He is referring to the three covenants connected with the exodus: one at Sinai (Horeb), one on the plains of Moab, and one at the mountains Gerizim and Ebal [HNTC, ICC2], as well as the covenant with Abraham [ICC2]. It is the original covenant with the people of Israel, which was renewed at various times [ICC1]. There were various times that God affirmed and reaffirmed his covenant with his people and their leaders [NTC].

2. He is referring to the old covenant and the new covenant [WBC].
3. The two words, 'covenants' and 'promises' mutually interpret one another, such that the covenants referred to should be understood in terms of the promises, similar to the way he uses the phrase 'covenants of promise' in Eph 2:12. The promises of the covenant have to do with salvation [BECNT].

QUESTION—Does νομοθεσία refer to the act of giving the law, or of the law itself?
1. It is the law itself [AB, Ho, ICC2], the Mosaic legislation [TNTC]. It is more or less equivalent to νόμος 'law' [ICC2].
2. It is the giving of the law [HNTC, ICC1, LN, NICNT]. He is focusing on the law as something having been given by God [NICNT]. The giving of the law was accompanied by awe and splendor [ICC1].
3. There is no real difference between the two, and his choice of νομοθεσία is probably due to stylistic reasons, so that it would sound more like υἱοθεσία [WBC]. It is both the gift that the law is, as well as the act of giving it [Gdt].

QUESTION—What specifically is the λατρεία 'worship'?
1. It is the worship in the temple [BECNT, Gdt, HNTC, Ho, ICC1, Mu, NAC, SSA, St, TH, TNTC, WBC] and the tabernacle [BECNT, Ho, Mu, SSA, TNTC], and the sacrificial system in particular [NICNT]. This noun refers to the awesome worship in the temple as ordained by God himself, so strikingly different from and superior to the worship of the pagans all around them [AB].
2. It is Israel's worship of God spoken of generally [ICC2, NTC]. While he is primarily thinking of the sacrificial system of worship in the tabernacle and temple, it would also include worship in the synagogue and the home [ICC2]. This true worship stands in contrast to whatever ways human beings have devised in their own thinking to worship God [ICC2].

QUESTION—What are the promises he refers to here?
They are the promises to Abraham and the patriarchs [AB, ICC2, NICNT], as well as to Moses and David [AB], and generally to all the promises God gave to Abraham and his descendants [Mor, NTC, TNTC]. It refers to the messianic promises [HNTC, ICC1, Mor, Mu, SSA, St, TNTC], the promises of Christ and his kingdom [Ho]. It refers to the promises to Abraham of the land and of the blessing of the nations [WBC]. It refers to the many OT promises of salvation and deliverance [TH]. Eschatological and messianic promises would also be included here [ICC2]. It includes greater blessings which are still to come [Gdt]. The promises of the covenant include the promise of salvation [BECNT].

9:5 whose are the fathers[a] and from whom (comes)[b] the Christ[c] according-to (the) flesh,[d]

LEXICON—a. πατήρ (LN 10.20): 'ancestor, forefather' [LN]. This plural noun is translated 'the fathers' [BECNT, ICC2, NICNT, NTC, WBC; KJV,

NASB], 'the fathers of the race' [HNTC], 'the patriarchs' [AB; NET, NIV, NRSV, REB], 'ancestors' [GW], 'famous ancestors' [CEV], 'famous Hebrew ancestors' [TEV], 'great ancestors' [NCV]. The phrase ὧν οἱ πατέρες 'whose are the fathers' is also translated 'Abraham, Isaac, and Jacob are their ancestors' [NLT]. This word implies that these ancestors are very important [TH].
   b. There is no lexical entry for this word in the Greek text. The implied verb is represented in translation as 'comes' [AB; NRSV], 'came' [WBC; KJV, NET, REB], 'is' [BECNT, ICC2, NICNT, NTC; NASB], 'is descended' [GW], 'springs' [HNTC], 'is traced' [NIV], not explicit [CEV, NCV, NLT, TEV].
   c. Χριστός (LN 53.82) (BAGD 1. p. 887): 'Christ' [BAGD, LN], 'Messiah' [BAGD, LN]. The phrase ὁ Χριστός is translated as having the definite article: 'the Christ' [BECNT, WBC; NASB, NET], 'the Christ himself' [HNTC], 'the Messiah' [AB, NICNT; GW, NRSV, REB]; as not having the definite article: 'Christ' [ICC2, NTC; KJV, NCV, NIV, TEV], 'Jesus Christ' [CEV], 'Christ himself' [NLT].
   d. The phrase κατὰ σάρκα 'according to the flesh' [NICNT; NASB, NRSV], is also translated 'according to his human nature' [GW], 'as concerning the flesh' [KJV], 'by natural descent' [AB; REB], 'by human descent' [NET], 'insofar as the flesh is concerned' [BECNT, WBC], 'so far as the flesh is concerned' [ICC2], 'as far as his human nature is concerned' [NTC; NLT], 'on the human side' [HNTC], 'as a human being' [TEV], 'human ancestry of' [NIV], not explicit [CEV, NCV].
QUESTION—Who are the 'fathers'?
   He is referring to Abraham, Isaac, and Jacob [AB, BECNT, Ho, ICC2, Mor, Mu, NICNT, SSA, St, TH, TNTC], as well as the twelve sons of Jacob [ICC2, St, TNTC], and other figures such as Joshua, Samuel, and David [St]. It refers to the patriarchs and the wilderness generation [WBC]. It is not limited just to them, however [ICC2, Mor], and possibly might also include the people who came out of Egypt during the exodus [NICNT], and possibly other well-known figures from the OT such as David [ICC2, Mu]. They are all the devout ancestors involved in the history of redemption [Mu, NTC].
QUESTION—Who is the antecedent of the phrase 'from whom'?
   While Paul describes all the other privileges as belonging *to* the people of Israel, when he mentions the Messiah he switches to ἐξ *'from'* to indicate a shift in the relationship, to show Christ *coming from* them as opposed to *belonging to* them [Mu]. The people of Israel are his origin, but he does not belong exclusively to them in terms of his destination [Gdt].
   1. The Christ comes from the people of Israel [AB, BECNT, Gdt, HNTC, Ho, ICC2, Mu, NAC, NICNT, NTC, SSA, St, WBC; NCV, NLT, TEV].
   2. The Christ comes from the fathers, that is, the patriarchs [CEV, GW].

the-one being over^a all God blessed^b forever^c amen.

LEXICON—a. ἐπί with genitive (LN 37.9) (BAGD I.1.b.α. p. 286): 'over' [AB, BAGD, BECNT, HNTC, ICC2, LN, NICNT, NTC, WBC; all versions except REB], 'above' [REB]. The phrase ὁ ὢν ἐπὶ πάντων 'the one being over all' is also translated 'is…over everything' [GW, NCV], 'the one who rules over everything' [NLT], 'who rules over all' [CEV, TEV], 'who stands over the whole process' [HNTC], 'supreme above all' [REB]. This preposition marks the object over which someone exercises a control or authority [LN].

b. εὐλογητός (LN 33.362) (BAGD p. 322): 'blessed' [BAGD, BECNT, HNTC, ICC2, NICNT, WBC; GW, KJV, NASB, NET, NRSV, REB], 'blest' [AB, NTC], 'praised' [BAGD; CEV, NIV, TEV], 'to be praised' [LN]. The phrase θεὸς εὐλογητὸς εἰς τοὺς αἰῶνας 'God blessed forever' is also translated 'he is God…and is worthy of eternal praise' [NLT], '(who is) God…praise him forever' [NCV], 'may God…be blessed forever' [REB]. This adjective describes someone as being worthy of praise or commendation [LN].

c. The phrase εἰς τοὺς αἰῶνας is translated 'forever' [AB, BECNT, HNTC, ICC2, NICNT, NTC, WBC; CEV, GW, KJV, NASB, NCV, NET, NIV, NRSV, REB, TEV], 'eternal' [NLT].

QUESTION—To whom does 'the one' refer?

1. It refers to Christ, and is an affirmation of Christ's sovereignty, deity, and blessedness [AB, BECNT, Gdt, GNT, Ho, ICC2, Mor, Mu, NAC, NTC, SSA, St, TNTC; KJV, NCV, NLT, NRSV].

   1.1 Paul is saying that Christ is over all, that he is God, and that he is blessed forever [AB, BECNT, Gdt, ICC1, ICC2, Mor, Mu, NICNT, NTC, SSA; KJV, NASB, NLT, NRSV].

   1.2 Paul is saying that Christ is God over all, and is blessed forever [Ho, TNTC; GW, NCV, NET, NIV].

2. It refers to God the Father; after saying that Christ is physically descended from Israel, Paul then begins a new sentence with a new subject, which is a doxology to God who is over all and is blessed forever [HNTC, WBC; CEV, REB, TEV].

QUESTION—To what or whom does πάντων 'all' refer?

1. It refers to 'things'; Christ is supreme over all things [BECNT, Gdt, ICC1, NICNT, SSA, WBC], including history [BECNT]. He is supreme over the universe [Ho].

2. It refers to all people, Jews and Gentiles alike [AB].

QUESTION—What is the function of ἀμήν 'amen'?

It is the normal congregational response to a doxology [Mor]. It is a proper conclusion to the doxology just spoken, but also to the list of Israel's blessings [TNTC]. It is the usual ending to a prayer [AB]. It is used here to give solemn assent to what has just been said [Ho]. It affirms that what he has just said is true, and marks a section boundary [SSA].

DISCOURSE UNIT—9:6–33 [Mu]. The topic is the vindication of God's righteousness and faithfulness.

DISCOURSE UNIT—9:6–29 [AB, ICC1, ICC2, Mor, NICNT, NTC, TNTC, WBC]. The topic is Israel's failure not contrary to God's direction of history [AB], the justice of the rejection [ICC1], unbelief and disobedience of men are shown to be embraced within the work of divine mercy [ICC2], God's sovereign freedom [Mor], defining the promise: God's sovereign election [NICNT], God's sovereign choice [TNTC], the call of God [WBC].

DISCOURSE UNIT—9:6–24 [Ho]. The topic is the rejection of Jews and the calling of Gentiles.

DISCOURSE UNIT—9:6–18 [NTC]. The topic is divine election and rejection.

DISCOURSE UNIT—9:6–13 [AB, HNTC, ICC1, Mor, NICNT, WBC]. The topic is God's promises to Israel stem from his gratuitous election of them as his people, hence his word has not failed [AB], God's elective purpose [HNTC], the rejection of Israel not inconsistent with the divine promises [ICC1], God works by election [Mor], the Israel within Israel [NICNT], the character of God's free choice [WBC].

9:6 **But (it is) not that^a the word^b of-God has-failed.^{c} For not all the-ones from^d Israel these (are) Israel;**

LEXICON—a. The phrase οὐχ οἷον δὲ ὅτι is a mixture of two idioms. It is translated 'but it is not that' [ICC2], 'now it is not that' [NICNT], 'it is not that' [NCV], 'it is not as though' [AB; NET, NIV, NRSV], 'but it is not as though' [HNTC, NTC, WBC; NASB], 'now it is not as though' [GW], 'not as though' [KJV], 'but it is by no means the case' [BECNT], 'it cannot be said that' [CEV], 'it cannot be that' [REB], 'I am not saying that' [TEV]. The clause οὐχ οἷον δὲ ὅτι ἐκπέπτωκεν ὁ λόγος τοῦ θεοῦ 'but it is not that the word of God has failed' is also translated 'Well then, has God failed to fulfill his promise to Israel?' [NLT].

b. λόγος (LN 33.98) (BAGD 1.b.α. p. 478): 'word' [AB, BAGD, BECNT, HNTC, ICC2, LN, NICNT, NTC, WBC; GW, KJV, NASB, NET, NIV, NRSV, REB], 'promise' [BAGD; CEV, NCV, NLT, TEV]. This noun denotes that which has been stated or said, with primary focus upon the content of the communication [LN].

c. perf. act. indic. of ἐκπίπτω (LN 75.7) (BAGD 3.b. p. 244): 'to fail' [AB, BAGD, BECNT, HNTC, ICC2, LN, NICNT, NTC, WBC; GW, NASB, NCV, NET, NIV, NLT, NRSV, TEV], 'to have proved false' [REB], 'to have taken none effect' [KJV]. The clause '(it is) not that the word of God has failed' is translated 'it cannot be said that God broke his promise' [CEV], 'has God failed to fulfill his promise to Israel?' [NLT]. The verb means to become inadequate for some function [LN].

d. ἐκ (LN 89.3) (BAGD 3.d. p. 235): 'from' [AB, BAGD, BECNT, LN], 'descended from' [HNTC, WBC; GW, NASB, NET, NIV], 'of' [BAGD, ICC2, LN, NICNT, NTC; CEV, KJV, NCV]. The phrase οἱ ἐξ Ἰσραήλ 'the ones from Israel' is also translated 'the descendants of Israel' [AB], 'the offspring of Israel' [REB], 'the people of Israel' [TEV], 'born into the nation of Israel' [NLT], 'Israelites' [NRSV].

e. The phrase οὗτοι Ἰσραήλ 'these (are) Israel' [BECNT, NICNT], is also translated 'are truly Israel' [AB, HNTC; NET, REB], 'are Israel' [ICC2, NTC, WBC; KJV, NASB, NIV], 'is part of Israel' [GW], 'are the people of God' [TEV], 'are the true people of God' [CEV], 'are truly God's people' [NCV], 'are truly members of God's people' [NLT], 'truly belong to Israel' [NRSV].

QUESTION—What relationship is indicated by δέ 'but'?

Most of the translations begin a new paragraph here [AB, BECNT, HNTC, ICC2, NICNT, NTC, WBC; all versions], and many do not translate the conjunction [AB; CEV, NCV, NET, NIV, NRSV, REB, TEV]. This conjunction indicates a transition from the preceding five verses of introduction to the body of Paul's argument which goes through to 11:32 [NICNT]. This transition is indicated by translating δέ as 'now' [NICNT; GW]. Although the primary relationship is a transition to the body of Paul's argument, there is some contrast [ICC1], and many translate δέ as 'but' [WBC]. The conjunction indicates a contraexpectation of an implied concession: '*most of my fellow Israelites rejected Christ*, but/yet this does not prove that God has failed to do what he promised' [SSA].

QUESTION—What is the meaning of ὁ λόγος τοῦ θεοῦ 'the word of God'?

It refers to God's promises [AB, BECNT, HNTC, Ho, ICC1, Mor, Mu, NAC, NICNT, NTC, SSA, St, TH; CEV, NCV, NLT, TEV]. It is his promises to Israel [Mor, NTC, St, WBC], the promise to bless Israel [NAC], the promise of salvation for Israel [BECNT, NICNT], God's promises to Israel and the patriarchs [AB], his promise to Abraham, including that of salvation through Christ [Ho], his promise of election [WBC]. It refers to God's stated purposes of grace in election [ICC2]. It refers to God's promise to Abraham, Isaac, and Jacob to bless their descendants [SSA]. It is God's word of promise in the covenants; Paul is saying that God's covenant has not been nullified [Mu]. This phrase is parallel to 'the oracles of God' in 3:2 [BECNT].

QUESTION—What relationship is indicated by γάρ 'for'?

Paul is addressing an error that was common among Jewish people in his time, which is that they would be saved by virtue of being born a Jew [BECNT, Ho, ICC1, Mor, NICNT, WBC].

1. This conjunction indicates the first grounds for his denial that Israel's unbelief nullified God's promises to Israel [ICC2, Mor, NICNT, TH]: I am not saying that the promise of God has failed, (it has not failed) since not all who belong to Israel in a physical sense belong to Israel in a spiritual sense.

2. It introduces 9:6b as the first explanation of his statement in 9:6a that the word of God has not failed, which he will develop until the end of 11:32 [BECNT].
3. This conjunction indicates the first grounds for the conclusion in 9:8 [SSA]: since not all the descendants of Israel are considered by God to be his true descendants, it is only those born as children of the promise that are reckoned as his descendants.

QUESTION—What is meant by Paul's statement that not all those of Israel are Israel?

1. Not all of those who are of Israel in the physical sense are Israel in the spiritual sense [BECNT, ICC1, ICC2, Mor, NICNT, WBC], the believing remnant within ethnic Israel [NICNT]. The first reference to 'Israel' is all of physical, ethnic Israel, and the second reference to 'Israel' is a smaller group within the first, the remnant [Mor]. Not all ethnic Jews are Jews of faith; God's promises are not tied to physical descent but are for those of Israel who will come to faith [AB]. Not all descendants of Israel are truly God's people, belonging to the true Israel [BECNT, Ho]. Within the larger nation of Israel there is a smaller 'Israel', consisting of believing Israelites who are willing and obedient witnesses of God's grace and truth [ICC2].
2. Not all the chosen people of God are descended from Israel; that is, some are Gentiles [TH].

QUESTION—Does the phrase ἐξ Ἰσραήλ 'from Israel' refer specifically to the patriarch Jacob or more generally to Israel as a nation?

1. It refers to the patriarch Jacob, who is also called Israel [Ho].
2. It refers to the nation of Israel [Gdt, NICNT].
3. It refers both to Jacob as well as to the nation [SSA]: who are descended from Jacob and who call themselves the people of Israel.

QUESTION—Does Paul's statement 'these are Israel' refer to all who believe in Christ, whether Jew or Gentile, or only to Jewish believers?

1. It refers to Jewish believers [AB, BECNT, ICC1, ICC2, Mor, Mu, NICNT, WBC]. Even though he uses the phrase 'the Israel of God' in Galatians 6:16 to describe all believers, here he is dealing with the issue of whether God's promises to ethnic Israel will be fulfilled [BECNT].
2. It refers to all believers [Ho, TH].

9:7 nor that/because they-are (the) seed[a] (of) Abraham all (the) children[b]

LEXICON—a. σπέρμα (LN 10.29) (BAGD 2.b. p. 762): 'seed' [BECNT, HNTC, ICC2, NICNT, NTC, WBC; KJV], 'posterity' [BAGD, LN], 'descendants' [BAGD, LN; NASB, NCV, NIV, NLT, REB, TEV], '(every) descendant' [GW], 'true descendants' [NET, NRSV], 'offspring' [AB, LN], not explicit [CEV]. This noun denotes posterity, with emphasis upon the ancestor's role in founding the lineage [LN].

b. τέκνον (LN 10.28) (BAGD 1.a.α., 2.e. p. 808): 'child' [BAGD], 'children' [AB, BECNT, HNTC, ICC2, NICNT, NTC, WBC; KJV,

NASB, NCV, NET, NIV, NLT, NRSV, TEV], 'true children' [REB], 'offspring' [LN], 'descendant(s)' [LN; CEV], not explicit [GW].

QUESTION—What relationship is indicated by οὐδ' ὅτι 'nor that/because'?

(Note that the answer to this question is closely related to the following question concerning which of the terms σπέρμα 'seed', and τέκνα 'children' is the more specific and which is the more general. Those who take οὐδ' ὅτι as indicating a causal relationship also take σπέρμα as the more general term and τέκνα as the more specific, referring to the true spiritual offspring of Abraham. Those who take οὐδ' ὅτι as introducing an object clause take τέκνα as more general and σπέρμα as the more specific term.)

1. It indicates a causal relationship that is being denied [AB, ICC2, NTC; KJV]: nor *just because* they are seed are they children [AB, ICC2, NTC; KJV, NASB, NIV]. It is the second grounds for the conclusion in 9:8 that not all natural born descendants of Abraham are considered God's children [SSA]. It is a proof of the statement in 9:6; that is, not all of Jacob's descendants inherit the blessing, just as not all of Abraham's descendants received the rights of sonship [ICC1].
2. It introduces an object clause [BECNT, HNTC, NICNT, WBC; NET, NRSV]: nor *that* all the children are the seed. It is parallel to οὐχ…ὅτι in 6a [NICNT]. 'Seed' is used in the narrower sense that 'not all of Abraham's children are his true descendants' [NRSV].

QUESTION—In the contrast between σπέρμα 'seed', and τέκνα 'children', which is the more general and which is the more specific?

(Note that in the Greek text it is not clear which of the two nouns is the subject and which is the predicate nominative. That is, Paul is either saying that not all the children are the seed of Abraham, or that not all the seed of Abraham are children.)

1. The term σπέρμα 'seed' or 'descendants' is general, and τέκνα 'children' is specific: not all Abraham's descendants or 'seed' are his true children, i.e., heirs of the promise [AB, Ho, ICC1, ICC2, Mor, Mu, NTC; KJV, NASB, NCV, NIV, NLT, REB, TEV].
2. The term τέκνα 'children' is general, and σπέρμα 'seed' or 'descendants' is specific. Not all Abraham's children are his true descendants or 'seed', i.e., heirs of the promise [BECNT, HNTC, NICNT, WBC; NET, NRSV]. The term σπέρμα 'seed' is the predicate, and in both clauses the adjective 'all' modifies the subject [HNTC].

QUESTION—How does Paul use the terms σπέρμα 'seed', and τέκνα 'children' in 9:7–8?

1. The terms are not used in a consistent manner. That is, 'children' in 9:7 corresponds to 'children of God', 'children of the promise', and 'seed' in 9:8, and 'seed' in 9:7 corresponds to 'children of the flesh' in 9:8 [AB, Ho, ICC1, ICC2, Mor, Mu, NTC; KJV, NASB, NCV, NIV, NLT, REB, TEV]: that is, many of Abraham's seed are not truly his children, they are children of the flesh, but his true seed are children of the promise and children of God.

2. The terms are used in a consistent manner. That is, 'seed' (or 'descendants') in 9:7 corresponds with 'the children of God', 'the children of the promise', and 'your seed' in 9:8, and 'children' in 9:7 corresponds with 'children of the flesh' in 9:8 [BECNT, NICNT, WBC; NRSV]. That is, many of Abraham's children are children of the flesh, but his true seed are children of the promise and children of God.

QUESTION—Does the term 'children' refer to being children of Abraham or children of God?

   1. Paul is saying that not all are children of Abraham [AB, BECNT, HNTC, ICC2, Mu, NICNT, NTC, WBC; GW, NCV, NIV, NLT, NRSV, REB].

   2. Paul is saying that not all are children of God [TEV].

rather,[a] In[b] Isaac your seed[c] shall-be-called.[d]

LEXICON—a. ἀλλά (LN 89.125): 'but' [BECNT, ICC2, LN, NICNT, NTC, WBC; KJV, NASB, NCV, NRSV, REB], 'rather' [AB, HNTC; NET], 'instead' [LN], 'however' [GW], 'on the contrary' [LN; NIV], 'for the Scriptures say' [NLT], not explicit [CEV, TEV]. This conjunction marks contrast [LN].

b. ἐν (LN 90.56) (BAGD III.3.a. p. 261): 'in' [BECNT, NICNT, WBC; KJV], 'in relation to, in respect to' [LN], 'by' [CEV], 'through' [AB, HNTC, ICC2, NTC; GW, NASB, NET, NIV, NLT, NRSV, REB, TEV], 'from' [NCV]. This preposition marks an experiencer of an event [LN].

c. σπέρμα: 'seed' [BECNT, NICNT, NTC, WBC; KJV], 'offspring' [AB; NIV, NLT, NRSV, REB, TEV], 'descendants' [GW, NASB, NCV, NET], not explicit [CEV]. The phrase 'In Isaac your seed shall be called' is translated 'your descendants through Isaac shall be called your seed' [HNTC, ICC2].

d. fut. pass. indic. of καλέω (LN 33.129) (BAGD 1.a.δ. p. 399): 'to be called' [BAGD, LN], 'to be named' [BAGD]. The clause Ἐν Ἰσαὰκ κληθήσεταί σοι σπέρμα 'In Isaac your seed shall be called' is translated 'in Isaac your seed shall be called' [BECNT, NICNT, WBC; KJV], 'it is through Isaac that your offspring shall be named' [AB], 'your descendants through Isaac shall be called your seed' [HNTC, ICC2], 'it is through Isaac that your seed will be reckoned' [NTC], 'through Isaac your descendants will carry on your name' [GW], 'through Isaac your descendants will be named' [NASB], 'the descendants I promised you will be from Isaac' [NCV], 'it is through Isaac that your offspring will be reckoned' [NIV], 'Isaac is the son through whom your descendants will be counted' [NLT], 'through Isaac your descendants will be counted' [NET], 'it is through Isaac that descendants shall be named for you' [NRSV], 'it is through the line of Isaac's descendants that your name will be traced' [REB], 'it is through Isaac that you will have the descendants I promised you' [TEV]. This verb means to speak of a person or object by a proper name [LN].

QUESTION—What is the sense of the verb κληθήσεται 'called'?
1. It means to name or identify [AB, Gdt, Ho, ICC1, ICC2, NTC, TH].
2. Paul uses the term 'call' with its normal meaning of naming or identifying, but in this context he also uses it to imply God's effectual call, bringing about what he has ordained [BECNT, NICNT, WBC]. Its meaning includes the sense of God's call as found in other passages in Romans [WBC]. The emphasis here is that the one who has the name really is what his name declares about him [BAGD, Mor].

9:8 that is, not the children^a of-the flesh^b these (are the) children of-God
LEXICON—a. τέκνον. This plural noun is translated as 'children' in both its occurrences in this sentence [AB, BECNT, HNTC, ICC2, NICNT, NTC, WBC; GW, KJV, NASB, NET, NIV, NRSV, REB, TEV]. It is translated 'descendants' in the first occurrence and 'children' in the second occurrence [NCV, NLT], not explicit [CEV].
b. σάρξ (LN 58.10) (BAGD 4. p. 743). The phrase τῆς σαρκός 'of the flesh' [AB, ICC2, NICNT, WBC; KJV, NASB, NET, NRSV], is also translated 'of flesh' [BECNT], 'of Abraham's flesh' [HNTC], 'of Abraham by natural descent' [REB], 'Abraham's physical (descendants)' [NLT], 'Abraham's true (children)' [NCV], 'natural (children)' [NTC; NIV], 'born by natural descent' [GW], 'born in the usual way' [TEV], not explicit [CEV]. This noun denotes human nature, particularly in reference to the physical aspect of human life [LN].
QUESTION—What is the function of τοῦτ' ἔστιν 'that is'?
Drawing from the quotation cited in 9:7b, it introduces a conclusion [Ho, NICNT], or an explanation [Mor, Mu, WBC]. It introduces a general principle concluded from 9:7 [Gdt, ICC1, ICC2, SSA].
QUESTION—What does τῆς σαρκός 'of the flesh' imply here?
1. It refers that which is natural, that is, to physical descent [AB, BECNT, Gdt, HNTC, Ho, ICC1, ICC2, Mu, NAC, NICNT, NTC, SSA, TH, WBC]. It has a somewhat negative quality to it [WBC].
2. It refers to that which comes from a merely human attempt to bring about the outcome of the divine promise [Mor].

rather^a the children of-the promise^b are-reckoned^c as seed.^d
LEXICON—a. ἀλλά (LN 89.125): 'rather' [NET], 'but' [AB, BECNT, ICC2, LN, NICNT, NTC, WBC; KJV, NASB, NIV, NRSV], 'instead' [LN; GW, TEV], 'on the contrary' [LN], not explicit [HNTC; CEV, NCV, NLT, REB]. This conjunction marks contrast [LN].
b. ἐπαγγελία (LN 33.288) (BAGD 2.a. p. 280): 'promise' [AB, BAGD, BECNT, HNTC, ICC2, LN, NICNT, NTC, WBC; GW, KJV, NASB, NET, NIV, NLT, NRSV], not explicit [CEV]. The phrase 'children of the promise' is translated 'those who become God's children because of the promise God made to Abraham' [NCV], 'children born of the promise' [AB], 'children born by the promise' [GW], 'children who come by promise' [HNTC], 'the children born through God's promise' [REB], 'the

children born as a result of God's promise' [TEV]. This noun denotes the content of what is promised [LN].
- c. pres. pass. indic. of λογίζομαι (LN 31.1) (BAGD 1.b. p. 476): 'to be reckoned' [AB, BECNT, NICNT, NTC, WBC; REB], 'to be considered' [BAGD, LN; GW, NLT, NRSV], 'to be regarded' [LN; NASB, NIV, TEV], 'to be counted' [HNTC, ICC2; KJV, NET], 'to be looked upon' [BAGD], not explicit [CEV, NCV]. This verb means to hold a view or have an opinion with regard to something [LN].
- d. σπέρμα: 'seed' [BECNT, ICC2, NICNT, NTC, WBC; KJV], 'his seed' [HNTC], 'Abraham's offspring' [AB; NIV], 'Abraham's children' [NLT], 'descendants' [NASB, NET, NRSV], 'true descendants' [TEV], 'Abraham's descendants' [GW, REB], not explicit [CEV, NCV].

QUESTION—What does Paul mean by the phrase 'children of promise'?

Just as Isaac was born as a result of God's promise of intervention, and not as a result of natural processes, so also believers are God's true children because of a spiritual or supernatural birth [BECNT, Ho, Mor, NICNT]. They are also heirs of God's promise of blessing to Abraham [Ho]. They are those who have been given God's promises of salvation [BECNT]. They are those whose birth is due to God's action, and not to some natural process [NTC]. Their origin and identity are based on God's promise; they are also the ones to whom the promise is given and in whom that promise will have its effect [Mu]. The blessings of the covenant with God come not in relation to physical heredity or law, but in terms of promise [WBC]. It refers to those born as a result of a promise or according to a promise, though it could also refer to those to whom the promise was given [SSA].

9:9 For this (is)[a] the word[b] of-promise,[c] According-to this time[d] I-will-come and a son will-be[e] to Sarah.

LEXICON—a. There is no lexical entry for this word in the Greek text. It is represented in translation as 'is' [BECNT, ICC2, NICNT, NTC, WBC; KJV, NASB], 'was' [NCV, TEV], 'so runs (the promise)' [AB], '(the promise) runs' [HNTC; REB], not explicit [CEV, NLT].
- b. λόγος (LN 33.98) (BAGD 1.b.α. p. 478): 'word' [BAGD, BECNT, ICC2, LN, NICNT, WBC; KJV, NASB], 'language' [NTC], not explicit [AB, HNTC; CEV, GW, NCV, NET, NIV, NLT, NRSV, REB]. The phrase ἐπαγγελίας ὁ λόγος 'the word of promise' is also translated 'God's promise was made in these words' [TEV], 'this is what the promise said' [GW, NRSV], 'this is what the promise declared' [NET], 'this is how the promise was stated' [NIV], '(a) word of promise is this word' [ICC2], 'God had promised' [NLT]. This noun denotes that which has been stated or said, with primary focus upon the content of the communication [LN].
- c. ἐπαγγελία (LN 33.288) (BAGD 2.a. p. 280): 'promise' [AB, BAGD, BECNT, HNTC, ICC2, LN, NICNT, NTC, WBC; GW, KJV, NASB, NET, NIV, NRSV, REB], 'God's promise' [NCV, TEV], 'God...

promised' [CEV], 'God had promised' [NLT]. This noun denotes the content of what is promised [LN].
d. καιρός (LN 67.1) (BAGD 1. p. 395): 'time' [BAGD, LN]. The phrase κατὰ τὸν καιρὸν τοῦτον 'according to this time' is also translated 'at this time' [BAGD, BECNT, HNTC, WBC; CEV, KJV, NASB], 'about this time' [NICNT; NRSV], 'at the appointed time' [NTC; NIV], 'at the time appointed' [AB], 'at the right time' [GW, NCV, TEV], 'at this season' [ICC2], 'in due season' [REB], 'about a year from now' [NET], 'about this time next year' [NLT]. This noun denotes points of time consisting of occasions for particular events [LN].
e. The phrase ἔσται τῇ Σάρρᾳ υἱός 'a son will be to Sarah' is also translated 'Sarah will have a son' [AB, NTC; GW, NCV, NET, NIV, NLT, TEV], 'Sarah shall have a son' [BECNT, HNTC, ICC2, NICNT, WBC; KJV, NASB, NRSV, REB], 'you will already have a son' [CEV].

QUESTION—What is the function of γάρ 'for'?
It introduces his explanation of what he meant by the word 'promise' in 9:8 [Mor, NICNT, SSA].

QUESTION—Why does ἐπαγγελίας comes first in the sentence?
It is placed first to show emphasis [AB, ICC1, ICC2, Mor, NICNT, SSA, WBC].

9:10 And[a] not only (this), but likewise[b] (with) Rebecca conceiving[c] from one, our father Isaac;

LEXICON—a. δέ (LN 89.94): 'and' [LN]. The phrase οὐ μόνον 'not only this' [ICC2, NICNT, NTC; KJV, NASB], is also translated 'not only that' [AB; NET, NIV], 'not only (did Abraham…)' [BECNT], 'not only so' [WBC], 'this is not all' [TEV], 'that is not all' [NCV, REB], 'nor is that all' [NRSV], 'further' [HNTC], not explicit [CEV, GW, NLT].
b. καί (LN 89.93): 'also' [BECNT, ICC2, LN, NICNT, NTC, WBC; KJV, NASB], 'even' [AB], 'something similar had happened' [NRSV], not explicit [HNTC; CEV, GW, NCV, NET, NIV, NLT, REB, TEV].
c. κοίτη (LN **23.50**) (BAGD 2.b. p. 440): 'to be pregnant' [LN]. The phrase ἐξ ἑνὸς κοίτην ἔχουσα 'conceiving from one' is translated 'conceived from one man' [BECNT], 'conceived children by one man' [NET], 'conceived twins by one man' [NASB], 'conceived children by one husband' [NRSV], 'conceived both her sons at one time by one and the same man' [ICC2], 'conceived (her two sons) at one time by one and the same husband' [NTC], 'conceived through intercourse with one man' [HNTC], 'conceived children in one act of intercourse' [NICNT], 'conceived by the one act of sexual intercourse' [WBC], 'became pregnant by…' [GW], 'was pregnant by one man' [LN], 'had children by one and the same man' [AB], 'Rebekah's sons had the same father' [NCV], 'Rebecca's two sons had the same father' [TEV], 'Rebekah's children had one and the same father' [NIV], 'Rebecca's children had one

and the same father' [REB], not explicit [CEV, NLT]. When used with the verb ἔχω this noun denotes being in a state of pregnancy [LN].

QUESTION—What is the function of οὐ μόνον δέ 'and not only this'?

It introduces an argument that strengthens and confirms what has just been said in the previous paragraph [BECNT, Ho, ICC1, ICC2, Mor, NICNT, NTC, SSA, WBC].

QUESTION—What is meant by the euphemism ἐξ ἑνὸς κοίτην ἔχουσα 'conceiving from one'?

1. It means that she conceived by one man, Isaac [AB]. It is translated this way by KJV, NASB, NCV, NET, NIV, NRSV, REB, TEV.
2. It means that she conceived by one act of sexual union [BAGD, BECNT, HNTC, ICC2, Mor, NAC, NICNT, NTC, WBC]. The noun κοίτη, which normally means 'bed' and is used to refer to the marriage bed (and therefore sexual union), here seems to refer to the semen itself, and thus one act of receiving semen, that is, one act of sexual intercourse [BAGD, ICC2, Mor, NICNT, WBC]. It refers not just to sexual union with only one man, but to her conception of both sons through a single act of sexual union [BECNT, ICC2, NAC, NICNT, NTC, WBC]. It emphasizes that with respect to birth, there was no difference between the two sons [Mor]. Their origin is in the same moment of conception [HNTC].

9:11 For/and[a] not-yet[b] having-been-born nor having-done either good[c] or evil,[d]

LEXICON—a. γάρ (LN 89.23, 91.1): 'for' [BECNT, ICC2, LN, NICNT, NTC, WBC; KJV, NASB], not explicit [AB, HNTC; CEV, GW, NCV, NET, NIV, NLT, NRSV, REB, TEV]. This conjunction can mark the reason or cause between events [LN (89.23)], or it can mark a new sentence and the conjunction is often best translated 'and' or left untranslated [LN (91.11)].

b. μήπω (LN 67.129) (BAGD p. 519): 'not yet' [BAGD, LN, NICNT, WBC; KJV, NASB], 'still not' [LN], 'still (unborn)' [ICC2], 'were not' [BECNT], 'before' [AB, HNTC, NTC; CEV, GW, NCV, NET, NIV, NLT, NRSV, REB], not explicit [TEV]. This adverb marks the negation of extending time up to and beyond an expected point [LN].

c. ἀγαθός (LN 88.1): 'good' [AB, BECNT, HNTC, ICC2, LN, NICNT, NTC, WBC; all versions]. This adjective describes positive moral qualities of the most general nature [LN].

d. φαῦλος (LN 88.116) (BAGD 1. p. 854): 'evil' [AB, BAGD, BECNT, HNTC, LN, NICNT, WBC; KJV], 'bad' [BAGD, ICC2, LN, NTC; CEV, GW, NASB, NCV, NET, NIV, NLT, NRSV, TEV], 'ill' [REB], 'worthless, base' [BAGD]. This adjective describes someone or something as being evil in the sense of moral baseness [LN].

QUESTION—How is this verse related to its context?

Verses 9:11–12a are a parenthetical thought [Gdt, ICC1, NICNT]. Verse 9:10 'but likewise with Rebecca conceiving from one, our father Isaac', is left unfinished [ICC1, ICC2, NICNT], and a new thought is added in

9:11–12a that is not necessary for the argument being developed in this section, which is that Jewish descent did not of itself imply a right to inherit the promise. Then the interrupted sentence of 9:10 is finished in 9:12b with a change in the grammatical structure, 'it was said to her that the older will serve the younger' [ICC1, NICNT]. Verse 9:11a describes the circumstances in which the prophetic message stated in 9:12b occurred; 9:11b-12a is a purpose clause that gives a rationale as to why this message was spoken to her when it was, which is to show God's sovereignty [NICNT]. Many translations combine and rearrange the clauses in verses 11–12 to smooth out this interruption [CEV, GW, NASB, NCV, NET, NIV, REB, TEV]. Some translations include the phrase 'not from works but from the one calling' (9:12a) in verse 11, leaving only 9:12b in verse 12 [CEV, NASB, NET, REB].

QUESTION—What relationship is indicated by the conjunction the γάρ 'for/and'?

1. It indicates the reason that Rebecca and her children also give a striking example of God's sovereignty, which is that the decision concerning her children was made even before their birth [Ho, SSA].
2. It indicates another ground for saying that those who were born as a result of what God promised are those whom God considers to be his children [SSA].
3. It indicates a new point that Paul introduces in order to add another point that came to his mind [ICC1, NICNT]. This describes the circumstances in which the word of prophecy was spoken to Rebecca [ICC2, NICNT].

so-that[a] the purpose[b] of-God according-to[c] election[d] might-stand,[e]

LEXICON—a. ἵνα (LN 89.59): 'so that' [LN; GW, NCV, NET, NRSV], 'in order that' [AB, BECNT, HNTC, ICC2, NICNT, NTC, WBC; NASB, NIV, REB, TEV], 'that' [KJV], 'for the purpose of, in order to' [LN]. This conjunction is translated as a verb phrase: '(the Lord said this) to show that' [CEV], '(this message) shows that' [NLT].

b. πρόθεσις (LN 30.63) (BAGD 2.b. p. 706): 'purpose' [AB, BAGD, BECNT, HNTC, ICC2, LN, NICNT, NTC, WBC; KJV, NASB, NET, NIV, NRSV, REB, TEV], 'plan' [LN; GW, NCV, NLT]. The phrase 'the purpose of God' is translated '(to show that) he makes his own choices' [CEV]. This noun denotes that which is planned or purposed in advance [LN].

c. κατά with accusative (LN 89.4) (BAGD II.7.c. p. 408): 'according to' [NICNT, NTC; KJV, NASB, NLT], 'in relation to' [LN], 'in' [AB; NET, NIV], 'in terms of' [WBC], 'based on' [TEV], 'with regard to' [LN], 'of' [BAGD; NRSV], 'a matter of (his choice)' [GW, REB], not explicit [CEV, NCV].

d. ἐκλογή (LN **30.92**) (BAGD 1. p. 243): 'election' [AB, BAGD, NICNT, NTC, WBC; KJV, NET, NIV, NRSV], 'electing (purpose)' [BECNT, ICC2], 'elective (purpose)' [HNTC], 'choice' [LN; GW, NASB, REB,

TEV]. The phrase 'the purpose of God according to election' is also translated 'the electing purpose of God' [BECNT], 'God's elective purpose' [HNTC], 'God's electing purpose' [ICC2], 'he makes his own choices' [CEV], 'God chooses according to his own plan' [NLT], '(he was the one) God wanted to call' [NCV]. This noun denotes a special choice based upon significant preference, often implying a strongly favorable attitude toward what is chosen [LN].

 e. pres. act. subj. of μένω (LN 13.89) (BAGD 1.c.β. p. 504): 'to stand' [ICC2, NTC, WBC; KJV, NASB, NET, NIV], 'to stand firm' [HNTC; REB], 'to remain' [BAGD, LN, NICNT; GW], 'to continue' [BAGD, LN; NRSV], 'to persist' [AB], 'to prevail' [BECNT], not explicit [CEV, NCV, NLT, TEV]. This verb means to continue to exist [LN].

QUESTION—What is the relationship between πρόθεσις 'purpose' and κατ' ἐκλογήν 'according to election'?

The phrase κατ' ἐκλογήν modifies πρόθεσις 'purpose' [BECNT, HNTC, Ho, ICC2, SSA]. It is God's electing purpose [BECNT, HNTC, Ho, ICC2], God's purpose according to what he had determined [SSA]. Election is the means by which God carries out his purpose [Gdt, NICNT]. Electing purpose is purpose that grows out of election and fulfills the intent of the election [Mu, NTC], but it is also true to say that the election has a determinative purpose [Mu]. God's purpose operates on the basis of election and by a process of election [HNTC]. God's purpose is characterized by election [ICC2]. God's purpose was expressed in his choosing one of the two sons [TH].

QUESTION—What is implied in his use of the verb μένῃ 'might stand'?

This word stands in contrast to ἐκπέπτωκεν 'has fallen' in 9:6 [BECNT, ICC2, Mor, St, WBC]; God's purpose prevails and is not thwarted [BECNT]. God's purpose abides, or stands firm [Mu, NICNT]. It persists, it goes on, it proceeds [AB]. It stands firm and will be accomplished [ICC2]. It will be firmly established or recognized [SSA]. It is established and recognized for what it is, as *God's* purpose [Ho]. God's purpose continued to be based on the choice he had made [TH]. God's plan remains intact [Gdt].

9:12 **not from[a] works[b] but from[c] the-one calling,[d] it-was-said to-her that The older[e] will-serve[f] the younger,[g]**

LEXICON—a. ἐκ with genitive (LN 89.77) (BAGD 3.i. p. 235): 'from' [LN, WBC], 'by' [NET, NIV, NRSV], 'of' [KJV], 'out of' [NICNT], 'because of' [AB; CEV, NASB, NCV], 'based on' [BECNT; TEV], 'based (not) on' [NTC; GW, REB], 'based…(not) on' [GW], 'on' [ICC2], 'resting on' [HNTC], 'according to' [BAGD; NLT]. This preposition marks means as constituting a source [LN].

 b. ἔργον (LN 42.11) (BAGD 1.c.β. p. 308): 'act' [LN], 'deed' [BAGD, LN]. This plural noun is translated 'works' [BECNT, HNTC, NICNT, WBC; KJV, NASB, NET, NIV, NRSV], 'human works' [ICC2, NTC], 'good or bad works' [NLT], 'deeds' [AB], 'human deeds' [REB]. The phrase οὐκ ἐξ ἔργων 'not from works' is also translated 'it wasn't because of anything either of them had done' [CEV], 'based...not on anything people do' [GW], 'based...not on anything they had done' [TEV], 'not because of anything he did' [NCV]. This noun denotes that which is done, with possible focus on the energy or effort involved [LN].

c. ἐκ with genitive: 'from' [WBC], 'by' [NET, NIV, NRSV], 'of' [KJV], 'out of' [NICNT], 'because of' [NASB], 'on' [AB], 'based on' [BECNT; GW, TEV], 'based...on' [ICC2, NTC; REB], 'resting on' [HNTC], not explicit [CEV, NLT]. The phrase ἐκ τοῦ καλοῦντος 'from the one calling' is also translated 'he was chosen because he was the one God wanted to call' [NCV].

d. pres. act. participle of καλέω (LN 33.312) (BAGD 2. p. 399): 'to call' [BAGD, BECNT, HNTC, ICC2, LN, NICNT, NTC, WBC; KJV, NASB, NIV, NLT]. The phrase τοῦ καλοῦντος 'the one calling' is also translated 'his call' [AB; NRSV], 'God's call' [GW], 'the call of God' [REB], 'his calling' [NET]. The phrase 'but from the one calling' is translated '(he was the one) God wanted to call' [NCV], 'he calls people' [NLT], '(the Lord said this to show that) he makes his own choices' [CEV], 'God's choice was based on his call' [TEV]. This verb means to urgently invite someone to accept responsibilities for a particular task, implying a new relationship to the one who calls [LN]. This word combines the meaning of the words 'summon' and 'invite' [BAGD].

e. μείζων (LN **67.102**) (BAGD 2a.α. p. 497): 'older' [AB, BAGD, BECNT, LN; NASB, NCV, NET, NIV, TEV], 'older son' [CEV, NLT], 'older child' [GW], 'elder' [ICC2, NTC, WBC; KJV, NRSV, REB], 'greater' [HNTC, NICNT].

f. fut. act. indic. of δουλεύω (LN 35.27) (BAGD 1.a. p. 205): 'to serve' [AB, BECNT, HNTC, ICC2, LN, NICNT, NTC, WBC; all versions except REB], 'to be servant to' [REB], 'to be subjected to' [BAGD]. This verb means to serve, normally in a humble manner and in response to the demands or commands of others [LN].

g. ἐλάσσων (LN **67.116**) (BAGD p. 248): 'younger' [AB, BAGD, BECNT, ICC2, LN, NTC, WBC; KJV, NASB, NCV, NET, NIV, NRSV, REB, TEV], 'the younger one' [CEV, GW], 'your younger son' [NLT], 'the less' [HNTC], 'the lesser' [NICNT].

QUESTION—In what sense does he use the term 'works'?
1. He is referring to actions or deeds in general [AB, BECNT, ICC2, Mor, NICNT, SSA, TH].
2. He is referring to works of the law as a Jewish expression of keeping the covenant [WBC].

9:13 just-as[a] it-is-written,[b] Jacob I-loved,[c] but Esau I-hated.[d]

LEXICON—a. καθώς (LN 64.14) (BAGD p. 387): 'just as' [BAGD, BECNT, LN, NICNT; NASB, NET, NIV], 'as' [NTC, WBC; KJV, NCV, NRSV, TEV], 'even as' [ICC2], 'as again' [HNTC], 'as it stands' [AB], not

explicit [GW, NLT]. The phrase 'just as it is written' is translated 'that's why the Scriptures say' [CEV], 'that accords with the text of scripture' [REB]. This adverb marks similarity in events and states, with the possible implication of something being in accordance with something else [LN].
- b. perf. pass. indic. of γράφω (LN 33.61) (BAGD 2.c. p. 166): 'to be written' [BAGD, LN]. The verb γέγραπται 'it is written' [AB, BECNT, HNTC, ICC2, NICNT, NTC, WBC; KJV, NASB, NET, NIV, NRSV] is also translated 'the Scriptures say' [CEV, GW], 'the Scripture says' [NCV], 'the scripture says' [TEV], 'in the words of the Scriptures' [NLT], '(that accords with) the text of scripture' [REB].
- c. aorist act. indic. of ἀγαπάω (LN 25.43) (BAGD 1.b.α. p. 4): 'to love' [AB, BAGD, BECNT, HNTC, ICC2, LN, NICNT, NTC, WBC; all versions except CEV], 'to like' [CEV]. This aorist verb is translated as perfect: 'I have loved' [NRSV], 'have I loved' [ICC2, WBC; KJV].
- d. aorist act. indic. of μισέω (LN 88.198) (BAGD 1. p. 522): 'to hate' [AB, BAGD, BECNT, HNTC, ICC2, LN, NICNT, NTC, WBC; all versions except CEV, NLT], 'to reject' [NLT]. The phrase 'Jacob I loved, but Esau I hated' is translated 'the Lord liked Jacob more than Esau' [CEV]. This aorist verb is translated as perfect: 'I have hated' [NRSV], 'have I hated' [ICC2, WBC; KJV]. This verb implies aversion and hostility [LN].

QUESTION—What is implied, if anything, by the fact that 'Jacob' precedes the verb ἠγάπησα 'I loved', of which it is the object?
1. Paul has altered the word order of the passage in Malachi for the sake of emphasis [AB, BECNT], stressing that it is Jacob who is chosen by God [BECNT].
2. The change is stylistic, to match the word order of the second clause [NICNT].

QUESTION—What is intended or implied by the term ἐμίσησα 'I have hated'?
'Love' and 'hate' refer to election and rejection [Gdt, ICC1, ICC2, Mor, NAC, NICNT, NTC, TH, WBC]. God has rejected and excluded Esau from his gracious purposes, though, like Ishmael, he is still the object of God's love and care [ICC2]. In this passage 'love' and 'hate' are not emotions but actions of choosing or rejecting [NICNT]. The term 'hate' may have some wrong connotations when used of God [St, TH]. There is an emotional aspect of hating that does not apply to God in all respects [Mor]. God's hate is holy, and does not include malice or vindictiveness [Mu].
1. God did not actually hate Esau; rather, this is a Semitic idiom in which the comparison is strengthened by stating it absolutely [NAC]. It is a hyperbole, meaning that God loved him less, and did not choose him [AB, Ho, SSA]. It is a Hebrew way of showing preference for one over another [St, WBC].
2. Although the idiom in Hebrew means that God preferred Jacob to Esau, Paul may have taken it literally [HNTC]. There is an emotional component here, with moral sympathy toward Jacob and moral antipathy

toward Esau [Gdt]. God is jealous for his own honor with a holy hatred that includes disapproval, disfavor, and displeasure, with a certain degree of vehemence [Mu].

QUESTION—Is Paul discussing the fate of individuals or only of the role of nations in salvation history?
1. He is speaking both of corporate and individual election [BECNT, Gdt, Ho, Mu, NAC, NICNT, NTC, St]. His emphasis, however, is more on their destiny as individuals [NAC, NICNT].
2. He is speaking in terms of the roles that nations play in salvation history [AB, Gdt, ICC2, Mor]. It does not refer to being chosen for salvation [Gdt, ICC1, Mor], but for service [Mor], or to higher privilege [ICC1]. In the Bible it is common when speaking of nations to find an oscillation between individual and corporate personality; here Paul focuses on the two nations [TNTC].

DISCOURSE UNIT—9:14–29 [HNTC, ICC1, ICC2]. The topic is God's sovereignty [HNTC], the rejection of Israel not inconsistent with the divine justice [ICC1], unbelief and disobedience of men embraced within divine mercy [ICC2].

DISCOURSE UNIT—9:14–23 [AB, NICNT, WBC]. The topic is God's sovereign freedom even uses indocility to his purpose [AB], objections answered: the freedom and purpose of God [NICNT], those not chosen are still within the purpose of God [WBC].

DISCOURSE UNIT—9:14–18 [Mor]. The topic is God's purpose is mercy.

9:14 What then shall-we-say?[a] Not[b] injustice[c] with God? Never may-it-be![d]

LEXICON—a. The sentence Τί οὖν ἐροῦμεν 'What then shall we say' [AB, BECNT, HNTC, ICC2, NICNT, NTC, WBC; NIV], is also translated 'What shall we say then' [KJV, NASB, NET], 'What shall we say to that' [REB], 'What then are we to say' [NRSV], 'So what should we say about this' [NCV]. The clauses Τί οὖν ἐροῦμεν; μὴ ἀδικία παρὰ τῷ θεῷ; 'What then shall we say? Not injustice with God?' are translated as one clause: 'Shall we say, then, that God is unjust?' [TEV], 'Are we saying that God is unfair?' [CEV], 'Are we saying then that God is unfair?' [NLT], 'What can we say—that God is unfair?' [GW]. This question is evidence of Paul's use of the diatribe question-and-answer rhetorical style [BECNT, HNTC, NICNT].
b. μή (LN 69.15) (BAGD C.1. p. 517): This word introduces a question for which a negative answer is expected [BAGD, LN]. This function is represented in translation as 'There is no…is there?' [NICNT, NTC, WBC; NASB], 'God is not…is he?' [BECNT], not explicit [AB, HNTC, ICC2; CEV, GW, KJV, NCV, NET, NIV, NLT, NRSV, REB, TEV].
c. ἀδικία (LN 88.21) (BAGD 2. p. 18): 'injustice' [BAGD, NTC, WBC; NASB, NET, NRSV, REB], 'unrighteousness' [HNTC, ICC2, LN, NICNT; KJV]. This noun is translated as an adjective pertaining to God:

'unjust' [AB; NIV, TEV], 'unrighteous' [BECNT], 'unfair' [CEV, GW, NCV, NLT].
d. aorist mid. (deponent = act.) optative of γίνομαι (LN 13.107) (BAGD I.3.a. p. 158): 'to come to be' [LN], 'to happen' [BAGD, LN]. The phrase μὴ γένοιτο 'Never may it be' [NASB], is also translated 'Certainly not' [AB, BECNT, WBC; CEV, REB], 'Absolutely not' [NET], 'No, indeed' [HNTC], 'God forbid' [ICC2; KJV], 'By no means' [NICNT; NRSV], 'Not at all' [NTC; NIV, TEV], 'In no way' [NCV], 'Of course not' [NLT], 'That's unthinkable' [GW]. The following punctuate this with an exclamation mark: AB, ICC2, NTC, WBC; CEV, GW, NASB, NET, NIV, NLT, NRSV, REB. See this expression also at 3:4, 6, 31, 6:2, and 6:15.

QUESTION—What would be the nature of the injustice or unrighteousness?
1. Paul is asking whether it might be unjust for God to deal with people in a way that is based on his own choice, as opposed to their works [Gdt, ICC1, ICC2]. Paul is raising the question of whether or not it is unjust of God to deal differently with unborn twin infants, showing favor to one and not to the other [HNTC]. He is asking if it is unfair to Esau for God to choose Jacob [NAC]. He is raising the question of whether God is just when judged by the standard of faithfulness to his own character [NICNT]. He is raising the question of whether or not election is unjust [Ho, SSA, St]. He is saying that it is not unjust for God to condemn some just because he shows mercy to others, since he doesn't owe mercy to anyone [Mor].
2. The question is not a question of justice, but of *righteousness*, that is, whether or not God has been faithful to his covenant promise [WBC]. Paul is asking what should be said about God's promise and gracious election, and about how God is dealing with Israel compared with how he dealt with them in the past [AB].
3. The question may arise as to whether Paul is doing injustice to God by his reasoning about God's sovereignty from 9:6–13 [NTC].

9:15 For[a] he-says to Moses, I-will-have-mercy[b] on-whom I-have-mercy[c] and I-will-have-compassion[d] on-whom I-have-compassion.[e]

LEXICON—a. γάρ (LN 89.23): 'for' [AB, BECNT, HNTC, ICC2, LN, NICNT, NTC, WBC; KJV, NASB, NET, NIV, NLT, NRSV, TEV], 'because' [LN], 'for example' [GW], not explicit [CEV, NCV, REB].
b. fut. act. indic. of ἐλεέω (LN 88.76) (BAGD p. 249): 'to have mercy on' [BAGD, BECNT, HNTC, ICC2, LN, NICNT, NTC, WBC; KJV, NASB, NET, NIV, NRSV, TEV], 'to show mercy' [AB, BAGD, LN; NLT, REB], 'to show kindness' [NCV], 'to be kind' [GW], 'to have pity' [CEV], 'to be merciful toward' [LN]. This verb means show kindness or concern for someone in serious need [LN].
c. pres. act. subj. of ἐλεέω. The phrase ὃν ἂν ἐλεῶ 'on whom I have mercy' [ICC2, NTC, WBC; NASB, NET, NIV, NRSV], is also translated 'on

whomever I have mercy' [BECNT, NICNT], 'on whomsoever I do have mercy' [HNTC], 'to whom I will show mercy' [REB], 'on whom I will have mercy' [KJV], 'to whomever I will' [AB], 'on anyone he wants to' [CEV], 'to anyone I want to' [GW], 'to anyone I choose' [NLT], 'to anyone to whom I want to show kindness' [NCV], 'on anyone I wish' [TEV].

d. fut. act. indic. of οἰκτίρω (LN **88.80**) (BAGD p. 562): 'to have compassion on' [AB, BECNT, NICNT, NTC; KJV, NASB, NRSV], 'to show compassion' [BAGD, LN, WBC; NLT], 'to have mercy' [**LN**], 'to have mercy on' [CEV, NET, NIV, TEV], 'to show mercy' [NCV], 'to be merciful' [GW], 'to pity' [HNTC], 'to have pity on' [ICC2; REB]. This verb means to show mercy and concern, with the implication of sensitivity and compassion [LN].

e. pres. act. subj. of οἰκτίρω. The phrase ὃν ἂν οἰκτίρω 'on whom I have compassion' [NTC; NASB, NET, NIV, NRSV], is also translated 'on whomever I have compassion' [BECNT, NICNT], 'on whom I will have compassion' [KJV], 'to whom I show compassion' [WBC], 'on whom I will have pity' [REB], 'on whom I have pity' [ICC2], 'whomsoever I do pity' [HNTC], 'on whomever I will' [AB], 'to anyone to whom I want to show mercy' [NCV], 'to anyone I want to' [GW], 'on anyone I wish' [TEV], 'to anyone I choose' [NLT], 'on anyone he wants to' [CEV].

QUESTION—What relationship is indicated by γάρ 'for'?

It indicates grounds for his assertion in 9:14 concerning God's justice [BECNT, Ho, ICC1, ICC2, Mor, Mu, NICNT, SSA, WBC]. It introduces the reason that God is not, in fact, unrighteous, which is that he is sovereign, and is therefore free to show mercy to whomever he wishes [BECNT, Ho]. It introduces a summary of all that has been said in 9:6–13 about God's gracious mercy [AB]. He will now explain how election and rejection relate to God's truth and righteousness [WBC].

QUESTION—What difference, if any, is there between 'have mercy' and 'have compassion'?

1. There is very little difference [Mor, Mu, SSA], but the use of both of them together adds emphasis to Paul's statement [Mor, SSA].
2. The first emphasizes the internal feeling, and the second the outward expression of or action about that internal feeling [Gdt, Ho, ICC1].

9:16 Therefore[a] then[b] not of-the-one willing[c] nor of-the-one running,[d] but of-God the-one having-mercy.[e]

LEXICON—a. ἄρα (LN 89.46) (BAGD 4. p. 104): 'so' [BAGD], 'so then' [LN], 'consequently, as a result' [BAGD, LN].

b. οὖν (LN 89.50): 'then' [LN], 'so, consequently' [BAGD, LN], 'therefore' [LN]. The phrase ἄρα οὖν 'therefore then' is translated 'so' [AB; NCV, NLT, NRSV], 'therefore' [BECNT; GW], 'so then' [HNTC, ICC2, NTC, WBC; KJV, NASB, NET, TEV], 'therefore' [NICNT; NIV], 'then' [CEV], 'thus' [LN].

c. pres. act. participle of θέλω (LN 25.1) (BAGD 2.p. 355): 'to will' [BAGD, BECNT, NICNT, WBC; KJV, NASB], 'to exercise his will' [HNTC], 'to wish' [BAGD, LN], 'to want, to desire' [LN], not explicit [AB]. The phrase τοῦ θέλοντος 'of the one willing' is also translated 'human willing' [AB], 'man's willing' [ICC2], '(man's) will' [NTC], 'a person's desire' [GW], 'man's desire' [NIV], 'human desire' [NET], 'human will' [NRSV, REB], 'what people want' [CEV, NCV], 'what man wants' [TEV], 'we can neither choose it' [NLT]. This verb means to desire to have or experience something [LN].

d. pres. act. participle of τρέχω (LN **68.61**) (BAGD 2.a. p. 825): 'to run' [BAGD], 'to attempt to do' [LN], 'to strive to advance' [BAGD]. The phrase τοῦ τρέχοντος 'the one running' is also translated 'the one who runs' [BECNT, WBC], 'the person who runs' [NTC], 'the man who runs' [NASB], 'him that runneth' [KJV], 'a man's running' [ICC2], 'like an athlete who runs to his goal' [HNTC], 'human effort' [AB; REB], 'a person's/man's effort' [GW, NIV], 'human exertion' [NET, NRSV], 'man's exertion' [NTC], 'what people try to do' [NCV], 'what we humans do' [TEV]. The phrase οὐδὲ τοῦ τρέχοντος 'nor of the one running' is also translated 'nor can we work for it' [NLT]. This verb means to try to do something [LN].

e. pres. act. participle of ἐλεάω (a variant spelling of ἐλεέω) (LN 88.76) (BAGD p. 249): 'to have mercy on, to show mercy' [BAGD, LN], 'to be merciful toward' [LN]. The phrase τοῦ ἐλεῶντος θεοῦ 'of God the one having mercy' is also translated 'on God's mercy' [AB, NTC; CEV, GW, NIV, REB, TEV], 'on the merciful God' [HNTC], 'on God who has mercy' [NASB], 'on God who shows mercy' [NET, NRSV], 'of God's showing mercy' [ICC2], 'from God who shows mercy' [BECNT], 'of the God who shows mercy' [NICNT], 'of God who shows mercy' [WBC], 'of God that sheweth mercy' [KJV], 'God will choose the one to whom he decides to show mercy' [NCV], 'so it is God who decides to show mercy' [NLT]. This verb means to show kindness or concern for someone in serious need [LN].

QUESTION—What relationship is indicated by the phrase ἄρα οὖν 'therefore then'?

It indicates a conclusion to be drawn from the Exodus passage just quoted in 9:15 [BECNT, Gdt, HNTC, Ho, ICC1, ICC2, Mor, NICNT, TH, WBC], and also repeats what has been said in 9:11–12 [BECNT, WBC]. If God's mercy and compassion are based entirely on his own choice, then it flows logically that it is not based on what human beings want or on what they do [Ho].

QUESTION—What is it that is not a matter of willing or running, and that is the implied subject this sentence?

The subject is God's granting of mercy [HNTC, ICC1, ICC2, Mor, Mu, TNTC]. It is his mercy in choosing certain people for salvation [NICNT]. It is God's election [SSA, TH, WBC]. The subject is God's election and mercy that bring salvation and everlasting life [NTC]. The subject is attaining

God's favor and being admitted to his kingdom [Ho]. It is the receiving of God's saving promises [BECNT]. The subject is God's gifts, and particularly the gift of salvation [Gdt].

QUESTION—What relationship is indicated by the genitive participial phrases 'of the one wishing' and 'of the one running'?

They indicate the reason for God's mercy; God's bestowal of mercy does not originate in human plan or effort [AB, HNTC, ICC2, Mor, NICNT]. God is merciful to people simply because he is merciful [ICC2]. The reason God is merciful to some is that he has chosen to do so (9:15) [SSA], he has elected them [BECNT, Ho], and he has called them [BECNT].

QUESTION—What is meant by the metaphor of 'running'?

'Willing' is the desire or purpose to do something, and 'running' is carrying out that desire [NICNT]. It speaks generally of human effort [BECNT, NAC, TH], of striving [HNTC, St], of exertion [Mor, Mu, NTC]. It speaks of day to day conduct, and in particular to the lifestyle of a devout Jewish person [WBC]. The two together speak of all that a person is capable of doing [NICNT, WBC], of human motivation and action [WBC]. It refers to good works that would presumably be meritorious [Gdt], of trying hard to be acceptable to God [SSA].

9:17 For[a] the scripture says to Pharaoh[b] that[c] For this-very-reason[d] I-raised-up[e] you

LEXICON—a. γάρ (LN 89.23): 'for' [AB, BECNT, HNTC, ICC2, LN, NICNT, NTC, WBC; KJV, NASB, NET, NIV, NLT, NRSV, REB, TEV], 'because' [LN], 'for example' [GW], not explicit [CEV, NCV].

b. Φαραώ (LN 93.373) (BAGD 853): 'Pharaoh' [AB, BAGD, BECNT, HNTC, ICC2, LN, NICNT, NTC, WBC; GW, KJV, NASB, NET, NIV, NLT, NRSV, REB]. The title 'Pharaoh' is translated 'king of Egypt' [CEV, NCV, TEV]. This is a title used as a proper name of the Egyptian king [BAGD, LN].

c. ὅτι (LN 90.21): 'that' [AB, HNTC, ICC2, LN, NTC], not explicit [BECNT, NICNT, WBC; all versions except KJV]. This conjunction may be used to introduce direct discourse, in which case it would not be rendered in English but would be represented by quotation marks [BAGD (2. p. 589)].

d. εἰς αὐτὸ τοῦτο: This phrase is translated 'for this very reason' [AB, BECNT, NICNT], 'for this very purpose' [HNTC, ICC2, NTC; NASB, NET, NIV, REB], 'for this purpose' [WBC], 'for the very purpose of' [NLT, NRSV], 'even for this same purpose' [KJV], 'for this reason' [GW, NCV], not explicit [CEV, TEV].

e. aorist act. indic. of ἐξεγείρω (LN **13.83, 87.38**) (BAGD 4. p. 273): 'to raise up' [AB, BECNT, HNTC, ICC2, LN (87.38), NICNT, NTC, WBC; KJV, NASB, NET, NIV, NRSV, REB], 'to cause to be' [LN (13.83)], 'to cause to appear, to bring into being' [BAGD]. The phrase ἐξήγειρά σε 'I raised up you' is also translated 'I let you become king' [CEV], 'I made you king' [NCV, TEV], 'I have appointed you' [NLT], 'I have put you here' [GW]. This aorist tense verb is translated as perfect tense: 'I have raised' [NICNT; NET, NRSV, REB], 'have I raised' [AB, ICC2, NTC; KJV], 'I have appointed' [NLT]. This verb can mean to cause to come into existence [LN (13.83)], or to cause someone to have a higher position or status [LN (87.38)].

QUESTION—What relationship is indicated by γάρ 'for'?
1. It introduces additional grounds for his assertion in 9:14 that God is righteous [BECNT, Ho, ICC2, Mor, Mu, NICNT, SSA], and is parallel with the γάρ 'for' in 9:15 [ICC2]. He is still dealing with the issue of God's justice [Ho].
2. It introduces a further development in 9:17–18 of what he has been saying in 9:16 [WBC].
3. It introduces an example of the way God hardens [Gdt].

QUESTION—What is the meaning of the verb phrase ἐξήγειρά σε 'I have raised you up'?
1. God raised Pharaoh up in the sense of causing him to be king [BECNT, Ho, ICC1, ICC2, Mor, Mu, NAC, NICNT, SSA, TH]. God appointed Pharaoh to this important role in salvation history [NICNT]. His appearance in history was due to God's will [BECNT, Ho, ICC2, Mor, Mu]. God brought Pharaoh to this particular time, place, and position [Gdt], to this stage in history [St]. For his own purposes God caused Pharaoh to appear at that point in history and in that position [Ho]. He raised him to his position as king and preserved him despite his disobedience [TNTC].
2. God spared Pharaoh from death during the previous plagues, such that he remained or stood until that point [NTC].

that[a] I-might-show[b] in[c] you my power[d] and that my name might-be-proclaimed[e] in[f] all[g] the earth.[h]

LEXICON—a. ὅπως (LN 89.59) (BAGD 2.a.α. p. 577): 'that' [AB, HNTC, ICC2, NTC; KJV, NET, NIV], 'in order that' [BAGD, BECNT, WBC], 'so that' [LN, NICNT; CEV], 'in order to' [LN; TEV], 'to (with infinitive)' [GW, NASB, NCV, REB], not explicit [NLT, NRSV].
  b. aorist mid. subj. of ἐνδείκνυμαι (LN 28.51) (BAGD 1. p. 262): 'to show' [BAGD, BECNT, ICC2, LN; CEV, KJV, NCV, TEV], 'to demonstrate' [BAGD, HNTC, LN, NICNT, WBC; GW, NASB, NET], 'to display' [AB, NTC; NIV], 'to exhibit' [REB], 'to cause to be known' [LN]. This verb is translated as a participle: 'of displaying' [NLT], 'of showing' [NRSV]. This verb means to cause to be made known, with possible emphasis upon the means [LN].
  c. ἐν with dative (LN 90.6): 'in' [BECNT, HNTC, ICC2; KJV, NASB, NCV, NET, NIV, NLT, NRSV, REB], 'through' [AB, NICNT, NTC, WBC; GW], 'by, from' [LN]. The phrase 'that I might show in you my

power' is also translated 'so that I could show you my power' [CEV], 'in order to use you to show my power' [TEV].
d. δύναμις (LN 76.1, 76.7) (BAGD 1. p. 207): 'power' [AB, BAGD, BECNT, HNTC, ICC2, LN (76.1), NICNT, NTC, WBC; all versions], 'might' [BAGD], 'mighty deed, miracle' [LN (76.7)]. This verb can mean the potentiality to exert force in performing some function [LN (76.1)], or a deed or act manifesting great power, with the implication of some supernatural force [LN (76.7)].
e. aorist pass. subj. of διαγγέλλω (LN 33.207) (BAGD 1. p. 182): 'to be proclaimed' [AB, BECNT, HNTC, ICC2, LN, NICNT, NTC, WBC; NASB, NET, NIV, NRSV], 'to be proclaimed far and wide' [BAGD], 'to be declared' [KJV], 'to be praised' [CEV]. The phrase 'that my name might be proclaimed' is also translated 'to spread my name' [GW], 'to spread my fame' [NLT, REB, TEV], 'so that my name will be talked about' [NCV]. This verb means to announce extensively and publicly [LN].
f. ἐν with dative (LN 83.13): 'in' [BECNT, HNTC, ICC2, LN, NICNT, NTC, WBC; NCV, NET, NIV, NRSV], 'over' [AB; REB, TEV], 'throughout' [GW, KJV, NASB, NLT], 'on' [CEV].
g. πᾶς (LN **63.2**) (BAGD 1.c.α. p. 631): 'all' [AB, BAGD, BECNT, HNTC, ICC2, LN, NICNT, NTC, WBC; KJV, NCV, NET, NIV, NRSV, REB], 'the whole' [BAGD; NASB, TEV], not explicit [GW, NLT]. The clause 'that my name might be proclaimed in all the earth' is translated 'so that I could...be praised by all people on earth' [CEV]. This adjective describes something as being entire or whole, with focus on the totality [LN].
h. γῆ (LN 1.39): 'earth' [AB, BECNT, HNTC, ICC2, LN, NICNT, NTC, WBC; all versions except TEV], 'world' [LN; TEV]. This noun denotes the surface of the earth as the dwelling place of mankind, in contrast with the heavens above and the world below [LN].

QUESTION—What is the power referred to here?

It is God's saving power [HNTC, ICC2, NICNT, WBC]. Paul uses the term here in the same sense he used it in 1:16, which is God's power for salvation [ICC2]. It is God's power for judgment, as expressed against Pharaoh and the Egyptians [NTC]. It is the power God showed in all he did to the Egyptians before the exodus [SSA]. It is God's saving power as well as his power to judge his enemies [BECNT, Gdt, Mor, NICNT]. It is God's saving power, by which he struck Pharaoh and Egypt and delivered Israel [Mu, NAC].

QUESTION—What is meant by God showing his power ἐν σοί 'in you'?

1. The preposition ἐν indicates that God was using his dealings with Pharaoh as a means to show his power to everyone [AB, ICC2, NICNT, NTC, SSA, TH, WBC; GW, TEV]: I will demonstrate *through* you my power. God showed his power by the miracles he worked in opposing Pharaoh [SSA].

2. The preposition ἐν indicates the one who experiences God's action [CEV]: I might show you my power.

QUESTION—What does 'name' signify here?

It represents God's fame or reputation, or the power he exercises [SSA]. It is his greatness [NTC], or his glory [Mor]. It parallels and overlaps with δύναμις 'power', which is his power to save his people, but also speaks of his merciful character [WBC]. It represents God's self-revelation of his own character and glory [ICC2]. It is his character [BECNT, NAC]. In this instance it is the news of God's great act of deliverance [HNTC], his character as the one who delivered Israel from its bondage [NAC]. God revealed his name as the Merciful One in 9:15 and in this verse where 'power' and 'name' are used in parallel and overlapping statements, the proclamation of God's name refers to God's powerful defense of his people when they were threatened by the mighty Pharaoh [WBC]. It is knowledge about God generally [TH].

9:18 Therefore then[a] he-has-mercy on-whom he-wills,[b] and/but[c] whom he-wishes he-hardens.[d]

LEXICON—a. The phrase ἄρα οὖν 'therefore then' is translated 'therefore' [AB, BECNT, NICNT; GW, KJV, NIV], 'thus' [REB], 'so then' [HNTC, ICC2, NTC, WBC; NASB, NET, NRSV, TEV], 'so' [NCV], 'so you see' [NLT], not explicit [CEV].

b. pres. act. indic. of θέλω (LN 25.1) (BAGD 2. p. 355): 'to will' [AB, BAGD, BECNT, HNTC, ICC2, NTC, WBC; KJV], 'to wish' [BAGD, LN, NICNT; TEV], 'to choose' [NET, NLT, NRSV, REB], 'to want' [GW, NCV, NIV], 'to desire' [NASB]. The sentence 'Therefore then he has mercy on whom he wills, and/but whom he wills he hardens' is also translated 'Everything depends on what God decides to do, and he can either have pity on people or make them stubborn' [CEV]. This verb means to desire to have or experience something [LN].

c. δέ (LN 89.94, 89.124): 'and' [AB, BECNT, HNTC, ICC2, LN (89.94), NICNT, NTC; KJV, NASB, NCV, NET, NIV, NLT, NRSV, TEV], 'but' [LN (89.124), WBC; REB], 'either…or' [CEV], not explicit [GW].

d. pres. act. indic. of σκληρύνω (LN **88.226**) (BAGD 1.b. p. 756): 'to harden' [BAGD, BECNT, HNTC, ICC2, NICNT, NTC, WBC; KJV, NASB, NET, NIV], 'to harden the heart of' [AB; NRSV], 'to make stubborn' [**LN**; CEV, GW, NCV, REB, TEV], 'to make obstinate' [LN]. The phrase ὃν δὲ θέλει σκληρύνει 'whom he wills he hardens' is also translated 'he chooses to harden the hearts of others so they refuse to listen' [NLT]. This verb means to cause to be stubborn and obstinate, especially with regard to the truth [LN].

QUESTION—What relationship is indicated by the phrase ἄρα οὖν 'therefore then'?

It introduces Paul's conclusion to the entire paragraph from 9:14 through 9:17 [BECNT, Ho]. It introduces the principle Paul that underlies what Paul has just been saying, which is that God's will is what is most important [Mor]. It introduces a summary of 9:15 concerning God's sovereignty and freedom in his dealings with human beings to accomplish his purposes [AB]. It introduces a conclusion to be drawn from 9:17, which is closely related to the thought of 9:15 [Gdt, ICC2, SSA]. It introduces a summary of the argument of 9:17 [ICC1]. It introduces a second conclusion drawn from 9:15, and is parallel to and coordinate with 9:16 [WBC].

QUESTION—What is meant by 'hardening'?

It is to make someone stubborn [AB, Ho, SSA, St, TH, WBC], obstinate [AB, TH], unyielding, and unresponsive [WBC]. It is to make a person spiritually insensitive [BECNT, NICNT], insensitive in conscience and mentally blind [Ho], inflexible, and unable to be saved [BECNT]. It means to turn away from what is true, just, and useful to that which is evil [Gdt].

QUESTION—What is Paul saying about God's role in the hardening of Pharaoh's heart?

1. God hardens those who first harden themselves [AB, Gdt, Mor, NAC, NTC, St]. The way God deals with a person takes into account his knowledge of the moral condition of the person [Gdt].
2. God's hardening precedes and causes the hardening of Pharaoh's heart [BECNT, Ho, NICNT]. Paul is clearly stressing God's initiative in this hardening [NICNT, WBC]. God did not make Pharaoh wicked, he only withheld grace from him that would have changed him, giving him up to the wickedness that was in his own heart [Ho, Mu].

QUESTION—Does this hardening apply to the salvation of individuals, or only with reference to an individual's role in salvation history?

1. It is relevant to the salvation of individuals, as well as to their role in salvation history [NICNT]. Paul uses singular forms such as ὅv 'whom' throughout the discussion; also, the contrasts of hardening and mercy in 9:18 are antithetical, with no suggestion that someone who has been hardened receives God's mercy, so that those who died without Christ have no hope [BECNT]. Pharaoh's hardness of heart led to everlasting punishment [NTC].
2. It is relevant to their role in salvation history [HNTC, ICC2], but not to their own final spiritual condition, as both the hardening and his having mercy are aspects of the outworking of his greater purpose of showing mercy [ICC2]. Paul is not focusing on eternal reprobation, and his argument here should be seen within the larger context of his discussion of God's mercy [WBC].

DISCOURSE UNIT—9:19–29 [Mor, NTC; CEV, NRSV, TEV]. The topic is God's wrath and mercy [Mor, NTC; NRSV], God's anger and mercy [CEV, TEV].

9:19 Then[a] you-will-say to-me, Why[b] does-he-find-fault[c] still?[d] For who has-resisted[e] his will?[f]

TEXT—Some manuscripts include another οὖν 'then' after τί 'Why'. It is included in brackets by GNT but not mentioned in the critical apparatus. It is included and translated 'then' by AB, NICNT; NCV, NIV, NRSV, REB. NICNT accepts it as a legitimate textual reading, but its inclusion by the others may be for stylistic rather than textual reasons.

LEXICON—a. οὖν (LN 89.50): 'then' [ICC2, LN, NICNT, NTC, WBC; KJV, NASB, NET, NRSV, REB], 'well then' [NLT], 'so' [LN; NCV], 'so then' [LN], 'therefore' [AB, BECNT], 'but' [TEV], 'of course' [HNTC], 'accordingly' [LN], not explicit [CEV, GW, NIV]. This particle marks result, often implying the conclusion of a process of reasoning [LN].

b. τί (LN 92.15): 'why' [AB, BECNT, HNTC, ICC2, LN, NICNT, NTC, WBC; all versions except CEV, TEV], 'how' [CEV, TEV].

c. pres. mid. (deponent = act.) indic. of μέμφομαι (LN **33.431**) (BAGD p. 502): 'to find fault' [AB, BAGD, BECNT, NICNT, NTC, WBC; GW, KJV, NASB, NET, NRSV, REB, TEV], 'to blame' [BAGD, ICC2, **LN**; CEV, NCV, NIV, NLT], 'to accuse' [LN], 'to make complaint' [HNTC]. The question 'Why then does he find fault still?' is translated 'Then why does God blame us for our sins?' [NCV], 'Why does God blame people for not responding?' [NLT], 'Why does God still find fault with anyone?' [GW], 'How can God find fault with anyone?' [TEV]. This verb means to bring accusation against someone on the basis that the person in question is clearly to blame [LN].

d. ἔτι (LN **89.135**) (BAGD 2.c. p. 316): 'still' [AB, BAGD, BECNT, HNTC, ICC2, NICNT, NTC, WBC; GW, NASB, NET, NIV, NRSV], 'yet' [KJV], 'nevertheless' [LN], not explicit [CEV, NCV, NLT, REB, TEV].

e. perf. act. indic. of ἀνθίστημι (LN 39.18) (BAGD 2. p. 67): 'to resist' [AB, BAGD, HNTC, LN, WBC; GW, KJV, NET, NRSV, REB, TEV], 'to fight' [NCV], 'to oppose' [BAGD], 'to withstand' [BAGD]. This perfect tense verb is translated as present: 'resists' [BECNT, NICNT; NASB, NIV], 'is resisting' [ICC2, NTC]. The clause 'For who has resisted his will?' is translated '(How can God blame us,) if he makes us behave in the way he wants us to?' [CEV], 'Haven't they simply done what he makes them do?' [NLT], 'Who can resist whatever God wants to do?' [GW]. This verb means to resist by actively opposing pressure or power [LN].

f. βούλημα (LN **30.57**, 25.4) (BAGD p. 146): 'will' [AB, BAGD, BECNT, HNTC, ICC2, LN (25.4), NICNT, NTC, WBC; all versions except CEV, GW, NLT], 'plan' [**LN** (30.57)], 'purpose' [LN (30.57)]. This noun denotes that which has been purposed and planned [LN].

QUESTION—Is Ἐρεῖς μοι οὖν 'Then you-will-say to-me' to be understood as a question or as a statement?
1. It is a statement: You will say to me [BECNT, HNTC, ICC2, NICNT, NTC, SSA; all versions]. Paul continues in the diatribe style [AB, BECNT, NICNT, SSA, WBC].
2. It is a question: Will you say to me? [AB].

QUESTION—How is the perfect tense of ἀνθέστηκεν 'has resisted' to be understood?
It is to be understood as having a present tense meaning: Who ever resists it? [AB, BECNT, Gdt, Ho, ICC1, ICC2, Mu, WBC; NASB, NIV]. The perfect is 'gnomic', stating what is always the case [BECNT, NICNT]. It is the same as saying, 'Who *can* resist' [Gdt, HNTC, Ho; GW, NCV, NRSV, REB, TEV].

9:20 On-the-contrary[a] O man,[b] who are you the-one talking-back[c] to God?

LEXICON—a. μενοῦνγε (LN **89.128**) (BAGD p. 503): 'on the contrary' [BAGD, BECNT, LN, NICNT, WBC; NASB], 'but' [AB, NTC; CEV, NET, NIV, NRSV, TEV], 'yes, but' [HNTC], 'nay but' [KJV], 'nay, rather' [ICC2], 'No, don't say that' [NLT], not explicit [GW, NCV, REB]. This particle is a relatively emphatic marker of contrast [LN].
b. The phrase ὦ ἄνθρωπε 'O man' [BECNT, ICC2, NICNT, NTC; KJV, NASB, NIV], is also translated 'man' [WBC], 'a human being' [NRSV], 'a mere human being' [AB; NET, NLT], 'my dear sir' [HNTC], 'my friend' [CEV, TEV], 'you are only human' [NCV], not explicit [GW, REB].
c. pres. mid. (deponent = act.) participle of ἀνταποκρίνομαι (LN **33.413**) (BAGD p. 73): 'to answer back to' [AB, BAGD, BECNT, HNTC, NICNT, WBC; NASB], 'to answer God back' [ICC2; REB], 'to talk back to' [NTC; GW, NET, NIV, TEV], 'to reply against' [KJV], 'to question' [CEV], 'to argue with' [NLT, NRSV], 'to criticize in return' [LN]. The rhetorical question 'who are you the one talking back to God?' is translated as a statement: 'human beings have no right to question God' [NCV]. This verb means to answer with disapproval [LN].

QUESTION—What is implied by the question ὦ ἄνθρωπε, μενοῦνγε σὺ τίς εἶ 'On the contrary, who are you O man'?
The fact that 'O man' comes first in the sentence and τῷ θεῷ 'to God' comes last indicates that they stand in contrast to one another [Gdt, ICC2, NAC, NICNT, WBC]. God the creator cannot be judged by human creatures, as limited as their knowledge is [AB]. It emphasizes the fact that an objector is merely human and subordinate [NICNT], absolutely inferior to the creator [Gdt]. There is an emphatic contrast between human weakness and ignorance on the one hand and the majesty of God on the other [Mu]. The vocative ὦ ἄνθρωπε shows that the very question is presumptuous [BECNT], and σύ is emphatic [BECNT, Mu, NICNT].

QUESTION—What relationship is indicated by μενοῦνγε 'On the contrary'?
It indicates argumentation [BECNT, Mu]. It is a strong corrective [AB, ICC1, Mor, Mu, NICNT]. It introduces a repudiation of what has been said [Ho]. It indicates contrast and emphasis [SSA], and antithesis [WBC]. It is an intensifier: *more certainly still* [Gdt].

QUESTION—What is implied in the use of the verb ἀνταποκρίνομαι 'talking back'?
It indicates disputing and resisting [BECNT], contradicting [Mor], contention [NICNT, WBC].

The thing-formed[a] will- not -say to the-one forming,[b] Why did- you -make[c] me thus?[d]

LEXICON—a. πλάσμα (LN **58.12**) (BAGD p. 666): 'the thing formed' [BECNT; KJV], 'what is formed' [BAGD, LN; NIV], 'the thing molded' [ICC2; NASB], 'what is molded' [AB, NTC; NET, NRSV], 'that which is molded' [BAGD, NICNT], 'the thing made' [WBC], 'the thing that was created' [NLT], 'the model' [HNTC], 'the clay' [CEV], 'a clay pot' [TEV], 'the pot' [REB], 'an object' [GW, NCV]. This noun denotes that which is formed or molded [LN]. This word is found only here in the NT.

b. aorist act. participle of πλάσσω (LN **58.11**) (BAGD 1.a. p. 666): 'to form' [BAGD, BECNT, **LN**; KJV, NIV], 'to mold' [BAGD, ICC2, LN; NRSV], 'to make' [NCV, TEV], 'to create' [NLT]. The phrase 'the one forming' is translated as a noun '(its) molder' [AB, NTC], '(its) maker' [WBC; GW], 'the molder' [NICNT; NASB, NET], 'the modeler' [HNTC], 'the potter' [CEV, REB]. This verb means to give a particular form to something [LN].

c. aorist act. indic. of ποιέω (LN 42.29) (BAGD I.1.a.α.. p. 680): 'to make' [AB, BAGD, BECNT, HNTC, ICC2, LN, NICNT, NTC, WBC; all versions except CEV], 'to fashion' [LN], 'to shape' [CEV]. This verb means to produce something new, with the implication of using materials already in existence [LN].

d. οὕτως (LN 61.9) (BAGD 1.b. p. 597): 'thus' [BAGD, ICC2, LN, NTC, WBC; KJV], 'like this' [AB, HNTC; all versions except CEV, KJV], 'in this way' [LN, NICNT], 'this way' [BECNT], 'in this manner' [BAGD]. This sentence is translated 'Does the clay have the right to ask the potter why he shaped it the way he did?' [CEV].

QUESTION—Why would it not say this?
This is a rhetorical question that makes an emphatic negative statement and it means that it wouldn't have the right to criticize the one who made it [SSA]. A potter has absolute power over his clay to do what he wants [ICC1].

9:21 Or does- not the potter[a] -have authority[b] (over) the clay[c] to make[d] from[e] the same lump[f]

LEXICON—a. κεραμεύς (LN **6.129**) (BAGD p. 428): 'potter' [AB, BAGD, BECNT, HNTC, ICC2, LN, NICNT, NTC, WBC; all versions except

TEV], 'the man who makes the pots' [TEV]. This noun denotes one who makes earthenware vessels [LN].
b. ἐξουσία (LN 37.13, 37.35) (BAGD 1. p. 278): 'authority over' [BECNT, NICNT], 'power over' [KJV], 'right over' [HNTC, ICC2, WBC; NASB, NRSV], 'right' [AB, BAGD, NTC; CEV, NET, NIV, NLT, TEV], 'right to control' [LN (37.35)], 'control' [LN (37.13)]. The phrase ἐξουσίαν τοῦ πηλοῦ 'right over the clay' is translated 'the right to do whatever he wants with his clay' [GW], 'make anything he wants to make' [NCV], 'do what he likes with the clay. Is he not free to make...?' [REB]. This noun denotes a state of control over someone or something [LN (37.13)], or the right to control or govern over [LN (37.35)].
c. πηλός (LN **2.18**) (BAGD 1.a. p. 656): 'clay' [BAGD, BECNT, HNTC, ICC2, LN, NICNT, WBC; GW, KJV, NASB, NRSV, REB, TEV], not explicit [AB, NTC; CEV, NCV, NET, NIV, NLT]. This word is conflated with φύραμα 'lump' and translated 'lump of clay' [AB, NTC; CEV, GW, NET, NIV, NLT, TEV]. The use of the genitive case of this noun is translated '(have authority) over' [BECNT, HNTC, ICC2, NICNT, NTC; KJV, NASB, NRSV]. This noun denotes moistened earth of a clay consistency [LN].
d. aorist act. infin. of ποιέω (LN 42.29) (BAGD I.1.a.α. p. 680): 'to make' [AB, BAGD, BECNT, HNTC, ICC2, LN, NICNT, NTC, WBC; all versions], 'to fashion' [LN].
e. ἐκ with genitive object (LN 89.3): 'from' [BECNT, ICC2, LN, NICNT, WBC; GW, NASB, NET, TEV], 'out of' [AB, HNTC, NTC; CEV, NIV, NRSV, REB], 'of' [KJV]. The phrase 'to make from the same lump' is translated 'he can use the same clay to make' [NCV], 'to use the same lump of clay to make' [NLT]. This preposition marks the source from which someone or something is physically or psychologically derived [LN].
f. φύραμα (LN **79.92**) (BAGD p. 869): 'lump' [BAGD, BECNT, HNTC, ICC2, LN, NICNT, WBC; KJV, NASB, NRSV, REB], not explicit [NCV]. This word is conflated with πηλός 'clay' and translated 'lump of clay' [AB, NTC; CEV, GW, NET, NIV, NLT, TEV]. This noun denotes a three-dimensional object with irregular rounding contours [LN].

QUESTION—What is implied in the image of the potter?

Paul is depicting God as moral governor, not as creator [Ho, St]. It speaks of God in his function of choosing how he uses groups of people, not as creator [Gdt]. It describes God as shaper of history, and of the role of nations within history [WBC]. It emphasizes the disparity between the infinitely great God and his creation [St]. We must remember that when God exercises his rights as creator over men like a potter over clay, he is dealing with them not just as creatures but as *sinners* [Mu].

the (one)[a] **vessel**[b] **for honor**[c] **but (the other) for dishonor?**[d]

LEXICON—a. There is no lexical entry in the Greek text for the expression 'the one...the other', but it is implied by the use of the μέν...δέ construction which posits two contrasting elements in the sentence, and which is usually not translated into English. This contrast is represented in translation as 'one for...the other for' [TEV], 'one...for...another for' [AB, NTC, WBC; NASB, NET, NRSV], 'one...for...and another...for' [ICC2; NCV], 'one...for and another to' [NLT], 'one for...one for' [HNTC], 'some...for and some for' [NIV], 'one...unto...and another unto' [KJV], 'one to...the other for' [REB], 'both...and' [NICNT], 'or' [BECNT; GW]. The phrase 'the (one) vessel for honor but (the other) for dishonor' is translated 'a fancy bowl and a plain bowl' [CEV].

b. σκεῦος (LN 6.118) (BAGD 2. p. 754): 'vessel' [BAGD, BECNT, HNTC, ICC2, LN, NICNT, NTC, WBC; KJV, NASB, NET, REB], 'vase' [AB], 'bowl' [CEV], 'jar' [NLT], 'pots' [TEV], 'pottery' [NIV], 'object' [NRSV], 'something' [GW], 'thing' [NCV]. This noun is a highly generic term for any kind of jar, bowl, basket, or vase [LN].

c. τιμή (LN 87.4) (BAGD 2.b. p. 817): 'honor' [BAGD, BECNT, LN, NICNT, NTC; KJV], 'honorable service' [ICC2], 'honorable use' [WBC; NASB], 'noble purpose' [AB], 'noble purposes' [NIV], 'noble...use' [HNTC], 'special use' [NCV, NET, NRSV], 'special occasion' [GW], 'special occasions' [TEV], 'decoration' [NLT], 'to be treasured' [REB]. The phrase 'vessel for honor' is translated 'a fancy bowl' [CEV]. This noun denotes honor as an element in the assignment of status to a person [LN].

d. ἀτιμία (LN **87.71**) (BAGD p. 120): 'dishonor' [BAGD, BECNT, LN, NICNT, NTC; KJV], 'object of dishonor' [**LN**], 'dishonorable use' [WBC], 'ignoble use' [HNTC], 'common use' [AB; NASB, NIV, REB], 'ordinary use' [NET, NRSV, TEV], 'everyday use' [GW], 'daily use' [NCV], 'menial service' [ICC2], 'disgrace, shame' [BAGD]. The phrase '(vessel) for dishonor' is translated 'a plain bowl' [CEV], 'another (jar) to throw garbage into' [NLT]. This noun denotes a state of dishonor or disrespect as a negative cognate form of τιμή 'honor, respect' [LN].

QUESTION—What 'right' is being discussed here?

It is God's right to make, from the mass of humanity, some who will be saved, and others who will be punished [NICNT]. It is God's right to deal with sinners as he sees fit [Ho, Mu]. Though God has absolute authority over his creatures, Paul is not at all suggesting that God is capricious [ICC2]. Although God's power is absolute, he does not exercise it in a despotic or arbitrary way [NAC]. It is God's right to decide whether and how to use people in the service of his kingdom [Gdt]. It primarily speaks of God in his role as shaper of history, as opposed to shaping the lives of individuals [WBC].

ROMANS 9:21   49

QUESTION—What is implied by εἰς τιμὴν 'for honor'?
The vessel is reserved for some special function [TH]. It could describe a bowl that is elaborately decorated so as to be fit for a king's palace [WBC].
QUESTION—What is implied by the term ἀτιμίαν 'dishonor'?
  1. It implies menial use [AB, BECNT, ICC2], everyday use [TH], ordinary use [SSA]. It could describe the chamber pot of a lowly family [WBC]. It was made for menial use, but not destruction [AB, ICC2].
  2. It is used in parallel with 'wrath' and 'destruction' in 9:22–23 [Gdt, NICNT]. It implies dishonor, in keeping with the sharp contrasts throughout the rest of the passage [NTC].

9:22 But[a] what-if[b] God, wishing to show[c] (his) wrath[d] and to-make-known[e] (his) power[f]

LEXICON—a. δέ (LN 89.124): 'but' [HNTC, ICC2, LN, NICNT, WBC; NET, REB], 'yet' [AB], 'and' [BECNT, NTC], not explicit [all versions except NET, REB].
  b. εἰ (LN 89.65): 'what if' [AB, HNTC, ICC2, NICNT, NTC, WBC; KJV, NASB, NET, NIV, NRSV], 'if' [BECNT, LN; GW, REB], not explicit [CEV, NCV, NLT, TEV]. The phrase εἰ δέ 'but what if' [HNTC, ICC2, NICNT, WBC; NET] is also translated 'and what if' [NTC], 'yet what if' [AB], 'what if' [KJV, NASB, NIV, NRSV], 'but if' [REB], 'and if' [BECNT], 'if' [GW], not explicit [CEV, NCV, NLT, TEV]. This particle is a marker of a condition, real or hypothetical, actual or contrary to fact [LN].
  c. aorist mid. infin. of ἐνδείκνυμαι (LN **28.51**) (BAGD 1. p. 262): 'to show' [BAGD, NTC; CEV, KJV, NCV, NIV, NLT, NRSV, TEV], 'to show forth' [BECNT, HNTC, ICC2], 'to display' [AB; REB], 'to demonstrate' [BAGD, LN, NICNT, WBC; GW, NASB, NET], 'to cause to be known' [LN]. This verb means to cause to be made known, with possible emphasis upon the means [LN].
  d. ὀργή (LN 88.173) (BAGD 2.b. p. 579): 'wrath' [AB, BAGD, HNTC, ICC2, NICNT, NTC, WBC; KJV, NASB, NET, NIV, NRSV], 'anger' [BECNT, LN; CEV, GW, NCV, NLT, TEV], 'retribution' [REB]. This noun denotes a relative state of anger [LN].
  e. aorist act. infin. of γνωρίζω (LN 28.26) (BAGD 1. p. 163): 'to make known' [AB, BAGD, HNTC, ICC2, LN, NICNT, NTC, WBC; NET, NRSV], 'to make (his power) known' [KJV, NASB, NIV, REB, TEV], 'to reveal' [BAGD; CEV, GW], 'to show forth' [BECNT], 'to let people see' [NCV]. The phrase εἰ δὲ θέλων ὁ θεὸς...γνωρίσαι τὸ δυνατὸν αὐτοῦ 'But what if God, wishing...to make known his power' is translated 'God has the right to show his anger and his power' [NLT]. This verb means to cause information to be known by someone [LN].
  f. δυνατός (BAGD 2.d. p. 209). This adjective is translated as a noun: 'power' [AB, BECNT, HNTC, ICC2, NICNT, NTC, WBC; all versions].

QUESTION—What relationship is indicated by δέ 'but'?
1. It is adversative [AB, ICC1, ICC2, Mor, WBC]. Paul adds a further, slightly different thought [WBC]. Paul knows that his illustration in 9:21 about God being like a potter is not fully adequate for what he is saying here [ICC2]. Paul is saying that although God can do whatever he wants to those he creates, in view of his mercy a person still has no right to complain [Mor].
2. It is continuative [BECNT, Gdt, Mu, NICNT, NTC]. Paul is building on the illustration of the σκεῦος 'vessel' in 9:21 to explain why God makes some vessels for eschatological destruction and other ones for mercy [BECNT]. It transitions from the metaphor in 9:19–21 to the application of it [Gdt].

QUESTION—What relationship is indicated by εἰ 'if'?
The syntax and grammar in this passage are complex and difficult [BECNT, HNTC, Ho, TH], with some of the most difficult and obscure grammar in the book of Romans [TH], or even in all of Paul's writings [Mor, NAC].
1. Paul appears to have begun a conditional sentence without ever completing it, introducing a protasis without an apodosis [HNTC, Ho, ICC1, ICC2, Mor, Mu, NAC, NICNT, TH, WBC]. The εἰ is to be understood as 'what if' [AB, BECNT, HNTC, ICC1, ICC2, Mu, NICNT, NTC]. The 'what if' suggests a different way of viewing the issue, one that is actually true [HNTC, TH].
2. It introduces the protasis of a conditional sentence, in conjunction with 9:23 which constitutes a second protasis or condition. The apodosis would be drawn from the thought of 9:20–21 and 9:24 [Gdt].

QUESTION—What would be the implied apodosis of this conditional sentence?
The implied apodosis would be that no one has the right to question God's authority [NICNT], or to challenge God about his dealings with people [SSA]. The implied apodosis is that since God is as merciful and gracious as he is, no one should accuse him of injustice [AB]. The implied apodosis is that if God wants to be patient with people and if he wants to reveal his great mercy, then no one has the right to find fault with God about how he directs human destinies by bringing both Jew and Gentile into the kingdom [Gdt].

QUESTION—What relationship is indicated by the use of the participle θέλων 'wishing'?
1. It is concessive: although he wished…[AB, Gdt, ICC1, NAC, SSA; CEV, GW, NASB, NCV, NLT, TEV]. That is, although he wished to make his power known, God withheld punishment because of his mercy, and also to show his lovingkindness to the objects of his mercy [AB]. God is patient because he was giving people opportunity to repent [AB, ICC2, WBC].
2. It is causal: because he wished…[BECNT, HNTC, ICC2, Mor, Mu, NICNT, NTC, TH]. That is, because he wished to make his power known, God withheld punishment to give more opportunity to show his power in judgment [BECNT, Mu]. If God had destroyed Pharaoh and Egypt right

away, there would not have been opportunity to do the many miracles and judgments that he performed [NTC].
3. It describes what generally is true about God [WBC]. That is, he wishes to make his power known, etc.

endured[a] with[b] great patience[c] vessels[d] of-wrath[e] having-been-prepared[f] for destruction,[g]

LEXICON—a. aorist act. indic. of φέρω (LN **25.176**) (BAGD 1.c. p. 855): 'to endure' [AB, BAGD, HNTC, ICC2, **LN**; KJV, NASB, NET, NRSV], 'to put up with' [BAGD, LN; CEV], 'to tolerate' [REB], 'to bear' [BAGD, BECNT, NICNT, NTC, WBC; NIV], 'to be...patient with' [GW, NLT], 'to stay with' [NCV]. The clause ὁ θεὸς...ἤνεγκεν ἐν πολλῇ μακροθυμίᾳ 'God...endured with great patience' is translated 'he was very patient in enduring' [TEV]. This verb means to put up with annoyance or difficulty [LN].

b. ἐν with dative (LN 13.8): 'with' [AB, BECNT, HNTC, ICC2, LN, NICNT, NTC, WBC; KJV, NASB, NET, NIV, NRSV, REB], not explicit [CEV, GW, NCV, NLT, TEV]. This preposition marks a state or condition [LN].

c. μακροθυμία (LN 25.167) (BAGD 2.b.α. p. 488): 'patience' [BAGD, BECNT, LN, NICNT, NTC, WBC; NASB, NET, NIV, NRSV, REB], 'forbearance' [BAGD], 'longsuffering' [AB, HNTC, ICC2; KJV]. The phrase ἐν πολλῇ μακροθυμίᾳ 'with great patience' is translated 'patiently' [BAGD; CEV, NCV], 'extremely patient' [GW], 'very patient' [NLT, TEV]. This noun denotes a state of emotional calm in the face of provocation or misfortune and without complaint or irritation [LN].

d. σκεῦος (LN 6.118) (BAGD 2. p. 754): 'vessel' [BAGD, BECNT, HNTC, ICC2, LN, NICNT, NTC, WBC; KJV, NASB], 'vase' [AB], 'object' [NET, NIV, NRSV, TEV], not explicit [CEV, GW, NCV, NLT]. The genitive phrase σκεύη ὀργῆς 'vessels of wrath' is translated 'vessels that were objects of retribution' [REB]. This noun is a highly generic term for any kind of jar, bowl, basket, or vase [LN].

e. ὀργή (LN 88.173) (BAGD 2.b. p. 579): 'wrath' [AB, BAGD, BECNT, HNTC, ICC2, NICNT, NTC, WBC; KJV, NASB, NET, NRSV], 'his wrath' [NIV], 'anger' [LN], 'his anger' [GW, NLT, TEV], 'retribution' [REB], not explicit [CEV]. This noun is translated as a verb: '(those people) he was angry with' [NCV]. This noun denotes a relative state of anger [LN].

f. perf. pass. participle of καταρτίζω (LN 75.5) (BAGD 2.a. p. 418): 'to be prepared' [BECNT, HNTC, ICC2, NICNT, NTC; NASB, NET, NIV], 'to prepare' [BAGD], 'to be made ready' [WBC; NCV], 'to design, to create' [BAGD], 'to be fashioned' [AB], 'to be made' [NRSV], 'to be fit' [KJV, NLT], 'to be headed' [GW], 'to be due' [REB], 'to be doomed' [TEV], 'to deserve' [CEV].

g. ἀπώλεια (LN **20.31**) (BAGD 2. p. 103): 'destruction' [AB, BAGD, BECNT, HNTC, ICC2, LN, NICNT, NTC, WBC; all versions except CEV, NCV]. This noun is translated as a verb: 'to be destroyed' [CEV, NCV]. This noun denotes the destruction of persons, objects, or institutions [LN].

Question—How is the plural noun σκεύη 'vessels' used?

This is the same word used as 'vessels' in 9:21 and it is used here to maintain a connection with the illustration which referred to vessels, but here the context requires the reference to be to people [TH]. Some translations maintain the use of 'vessels' [AB, BECNT, HNTC, ICC2, NICNT, NTC, WBC; KJV, NASB], while others use words that refer to people: 'objects' [NET, NIV, NLT, NRSV, TEV], 'people' [GW, NCV], 'everyone' [CEV].

QUESTION—What relationship is indicated by the genitive construction σκεύη ὀργῆς 'vessels of wrath'?

They are the objects of God's wrath [AB, Gdt, Ho, ICC2, TH, TNTC, WBC; GW, NCV, NIV, NLT, NRSV, REB, TEV]. They are destined to receive God's wrath [Ho, Mor, NICNT]. They deserve God's wrath [ICC1]. They are instruments for the exhibition of God's wrath [Mu].

QUESTION—What is signified by the use of the perfect passive participle κατηρτισμένα 'prepared'?

1. It indicates a current condition [AB, Gdt, ICC1, ICC2, Mor, St, TH, TNTC]. They are completely fitted for destruction [Mor]. They are in the state of being fit only for discarding [AB]. They are close in time to that point, and even deserve it [TH]. It implies that they are being or have been prepared or fitted for final destruction as a judgment for their actions and character [WBC]. God does not make men wicked [Ho], nor does he create men to destroy them [Ho, Mor, St]. They are ripe for destruction [TNTC]. They are worthy to be destroyed, but it does not mean that they necessarily will be destroyed [ICC2].
2. It implies that they were created for the purpose of being destroyed. However, in the parallel between God's preparing vessels of mercy for glory ahead of time and his preparing vessels of wrath for destruction the emphasis is not equal [BECNT].

QUESTION—Who is the implied agent of the participle κατηρτισμένα 'prepared'?

1. God prepared them for destruction [BECNT, Ho, Mu, NICNT, WBC]. God prepared them for destruction, but that does not mean that he created them for destruction [Ho, WBC].
2. They prepared themselves [Mor, NAC, NTC, St]. They did it themselves with Satan's help [Mor, NTC]. Their lives and conduct have determined their destiny [NAC]. They prepare themselves for destruction by their own evil doing [St].
3. Comment regarding the identity of the agent is purposely omitted by some [AB, Gdt, ICC1, ICC2, Mu, SSA, TH]: they were fitted for eternal destruction. There are theological views that influence the interpretation

of the agent, whether the agent is God, themselves, or Satan, so the translation 'who are made for destruction' is given so as not to suggest an agent [SSA]. They were ripe or ready for a destruction that was soon to come, and they deserved it [TH].

QUESTION—Who are these vessels of wrath?

They are those who are impenitent and who will be lost eternally [BECNT, Ho, ICC1, NICNT, NTC]. They are the Jews, who have steadfastly resisted God throughout history [Gdt].

QUESTION—Do the vessels for honor or dishonor on the one hand and the vessels of wrath and vessels of mercy on the other hand relate to salvation?

1. His statement relates to God's dealings in salvation history; no potter would make a vessel in order to destroy it [AB, ICC2, WBC]. It does not seem that he is talking about eternal destruction [TH]. It is not at all clear whether the vessels for dishonor and the vessels of wrath are the same people [WBC].
2. His statement is also about eternal salvation [BECNT, Ho, ICC1, NICNT]. The vessels for dishonor and vessels of wrath are the same people [BECNT, Gdt, Ho, Mu, NICNT].

9:23 and in-order-to^a make-known^b the riches^c of-his glory^d

LEXICON—a. ἵνα (LN 89.59): 'in order to' [HNTC, ICC2, LN, NICNT, NTC; REB], 'to' [AB], 'in order that' [BECNT, WBC; NASB], 'that' [KJV], 'so that' [LN; NCV], 'for the purpose of' [LN]. The relation indicated or implied by this word is translated 'he did this by…' [CEV], 'he also wanted to…' [TEV], 'Can't God also…?' [GW], 'And what if he is willing to…?' [NET], 'What if he did this to…?' [NIV], 'and what if he has done so in order to…?' [NRSV], 'he does this to…' [NLT]. This particle marks purpose, with the frequent implication of some underlying reason [LN].

b. aorist act. subj. of γνωρίζω (LN 28.26) (BAGD 1. p. 163): 'to make known' [AB, BAGD, BECNT, HNTC, ICC2, LN, NICNT, NTC, WBC; KJV, NASB, NCV, NET, NIV, NRSV, REB], 'to make (to) shine (even brighter)' [NLT], 'to reveal' [BAGD; GW, TEV], 'to show' [CEV]. This verb means to cause information to be known by someone [LN].

c. πλοῦτος (LN 57.30) (BAGD 2. p. 674): 'riches' [AB, BECNT, ICC2, LN, NICNT, NTC; GW, KJV, NASB, NIV, NLT, NRSV], 'wealth' [BAGD, HNTC, LN, WBC; NET], 'full wealth' [REB], 'abundance' [BAGD, LN]. The phrase 'the riches of his glory' is translated 'how glorious he is' [CEV], 'his rich glory' [NCV], 'his abundant glory' [TEV]. This noun denotes an abundance of possessions exceeding the norm of a particular society [LN].

d. δόξα (LN 79.18) (BAGD 1.a. p. 203): 'glory' [AB, BAGD, BECNT, HNTC, ICC2, LN, NICNT, NTC, WBC; all versions except CEV], 'splendor' [LN]. The phrase 'the riches of his glory' is translated 'how glorious he is' [CEV]. This noun denotes the quality of splendid, remarkable appearance [LN].

QUESTION—What relationship is indicated by καὶ ἵνα 'and in order to'?

It introduces a purpose clause that counterbalances Paul's discussion of God's wrath, and those who are the objects of it, with what he wants to say about God's mercy and those who will be saved [Mor].

1. It depends on ἤνεγκεν 'he endured' [AB, HNTC, ICC1, Mu, NICNT, NTC, St, WBC]. He endured them in order to show his mercy to those whom he calls [AB, HNTC, ICC1, NICNT, NTC]. His great mercy to Israel would not have been seen if he had destroyed Pharaoh and Egypt sooner [NTC]. Καί gives emphasis to this third purpose clause; he endured them in order to show his wrath and his power, and *especially* his mercy to those whom he calls [NICNT]. He endured them in order to allow more opportunity for repentance, but also to make the final outpouring of wrath more dreadful, which will in turn reveal his glory even more to those upon whom he has mercy [St].

2. It depends on κατηρτισμένα 'having been prepared' [BECNT]. Those who are objects of his wrath are prepared for destruction in order to display in a greater way his mercy toward those being saved [BECNT].

3. It depends on ἤνεγκεν and κατηρτισμένα. He endured them in order to show his mercy to them and others, and reveals his wrath against sin to show its seriousness, proving how great his forgiving grace really is [ICC2].

4. It functions as does the εἰ 'if' of 9:22, introducing a second protasis of a conditional sentence, parallel to the clause beginning with εἰ δὲ θέλων ὁ θεός 'if God, willing...', and of which the apodosis is drawn from the thought of 9:20–21 and 9:24. That is, if God wants to be patient with people and if he wants to reveal his great mercy, then who are you to find fault with God about how he directs human destinies by bringing both Jew and Gentile into the kingdom? [Gdt].

QUESTION—What is the glory that Paul speaks of here?

1. The phrase τῆς δόξης 'of glory' is descriptive: glorious riches, which in this case is the riches of his mercy [AB, ICC2, Mor, NTC, SSA, WBC], or of the grace he gives [NAC], or the glorious way God acts to show mercy [SSA]. It is the splendor of God's love poured out on the vessels of honor and manifested in his mercy [Gdt]. It is God's excellence generally, but especially describes how great his mercy is [Ho]. It is the summary of all God's glorious attributes [NTC]. It is God's splendor which will be shown to and in those he has redeemed and transformed [St]. It is the sum of God's perfections, especially his mercy, manifested in all their splendor and fullness [Mu]. It recalls his self-revelation in Ex 33:18–19 as being merciful and compassionate [WBC].

2. The phrase τῆς δόξης 'of glory' is epexegetic, re-stating what the riches consist of: riches, that is, glory [NICNT].

upon/to[a] vessels[b] of-mercy[c] which he-prepared-beforehand[d] for[e] glory,[f]

LEXICON—a. ἐπί with accusative (LN 90.57) (BAGD III.1.b.ε. p. 289): 'upon' [BECNT, ICC2; NASB], '(lavished) upon' [NTC], 'on' [BAGD, LN, WBC; CEV, KJV, NET, NLT, REB], 'to' [LN, NICNT; GW, NCV, NIV], 'toward' [BAGD], 'for' [AB, BAGD, HNTC; NRSV]. The phrase 'to make known the riches of his glory upon' is translated 'to reveal his abundant glory, which was poured out on' [TEV]. This preposition marks an experiencer, often with the implication of an action by a superior force or agency [LN].

b. σκεῦος (LN 6.118) (BAGD 2. p. 754): 'vessel' [BAGD, BECNT, HNTC, ICC2, LN, NICNT, NTC, WBC; KJV, NASB], 'vase' [AB], 'object' [GW, NET, NIV, NRSV, TEV]. The phrase 'vessels of mercy' is translated 'the people who receive his mercy' [NCV], 'vessels that were objects of mercy' [REB], 'those to whom he shows mercy' [NLT].

c. ἔλεος (LN 88.76) (BAGD 2.b. p. 250): 'mercy' [AB, BAGD, BECNT, HNTC, ICC2, LN, NICNT, NTC, WBC; KJV, NASB, NET, NLT, NRSV, REB], 'his mercy' [GW, NCV, NIV, TEV]. The phrase 'to make known the riches of his glory upon vessels of mercy' is translated 'when he has pity on the people...' [CEV]. This noun denotes kindness or concern for someone in serious need [LN].

d. aorist act. indic. of προετοιμάζω (LN **77.4**) (BAGD p. 705): 'to prepare beforehand' [BAGD, BECNT, ICC2, NICNT, NTC, WBC; NASB, NET, NRSV], 'to prepare in advance' [LN; NIV], 'to prepare from the first' [REB], 'to prepare' [GW, NCV, NLT, TEV], 'to make ready in advance' [**LN**], 'to be prepared in advance' [NLT], 'to make ready beforehand' [HNTC], 'to fashion beforehand' [AB], 'to choose' [CEV]. The phrase 'which he prepared beforehand' is translated 'which he had afore prepared' [KJV]. This verb means to make ready or prepare in advance [LN].

e. εἰς with accusative (LN 89.57): 'for' [AB, BECNT, HNTC, ICC2, NICNT, NTC, WBC; GW, NASB, NET, NIV, NLT, NRSV, REB], 'for the purpose of' [LN], 'unto' [KJV]. This preposition is translated as a verb 'to share in' [CEV], 'to have' [NCV], 'to receive' [TEV]. This preposition marks intent, often with the implication of expected result [LN].

f. δόξα (LN 79.18) (BAGD 1.a. p. 203): 'glory' [BAGD, BECNT, HNTC, ICC2, LN, NICNT, NTC, WBC; GW, KJV, NASB, NET, NIV, NLT, NRSV, REB], 'such glory' [AB], 'his glory' [CEV, NCV, TEV], 'splendor' [LN].

QUESTION—What relationship is indicated by ἐπί 'upon/to'?

1. God wants to make known *to* those who are vessels of mercy how great the riches of his glory are for them [Mor, NICNT, SSA, St; NIV].
2. God wants to make known how great the riches of his glory are *upon* or *for* those who are vessels of mercy [AB, BECNT, Gdt, HNTC, ICC1, ICC2, NAC, NTC, WBC; NASB, NLT, NRSV, TEV].

2.1 He does this so that unbelievers might see his mercies to the others [NAC]. He does this so that Israel might see his mercies that are available to them if they will believe [AB]. He reveals his mercy for believers to unbelievers so they will want to repent, and he reveals his wrath upon sin and unbelief so that believers will appreciate the mercy they have received [ICC2].
2.2 He does this so that believers might see his mercies to them [HNTC].

QUESTION—What is the glory Paul speaks of here?

It is the glory believers will experience in heaven [Ho, ICC2, SSA], the final destiny of his redeemed ones [St]. It is the personal experience of the glorious presence of God, as in 5:2 and 8:18, but seen in the context of 8:28–30 [ICC2]. It is the state of future glory of which he spoke in 8:28–30 [AB, NTC]. It is eschatological glory, that is, future splendor in eternal life [BECNT]. 'Glory' parallels 'honor' in 9:21 [BECNT]. It is that glory that God bestows upon believers in eternal bliss [Mu].

DISCOURSE UNIT—9:24–29 [AB, NICNT, WBC]. The topic is God does not act arbitrarily: Israel's call, infidelity, and remnant are foreseen in what God announced in the Old Testament [AB], God's calling of a new people: Israel and the Gentiles [NICNT], those called include both Jews and Gentiles, as prophesied [WBC].

9:24 even/also[a] whom he-called,[b] us, not only from-among[c] (the) Jews but also from-among[d] (the) Gentiles,

LEXICON—a. καί (LN 89.93, 89.92): 'even' [AB, ICC2, LN (89.93), NTC; KJV, NASB, NET, NIV], 'including' [NRSV], 'also' [LN (89.93)], 'and' [LN (89.92)], not explicit [HNTC, NICNT; CEV]. The phrase καί...ἡμᾶς 'even/also...us' is translated 'also...namely us' [BECNT], 'also...even us' [ICC2], 'even us...also' [NTC; NASB, NIV], 'by which I mean us' [WBC], 'this is what God did for us' [GW], 'and we are those people' [NCV], 'we are those objects of mercy' [REB], 'for we are the people' [TEV], 'and we are among those' [NLT]. This conjunction can mark an additive relation that is not coordinate [LN (89.93)], or an additive relationship that is coordinate [LN (89.92)].

b. aorist act. indic. of καλέω (LN 33.312) (BAGD 2. p. 399): 'to call' [AB, BAGD, BECNT, HNTC, ICC2, LN, NICNT, NTC, WBC; all versions except CEV, NLT], 'to select' [NLT]. This word combines the meaning of the words 'summon' and 'invite' [BAGD]. The phrase καὶ ἐκάλεσεν ἡμᾶς 'even/also whom he called, us' is translated 'we are those chosen ones' [CEV]. This verb means to urgently invite someone to accept responsibilities for a particular task, implying a new relationship to the one who does the calling [LN].

c. ἐκ with genitive (LN 89.121) (BAGD 1.b. p. 234): 'from among' [AB, HNTC, ICC2, NICNT; NASB, REB, TEV], 'from' [BAGD, BECNT, LN (89.121), NTC, WBC; NCV, NET, NIV, NLT, NRSV], 'out of' [BAGD], 'of' [KJV]. The phrase 'not only from among (the) Jews but also from among (the) Gentiles' is translated 'whether Jews or Gentiles' [CEV], 'whether we are Jews or not' [GW]. This preposition marks dissociation in the sense of being 'independent from' someone or something [LN].

d. ἐκ with genitive (LN 89.121) (BAGD 1.b. p. 234).

QUESTION—What is the relation of 9:24 to the immediate context?
1. 9:22 and 9:23 are one sentence, and 9:24 through 9:25 are another sentence [BECNT].
2. 9:23 is one sentence, and 9:24 through 9:26 are another sentence, though 9:24 resumes the idea that was begun in 9:23 [AB].
3. 9:22 and 9:23 are one sentence, ending with a question mark, and 9:24 through 9:26 are another sentence [GNT, NICNT, WBC].
4. 9:22 through 9:24 are one sentence, ending with a question mark [HNTC, NTC]. There is a dash between 9:23 and 9:24, separating the thought somewhat [HNTC].
5. 9:22 through 9:26 are one sentence; a question mark occurs at the end of 9:24, but 9:25 begins with a dash and a lower case letter, indicating continuity with the previous two verses, after a pause, in a single long sentence [ICC2].

QUESTION—What is the syntactical relation of οὕς 'whom' and ἡμᾶς 'us' in this verse?
1. Continuing with what has been said in 9:23, οὕς 'whom' begins a relative clause dependent on the antecedent σκεύη 'vessels', and ἡμᾶς 'us' is in apposition to οὕς 'whom' [BECNT, Ho, ICC1, ICC2, Mor, NTC]: vessels, whom he also called, even us. This relative clause modifies and softens the harshness of what has been said in 9:19–21 [ICC1].
2. A new sentence begins, with οὕς 'whom' and ἡμᾶς 'us' both being objects of the verb ἐκάλεσεν 'he called' [NICNT, WBC]. The awkward phrasing gives emphasis to 'us' [WBC].

QUESTION—What relationship is indicated by καί 'even'?
1. καί means 'even' or 'namely' and identifies the vessels of mercy [BECNT, ICC2, SSA, TH]: God prepared the vessels of mercy for glory, those vessels being us who are from among the Jews and Gentiles.
2. καί means 'and' and indicates that there is an additional, coordinate fact [Gdt, ICC1, NICNT]: God prepared the vessels of mercy for glory, *and* he called us from among the Jews and Gentiles.
3. There is a coordinate relation: he revealed his glory and he also called us; but there is also an emphasis on 'us'. The deliberately awkward phrasing, 'whom also he called, us' is meant to make the reader to go slowly and perceive the emphasis on 'us', and it means 'by which I means *us*, whom he also called' [WBC].

QUESTION—To whom does the pronoun 'us' refer?
Paul includes his Roman readers as well as himself [ICC2, Mor, NTC]. The main point Paul is making is that it is only by God's mercy, and not by their merit that anyone is saved [NTC].

QUESTION—What is implied in Paul's use of the verb ἐκάλεσεν 'he called'?

It speaks of the effective call of God [BECNT, Ho, ICC2, Mor, Mu, NICNT, NTC, WBC]. Election is carried out by the effective call [WBC]. 'Call' is a thematic word in this epistle [NICNT, WBC]. After 'mercy', it is the principle thematic word in the passage [WBC]. It is the call of God, not natural descent, that constitutes the people of God, and which is the basis for anyone being included in the people of God [NICNT]. It is God's gracious call [AB]. The invitation is applied to the heart and life in such a way that it saves [NTC]. It means that he chose them [SSA].

QUESTION—What relationship is indicated by ἐκ 'from among'?

It indicates that there is an element of separation; God has not called all the Jews, but only certain ones from among them [Mor, NICNT, WBC].

DISCOURSE UNIT—9:25–33 [GW]. The topic is God chose people who are not Jewish.

9:25 as[a] he-[b] also -says in Hosea,[c] I-will-call[d] those (who are) not my people My people and the (one) not having-been-loved[e] Loved;

LEXICON—a. ὡς (LN 64.12) (BAGD II.4.a. p. 897): 'as' [AB, BAGD, BECNT, ICC2, LN, NICNT, WBC; all versions except CEV, NLT, TEV], 'just as' [NTC; CEV]. This word is used to introduce a Scripture quotation [BAGD]. The phrase ὡς λέγει 'as he says' is also translated 'this is what he says' [TEV], 'concerning the Gentiles, God says' [NLT], 'That this calling of Gentiles as well as Jews was intended is shown in Scripture, as God says' [HNTC]. This adverb marks a relatively weak relationship between events or states [LN].

b. There is no lexical entry for the word 'he', the subject of the verb being included in the verb itself. This is translated 'he' [AB, ICC2, NTC, WBC; KJV, NASB, NET, NIV, NRSV, REB, TEV], 'God' [HNTC; GW, NLT], 'the Lord' [CEV], 'Scripture' [NCV], 'it' [BECNT, NICNT].

c. 'Hosea' (LN 93.388): 'Hosea' [AB, BECNT, ICC2, LN, NICNT, NTC, WBC; GW, NASB, NCV, NET, NIV, NRSV, REB], 'Osee' [KJV], 'the book of Hosea' [HNTC; CEV, TEV], 'the prophecy of Hosea' [NLT].

d. fut. act. indic. of καλέω (LN 33.129) (BAGD 1.a.β. p. 399): 'to call' [AB, BAGD, BECNT, HNTC, ICC2, LN, NICNT, NTC, WBC; all versions except CEV]. The phrase 'I will call those (who are) not my people my people' is translated 'although they were not my people, I will make them my people' [CEV], 'I will say, "You are my people" to those I had called "not my people"' [NCV]. This verb means to speak of a person or object by means of a proper name [LN]. It combines the meaning of the words 'summon' and 'invite' [BAGD].

e. perf. pass. participle of ἀγαπάω (LN 25.43) (BAGD 1.d. p. 5): 'to be loved' [AB, BAGD, LN, NICNT; CEV, GW, NCV, NIV, NLT, TEV], 'to be unloved' [NET, REB], 'to be beloved' [BECNT, HNTC; KJV, NASB, NRSV]. The phrase οὐκ ἠγαπημένην ἠγαπημένην 'not having been loved Loved' is translated '(I will call those)...Unloved 'Beloved''

[ICC2], '(I will call) the not loved "loved"' [WBC], 'Not my loved one (I will call) My loved one' [NTC]. This verb means to have love for someone or something, based on sincere appreciation and high regard [LN].

QUESTION—Is there any significance in the fact that Paul alters 'I will say' in the LXX text of the Hosea passage to 'I will call'?

1. It speaks of the divine call [BECNT, Gdt, ICC2, Mor, NICNT, WBC]. Paul chooses this word to emphasize the effective call of God, already mentioned in 9:23 [NICNT]. The verb can be used with reference to giving a name or to calling someone to a particular role or task, and Paul is employing both senses here [AB]. The naming is effectual, one that brings about a change of condition [ICC2]. It continues Paul's theme of divine calling and choice [WBC]. It is God's call to salvation [Gdt].
2. It simply means 'to name', and does not bear the same meaning as other uses in Romans [ICC1]. It means to declare what someone is [SSA].

QUESTION—What is the significance of the change from the plural 'the people' in the first line of the quotation to the singular 'the (one)' in the second line?

The noun 'people' in the first line is masculine singular both in Greek and in the Hebrew of the Hosea passage Paul is citing, but in English 'people' is a plural noun. In the second line some versions refer to 'her' who was unloved (NASB, NET, NIV, NRSV), since the Greek participle ἠγαπημένην 'unloved' is feminine, corresponding to the feminine verb in Hebrew.

QUESTION—Why does Paul apply this text from Hosea, which is about Israel's restoration, to Gentiles?

There is a similar principle involved [Gdt, Ho, ICC1, Mu, TNTC, WBC]. Just as God could restore Israel, which had been rejected from the covenant, so also he could include Gentiles, who had been outside of the covenant [Gdt, Ho, ICC1, Mu, WBC]. Paul reasons that if there is hope for Israelites who were put outside the people of God because of their sin, then there is also hope for Gentiles who were outside naturally [Mor]. The promise to restore the rejected Israelites, who had been exiled to the dark realm of the Gentiles, also shows God's willingness to include the Gentiles in his salvation [ICC2]. The northern kingdom of Israel was unworthy of the restoration promised in the Hosea passage, and Paul applies this passage to the Gentiles in order to show how God chooses people who would otherwise be unworthy of such special privilege [AB]. The cause of the conversion of the Gentiles is the same as that of the restoration of Israel, which is the grace of the sovereign God [NTC]. Paul sees OT predictions about a renewed Israel as being fulfilled in the church [BECNT, NICNT]. Paul sees the church as forming the new people of God [BECNT].

9:26 and it-will-be[a] in the place[b] where it-was-said to-them, You (are) not my people, there they-will-be-called sons[c] of-(the) living[d] God.

LEXICON—a. fut. mid. (deponent = act.) indic. of εἰμί (LN 13.104) (BAGD I.4. p. 223): 'to be' [BECNT, LN, NICNT, WBC; NASB], 'to come to pass' [HNTC; KJV], 'to happen' [LN, NTC; NIV], 'to take place, to occur' [BAGD], not explicit [AB, ICC2; CEV, GW, NCV, NET, NLT, NRSV, REB, TEV].

  b. τόπος (LN **80.1**) (BAGD 2.d. p. 823): 'place' [BECNT, HNTC, LN, NICNT, WBC; KJV, NASB], 'very place' [AB, NTC; CEV, NET, NIV, NRSV, REB, TEV], not explicit [NCV]. The phrase 'in the place where' is translated 'instead of' [BAGD, ICC2], 'wherever (they were told)' [GW], 'once (they were told)' [NLT]. This noun denotes an area of any size [LN]. This word is used with a special meaning in this verse: 'instead of their being told..., there they shall be called...' [BAGD].

  c. υἱός (LN 9.4, 36.39) (BAGD 1.c.γ. p. 834): 'son' [BAGD, HNTC, ICC2, LN (9.4), NICNT, NTC, WBC; NASB, NET, NIV, REB, TEV], 'follower' [LN (36.39)]. This plural noun is translated 'sons and daughters' [BECNT], 'children' [AB; CEV, GW, KJV, NCV, NLT, NRSV]. This noun can be used to denote a person of a class or kind, specified by the following genitive construction [LN (9.4)], or as a figurative extension of the term denoting a father-son relationship, referring to one who is a disciple or follower of someone, with the implication of being like the one whom he or she follows [LN (36.39)].

  d. pres. act. participle of ζάω (LN 23.88) (BAGD 1.a.ε. p. 336): 'to live' [BAGD, LN]. This participle is translated as an adjective: 'living' [AB, BAGD, BECNT, HNTC, ICC2, LN, NICNT, NTC, WBC; all versions]. This is used to describe someone who is not subject to death [BAGD].

QUESTION—What is meant by the phrase 'in the place where'?

  1. Paul probably does not intend a specific geographical reference here [AB, BECNT, NAC, WBC]. Paul's focus is theological, not geographical [WBC]. It is a general statement; wherever people have not had the privilege of being God's people, they will now have the opportunity to be his people [NTC]. It speaks generally of the gathering of Gentiles that occurs throughout the world [BECNT, ICC1, Mu]. It refers to the whole world, where Gentiles had previously had to endure the reproach of not being God's people [ICC1]. Just as Israel of old was dispersed into exile in other lands, so also God is now calling people for himself from outside the land of Israel [Gdt, NICNT]. It speaks generally of other places, that is, Gentiles, who are now invited to be God's people [Mor]. Whereas Hosea spoke of the exiles returning to Jerusalem, Paul has transferred this call to the Gentiles, with no specific reference intended for 'place', which is just a part of the quotation [AB]. It refers to anywhere in the world that Gentiles become God's people [Ho, SSA]. The singular form of the LXX in Hosea, 'in the place', refers to the specific place of the northern kingdom of Israel, but Paul is referring to wherever Gentiles become

God's people, and this intention is shown by translating it 'in each place' [SSA].
  2. It means 'instead of' [BAGD, ICC2]: in place of or instead of being told they are not God's people.

QUESTION—What is implied in Paul's use of the verb κληθήσονται 'they shall be called'?
  1. It continues his emphasis on the effective call of God [BECNT, ICC2, Mor, NICNT]. What prevails is the call, not the situation [Mor].
  2. It means 'to be named', though the new names, which express aspects of the new, covenantal relationship, are correlative with the effectual call, and have saving significance [Mu].

QUESTION—What is meant by 'the living God'?
It indicates that God is the source of life, the one who gives life [TH]. It means that God is all powerful [SSA]. It contrasts God with lifeless idols [WBC].

9:27 But/and[a] Isaiah cries-out[b] concerning[c] Israel,
LEXICON—a. δέ (LN 89.124, 89.94): 'but' [BECNT, ICC2, LN (89.124), NICNT, NTC; REB], 'and' [AB, HNTC, LN (89.94); CEV, GW, KJV, NCV, NET, NLT, NRSV, TEV], not explicit [WBC; NASB, NIV].
  b. pres. act. indic. of κράζω (LN 33.83) (BAGD 2.b.α. p. 448): 'to cry out' [AB, BECNT, HNTC, ICC2, NICNT, NTC; NASB, NCV, NET, NIV, NLT, NRSV], 'to cry' [KJV], 'to call out' [BAGD], 'to shout' [LN], 'to proclaim' [WBC], 'to exclaim' [TEV], 'to say' [CEV, GW]. The phrase 'Isaiah cries out' is translated 'Isaiah makes this proclamation' [REB]. This term denotes urgent speech in this context [BAGD]. This verb means to shout or cry out, with the possible implication of the unpleasant nature of the sound [LN].
  c. ὑπέρ with genitive (LN 90.24) (BAGD 1.f. p. 839): 'concerning' [BAGD, BECNT, HNTC, ICC2, LN, NICNT, NTC, WBC; KJV, NASB, NIV, NLT, NRSV], 'about' [AB, BAGD, LN; CEV, GW, NCV, REB, TEV], 'on behalf of' [NET]. This noun denotes general content, whether of a discourse or mental activity [LN].

QUESTION—What relationship is indicated by δέ 'but/and'?
  1. It is contrastive [BECNT, Gdt, ICC2, Mor]. The fate of Israel is contrasted with that of the Gentiles [BECNT]. Hosea's word of promise is contrasted with Isaiah's threat [ICC2]. Whereas many Jews are now excluded, Gentiles are being included [Mor].
  2. It is additive, introducing additional grounds for what Paul has said in 9:22-24 [SSA].

QUESTION—What relationship is indicated by ὑπέρ 'concerning'?
  1. It means 'about' or 'concerning' [AB, BECNT, HNTC, ICC2, Mor, NICNT, NTC, SSA, WBC; all versions except NET].
  2. It means 'on their behalf' [NET].

3. It may mean 'over', as a threat hanging over the head of those to whom the prophet speaks [Gdt].

QUESTION—What is implied in the verb κράζει 'cries out'?

It implies a certain urgency and intensity [Mor, NAC, NICNT, WBC]. It marks the importance of what is being said [BECNT]. It is used to arouse attention [Mu]. It has a threatening tone [Gdt]. It is commonly used with reference to prophetic utterances [ICC2, NTC].

Even-if[a] the number of-the sons of-Israel would-be as[b] the sand[c] of-the sea,[d] (only)[e] the remnant[f] will-be-saved;[g]

LEXICON—a. ἐάν (LN 89.67): 'even if' [BECNT, WBC; TEV], 'if' [LN, NICNT], 'though' [HNTC, ICC2, NTC; KJV, NASB, NET, NIV, NLT, NRSV, REB], 'although' [GW], 'should' [AB], not explicit [CEV, NCV]. This adverb marks condition, with the implication of reduced probability [LN].

b. ὡς (LN 64.12) (BAGD II.3.b. p. 897): 'as' [AB, BAGD, BECNT, HNTC, ICC2, LN, NICNT, NTC, WBC; CEV, KJV, NASB, NET], 'as many as' [TEV], 'as numerous as' [GW, NLT], 'countless as' [REB], 'like' [BAGD, LN; NCV, NIV, NRSV].

c. ἄμμος (LN **2.28**) (BAGD p. 46): 'sand' [BAGD, BECNT, HNTC, ICC2, NICNT, NTC, WBC; KJV, NASB, NET, NIV, NLT, NRSV], 'sands' [AB; REB], 'grains of sand' [LN; CEV, GW, NCV, TEV]. This word is used figuratively here of that which cannot be counted [BAGD].

d. θάλασσα (LN 1.69) (BAGD 1.a. p. 350): 'sea' [AB, BAGD, BECNT, HNTC, ICC2, LN, NICNT, NTC, WBC; KJV, NASB, NCV, NET, NIV, REB, TEV], 'seashore' [BAGD; GW, NLT, NRSV], 'beach' [CEV]. The phrase τῆς θαλάσσης is translated 'of the sea' [AB, BECNT, HNTC, ICC2, NICNT, NTC, WBC; KJV, NASB, NET, NRSV, REB], 'on the seashore' [GW, NLT], 'by the sea' [NCV, NIV, TEV], 'along the beach' [CEV]. This noun denotes a generic collective term for all bodies of water, as contrasted with the sky and the land [LN].

e. There is no lexical entry for this word in the Greek text, but it is implied as introducing the apodosis of the concessive sentence. It is represented in translation as 'only' [BECNT, ICC2; GW, NET, NIV, NLT, NRSV, REB], '(only)' [NTC, WBC], 'but only' [CEV, NCV], 'yet only' [TEV], 'yet' [HNTC], not explicit [AB, NICNT; KJV, NASB].

f. ὑπόλειμμα (LN 63.22) (BAGD p. 845): 'remnant' [AB, BAGD, BECNT, ICC2, LN, NICNT, NTC, WBC; KJV, NASB, NET, NIV, NLT, REB], 'remnant of them' [HNTC; NRSV], 'a few of them' [NCV, TEV], 'a few who are left' [CEV], 'small part' [LN]. This noun denotes a relatively small part which continues to exist [LN]. This word is emphatic [TH]. It is found only here in the NT.

g. fut. pass. indic. of σῴζω (LN 21.27) (BAGD 3. p. 798): 'to be saved' [AB, BAGD, BECNT, HNTC, ICC2, LN, NICNT, NTC, WBC; all versions]. This word can be used in two senses here, meaning to escape or be preserved, or to receive salvation. That is, those few who escape and are preserved are the ones who receive messianic salvation [BAGD]. This verb means to cause someone to experience divine salvation [LN].

QUESTION—What is meant by the verb σωθήσεται 'will be saved'?

It speaks of salvation [BECNT]. They are those Jews who accept Christ [AB], who return to God and are saved [Mor, NTC]. They are preserved, and also have salvation [BAGD].

QUESTION—What is the importance of the definite article 'the' with 'remnant'?

The article is significant [Gdt, Mor]. It is not an accidental leftover, but *the* remnant [Mor]. The remnant is something that is known [Gdt].

QUESTION—Is Paul being positive or negative about Israel's future prospects?
1. It is basically a positive statement [WBC]. It offers a ray of hope [AB, NTC]. It includes elements both of judgment and of hope [NICNT].
2. It is rather negative, in that *only* a remnant will be saved, and all others excluded [Mor]. The fact that only a remnant is saved, and that the rest experience wrath, serves to emphasize how great God's mercy is to the remnant [BECNT, Mu].

9:28 for finishing[a] and bringing-about-swiftly[b] he-will-carry-out[c] (his) sentence[d] on[e] the earth.

TEXT—Instead of συντέμνων 'bringing about swiftly', some manuscripts have συντέμνων εν δικαιοσύνῃ ὅτι λόγον συντετμημένον 'and cut it short in righteousness, because a short work' etc. GNT selects the shorter reading with an A rating, indicating that the text is certain. The longer reading is taken by KJV only.

LEXICON—a. pres. act. participle of συντελέω (LN **68.22**) (BAGD 2. p. 792): 'to carry out' [BAGD], 'to finish, to complete, to end' [LN], 'to accomplish' [BAGD, LN]. See the following word in item b. for translations of the phrase συντελῶν καὶ συντέμνων 'finishing and bringing about swiftly'. This verb means to successfully finish some activity, and here it could be translated 'he will accomplish what he has said', or with that meaning being implied, translated as 'he will settle the account' [LN]. The subject of the verb is 'the Lord'.

b. pres. act. participle of συντέμνω (LN **67.72**) (BAGD p. 792): 'to cut short' [NICNT, WBC], 'to cut short, to shorten, to bring to an end' [LN], 'to cut short (the time)' [**LN**]. The phrase συντελῶν καὶ συντέμνων 'finishing and bringing about swiftly' is translated 'accomplishing it and determining it' [HNTC], 'completing it and cutting it short' [NICNT], 'he will finish (the work), and cut it short' [KJV]. The two participles are also translated to show the manner in which the Lord will carry out his sentence: 'in a decisive way' [BECNT], 'with rigor and dispatch' [AB], 'with speed and finality' [NIV], 'quickly and with finality' [NLT], 'complete and cut short' [WBC], 'complete and decisive' [ICC2], 'summary and final' [REB], 'quickly and completely' [NCV],

'completely and quickly' [NTC; NET], 'completely and decisively' [GW], 'quickly and decisively' [NRSV], 'thoroughly and quickly' [NASB], 'quickly settle his full account' [TEV], 'he will be quick and sure (to do)' [CEV]. This verb means to cause something of duration to come to an abrupt end, with the implication of that being sooner than expected [LN]. It is found only here in the NT.
  c. fut. act. indic. of ποιέω (LN 42.7): 'to carry out' [AB, LN, NTC; GW, NIV, NLT], 'to accomplish' [BECNT, ICC2], 'to execute' [NASB, NET, NRSV], 'to perform' [NICNT, WBC], 'to do' [CEV], 'to make' [KJV], 'to bring (his word) to pass' [HNTC], not explicit [REB]. This verb means to do or perform, and can be used generically for almost any type of activity [LN].
  d. λόγος (LN 56.7) (BAGD 1.b.α. p. 478): 'a sentence' [ICC2], 'his sentence' [AB, NTC; GW, NET, NIV, NLT, NRSV], 'the Lord's sentence' [REB], 'his word' [BECNT, HNTC, NICNT, WBC; NASB], 'accusation' [LN]. The phrase 'he will carry out his sentence' is translated 'the Lord will be...sure to do...what he has warned he will do' [CEV], 'the Lord will...punish the people' [NCV], 'the Lord will settle his full account' [TEV]. This noun denotes a formal declaration of charges against someone in court [LN].
  e. ἐπί with genitive (LN 83.46): 'on' [AB, LN, NICNT, NTC, WBC; CEV, GW, NCV, NET, NIV, NRSV, REB], 'upon' [BECNT, HNTC, ICC2, LN; KJV, NASB, NLT], 'with' [TEV].
QUESTION—What relationship is indicated by γάρ 'for'?
  It introduces 9:28 as the grounds for what he has just said [BECNT]. It introduces 9:28 as the reason for what has just been said in 9:27; that is, only a small part will be saved because of how completely God will punish the people of the land [SSA].
QUESTION—What area of meaning is intended by λόγος 'sentence'?
  1. It is a judicial sentence that will be executed [AB, Gdt, ICC2, NTC; GW, NET, NIV, NLT, NRSV, REB]. It is his threat of judgment [Ho, SSA], his decree of judgment [Mu].
  2. It refers to God's promises, which will be fulfilled [BAGD].
  3. It refers both to God's warnings as well as to God's promises to Israel, which will be fulfilled [WBC].
QUESTION—What is meant by this statement?
  1. Judgment will be complete and decisive [BECNT, Gdt, ICC1, ICC2, Mor, NICNT, NTC, SSA, TH]. It will be accomplished with dispatch [Mu, NAC, NTC], thoroughness [Mu, NAC, NTC], and vigor [NTC].
  2. There is a cutting short or limitation in some sense to the fulfillment of God's promise, either that the promises will be fulfilled in a limited way or for a limited number from the remnant of Israel [AB]. It will be fulfilled for only a part of Israel [WBC].

9:29 And just-as[a] Isaiah predicted,[b] Unless[c] the Lord of-hosts[d] had-left[e] seed[f] to-us,

LEXICON—a. καθώς (LN 64.14) (BAGD 1. p. 391): 'just as' [BAGD, BECNT, LN, NICNT; NASB, NET, NIV], 'as' [AB, ICC2, NTC, WBC; KJV, NCV, NRSV, REB, TEV], not explicit [CEV, GW, NLT]. The word καθώς 'just as' is translated 'this accords further with what (Isaiah said)' [HNTC]. This adverb marks similarity in events and states, with the possible implication of something being in accordance with something else [LN].
  b. perf. act. indic. of προεῖπον (the aorist form of προλέγω) (LN 33.281, 33.423) (BAGD 1. p. 704): 'to predict' [AB, LN (33.281), NTC; GW, NET, NRSV], 'to warn' [LN (33.423)], 'to foretell' [BAGD, BECNT, ICC2, NICNT; NASB], 'to proclaim beforehand' [BAGD], 'to say beforehand' [WBC], 'to say before' [KJV, TEV], 'to say earlier' [HNTC], 'to say previously' [NIV, REB], 'to say in another place' [NLT], 'to say' [CEV, NCV]. This verb means to say in advance what is going to happen [LN].
  c. εἰ μή (LN 89.131): 'unless' [BECNT; NIV], 'except' [WBC; KJV, NASB], 'except that' [LN], 'if…had not' [AB, HNTC, NICNT, NTC; CEV, GW, NET, NLT, NRSV, REB, TEV], 'had not' [ICC2]. The clause 'unless…we would have become as…' is translated 'the Lord allowed…otherwise we would have become…' [NCV]. This expression marks contrast by designating an exception [LN].
  d. Σαβαώθ (LN **12.8**) (BAGD p. 738). This is a transliteration of a Hebrew plural noun. It is translated 'of Hosts' [AB, BAGD, BECNT, ICC2, NICNT, NTC; NRSV, REB], 'of Heaven's Armies' [NLT], 'of Armies' [GW, NET], 'Sabaoth' [HNTC], 'of Sabaoth' [WBC; KJV, NASB], 'almighty' [**LN**; NIV, TEV], 'all powerful' [LN; CEV, NCV]. This is a Greek transliteration of a Hebrew word meaning 'armies' which is used with κύριος 'Lord' as a title for God, and denotes one who has overwhelming power [LN].
  e. aorist act. indic. of ἐγκαταλείπω (LN **13.92**) (BAGD 1. p. 215): 'to leave' [AB, BECNT, HNTC, ICC2, LN, NICNT, NTC, WBC; GW, KJV, NASB, NET, NIV, NRSV, REB, TEV], 'to leave behind' [BAGD], 'to cause to remain' [LN], 'to spare' [CEV, NLT]. The clause 'unless the Lord of hosts had left seed to us' is translated 'the Lord All-Powerful allowed a few of our descendants to live' [NCV]. This verb means to cause something or someone to continue to exist, normally referring to a small part of a larger whole [LN].
  f. σπέρμα (LN 10.29) (BAGD 2.a. p. 761): 'seed' [BECNT, HNTC, ICC2, NICNT, NTC, WBC; KJV], 'posterity' [LN; NASB], 'offspring' [AB, LN], 'descendants' [LN; NET, NIV, REB], 'our descendants' [CEV], 'some descendants' [GW, TEV], 'a few of our descendants' [NCV], 'a few of our children' [NLT], 'survivors' [BAGD, LN; NRSV]. This noun

denotes posterity, with emphasis upon the ancestor's role in founding the lineage [LN].

QUESTION—What is meant by κύριος Σαβαώθ 'Lord of hosts'?

The Hebrew word 'Sabaoth' means 'host' or 'army' in the sense of any multitude orderly arranged, so it could refer to an army of men or angels, or to the arrangement of the stars or even of the whole universe [Ho]. It means that he is lord of all [Mor], of the whole heavens and all they contain [Ho]. The genitive construction, 'Lord of the hosts' means the Lord *who controls everything in heaven* [SSA]. Some translate this title without the idea of an army and simply say 'the Lord All-Powerful' [CEV, NCV], 'the Lord Almighty' [NIV, NLT, TEV].

QUESTION—Who are the σπέρμα 'seed' that he refers to here?

1. They are the true children of Abraham spoken of earlier [BECNT, HNTC, Mu, WBC], the remnant spoken of in the previous verse [AB, BECNT, Mu]. It refers to the 'seed' mentioned in 9:7–8 [NICNT, WBC]. These are the Israelites who are Abraham's true children and God's true children [BECNT, HNTC, Mu]. While 'remnant' is depressing, 'seed' can embrace all nations, Gentile and Jew [WBC]. It includes an element of hope for Israel [NICNT].
2. The image here is of seed reserved for sowing [Gdt, Ho]. A glorious future will spring and grow from that remnant [Gdt]. The noun 'seed' implies that God is the sower and that there is hope for the future [NTC]. It is used in a sense different from 9:7–8, here to express the idea that the survivors will be few, but with the prospect for new growth [ICC2, Mor].

we- would -have-become[a] like Sodom and we- would -have-been-made-like[b] Gomorrah.

LEXICON—a. aorist pass. (dep. = act.) indic. of γίνομαι (LN 13.48): 'to become' [BECNT, HNTC, ICC2, LN, NICNT, WBC; NASB, NET, NIV, REB, TEV], 'to be' [GW, KJV], 'to fare' [AB, NTC; NRSV], not explicit [CEV, NCV, NLT].

b. aorist pass. indic. of ὁμοιόω (LN 64.4) (BAGD 1. p. 567): 'to be made like' [AB, ICC2, NICNT, NTC; KJV, NRSV], 'to be like' [LN; GW, NIV, TEV], 'to become like' [BECNT, HNTC], 'to be the same as' [WBC], 'to resemble' [NASB, NET], 'to be destroyed like' [CEV], 'to be completely destroyed like' [NCV], 'to be wiped out like' [NCV]. The clause 'we would have become like Sodom and we would have been made like Gomorrah' is translated 'we should have become like Sodom, and no better than Gomorrah' [REB], 'we would have been destroyed like the cities of Sodom and Gomorrah' [CEV], 'we would have been completely destroyed like the cities of Sodom and Gomorrah' [NCV]. This verb means to be like or similar to something else [LN].

QUESTION—What is implied by the comparison to Sodom and Gomorrah?

It speaks of total destruction [ICC2, Mor, SSA], of annihilation [Gdt, ICC1, NICNT], of destruction by God's wrath [AB], of eschatological judgment

[WBC], of judgment with no survivors [SSA]. The fact that anybody is saved is a miracle of God's grace [BECNT, ICC2].

DISCOURSE UNIT—9:30–11:36 [BECNT]. The topic is God's righteousness to Israel and the Gentiles.

DISCOURSE UNIT—9:30–11:10 [BECNT]. The topic Israel's rejection of God's saving righteousness.

DISCOURSE UNIT—9:30–10:21 [AB, ICC1, ICC2, Mor, NAC, NICNT, TNTC, WBC; NET, NIV]. The topic is Israel's failure is derived from its own refusal [AB], Israel is without excuse, but in the light of Scripture we may hope that the fact that the Gentiles believe will provoke Israel to jealousy [ICC2], human responsibility [Mor], the cause of Israel's rejection [NAC], understanding Israel's plight: Christ as the climax of salvation history [NICNT], human responsibility [TNTC], the word of faith [WBC], Israel's rejection culpable [NET], Israel's unbelief [NIV].

DISCOURSE UNIT—9:30–10:13 [ICC1, NICNT]. The topic is Israel itself to blame for its rejection [ICC1], Israel, the Gentiles, and the righteousness of God [NICNT].

DISCOURSE UNIT—9:30–10:4 [WBC; NLT, NRSV]. The topic is Israel has misunderstood God's righteousness [WBC], Israel's unbelief [NLT, NRSV].

DISCOURSE UNIT—9:30–33 [AB, HNTC, Mor, NICNT, NTC, TNTC]. The topic is Israel has stumbled in its pursuit of uprightness [AB], why Israel stumbled [HNTC], the stumbling stone [Mor, TNTC], the righteousness of God and the law of righteousness [NICNT], conclusion [NTC].

9:30 What then shall we say?[a] That Gentiles,[b] the-ones not -pursuing[c] righteousness[d] received righteousness, but a righteousness from[e] faith,

LEXICON—a. The question Τί οὖν ἐροῦμεν; is translated 'What then shall we say?' [AB, HNTC, ICC2, NICNT, NTC, WBC; NIV], 'What shall we say then?' [BECNT; KJV, NASB, NET], 'What then are we to say?' [NRSV], 'Then what are we to say?' [REB], 'So what can we say?' [GW], 'What does all of this mean?' [CEV, NLT], 'So what does all this mean?' [NCV], 'So we say that…' [TEV].

    b. ἔθνη (LN 11.37): 'Gentiles' [AB, BECNT, HNTC, ICC2, NICNT, NTC, WBC; all versions except GW, NCV], 'non-Jewish people' [GW], 'those who are not Jews' [NCV], 'heathen, pagans' [LN]. This plural noun, which has no definite article, is translated without the article: 'Gentiles' [AB, HNTC, ICC2, NICNT, NTC, WBC; NASB, NRSV, REB]; as having the article: 'the Gentiles' [BECNT; CEV, KJV, NET, NIV, NLT, TEV]. This noun denotes those who do not belong to the Jewish or Christian faith [LN].

    c. pres. act. participle of διώκω (LN **68.66**) (BAGD 4.b. p. 201): 'to pursue' [AB, BECNT, ICC2, NICNT, NTC, WBC; NASB, NET, NIV], 'to follow

after' [KJV], 'to try to follow' [NLT], 'to make effort after' [REB], 'to strive for' [LN; NRSV], 'to make (righteousness) their aim' [HNTC]. This verb means to do something with intense effort and with definite purpose or goal [LN].
  d. δικαιοσύνη (LN 88.13) (BAGD 3. p. 197): 'righteousness' [BAGD, BECNT, HNTC, ICC2, LN, NICNT, NTC, WBC; KJV, NASB, NET, NIV, NRSV, REB], 'uprightness' [AB], God's standards [NLT]. The phrase 'the Gentiles, who were not seeking righteousness' is translated 'the Gentiles were not trying to be acceptable to God' [CEV], 'non-Jewish people who were not trying to gain God's approval' [GW], 'those who are not Jews were not trying to make themselves right with God' [NCV], 'the Gentiles, who were not trying to put themselves right with God' [TEV], 'the Gentiles were not trying to follow God's standards' [NLT]. This noun denotes the act of doing what God requires [LN].
  e. ἐκ with genitive (LN 90.16): 'from' [LN, WBC], 'of' [ICC2; KJV], 'by' [BECNT, LN, NTC; NASB, NET, NIV, NLT], 'through' [NRSV, TEV], 'based on' [AB, NICNT; GW, REB], 'which rests on' [HNTC], 'because of' [NCV]. The phrase 'the Gentiles…received righteousness, but a righteousness from faith' is translated 'the Gentiles…found that he would accept them if they had faith' [CEV], 'it was by faith that this took place' [NLT]. This preposition marks the source of an activity or state, with the implication of something proceeding from or out of the source [LN].

QUESTION—What is the function of this question Τί οὖν ἐροῦμεν; 'What then shall we say?'

Paul tries to anticipate and answer wrong assumptions about what he has said [BECNT], and also transitions to the next phase of his reasoning [AB, BECNT]. He is asking what we should conclude from what he has just been discussing [Ho, ICC2, SSA, St]. It introduces a summary of what he has been saying [HNTC, ICC1, Mor, NAC, NTC, TH]. It introduces the implication of what he has said in 9:6–29 [NICNT]. He has already dismissed the idea that God has annulled his word, and now transitions to the solution of the question of Israel's rejection [Gdt].

QUESTION—Should the sentence that begins ὅτι ἔθνη 'That Gentiles…' be understood as a statement or as a question?
  1. It is a statement [Gdt, HNTC, Ho, ICC1, ICC2, Mor, Mu, NAC, NICNT, SSA, St, WBC]. It is translated as a statement by all versions.
  2. It is a question that further explains the first question Τί οὖν ἐροῦμεν; 'What then shall we say? That Gentiles who did not pursue…?' [AB].

QUESTION—Is there an implied definite article with 'Gentiles'?
  1. There is no implied definite article [Gdt, HNTC, ICC1, ICC2, Mor, NICNT, NTC, SSA, St, WBC]. It refers to some Gentiles, not all [AB, ICC1, ICC2, WBC]. 'Gentile' is descriptive, referring to people who have this characteristic [Gdt]. Gentiles as a whole were not included [HNTC]. The emphasis is not on the number of Gentiles, but on the fact that they are Gentiles as opposed to Jews [NICNT].

2. It is translated as having a definite article by BECNT, but he does not comment on the issue.

QUESTION—What is the sense of the participle διώκοντα 'pursuing'?

It represents a quest characterized by zeal and energy [ICC2], by earnest effort [Mor]. It means to try to find something [SSA]. It is based on the metaphor of a runner in a race [AB, Ho, ICC1]. The main thought is that of pursuing a goal, which is more general than the idea of racing [WBC].

QUESTION—What does he mean when he says that Gentiles were not pursuing righteousness?

There were Gentiles who pursued moral uprightness, but not a right standing before God [ICC2, Mor, NICNT]. It was not that there were no Gentiles who lived a moral life, but that the righteousness they sought was not justification in the sense of a right relation to God [Gdt, Mu]. They weren't looking for a way by which they would be declared righteous in God's sight [SSA], or put into a harmonious relation to God [AB, HNTC]. There were Gentiles who were moral, but Paul's idea of 'righteousness' is defined by being in covenant relationship with God, which by definition excluded the Gentiles [WBC]. Prior to the coming of the gospel, Gentiles lived in moral and spiritual darkness [NTC]. Pagans were godless and self-centered [St].

QUESTION—What relationship is indicated by δέ 'but'?

It is explicative, introducing an explanation about the kind of righteousness he is talking about [Gdt, Mor].

QUESTION—What is meant by 'faith' that he speaks of here?

They put their trust in Christ [TH]. They trusted in what Christ did for them, believing that he died for their sin [SSA]. This faith came through the preaching of the gospel [HNTC].

9:31 **but[a] Israel seeking[b] a law[c] of[d] righteousness did not attain[e] (the) law.**

TEXT—Instead of εἰς νόμον οὐκ ἔφθασεν 'did not attain (the) law', some manuscripts have εἰς νόμον δικαιοσύνης οὐκ ἔφθασεν 'did not attain (the) law of righteousness'. GNT does not mention this alternative. Only KJV adopts this reading.

LEXICON—a. δέ (LN 89.124): 'but' [BECNT, HNTC, ICC2, LN, NICNT; KJV, NASB, NET, NIV, NLT, NRSV], 'whereas' [AB, WBC; REB], 'while' [TEV], 'however' [NTC], not explicit [CEV, GW, NCV]. This conjunction marks contrast [LN].

b. pres. act. participle of διώκω (LN 68.66) (BAGD 4.b. p. 201): 'to seek' [TEV], 'to strive toward' [LN], 'to strive for' [BAGD; NRSV], 'to pursue' [AB, BAGD, BECNT, ICC2, NICNT, WBC; NASB, NET, NIV], 'to be in pursuit of' [NTC], 'to try to follow' [NCV], 'to try' [CEV], 'to try to gain (God's approval)' [GW], 'to try so hard' [NLT], 'to seek after' [BAGD], 'to follow after' [KJV], 'to make great efforts after' [REB]. The phrase 'Israel seeking a law' is translated 'Israel, whose aim is the law' [HNTC].

c. νόμος (LN 33.333): 'law' [LN]. This noun, which lacks the definite article, is translated as not having the article: 'a law' [AB, HNTC, NICNT; NASB, NCV, NET, NIV, REB, TEV]; as having the article: 'the law' [BECNT, ICC2, NTC, WBC; CEV, KJV, NLT, NRSV], 'Moses' Teachings' [GW]. This noun denotes a formalized rule (or set of rules) prescribing what people must do [LN].

d. There is no lexical entry for this word in the Greek text. It reflects the genitive case of the word 'righteousness'. The phrase νόμον δικαιοσύνης 'a law of righteousness' [NICNT; NASB, NET, NIV, REB], is also translated 'a law of uprightness' [AB], 'the law of righteousness' [ICC2, NTC, WBC; KJV], 'the law for righteousness' [BECNT], 'a law purporting to give righteousness' [HNTC], 'the righteousness that is based on the law' [NRSV]. The phrase 'Israel seeking a law of righteousness' is translated 'the people of Israel…were trying to be acceptable by obeying the Law' [CEV], 'the people of Israel tried to gain God's approval by obeying Moses' Teachings' [GW], 'the people of Israel tried to follow a law to make themselves right with God' [NCV], 'but the Jews, who tried so hard to get right with God by keeping the law' [NLT], 'God's people, who were seeking a law that would put them right with God' [TEV].

e. aorist act. indic. of φθάνω (LN **13.16**) (BAGD 2. p. 857): 'to attain' [BAGD, LN], 'to achieve' [LN], 'to reach' [BAGD]. The phrase 'did not attain the law' is translated 'did not attain it' [**LN**; NET; similarly NIV], 'did not attain the Law' [BECNT], 'has not attained to that Law' [HNTC, NTC], 'has not attained to the law (of righteousness)' [KJV], 'but never attained to it' [REB], 'did not arrive at that law' [NASB], 'but did not reach their goal' [GW], 'has not reached the law' [WBC], 'never reached that Law' [HNTC], 'but they did not succeed' [NCV], 'did not succeed in fulfilling that law' [NRSV], 'never succeeded' [NLT], 'did not find it' [TEV], 'did not achieve that law' [ICC2], 'did not achieve it' [AB], 'were not acceptable to God' [CEV]. There is a contrast between seeking the law and not attaining the law, and that is why some translations have provided the conjunction 'but' [TH]. This verb means to attain or arrive at a particular state [LN].

QUESTION—What relationship is indicated by the use of the participle διώκων 'seeking'?

It is concessive; although they pursued they did not attain [BECNT, SSA; NET]. It is descriptive; the participle should not be taken as indicating the reason they did not succeed, it simply describes their committed lifestyle as devout members of Israel [WBC].

QUESTION—What relationship is indicated by the genitive construction νόμον δικαιοσύνης 'a law of righteousness'?

1. It means a law that could give righteousness; they were not seeking righteousness as such, but were seeking the law in its many details, and in so doing missed the spirit of it [Gdt]. It is a law that could lead to uprightness [AB], one that would put them right with God [TH]. It is a law

that promised a right status before God [ICC2, NAC], but God intended that what the law would show them was that the way of attaining righteousness is *faith* [ICC2, Mor]. It is a law that purports to give righteousness, although in actuality it is not able to do so [HNTC]. It is a law whose object is righteousness and that promises righteousness if its demands are met [NICNT]. It is a law that defines righteousness, being the standard that tells what God requires of the people in covenant with him [WBC]. Their goal was not righteousness, but a law that would bring them righteousness [TH]. It is a law that would be a basis for being declared righteous [SSA]. The concept of a law which promises righteousness is essentially the same as a righteousness that comes as a result of obeying the law [NAC]. It refers to the Mosaic law that the people of Israel followed [AB, HNTC, ICC2, NAC, NICNT, SSA, TH, WBC; CEV, GW].
2. It is a rule of life that would produce righteousness [ICC1]. It is the principle, institution, order, or rule that was concerned with justification, namely, their religion [Mu].

QUESTION—What does Paul mean by saying that they were seeking a law of righteousness?

They sought a righteous status before God by means of following what the law of Moses requires [ICC2, TH]. He is saying that they were seeking to be justified by their own righteousness [Ho]. They sought to be made right with God by their keeping the Mosaic law [AB, HNTC, NAC, NICNT]. They focused on the law because they thought they could attain righteousness through it [NICNT]. To attain the law is to live up to its demands [WBC]. They were seeking to attain a state of righteousness in God's sight by observing the entire law [NTC]. They were pursuing a legal righteousness, the path of acceptance with God that is based on law-keeping [TNTC]. They sought a rule of life that would produce righteousness [ICC1]. They pursued the institution that was concerned with justification, namely, their religion [Mu].

9:32 **Why?ᵃ Because not fromᵇ faith but asᶜ fromᵈ works;ᵉ**

TEXT—Instead of ἔργων 'works', some manuscripts have ἔργων νόμου 'works of the law'. GNT selects the reading 'works' with a B rating, indicating that the text is almost certain. The reading 'works of the law' is taken by KJV only.

LEXICON—a. The phrase διὰ τί is translated 'Why?' [BECNT, HNTC, ICC2, NTC; GW, NASB], 'Why so?' [WBC], 'Why was this?' [AB; REB], 'And why not?' [CEV, TEV], 'Why not?' [NET, NIV, NLT, NRSV], 'Wherefore?' [KJV], 'For what reason?' [NICNT], not explicit [NCV].
  b. ἐκ with genitive (LN 90.16): 'from' [LN, WBC], 'by' [BECNT, HNTC, LN, NTC; KJV, NASB, NET, NIV], 'by having' [CEV], 'with' [AB], 'on' [GW], 'on the basis of' [ICC2, NICNT; NRSV], 'to be based on' [REB], 'to depend on' [TEV]. The phrase 'not from faith' is translated

'instead of trusting in him' [NLT], 'instead of trusting in God to make them right' [NCV]. This preposition marks the source of an activity or state, with the implication of something proceeding from or out of the source [LN].
- c. ὡς (LN 64.12) (BAGD III.3. p. 898): 'as' [BECNT, ICC2, LN; KJV], 'as if' [AB, HNTC, NICNT, WBC; NET, NIV, NRSV], 'as though' [NASB], 'by' [NTC; CEV, NCV, NLT], not explicit [NCV, NLT]. The phrase ὡς ἐξ ἔργων 'as from works' is translated 'they relied on their own efforts' [GW], 'their efforts were...based on...deeds' [REB], 'they (did not) depend (on faith) but on what they did' [TEV].
- d. ἐκ with genitive (LN 90.16): 'from' [BECNT, LN, WBC], 'by' [AB, HNTC, LN; CEV, KJV, NASB, NCV, NET, NIV, NLT], 'on the basis of' [ICC2, NICNT], 'to be based on' [NRSV, REB], 'to depend on' [TEV], 'to rely on' [GW], 'by relying on' [NTC].
- e. ἔργον (LN 42.11) (BAGD 1.c.β. p. 308): 'act' [LN], 'deed' [BAGD, LN]. This plural noun is translated 'works' [BECNT, HNTC, ICC2, NICNT, WBC; NASB, NET, NIV, NRSV], 'their works' [NTC], 'deeds' [AB; REB], 'their own efforts' [GW], 'the things they did' [NCV], 'what they did' [TEV], 'the works of the law' [KJV], 'keeping the law' [NLT], 'obeying the Law' [CEV]. This noun denotes that which is done, with possible focus on the energy or effort involved [LN].

QUESTION—What is the implied verb in the verbless phrase ὅτι οὐκ ἐκ πίστεως ἀλλ' ὡς ἐξ ἔργων 'because not from faith but as from works'?

The implied thought would be the finite verb 'they pursued' [AB, HNTC, ICC2, Mor, NAC, NTC, SSA, WBC], or the participle 'seeking' [Gdt].

QUESTION—Who is the object of the faith Paul is talking about here?
1. It is faith in God [CEV]. It is trusting God [NCV, NLT], to make them right [NCV], as a way to get right with him [NLT]. It is trusting God to provide a way to save them [SSA].
2. It is faith in Christ [AB].

QUESTION—What relationship is indicated by the phrase ἀλλ' ὡς 'but as'?

It means 'as if it were possible' to do so by works [Gdt, HNTC, Ho, ICC2, Mor, NICNT]. It indicates that this is Israel's view of things [ICC1, TH, WBC], that righteousness is something that is exclusively theirs through their covenant relationship with God [WBC]. It indicates that this method of being put right with God could not have been successful [ICC2, SSA]. Their attempt to be right with God was 'not based on faith but, mistakenly, on deeds' [REB].

they-stumbled-against[a] the stone[b] of-stumbling,[c]

LEXICON—a. aorist act. indic. of προσκόπτω (LN 25.182) (BAGD 2.a. p. 716): 'to stumble against' [HNTC, ICC2], 'to stumble over' [AB, NICNT, NTC, WBC; GW, NASB, NCV, NET, NIV, NLT, NRSV, TEV], 'to stumble on' [BECNT], 'to stumble at' [KJV], 'to fall over' [CEV], 'to trip over' [REB], 'to take offense (at)' [BAGD, LN]. This verb means to

strike one's foot against something as one walks and in this way to lose one's balance temporarily [LN].
b. λίθος (LN 2.24) (BAGD 2. p. 474): 'stone' [AB, BAGD, BECNT, HNTC, ICC2, LN, NICNT, NTC, WBC; all versions except GW], 'rock' [GW]. This noun denotes a piece of rock, whether shaped or natural [LN].
c. πρόσκομμα (LN **15.229**) (BAGD 1.a. p. 716): 'stumbling' [BAGD, BECNT, ICC2, NICNT, WBC], 'that which causes stumbling' [LN], 'offense' [BAGD], not explicit [REB]. The phrase 'the stone of stumbling' is translated 'the stumbling stone' [AB, NTC; NASB, NET, NIV, NRSV, TEV], 'that stumblingstone' [KJV], 'the stone set for stumbling' [HNTC], 'the stone that causes people to stumble' [NCV], 'the stone that makes people stumble' [CEV], 'the rock that trips people' [GW], 'the great rock in their path' [NLT]. This noun denotes that which causes someone to stumble [LN].

QUESTION—What is the relation between the two clauses 'because not...works' and 'they stumbled...of stumbling'?

The lack of a linking word indicates the solemnity of what he is saying in the second clause [ICC2, WBC].

1. There should be a 'therefore' between them; the second clause states the consequence of what he has stated in the first one [BECNT].
2. The second clause states the underlying reason for what has been stated in the first clause [NTC, TH].

9:33 **just-as it-is-written, Look,[a] I-place[b] in Zion a stone of-stumbling and a rock of-offence,[c]**

LEXICON—a. ἰδού (LN 91.13): 'look' [AB, LN; CEV, TEV], 'see' [NIV, NRSV], 'behold' [BECNT, HNTC, ICC2, NICNT, NTC, WBC; KJV, NASB], 'look' [NET], 'here' [REB], not explicit [GW, NCV, NLT]. This particle is a prompter of attention, serving also to emphasize the following statement [LN].

b. pres. act. indic. of τίθημι (LN 85.32) (BAGD I.1.a.α. p. 815): 'to place' [BAGD, LN, NICNT, WBC; CEV, GW, NLT, TEV], 'to lay' [BAGD, BECNT, HNTC, ICC2, NTC; KJV, NASB, NET, NIV, NRSV, REB], 'to put' [BAGD, LN; NCV], 'to set' [AB]. This verb means to put or place something in a particular location [LN].

c. σκάνδαλον (LN 25.181) (BAGD 2. p. 753): 'offense' [BECNT, ICC2, LN, NICNT, NTC, WBC; KJV, NASB], 'what causes offense' [LN], 'temptation to sin, enticement to apostasy' [BAGD]. The phrase 'a rock of offence' is translated 'a rock to trip over' [AB], 'a rock for tripping' [HNTC], 'a rock to stumble against' [REB], 'a stone to make people (stumble and) fall' [CEV], 'a rock that makes them fall' [NCV, NIV, NLT], 'a rock that will make them fall' [NET, NRSV, TEV], 'a large rock that people find offensive' [GW]. This noun denotes that which causes offense and thus arouses opposition [LN].

QUESTION—What does Zion refer to?

It is the name for the hill on which Jerusalem is build, but represents Jerusalem and then the nation of Israel [SSA].

QUESTION—What or who is the stone of stumbling?

This stone is a metaphor that refers to Christ [AB, Gdt, HNTC, Ho, ICC1, ICC2, Mor, Mu, NICNT, NTC, St, TH, WBC]. The Jewish audience already understood that this passage referred to the coming Messiah [SSA]. The term 'stone' had been used of Christ in the Gospel passages about the stone that the builders rejected [ICC1]. People 'stumble' over the plan of salvation that he revealed [Ho]. It is the gospel of Christ [TNTC]. Christ's obscurity and suffering were offensive to the Jews [HNTC]. It is Christ's death on the cross, which was disgusting to them [SSA]. It is justification by faith [NAC].

QUESTION—What is the difference, if any, between πρόσκομμα 'stumbling', and σκάνδαλον 'offense'?

1. They are a doublet, meaning basically the same thing [SSA]. They are near synonyms [WBC].
2. Πρόσκομμα is the shock of the moral conflict between Israel and its Messiah, the way they falsely judged him and his ministry; σκάνδαλον is the fall coming from their unbelief, which is their rejection of him and of God himself through him [Gdt].

and the-one believing[a] on[b] him[c] will- not -be-ashamed.[d]

LEXICON—a. pres. act. participle of πιστεύω (LN 31.85) (BAGD 2.a.γ. p. 661): 'to believe (in/on)' [AB, BAGD, BECNT, HNTC, ICC2, LN, NICNT, WBC; GW, KJV, NASB, NET, NRSV, TEV], 'to trust' [BAGD, LN; NCV, NIV, NLT], 'to put one's trust' [NTC], 'to have faith' [CEV, REB]. This verb means to believe to the extent of complete trust and reliance [LN].

b. ἐπί with dative (LN 90.57) (BAGD II.1.b.γ. p. 287): 'on' [BAGD, ICC2, LN, NICNT; KJV], 'upon' [HNTC], 'in' [AB, BAGD, BECNT, NTC, WBC; all versions except KJV]. This preposition marks an experiencer [LN].

c. αὐτός (LN 92.11). This pronoun is masculine because it refers to the λίθος 'stone', which is grammatically masculine. It is translated as referring to a person: 'him' [AB, BECNT, ICC2, NTC; GW, KJV, NASB, NCV, NET, NIV, NLT, NRSV, TEV], 'that one' [CEV], 'me' [WBC]; as referring to the stone as an object: 'it' [HNTC, NICNT; REB].

d. fut. pass. indic. of καταισχύνω (LN 25.194) (BAGD 3.b. p. 411): 'to be ashamed' [GW, KJV], 'to be put to shame' [AB, BAGD, BECNT, HNTC, ICC2, LN, NICNT, NTC, WBC; NET, NIV, NRSV, REB], 'to be disappointed' [BAGD; CEV, NASB, NCV, TEV], 'to be disgraced' [NLT]. This verb means to cause someone to be much ashamed [LN].

QUESTION—What is the relationship of this clause to the first clause, which begins with 'Look'?

It is a contraexpectation; that is, although Christ is a cause of offense to some, yet others believe in him and won't be disillusioned or disappointed in their hope [SSA].

QUESTION—What is the meaning of the verb καταισχύνω 'be ashamed' in this context?

They will have vindication at the final judgment [BECNT, WBC]. They won't be condemned when they stand before God in the final judgment [Mor]. They won't be disillusioned in what they had hoped for [Mu, SSA, TNTC].

DISCOURSE UNIT—10:1–21 [Ho, Mu, St; GW]. The topic is the rejection of the Jews as the particular people of God, and the extension of the offers of salvation to all nations [Ho], the righteousness of faith [Mu], Israel's fault: God's dismay over her disobedience [St], if you believe you will be saved [GW].

DISCOURSE UNIT—10:1–13 [HNTC, Mor, NTC, TNTC]. The topic is the righteousness of men and the righteousness of God [HNTC], two ways of righteousness [Mor, TNTC], self-righteousness versus the righteousness that comes from God and is appropriated by faith [NTC].

DISCOURSE UNIT—10:1–4 [AB, NICNT]. The topic is uprightness comes from faith in Christ, who is the end of the Law [AB], the righteousness of God and their own righteousness [NICNT].

10:1 **Brothers,[a] the desire[b] of-my heart[c] and (my) prayer[d] to God for them (is) for[e] their salvation.[f]**

LEXICON—a. ἀδελφός (LN 11.23): 'fellow believer, Christian brother' [LN]. This plural noun is translated 'brothers' [AB, NTC, WBC; NIV], 'my brothers', [TEV], 'brethren' [HNTC, ICC2; KJV, NASB], 'brothers and sisters' [BECNT, NICNT; GW, NCV, NET, NRSV], 'dear brothers and sisters' [NLT], 'friends' [CEV, REB]. This noun denotes a close associate of a group of persons having a well-defined membership [LN]. The position of this word in the sentence shows emphasis [ICC1, Mor]. Its use by Paul is always emphatic [ICC1].

 b. εὐδοκία (LN **25.8**) (BAGD 3. p. 319): 'desire' [AB, BAGD, BECNT, ICC2, LN, NICNT, NTC, WBC; GW, KJV, NASB, NET, NIV, NRSV, REB], 'wish' [BAGD; CEV], 'will' [HNTC]. This noun is translated as a verb: 'to wish' [TEV]. The phrase ἡ εὐδοκία τῆς ἐμῆς καρδίας 'the desire of my heart' is translated 'the thing I want most' [NCV], 'the longing (of my heart)' [NLT], 'my deepest wish' [CEV], 'what I wish for with all my heart' [**LN**]. This noun denotes that which is desired on the basis of its appearing to be beneficial [LN]. This word expresses the depth of Paul's affection for them [Mor].

c. καρδία (LN 26.3) (BAGD 1.b.ε. p. 404): 'heart' [BAGD, BECNT, HNTC, ICC2, LN, NICNT, NTC, WBC; all versions except CEV, NCV], not explicit [CEV, NCV]. The use of this word indicates the depth and sincerity of what Paul is saying [WBC]. This noun denotes the source of a person's psychological life, especially one's thoughts [LN].

d. δέησις (LN 33.171) (BAGD p. 172): 'prayer' [AB, BAGD, BECNT, ICC2, LN, NICNT, NTC, WBC; CEV, GW, KJV, NCV, NET, NIV, NLT, NRSV, REB], 'request, plea' [LN], 'supplication' [HNTC]. This noun is translated as a verb: 'to pray' [TEV]. This noun denotes that which is asked with urgency based on presumed need [LN].

e. ὑπέρ with genitive object (LN 90.24): 'for' [BECNT, NICNT, WBC; NET, REB], 'concerning, about' [LN], not explicit [AB, HNTC, ICC2, NTC; CEV, GW, KJV, NCV, NIV, NLT, NRSV, TEV]. This preposition marks general content, whether of a discourse or mental activity [LN].

f. σωτηρία (LN 21.25, 21.26) (BAGD 2. p. 801): 'salvation' [AB, BAGD, BECNT, LN, NICNT, WBC; NASB, NET, REB]. This noun is translated as a verb: 'to be saved' [HNTC, ICC2, NTC; CEV, GW, KJV, NCV, NIV, NLT, NRSV, TEV]. This noun denotes the process of being saved or the state of having been saved [LN].

QUESTION—What relationship is indicated by μέν (untranslated) in the phrase Ἀδελφοί, ἡ μὲν εὐδοκία 'Brothers, the desire…'?

1. It strengthens the impact of what Paul is saying [HNTC, TH]. Paul is saying that, despite the fact of God's election and the predictions of Scripture about Jewish unbelief, he still earnestly desires their salvation [HNTC].
2. It means to 'the degree that it depends on what I want' [ICC2, WBC].
3. It sets up a contrast, the antithesis of which is in 10:3; that is, he prays for their salvation, but they are missing it [ICC1].

10:2 For I-bear- them -witness[a] that they-have a zeal[b] (for)[c] God but not according-to[d] knowledge;[e]

LEXICON—a. pres. act. indic. of μαρτυρέω (LN 33.262) (BAGD 1.a. p. 492): 'to bear witness' [BAGD, HNTC, ICC2, WBC;], 'to witness' [LN], 'to testify' [AB, BAGD, BECNT, NICNT, NTC; NET, NIV, NRSV, REB], 'to know' [CEV, NLT], 'to assure (you)' [GW], 'to be able to assure (you)' [TEV], 'to bear record' [KJV], 'to be able to say' [NCV]. This verb means to provide information about a person or an event concerning which the speaker has direct knowledge [LN].

b. ζῆλος (LN **25.46**) (BAGD 1. p. 337): 'zeal' [AB, BAGD, BECNT, ICC2, NICNT, NTC, WBC; KJV, NASB, NRSV, REB], 'enthusiasm' [HNTC; NLT]. The phrase 'they have a zeal for God' is translated 'they are zealous for God' [NET, NIV], 'they are deeply devoted to God' [LN; GW, TEV], 'they really try to follow God' [NCV], 'they love God' [CEV]. This noun denotes having a deep concern for or devotion to

someone or something [LN]. Its position in the clause shows emphasis [ICC2].
c. There is no lexical entry for the preposition 'for' in the Greek text, the relation between 'zeal' and 'God' being indicated by the use of the genitive case of 'God'. This relation is translated 'for' [AB, BECNT, HNTC, ICC2, NICNT, NTC, WBC; NASB, NET, NIV, NLT, NRSV, REB], 'to' [GW, TEV], 'of' [KJV], not explicit [CEV, NCV].
d. κατά with accusative object (LN 89.8) (BAGD II.5.a.γ. p. 407): 'according to' [BAGD, BECNT, ICC2, NICNT; KJV], 'in accordance with' [LN, WBC; NASB], '(not) based on' [NTC; NIV, TEV], 'in line with' [NET], not explicit [AB, HNTC; CEV, GW, NCV, NLT, NRSV, REB]. This preposition marks a relation involving similarity of process [LN].
e. ἐπίγνωσις (LN **28.18**) (BAGD p. 291): 'knowledge' [BAGD, BECNT, ICC2, LN, NICNT, NTC, WBC; KJV, NASB, NIV, TEV], 'understanding' [HNTC]. The phrase 'not according to knowledge' is translated 'not well informed' [AB], 'they don't understand' [CEV], 'they are misguided' [GW], 'they do not know the right way' [NCV], 'their zeal is not in line with the truth' [NET], 'it is misdirected zeal' [NLT], 'it is not enlightened' [NRSV], 'it is an ill-informed zeal' [REB]. This noun denotes the content of what is definitely known [LN].

QUESTION—What relationship is indicated by γάρ 'for'?

It indicates that what follows is the reason or basis for the concern Paul expressed for his own people in the previous verse [AB, Ho, ICC1]. It indicates 10:2 as the reason that he prays for them earnestly, which is that they have such a zeal for God [BECNT, ICC2], although this may not be the only reason [ICC2]. It indicates why Paul is so grieved [ICC1]. It indicates the situation that underlies Paul's concern for the Jews [SSA]. The reason the Jews have not found salvation is that, although they had plenty of zeal, their knowledge was lacking [NICNT].

QUESTION—What was this zeal for God?

It was a strong desire to live in a way that is in according with God's will [NTC]. It was religious sincerity, but without knowledge it became fanaticism [St]. It was their attachment to the worship of God and the ceremonies involved, and intensified by numerous persecutions at the hands of Gentiles over the years [Gdt]. They had zeal for their law, their traditions, and even for their own merits [Ho]. It was a passionate and overwhelming concern to do the will of God and a depth of dedication to the covenant with him [WBC]. It was their religious interest [Mu]. They gave themselves to God with a devoted and courageous zeal [HNTC]. They sought God zealously [SSA]. Their zeal was fervent, concentrated, and tenacious [ICC2]. The Jew prided himself in this zeal more than anything else [ICC1].

QUESTION—How was their zeal an ignorant one?

Despite the fact that they were so dedicated and careful in their obedience, their ignorance was actually obstinate and perverse, and missing the most important point [ICC2]. They lacked the higher knowledge, which is the true knowledge of God, and the moral discernment that enables one to learn the right way [ICC1]. They failed to discern the true meaning and the moral goal and intent of their law and rituals [Gdt]. While they did have some knowledge of God, they lacked correct knowledge and understanding and were unwise [Ho]. They had no insight into how God provides righteousness [NAC]. They didn't recognize how God's righteousness is bestowed, and they were too nationalistic [WBC]. They failed to acknowledge God's gift of righteousness [NTC]. They did not recognize how God was working out his plan in the world [NICNT]. Their ignorance was without excuse, because they should have known [Mor].

10:3 for not-knowing[a] the righteousness[b] of-God and seeking[c] to-establish[d] their-own, to the righteousness of-God they-did- not -submit.[e]

LEXICON—a. pres. act. participle of ἀγνοέω (LN 28.13, 32.7) (BAGD 2. p. 11): 'to not know' [BAGD, LN, WBC; NASB, NCV, NIV, TEV], 'to not understand' [HNTC; GW, NLT], 'to be ignorant of' [BECNT, LN (28.13), NICNT; KJV, NRSV], 'to fail to understand' [LN (32.7)], 'to be unaware' [AB], 'to fail to recognize' [ICC2], 'to fail to acknowledge' [NTC], 'to ignore' [NET, REB], not explicit [CEV]. This participle is the first word in the sentence, showing emphasis [TH]. This verb means to not have information about something or to not be able to understand [LN]. It could also be translated 'disregarding' [WBC].

b. δικαιοσύνη (LN 88.13) (BAGD 3. p. 197): 'righteousness' [BAGD, BECNT, HNTC, ICC2, LN, NICNT, NTC, WBC; KJV, NASB, NET, NIV, NRSV, REB], 'uprightness' [AB]. The phrase 'the righteousness of God' is translated 'what makes people acceptable to God' [CEV], 'how to receive God's approval' [GW], 'the way that God makes people right with him' [NCV], 'God's way of making people right with himself' [NLT], 'the way in which God puts people right with himself' [TEV]. This noun denotes the act of doing what God requires [LN].

c. pres. act. participle of ζητέω (LN 25.9) (BAGD 2.b.γ. p. 339): 'to strive for' [BAGD], 'to desire' [BAGD, LN], 'to wish' [BAGD], 'to seek to' [AB, BECNT, HNTC, ICC2, NICNT, NTC, WBC; NASB, NET, NIV, NRSV], 'to try to' [CEV, GW, NCV, REB, TEV], 'to go about to' [KJV], 'to cling to (their own way)' [NLT]. This verb means to desire (and attempt) to have or experience something [LN].

d. aorist act. inf. of ἵστημι (LN **76.21**) (BAGD I.2.a. p. 382): 'to establish' [BAGD, BECNT, HNTC, ICC2, LN, NICNT, NTC, WBC; KJV, NASB, NET, NIV, NRSV], 'to keep' [NLT], 'to make valid' [BAGD], 'to set up' [AB; GW, REB, TEV], 'to be acceptable' [CEV], 'to make (themselves)' [NCV]. This verb means to establish as validated and in force [LN].

e. aorist pass. indic. of ὑποτάσσω (LN 37.31) (BAGD 1.b.β. p. 848). This passive verb is translated as active: 'to submit to' [AB, HNTC, ICC2, NICNT, NTC; KJV, NET, NIV, NRSV, REB, TEV], 'to refuse to trust'

[CEV], 'to accept' [GW, NCV], 'to obey' [BAGD]; as middle: 'to subject oneself' [BAGD, BECNT, LN, WBC; NASB]. The phrase 'they did not submit' is translated 'refusing to accept' [NLT]. This verb means to bring something under the firm control of someone [LN].

QUESTION—What relationship is indicated by γάρ 'for'?

It indicates an explanation as to what Paul meant by what was just said in the previous verse about their zeal [AB, BECNT, Mu, SSA, TH]. It indicates an explanation as to why their zeal was uninformed [ICC1, ICC2, Mu, NICNT]. It indicates the grounds for the statement that their zeal was uninformed [Mor].

QUESTION—What relationship is indicated by the participles ἀγνοοῦντες 'not knowing' and ζητοῦντες 'seeking'?

1. They explain what it means to have a zeal that is without knowledge [AB, Gdt, ICC2]. The main clause following the two participial clauses states the disobedience that resulted from that ignorance [ICC2]. It explains why they had zeal without knowledge [ICC1].
2. They are causal, indicating why the people of Israel did not submit themselves to God's righteousness [BECNT, HNTC, SSA, WBC]. Not submitting to the righteousness of God is both a consequence of their ignorance of his righteousness as well as an extension of it [WBC].

QUESTION—What is 'the righteousness of God' in this context?

1. It is the righteousness that comes from God [Gdt, HNTC, Ho, ICC1, Mor, NAC, NTC, St, TH]. It is a right standing with God that comes from God [Mor], and is his gift [HNTC], a righteousness that has God as its author and is based on what Christ has done in his atoning work [NTC]. It is the way God makes or declares people to be righteous [SSA].
2. It is God's righteousness at work as an active power [AB, BECNT, Mu, NICNT, WBC]. It is God's own uprightness as well as his active acquitting power [AB]. It is God's own righteousness which is powerfully active as God's provision to meet man's fundamental need, which is justification [Mu]. It is God's gracious power that accepts and sustains those who believe [WBC]. It is God's saving righteousness, which includes his work of transformation [BECNT]. It is God's dynamic action by which he brings people into right relationship with himself [NICNT].

QUESTION—In what way were they trying to establish their own righteousness?

1. They were trying to make themselves right before God [AB, BECNT, HNTC, Ho, ICC1, Mu, NAC, NICNT, St, TH]. They tried to make themselves upright by doing what the law requires [AB, Gdt, NAC], by being perfectly obedient to the law [HNTC], by good works [BECNT, St], and religious observances [St], by human character and works [Mu], by human effort [NICNT]. In seeking a righteousness they had earned they were refusing to let grace be grace [ICC2]. They did not comprehend that human righteousness can never satisfy God's just requirements [HNTC,

St]. They trusted in their own merits and advantages as the basis for which God would accept them [Ho].
2. Disregarding how God puts people right with him by faith, they focused only on their own status within the covenant with God, but this had the effect in their thinking of excluding the Gentiles from a right relation to God. The contrast implied in 'their own' is not a contrast between their own righteousness, accomplished by themselves, as opposed to God's righteousness, but their own righteousness as opposed to anyone else's, meaning that they saw right relation with God as something that was exclusively theirs and not shared by any other people [WBC].

10:4 **For Christ is the end[a] of-(the) law[b] for[c] righteousness[d] for/to[e] all those-believing.**

LEXICON—a. τέλος (LN 67.66, 89.55) (BAGD 1.a., c. p. 811): 'end' [AB, BAGD (1.a.), BECNT, HNTC, ICC2, LN (67.66), WBC; KJV, NASB, NET, NIV, NRSV, REB, TEV], 'termination, cessation' [BAGD (1.a.)], 'culmination' [NICNT], 'goal' [BAGD (1.c.), LN (89.55), NTC], 'purpose' [BAGD (1.c.), LN (89.55)], 'intent' [LN (89.55)], 'fulfillment' [GW]. The phrase 'end of the law' is translated as a verbal phrase 'makes the Law no longer necessary' [CEV], '(Christ) ended the law' [NCV], '(Christ) has already accomplished the purpose for which the law was given' [NLT]. This noun denotes a point of time marking the end of some period of time [LN (67.66)], or it denotes the purpose for bringing about some result [LN (89.55)], or it denotes the termination of the law [BAGD (1.a.)], and perhaps at the same time the goal of the law [BAGD (1.c.)]. It is placed first in the sentence for emphasis [BECNT].

b. νόμος (LN 33.55, 33.333) (BAGD 3. p. 542): 'the Law' [LN (33.55); CEV], 'law' [AB, BECNT, HNTC, ICC2, LN (33.333), NICNT, NTC, WBC; KJV, NASB, NCV, NET, NIV, NLT, NRSV, TEV], 'the law of Moses' [BAGD], 'Moses' Teachings' [GW]. This noun can denote the first five books of the Old Testament [LN (33.55)], or a formalized rule prescribing what people must do [LN (33.333)].

c. εἰς with accusative object (LN 90.23, 89.57, 89.48): 'for' [KJV, NASB], 'concerning, about' [LN (90.23)], 'for the purpose of, in order to' [LN (89.57)], 'to cause, with the result that' [LN (89.48); NET], 'so that' [AB, ICC2, NICNT, NTC; GW, NCV, NIV, TEV], 'with reference to' [BECNT], 'as a means to' [WBC], not explicit [HNTC; CEV, NLT, NRSV]. The phrase 'for righteousness' is translated 'brings righteousness' [REB]. This preposition marks content as a means of specifying a particular referent [LN (90.23)], or can mark intent (with expected result) [LN (89.57)], or can mark result, with the probable implication of a preceding process [LN (89.48)].

d. δικαιοσύνη (LN 88.13) (BAGD 3. p. 197): 'righteousness' [BAGD, BECNT, HNTC, ICC2, LN, NICNT, NTC, WBC; KJV, NASB, NET, NIV, NRSV, REB], 'uprightness' [AB], not explicit [CEV, GW, NCV].

The phrase 'for righteousness' is translated 'made right with God' [NLT], 'put right with God' [TEV]. This noun denotes the act of doing what God requires [LN].
e. There is no lexical entry for the preposition 'for/to' in the Greek text, the dative case of the participle πιστεύοντι being used to express the relation between it and the subject of the sentence τέλος 'end'. This relation is translated 'for' [AB, HNTC, NICNT, NTC, WBC; CEV, NET, NIV, NRSV, REB], 'to' [BECNT, ICC2; KJV, NASB], not explicit [GW, NCV, NLT].

QUESTION—What relationship is indicated by γάρ 'for'?
1. It relates to what he has said in 10:3 [AB, BECNT, ICC2, Mor, Mu, NICNT, WBC]. It indicates 10:4 as a further explanation of what he has just said in 10:3 [AB, ICC2, WBC]. It indicates an explanation of what it means that they did not submit to God's righteousness [ICC2]. It indicates the grounds for what Paul implied in 10:3, that the Jews were wrong about how they were looking for righteousness [Mor]. It indicates the grounds for his statement in 10:3 that it is not man's righteousness but God's that God has instituted as the way of salvation [Mu]. An unstated proposition must be supplied; either *the Jews were wrong* for their failure to submit to God's righteousness because Christ is the end of the law, or *believers have submitted* to God's righteousness because Christ is the end of the law [BECNT]. The Jews were wrong to pursue a righteousness of their own because Christ has brought a culmination to the law and made righteousness available for believers [NICNT].
2. It indicates a reason for what he says in 10:2 concerning why the Jews were wrong in having failed to submit to God's law, which is that their zeal was 'without knowledge' [ICC1, SSA].

QUESTION—What is meant by νόμος 'law'?
1. It is the law of Moses [AB, BECNT, HNTC, Ho, ICC2, Mor, NAC, NICNT, NTC, SSA, St, TH, TNTC, WBC]. It is the whole rule of human duties, including the law of Moses for the Jews [Ho].
2. It is law generally, or as a principle [ICC1, Mu]. It is law as commandment requiring obedience [Mu]. This refers to any legal requirements used as a method for obtaining righteousness [ICC1].

QUESTION—What does τέλος 'end' mean in the phrase 'Christ is the end of the law' and how is this related to the prepositional phrase εἰς δικαιοσύνην παντὶ τῷ πιστεύοντι 'for righteousness for all who believe'?
(The reader should note that understanding and interpreting this verse is quite challenging and various opinions have been expressed throughout the history of the church. It is considered to express a very significant statement of Paul's theology regardless of what position one takes.)
1. Christ brings about the ending or termination of the law as a way of attaining righteousness [BECNT, Gdt, Ho, ICC1, Mor, Mu, NAC, SSA, St, TH; CEV, NCV, NET, NRSV, REB, TEV]. Christ makes the law no longer necessary [CEV].

1.1 Righteousness was the purpose of this termination [Ho, ICC1, NAC, St, WBC; NCV, NIV, NRSV]. Christ has brought the law to an end so that righteousness may be available to all who believe [NAC]. Christ has abrogated the law by fulfilling its demands [Ho].
1.2 Righteousness is the result of this termination [Gdt, TH; NET, REB, TEV]. Because Christ has brought the law to an end, God puts people who believe right with himself [TH].
1.3 Righteousness was both the purpose and result of this termination; Christ put an end to the economy of law to make righteousness available, and now it is offered to and given to believers [Gdt].
1.4 Attaining righteousness was the purpose for which some people used the law, but that has now come to an end [BECNT, Mor, Mu, SSA, WBC]. For believers, Christ brings an end to using the law to attain righteousness [BECNT]. Christ brought an end to the law's perceived function as a way of attaining righteousness [Mor, SSA]. Paul is saying that Christ has brought an end to the law's perceived function of granting Israel an exclusive access to relationship with God [WBC].
2. Christ is the goal of the law, bringing righteousness as a result [AB, ICC2, NTC]. The OT law was given to establish love, and Christ is the goal, meaning, and substance of that law [NTC]. Christ is the goal and fulfillment of the law because faith in him brings about the kind of love that is the fulfillment of the law, righteousness now being the result of what Christ has accomplished [AB]. The aim, intent, and real meaning of the law is found in Christ, with the result being that righteousness is now available for those who believe in Christ [ICC2].
3. Christ is both the goal and the termination of the law [HNTC, NICNT, TNTC]. The OT law is perfectly fulfilled in Christ, so it should no longer be seen as a means for acquiring a righteous status before God [TNTC]. Instead of destroying the law, Christ puts an end to it by realizing all that it stands for [HNTC]. If Paul is continuing the analogy of a race (begun with the word 'pursue' in 9:30-31), then his use of τέλος could be a continuation of that analogy, since the race is ended when the goal is reached. That is, Christ has brought the era of the law to an end and is himself what the law was pointing toward [NICNT].
3.1 Christ has realized righteousness for every believer, with the result that he has brought about the end of the law as the order of relations between God and man [HNTC].
3.2 Christ has brought about the end of the law, doing so for the purpose of bringing righteousness to all who believe [NICNT].

DISCOURSE UNIT—10:5–21 [CEV, NLT, NRSV, TEV]. The topic is anyone can be saved [CEV], salvation is for everyone [NLT], salvation is for all [NRSV, TEV].

DISCOURSE UNIT—10:5–13 [AB, NICNT, WBC]. The topic is the gospel and law [NICNT], the righteous from the law and the righteous from faith

[WBC], the new way of uprightness, open to all, is easy and near at hand, as Scripture shows [AB].

10:5 For Moses writes-about[a] the righteousness from[b] (the) law that[c] The man doing[d] (these) things shall-live by[e] them.

TEXT—Textual questions in this verse are rather complex. The GNT (UBS 4th edition), Nestle-Aland 26th and 27th editions, and most contemporary versions accept the reading Μωϋσῆς γὰρ γράφει τὴν δικαιοσύνην τὴν ἐκ [τοῦ] νόμου ὅτι ὁ ποιήσας αὐτὰ ἄνθρωπος ζήσεται ἐν αὐτοῖς, 'For Moses writes about the righteousness from (the) law that The man doing (these) things shall live by them'. Some manuscripts have the alternative reading (or minor variations of it) Μωϋσῆς γὰρ γράφει ὅτι τὴν δικαιοσύνην τὴν ἐκ νόμου ὁ ποιήσας ἄνθρωπος ζήσεται ἐν αὐτῇ, 'For Moses writes that The man doing the righteousness from (the) law shall live by it'. GNT does not mention this second alternative. It is the reading taken by Nestle-Aland 25th edition, but in subsequent editions Nestle-Aland has accepted the first option listed above. The second reading is taken only by ICC2 and NASB.

LEXICON—a. pres. act. indic. of γράφω (LN 33.61) (BAGD 2.c. p. 167): 'to write about' [BAGD, LN, NICNT; GW, NCV, NET, TEV], 'to write thus of' [AB], 'to write concerning' [BECNT; NRSV], 'to write of' [HNTC; REB], 'to write that' [NLT], 'to describe (in this way)' [NTC; NIV], 'to write with reference to' [WBC], 'to say that' [CEV], 'to describe' [KJV]. ICC2 and NASB also translate 'to write that', but this reflects their acceptance of the variant reading that includes ὅτι 'that' after γράφει 'writes'.

b. ἐκ with genitive object (LN 89.77, 90.16, 89.3): 'from, by means of' [LN (89.77)], 'from' [LN (89.3)], 'from, by' [LN (90.16); TEV], 'through' [REB]. This preposition is translated as a phrase: 'that is by' [NTC; NET, NIV], 'that is from' [BECNT], 'that comes from' [AB; NRSV], 'which is of' [ICC2; KJV], 'which is from' [WBC], 'which has its roots in' [HNTC], 'that is based on' [NICNT; NASB], 'attained through' [REB], 'by obeying' [CEV, TEV], 'by following' [GW, NCV], not explicit [NLT]. This preposition marks means as constituting a source [LN (89.77)], or the source of an activity or state [LN (90.16)], or the source from which someone or something is physically or psychologically derived [LN (89.3)].

c. ὅτι (LN 90.21): 'that' [HNTC, ICC2, LN; KJV, NASB], not explicit [NLT]. This adverb marks discourse content, whether direct or indirect [LN]. This discourse marker indicates that what follows is a citation from Scripture [AB, BECNT, NICNT, NTC, WBC; CEV, GW, NCV, NET, NIV, NRSV, REB, TEV].

d. aorist act. participle of ποιέω (LN 90.45): 'to do' [AB, BECNT, HNTC, ICC2, LN, NICNT, NTC, WBC; CEV, KJV, NET, NIV, NRSV], 'to practice' [LN; NASB], 'to perform' [LN], 'to obey' [GW, NCV, TEV],

'to keep' [REB]. This verb is translated as a noun: 'obedience' [NLT]. This verb marks an agent relation with a numerable event [LN].
  e. ἐν with dative object (LN 89.76): 'by' [BECNT, HNTC, LN, NTC; KJV, NASB, NET, NIV, NRSV, REB], 'by means of, through' [LN], 'in' [AB, ICC2, NICNT, WBC], 'because of' [NCV]. This word is translated by a phrase 'you must do all that the Law commands' [CEV], '…because of the laws he obeys' [GW], not explicit [NLT, TEV]. This preposition marks the means by which one event makes another event possible [LN].

QUESTION—What relationship is indicated by γάρ 'for'?
  It indicates an explanation of what is said in 10:4 [AB, ICC2]. It indicates grounds for what has been said in 10:4 [BECNT, Mor]. 10:5-8 also contrasts the attempt to gain righteousness from the law with trusting Christ for it [BECNT]. It indicates 10:5-8 as an explanation of the relation between righteousness and faith, and what that would mean, with 10:5 giving the negative aspect of the argument and 10:6-8 giving the positive aspect [NICNT]. It indicates 10:5-13 as an explanation of what is said in 10:4 [ICC2]. It indicates 10:5 as an elaboration or explanation of what has been said in 10:2-4 [WBC]. It builds on 10:4, which is both an important idea in Paul's theology and also is a crucial transition to what follows, but it primarily indicates 10:5-13 as evidence or grounds for what Paul has been saying in 9:30-33 about being declared righteous by keeping the law [SSA].

QUESTION—What is the 'righteousness from the law'?
  1. It is a negative conception and is in contrast to a righteousness gained by faith [BECNT, Ho, NAC, NICNT, SSA, TNTC]. It is tied to the law and one's own works [ICC1, NICNT]. It is a righteousness demanded by the law, but one that no one can attain [BECNT].
  2. It is the righteousness of Christ by which he fulfilled all the law's demands, and thus secured a righteous status and blessing for himself, and eternal life for those who trust him [ICC2, NTC].
  3. It is righteousness as understood by Jewish people, that is, a righteousness that consists of having and observing the law, and therefore restricted to the Jewish people as people of the covenant and excluding all others as being outside the covenant [WBC].

QUESTION—What relationship is indicated by ἐν 'by'?
  It is instrumental [Ho, NICNT, NTC, SSA, TH]; the person who does the things required by the law will find life by doing those things [AB, Ho, SSA, TH]. The Jewish person who wants to live a life sustained by God within the covenant God gave them will do so by living in accordance with the way prescribed by the law [WBC].

QUESTION—Is the phrase ζήσεται ἐν αὐτοῖς 'shall live by them' intended to convey a hopeful promise or an impossible demand?
  1. For those who want to establish their own righteousness by fulfilling the demands of the law, it sets forth an impossible demand [BECNT, Ho, ICC2, Mu, NAC, NICNT, SSA, St, TNTC]. Those who seek to attain righteousness through the law will only fail [HNTC]. Paul is warning that

seeking to establish a relationship with God through law is doomed to fail, because human inadequacy is such that law has never been an avenue to eternal life [NICNT].
2. The law sets forth both an impossible demand as well as a hopeful promise [Gdt, Mor]. On the one hand, the Jewish people should have recognized that they could not do all the law demanded, but on the other hand, the law reveals God's grace for those who look to him in trust [Gdt, Mor].
3. It speaks of what Christ has in fact achieved, having perfectly fulfilled the law's requirements and granting eternal life to those who follow him [ICC2, NTC].
4. It is intended in a positive light, in that it prescribes the way that Israel was to live within the covenant, and not as a way of meriting or earning righteousness or eternal life [WBC].

10:6 **But the righteousness from[a] faith[b] speaks thus,[c]**

LEXICON—a. ἐκ with genitive object (LN 89.77): 'from' [AB, LN, WBC], 'that comes from' [NRSV], 'that comes by' [REB], 'by means of' [LN, NTC; NET, NIV], 'of' [BECNT, ICC2; KJV], 'based on' [NICNT; GW, NASB], 'through' [NCV, TEV]. The phrase 'the righteousness from faith' is translated 'the righteousness which has its root in faith' [HNTC], '(people whose) faith makes them acceptable to God' [CEV], 'God's approval which is based on faith' [GW], 'being made right through faith' [NCV], 'faith's way of getting right with God' [NLT], 'being put right with God through faith' [TEV]. This preposition marks means as constituting a source [LN].

b. πίστις (LN 31.85, 31.102) (BAGD 2.d.α. p. 663): 'faith' [AB, BAGD, BECNT, HNTC, ICC2, LN (31.85), NICNT, NTC, WBC; all versions], 'Christian faith' [LN (31.102)]. This noun denotes complete trust and reliance [LN (31.85)], or belief in the good news of Jesus Christ with the result of becoming a follower [LN (31.102)].

c. οὕτως (LN **61.10**) (BAGD 2. p. 598): 'thus' [AB, HNTC, ICC2, WBC], 'in this way' [BAGD; BECNT], 'the following' [**LN**], 'as follows' [LN], 'in this manner' [NICNT], 'on this wise' [KJV], not explicit [NTC; CEV, GW, NET, NIV, NLT, NRSV, REB]. The phrase 'speaks thus' is translated 'this is what the Scripture says' [NCV], 'what the Scripture says…is this' [TEV]. This adverb refers to that which follows [LN].

QUESTION—What relationship is indicated by δέ 'but'?

It is contrastive [AB, BECNT, HNTC, Ho, ICC2, Mor, NICNT, NTC, SSA, TH, WBC].
1. It contrasts the two ways of obtaining the state of being righteousness before God: by obeying the Law or by having faith in Christ [AB, BECNT, HNTC, Ho, Mor, NICNT, SSA, St, TH].
2. It contrasts the righteousness earned by Christ's obedience with the righteousness granted to those who believe in him [ICC2, NTC].

3. It contrasts two kinds of righteousness: the concept of righteousness the Jews thought they obtained by following the Law and maintaining loyalty to God's covenant, and the concept of righteousness before God that Christians obtain by believing in Christ [WBC].

QUESTION—What relationship is indicated by ἐκ 'from'?

It indicates the source, basis, or means of righteousness [AB, BECNT, HNTC, Ho, ICC2, Mor, NAC, NICNT]. It indicates the basis of righteousness [BECNT, ICC2, NAC, NICNT]. Righteousness comes from faith [AB], has its root in faith [HNTC]. Faith does not create this righteousness, but it is the means by which it is received [Mor].

QUESTION—Who is speaking in this passage?

1. The attribute of righteousness is personified so as to be the speaker [AB, Ho, ICC1, ICC2, Mu, NICNT, NTC, WBC; KJV, NASB, NET, NIV, NRSV, REB]: righteousness speaks. The OT sometimes personifies activities and concepts that are closely related to God, such as Wisdom in Proverbs 8 or the Word in Isaiah 55 [NICNT]. The words Μὴ εἴπῃς ἐν τῇ καρδίᾳ σου 'Don't say in your heart' only occur in the LXX in Isaiah 8:17 and 9:4, both of which warn the people of Israel that the blessings they will receive from God will not be due to their efforts or their righteousness [ICC2, NICNT], and Paul's use of the phrase as an introductory formula is an implied criticism of his Jewish contemporaries' pursuit of their own righteousness [NICNT].
2. The Scriptures are the speaker in the sense that the words are quoted from them [GW, NCV, TEV]: the Scriptures say.
3. People who have been declared to be righteous are the speakers [SSA; CEV]. The personification can be avoided by making the agent generic and also include the source of the words: 'anyone who has been declared righteous by believing in Christ can say to anyone as Moses said' [SSA].

Don't say in your heart,^a Who will-go-up^b into heaven?^c That is, to-bring-Christ -down;^d

LEXICON—a. καρδία (LN 26.3) (BAGD 1.b.β. p. 403): 'heart' [AB, BECNT, HNTC, ICC2, LN, NICNT, NTC, WBC; KJV, NASB, NET, NIV, NLT, NRSV], not explicit [CEV]. The phrase 'say in your heart' is translated 'say to yourself' [BAGD; NCV, REB], 'ask yourself' [GW, TEV]. This noun denotes the source of a person's psychological life, especially one's thoughts [LN].

b. future mid. (deponent = act.) indic. of ἀναβαίνω (LN 15.101) (BAGD 1.a.β. p. 50): 'to go up' [AB, BAGD, WBC; CEV, GW, NCV, NLT, REB, TEV], 'to ascend' [BAGD, BECNT, HNTC, ICC2, NICNT, NTC; KJV, NASB, NET, NIV, NRSV]. This verb means to move in an upward direction [LN].

c. οὐρανός (LN 1.11) (BAGD 2.b. p. 595): 'heaven' [AB, BAGD, BECNT, HNTC, ICC2, LN, NICNT, NTC, WBC; all versions]. This noun denotes the supernatural dwelling place of God and other heavenly beings [LN].

d. aorist act. infin. of καταγω (LN 15.175) (BAGD p. 410): 'to bring down' [AB, BAGD, BECNT, HNTC, ICC2, LN, NICNT, NTC, WBC; all versions]. This verb means to lead or to bring down [LN].

QUESTION—What feeling is being expressed by this question?

The two questions express doubt or unbelief [Gdt, Ho, Mu, SSA, TNTC].

1. The question is posed as though it were by someone who discounted the incarnation or the resurrection of Christ [Mu, TNTC], or who assumes the resurrection and ascension of Christ are impossible [Ho]. It is something that might possibly be posed by someone critical or doubtful of what Paul has been teaching [SSA].
2. The question is posed as though it were by Christians who believe Christ's incarnation and resurrection, but who don't fully understand their efficacy and effect [Gdt].

QUESTION—Is there any significance in the difference between γράφει 'writes' in 10:5 and λέγει 'says' in this verse?

1. There is no implied contrast [BECNT, ICC2, NICNT]. Paul uses both verbs to introduce OT citations [BECNT, NICNT].
2. There is some contrast implied between Moses and the era of the written law on the one hand, which is represented by γράφει 'writes', and the era of the Spirit on the other hand, which has superseded the era of the law, as represented by λέγει 'says' [AB, WBC].

QUESTION—What is Paul's intent in using the quotation from Deut. 30:11–14?

Going up into heaven or going down into the abyss were proverbial expressions representing something that is not possible [Ho, Mor, NICNT].

1. Paul's interpretation and application are harmonious with the essence of the Deuteronomy passage [BECNT, ICC2, Mor, NICNT, NTC, WBC].
   1.1 Paul is saying that, just as the message of Moses was accessible in the sense of being readily knowable, so also Christ and the message of the gospel are readily accessible [Ho, Mu, St]. The Deuteronomy passage is a context of grace, in that God graciously made all they needed to know readily available [Mu].
   1.2 Paul is giving the basic thought of the Deuteronomy passage, which is in harmony with his understanding of justification by faith: the impossibility of fulfilling all the requirements of the law is balanced by the grace of God [Gdt, Mor], and by the fact that Jesus Christ has in fact fulfilled the law [Gdt]. The Jews unfortunately failed to see that grace [Mor]. Paul is able to take a passage about the law and apply it to faith because he views the Deuteronomy 30 passage as expressing God's grace in establishing relationship with Israel, bringing his word near them so they might know him, just as he has now brought Christ to people as his word of revelation. In this way Paul applies the principle of grace in God's revelation: just as the OT Israelite could not plead ignorance of God's will, neither can Paul's contemporaries, Jew or Gentile, plead ignorance of God's revelation in Christ [NICNT].

1.3 The law spoken of in the Deuteronomy 30 passage was a gift of divine grace just as the incarnation of the Son of God was, and because Christ is the goal and fulfillment of the law there is a close inner connection between them, thus enabling Paul to apply this OT passage to Christ [ICC2]. Paul uses the Deuteronomy passage because it emphasizes God's grace in his gifts to Israel, gifts which were not merited by their righteousness or their works [NTC].

1.4 Paul is contrasting the Lev. 18:5 passage, which describes righteousness in terms of the rituals and practices defining Israel's national identity, with Deut. 30:11–14, which describes a righteousness that is by faith, springing from a deeper level of obedience, and which is similar to the gospel he proclaims [WBC].

1.5 The context of the Deuteronomy 30 passage is that in chapter 29 Moses stated that the generation he was addressing would *not* listen, and that God's disciplinary measures would be necessary. Chapter 30 then refers to the condition *after* they are restored, and will have been given hearts to hear and obey God. Paul is thus able to apply this to the contemporary situation in that the condition of Deuteronomy 30 has been fulfilled in the coming of Christ, who has enabled people to keep the law [BECNT].

2. Paul is borrowing wording from the Deuteronomy passage, concerning law, to make his own point about faith [AB, HNTC, Ho, ICC1, NAC, TNTC]. Paul's point is that, because Christ has come into the world and has risen from the dead, a person only needs to accept what has been done by faith in order to be made right with God [AB]. Paul is not citing the passage as a proof-text; he is using wording from it that had become proverbial and was in common use [ICC1]. (Note that this position is very similar to 1.1, the point of contact being that Paul is using language from a passage in which Moses talks about the accessibility of the law to describe the accessibility of the gospel.)

QUESTION—What is the function of τοῦτ' ἔστιν 'that is'?

It indicates Paul's interpretation or explanation of the passage he has cited [BECNT, Ho, ICC1, ICC2, SSA]. It indicates his explanatory comment about the OT text to apply it to his current situation [NICNT].

QUESTION—Why does Paul suggest that someone might want to bring Christ down from heaven or up from the abyss?

A person might disparagingly say this as though to say that someone would need to go to great lengths to get God's message, ignoring the fact that God's message has come in the person of Christ; but no one needs to go up to heaven and bring down Christ to give us the message of salvation, and no one needs to go down to the place of the dead to bring up Christ to give us that message [SSA]. The questions asking who will go into heaven or down into the abyss are the expressions of unbelief that deny that Christ has come down or been raised from the dead [Ho, Mu, NTC], or which overlook the role his incarnation and resurrection have played in the outworking of salvation for believers [Gdt]. Just as the Deut. passage sets aside any excuse for an Israelite not responding to God's law in the trust, gratitude, and love for others that it demands, so also there is no excuse for failing to recognize the Messiah God has sent them [ICC2]. In searching for the source of our righteousness, it is not necessary to go up to heaven to bring Christ down, because he already became a man and lived among us. Even though he was put to death, it isn't necessary to search for him in the place of the dead since he has risen from the dead [ICC1]. For someone to obtain righteousness by faith it does not depend on Christ's continued presence on earth since the gospel is the word the apostles preach [WBC].

10:7 Or, Who will-go-down[a] into the abyss?[b] That is, to bring-up[c] Christ from-among dead (persons).

LEXICON—a. future mid. (deponent = act.) indic. of καταβαίνω (LN 15.107) (BAGD 1.a.δ. p. 408): 'to go down' [AB, BAGD, LN, WBC; CEV, GW, NCV, NET, NLT, REB, TEV], 'to descend' [BECNT, HNTC, ICC2, LN, NICNT, NTC; KJV, NASB, NIV, NRSV]. This verb means to move down, irrespective of the gradient [LN].

  b. ἄβυσσος (LN **1.20**) (BAGD 2. p. 2): 'abyss' [AB, BAGD, BECNT, HNTC, ICC2, LN, NICNT, NTC, WBC; NET, NRSV, REB], 'underworld' [BAGD], 'the world of the dead' [CEV], 'the place of the dead' [NLT], 'the depths' [GW], 'the deep' [KJV, NIV], 'the world below' [NCV, TEV]. This noun denotes a location of the dead [LN].

  c. aorist act. indic. of ἀνάγω (LN 15.176) (BAGD 1. p. 53): 'to bring up' [AB, BAGD, HNTC, ICC2, LN, NICNT, NTC, WBC; KJV, NASB, NCV, NET, NIV, NRSV, REB, TEV], 'to lead up' [LN], 'to raise' [BECNT; CEV], 'to bring back' [GW, NLT]. This verb means to bring or lead up [LN].

QUESTION—What is the abyss?

It speaks of the realm of the dead [BECNT, Gdt, HNTC, Ho, ICC2, Mor, Mu, NICNT, NTC, SSA, TH], of the underworld [ICC1, NICNT, WBC], the depths of the earth as representing Sheol, the place of the dead [ICC2]. Paul uses it here as being the opposite of heaven [Gdt, Mor]. Paul uses it here to refer both to the depths of the sea, in contrast to the sky and earth, as well as to the netherworld [AB]. This is Paul's only use of this word [AB].

10:8 But[a] what does-it-say? The word[b] is near[c] to-you in your mouth and in your heart, that is, the word[d] of-faith[e] that we-preach.[f]

LEXICON—a. ἀλλά (LN 89.125): 'but' [AB, BECNT, ICC2, LN, NICNT, NTC, WBC; KJV, NASB, NET, NIV, NRSV], 'no' [HNTC], 'however' [GW], 'and' [REB], 'in fact' [NLT], not explicit [CEV, NCV, TEV]. This conjunction marks an emphatic contrast [LN].

  b. ῥῆμα (LN 33.98) (BAGD 1. p. 735): 'word' [AB, BAGD, BECNT, HNTC, ICC2, LN, NICNT, NTC, WBC; KJV, NCV, NET, NIV, NRSV, REB], 'message' [LN; CEV, GW, NLT, TEV]. This noun denotes that which has been stated or said, with primary focus upon the content of the communication [LN].

c. ἐγγύς (LN 83.26) (BAGD 3. p. 214): 'near' [AB, BAGD, BECNT, HNTC, ICC2, LN, NICNT, WBC; CEV, GW, NASB, NCV, NET, NIV, NRSV, REB, TEV], 'close' [BAGD, NTC], 'nigh' [KJV]. This word is translated as a phrase: 'very close at hand' [NLT]. This preposition marks a position relatively close to another position [LN].
d. ῥῆμα (LN 33.98) (BAGD 1. p. 735): 'word' [AB, BAGD, BECNT, HNTC, ICC2, LN, NICNT, NTC, WBC; KJV, NET, NIV, NRSV, REB], 'message' [LN; CEV, GW, NLT, TEV], 'teaching' [NCV].
e. πίστις (LN 31.85, 31.102) (BAGD 2.d.α. p. 663): 'faith' [AB, BAGD, BECNT, HNTC, ICC2, LN (31.85), NICNT, NTC, WBC; all versions except NLT], 'Christian faith' [LN (31.102)]. The phrase 'the word of faith that we preach' is translated 'And that message is the very message about faith that we preach' [NLT]. This noun denotes complete trust and reliance [LN (31.85)], or belief in the good news of Jesus Christ with the result of becoming a follower [LN (31.102)].
f. pres. act. indic. of κηρύσσω (LN 33.256) (BAGD 2.b.β. p. 431): 'to preach' [AB, BAGD, BECNT, HNTC, ICC2, LN, NICNT, NTC, WBC; CEV, KJV, NASB, NET, NLT, TEV], 'to proclaim' [BAGD; NIV, NRSV, REB], 'to spread' [GW], 'to tell' [NCV]. This verb means to publicly announce religious truths and principles while urging acceptance and compliance [LN].

QUESTION—What is the subject of the verb λέγει 'does it say'?

The subject is the righteousness based on faith [ICC2, NICNT, NTC, WBC].

QUESTION—In what sense is the adjective 'near' used here?

It is easily accessible [Mu, St]. The message is very accessible in the sense that people can talk about it and think about it [SSA]. It can be known and talked about, so it is not remote or obscure, but also God is near with his grace and help [Gdt]. Faith is as close as the mouth and the heart [BAGD]. The obedience of faith that comes from the heart is not something unattainable [WBC], it is simple and easy [Ho]. It is close to the one who would believe, and belief is the expected reaction to hearing this message [AB]. The message about the righteousness that comes from faith can be known and understood; it also causes God's law to come near in the sense of being written on human hearts [NICNT]. God himself had drawn near to his people through his gracious promises, assurances, and warnings [NTC]. Just as God graciously stooped down to reveal himself to Israel in his word, which was accessible to them, so also he has given himself to humankind in Jesus Christ, who is closely connected to the law of God [ICC2]. It is readily available to anyone through simple belief and confession [NAC]. It is something that is immediately possible [HNTC].

QUESTION—What is the function of τοῦτ' ἔστιν 'that is'?

It indicates his explanation of the meaning of a τὸ ῥῆμα 'the word' [ICC1, ICC2].

QUESTION—How are the nouns related in the genitive construction τὸ ῥῆμα τῆς πίστεως 'the word of faith'?
1. It is the word or message that calls for faith [ICC2, Mor, NICNT, NTC, TH], the message to which faith is directed [Mu, TNTC], the message that stimulates faith [NAC], the message which proclaims faith as the principle of righteousness [ICC1].
2. It is the message that is believed, the objective content of Christian faith [AB].
3. It is the message that calls for faith as well the message that proclaims the faith that is believed [BECNT, WBC]. It is the word characterized by faith and that calls for faith [WBC]. There is little difference between 'the message concerning faith' and 'the message that is to be believed'; it is the message that people must believe in Christ [SSA].

QUESTION—Is the 'we' inclusive of the readers or exclusive?
It is exclusive [ICC2, Mor, Mu, SSA, St]. He is speaking of the message that the apostles preach [Mu, NICNT, St], that Paul and his companions [Mor], or that he and other Christian preachers preach [ICC2, SSA].

10:9 **That/because[a] if you-confess[b] with[c] your mouth[d] (that) Jesus (is) Lord[e]**

LEXICON—a. ὅτι (LN 91.15, 89.33): 'that' [HNTC, LN (91.15); KJV, NASB, NIV], 'that is, namely' [BECNT, LN (91.15)], 'because' [LN (89.33), NTC, WBC; NET, NRSV], 'for' [ICC2, LN (89.33), NICNT; NLT], not explicit [CEV, GW, NCV, REB, TEV]. This adverb marks identificational and explanatory clauses [LN (91.15)], or cause or reason based on an evident fact [LN (89.33)].
b. aorist act. subj. of ὁμολογέω (LN 33.275) (BAGD 4. p. 568): 'to confess' [BAGD, BECNT, HNTC, ICC2, LN, NICNT, WBC; KJV, NASB, NET, NIV, NLT, NRSV, TEV], 'to acknowledge' [BAGD], 'to declare publicly' [BAGD], 'to declare' [GW], 'to profess' [AB], 'to (honestly) say' [CEV], 'to say' [NCV]. This verb is translated as a noun: 'confession' [NTC; REB]. This verb means to acknowledge a fact publicly, often in reference to previous bad behavior [LN].
c. ἐν with dative object (LN 89.76, 90.10): 'with' [AB, BECNT, HNTC, ICC2, LN (90.10), NICNT, WBC; KJV, NASB, NET, NIV, NLT, NRSV], 'by means of, by' [LN (89.76)]. The phrase 'with your mouth' is translated 'if on your lips is the confession' [NTC], 'if you use (your mouth)' [NCV], not explicit [CEV, GW, REB, TEV]. This preposition marks the means by which one event makes another event possible [LN (90.76)], or an immediate instrument [LN (90.10)].
d. στόμα (LN 8.19, 33.74): 'mouth' [BECNT, HNTC, ICC2, LN (8.19), NICNT, WBC; KJV, NASB, NCV, NET, NIV, NLT], 'lips' [AB, NTC; NRSV, REB], 'speech' [LN (33.74)], not explicit [CEV, GW, TEV].
e. κύριος (LN 12.9) (BAGD 2.a. p. 459, 2.c.γ. p. 460): 'Lord' [AB, BAGD, BECNT, HNTC, ICC2, LN, NICNT, NTC, WBC; all versions]. The

phrase 'confess…(that) Jesus is Lord' is translated 'confess…the Lord Jesus' [KJV]. This noun denotes one who exercises supernatural authority over mankind [LN].

QUESTION—What relationship is indicated by ὅτι 'that'?
1. It means 'that', and is a discourse marker indicating the content of the message of faith that they preach [AB, BECNT, HNTC, Ho, Mor, Mu, SSA, TH; probably ICC1, St; KJV, NASB, NIV].
2. It means 'because' or 'for', and indicates the grounds for his statement that the word is near to them [ICC2, NICNT, NTC, WBC; NET, NLT, NRSV]. Paul explains why the word of faith is near, which is that it requires only a simple response [ICC2, NICNT, NTC, WBC].

QUESTION—What is meant by confessing with the mouth that Jesus is Lord?
It is a public declaration [SSA, TH]. It is a solemn public profession of faith in Christ and commitment to him [Mor]. It is the outward expression of the inner faith response [NICNT]. This profession means that Christ is obviously more than a rabbi, he is a heavenly being [HNTC, Mor]. It is to identify oneself as belonging to Jesus Christ [WBC]. It is to profess publicly one's belief in Jesus' resurrection [NAC, NICNT], his deity [Ho, Mor, NAC, SSA], and his lordship [NICNT, SSA]. It is to confess the full extent of his lordship [Ho], to acknowledge his incarnation, death, resurrection, exaltation, and universal dominion [Mu]. It may refer to a baptismal confession [HNTC, TNTC]. It is a doctrinal profession [BECNT].

and believe[a] in[b] your heart[c] that God raised[d] him from-among dead (persons), you-will-be-saved;[e]

LEXICON—a. aorist act. subj. of πιστεύω (LN 31.35) (BAGD 1.a.β. p. 660): 'to believe' [AB, BAGD, BECNT, HNTC, ICC2, LN, NICNT, WBC; all versions except REB]. The phrase 'if you believe in your heart' is translated 'if in your heart is the faith' [NTC], 'if the faith…is in your heart' [REB]. This verb means to believe something to be true and, hence, worthy of being trusted [LN].
b. ἐν with dative object (LN 90.10, 83.13): 'in' [AB, BECNT, ICC2, LN (83.13), NICNT, NTC, WBC; KJV, NASB, NCV, NET, NIV, NLT, NRSV, REB], 'with' [HNTC, LN (90.10); CEV], not explicit [GW, TEV]. This preposition marks an immediate instrument [LN (90.10)], or a position defined as being within certain limits [LN (83.13)].
c. καρδία (LN 26.3) (BAGD 1.b.α. p. 403): 'heart' [AB, BAGD, BECNT, HNTC, ICC2, LN, NICNT, NTC, WBC; all versions except GW, TEV], not explicit [GW, TEV]. This noun denotes the source of a person's psychological life, especially one's thoughts [LN].
d. aorist act. indic. of ἐγείρω (LN 23.94) (BAGD 1.a.β. p. 214): 'to raise' [AB, BAGD, BECNT, HNTC, ICC2, NICNT, NTC, WBC; all versions except GW], 'to bring back to life' [GW], 'to raise to life, to make live again' [LN]. This verb means to cause someone to live again after having once died [LN].

ROMANS 10:9

e. fut. pass. indic. of σῴζω (LN 21.27) (BAGD 2.b. p. 798): 'to be saved' [AB, BAGD, BECNT, HNTC, ICC2, LN, NICNT, NTC, WBC; all versions except REB]. The clause 'you will be saved' is translated 'you will find salvation' [REB]. This verb means to cause someone to experience divine salvation [LN].

QUESTION—What is implied by this second clause beginning with 'and believe in your heart'?

1. Inward belief and outward profession are two aspects of one reality [NAC, WBC]. They are not separable [BECNT, St, TNTC], and no distinction is intended between the two [HNTC]. Professing Jesus' lordship openly as well as really believing are two related but separate aspects of faith [AB]. He is talking about the outward and inward aspects of faith; the state of the heart and the outward conduct are both important [Mor]. Heartfelt belief is the essential requirement for salvation, of which the confession is the outward expression, not some second requirement [NICNT]. While the content of what is believed in the heart and of what is confessed with the mouth are stated in different terms, they are essentially the same thing, and one interprets the other [ICC2]. The verbal confession and the heart belief are not listed in order of how they are experienced; Paul is simply following the wording of the OT passage he is quoting [ICC2, NAC, NTC]. The verb may refer to the initial act of believing [NAC, WBC].

2. The believing and confessing are two separate events [ICC1, Mu]. Faith leads to righteousness and confession leads to salvation, but the two must both be present for either to be effective [Mu]. Belief, and the change of heart that must necessarily accompany it, will bring righteousness, and the profession of faith made at baptism will start the believer on the way that leads to salvation at the last day [ICC1].

QUESTION—What is meant or implied by 'believe in your heart'?

It is the inward faith and conviction that will prompt total dedication to God [AB]. It is a belief that takes hold of the entire inner being [Mor]. It is a heart conviction [BECNT]. It speaks of the inner response [NICNT]. The heart is conceived of as the center of the entire life, encompassing the mind, the will, and the emotions [Mu, NTC]. It is a belief that is both emotional and deeply motivating [WBC]. True belief will be accompanied by a change of heart [ICC1]. The heart is the seat of the religious consciousness as well as its source [Mu], the whole of the inner being, including the affections and the mind [Ho].

QUESTION—What is implied by the requirement of believing that God raised Jesus from the dead?

This implies that Jesus died but God resurrected him [SSA]. This focus on his resurrection does not detract from Christ's death for our sins, because the resurrection bears witness to the efficacy of his death [NICNT]. His resurrection indicates his triumph over death [ICC1]. His resurrection is the basis for believing that Jesus is Lord [Gdt, TH], and proves that he is Lord [NTC]. By raising Christ from the dead, God decisively and irrevocably seals him as the eternal Lord [ICC2]. It shows that he is triumphant over the forces of evil [Mor]. The resurrection proves that he is the son of God [NAC]. When God resurrected Jesus, he publicly acknowledged that Jesus was all that he claimed to be and that he accepted all that Jesus had done to save us from our sins [Ho]. Jesus' resurrection demonstrates that in him God has inaugurated the age to come and that he is now the source of supernatural life [HNTC]. His resurrection and his lordship are inseparable corollaries, and to affirm one is to affirm the other [BECNT, WBC].

QUESTION—What is meant by the use of the future tense of the verb 'will be saved'?

1. It primarily points to future salvation [BECNT, HNTC, ICC1, ICC2, Mor, TNTC, WBC], the life of the coming age [Mor], the eschatological salvation of eternal life [ICC2], the eschatological end result of the process [WBC], being saved at the last day [HNTC].
2. It is a logical use of the future tense, and does not primarily refer to any particular point in time [NICNT].

10:10 For^a with-(the)-heart^b it-is-believed^c resulting-in^d righteousness,^{e}

LEXICON—a. γάρ (LN 89.23): 'for' [AB, BECNT, HNTC, ICC2, LN, NICNT, NTC, WBC; KJV, NASB, NET, NIV, NLT, NRSV, REB, TEV], not explicit [CEV, GW, NCV]. This conjunction marks cause or reason between events [LN].

b. καρδία (LN 26.3) (BAGD 1.b.α. p. 403): 'heart' [BAGD, LN]. The relationship indicated by the dative case of this word is translated 'with (the heart)' [BECNT, ICC2, NICNT, NTC, WBC; KJV, NASB, NCV, NET, NIV, NRSV], 'of (the heart)' [AB], 'in (the heart)' [HNTC; NLT, REB], not explicit [CEV, GW, TEV]. This noun denotes the source of a person's psychological, life especially one's thoughts [LN].

c. pres. pass. indic. of πιστεύω (LN 31.35) (BAGD 1.a.β. p. 660). This passive verb is translated as active: 'to believe' [BAGD, BECNT, ICC2, LN (31.35), NICNT, WBC; all versions except REB, TEV]. This verb is translated as a noun: 'faith' [AB, HNTC, NTC; REB, TEV]. The passive voice here may express something of an impersonal nuance: 'one believes, one confesses' [Mu, NICNT, TH]. This verb means to believe something to be true and, hence, worthy of being trusted [LN].

d. εἰς with accusative object (LN 89.48) (BAGD 4.e. p. 229): 'resulting in' [NASB], 'with the result that, so that as a result, to cause' [LN], 'to' [BAGD; REB], 'leading to' [NTC], 'leads to' [AB], 'so as to receive' [BAGD], 'unto' [ICC2; KJV], 'for' [NICNT, WBC], not explicit [BECNT; CEV, GW, NCV, NET, NIV, NLT, NRSV, TEV]. This clause is translated 'such faith of the heart leads to uprightness' [AB]. This preposition is translated as the infinitive verb 'to produce' [HNTC]. This preposition marks result, with the probable implication of a preceding process [LN].

e. δικαιοσύνη (LN 88.13) (BAGD 3. p. 197): 'righteousness' [BAGD, BECNT, HNTC, LN, NICNT, NTC, WBC; KJV, NASB, NET, REB], 'uprightness' [AB], 'justification' [ICC2], not explicit [CEV, GW, NCV, NLT, TEV]. This noun is translated as a passive verb: 'to be justified' [NIV, NRSV]. It denotes the act of doing what God requires [LN].

QUESTION—What relationship is indicated by γάρ 'for'?

It gives grounds for the statement in the previous verse [Ho, ICC1, ICC2]. It gives grounds for this assertion that faith and confession are all that is necessary for a person to be saved [Ho]. It indicates additional explanation of what has just been said [Mor, SSA]. This is an amplification of the confession and inward belief in 10:9, not a reason for it [SSA]. This serves to emphasize the double aspect of saving faith [WBC].

and^a with-the mouth^b it-is-confessed^c resulting-in^d salvation.^e

LEXICON—a. δέ (LN 89.94): 'and' [BECNT, HNTC, ICC2, LN, NICNT, NTC, WBC; all versions except CEV, TEV], not explicit [AB; CEV, TEV]. This conjunction marks an additive relation, but with the possible implication of some contrast [LN].

b. στόμα (LN 8.19, 33.74): 'mouth' [BECNT, HNTC, ICC2, LN (8.19), NICNT, WBC; KJV, NASB, NCV, NET, NIV, NLT, NRSV], 'speech' [LN (33.74)], 'lips' [AB, NTC; REB], 'confession' [TEV], not explicit [CEV, GW].

c. pres. pass. indic. of ὁμολογέω (LN 33.275) (BAGD 4. p. 568). This passive verb is translated as active: 'to confess' [BAGD, BECNT, LN, NICNT, WBC; KJV, NASB, NET, NIV, NLT, NRSV], 'to tell' [CEV], 'to declare' [GW], 'to say' [NCV]. This verb is translated as a noun: 'confession' [HNTC, ICC2, NTC, WBC; REB, TEV], 'profession' [AB]. This verb means to acknowledge a fact publicly, often in reference to previous bad behavior [LN].

d. εἰς with accusative object (LN 89.48) (BAGD 4.e. p. 229): 'resulting in' [NASB], 'issuing in' [NTC], 'to' [AB, BAGD, NTC; REB], 'so as to receive' [BAGD], 'with the result that, so that as a result, to cause' [LN], 'unto' [ICC2; KJV], 'for' [NICNT, WBC], not explicit [BECNT; CEV, GW, NCV, NET, NIV, NLT, NRSV, TEV]. This preposition is translated as the infinitive verb 'to produce' [HNTC]. This preposition marks result, with the probable implication of a preceding process [LN].

e. σωτηρία (LN 21.25) (BAGD 2. p. 801): 'salvation' [AB, BAGD, BECNT, HNTC, ICC2, LN, NICNT, NTC, WBC; KJV, NASB, NET, REB]. This noun is translated as an active verb: 'to save' [CEV]; as a passive verb: 'to be saved' [GW, NCV, NIV, NLT, NRSV, TEV]. This noun denotes a state of having been saved [LN].

QUESTION—Are the actions of believing and confessing viewed as two separate acts or events, or as two aspects of one and the same act?

1. They are two aspects of the same thing [AB, HNTC, Mor, NAC, TH, TNTC, WBC], of one act of adhering to Christ [AB], of one saving

experience [Mor]. The order of confession and faith in 10:9 is now reversed to their more natural order of inward belief being expressed by the open confession of that belief [WBC], but the two actions are like the two sides of one coin [TH, WBC]. Belief in the heart precedes the confession, which grows out of belief [BECNT]. Both actions lead to both results [SSA]. Inward faith and outward profession belong together, and their content must be merged [St].
2. They are two conditions for salvation [Gdt]. Both are necessary, but they are viewed as being distinct, and the outcomes as being distinct [Mu].

QUESTION—Are righteousness and salvation viewed as separate matters?
1. This is a rhetorical formulation and he is not trying to stress any difference between the two [AB, BECNT, HNTC, NAC, NICNT]. Both are the result of believing with the heart and confessing with the mouth [NICNT]. Righteousness is synonymous here with salvation, which is the outcome of both confession and faith [NTC, WBC]. They cannot be distinguished [TNTC], there is no significant difference [St]. No difference is intended between the two, as both refer to salvation [ICC2].
2. There is some distinction [Mu]. Justification occurs in this life as a result of believing, but salvation is the final culmination in glory of the whole process of believing, confessing, and persevering in faith [Gdt].

10:11 For the Scripture says, All[a] those-believing[b] on[c] him will- not -be-ashamed[d]

LEXICON—a. πᾶς (LN 59.23) (BAGD 1.c.γ. p. 632): 'all' [LN]. The phrase Πᾶς…οὐ 'all…(will) not' is translated 'No one…(will)' [AB, HNTC, NICNT, NTC; CEV, NRSV, REB], 'everyone …(will)' [BECNT, ICC2, WBC; NET], 'whoever' [GW, NASB, TEV], 'whosoever' [KJV], 'anyone' [NCV, NIV, NLT]. This adjective denotes the totality of any object, mass, collective, or extension [LN].
b. aorist pass. participle of πιστεύω (LN 31.35) (BAGD 1.d. p. 661): 'to believe' [AB, BAGD, BECNT, HNTC, ICC2, LN, NICNT, WBC; GW, KJV, NASB, NET, NRSV, TEV], 'to put one's trust in' [NTC], 'to trust' [NCV, NIV, NLT], 'to have faith' [CEV, REB]. This verb means to believe something to be true and, hence, worthy of being trusted [LN].
c. ἐπί with dative object (BAGD II.1.b.γ. p. 287): 'on' [BAGD, ICC2, NICNT; KJV], 'in' [AB, BAGD, BECNT, HNTC, NTC, WBC; GW, NASB, NCV, NET, NIV, NLT, NRSV, REB, TEV], not explicit [CEV].
d. fut. pass. indic. of καταισχύνω (LN 25.194) (BAGD 3.b. p. 411): 'to be put to shame' [AB, BECNT, HNTC, ICC2, LN, NICNT, NTC, WBC; NET, NIV, NRSV, REB], 'to be disappointed' [BAGD; CEV, GW, NASB, NCV, TEV], 'to be ashamed' [KJV], 'to be disgraced' [LN; NLT]. This verb means to cause someone to be very ashamed [LN].

QUESTION—What relationship is indicated by γάρ 'for'?
It indicates the grounds for what he has just said about faith [BECNT, Ho, ICC1, ICC2, Mor, SSA]. It supports the statement that faith leads to

justification [ICC2], to salvation [Ho, ICC1]. It indicates grounds for and further explanation of his interpretation of the Deut. 30 passage [WBC].

QUESTION—What does it mean not to be ashamed?

At the time of judgment the believer will be delivered [NICNT], or vindicated [BECNT]. At the judgment the person who believes will have justification and salvation [SSA]. The person who has believed will not be deceived in what he hopes for [Gdt]. Some commentaries and versions focus on how the person will be regarded by others: he will not be put to shame [AB, BECNT, HNTC, ICC2, LN, NICNT, NTC, WBC; NET, NIV, NRSV, REB], or be brought to disgrace [WBC; NLT]. Some focus on how the person will feel on the day of judgment: he will not be let down [TNTC], or be disappointed [BAGD; CEV, GW, NASB, NCV, TEV].

10:12 For there-is no distinction[a] of[b] Jew and Greek, for the same (one is) Lord of[c] all, being-generous[d] toward[e] all those-calling-on[f] him;

LEXICON—a. διαστολή (LN **58.42**) (BAGD p. 188): 'distinction' [AB, BAGD, BECNT, HNTC, ICC2, LN, NICNT, NTC, WBC; NASB, NET, NRSV, REB], 'difference' [BAGD, LN; GW, KJV, NCV, NIV, TEV], not explicit [CEV]. The clause 'there is no distinction' is translated 'are the same in this respect' [NLT]. This noun denotes a clear or marked distinction [LN].

b. There is no lexical entry for this word in the Greek text, the relation between 'distinction' and the proper nouns 'Jew' and 'Greek' being indicated by the genitive case of 'Jew' and 'Greek'. This is represented in translation as '(difference/distinction) between' [AB, BECNT, HNTC, ICC2, NICNT, NTC, WBC; all versions except CEV, NLT], not explicit [CEV, NLT].

c. There is no lexical entry for this word in the Greek text, the relation between 'Lord' and 'all' being indicated by the genitive case of 'all'. This is represented in translation as 'of' [AB, BECNT, HNTC, ICC2, NICNT, NTC, WBC; NASB, NCV, NET, NIV, NRSV, REB, TEV], 'over' [KJV], not explicit [CEV, GW, NLT].

d. pres. act. participle of πλουτέω (LN **57.104**) (BAGD 2. p. 674): 'to be generous' [LN; CEV, NRSV], 'to give generously' [LN; NLT], 'to be rich (toward/to/unto)' [BAGD, ICC2, WBC; KJV], 'to bestow' [AB, NICNT], 'to dispense' [BECNT], 'to abound' [HNTC; NASB], 'to bless' [NTC; NET, NIV, TEV], 'to give' [GW, NCV], not explicit [REB]. This verb means to give generously of one's wealth [LN].

e. εἰς with accusative object (LN 90.59) (BAGD 4.g. p. 229): 'toward' [ICC2, LN], 'to' [BECNT, HNTC, LN, WBC; CEV, GW, NCV, NLT, NRSV], 'for' [BAGD, LN; NASB], 'on' [AB, NICNT], 'unto' [KJV], not explicit [NTC; NET, NIV, REB, TEV]. This preposition marks an involved experiencer [LN].

f. pres. mid. participle of ἐπικαλέομαι (LN 33.176) (BAGD 2.b. p. 294): 'to call on' [BAGD, BECNT, NTC; NET, NIV, NLT, NRSV, REB], 'to call upon' [AB, BAGD, HNTC, LN, NICNT, WBC; KJV, NASB], 'to call to' [TEV], 'to invoke' [ICC2], 'to ask for help' [CEV], 'to pray to' [GW], 'to trust in' [NCV]. This verb means to call upon someone to do something, normally implying an appeal for aid [LN]. Calling on him is the equivalent of praying to him [TH]. This refers to asking either the Father or the Son for help or intervention [NICNT].

QUESTION—What relationship is indicated by γάρ 'for', which begins this sentence?

It indicates the grounds for his statement that no one who trusts in Christ will be ashamed [ICC2, NTC]. It continues the logical sequence of his argument [Gdt, Mor]. It indicates an explanation for his statement that the gospel applies to all people [BECNT, ICC1]. It indicates an elaboration of the implications of πᾶς 'all' in 10:11 [Ho, Mu, WBC]. It indicates 10:12-13 as grounds for what is being claimed in 10:9-10 [SSA]. It indicates the conclusion drawn from the concept that salvation is free [Gdt].

QUESTION—What is meant by his statement that there is no distinction between Jew and Greek?

Here Ἕλληνος 'Greek' [GW, KJV, NASB, NET, NRSV, REB] is used to refer to anyone who is not a Jew [NCV, SSA], that is, a Gentile [BECNT, Gdt, HNTC, Ho, ICC1, ICC2, Mor, NAC, NICNT, SSA, TH, WBC; CEV, NIV, NLT, TEV]. The opportunity to receive uprightness through faith is given to all alike [AB]. There is no difference with respect to how a person is saved [NAC, NTC, TH]. God treats them both alike [SSA]. Despite very real cultural, racial, and religious differences between Jews and Gentiles, there is only one way of salvation [Mor]. Jews and Gentiles are alike with respect to sin, judgment, the Lord's rule over them, and the grace offered to them [NICNT]. All are sinners, and all are saved the same way [Ho]. All are sinners, and all can share in righteousness through faith [ICC2, Mu]. All have sinned, all have the same lord, and all can enjoy God's blessings [HNTC]. Faith is the only method of salvation for anyone, whether they are Jew or Gentile [ICC1]. The covenant privileges have been expanded to include all people, not just Jews, and on the same basis, which is faith [WBC]. God's righteousness, saving mercy, and pardon are available to all alike [TNTC]. Those distinctions are not abolished, but they are made irrelevant [St]. It was the law that separated Jew and Gentile, and now that the this has been removed by the work of the Messiah, mankind is now only one social body [Gdt].

QUESTION—To whom does the title 'Lord' refer?

It refers to Jesus Christ [AB, BECNT, Gdt, HNTC, Ho, ICC1, ICC2, Mor, Mu, NAC, NICNT, NTC, St, WBC]. In 10:9 Jesus is called the Lord, so 'him' in 10:11 refers to Jesus, as does 'the Lord' in this verse [NICNT]. It is significant that the term 'call upon', normally used of prayer to deity, is applied to Christ [ICC1, Mor].

QUESTION—What relationship is indicated by the second γάρ 'for'?
It takes Paul's argument yet another stage further [Mor]. It supports the first statement in this verse [ICC1, ICC2]. It explains why distinctions between the two groups were irrelevant [BECNT]. The same method of salvation applies to all people because it is the same Lord who has redeemed them [ICC1]. It indicates a second elaboration of the implications of πᾶς 'all' in 10:11 [WBC]. It indicates 10:12b-c as an amplification of the statement in 10:12a that God treats Jews and Gentiles alike. [SSA].

QUESTION—What is implied by the phrase πλουτῶν εἰς 'being generous toward'?
The resources that God makes available to his people through his son are unlimited [NICNT]. God is generous beyond our comprehension [NTC]. Christ gives generously to those who call on him [ICC2]. The wealth is that of spiritual blessings [ICC1]. He helps from his abundant resources [Ho, WBC]. He blesses richly [NAC, St]. It speaks of his resources of goodness and glory [HNTC], of his beneficence [BECNT], of his abundant blessings [SSA]. It speaks of the readiness and fullness by which he accepts anyone who will call upon him [Mu]. He communicates the blessings of salvation to all believers equally [Gdt].

10:13 For all[a] who would call-on[b] the name[c] of-the Lord will-be-saved.[d]

LEXICON—a. πᾶς (LN 59.23) (BAGD 1.c.γ. p. 632): 'all' [LN; CEV], 'everyone' [AB, BAGD, BECNT, ICC2, NICNT, NTC, WBC; NET, NIV, NLT, NRSV, REB, TEV], 'whoever' [BAGD; GW, NASB], 'whosoever' [HNTC; KJV], 'anyone' [NCV]. This adjective denotes the totality of any object, mass, collective, or extension [LN].
   b. aorist mid. subj. of ἐπικαλέομαι (LN 33.176) (BAGD 2.b. p. 294): 'to call on' [BAGD, BECNT, NICNT, NTC; NCV, NET, NIV, NLT, NRSV, REB], 'to call upon' [AB, BAGD, HNTC, LN, WBC; KJV, NASB], 'call out to' [CEV, TEV], 'to invoke' [ICC2], 'to pray (in the name of)' [GW]. The phrase 'all who would call on the name of the Lord' is translated 'whoever prays in the name of the Lord' [GW], 'anyone who calls on the Lord' [NCV], 'all who call out to the Lord' [CEV], 'everyone who calls out to the Lord for help' [TEV]. This verb means to call upon someone to do something, normally implying an appeal for aid [LN].
   c. ὄνομα (LN 33.126) (BAGD I.4.b. p. 571): 'name' [AB, BAGD, BECNT, HNTC, ICC2, NICNT, NTC, WBC; GW, KJV, NASB, NET, NIV, NLT, NRSV, REB], not explicit [CEV, NCV, TEV]. This noun denotes the proper name of a person or object [LN].
   d. fut. pass. indic. of σῴζω (LN 21.27) (BAGD 2.b. p. 798): 'to be saved' [AB, BAGD, BECNT, HNTC, ICC2, LN, NICNT, NTC, WBC; all versions]. This verb means to cause someone to experience divine salvation [LN].

QUESTION—What relationship is indicated by γάρ 'for'?
It carries the argument yet another step along by introducing a Scripture citation [Mor]. It indicates a summary and close of his argument in this section [ICC1]. It indicates yet a third elaboration of the implications of πᾶς 'all' in 10:11 [WBC]. It supports his assertion that those who call on him will experience his goodness and riches [BECNT]. It indicates a passage from the prophet Joel as grounds for the statement he has just made [SSA].

QUESTION—What does it mean to 'call on the name' of the Lord?
'The name of the Lord' refers to the Lord himself since the name represented what a person is [TH]. Some translate this expression simply as 'the Lord' [SSA; CEV, NCV, TEV]. This is a quotation from the prophet Joel (3:5), where 'the Lord' refers to God [SSA]. The quotation is applied to Christ, so the salvation here refers to Christian salvation [Mor, Mu, NICNT, St, WBC]. Calling on the name of the Lord is to invoke Christ in prayer [BECNT, Ho, ICC1, ICC2, Mor]. It is to cry out to Christ with a deep sense of need as well as with a conviction that he can be trusted to help [Mor]. It is to call upon Christ for salvation [Mu, NICNT, St]. It is also an act of worship [Ho, Mu]. It is the cry of confession that Jesus is Lord [NAC].

QUESTION—What is the salvation spoken of here?
Paul is speaking of salvation in the sense of the final outcome of all things [ICC1, Mor].

DISCOURSE UNIT—10:14–21 [AB, HNTC, ICC1, Mor, NICNT, NTC, TNTC, WBC]. The topic is Israel has not responded to this preached word [AB], Israel's unbelief inexcusable [HNTC], Israel's unbelief not excused by want of opportunity [ICC1], worldwide proclamation [Mor], Israel's accountability [NICNT], Israel is responsible for its own rejection; that rejection is not arbitrary [NTC], the world-wide proclamation [TNTC], Israel's failure to respond to the gospel [WBC].

10:14 How[a] then[b] would-they-call-on (one) in whom they have- not -believed?[c]

LEXICON—a. πῶς (LN 92.16) (BAGD 1.e. p. 732): 'how' [AB, BAGD, BECNT, HNTC, ICC2, LN, NICNT, NTC, WBC; all versions except NCV], not explicit [NCV]. This adverb is an interrogative reference to means [LN].
  b. οὖν (LN 89.50) (BAGD 1.c.γ. p. 593, 4. p. 593): 'then' [BAGD (1.c.γ.), BECNT, LN, NTC; KJV, NASB, NIV], 'therefore' [NICNT, WBC], 'but' [AB, BAGD (4.), LN (89.127); GW, NCV, NLT, NRSV, REB, TEV], 'however' [BAGD (4.)], not explicit [ICC2; CEV, NET]. This word is translated by an entire sentence: 'This, however, evokes a new series of questions' [HNTC]. This conjunction marks result, often implying the conclusion of a process of reasoning [LN].
  c. aorist act. indic. of πιστεύω (LN 31.35) (BAGD 1.d. p. 661): 'to believe (in)' [AB, BAGD, BECNT, HNTC, ICC2, LN, NICNT, WBC; KJV, NASB, NCV, NET, NIV, NLT, NRSV, TEV], 'to have faith (in)' [NTC;

CEV, REB]. The phrase εἰς ὅν 'in whom' is the object of this verb [ICC2, Mor, Mu, NICNT, WBC]. This verb means to believe something to be true and, hence, worthy of being trusted [LN].

QUESTION—What is the rhetorical purpose and structure of 10:14–21?
1. Paul is dealing with the question of why Jews generally have not believed the gospel; through a series of four questions posed in 10:14–15, he raises the question of whether or not they have heard the news through authorized messengers, and asserts at the end of 10:15 that they have heard, but were disobedient. He then raises two more possible objections in 10:18–19 about whether Israel really heard and understood, to which he answers that they in fact did hear and understand, but did not believe [HNTC, ICC1].
2. Using the diatribe format to justify God's actions with respect to his people, Paul raises four objections about the unbelief of the Jews, and then answers them. The four objections are: (1) Were duly appointed messengers sent? (2) Why didn't everyone believe? (3) Did Israel hear the message? and (4) Did they really understand? Paul answers that the heralds have gone out, the message was preached and heard, Israel understood, but they did not believe because they were obstinate [AB].
3. In 10:14–15 Paul anticipates an objection from Jewish people to the effect that they can't be expected to believe if they haven't heard about Christ, to which he responds in 10:16 that they have heard, and supports that in 10:17 with the proposition that in fact even some Jews have heard and believed. Then in 10:18–21 he poses two questions that might arise about the Jews having heard the gospel, and answers those as well [SSA].

QUESTION—What relationship is indicated by οὖν 'then'?
1. It indicates a logical progression in Paul's argument [HNTC, ICC1, Mu, NICNT]. It indicates an analysis of what is involved in calling on the name of the Lord mentioned in the two previous verses [Mu]. It indicates a series of rhetorical questions probing what conditions are necessary for people to be able to call upon the name of the Lord [HNTC, NICNT]. It sums up and draws a conclusion from what has just been argued, and indicates another step in the argument; that is, what conditions are necessary for salvation, and have they been met? [ICC1].
2. It is contrastive, introducing a series of rhetorical questions raised as possible objections to what Paul has been saying [AB, SSA]. It indicates the rhetorical questions, but may also express an element of contrast [Mor]. It is translated as introducing a contrastive idea by GW, NCV, NLT, NRSV, REB, TEV.

QUESTION—What is the function of this series of rhetorical questions in 10:14–15?
Paul is preparing for the premise of 10:16, concerning the fact that not all of them believed the gospel [Mu], or obeyed it [HNTC], or called upon the Lord [TH]. He is preparing for his accusation in 10:16 and 10:21 that Israel is responsible for its rejection by God, and that anyone who rejects God's

messenger rejects God himself [NTC]. In 10:14–15 Paul anticipates an objection from Jewish people to his arguments presented so far, namely, that he should not expect Jewish people to believe in Jesus if they have not heard the gospel from messengers sent by God and understood it. Paul's answer follows in 10:16 ff. that, in fact, Jewish people have heard, but if they don't comprehend it, it is because they have refused to believe [SSA]. Paul is probing what it conditions are necessary for people to be able to call upon the name of the Lord [NICNT].

QUESTION—What is the relation of these rhetorical questions to one another?

They are a chain or sequence of logically related ideas, one naturally following on the other and drawing a conclusion from it [BECNT, HNTC, ICC2, Mu, NICNT, NTC, SSA, St, TH]. The links are in reverse order of occurrence [St, TH].

QUESTION—Who would be the implied subject of the verbs?
1. The subject of the verbs is the Jews [AB, HNTC, ICC2, SSA, TH]. What Paul says is true generally for all people, but he is focusing particularly on the Jews [ICC1, Mor].
2. Paul is speaking of people generally, but he is also thinking of Israel in particular [NICNT, NTC, St].
3. What he is saying is generally true of all people [BECNT, Mu]. Paul's direct concern here is the Gentiles [Ho].

And how would-they-believe-in[a] (one) whom they-did- not -hear?[b] And how would-they-hear apart-from[c] preaching?[d]

LEXICON—a. aorist act. subj. of πιστεύω. See above. The phrase 'how would they believe in' is translated 'how can they believe in' [AB; GW, NIV, NLT, TEV], 'how shall they believe in' [BECNT, NICNT, WBC; KJV, NASB], 'how are they to believe in' [HNTC; NET, NRSV], 'how could they believe in' [ICC2], 'how can they have faith in' [NTC], 'how can people have faith in' [CEV], 'how could they have faith in' [REB], 'before they can believe in' [NCV]. This verb means to believe something to be true and, hence, worthy of being trusted [LN].

b. aorist act. indic. of ἀκούω (LN 33.212) (BAGD 1.b.α. p. 32): 'to hear' [BAGD, BECNT, HNTC, ICC2, LN, NICNT, NTC, WBC; all versions], 'to listen' [AB], 'to receive news' [LN]. The phrase οὗ οὐκ ἤκουσαν 'of whom they did not hear' is translated 'whom they had not heard' [NICNT], 'of whom they have never heard' [KJV, NIV, NRSV], 'they must hear about him' [NCV], 'one they have not heard of' [NET], 'have never heard about him' [NLT], 'without having heard of him' [REB], 'have never heard (the message)' [TEV], 'have never heard about him' [CEV]. This verb means to receive information about something, normally by word of mouth [LN].

c. χωρίς (LN 89.120) (BAGD 2.a.β. p. 890): 'apart from' [BAGD, LN], 'without' [BAGD, BECNT, HNTC, ICC2, LN, NICNT, NTC, WBC; KJV, NASB, NET, NIV, NRSV, REB], 'unless through' [AB], 'unless'

[CEV, NLT]. The sentence 'And how would they hear apart from preaching?' is translated 'How can they hear if no one tells the Good News?' [GW], 'and for them to hear about the Lord, someone must tell them' [NCV], 'and how can they hear if the message is not proclaimed?' [TEV]. This preposition marks negatively linked elements [LN].
  d. pres. act. participle of κηρύσσω (LN **33.256**) (BAGD 2.b.β. p. 431): 'to preach' [BAGD, LN, WBC; NET, NIV], 'to proclaim' [BAGD]. This verb is translated as a noun: 'preacher' [AB, BECNT, ICC2, NICNT, NTC; KJV, NASB]; as a phrase: 'someone preaching' [WBC], 'someone to make proclamation' [HNTC]. The phrase 'apart from preaching' is translated 'unless someone tells them' [CEV], 'without someone to spread the news' [REB], 'without someone to proclaim him' [NRSV], 'without a preacher' [KJV, NASB], 'if the message is not proclaimed' [TEV], 'if no one tells the Good News' [GW], '(for them to hear about the Lord,) someone must tell them' [NCV]. This verb means to publicly announce religious truths and principles while urging acceptance and compliance [LN].

QUESTION—What relationship is indicated by the genitive pronoun οὗ in the phrase οὗ οὐκ ἤκουσαν 'whom they did not hear'?

1. It is an objective genitive and means to hear *him*, not hear *about* him [AB, BECNT, HNTC, ICC1, ICC2, Mor, Mu, NTC, St, TH, WBC]. They either need to hear him, or to hear what he speaks through his messengers [ICC1, Mu, NTC]. Christ himself speaks when the gospel is proclaimed [Mu]. People must hear either Christ himself or Christ speaking through his preachers [HNTC]. Christ is in fact present in his preachers when they proclaim their message [Mor].

2. It means to hear *about* him [Gdt, NAC, NICNT, SSA]. Christ is heard when the message of the gospel is heard [NICNT]. The relative pronoun is a metonymy, in which 'whom' refers to 'the message about Christ' since no one would argue that it was necessary to hear Christ's actual voice [SSA]. It is translated as meaning that they need to hear about him by CEV, KJV, NCV, NET, NIV, NLT, NRSV, REB.

10:15 And how would-they-preach[a] unless[b] they-are-sent?[c]

LEXICON—a. aorist act. subj. of κηρύσσω. (LN **33.256**) (BAGD 2.b.β. p. 431): 'to preach' [AB, BAGD, BECNT, ICC2, LN, NICNT, NTC, WBC; KJV, NASB, NET, NIV], 'to make proclamation' [HNTC], 'to tell' [CEV, GW, NCV, NLT], 'to proclaim' [NRSV, TEV], 'to spread (the news)' [REB]. This verb means to publicly announce religious truths and principles while urging acceptance and compliance [LN].
  b. ἐὰν μή: 'unless' [AB, BECNT, HNTC, ICC2, NICNT, NTC, WBC; NASB, NET, NIV, NRSV], 'except' [KJV], 'without (being sent)' [CEV, NLT, REB]. The phrase 'unless they are sent' is translated 'if no one sends them' [GW], 'that person must be sent' [NCV], 'if the messengers are not sent out' [TEV].

c. aorist pass. subj. of ἀποστέλλω (LN 15.66): 'to be sent' [AB, BECNT, HNTC, ICC2, LN, NICNT, WBC; CEV, KJV, NASB, NCV, NET, NIV, NLT, NRSV, REB], 'to be sent out' [TEV], 'to be commissioned' [NTC]. This passive verb is translated as active: '(if no one) sends them' [GW]. This verb means to cause someone to depart for a particular purpose [LN].

QUESTION— Who are the ones who are sent and who sent them?

The verb ἀποστέλλω 'send' is cognate to the noun 'apostle', and alludes to the apostles [AB, Gdt, WBC], who are the origin of the testimony of the church [AB]. Paul may be referring specifically to himself and other apostles here [St].

1. He means that they are commissioned by Christ to be his spokesmen [HNTC, ICC2, Mu, NTC, WBC].
2. God has authorized and commissioned preachers [ICC2], and has sent them [NICNT]. The preacher is a herald of God, who is the divine monarch [AB]. The objection that might be raised is that preachers have not been sent by God, but should be, to which Paul will respond that God in fact has done so [SSA].

Just-as it-has-been-written[a] How beautiful/timely[b] (are) the feet of-those-proclaiming[c] the good-things.[d]

TEXT—Some manuscripts include τῶν εὐαγγελιζομένων εἰρήνην 'of those preaching peace' after πόδες 'feet'. It is omitted by GNT with an A rating, indicating that the text is certain. It is included only by KJV.

LEXICON—a. The phrase 'just as it has been written' is translated 'as it stands written' [AB], 'just as it is written' [BECNT, NICNT; NASB], 'as it is written' [HNTC, NTC, WBC; KJV, NET, NIV, NRSV], 'it is written' [NCV], 'the Scriptures say' [CEV], 'as Scripture says' [GW, REB], 'as the scripture says' [TEV], 'that is why the Scriptures say' [NLT], 'relevant here is the testimony of (the scripture)' [ICC2].

b. ὡραῖος (LN **67.3**, 79.10) (BAGD 1. p. 896): 'beautiful' [BECNT, HNTC, ICC2, LN (79.10), NTC; CEV, GW, KJV, NASB, NCV, NIV, NLT, NRSV], 'lovely' [LN (79.10)], 'timely' [AB, **LN** (67.3), NICNT, WBC; NET], 'happening at the right time' [BAGD, LN (67.3)], 'welcome' [REB], 'wonderful' [TEV]. This adjective describes a point of time which is particularly appropriate [LN (67.3)], or something that is beautiful, often with the implication of appropriateness [LN (79.10)].

c. pres. mid. participle of εὐαγγελίζω (LN 33.215) (BAGD 2.a.β. p. 317): 'to proclaim, to preach' [BAGD], 'to tell the good news, to announce the gospel' [LN]. The phrase τῶν εὐαγγελιζομένων [τὰ] ἀγαθά 'those proclaiming the good things' is translated 'those who bring good news of good things' [HNTC, ICC2], 'those who bring good news' [AB, NICNT, NTC; NIV, NRSV], 'them that...bring glad tidings' [KJV], 'those who proclaim the good news' [BECNT; NET], 'those who preach good news' [WBC], 'messengers who bring good news' [NLT, TEV], 'the messengers of good news' [REB], 'the messengers who announce the Good News'

[GW], 'who comes to bring good news' [NCV], 'someone coming to preach the good news' [CEV].

QUESTION—What idea or proposition is Paul supporting by this quotation from Isaiah?

Having proved logically that the gospel should be preached to all people, he now uses the quotation from Isaiah to support that [Ho]. It speaks of the sanctity, privilege, and dignity of being Christ's spokesman as a preacher of his message, as well as of the character of the message itself [Mu]. It implies that such preachers have in fact been sent [AB, BECNT, HNTC, ICC1, ICC2, NICNT].

QUESTION—Why does he speak about the feet of the ones who proclaim good things?

The noun 'feet' is a metonymy, representing the actions of sending and going [BECNT, SSA]. The feet may imply travel [WBC]. It is a metonymy in which the part of the body, the 'feet', not only stands for the person connected with the feet, but also stands for the action of the person in moving and arriving at a destination [SSA]. Some versions include in the translation the function of the feet: 'the feet of the messengers' [GW, NLT, REB], 'the feet of those who bring' [NASB, NIV, NRSV], 'even the feet of someone coming to preach' [CEV]. Some versions omit the reference to the feet and translate the idea of movement: 'how wonderful is the coming of messengers who bring' [TEV], 'how beautiful is the person who comes to bring' [NCV], 'how timely is the arrival of those' [NET].

QUESTION—Is he saying that their feet are beautiful or that they are timely?

1. The adjective ὡραῖος means beautiful [ICC1, NAC, St]: how beautiful are the feet. This is a metaphor to describe their coming as being wonderful [TH]. Their message was welcome [ICC1, NAC, St], bringing joy to the hearers [Gdt], so their approach was delightful [Ho].
2. The adjective ὡραῖος means timely [AB, Gdt, Mor, NICNT, NTC, WBC]: how timely are the feet, that is, their coming. It means that an event which such a person announces is opportune, happening or coming at the right time [BAGD, LN (67.3)], such as the harvest season [WBC]. The news they brought was timely [AB, Mor, NICNT, NTC, WBC]. It is like something blooming in the correct season or like something long-awaited [NTC].
3. It means that their coming was swift-footed or timely, but it also says something about the character of the message, that it was beautiful or welcome [Mu].

10:16 But[a] not all obeyed[b] the gospel.[c] For Isaiah says, Lord, who believed our report?[d]

LEXICON—a. ἀλλά (LN 89.125): 'but' [BECNT, ICC2, LN, NICNT, NTC, WBC; GW, KJV, NCV, NET, NIV, NLT, NRSV, TEV], 'yet' [AB, HNTC; CEV], 'however' [NASB], not explicit [REB]. This conjunction marks emphatic contrast [LN].

b. aorist act. indic. of ὑπακούω (LN 36.15) (BAGD 1. p. 837): 'to obey' [BAGD, BECNT, ICC2, LN, NICNT, WBC; KJV, NET, NRSV], 'to heed' [AB; NASB], 'to become obedient' [HNTC], 'to accept' [NTC; NCV, NIV, TEV], 'to believe' [CEV, GW], 'to welcome' [NLT], 'to respond' [REB]. This verb means to obey on the basis of having paid attention to someone or something [LN].

c. εὐαγγέλιον (LN 33.217) (BAGD 1.a. p. 318): 'gospel' [AB, BAGD, BECNT, LN, NICNT, WBC; KJV], 'good news' [BAGD, HNTC, ICC2, LN, NTC; GW, NCV, NET, NIV, NLT, NRSV, REB, TEV], 'the message' [CEV], 'glad tidings' [NASB]. This noun denotes the content of good news [LN].

d. ἀκοή (LN **24.57**) (BAGD 2.b. p. 31): 'report' [BAGD, BECNT, NICNT, WBC; KJV, NASB, NET], 'message' [AB, ICC2, LN, NTC; GW, NIV, NLT, NRSV, TEV], 'account, preaching' [BAGD]. This word is translated by the phrase 'what they heard from us' [HNTC], 'what we said' [CEV], 'what we told them' [NCV], 'when they heard us' [REB]. This noun denotes that which is heard by someone [LN].

QUESTION—What relationship is indicated by ἀλλά 'but'?

It is a strong adversative, expressing the opposite of what one might expect [Gdt, Mor]. Whereas faith and salvation should have resulted, unbelief resulted instead [Gdt].

1. It indicates what is a missing link for many people in the chain of requirements for salvation that he has been describing. Although the other conditions for salvation were met, what was lacking was faith on the part of those who heard the message [ICC2, NICNT].
2. The first clause 'not all believed' states an objection to what has just been said: if the gospel really were ordained by God, it would have been more successful, and people would have believed. The second clause in this verse is Paul's answer to this objection [AB, ICC1].
3. It indicates 10:16 as a response to what has been said in 10:14–15, not to single out any particular missing link in the chain, but simply to say that the process has failed, at least for some [WBC].
4. It indicates what would be the protasis of an implied conditional proposition; that is, it was the will of God for all people to hear the gospel, even though some did not believe [Ho].
5. It indicates Paul's rebuttal to the possible objections raised in 10:14–15 [SSA].

QUESTION—What does he mean by 'not all'?

1. It is a meiosis, or understatement [BECNT, ICC1, ICC2, Mor, NTC, St]. It was actually the majority of the Jews who were disobedient [BECNT, Mu, NICNT], and did not accept the gospel [NTC]. Although the gospel was finding acceptance in the world, most Jews did not accept it [Gdt]. It is a litotes, a negation of an opposite, and means 'very few' [NAC, NICNT]. It echoes the 'not all' of 9:6 where he says 'not all' Israelites are truly Israelites [NICNT]. It echoes the τινες 'some' of 3:3 [ICC2].

2. It is an antithesis to the 'all' in 10:13, and does not specify any quantity [WBC].

QUESTION—What relationship is indicated by γάρ 'for'?

It indicates a clarification; Paul clarifies the point he has made by saying that faith does not necessarily result from hearing the preached message [BECNT]. It indicates an explanation of why it is not so strange that someone who hears the gospel would not respond, which is that Isaiah has even foretold such things [Gdt, Mor]. It introduces the Isaiah passage in answer to the objection that unbelief implies that messengers had not been sent, because in fact they have, as even Isaiah prophesied [ICC1, SSA]. It indicates a reason for the fact that not all believed [NTC]. It indicates a scriptural confirmation to what is said in the first part of the verse [ICC2, WBC].

QUESTION—What is the answer anticipated by the rhetorical question quoted from Isaiah?

It implies that few Jews have believed [BECNT, Mor, Mu, NTC, SSA], though many should have done so [Mor]. Just because they didn't believe does not mean that the message wasn't preached to them [AB].

10:17 So-then[a] faith[b] (comes)[c] from[d] hearing[e] and hearing (comes) through[f] (the) word[g] of-Christ.

TEXT—Instead of Χριστοῦ 'of Christ', some manuscripts have θεοῦ 'of God'. GNT selects the reading 'of Christ' with an A rating, indicating that the text is certain. The reading 'of God' is taken only by KJV.

LEXICON—a. ἄρα (LN 89.46) (BAGD 4. p. 104): 'so then' [BAGD, WBC; KJV, REB, TEV], 'so' [BAGD, LN; GW, NASB, NCV, NLT, NRSV], 'then' [AB, HNTC, LN], 'therefore' [BECNT, NICNT], 'consequently' [LN, NTC; NET, NIV], 'it is implied that' [ICC2], not explicit [CEV]. This conjunction marks result as an inference from what has preceded [LN].

b. πίστις (LN 31.85, 31.102) (BAGD 2.d.α. p. 663): 'faith' [AB, BAGD, BECNT, HNTC, ICC2, LN (31.85), NICNT, NTC, WBC; all versions], 'Christian faith' [LN (31.102)]. This noun denotes complete trust and reliance [LN (31.85)], or belief in the good news of Jesus Christ with the result of becoming a follower [LN (31.102)].

c. There is no lexical entry for this work in the Greek text, but it is implied. It is represented in translation as 'comes' [AB, BECNT, HNTC, ICC2, NICNT, NTC, WBC; GW, NASB, NCV, NET, NIV, NLT, NRSV, TEV], 'cometh' [KJV], 'does come' [REB], not explicit [CEV].

d. ἐκ with genitive object (LN 90.12): 'from' [AB, BECNT, NICNT, NTC, WBC; GW, NASB, NCV, NET, NIV, NLT, NRSV, REB, TEV], 'by' [LN; KJV], 'as a result of' [HNTC, LN], 'of' [ICC2], not explicit [CEV]. This clause is translated 'No one can have faith without hearing' [CEV]. This preposition marks instrument, with the added implication of result [LN].

e. ἀκοή (LN 24.52): 'hearing' [BECNT, HNTC, ICC2, LN, NICNT, NTC, WBC; CEV, GW, KJV, NASB, NCV, NIV, NLT, REB, TEV], 'what is heard' [AB; NET, NRSV].

f. διά with genitive object (LN 89.76): 'through' [AB, BECNT, HNTC, ICC2, LN, NICNT, NTC, WBC; NET, NIV, NRSV, REB, TEV], 'by' [LN; KJV, NASB], 'by means of' [LN], not explicit [CEV, GW, NCV, NLT]. This preposition marks the means by which one event makes another event possible [LN].

g. ῥῆμα (LN 33.98) (BAGD 1. p. 735): 'word' [AB, BAGD, BECNT, HNTC, ICC2, LN, NICNT, NTC, WBC; KJV, NASB, NET, NRSV, REB], 'message' [LN; CEV, GW, NIV, TEV], 'Good News' [NCV, NLT]. This noun denotes that which has been stated or said, with primary focus upon the content of the communication [LN].

QUESTION—What relationship is indicated by ἄρα 'so then'?
1. It indicates a summary of what he has said in 10:14-15 [BECNT, HNTC, NICNT, WBC], as well as a conclusion [Mor, NTC], and a transition back to that topic [Gdt, HNTC, NICNT]. It indicates a conclusion of what is implied in his quotation from Isaiah and an application of that to the topic he is addressing [ICC2]. It indicates a parenthetical comment that draws a conclusion from what has been said, which is that the message has at least been heard [ICC1].
2. It indicates a further proof that Jewish people have heard the gospel, which is that some of them *are* hearing and *are* believing the message [SSA].

QUESTION—What does he mean by πίστις 'faith'?
It is personal commitment [AB]. It is a wholehearted commitment of oneself to God and submission to Christ's lordship [BECNT]. Obedience and commitment of the whole person is essential, as faith is entrusting oneself to God and holding nothing back [WBC]. Obedience requires faith, and faith requires obedience [ICC2].

QUESTION—What is meant by 'faith comes by hearing'?
People believe in Christ as a response to hearing a message that has been preached about him [Mu, SSA]. There must be a response to hearing a preached message, as the gospel does not arise spontaneously from within a person [AB, BECNT]. Hearing is the intermediate step or 'hinge' between the message being spoken and its being believed [ICC2]. The message awakens faith and makes it possible [NAC]. Faith must rest on the message that is preached, and without that message there is no basis for faith [Ho].

QUESTION—What is the relationship between the nouns in the genitive phrase διὰ ῥήματος Χριστοῦ 'through the word of Christ'?
1. The genitive is objective [AB, BECNT, ICC1, NICNT, SSA, TH, TNTC, WBC]. It is the word or message about Christ [AB, BECNT, ICC1, TH, WBC], the gospel of the crucified and resurrected Lord [BECNT], the message about the lordship and resurrection of Jesus Christ [NICNT].

2. The genitive is subjective; it is the word or message that Christ speaks [ICC2], either directly or through his messengers [HNTC, ICC2, NAC]. Christ speaks through his messengers [NAC].
3. It is the message about Christ, the gospel, but is also the message that Christ speaks [Mu, NTC, WBC]. It comes from Christ but is also about Christ [NTC].

10:18 But[a] I-say, Did-they- not -hear?[b]
LEXICON—a. ἀλλά (LN 89.125): 'but' [AB, BECNT, HNTC, ICC2, LN, NICNT, NTC, WBC; all versions except REB], 'then' [REB]. This conjunction marks emphatic contrast [LN].
   b. aorist act. indic. of ἀκούω (LN 33.212) (BAGD 3.a. p. 32): 'to hear' [AB, BECNT, HNTC, ICC2, LN, NICNT, NTC, WBC; all versions], 'to receive news' [LN], 'to learn about, be informed about' [BAGD]. The question μὴ οὐκ ἤκουσαν; is translated 'Did they not hear?' [HNTC, ICC2; NIV], 'have they not heard?' [NICNT; KJV, NET, NRSV], 'Didn't they hear that message?' [GW], 'Didn't people hear the Good News?' [NCV], 'is it the case that they have not heard?' [WBC], 'Can it be that they have not heard?' [AB, NTC], 'Can it be that they never heard?' [REB], 'Is it true that they did not hear the message?' [TEV], 'have the people of Israel actually heard the message?' [NLT], 'surely they have never heard, have they?' [NASB], '(But am I saying that) the people of Israel did not hear?' [CEV], 'Israel has certainly heard' [BECNT]. This verb means to receive information about something [LN].
QUESTION—What kind of answer does μὴ οὐκ anticipate?
   It anticipates an affirmative answer: yes, they did hear [BECNT, ICC2, Mu, NAC, NICNT, SSA, WBC].
QUESTION—What is the relation of ἤκουσαν 'did they hear' with what has already been said?
   Paul has used the verb ἀκούω 'hear' twice in 10:14-17, and the close cognate ὑπακούω 'to obey' in 10:16, and the cognate noun ἀκοή, translated 'report' in 10:16 and 'hearing' in 10:17 [BECNT, WBC]. This is a play on words that is obvious in Greek but not in English [BECNT, WBC].

On-the-contrary,[a] Into all the earth[b] their message[c] went-out[d]
LEXICON—a. μενοῦνγε (LN 89.128) (BAGD p. 503). This word is translated 'on the contrary' [BAGD, LN, WBC], 'of course' [AB], 'rather' [BAGD], 'of course they did' [NTC; NIV, REB, TEV], 'Certainly they did!' [GW], 'Yes, they heard' [NCV], 'Yes indeed' [BECNT], 'Yes, verily' [KJV], 'Yes, they have' [NET, NLT], 'Why listen:' [HNTC], 'They did indeed' [ICC2], 'Indeed they have' [NICNT; NASB, NRSV]. In connection with the first clause this word is translated, 'But am I saying that the people of Israel did not hear? No, I am not!' [CEV]. This particle is a relatively emphatic marker of contrast [AB, ICC1, LN, TH].
   b. γῆ (LN 1.39): 'earth' [AB, BECNT, HNTC, ICC2, LN, NICNT, NTC, WBC; CEV, KJV, NASB, NET, NIV, NLT, NRSV], 'world' [LN; GW,

NCV, REB, TEV]. This noun denotes the earth as the dwelling place of mankind [LN].
c. φθόγγος (LN **33.104**) (BAGD p. 857): 'message' [LN; CEV, NCV, NLT], 'utterance' [HNTC, LN], 'sound' [BAGD, NTC, WBC; KJV], 'voice' [AB, ICC2, NICNT; GW, NASB, NET, NIV, NRSV, REB], 'report' [BECNT]. This word is translated 'The sound of their voice' [TEV]. This noun denotes an utterance, with possible focus upon the clarity of the verbal sounds [LN].
d. aorist act. indic. of ἐξέρχομαι (LN 15.7) (BAGD 2.b.α. p. 275): 'to go out' [BAGD, BECNT, HNTC, ICC2, NTC, WBC; GW, NASB, NCV, NET, NIV, NRSV, TEV], 'to go' [LN; KJV, NLT], 'to go forth' [AB, NICNT], 'to announce' [CEV], 'to sound' [REB]. This verb means to move from one place to another [LN]. This aorist verb is translated as perfect tense: 'has gone out' [HNTC, WBC; GW, NASB, NET, NIV, NRSV], 'has gone throughout (the earth)' [NLT], 'has gone forth' [AB, NICNT], 'is gone out' [ICC2], 'has sounded' [REB].

QUESTION—How does the passage from Psalm 19 relate to Paul's argument?

The preaching of the gospel by Christian preachers all over the world is like the widespread nature of the witness of creation [AB, BECNT, Gdt, HNTC, ICC1, ICC2, Mu, NAC, NICNT, NTC, St]. He is implying that the spread of the gospel is as world-wide as the lights in the heavens [Ho, NAC, TNTC]. The witness of the created order symbolizes the witness of the church [St]. Just as people everywhere can know about God from observing the stars, so also Jews everywhere can know the gospel because it has been preached all over the world [SSA]. Paul is saying that the special revelation of the message of Jesus Christ is sounding forth all around the world in the same way as the general revelation described in Psalm 19; this is not an artificial comparison because although this line quoted from Psalm 19 speaks of general revelation, such as through creation, the second half of that psalm speaks of special revelation, such as through God's words, which is what the gospel is [Mu]. Paul does not cite Psalm 19 as a proof text or prophecy, but borrows the language of the psalm to describe the spread of the gospel, which is also a testimony [WBC]. Paul uses the wording of Psalm 19:1-6, which describes how general revelation has reached all the earth, to describe the spread of the gospel all over the earth [Ho, NICNT]. The wide and rapid spread of the gospel in the first century was amazing [NTC].

and their words[a] to the ends[b] of-the world.[c]

LEXICON—a. ῥῆμα (LN 33.98) (BAGD 1. p. 735): 'word' [AB, BAGD, BECNT, HNTC, ICC2, LN, NICNT, NTC, WBC; GW, KJV, NASB, NCV, NET, NIV, NLT, NRSV, REB, TEV], 'message' [LN], 'it' (referring to the previous 'message') [CEV]. This noun denotes that which has been stated or said, with primary focus upon the content of the communication [LN].

b. πέρας (LN **80.6**) (BAGD 1. p. 644): 'end' [BAGD, BECNT, HNTC, ICC2, LN, NICNT, NTC, WBC; GW, KJV, NASB, NET, NIV, NRSV, REB, TEV], 'limit' [BAGD, LN], 'bounds' [AB], 'all over' [CEV], 'everywhere' [NCV], 'all' [NLT]. This noun denotes the limit as the distant end of a space [LN].

c. οἰκουμένη (LN 1.39) (BAGD 1.a. p. 561): 'the world' [AB, BAGD, HNTC, LN; CEV, KJV, NASB, NET, NIV, NLT, NRSV], 'the inhabited world' [ICC2, NICNT, NTC, WBC], 'the earth' [LN; GW, NCV, REB, TEV], 'the inhabited earth' [BAGD, BECNT]. This noun denotes the dwelling place of mankind [LN].

QUESTION—Is Paul claiming that everyone in the world has heard the gospel?

Paul is using hyperbole [NICNT, SSA, St, WBC]; the gospel had not been preached to all people individually, but representatively to many nations throughout the Roman world [NICNT]. Paul is not saying that everyone everywhere has already heard the gospel, just that the message has been spread very widely [BECNT]. He is saying that the gospel has been preached very widely, not that the task of preaching to the nations has been completed [ICC2]. The gospel had been preached wherever there were Jewish communities [St]. He is saying that the gospel is being spread throughout the world, and that no one can say that the Jews did not hear it [Mu]. It had gone to most parts of the Mediterranean world where Jews lived [TNTC]. No Jew anywhere could plead ignorance about this message [Gdt]. Not everyone had heard, but the character of the gospel is universal [ICC1]. Probably most of the Jews in the Roman empire, with the possible exception of Spain, had at least heard something about the gospel of Christ [WBC].

10:19 But I-say, Did Israel not understand?[a] First[b] Moses says I-will-make- you -jealous[c] by (those) not a nation,[d]

LEXICON—a. aorist act. indic. of γινώσκω (LN 32.16): 'to understand' [AB, NTC; CEV, NCV, NET, NIV, NLT, NRSV, REB, TEV], 'to come to understand' [LN], 'to comprehend' [LN], 'to know' [BECNT, HNTC, NICNT, WBC; KJV, NASB]. This verb is translated as a noun: 'knowledge' [ICC2]. The question μὴ Ἰσραὴλ οὐκ ἔγνω; 'Did Israel not understand?' [NIV, NRSV] is also translated 'Did the people of Israel not understand?' [TEV], 'Didn't the people of Israel understand?' [NCV], 'didn't Israel understand?' [NET], 'Can it be that Israel did not understand?' [AB, NTC], 'Did the people of Israel understand or not?' [CEV], 'Didn't Israel understand that message?' [GW], 'did the people of Israel really understand?' [NLT], 'Can it be that Israel never understood?' [REB], 'Did not Israel know?' [KJV], 'Did Israel really not know?' [HNTC], 'Israel certainly knew, didn't it?' [BECNT], 'has not Israel known?' [NICNT], 'is it the case that Israel has not known?' [WBC], 'surely Israel did not know, did they?' [NASB], 'was Israel without knowledge?' [ICC2]. This verb means to come to an understanding as the result of ability to experience and learn [LN].

b. πρῶτος (LN 67.18) (BAGD 1.a. p. 725): 'first' [HNTC, ICC2, NICNT, NTC, WBC; GW, KJV, NASB, NCV, NET, NIV, NRSV, REB, TEV], 'earlier' [BAGD], 'formerly' [LN], 'first of all' [AB, BECNT], 'even in the time of' [NLT], not explicit [CEV]. This adjective describes a point of time earlier in a sequence [LN].

c. fut. act. indic. of παραζηλόω (LN **88.164**) (BAGD p. 616): 'to make jealous' [AB, BAGD, ICC2, **LN**, NICNT; CEV, GW, NASB, NCV, NET, NRSV, TEV], 'to provoke to jealousy' [BAGD, BECNT, WBC; KJV], 'to cause to be envious' [LN], 'to stir up to envy' [HNTC], 'to stir one to envy' [REB], 'to make envious' [NTC; NIV], 'to rouse one's jealousy' [NLT]. This verb means to cause someone to feel strong jealousy or resentment against someone [LN].

d. ἔθνος (LN 11.55): 'nation' [AB, BECNT, HNTC, ICC2, LN, NICNT, WBC; all versions except KJV], 'people' [KJV]. The phrase 'those not a nation' is translated 'a not nation' [WBC], 'a so-called nation' [TEV], 'people who are nation of nobodies' [CEV], 'them that are no people' [KJV]. This noun denotes the largest unit into which the people of the world are divided on the basis of their constituting a socio-political community [LN].

QUESTION—What kind of answer does μὴ...οὐκ anticipate?

It anticipates an affirmative answer: yes, they did [BECNT, Gdt, ICC2, Mu, NICNT, TH, WBC].

QUESTION—What is implied by his use of the term 'Israel'?

It calls to mind Israel's religious privilege, its election, and its prophets to underscore the fact that they should have believed [ICC1, ICC2]. His use of the name Israel helps underscore his point, because Israel has received much revelation from God through the prophets about his plans and his purposes [NICNT]. 'Israel' speaks of their election and their covenant relation to God [WBC].

QUESTION—What was it that they knew or understood?

1. They knew the gospel message [AB, ICC1, NAC, NTC, SSA, St, TH]. Not only have they heard the message of salvation, they should have understood the Biblical theme of God's righteousness and mercy [HNTC]. They knew their own scriptures and had heard the gospel message, so they should have known what to expect that God would do [WBC].

2. They knew that God could act in such a way as to include the Gentiles and judge Israel [NICNT]. They understood that the kingdom would be taken from them and offered to others who would produce spiritual fruit [Mu]. They knew that the Gentiles would be accepted into the people of God and Israel would resist [BECNT]. They knew that the Gentiles were to be called and they would be rejected [Ho]. They knew of the universality of the gospel [Gdt].

QUESTION—What relationship is indicated by πρῶτος 'first'?

Moses was the first to tell of Israel's being provoked to jealousy [Mu, NICNT, SSA]. Moses is the first to testify that Israel indeed knew [ICC2], they knew even as early as Moses [ICC1]. Moses' message came before that of the prophets [HNTC, Ho]. Paul quotes first from Moses [Gdt, St]. It also refers to the fact that God has given this testimony from the very beginning of his recorded words [Gdt].

QUESTION—What is meant or implied by the phrase 'not a nation'?

It picks up on the wording of 9:25–26 where those who are 'not my people' become God's people [ICC2, NICNT, St, TNTC]. It refers back to Deut. 32:21 where God says that he will provoke his people to jealousy by those who are not his people [Gdt]. The Gentiles were not a nation in the sense that they had not received all the blessings and privileges that the nation Israel had received [NTC, SSA]. Relative to Israel the Gentiles are strangers and aliens, and had not received the covenant favor that Israel had received [Mu]. Because Israel provoked God by worshipping that which is not God, he will provoke them by what is, to them, no people [NICNT].

by a nation without-understanding^a I-will-make- you -angry.^b

LEXICON—a ἀσύνετος (LN 32.49) (BAGD 1. p. 118): 'without understanding' [BECNT, LN, NICNT; NASB], 'foolish' [AB, BAGD, ICC2, LN; KJV, NLT, NRSV, REB], 'senseless' [BAGD, HNTC, LN, NTC, WBC; NET], '(people) who don't understand a thing' [CEV], '(a nation) that doesn't understand' [GW, NCV], '(a nation) that has no understanding' [NIV], '(a nation) of fools' [TEV]. The last clause is translated 'I will provoke your anger through the foolish Gentiles' [NLT]. This adjective describes something as lacking capacity for insight and understanding [LN].

b. fut. act. indic. of παροργίζω (LN **88.177**) (BAGD p. 629): 'to make angry' [BAGD, BECNT, ICC2, LN, NICNT, NTC, WBC; CEV, GW, NCV, NIV, NRSV, TEV], 'to anger (someone)' [KJV, NASB], 'to provoke one's anger' [AB], 'to provoke to anger' [HNTC; NET, NLT], 'to rouse (someone's) anger' [REB]. This verb means to cause someone to become provoked or quite angry [LN].

QUESTION—What is the point that Paul is making by this statement?

If Gentiles, who were darkened theologically, could understand the gospel, Jews could certainly have understood it [Mor, NAC]. Israel is responsible for their unbelief because they had received enough understanding of the way of salvation [NTC]. Their own scriptures should have enabled them to see God at work in the gospel [NICNT]. It was to Israel's shame that they didn't believe, whereas Gentiles did believe [HNTC]. If Gentiles who did not have Israel's privilege in terms of knowing God actually did come to know, then Israel cannot claim not to have known [ICC2]. Israel has no excuse for unbelief [St, WBC]; they are simply stubborn [St]. If the ignorant and corrupt Gentiles can receive God's light, the only reason for the Jews not doing so is that they are so stubborn and proud [Gdt]. They should have known from their own scriptures what to expect [WBC].

10:20 And Isaiah is-very-bold[a] and says, I-was-found[b] by those not seeking[c] me, I-became manifest[d] to-those not asking-for[e] me.

LEXICON—a. pres. act. indic. of ἀποτολμάω (LN **25.163**) (BAGD p. 101): 'to be very bold' [BECNT, ICC2, LN, NTC, WBC; KJV, NASB, NCV, NET, NRSV], 'to make bold' [AB, HNTC], 'to be daring' [REB], 'to be bolder' [TEV]. This verb is translated as an adverb: 'boldly (says)' [NICNT; GW, NIV, NLT]; as an adjective: 'fearless' [CEV]. This verb means to be particularly bold or daring in what one does [LN]. It occurs only here in the NT.

b. aorist pass. indic. of εὑρίσκω (LN 27.27) (BAGD 2. p. 325): 'to be found' [AB, BAGD, BECNT, HNTC, ICC2, LN, NICNT, WBC; all versions except KJV], 'to be discovered' [BAGD, LN], 'to be made manifest' [KJV]. This passive verb is translated as active: 'to find' [NTC]. This verb is translated by the phrase 'I let myself be found' [ICC2]. This verb means to learn the location of something, either by intentional searching or by unexpected discovery [LN].

c. pres. act. participle of ζητέω (LN 27.41) (BAGD 1.a.β. p. 338): 'to seek' [AB, BAGD, BECNT, HNTC, ICC2, NICNT, NTC, WBC; KJV, NASB, NET, NIV, NRSV], 'to look for' [BAGD, LN; CEV, GW, NCV, NLT, REB, TEV], 'to try to find' [LN]. This verb means to try to learn the location of something by searching for it [LN].

d. ἐμφανής (LN **28.35**) (BAGD p. 257): 'visible' [BAGD], 'revealed' [BAGD, BECNT, NTC, WBC; GW, NIV, REB], 'well known' [LN; NET], 'evident' [LN]. The verb phrase ἐμφανὴς ἐγενόμην 'I became manifest' [NASB] is also translated 'I was made manifest' [KJV], 'I made myself manifest' [ICC2], 'I appeared' [HNTC; CEV, TEV], 'I showed myself' [AB; NLT], 'I have shown myself' [NRSV], 'I made myself known' [NCV], 'I became well known' [NET], 'I revealed myself' [NTC; NIV, REB], 'I have revealed myself' [BECNT, WBC], 'I was revealed' [GW]. It is also translated as future: 'I will make myself manifest' [NICNT].

e. pres. act. participle of ἐπερωτάω (LN 33.161) (BAGD 1.c. p. 285): 'to ask for' [AB, LN, NICNT, NTC, WBC; GW, NASB, NET, NIV, NLT, NRSV, TEV], 'to ask' [BAGD], 'to ask about' [CEV, REB], 'to ask after' [KJV], 'to request' [LN], 'to inquire' [BECNT, HNTC, ICC2]. The two sections of the quotation have been reordered in NCV: 'I was found by those who were not asking me for help. I made myself known to people who were not looking for me.' This verb means to ask for, usually with the implication of an underlying question [LN].

QUESTION—What does he imply by the verb ἀποτολμᾷ 'is very bold'?

What Isaiah has said is very bold [BECNT, WBC] or astonishing [ICC2]. Isaiah foretold this very plainly and forthrightly [Ho, Mu], unambiguously [Gdt]. Isaiah spoke more boldly than Moses did in this matter [HNTC, TNTC; TEV]. Isaiah's statement is even more incisive [NTC], more clear

[NICNT], more likely to provoke anger [SSA]. Isaiah was bold when he stood up to the people of his own day [ICC1].

10:21 But concerning[a] Israel he-says, All the day[b] I-stretched-out[c] my hands[d] to a people[e] disobeying[f] and rebelling.[g]

LEXICON—a. πρός (LN 90.25) (BAGD III. 5. a. p. 710): 'concerning' [ICC2, NTC, WBC; NIV, TEV], 'about' [BAGD, LN, NICNT; CEV, GW, NCV, NET], 'regarding' [NLT], 'of' [AB, HNTC; NRSV, REB], 'as for' [NASB], 'to' [BECNT, LN; KJV], 'with reference to' [BAGD]. This preposition marks content, particularly when persons are involved and/or the context suggests some type of response being made [LN].

b. ἡμέρα (LN 67.178) (BAGD 2. p. 346): 'day' [AB, BAGD, BECNT, HNTC, ICC2, LN, NICNT, NTC, WBC; all versions]. The phrase Ὅλην τὴν ἡμέραν 'all the day' [WBC] is also translated 'all day long' [AB, BECNT, NTC; CEV, GW, KJV, NCV, NET, NIV, NLT, NRSV, REB, TEV], 'all day' [HNTC], 'all the day long' [ICC2, NICNT; NASB]. This noun denotes a full day, which according to Hebrew reckoning began at sunset and ended at the following sunset [LN].

c. aorist act. indic. of ἐκπετάννυμι (LN 16.19) (BAGD p. 243): 'to stretch out' [BECNT, HNTC, ICC2, LN, NTC, WBC; GW, NASB, REB], 'to hold out' [AB, BAGD, NICNT; NET, NIV, NRSV, TEV], 'to reach out' [CEV], 'to extend' [LN], 'to stretch forth' [KJV], 'to stand ready (to accept)' [NCV], 'to open (my arms)' [NLT]. This verb means to cause an object to extend in space (for example, by becoming straight, unfolded, or uncoiled) [LN]. This word occurs only here in the NT.

d. χείρ (LN 8.30): 'hand' [AB, BECNT, HNTC, ICC2, LN, NICNT, NTC, WBC; GW, KJV, NASB, NET, NIV, NRSV, REB, TEV], 'arm' [NLT], not explicit [CEV, NCV]. This noun denotes a hand or any relevant portion of the hand, including, for example, the fingers [LN].

e. λαός (LN 11.55): 'people' [AB, BECNT, HNTC, ICC2, LN, NICNT, NTC, WBC; all versions except NLT], 'nation' [LN]. The clause is translated 'All day long I opened my arms to them' which refers back to 'regarding Israel' at the beginning of the verse [NLT]. This noun denotes the largest unit into which the people of the world are divided on the basis of their constituting a socio-political community [LN].

f. pres. act. participle of ἀπειθέω (LN 36.23, 31.107) (BAGD 2. p. 82): 'to disobey' [BAGD, LN (36.23); NCV], 'to be disobedient' [BAGD], 'to refuse to believe' [LN (31.107)], 'to refuse to obey' [CEV]. This participle is translated as an adjective: 'disobedient' [AB, BECNT, HNTC, ICC2, NICNT, NTC, WBC; GW, KJV, NASB, NET, NIV, NLT, NRSV, REB, TEV]. This verb means to refuse to comply with the demands of some authority [LN (36.23)], or to refuse to believe the Christian message [LN (31.107)].

g. pres. act. participle of ἀντιλέγω (LN 33.455) (BAGD 2. p. 74): 'to oppose' [BAGD, LN], 'to refuse' [BAGD], 'to be stubborn' [CEV]. This participle is translated as an adjective: 'disobedient' [BAGD], 'defiant' [AB; REB], 'recalcitrant' [BECNT], 'contradicting' [HNTC], 'gainsaying' [ICC2; KJV], 'obstinate' [NICNT, NTC, WBC; NASB, NIV], 'rebellious' [GW, NLT, TEV], 'stubborn' [NCV, NET], 'contrary' [NRSV]. This verb means to speak against something or someone [LN].

QUESTION—What relationship is indicated by πρός 'to'?
1. God speaks about or concerning Israel [AB, HNTC, ICC2, Mor, NTC, SSA, WBC; CEV, GW, NASB, NCV, NET, NIV, NLT, NRSV, REB].
2. God speaks to Israel [BECNT, Gdt, ICC1, NICNT; KJV]. Although NICNT translates 'about', it comments that here the word means 'to'.

QUESTION—What relationship is indicated by δέ 'but'?
It is contrastive [NICNT, SSA; KJV, NCV, NET, NIV, NLT, NRSV, TEV]. Whereas in the previous verse he applies Isaiah 65:1 to Gentiles, here he applies Isaiah 65:2 to the Jews [NICNT].

QUESTION—What is implied by the gesture of extending the hands?
It is a gesture of welcome and invitation [AB, Ho]. It expresses God's patience as well as his invitation to them [NTC]. It is an invitation to return [SSA, St]. It expresses God's tender concern [Mor]. God pleads with Israel [HNTC]. It is a gesture of entreaty, and of God's overture of mercy [Mu]. It expresses a genuine longing on God's part for the people to respond in faith [BECNT]. It is a gesture of pleading love, or at least of welcome [NAC]. God is reaching out to offer grace to Israel [NICNT]. It is a gesture of appeal, of welcome, and of friendship [ICC2]. God offers peace and reconciliation [TH]. God calls to them with the tenderness of a mother [ICC1]. It is anthropomorphic (describing God's actions and gestures in terms of human ones) [Mor].

QUESTION—What is implied by Paul's statement here about Israel's resistance to God?
Israel has merited the judgment that happened to them [NTC]. They flatly refused God's gracious invitation and are fully responsible [Mor]. In chapter nine he discusses predestination, and here he discusses Israel's responsibility for their own unbelief, both of which are true [BECNT, Mor]. Israel's obstinacy caused them to miss God's saving help [NTC]. Their disobedience is inexcusable [Mu]. Israel's disobedience and unbelief is as paradoxical as the Gentiles' faith [HNTC]. Israel's rejection came from their willful disobedience [NAC]. Israel wanted to keep a monopoly on God's grace, but having become blinded by their privileges, they are completely without excuse for having missed salvation [Gdt]. Divine predestination does not negate human responsibility; disobedience is still disobedience [WBC]. God only rejects those who refuse him [Ho].

DISCOURSE UNIT—11:1–36 [AB, ICC2, Mor, Mu, NAC; GW]. The topic is Israel's failure is partial and temporary [AB], God has not cast off his people [ICC2], God's promises will be fulfilled [Mor], the restoration of Israel [Mu], some alleviating factors [NAC], God's continuing love for Jewish people [GW].

DISCOURSE UNIT—11:1–32 [St, WBC; NCV]. The topic is Israel's future: God's long-term design [St], the mystery of God's faithfulness [WBC], God shows mercy to all people [NCV].

DISCOURSE UNIT—11:1–29 [TNTC]. The topic is God's purpose for Israel.

DISCOURSE UNIT—11:1–12 [TNTC; TEV]. The topic is Israel's alienation is not final [TNTC], God's mercy on Israel [TEV].

DISCOURSE UNIT—11:1–10 [AB, HNTC, Ho, ICC1, Mor, Mu, NAC, NICNT, NTC, WBC; CEV, NRSV]. The topic is Israel's hardening is partial [AB], the remnant [HNTC], the rejection of Israel is not total [Ho], the rejection of Israel is not complete [ICC1], the remnant of Israel [Mor; NIV], the remnant and the remainder [Mu], the rejection is not total [NAC], summary: Israel, the elect and the hardened [NICNT], the election of Israel's minority or remnant versus the hardening of its majority [NTC], the remnant according to grace—and the others [WBC], God has not rejected his people [CEV], Israel's rejection is not final [NRSV].

11:1 I-say[a] then,[b] God did- not -reject[c] his people[d] (did he)?[e]
LEXICON—a. pres. act. indic. of λέγω (LN 33.69): 'to say' [BECNT, LN, NICNT; CEV, KJV, NASB], 'to ask' [AB, HNTC, ICC2, NTC, WBC; GW, NCV, NET, NIV, NLT, NRSV, REB, TEV]. This verb means to speak or talk, with apparent focus upon the content of what is said [LN].
  b. οὖν (LN 89.50): 'then' [AB, BECNT, ICC2, LN, NTC; KJV, NASB, NIV, NLT, NRSV, REB, TEV], 'so' [LN; GW, NCV, NET], 'therefore' [LN, NICNT, WBC], 'consequently, accordingly, so then' [LN], 'with all this in mind' [HNTC], not explicit [CEV]. This conjunction marks result, often implying the conclusion of a process of reasoning [LN].
  c. aorist mid. (deponent = act.) indic. of ἀπωθέομαι (LN 15.46) (BAGD 2. p. 103): 'to reject' [AB, BAGD, BECNT, NICNT, NTC; GW, NASB, NET, NIV, NLT, NRSV, REB, TEV], 'to cast off' [HNTC, ICC2], 'to cast away' [KJV], 'to repudiate' [BAGD, WBC], 'to turn one's back' [CEV], 'to throw out' [NCV], 'to push away, to thrust aside' [LN]. This aorist verb is translated using the English perfect tense: 'has rejected' [AB, BECNT, HNTC, ICC2, NICNT, WBC; CEV, GW, KJV, NASB, NET, NLT, NRSV, REB]. This verb means to use force in pushing or thrusting someone or something away or aside [LN].
  d. λαός (LN 11.55, 11.12): 'people' [AB, BECNT, HNTC, ICC2, LN (11.55), NICNT, NTC, WBC; all versions], 'people of God' [LN (11.12)]. The phrase τὸν λαὸν αὐτοῦ 'his people' is also translated 'his people Israel' [GW], 'his own people, the nation of Israel' [NLT]. This noun denotes the largest unit into which the people of the world are divided on the basis of their constituting a socio-political community [LN (11.55)], or people who belong to God [LN (11.12)].
  e. These words are not in the Greek text, but are supplied in the English translation to indicate the fact that the question introduced by μή 'not'

expects a negative answer [AB, BECNT, Gdt, ICC1, ICC2, Mu, NICNT, TNTC, WBC; NASB, NET]. This is represented in translation as 'has God rejected?' [AB; GW, NLT, NRSV, REB], 'has God cast off?' [HNTC, ICC2], 'has God repudiated?' [WBC], 'hath God cast away?' [KJV].

QUESTION—What is the sense of the verb λέγω 'I say'?

It actually introduces a question [AB, HNTC, Ho, ICC2, NAC, NTC, WBC], one that Paul wants the readers themselves to consider and answer [NTC]. It is a way of raising a question that a Jewish person might raise in response to what Paul is saying [SSA].

QUESTION—What relationship is indicated by οὖν 'then'?

It introduces a question about what conclusion is to be drawn from what he has said [Gdt, Ho, ICC2, Mor, NICNT, NTC, WBC]. It builds on what he has in 10:18–21 [WBC], or even in 10:14–21 [HNTC, NICNT]. It follows from what he has said in 10:21 about Israel's disobedience and stubbornness [NICNT, NTC], which in turn summarizes the whole of his discussion in 9:30–10:21 [BECNT, NICNT], or in all of chapters 9 and 10 [Gdt]. It follows generally on what he has been saying, but not on any one specific point [Mor].

QUESTION—Was there any sense in which God had rejected Israel?

The wording of Paul's question is taken from several OT texts such as Ps. 94:14 and 1 Sam. 12:22 that assert that God will not reject his people [AB, BECNT, ICC2, NICNT, NTC, St, TNTC], as well as Lam. 3:31 [WBC]. The fact that God chose them means that it is not possible that he would reject them [BECNT, ICC1, ICC2, Mu, St, WBC]. The question implies that if God has rejected his people, then he has broken his promises recorded in chapter 10 [ICC2]. God has declared that his covenant with them cannot be broken [St]. In a certain limited sense God has rejected them, but not altogether [NTC]. In chapter nine Paul says that God's rejection of Israel was partial, but not complete; in chapter ten he says that it was not arbitrary, but based on their actions [NTC]; and here in chapter eleven he says that it is not total [Ho, Mu, NTC, St] nor final [Ho, Mu, St]. Paul's point is that God has not rejected *all* Jews [SSA]. The promises that God will not reject his people are not directed toward the nation in general, but toward the spiritual Israel, the elect [Ho].

Never-may-it-be![a] For[b] I[c] also am an Israelite,[d] of-(the) seed[e] of-Abraham, (the) tribe[f] of-Benjamin.

LEXICON—a. aorist mid. (deponent = act.) optative of γίνομαι (LN 13.107) (BAGD I.3.a. p. 158): 'to come to be' [LN], 'to occur or to happen' [LN]. The phrase μὴ γένοιτο 'Never may it be!' is translated 'Certainly not!' [AB, BECNT, HNTC; CEV, TEV], 'God forbid!' [ICC2; KJV], 'By no means!' [NICNT; NIV, NRSV], 'Of course not!' [NTC; NLT, REB], 'Not at all!' [WBC], 'That's unthinkable!' [GW], 'May it never be!' [NASB],

'no!' [NCV], 'absolutely not!' [NET]. This verb means to happen, with the implication that what happens is different from a previous state [LN].
- b. γάρ (LN 89.23) (BAGD 1.b. p. 151): 'for' [BECNT, ICC2, LN, NICNT, WBC; KJV, NASB, NET], 'because' [LN], 'why, (I myself)' [HNTC, NTC], 'consider this' [GW], 'remember that' [NLT], not explicit [AB; CEV, NCV, NIV, NRSV, REB, TEV]. This conjunction marks cause or reason between events [LN].
- c. ἐγώ (LN 92.1): 'I' [BECNT, LN; CEV], 'I indeed' [LN], 'I myself' [AB, HNTC, ICC2, NTC; GW, NCV, NIV, NLT, NRSV, REB, TEV], 'even I' [NICNT], 'I too' [WBC; NASB, NET], 'I also' [KJV]. This pronoun denotes a reference to the speaker (with emphasis) [LN].
- d. Ἰσραηλίτης (LN 93.183) (BAGD p. 381): 'Israelite' [AB, BECNT, HNTC, ICC2, LN, NICNT, NTC, WBC; GW, KJV, NASB, NCV, NET, NIV, NRSV, REB, TEV], 'of the people of Israel' [CEV], 'a Jew' [NLT]. This noun denotes the ethnic name of a person belonging to the nation of Israel [LN].
- e. σπέρμα (LN 10.29) (BAGD 2.b. p. 761): 'seed' [BECNT, HNTC, ICC2, NICNT, NTC, WBC; KJV], 'posterity' [BAGD, LN], 'descendant' [AB, BAGD, LN; CEV, GW, NASB, NET, NIV, NLT, NRSV, TEV], 'family' [NCV], 'offspring' [LN], 'children' [BAGD], 'stock' [REB]. This noun denotes posterity, with emphasis upon the ancestor's role in founding the lineage [LN].
- f. φυλή (LN 10.2) (BAGD 1. p. 868): 'tribe' [AB, BAGD, BECNT, HNTC, ICC2, LN, NICNT, NTC, WBC; all versions]. This noun denotes a subgroup of a nation which is regarded as being more closely related biologically than the entire nation [LN].

QUESTION—What relationship is indicated by γάρ 'for'?
1. This conjunction indicates the reason why it cannot be said that God has rejected his people [AB, BECNT, Gdt, HNTC, Ho, ICC2, NAC, NICNT, NTC, SSA, St, TH, TNTC]. God has not rejected *all* Israelites, as proved by the fact that Paul is a believer [SSA]. Paul knows from his own experience as an Israelite that God has not rejected Israel [AB]. Paul himself is part of the elect remnant [BECNT]. The call of Paul, an Israelite, as apostle to the Gentiles shows that God has not rejected his people [ICC2].
2. This conjunction indicates the reason for his feeling of horror at the suggestion that God would forsake his people [ICC1, Mu, WBC]. Paul speaks from a Jewish viewpoint, in which it would be unconceivable to imagine that God would reject his people [ICC1, WBC]. Paul's feelings as an Israelite would make him disloyal if he thought God would reject his people [ICC1].
3. This includes both of the above [Mu]. Paul is saying the he is an example of an Israelite that God has saved, and also that as an Israelite it would be inconceivable for him to imagine that God would reject his people [Mu].

QUESTION—Why does Paul go on to add that he is descended from Abraham and Benjamin?
1. It underscores his identity as an Israelite, but nothing specific beyond that [BECNT, ICC2, NICNT, NTC, WBC].
2. Abraham was the great example of faith, and Benjamin had special significance as the only son of Jacob born in the promised land, and his was the only tribe that remained loyal to Judah [Mor]. Of the tribes, Benjamin was viewed as the most Israelite, and was the tribe from which Paul's namesake in Hebrew, Saul, the warrior king, came [AB]. Benjamin was the only tribe left with Judah in the restored nation after the exile [Ho, ICC1]. Claiming descent from Abraham means that he is not just a proselyte, but a true Israelite [Ho].

11:2 God did- not -reject his people whom he foreknew.[a]
LEXICON—a. aorist act. indic. of προγινώσκω (LN 30.100, 28.6) (BAGD p. 703): 'to foreknow' [AB, BECNT, HNTC, ICC2, NICNT, NTC, WBC; KJV, NASB, NET, NIV, NRSV], 'to know (long ago)' [GW], 'to choose' [NCV, NLT, TEV], 'to acknowledge' [REB], 'to know beforehand, to have foreknowledge' [BAGD, LN (28.6)], 'to choose beforehand' [BAGD, LN (30.100)], 'to select in advance' [LN (30.100)]. This verb is translated as a noun phrase: 'his chosen people' [CEV]. This verb means to choose or select in advance of some other event [LN (30.100)], or to know about something before it happens [LN (28.6)].
QUESTION—To whom does τὸν λαὸν αὐτοῦ ὃν προέγνω 'his people whom he foreknew' refer?
1. It refers to Israel as a whole [AB, BECNT, Gdt, ICC1, ICC2, Mu, NAC, NICNT, NTC, SSA, St, WBC]. The relative clause 'whom he foreknew' defines the people and also indicates a reason for saying that God did not reject his people [ICC1, ICC2, NICNT].
2. It refers to the elect within Israel itself [Ho].
QUESTION—How is the term 'foreknew' used here?
1. It means that God chose them [AB, BECNT, HNTC, Ho, ICC1, ICC2, Mor, Mu, NAC, NICNT, SSA, St, WBC]. He chose them, but he also knew beforehand that they would not always be faithful [WBC]. God's graciously electing Israel means that he will not reject them, since his choice of them is not based on anything they are or do [NICNT]. He chose them for special blessing, but that does not mean they will all experience salvation [Mor, NICNT, SSA]. This verb speaks of God's covenant love for his people [BECNT, Mu], and is the antonym of ἀπώσατο 'rejected' [BECNT].
2. It means that God knew in advance who it was that would believe [Gdt].

Or do-you(pl)- not -know[a] what the Scripture says about[b] Elijah, as[c] he-pleads[d] to-God against[e] Israel?
LEXICON—a. perf. (with pres. meaning) act. indic. of οἶδα (LN 28.1) (BAGD 1.f. p. 556): 'to know' [AB, BAGD, BECNT, HNTC, ICC2, LN, NICNT,

NTC, WBC; GW, NASB, NCV, NET, NIV, NRSV, REB, TEV], 'to remember' [CEV], 'to realize' [NLT]. The phrase 'do you not know' is translated 'Wot ye not' [KJV]. This verb means to possess information about something [LN].

b. ἐν (LN 90.23): 'about' [LN; NCV, NET], 'concerning, with respect to, with reference to' [LN], 'about this' [NLT], 'in the passage about' [AB, BECNT; NASB, NIV], 'in the section about' [ICC2, NICNT, NTC, WBC], 'in the story of' [HNTC; REB], 'of (Elias/Elijah)' [KJV, NRSV]. The phrase 'what the Scripture says about Elijah' is translated 'what Elijah says in the Scripture passage' [GW], 'what the scripture says in the passage where Elijah...' [TEV], 'what the Scriptures say about this? Elijah...' [NLT], 'reading in the Scriptures how Elijah...' [CEV]. This preposition marks content as a means of specifying a particular referent [LN].

c. ὡς (LN 89.86) (BAGD I.2.d. p. 897): 'how' [AB, BAGD, BECNT, HNTC, ICC2, LN, NICNT, NTC, WBC; CEV, KJV, NASB, NCV, NET, NIV, NRSV, TEV], 'when' [GW], not explicit [NLT, TEV]. This conjunction marks an event indicating how something took place [LN].

d. pres. act. indic. of ἐντυγχάνω (LN 33.169) (BAGD 1. p. 270): 'to plead' [AB, ICC2, LN; NASB, NET, NRSV, REB, TEV], 'to appeal to' [BAGD, HNTC, LN, NICNT, WBC; NIV], 'to petition' [LN], 'to intercede' [BECNT], 'to make intercession to' [KJV], 'to pray to' [NCV]. The phrase ἐντυγχάνει...κατά 'pleads against' is translated 'complained about' [NTC; CEV, NLT; similarly GW]. This verb means to ask for something with urgency and intensity [LN].

e. κατά with genitive object (LN 90.31) (BAGD I.2.b.β. p. 405): 'against' [AB, BAGD, BECNT, HNTC, ICC2, LN, NICNT, WBC; KJV, NASB, NCV, NET, NIV, NRSV, REB, TEV], not explicit [NTC; CEV, GW, NLT]. This preposition marks opposition, with the possible implication of antagonism [LN].

QUESTION—What is implied in the question ἢ οὐκ οἴδατε 'or do you not know'?

He assumes they will know the passage he cites as well as its implications [NICNT]. He is implying that they should know this story [Mu, NTC]. He wants them to bear something in mind, which they may or may not have realized previously [SSA]. He is implying that if they think God will reject his people, they must be ignorant of Elijah's experience [Mor]. This phrase introduces the grounds for his assertion that God has not rejected his people [BECNT].

11:3 Lord, they-killed[a] your prophets,[b] they-destroyed[c] your altars,[d] and I alone[e] was-left-remaining[f] and they seek[g] my life.

LEXICON—a. aorist act. indic. of ἀποκτείνω (LN 20.61): 'to kill' [AB, BECNT, HNTC, ICC2, LN, NICNT, NTC, WBC; all versions]. This verb

means to cause someone's death, normally by violent means, with or without legal justification [LN].
b. προφήτης (LN 53.79): 'prophet' [AB, BECNT, HNTC, ICC2, LN, NICNT, NTC, WBC; all versions]. This noun denotes one who proclaims inspired utterances on behalf of God [LN].
c. aorist act. indic. of κατασκάπτω (LN 20.56) (BAGD p. 418): 'to destroy' [ICC2, LN; CEV, NCV], 'to tear down' [AB, BAGD, BECNT, LN, NICNT, WBC; GW, NASB, NIV, NLT, REB, TEV], 'to dig down' [HNTC; KJV], 'to demolish' [NTC; NET, NRSV]. This verb means to tear down or destroy by digging down into or under [LN].
d. θυσιαστήριον (LN 6.114) (BAGD 1.c. p. 366): 'altar' [AB, BAGD, BECNT, HNTC, ICC2, LN, NICNT, NTC, WBC; all versions]. This noun denotes any type of altar or object where gifts may be placed and ritual observances carried out in honor of supernatural beings [LN].
e. μόνος (LN **58.50**) (BAGD 1.a.α. p. 527): 'alone' [AB, BAGD, BECNT, HNTC, ICC2, LN, NICNT, WBC; KJV, NASB, NET, NRSV, REB], 'only one' [LN, NTC; CEV, GW, NIV, NLT, TEV], 'only prophet' [NCV]. This adjective describes the only entity in a class [LN].
f. aorist pass. indic. of ὑπολείπω (LN **85.66**) (BAGD p. 845): 'to be left' [AB, BAGD, BECNT, HNTC, ICC2, LN, NICNT, NTC, WBC; all versions], 'to remain' [BAGD, LN]. This verb means to be left behind [LN]. This word is used only here in the NT.
g. pres. act. indic. of ζητέω (LN 20.66) (BAGD 2.b.δ. p. 339): 'to seek' [BAGD, LN]. The idiom ζητοῦσιν τὴν ψυχήν μου 'they seek/are-seeking my life' [AB, BAGD, BECNT, HNTC, ICC2, NICNT, NTC, WBC; NASB, NET, NRSV, REB] is also translated 'they're trying to take my life' [GW], 'they are trying to try to kill me' [NCV, NIV, NLT, TEV], 'they want to kill me' [CEV]. The idiom 'to seek the life' means to desire or intend to kill [LN].

11:4 But what does- the divine-reply[a] -say to him? I-left[b] for-myself seven-thousand men,[c]

LEXICON—a. χρηματισμός (LN **28.40**) (BAGD p. 885): 'divine revelation' [**LN**], 'divine statement or answer' [BAGD], 'revelation from God' [LN]. The phrase 'what does the divine reply say to him' is translated 'what does the divine answer say to him' [ICC2, NICNT; similarly WBC], 'what does the divine oracle say to him' [HNTC], 'what saith the answer of God unto him' [KJV], 'what is/was the divine reply to him' [AB; NRSV], 'what is/was the divine response to him' [BECNT; NASB, NET], 'what was the divine word to him' [REB], 'what is/was God's reply to him' [NTC; NIV], 'what was God's reply' [GW], 'what answer did God give him' [TEV; similarly NCV], 'do you remember God's reply' [NLT], 'the Lord told Elijah' [CEV]. This noun denotes the content of a divine revelation or utterance [LN]. This word is used only here in the NT.

b. aorist act. indic. of καταλείπω (LN 13.92) (BAGD 1.c. p. 413): 'to leave, to cause to remain, to leave to exist' [LN], 'to leave over, to keep' [BAGD]. The phrase 'left for myself' is translated 'have reserved for myself' [AB; KJV, NIV], 'have left to myself' [BECNT], 'have left myself' [HNTC, ICC2; REB], 'have left for myself' [NICNT, NTC], 'have kept for myself' [WBC; GW, NASB, NET, NRSV, TEV], 'still have' [CEV], 'have left' [NCV], 'No, I have' [NLT]. This verb means to cause to continue to exist, normally referring to a small part of a larger whole [LN].

c. ἀνήρ (LN 9.24, 9.1): 'man' [LN (9.24)], 'person' [LN (9.1)]. This plural noun is translated 'men' [AB, BECNT, HNTC, ICC2, NICNT, NTC, WBC; KJV, NASB, REB, TEV], 'others' [NLT], 'followers' [CEV], 'people' [GW, NCV, NET], not explicit [NIV, NRSV]. This noun denotes an adult male person of marriageable age [LN]. The relative pronoun οἵτινες 'who', indicates that they were 'of such a character' that they did not do this, that is, bend the knee to Baal [Mor].

QUESTION—What is the logic of Paul's argument here?

Paul is saying that in his day, just as in Elijah's day, a remnant of Israelites believe [BECNT, ICC1, NTC, SSA, St]. In a time when the nation is in decay God chooses and preserves a remnant, he has not cast off the entire nation [Mor]. Like Elijah, Paul knows he is part of a remnant that God has chosen [AB]. The fact that God preserved a remnant during Elijah's day is the basis for hoping that he is doing the same in Paul's day [NICNT, WBC]. Just as in Elijah's day there is still a remnant that has been chosen by grace to fulfill God's purposes [St].

1. The correlation intended is not between Paul and Elijah, but between Israel of old and Israel of Paul's day; that is, a remnant is saved, but the rest are apostate [BECNT].
2. Paul also personally identifies with Elijah, who stood virtually alone in his day [NICNT, WBC].

QUESTION—Does the term ἀνήρ refer specifically to males or to people in general?

It refers to the men, and therefore there would be more people if the women and children were counted [ICC2, NTC, WBC].

QUESTION—What is implied by ἐμαυτῷ 'for myself'?

They belong to God [Ho, SSA], they are his very own [Ho]. It strengthens the sense of God's intervention [Mor, WBC], and his covenant faithfulness [WBC]. Paul has added this phrase to his citation from the OT passage, as it is not in the Hebrew or the LXX [Ho, Mor]. It emphasizes that this remnant is set apart by God himself for his own gracious purposes [Gdt, Mu].

QUESTION—Does the figure of seven thousand represent an unexpectedly large number or a pitifully small number?

1. It was only a remnant, but that remnant was significant [Mor, NTC], or substantial [WBC]. It was much more than Elijah would have imagined [Mu, NTC]. The number is significant when compared to only one person,

which is all Elijah saw [SSA]. The faithful are a substantial portion [HNTC]. It was small compared to the whole population, but larger than what may have appeared, humanly speaking [Ho].
  2. It symbolizes a fairly small number of people [BECNT].
QUESTION—Is the figure 'seven thousand' to be understood symbolically or as an actual figure?
  These seven thousand are not prophets, but worshippers of God [Gdt, Mor].
  1. The number is symbolic [BECNT, ICC2]. The number seven represents completeness in the Bible and in Jewish thought [ICC2].
  2. The number is symbolic, but there were at least that many in actuality [NTC]. If it is symbolic it symbolizes the complete number of the chosen people of God [Mor, WBC].
  3. It is an actual number; Paul simply cites the text, but probably does not intend any symbolic meaning [NICNT].

who did- not -bend[a] (the) knee[b] to Baal.[c]
LEXICON—a. aorist act. indic. of κάμπτω (LN 53.61) (BAGD 1. p. 402): 'to bend' [AB, BAGD, ICC2], 'to bow' [BAGD, BECNT, HNTC, NICNT, NTC, WBC; KJV, NASB, NET, NIV, NRSV], 'to kneel' [REB], 'to kneel to worship' [GW]. This word is conflated with the following word 'knee' and translated 'to worship' [LN; CEV, TEV], 'to bow before' [LN], 'to bow down' [NCV, NLT]. Kneeling is a symbol of submitting or recognizing someone's lordship [Mor]. This verb means to bend or bow the knee as a symbol of religious devotion [LN].
  b. γόνυ (LN 8.47) (BAGD p. 165): 'knee' [AB, BAGD, BECNT, HNTC, ICC2, LN, NICNT, NTC, WBC; KJV, NASB, NET, NIV, NRSV], not explicit [CEV, NCV, NLT, TEV]. This noun is translated as a verb: 'to kneel' [GW, REB].
  c. Βάαλ (LN 93.56) (BAGD p. 129): 'Baal' [AB, BAGD, BECNT, HNTC, ICC2, LN, NICNT, NTC, WBC; all versions]. This noun denotes a Semitic deity [LN].
QUESTION—In the phrase τῇ Βάαλ 'the Baal' why does the masculine noun Baal have a feminine definite article?
  The feminine article is used because Jews would avoid using the name 'Baal' by saying the word 'shame', which is feminine in both Hebrew and in Greek; this substitution would be marked in Greek written texts by using the feminine definite article [AB, BECNT, ICC1, ICC2, Mor, NICNT, TNTC, WBC]. This practice indicates contempt for the false god [Mor].

11:5 Thus[a] also therefore in[b] the now time[c]
LEXICON—a. οὕτως (LN 61.9) (BAGD 1.b. p. 597): 'thus' [BAGD, LN], 'so, in this way' [LN]. The phrase 'thus also therefore' is translated 'so also' [HNTC], 'so, as there were then' [GW], 'even so then' [KJV], 'so then too' [ICC2], 'in the same way then' [NASB], 'so in the same way' [NET], 'so too' [AB, NTC; NIV, NRSV], 'in just the same way' [REB], 'in the same way, therefore', [BECNT], 'in this manner, therefore' [NICNT],

'thus therefore also' [WBC], 'it is the same' [CEV, NCV, NLT, TEV]. This adverb marks reference to that which precedes [LN].
  b. ἐν (LN 67.136): 'in' [BECNT, ICC2, WBC], 'at' [AB, HNTC, NICNT, NTC; KJV, NASB, NET, NIV, NRSV, REB], 'for' [LN], 'during, within' [LN], not explicit [CEV, GW, NCV, NLT, TEV]. This preposition marks the extent of time within a unit [LN].
  c. καιρός (LN 67.78) (BAGD 1. p. 394): 'time' [AB, BAGD, BECNT, HNTC, ICC2, LN, NICNT, NTC, WBC; KJV, NASB, NET, NIV, NRSV, REB], 'period of time' [LN], not explicit [CEV, GW, NCV, NLT, TEV]. The phrase ἐν τῷ νῦν καιρῷ 'in the now time' is translated 'in the present time' [BECNT, WBC], 'at the present time' [AB, HNTC, ICC2, NICNT, NTC; NASB, NET, NIV, NRSV, REB], 'at this present time' [KJV], 'now' [GW]. This noun denotes an indefinite unit of time [LN].

QUESTION—What relationship is indicated by οὖν 'therefore'?
This conjunction indicates the conclusion to be derived from the example of Elijah [BECNT, SSA, WBC]. It introduces an application to be made based on the account he has cited [ICC1, ICC2, Mor, TH].

QUESTION—What relationship is indicated by οὕτως 'thus'?
What is happening in the present happened as well in Elijah's day [Gdt, Mor]. This is an example of the way God typically works [BECNT, WBC]. It emphasizes the similarity between the current situation and what happened long ago, which is that true believers were few [SSA]. The principle of election and grace has application across the centuries [BECNT]. The Elijah narrative is relevant to the situation of Paul's day [ICC2].

QUESTION—What is the significance of Paul's use of the phrase ἐν τῷ νῦν καιρῷ 'in the now time'?
It is associated with the eschatological age of fulfillment [NICNT, WBC]. Four of the five other times he uses this phrase are in texts referring to the eschatological age of fulfillment, which is what he intends here [NICNT].

there-has-come-to-be[a] a remnant[b] according-to[c] election[d] of-grace;[e]
LEXICON—a. perf. act. indic. of γίνομαι (LN 13.80) (BAGD II.5. p. 160): 'to come to be' [NASB], 'to come into being' [AB, HNTC, NICNT, NTC; REB], 'to be' [BECNT, ICC2, WBC; CEV, GW, KJV, NCV, NET, NIV, NRSV, TEV], 'to exist' [BAGD]. The phrase 'there has come to be a remnant' is translated 'a few of the people of Israel have remained faithful' [NLT]. This verb means to come into existence [LN]. The perfect tense indicates an action bringing about a situation that is still in effect [Mor, WBC].
  b. λεῖμμα (LN **63.22**) (BAGD p. 470): 'remnant' [AB, BAGD, BECNT, HNTC, ICC2, LN, NICNT, NTC, WBC; KJV, NASB, NET, NIV, NRSV, REB], 'small part' [LN], 'small number' [LN]. This noun is translated as a phrase: 'a few of the people of Israel have remained faithful' [NLT], 'a few of them are still his followers' [CEV], 'a small number left of those whom (God has chosen)' [TEV], 'a few people that (God has chosen)'

[NCV], 'a few left that (God has chosen)' [GW]. This noun denotes a relatively small part which continues to exist [LN]. This word, which is a cognate of the verb καταλείπω 'to leave', occurs only here in the NT.

c. κατά with accusative object (LN 89.8) (BAGD II.5.a.δ. p. 407): 'in accordance with' [BAGD, LN, WBC], 'in relation to' [LN], 'according to' [BAGD, BECNT, ICC2; KJV, NASB], 'based on' [HNTC, NICNT], 'because of' [NLT, TEV], not explicit [AB, NTC; CEV, GW, NCV, NET, NIV, NRSV, REB]. This preposition marks a relation involving similarity of process [LN].

d. ἐκλογή (LN 30.92) (BAGD 1. p. 243): 'election' [BAGD, HNTC, ICC2, NICNT, WBC; KJV], 'choice' [LN; NASB], not explicit [BECNT; CEV]. This noun is translated as a verb: 'to be chosen' [AB, NTC; GW, NCV, NET, NIV, NRSV, REB], 'to choose' [NLT, TEV]. This noun denotes a special choice based upon significant preference, often implying a strongly favorable attitude toward what is chosen [LN].

e. χάρις (LN 88.66) (BAGD 2.a. p. 877): 'grace' [AB, BAGD, BECNT, ICC2, LN, NICNT, NTC, WBC; KJV, NCV, NET, NIV, NLT, NRSV, REB, TEV], 'kindness' [LN; GW, NLT]. This noun is translated as a noun phrase: 'gracious act' [HNTC], 'gracious choice' [NASB], 'grace, his undeserved kindness' [NLT]. It is translated as a verb phrase: 'to be kind' [CEV]. This noun denotes kindness shown to someone, with the implication of graciousness on the part of the one showing such kindness [LN].

QUESTION—What relationship is indicated by the genitive phrase ἐκλογὴν χάριτος 'election of grace'?

The genitive χάριτος 'of grace' describes the election; the election is gracious [BECNT, Ho, ICC2, Mu, NICNT], that is, it is characterized by grace [HNTC]. God's election depended on his own choice and not on anything Israel had done [WBC]. It excludes any role for works [BECNT]. God's choosing them was based on his kindness [Ho, SSA, TH]. It is an act of free favor [ICC1]. The choice was made on the basis of God's benevolence, not on the basis of their faithfulness to the law [AB], or any other merit [Ho].

QUESTION—To whom does the phrase ἐκλογὴν χάριτος 'election of grace' apply?

1. It refers to Jewish believers in Christ [AB, BECNT, HNTC, ICC1, ICC2, Mor, Mu, NAC, NICNT, SSA, St, TNTC, WBC].
2. It refers to the whole of Israel, who in God's grace and foreknowledge, were chosen for their role in the plan of salvation, and from whom God has always left a remnant of true believers [Gdt].

11:6 and[a] if (it is) by-grace,[b] no-longer[c] (is it) from[d] works,[e]

LEXICON—a. δέ (LN 89.94): 'and' [AB, BECNT, LN, NICNT, NTC; KJV, NCV, NET, NIV, NLT], 'but' [HNTC, ICC2, WBC; NASB, NRSV,

REB], not explicit [CEV, GW, TEV]. This conjunction marks an additive relation, but with the possible implication of some contrast [LN].

b. The relation indicated by the dative case of this noun is translated 'by grace' [AB, BECNT, HNTC, ICC2, NICNT, NTC, WBC; KJV, NASB, NET, NIV, NRSV, REB], 'because of grace' [CEV], '(chosen) by God's kindness' [GW], '(he chose them) by grace' [NCV], 'through God's kindness' [NLT], '(his choice is) based on his grace' [TEV]. This relation is called 'dative of manner' [NICNT].

c. οὐκέτι (LN 67.130) (BAGD 2. p. 592): 'no longer' [AB, BECNT, LN, NICNT, NTC, WBC; NASB, NET, NIV, NRSV], 'it does not (depend on)' [HNTC], 'it is not' [ICC2; NCV, NLT], 'and not' [CEV], 'not' [TEV], 'then not' [BAGD], '(they) weren't (chosen)' [GW], 'no more' [KJV], 'it does not rest on' [REB]. This adverb marks the extension of time up to a point but not beyond [LN].

d. ἐκ (LN 89.25) (BAGD 3.f. p. 235): 'from' [WBC], 'because of' [LN; CEV, GW], 'by' [AB, BECNT, NTC; NET, NIV, NLT], 'depend on' [HNTC], 'rest on' [REB], 'on the basis of' [ICC2, NICNT; NASB, NRSV], 'of' [KJV], 'for' [NCV], 'on' [TEV]. This preposition marks cause or reason, with focus upon the source [LN].

e. ἔργον (LN 42.11, 42.42) (BAGD 1.c.β. p. 308): 'work' [BECNT, HNTC, ICC2, LN (42.42), NICNT, NTC, WBC; KJV, NASB, NET, NIV, NRSV], 'good work' [NLT], 'deed' [AB, BAGD, LN (42.11); REB], 'act' [LN (42.11)], 'anything they have done' [CEV], 'anything they did' [GW], 'the things they have done' [NCV], 'what they have done' [TEV]. This noun denotes that which is done, with possible focus on the energy or effort involved [LN (42.11)], or that which one normally does [LN (42.42)].

QUESTION—What relationship is indicated by εἰ 'if'?

The preposition εἰ 'if' indicates a condition that is assumed to be true [Mor, SSA, TH], and this clause functions as the grounds for the statement that God no longer elects his people because of their works [NICNT, SSA].

QUESTION—What is implied by his use of οὐκέτι 'no longer'?

The use is logical, not temporal [BAGD, BECNT, Gdt, HNTC, Ho, ICC2, SSA, WBC]. It never was by works [BECNT, Mor]. When people recognize that salvation is by grace there is no longer any place for works [Mor]. Christian people no longer believe what the rabbinical Jews taught and believed about salvation through human merit [NTC].

QUESTION—What does ἔργων 'works' refer to?

1. It is anything that people do [BECNT, Mor, Mu, NICNT, TH]. It is meritorious achievement [ICC1, ICC2], human will or performance [Mu]. While it includes the works of the law, it is much broader than that, encompassing all human efforts [NICNT]. God's choice is an eternal one, prior to all works and not based on foreknowing any such works [BECNT, HNTC, Ho, Mor]. Grace and meritorious works are mutually exclusive [NAC, St].

2. It is specifically the works of the law, that is, the rituals and customs that defined them religiously and ethnically, and which they believed would qualify them to be in God's covenant community [WBC].

otherwise[a] grace becomes[b] no-longer[c] grace.

TEXT—At the end of this sentence some manuscripts include 'but if by works, then it is no more grace; otherwise work is no more work'. It is omitted by GNT with an A rating, indicating that the text is certain. It is included by KJV only.

LEXICON—a. ἐπεί (LN 89.32) (BAGD 2. p. 284): 'otherwise' [HNTC, NICNT; GW, KJV, NASB, NET, NRSV], 'for otherwise' [BAGD], 'since otherwise' [WBC], 'since (if it were)' [NTC], 'if it were' [NIV], 'then' [BECNT, ICC2; TEV], 'for in that case' [NLT], 'for' [AB], 'or' [REB], 'because, since, for, inasmuch as' [LN], not explicit [CEV, NCV]. This adverb marks cause or reason, often with the implication of a relevant temporal element [LN].

b. pres. mid. or pass. (deponent = act.) indic. of γίνομαι (LN 13.48, 13.3): 'to become' [LN (13.48)], 'to be' [BECNT, HNTC, ICC2, LN (13.3), NICNT, NTC, WBC; GW, KJV, NASB, NCV, NET, NIV, NLT, NRSV, TEV], 'to cease to be' [AB; REB], 'to happen' [CEV]. This verb means to come to acquire or experience a state [LN (13.48)], or to possess certain characteristics, with the implication that they were acquired [LN (13.3)].

c. οὐκέτι. The phrase 'grace becomes no longer grace' is translated 'grace would cease to be grace' [AB], 'grace is no longer grace' [BECNT], 'grace would no longer be grace' [HNTC, NICNT, NTC, WBC], 'grace would no more be grace' [ICC2], 'God's grace would not be what it really is—free and undeserved' [NLT], 'it could not have happened except for God's kindness' [CEV], 'God's gift of grace would not really be a gift' [NCV].

QUESTION—What meaning is intended by the adverb οὐκέτι 'no longer'?
It is logical, not temporal [HNTC, ICC2, NICNT, TH, WBC].

11:7 What then?[a] What Israel seeks,[b] this it did- not -attain,[c]

LEXICON—a. The phrase τί οὖν 'what then?' [HNTC, ICC2, NICNT, NTC, WBC; KJV, NASB, NET, NIV, NRSV, TEV], is also translated 'So then what?' [AB], 'What then is the outcome?' [BECNT], 'So what does all this mean?' [GW], 'So this is what has happened:' [NCV], 'So this is the situation:' [NLT], 'What follows?' [REB], 'this means that' [CEV].

b. pres. act. indic. of ἐπιζητέω (LN 25.9) (BAGD 2.a. p. 292): 'to seek' [AB, BECNT, HNTC, ICC2, NICNT, NTC, WBC; CEV, KJV, NASB, NET, NIV, NRSV, REB], 'to strive for' [BAGD; GW], 'to look for' [NLT, TEV], 'to desire' [LN], 'to wish, wish for' [BAGD]. The phrase 'what Israel seeks' is translated 'although the Israelites tried to be right (with God)' [NCV]. This verb means to desire to have or experience something, with the probable implication of making an attempt to realize

one's desire [LN]. This compound verb form is strengthened by the prefix ἐπι- [Mor, WBC].
  c. aorist act. indic. of ἐπιτυγχάνω (LN **90.61, 57.60**) (BAGD p. 304): 'to attain' [BAGD, HNTC, LN (57.60), NICNT; REB], 'to obtain' [BECNT, ICC2, **LN** (57.60), NTC, WBC; KJV, NASB, NET, NIV, NRSV], 'to find' [CEV, NLT, TEV], 'to achieve' [AB; GW], 'to succeed' [NCV], 'to experience' [**LN** (90.61)]. This verb means to experience some happening [LN (90.61)], or to acquire or gain what is sought after [LN (57.60)].

QUESTION—What is the function of τί οὖν 'What then?'

It introduces a logical conclusion that should follow from what has been said [BECNT, ICC2, Mor, Mu, NTC, SSA]. He is returning to the issue raised in 9:30–31 about Israel's having failed to attain right standing with God [NTC]. It calls attention to the conclusion Paul is about to draw, which is that since only some of the people of Israel are chosen by God for salvation, most of them did not find the righteousness they were seeking [SSA]. Paul typically uses this expression to keep an argument moving along; here he picks up on what he has said in 9:31 and 10:3, and goes on to conclude that the corollary of one person being elected is that another is hardened [WBC]. It introduces a conclusion that he will draw based on what he has said in 11:1–6 [ICC2, Mu], or 11:2–6 [ICC1]. It introduces a conclusion that he will draw about 'the remnant' based on what he has said in 11:2b–6, which is that it is because of God's election that there is even a remnant left [NICNT]. It introduces a conclusion that he will draw from the entire discussion in 9:30–11:6 about Israel's failure to attain the righteousness that it sought [BECNT]. After his digression about grace in 11:6 he now returns to the main thought about election [HNTC]. It introduces the question of what in fact has actually happened, if it is true that Israel has not been rejected [Gdt].

QUESTION—What was it that Israel was seeking?
  1. They were seeking a right standing with God [AB, BECNT, Gdt, HNTC, Ho, ICC1, ICC2, Mor, Mu, NAC, NICNT, St, TH]. They sought a righteousness based on personal merit [NAC]. They sought justification and an acceptance with God that would provide entrance into his kingdom [Ho].
  2. They were seeking the benefits of continuing in their covenant relationship with God, which would include being vindicated on the last day [WBC].

but the election[a] did-attain; the rest[b] were hardened.[c]

TEXT—Instead of ἐπωρώθησαν 'were hardened', some manuscripts have ἐπηρώθησαν 'were blinded'. GNT does not mention this alternative. Only KJV reads 'were blinded'.

LEXICON—a. ἐκλογή (LN **30.93**) (BAGD 2. p. 243): 'the election' [KJV], 'election' [BECNT], 'the elect' [HNTC, ICC2, NICNT, NTC, WBC; NET, NIV, NRSV], 'the selected' [BAGD], 'the chosen' [AB, LN], 'those who were chosen' [NASB], 'the ones God chose' [NCV], 'the ones God

has chosen' [NLT], 'the chosen few' [REB], 'the small group that God chose' [TEV], 'only a chosen few' [CEV], 'those whom God has chosen' [GW]. This noun denotes that which has been chosen [LN].
b. λοιπός (LN 63.21) (BAGD 2.b.α. p. 480): '(the) rest' [BECNT, HNTC, ICC2, LN, NICNT, WBC; CEV, GW, KJV, NASB, NET, NLT, NRSV, REB, TEV], '(the) other' [AB, BAGD, LN, NTC; NCV, NIV]. This word is translated by a noun phrase: 'the hearts of the rest' [NLT]. This adjective describes the part of a whole which remains or continues, and thus constitutes the rest of the whole [LN].
c. aorist pass. indic. of πωρόω (LN **27.51**) (BAGD p. 732): 'to be hardened' [BAGD, BECNT, HNTC, ICC2, NICNT, NTC, WBC; NASB, NET, NIV, NLT, NRSV, REB], 'to be stubborn' [CEV], 'to be closed' [GW], 'to be blinded' [KJV], 'to be made blind' [BAGD], 'to be made stubborn' [NCV], 'to grow deaf' [TEV], 'to be made obtuse' [AB], 'to cause to be completely unwilling to learn' [**LN**], 'to cause the mind to be closed' [LN]. This verb means to cause someone to be completely unwilling to learn or accept new information [LN]. The use of the aorist tense here is generally understood as being inceptive, focusing on the beginning of the action [TH].

QUESTION—Why does Paul use the abstract noun ἐκλογή 'the election' instead of 'the elect'?

It is simply a metonymy in which 'the election' represents 'the elect' [NTC], in which the abstract represents the concrete [AB, ICC2, Mu]. It probably focuses more on the concept of election itself than on those who are elected [ICC1, Mor, Mu]. It focuses on God's initiative in the electing [NICNT], on God's action [BECNT, ICC2], which accomplishes what Israel cannot [BECNT], and is the cause of their very existence [ICC2].

QUESTION—To whom does 'the election' refer?
1. It refers here to Jews who are among those chosen for salvation [AB, HNTC, ICC1, ICC2, Mu, NICNT, SSA, St].
2. It refers to all the elect, whether Jew or Gentile [BECNT, Mor, NAC, WBC]. It refers primarily to believing Jews, but may also include Gentile Christians as well [NAC, WBC].

QUESTION—To whom does 'the rest' refer?

It refers to unbelieving Jews [AB, BECNT, HNTC, ICC1, ICC2, NAC, NICNT, SSA, St].

QUESTION—What does ἐπωρώθησαν 'were hardened' mean here?

They were made spiritually insensitive [Mor, NICNT, SSA], unable to perceive the truth [SSA]. They didn't comprehend or believe [WBC]. They were insensitive to God's revelation and to the Holy Spirit [NAC], insensitive to the truth of the gospel and how excellent it is [Ho]. It is to be deprived of the ability to understand what is true or false, or to be touched by what is good or from God [Gdt]. Although the hardening of the nation of Israel is temporary, from 9:22–23 we learn that the hardening of individuals permanently binds people in the sins they themselves have chosen [NICNT].

QUESTION—Who or what is the agent of this passive verb ἐπωρώθησαν 'were hardened'?
1. God himself hardened them [AB, BECNT, HNTC, Ho, ICC2, Mu, NAC, NICNT, SSA, St, TH, TNTC, WBC]. Since 9:18 and 11:8 indicate that God is the agent of the hardening mentioned there, it is implied that he is also the agent here [NICNT]. Their religious zeal was actually turned to sin [HNTC]. The fact that God hardens them does not excuse them from responsibility for their own sin [BECNT].
   1.1 The unbelief caused the hardening; that is, they were hardened by God as a judgment for their refusing to obey him [Ho, Mu, NAC, St, TH, TNTC]. They refused the way of faith, and as a consequence could no longer hear God, because disobedience hardens people spiritually [NAC]. Their spiritual insensitivity was self-induced, and then became a divine judgment in which God gave them up to their own stubbornness [St]. They were abandoned to their own hardness of heart [Ho]. Their spiritual insensitivity came as a judicial punishment for not heeding God's word [TNTC].
   1.2 The hardening caused the unbelief [BECNT].
   1.3 Disobedience comes as a result of being hardened, and being hardened comes as a result of being disobedient; these processes go on simultaneously [HNTC].
2. They were hardened by their own sin [Gdt, ICC1, Mor]. They did not fail because they had been hardened; they were hardened because they failed [ICC1, Mor].

11:8 Just-as[a] it-is-written,[b] God gave[c] them a spirit[d] of-stupor,[e]

LEXICON—a. καθώς (LN 64.14): 'just as' [BECNT, LN; CEV, NASB], 'as' [AB, HNTC, NTC, WBC; GW, NCV, NET, NIV, NLT, NRSV, REB, TEV], 'even as' [ICC2, NICNT], 'according as' [KJV]. This conjunction marks similarity in events and states, with the possible implication of something being in accordance with something else [LN].
   b. perf. pass. indic. of γράφω (LN 33.61) (BAGD 2.c. p. 166): 'to be written' [AB, BAGD, BECNT, HNTC, ICC2, LN, NICNT, NTC, WBC; KJV, NASB, NCV, NET, NIV, NRSV, REB]. The phrase 'just as it is written' is translated '(just) as the Scripture/s say/s' [CEV, GW, NLT, TEV].
   c. aorist act. indic. of δίδωμι (LN 90.90): 'to give' [BECNT, HNTC, ICC2, NICNT, NTC, WBC; GW, KJV, NASB, NCV, NET, NIV, NRSV], 'to grant' [AB], 'to make (someone) experience, to cause' [LN]. This verb means to cause people to undergo some experience, with the probable implication of something which is in retribution for something done [LN].
   d. πνεῦμα (LN 30.6) (BAGD 7. p. 678): 'spirit' [AB, BAGD, BECNT, HNTC, ICC2, NICNT, NTC, WBC; GW, KJV, NASB, NET, NIV, NRSV], 'mind' [NCV], 'senses' [REB], 'minds and hearts' [TEV], 'disposition, attitude, way of thinking' [LN], not explicit [CEV, NLT].

This noun denotes an attitude or disposition reflecting the way in which a person thinks about or deals with some matter [LN].
e. κατάνυξις (LN 30.19) (BAGD p. 415): 'stupor' [AB, BAGD, BECNT, NICNT, NTC; NASB, NET, NIV], 'slumber' [HNTC; KJV], 'torpor' [ICC2, WBC], 'deep sleep' [GW], 'bewilderment' [LN], 'not being able to think' [LN]. The clause 'God gave them a spirit of stupor' is translated 'God made them so stupid' [CEV], 'God gave people a dull mind so they could not understand' [NCV], 'God has put them into a deep sleep' [NLT], 'God gave them a sluggish spirit' [NRSV], 'God has dulled their senses' [REB], 'God made their minds and hearts dull' [TEV]. This noun denotes a state of not being able to think satisfactorily because of complete bewilderment and stupor [LN]. This word occurs only here in the NT.

QUESTION—What passage is being quoted?
He is drawing from Deut 29:4 and Is 29:10 [AB, BECNT, Ho, ICC1, Mu, NICNT, SSA, St, TH, TNTC, WBC], as well as Ps 69:22–23 [AB, NICNT].

QUESTION—What is a spirit of stupor?
It is the inability to think satisfactorily [LN]. Just as a sleeping person is insensitive to external stimuli, these people are dull and apathetic morally and mentally [NTC]. They are blind to spiritual things [NICNT]. They are in a state of insensibility [ICC2, Mor, SSA], of apathy [SSA], of stupefaction [Mor], of spiritual insensitivity [ICC1, NAC, St]. They are perverse and spiritually blind [AB]. They can't see or understand truth [BECNT]. It is an inability to understand that which is spiritual in nature [TH].

eyes[a] to-see[b] not and ears[c] to-hear[d] not until the day of-today.[e]

LEXICON—a. ὀφθαλμός (LN 8.23, 32.24) (BAGD 2. p. 599): 'eye' [AB, BAGD, BECNT, HNTC, ICC2, LN (8.23), NICNT, NTC, WBC; all versions except TEV], 'understanding' [LN (32.24)]. The phrase 'eyes to see not' is translated 'they cannot see' [TEV]. This noun denotes capacity to understand as the result of perception [LN (32.24)].
b. pres. act. infin. of βλέπω (LN 32.11, 24.7) (BAGD 2. p. 143): 'to see' [AB, BECNT, HNTC, LN (32.11, 24.7), NICNT, NTC, WBC; GW, KJV, NASB, NCV, NET, NIV, NLT, NRSV, TEV], 'to be able to see' [BAGD], 'to understand, to perceive, to recognize' [LN (32.11)]. The verb phrase 'to see not' is translated as an adjective: 'blind' [ICC2; CEV, REB]. This verb means to come to understand as the result of perception [LN (32.11)], or to see, frequently in the sense of becoming aware of or taking notice of something [LN (24.7)].
c. οὖς (LN 8.24) (BAGD 2. p. 595): 'ear' [AB, BAGD, BECNT, HNTC, ICC2, LN, NICNT, NTC, WBC; all versions except TEV]. The phrase 'ears to hear not' is translated 'they cannot hear' [TEV].
d. pres. act. infin. of ἀκούω (LN 24.52, 32.1): 'hear' [AB, BECNT, HNTC, LN (24.52), NICNT, NTC, WBC; GW, KJV, NASB, NCV, NET, NIV, NLT, NRSV, TEV], 'understand' [LN (32.1)]. The verb phrase 'to hear

not' is translated as an adjective: 'deaf' [ICC2; CEV, REB]. This verb means to hear and understand a message [LN (32.1)].

e. σήμερον (LN 67.205) (BAGD p. 749): 'today' [BAGD, LN]. The idiomatic expression ἕως τῆς σήμερον ἡμέρας 'until the day of today' is translated 'until this very day' [BECNT, WBC], 'until the present day' [NICNT], 'even to this day' [AB], 'unto this very day' [ICC2], 'to this very day' [NTC; NET, NIV, TEV], 'to this day' [GW, NLT], 'up to this day' [HNTC], 'unto this day' [KJV], 'down to this very day' [NASB, NRSV], 'this continues until today' [NCV], 'and so it is to this day' [REB], 'still' [CEV]. This noun denotes the same day as the day of a discourse [LN].

QUESTION—What relationship is indicated by the negated articular infinitives τοῦ μὴ βλέπειν 'to see not' and τοῦ μὴ ἀκούειν 'to hear not'?

In this passage they describe traits or attributes [Mor, NICNT, SSA]: not seeing, not hearing.

QUESTION—What is the significance of Paul's phrase ἕως τῆς σήμερον ἡμέρας 'until the day of today'?

While it implies an enduring condition up to the present day, it also implies that the hardening won't last indefinitely [ICC2]. When Moses originally spoke these words to the people of Israel, it was with the understanding that it would not be a permanent condition, but would eventually be changed by God, which is also what Paul sees for the people of Israel of his day [BECNT]. As Stephen testified before his martyrdom, they have been spiritually obstinate from the very beginning [ICC1, Mu]. The phrase is intended to be emphatic here, and that is why TEV places it at the beginning of the clause [TH].

11:9 David also says, May- their table[a] -become[b] for a snare[c] and for a trap[d]

LEXICON—a. τράπεζα (LN 6.113) (BAGD 2. p. 824): 'table' [AB, BAGD, BECNT, HNTC, ICC2, LN, NICNT, NTC, WBC; GW, KJV, NASB, NET, NIV, NLT, NRSV, REB], 'feasts' [NCV, TEV]. The phrase 'may their table become' is translated 'turn their meals' [CEV]. This noun denotes a generic expression for any type of table [LN].

b. aorist pass. impera. of γίνομαι (LN 13.48) (BAGD I.4.a. p. 159): 'to become' [BAGD, BECNT, HNTC, ICC2, LN, NICNT, NTC, WBC; GW, NASB, NET, NIV, NLT, NRSV], 'to be' [AB; REB], 'to turn' [CEV], 'to be made' [KJV]. The phrase 'to become a snare and a trap' is translated, 'to trap and cause their ruin' [NCV], 'to be caught and trapped' [TEV]. This verb means to come to acquire or experience a state [LN]. The preposition εἰς 'to, into' precedes each of the four predicate nouns to mark the change of state or condition indicated by the verb 'to become', but this is not represented in English versions because of considerations of English style.

c. παγίς (LN 6.23, **37.15**) (BAGD 2. p. 602): 'snare' [AB, BAGD, HNTC, ICC2, LN (6.23), NICNT, NTC, WBC; KJV, NASB, NET, NIV, NLT, NRSV, REB], 'trap' [BAGD, BECNT, LN (6.23); GW], 'means for gaining control over (someone)' [**LN** (37.15)], not explicit [CEV, TEV]. The noun 'snare/trap' is translated as a verb: 'to trap' [NCV], 'to be caught' [TEV]. This noun denotes an object used for trapping or snaring birds [LN (6.23)], or it is used figuratively for a means of gaining control and implies an element of surprise [LN (37.15)].
   d. θήρα (LN **6.24**) (BAGD p. 360): 'trap' [AB, BAGD, HNTC, ICC2, LN, NICNT, NTC; CEV, KJV, NASB, NET, NIV, NLT, NRSV, REB], 'snare' [BECNT, LN], 'net' [BAGD, WBC; GW], 'ruin' [NCV]. The noun 'trap' is translated as a verb: 'to trap' [TEV]. This word occurs only here in the NT. This noun denotes an instrument used for trapping, especially animals other than birds [LN].

QUESTION—How could a table become a snare?

The common idea in these idioms seems to be that of having a false sense of security in something that one would normally be able to trust [SSA]. What they trusted actually became the cause of their falling [BECNT]. What should have nourished unexpectedly became a source of difficulty [Mor]. Even the good things they enjoy may turn out to be a snare to them [ICC2, Mu, St], such as the sense of community, well-being, and security that one experiences at home [St]. Paul is speaking in general terms, and does not intend to apply the particular details of the passage he is citing, such as the table or the bending of the back, to the Jewish non-believers he is describing [BECNT, ICC2, NICNT]. Paul refers to Jewish emphasis on ritual purity, especially when eating meals, that was so important for his fellow Pharisees; this emphasis on such ritual practices as a way of maintaining their standing within the covenant community was a snare for them [WBC]. It refers to a tablecloth spread on the ground over which a person may trip; in the case of Israel, what was closest to them became the cause of stumbling [AB]. Table fellowship symbolizes the sense of Jewish unity that was created by the law and that was valued highly by the Jews [HNTC]. The image of feasting represents the fact that the trust they had placed in their position as God's elect and in the law and scripture has proved to be their downfall [ICC1]. Paul uses the table as a symbol of their ritual acts of worship in the Jewish system [Gdt]. Their very celebrations become their downfall [NAC].

and for a stumbling-stone[a] and for[b] retribution[c] to-them.

LEXICON—a. σκάνδαλον (LN **6.25**) (BAGD 1. p. 753): 'stumbling block' [AB, BECNT, ICC2, NICNT, NTC; KJV, NASB, NET, NIV, NRSV], 'offence' [HNTC], 'trap' [BAGD, LN, WBC], 'snare' [GW], 'downfall' [REB]. This noun is translated as a verb phrase: 'so that they will stumble' [CEV], '(let their feasts) cause them to stumble' [NCV], '(let their blessings) cause them to stumble' [NLT], 'may they fall' [TEV].

This noun denotes a trap, probably of the type that has a stick which causes the trap to shut when touched by an animal [LN].
b. εἰς (LN 89.57): 'for the purpose of, in order to' [LN]. In the four occurrences of εἰς 'for' in this verse, the first three indicate purpose, but this one indicates result [SSA]. None of these occurrences are translated explicitly by any commentary or versions. This preposition marks intent, often with the implication of expected result [LN].
c. ἀνταπόδομα (LN **38.20**) (BAGD p. 73): 'retribution' [AB, BAGD, ICC2, NICNT, NTC, WBC; NASB, NET, NIV, NRSV, REB], 'recompense' [HNTC, LN; KJV], 'recompense for what they have done' [**LN**], 'punishment' [GW], 'punishment for what they have done' [**LN**], 'repayment' [BECNT]. This noun is translated as a verb phrase: 'they will be given what they deserve' [CEV], 'cause them to be paid back' [NCV], 'may they be punished' [TEV]. This noun is translated as a clause: 'let them get what they deserve' [NLT]. This noun denotes the recompense, whether positive or negative, which is given to someone on the basis of or in exchange for what has been done. The context indicates clearly the negative aspect of the recompense [LN].

11:10 May- their eyes -be-darkened[a] (that they) see[b] not and may- their backs -be-bent[c] through all-(time).[d]

LEXICON—a. aorist pass. impera. of σκοτίζομαι (LN **32.44**) (BAGD 2. p. 757): 'to be darkened' [BAGD, BECNT, HNTC, ICC2, NICNT, NTC, WBC; KJV, NASB, NET, NIV, NRSV], 'to become darkened' [REB], 'to be dimmed' [AB], 'to become clouded' [GW], 'to be closed' [NCV], 'to go blind' [NLT], 'to be blinded' [TEV], 'to be incapable of perceiving, to not be able to understand' [LN]. The clause 'may their eyes be darkened that they see not' is translated 'Blindfold their eyes! Don't let them see.' [CEV], 'may they become unable to perceive' (literally 'may their understanding become unable to understand') [**LN**]. This verb means to become unable to perceive and thus unable to understand [LN].
b. pres. act. infin. of βλέπω (LN 32.11, 24.41) (BAGD 1.b. p. 143): 'to see' [BAGD, BECNT, HNTC, LN (32.11), NICNT, NTC; CEV, KJV, NASB, NET], 'to understand, to perceive' [LN (32.11)], 'to be able to see' [AB, ICC2, LN (24.41), WBC; GW, NCV, NIV, NLT, NRSV, TEV], 'to become blind' [REB]. The phrase, 'see not' is translated 'Don't let them see.' [CEV]. This verb means to come to understand as the result of perception [LN (32.11)], or to have the faculty of sight [LN (24.41)].
c. aorist act. impera. of συγκάμπτω (LN **24.94**) (BAGD p. 773): 'to be bent' [BECNT, NICNT; NIV, NLT, NRSV], 'to bend' [AB, BAGD, WBC; CEV, NASB], 'to bow down' [HNTC, ICC2, NTC; KJV, REB], 'to keep bent' [NRSV]. The idiom 'may their backs be bent for all time' is translated 'bend their backs forever, make them slaves forever, make them toil hard forever' [**LN** (8.40)], 'make them bend under their troubles at all times' [**LN** (24.94); TEV], 'bend their backs beneath a burden that will

never be lifted' [CEV], 'let them carry back-breaking burdens forever' [GW], 'let their backs be forever weak from trouble' [NCV]. The idiom 'to bend the back' means to be bent down with difficulties, to undergo particularly difficult hardships, or to be overwhelmed with trouble, and sometimes forced labor is implied [LN (24.94)]. This word occurs only here in the NT.

    d. The phrase διὰ παντός is translated 'forever' [HNTC, NTC; GW, NASB, NCV, NIV, NLT, NRSV], 'continually' [AB, BECNT, ICC2, NICNT, WBC; NET], 'that will never be lifted' [CEV], 'always' [KJV], 'unceasingly' [REB], 'at all times' [TEV].

QUESTION—What is being expressed by the image of the back bending?

It is a metonymy for slavery, the bent back representing a slave's having to bear a heavy load [SSA]. It is a symbol of bondage [HNTC], of oppression and slavery, of whatever is the opposite of liberty [WBC]. It symbolizes being weak from bearing a burden [AB, NAC], in this case, from having rejected the gospel [AB]. It can symbolize grief, fear, or oppression [St]. Some think it refers to oppression from slavery and others think it suggests grief, but it is not clear what it means here [NICNT].

QUESTION—What is to be understood by διὰ παντός 'through all (time)'?

It means 'continually', not 'forever' [AB, ICC2, WBC].

DISCOURSE UNIT—11:11–32 [BECNT, NICNT]. The topic is defining the promise: the future of Israel [NICNT], God's righteousness in his plan for Jews and Gentiles [BECNT].

DISCOURSE UNIT—11:11–24 [AB, HNTC, Ho, ICC1, Mor, Mu, NAC, NTC, WBC; CEV, NIV, NRSV]. The topic is that Israel's disbelief is temporary and providential [AB], the unfolding of God's plan [HNTC], restoration of Israel is desirable [Ho], the rejection of Israel not final [ICC1], the restoration of Israel [Mor], the fullness of Israel [Mu], the rejection is not final [NAC], engrafted branches [NTC; NIV], the hope of Israel's restoration [WBC], Gentiles will be saved [CEV], the salvation of the Gentiles [NRSV].

DISCOURSE UNIT—11:11–15 [NICNT]. The topic is God's purpose in Israel's rejection.

11:11 I-say[a] then,[b] they-did- not -stumble[c] such-that[d] they-fell[e] (did they)?[f]

LEXICON—a. pres. act. indic. of λέγω (LN 33.69): 'to say' [BECNT, LN, NICNT; KJV, NASB], 'to ask' [AB, ICC2, NTC, WBC; GW, NCV, NET, NIV, NRSV, REB, TEV], 'to repeat (my question)' [HNTC], not explicit [CEV, NLT]. This verb means to speak or talk, with apparent focus upon the content of what is said [LN]. This repeats the same phrase 'I say then' from 11:1.

    b. οὖν (LN 89.50): 'then' [AB, BECNT, HNTC, ICC2, LN, NTC; KJV, NASB, NET, REB, TEV], 'therefore' [LN, NICNT, WBC], 'again' [NIV], 'so, consequently, accordingly' [LN], not explicit [CEV, GW,

NCV, NLT, NRSV]. This conjunction marks result, often implying the conclusion of a process of reasoning [LN].
c. aorist act. indic. of πταίω (LN **88.291**) (BAGD 1. p. 727): 'to stumble' [AB, BAGD, BECNT, HNTC, ICC2, LN, NICNT, NTC, WBC; GW, KJV, NASB, NET, NIV, NLT, NRSV, REB, TEV], 'to sin' [**LN**], 'to fall' [CEV, NCV]. This verb is a figurative extension of 'to stumble' and means to fail to keep the law of God [LN].
d. ἵνα (LN 89.49): 'so as a result, that, so that' [LN], 'so as to' [AB, BECNT, HNTC, ICC2, NICNT, NTC, WBC; NASB, NIV, NRSV], 'so badly' [GW], 'that' [KJV], 'into' [NET], not explicit [CEV, NCV, NLT, REB, TEV]. This conjunction marks result, though in some cases implying an underlying or indirect purpose [LN].
e. aorist act. subj. of πίπτω (LN 13.97) (BAGD 2.a.β. p. 660): 'to fall' [BAGD, NICNT, NTC, WBC; KJV, NASB, NRSV, TEV], 'to fall irremediably' [AB], 'to fall permanently' [BECNT], 'to fall altogether' [HNTC], 'to fall irrevocably' [ICC2], 'to fall, never to get up again' [CEV], 'to fall beyond recovery' [NIV, NLT], 'to come to an end' [LN (13.97)], 'to be completely ruined' [BAGD]. This verb is translated as a noun: 'fall' [NCV, NET, REB]. The phrase 'such that they fell' is translated 'did that fall destroy them' [NCV], '(stumble) into an irrevocable fall' [NET], 'that it can't get up again' [GW], 'was their fall final' [REB], 'did they fall to their ruin' [TEV]. This verb means to cease to exist in a particular post or position [LN].
f. These words are not in the Greek text, but are supplied in English translation to indicate that the question introduced by μή 'not' expects a negative answer. In combination with the verb 'stumble' this is represented in translation as 'Did they stumble?' [AB, HNTC, NTC; NIV], '…has not stumbled…has it?' [BECNT], 'Have they stumbled?' [ICC2, WBC; KJV, NRSV], 'They have not stumbled…, have they?' [NICNT], 'Do I mean (that the people of Israel fell)?' [CEV], 'Has Israel stumbled?' [GW], 'They did not stumble…, did they?' [NASB, NET], 'When the Jews fell, did that fall destroy them?' [NCV], 'Did God's people stumble?' [NLT], 'When they stumbled, was their fall final?' [REB], 'When the Jews stumbled, did they fall to their ruin?' [TEV].

QUESTION—What is the function of λέγω οὖν 'I say then'?

It reintroduces his question raised at the beginning of the chapter about whether God had rejected Israel [HNTC]. It returns to the concerns expressed in similar questions raised in 10:18–19 and 11:1, and which would likely be raised by Jewish people [SSA]. It introduces a question that he uses to advance his argument to the next stage [Mor]. It introduces a question that refers back to what he has said about the stumbling stone [AB]. It introduces a question that naturally follows on his comment in 11:7 about the hardening of the portion of Israel [Gdt, NICNT]. The question is not whether the hardened people within Israel can still be saved, but whether Israel as a whole can be saved [NICNT]. It introduces a question that naturally follows on all that he has said in 9:30–11:10 [BECNT].

QUESTION—What is the stumbling Paul refers to here?

It is the Jews' rejection of Christ [Mu, NICNT], and the rejection of the righteousness that comes through faith in him [NICNT]. It is their having failed to believe in Christ [HNTC, NAC, SSA]. It is their rejection of the gospel [ICC2, NTC]. It is their failure to obtain salvation [BECNT].

QUESTION—What relationship is indicated by ἵνα 'such that'?

1. It indicates result; that is, have they stumbled with the result that they will not recover? [Gdt, HNTC, ICC1, ICC2, Mor, NAC, SSA, WBC]. If ἵνα were to be used to indicate purpose, the purpose would be the purpose of the subject of the verb, which in this case is Israel, but Israel would not stumble for the purpose of falling or not recovering [Mor, SSA].
2. It indicates both purpose and result; that is, Israel's stumbling did not result in permanent rejection because God has not willed that [NICNT]. It indicates result, but there is also an element of divine purpose implied [WBC].
3. It indicates purpose [BECNT, Ho, Mu]. God's purpose in their stumbling was not that they fall, but that salvation might go to the Gentiles [Ho, Mu]. God does not intend for their hardening to be permanent [BECNT].

QUESTION—What is implied in the verb πίπτω 'to fall'?

It would be to come to permanent and complete spiritual ruin [Ho, ICC2, NICNT, WBC], a permanent exclusion from the Messianic salvation [ICC1], a final and irreversible doom [NTC]. It would mean to fall away from God permanently [SSA], such that they could never experience salvation [HNTC], that they would be unable to recover [TH, TNTC], that they would be lost forever [Mor], so as to be cut off from the possibility of salvation [AB], so as to lose forever their status as God's people [Gdt]. He is asking if their hardened condition will be permanent and hopeless [St], irrevocable and irreversible [BECNT].

Never may-it-be!ᵃ Butᵇ byᶜ their transgressionᵈ

LEXICON—a. See this expression at 11:1. Here it is translated 'May it never be!' [NASB], 'Certainly not!' [AB, BECNT, HNTC; CEV], 'God forbid!' [ICC2; KJV], 'By no means' [NICNT; NRSV, TEV], 'Of course not!' [NTC; NLT], 'Not at all!' [WBC], 'That's unthinkable!' [GW], 'No!' [NCV], 'Absolutely not!' [NET], 'Not at all!' [NIV], 'Far from it!' [REB].

b. ἀλλά (LN 89.125): 'but' [BECNT, ICC2, LN, NICNT, WBC; KJV, NASB, NCV, NET, NRSV], 'instead, on the contrary' [LN], 'yet' [AB], 'rather' [NTC; NIV], not explicit [HNTC; CEV, GW, NLT, REB, TEV]. This is a strong adversative [Mor]. This conjunction marks emphatic contrast [LN].

c. There is no lexical entry for the preposition 'by' in the Greek text, but it is used to express the relationship indicated by the dative case of the noun

παράπτωμα 'transgression'. This relation is translated 'by' [HNTC, ICC2, WBC; GW, NASB, NET], 'through' [NICNT; KJV, NRSV, REB], 'because of' [AB, NTC; NIV], 'because' [TEV], 'by means of' [BECNT], not explicit [CEV, NCV, NLT].
  d. παράπτωμα (LN 88.297) (BAGD 2.a.β. p. 621): 'transgression' [BAGD, BECNT, LN; NASB, NET, NIV], 'sin' [BAGD, LN], 'trespass' [AB, ICC2, NICNT, NTC, WBC], 'stumble' [HNTC], 'stumbling' [NRSV], 'failure' [CEV, GW], 'fall' [KJV], 'mistake' [NCV], 'false step' [BAGD; REB], '(they were) disobedient' [NLT], 'they sinned' [TEV]. This noun denotes what a person has done in transgressing the will and law of God by some false step or failure [LN].
QUESTION—What relationship is indicated by the use of the dative case of 'transgression'?
  1. It indicates the cause or reason that salvation has come to Gentiles [AB, HNTC, ICC2, NICNT, NTC, SSA, TH; NIV, TEV]: because of their trespass. The normal instrumental meaning of the dative has moved over into a causal sense [ICC2, NICNT].
  2. It indicates the means by which salvation has come to Gentiles [BECNT, WBC; GW, NASB, NET].

salvation[a] (has come)[b] to-the Gentiles in-order-to[c] make- them -jealous.[d]
LEXICON—a. σωτηρία (LN 21.25) (BAGD 2. p. 801): 'salvation' [AB, BAGD, BECNT, HNTC, ICC2, LN, NICNT, NTC, WBC; all versions except CEV]. This noun is translated as a verb: 'to be saved' [CEV]. This noun denotes a state of having been saved [LN].
  b. There is no lexical entry for this verb in the Greek text, it is implied. It is represented in translation as 'has come' [AB, BECNT, HNTC, ICC2, NICNT, NTC; GW, NASB, NET, NIV, NRSV, REB, TEV], 'is coming' [WBC], 'is come' [KJV], 'brought' [NCV], not explicit [CEV]. The phrase 'salvation has come to the Gentiles' is translated 'God made salvation available to the Gentiles' [NLT].
  c. The relation indicated by εἰς τό with the infinitive is translated 'in order to' [BECNT, HNTC, ICC2, NICNT, WBC; NCV], 'for to' [KJV], 'so as to' [NRSV], 'he wanted' [NLT], not explicit [AB, NTC; CEV, GW, NASB, NET, NIV, REB, TEV].
  d. aorist act. infin. of παραζηλόω (LN 88.164) (BAGD p. 616): 'to make jealous' [AB, BAGD, ICC2, LN, NICNT; CEV, GW, NASB, NCV, NET, NRSV, TEV], 'to cause to be envious' [LN], 'to make envious' [NTC; NIV], 'to provoke to jealousy' [BAGD, BECNT, WBC; KJV], 'to provoke to envy' [HNTC], 'to become jealous' [NLT], 'to stir to envy' [REB]. This verb means to cause someone to feel strong jealousy or resentment against someone [LN].

QUESTION—How has the Jews' transgression caused salvation to come to the Gentiles?

Wherever he went Paul preached to the Jews first, but when they rejected it, he turned to the Gentiles [BECNT, Ho, ICC1, ICC2, NICNT, NTC, St, TNTC, WBC]. He may also be referring to Israel's rejection of Christ and their involvement in his crucifixion, which is the very basis of salvation [ICC2, WBC]. Jewish religious forms, which were offensive to Gentiles and would always have kept most Gentiles excluded from faith, are no longer relevant for people wanting to be reconciled with God, and therefore many more Gentiles can now come into the kingdom [Gdt]. Had the majority of the Jews embraced the Christian faith they would no doubt have insisted that the Gentiles observe Jewish rituals, and thus would have inhibited Gentiles from coming to Christ [Ho].

QUESTION—How would the Jews be made jealous?

They would be made jealous when they observe how God blesses the Gentiles who believe in Christ [SSA, St]. The Jews will see the Gentiles' fellowship with God and one another, and the joy and peace brought by the Holy Spirit, and will want the same for themselves [St]. When they see how the Gentiles have received righteousness by faith [AB, HNTC], the Jews would seek God's mercy for the same thing and stop trying to achieve righteousness by their works [HNTC]. When the Jews see the salvation that the Gentiles experience, they will be moved to have a passionate desire for the same thing [Mor]. When they see other people receiving God's mercy and goodness they will realize what they are missing and want the salvation they once rejected [ICC2]. When they see others enjoying the blessings that should have been theirs, they will want it themselves [Gdt]. They will see the Gentiles enjoying the messianic blessings that were intended for the Jews [NAC, TNTC].

11:12 Now[a] if their transgression (is)[b] riches[c] of-(the)-world[d]

LEXICON—a. δέ (LN 89.94, 89.124): 'now' [AB, NICNT, NTC; KJV, NASB, NET, NLT, NRSV], 'and' [BECNT, LN (89.94), WBC], 'but' [HNTC, ICC2, LN (89.124); CEV, NIV], not explicit [GW, NCV, REB, TEV]. This conjunction can mark contrast [LN (89.124)], or it can mark an additive relation, but with the possible implication of some contrast [LN (89.94)].

b. There is no lexical entry for this word in the Greek text. The implied verb is translated 'is' [BECNT; NASB], 'be' [KJV], 'means' [ICC2, NICNT, WBC; NET, NIV, NRSV, REB], 'has meant' [AB], 'has thus come to mean' [HNTC], 'brought' [NCV, TEV], not explicit [CEV, GW, NLT].

c. πλοῦτος (LN 57.30) (BAGD 2. p. 674): 'riches' [BECNT, ICC2, LN, NICNT, NTC, WBC; KJV, NASB, NET, NIV, NRSV], 'wealth' [BAGD, HNTC, LN], 'abundance' [BAGD, LN], 'enrichment' [AB; REB], not explicit [CEV]. This noun is translated as a verb: 'to make rich' [GW], 'to be enriched' [NLT]; as an adjective: 'rich (blessings)' [NCV, TEV]. This noun denotes an abundance of possessions exceeding the norm of a particular society [LN].

d. κόσμος (LN 9.23) (BAGD 4.a. p. 446): 'world' [AB, BAGD, BECNT, HNTC, ICC2, NICNT, NTC, WBC; GW, KJV, NASB, NCV, NET, NIV, NRSV, REB, TEV], 'world's people' [CEV], 'the Gentiles' [NLT]. The genitive κόσμου is translated 'of the world' [AB, HNTC; CEV, KJV, REB], 'for the world' [BECNT, ICC2, NICNT, NTC, WBC; NASB, NCV, NET, NIV, NRSV], 'to the world' [TEV], '(made) the world' [GW], '(if the) Gentiles' [NLT]. This noun denotes people associated with a world system and estranged from God [LN].

QUESTION—What relationship is indicated by εἰ 'if'?

It indicates a condition of fact: 'if, as is the case' [Mor, SSA].

QUESTION—What does ὁ κόσμος 'the world' represent here?

(Note that options 1 and 2 are essentially the same, since 'the whole world' in the context of Paul's argument would mean 'everyone else in the world', not just the Jews.)

1. Paul is referring to the Gentiles [BECNT, Gdt, ICC2, Mor, Mu, NICNT, SSA; CEV, NLT], whom God will bless richly [SSA]. The parallelism of 'the riches of the world' with the following 'riches of the Gentiles' shows that 'world' means the 'Gentile world' [NICNT]. 'The world' is synonymous with 'Gentiles', but is used here to signify ethnic universalism [Mu].
2. It refers to all people, all humankind [HNTC, WBC]. 'World' is parallel with 'Gentiles' and contrasts with the rest of Israel who sinned [WBC].
3. It refers to the whole *kosmos*, which would include all people. That is, Israel's failure has caused the *kosmos* to be able to share in the bounty of the messianic salvation, and more specifically, for the Gentiles to share in the rich heritage of Israel, which Israel itself has been missing [AB].

and their loss[a] riches of-(the) Gentiles,[b] how-much more[c] their fullness?[d]

LEXICON—a. ἥττημα (LN 13.22) (BAGD p. 349): 'loss' [AB; NCV, NIV], 'defeat' [BAGD, BECNT, ICC2, NICNT, NTC; NET, NRSV], 'failure' [LN, WBC; GW, NASB], 'spiritual poverty' [TEV], not explicit [NLT]. This noun is translated as a phrase, 'the cutting down of their numbers' [HNTC], 'sin and loss' [CEV], 'the diminishing of them' [KJV], 'the falling short' [REB]. This noun denotes a lack of attaining a desirable state or condition [LN].

b. ἔθνος (LN 11.55, 11.37): 'nation' [LN (11.55)]. This plural noun is translated 'Gentiles' [AB, BECNT, HNTC, ICC2, NICNT, NTC, WBC; KJV, NASB, NET, NIV, NRSV, REB, TEV], 'world's people' [CEV], 'people who are not Jewish' [GW], 'non-Jewish people' [NCV], 'the world' [NLT], 'heathen, pagan' [LN (11.37)]. This noun denotes those who do not belong to the Jewish or Christian faith [LN (11.37)].

c. The phrase πόσῳ μᾶλλον is translated 'how much more' [AB, BECNT, ICC2, NICNT, NTC, WBC; KJV, NASB, NET, NRSV, REB], 'so much

more' [HNTC], 'even more' [CEV], 'even richer' [GW], 'much richer (blessings)' [NCV], 'how much greater' [NIV, NLT, TEV].
d. πλήρωμα (LN 59.32) (BAGD 4. p. 672): 'fullness' [BECNT, ICC2, LN, NICNT, NTC, WBC; KJV, NIV], 'completeness' [LN], 'full number' [AB], 'full strength' [HNTC], 'full return' [CEV], 'inclusion (of Jewish people)' [GW], 'fulfillment' [BAGD; NASB], 'fulfilling' [BAGD], 'full restoration' [NET], 'full inclusion' [NRSV], 'full strength' [REB], not explicit [NCV, TEV]. This noun is translated as a verb phrase: 'finally accept' [NLT]. This noun denotes a total quantity, with emphasis upon completeness [LN].

QUESTION—What is the sense intended for ἥττημα 'loss'?

Paul may have chosen to use this word ending with -μα, for rhetorical reasons, to correspond with παράπτωμα 'transgression' and πλήρωμα 'fullness' [BECNT, WBC].

1. It represents a loss or defeat [AB, BECNT, Ho, ICC1, ICC2, Mor, Mu, NAC, NICNT, NTC, SSA, St]. It is a spiritual defeat [NICNT, SSA]. It is a defeat or loss such as an overthrow in battle, which occurred when the kingdom of God was taken from them [Mu].
2. It represents a diminishing of their numbers, in the sense of how many of them are experiencing salvation [Gdt, HNTC].
3. It represents a failure or loss; however, Paul's choice of this word has more to do with rhetorical balance than with precise meaning, since he wants a word ending with -μα to match παράπτωμα 'transgression' and πλήρωμα 'fullness' [WBC].

QUESTION—What is the sense of πόσῳ 'how much (more)'?

It is used in a lesser-to-greater argument to show how much greater one thing is than another [BECNT, Mu, NAC, NICNT, SSA, St, TH]. It is used in an exclamatory sense [SSA].

QUESTION—What is τὸ πλήρωμα 'the fullness'?

Paul may be using this word as much for rhetorical balance with the two other nouns ending in -μα as for precise meaning, using it to express a contrast with the idea of the remnant [WBC].

1. It is the full number of Jews who will come to believe [AB, BECNT, Ho, ICC1, ICC2, NAC, NTC, SSA, TNTC]. It is the full restoration of Israel to faith [Mu, NAC], and to their privileges and blessings [Mu].
1.1 It is the full number of the people of Israel returning to God in faith [Gdt, HNTC, TNTC], which would be all of the people of Israel who are alive when that event occurs [Gdt].
1.2 It is the elect remnant of Israel coming to its full strength in terms of their numbers throughout time, not at some point at the close of history [NTC].
1.3 It has the sense of *complement*; that is, when the Jews finally believe, they will bring to completion the whole number of the people of God [Ho].

2. It is the fullness of spiritual blessing that will be experienced when the full number of Israelites comes to salvation [Mu, NICNT]. It is the full measure of blessing [Ho].
3. It is Israel's being converted and restored, as well as significantly increasing in numbers [St].
4. It is the fulfilling of God's will [BAGD].

QUESTION—For whom will their fullness be an enrichment or benefit?
1. It will be a benefit to all people of the world [AB, HNTC, NTC, WBC]. This includes both Jews and Gentiles [WBC].
2. It will be a benefit to the Gentiles [Gdt, Ho, Mor, Mu, NICNT, St]. There will be gospel blessings far beyond those known by the Gentiles during Israel's time of apostasy [Mu].
3. It is ambiguous; Paul does not say [SSA].

DISCOURSE UNIT—11:13-24 [TNTC; TEV]. The topic is admonition to Gentile Christians [TNTC], the salvation of the Gentiles [TEV].

11:13 Now[a] I-speak[b] to-you(pl) Gentiles;

LEXICON—a. δέ (LN 89.124): 'now' [AB, BECNT, HNTC, NICNT; CEV, GW, NCV, NET, NRSV, TEV], 'but' [ICC2, LN (89.124); NASB], not explicit [NTC, WBC; KJV, NIV, NLT, REB]. This conjunction marks contrast [LN].
b. pres. act. indic. of λέγω (LN 33.69): 'to speak' [HNTC, ICC2, LN, NICNT, NTC, WBC; CEV, GW, KJV, NASB, NCV, NET, NRSV, REB, TEV], 'to talk' [LN; NIV], 'to turn' [AB], 'to say' [BECNT; NLT]. This verb means to speak or talk, with apparent focus upon the content of what is said [LN].

QUESTION—Why does Paul say 'I speak to you Gentiles'?
It introduces a parenthetical comment that is now addressed specifically to the Gentiles in his audience [AB, BECNT, Ho, ICC1, ICC2, WBC]. This also marks a shift of focus, as Paul is moving from exposition to exhortation [AB]. He is not starting a new paragraph or new thought; rather, he is continuing the same topic he has been addressing in the last two verses, but he wants to make sure that the Gentiles in his audience pay special attention to it [ICC1, ICC2]. Paul is getting the attention of Gentile readers, who might assume that all this discussion about the remnant of Israel has nothing to do with them [HNTC, Ho]. Paul has been talking about the salvation of Gentiles, and now wants to impress upon Gentiles the importance of the conversion of the Jews, even for the Gentiles' sake [Ho, Mu]. The fact that he is apostle to the Gentiles does not mean he has no concern for Jewish people [Ho]. Paul does not want his Gentile readers to assume that his ministry to them is only for the purpose of stimulating Jews to envy, but in fact it is intended to bring great blessing to the Gentiles as well when the Jews finally do believe in Christ [BECNT].
1. He has shifted from a answering series of questions that a Jew might raise to addressing the non-Jewish readers in Rome [SSA].

2. He has been addressing Gentiles all along [NAC].

QUESTION—Does this comment indicate anything about the ethnic make-up of the church in Rome?
   1. This comment indicates that the majority of the people in the Roman church were Gentiles [AB, Gdt, ICC1, Mu, NICNT, St, WBC].
   2. It does not indicate anything about whether or not the church was predominantly Gentile [BECNT, ICC2].

inasmuch- then[a] -as[b] I am apostle of[c] (the) Gentiles, I-glorify[d] my ministry,[e]
LEXICON—a. οὖν (LN 89.50): 'then' [LN, WBC; NASB, NRSV], 'so, therefore, consequently, accordingly, so then' [LN], 'precisely' [HNTC], 'therefore' [NICNT], not explicit [AB, BECNT, ICC2, NTC; CEV, GW, KJV, NCV, NET, NIV, NLT, REB, TEV]. This conjunction marks result, often implying the conclusion of a process of reasoning [LN].
   b. ὅσος (LN **78.52**) (BAGD III.3. p. 289). The phrase ἐφ' ὅσον is translated 'as' [AB, ICC2, NTC, WBC; CEV, GW, KJV, NASB, NIV, NRSV, TEV], 'as much as' [LN], 'in so far as' [BAGD, BECNT, NICNT], 'because' [HNTC], not explicit [NCV, NET, NLT, REB]. This adjective describes a degree of correlative extent [LN].
   c. There is no lexical entry for the preposition 'of' in the Greek text, the genitive case being used to express the relation between 'apostle' and 'Gentiles'. This relation is translated 'of' [AB, ICC2; KJV, NASB], 'to' [BECNT, NICNT, NTC, WBC; CEV, NCV, NET, NIV, NLT, NRSV, REB, TEV], '(sent) to' [GW], not explicit [HNTC].
   d. pres. act. indic. of δοξάζω (LN 87.24) (BAGD 1. p. 204): 'to glorify' [BECNT, ICC2, LN, NICNT; NRSV], 'to make much of' [AB, HNTC], 'to take pride in' [NTC; CEV, TEV], 'to magnify' [BAGD, WBC; KJV, NASB, NET], 'to bring honor to' [GW], 'to make the most of' [NCV], 'to make much of' [NIV, REB], 'to stress' [NLT]. This verb means to cause someone to have glorious greatness [LN].
   e. διακονία (LN 35.21) (BAGD 3. p. 184): 'ministry' [AB, BECNT, ICC2, LN, NICNT, NTC, WBC; GW, NASB, NET, NIV, NRSV, REB], 'task' [LN], 'office' [BAGD, HNTC; KJV], 'work' [CEV, NCV, TEV], not explicit [NLT]. This noun denotes the role or position of serving [LN].

QUESTION—What relationship is indicated by ἐφ' ὅσον 'inasmuch as'?
   It indicates the basis on which he makes the statement that follows [HNTC, ICC2, Mor, SSA, TH, WBC]. That is, because he is the apostle to the Gentiles, he can highly esteem the ministry God gave him [SSA]. He speaks in his capacity as apostle to the Gentiles [ICC2, WBC]. If as a Jew he earnestly desires to bring about the conversion of his people, he strives all the more to do it as apostle to the Gentiles, since the Jews' conversion will bring blessing to these Gentiles [Gdt].

QUESTION—What relationship is indicated by the phrase μὲν οὖν 'then'?
   Μέν is normally not translated in English, since it has no direct English equivalent.

1. It indicates that what follows is probably contrary to the readers' expectation [HNTC, ICC1, ICC2, Mor, NICNT, SSA]. The contrast follows in 11:14, which is that although the ministry that God appointed Paul to fulfill is a ministry to the Gentiles, he hopes that he can also cause some Jews to believe as well [HNTC, SSA]. Although Gentile Christians might argue that Paul's ministry to Gentiles shows that he has given up hope for the Jewish people, it is quite the opposite, as he hopes that his ministry to Gentiles will prompt some of them to believe [NICNT]. He did not want the Gentile believers in Rome to assume he had turned away from the Jewish people because of their unbelief [ICC2]. He did not want the Gentile believers in Rome to assume that, because of the attention he is giving to the unbelief of the Jews, he is disregarding his ministry among the Gentiles [ICC1].
2. It summarizes what has been said as he transitions to a new topic: so then, etc. [BECNT, WBC].

QUESTION—What does it mean for Paul to 'glorify' his ministry?

He tries very hard to carry out his responsibilities successfully [Gdt, Ho, ICC1]. He works zealously to fulfill his ministry [Gdt]. He esteems his ministry very highly [NTC, SSA, TNTC]. He is enthusiastic about his ministry [NTC]. He esteems his ministry very highly and he also works very hard to carry out his responsibilities successfully [AB, BECNT, ICC2, Mu, NICNT, St, WBC]. He exalts his office and zealously carries it out [Mu]. He tries to make his ministry well-known so that the impact on the Jews will be greater [HNTC].

11:14 if somehow[a] I-may-make-jealous[b] my kinsmen[c] and I-may-save[d] some[e] of-them.

LEXICON—a. The phrase εἴ πως 'if somehow' [BECNT; NASB, NET], is also translated 'if, in some way' [NICNT], 'in the hope that' [AB, ICC2, NTC, WBC; NIV], 'to see if (I may)' [HNTC], 'I hope in this way' [CEV], 'perhaps' [GW, TEV], 'if by any means' [KJV], 'in that way' [NCV], 'for I want somehow to' [NLT], 'in order to' [NRSV], '(yet always) in the hope of' [REB].
b. aorist act. subj. or fut. act. indic. of παραζηλόω (LN 88.164) (BAGD p. 616): 'to make jealous' [BAGD, ICC2, LN; CEV, GW, NCV, NLT, NRSV, TEV], 'to provoke to jealousy' [BAGD, BECNT, WBC; NET], 'to stir up to jealousy' [AB], 'to stimulate to jealousy' [NICNT], 'to move to jealousy' [NASB], 'to provoke to envy' [HNTC], 'to arouse to envy' [NTC; NIV], 'to stir to envy' [REB], 'to provoke to emulation' [KJV], 'to cause to be envious' [LN]. This verb and the one following are translated as subjunctive by AB, BECNT, HNTC, ICC2, NICNT, NTC, WBC; KJV, NASB, NET. This verb means to cause someone to feel strong jealousy or resentment against someone [LN].
c. σάρξ (LN **10.1**) (BAGD 4. p. 743): 'kinspeople' [NICNT], 'kindred' [ICC2, WBC], 'people' [AB, NTC; CEV, GW, NCV, NET, NIV, NRSV],

'flesh' [BECNT, HNTC; KJV], 'race' [LN; REB, TEV], 'ethnic group, nation' [LN], 'fellow countrymen' [BAGD; NASB], 'the people of Israel' [NLT]. This noun denotes a relatively large group of persons regarded as being biologically related [LN].

d. fut. act. indic. or aorist act. subj. of σώζω (LN 21.27) (BAGD 2.a.β. p. 798): 'to save' [AB, BAGD, BECNT, HNTC, ICC2, LN, NICNT, NTC, WBC; GW, KJV, NASB, NET, NIV, NLT, NRSV, REB, TEV], 'to be saved' [CEV, NCV]. This verb means to cause someone to experience divine salvation [LN].

e. τὶς (LN 92.12): 'some of them' [AB, BECNT, HNTC, ICC2, NICNT, NTC, WBC; all versions except CEV], 'some (of my own people)' [CEV], 'someone, anyone' [LN]. This adjective is pronominal and refers to someone or something indefinite, spoken or written about [LN].

QUESTION—What is being expressed by εἴ πως 'if somehow'?

It expresses a hope that Paul has [ICC2, Mor, NICNT, SSA, WBC]. It indicates the purpose for which Paul exalts his ministry [BECNT].

QUESTION—What is implied by his use of the word τὶς 'some'?

Paul's expectations of his impact on the Jewish people are rather modest [BECNT, Gdt, HNTC, ICC2, Mor, NAC, NICNT, St, WBC]. It suggests that he does not necessarily expect to live to see the return of Christ, since his work makes only a modest contribution to the salvation of Israel, which he considered inevitable before Christ should return [Gdt, Mor, NICNT].

11:15 For[a] if their rejection[b] (is)[c] the reconciliation[d] of-the world,

LEXICON—a. γάρ (LN 89.23): 'for' [AB, BECNT, HNTC, ICC2, LN, NICNT, NTC, WBC; KJV, NASB, NET, NIV, NLT, NRSV, REB, TEV], 'because' [LN], not explicit [CEV, GW, NCV]. This conjunction marks cause or reason between events [LN].

b. ἀποβολή (LN **34.38**) (BAGD 1. p. 89): 'rejection' [AB, BAGD, BECNT, HNTC, ICC2, LN, NICNT, NTC, WBC; GW, NASB, NET, NIV, NLT, NRSV, REB], '(the) casting away' [KJV]. This noun is translated as a verb: 'to reject' [CEV], 'to turn away' [NCV], 'to be rejected' [TEV]. This noun denotes the removal of someone from a particular association [LN].

c. There is no lexical entry for this verb in the Greek text, it is implied. It is represented in translation as 'is' [BECNT; NET, NIV, NRSV], 'be' [KJV, NASB], 'has meant' [AB; REB], 'has resulted' [HNTC], 'means' [ICC2, NICNT, NTC, WBC; GW], 'meant' [NLT], not explicit [CEV, NCV, TEV].

d. καταλλαγή (LN 40.1) (BAGD p. 414): 'reconciliation' [AB, BAGD, BECNT, HNTC, ICC2, LN, NICNT, NTC, WBC; NASB, NET, NIV, NRSV, REB], 'the reconciling of' [KJV]. This noun is translated as a verb: 'to be able to turn to him' [CEV], 'to be brought back to God' [GW], 'to become friends with other people in the world' [NCV], 'to offer salvation to the rest of the world' [NLT], 'to be changed from God's enemies into his friends' [TEV]. This noun denotes the reestablishment of proper friendly interpersonal relations after these have been disrupted or broken [LN].

QUESTION—What relationship is indicated by γάρ 'for'?

1. It indicates the reason for the statement he made in 11:13, which is that he seeks to stimulate Israel to jealousy because when they come to believe in Christ, blessing will come to the world [Gdt, ICC2, NICNT, WBC].
2. It indicates a further amplification of what Paul has been saying; that is, God brought many people to himself as a result of having rejected most of the Jews [SSA].
3. It moves his argument forward, but without any specific tie to anything that has been said [Mor].
4. It resumes the thought of 11:12 after his parenthetical comments in 11:13–14 [AB, ICC1].

QUESTION—What relationship is indicated by εἰ 'if'?

It indicates a condition of fact: 'if, as is the case' [Mor, SSA].

QUESTION—Who is the implied agent of the event 'rejection'?

1. God is the agent of the action; he has temporarily rejected the Jews [BECNT, ICC1, ICC2, Mor, Mu, NICNT, SSA, St, TH, WBC].
2. The Jews are the agent; they have rejected the gospel [AB].

QUESTION—In what way is the rejection of Israel the reconciliation of the world?

The result of the Jews being rejected is that God brought many other people to himself [ICC1, ICC2, NICNT, SSA, TH, WBC]. Here 'reconciliation' represents the death of Christ which caused reconciliation [ICC2, WBC]; it also represents the acceptance of that reconciliation by human beings [WBC]. Reconciliation is their being brought into fellowship with God as well as being brought into union with the commonwealth of Israel [Ho].

QUESTION—What does 'the world' represent here?

(Note that there may be little difference in the minds of the commentary authors between options 1.1 and 1.2.)

1. It refers to the people of the world.
1.1 It refers to the Gentiles [BECNT, Mu, NICNT, NTC, SSA, St, TH], all nations of the world [NTC].
1.2 It refers to all people [Ho, ICC2, WBC].
2. It refers to the whole universe [AB].

what (will be) (their) acceptance[a] if not[b] life from-among dead (ones)?[c]

LEXICON—a. πρόσλημψις (LN **34.34**) (BAGD p. 717): 'acceptance' [AB, BAGD, BECNT, HNTC, ICC2, LN, NICNT, NTC, WBC; GW, NASB, NET, NIV, NLT, NRSV, REB], 'the receiving' [KJV]. This noun is translated as a verb phrase: 'when God makes friends with Israel' [CEV], 'when God accepts the Jews' [NCV], 'when they are accepted' [TEV]. This noun denotes the acceptance of someone into an association [LN]. It is found only here in the NT.

b. The phrase εἰ μή is translated 'if not' [NICNT], 'but' [HNTC, ICC2, NTC; KJV, NASB, NET, NIV, NRSV], 'other than' [WBC], 'nothing less than' [AB; REB], 'except' [BECNT], 'even more wonderful' [NLT], not explicit [CEV, GW, NCV, TEV].
c. The phrase ζωὴ ἐκ νεκρῶν 'life from among dead ones' is translated 'life from the dead' [AB, BECNT, HNTC, ICC2, NICNT, NTC, WBC; KJV, NASB, NET, NIV, NRSV, REB], '(it will be like) bringing the dead back to life' [CEV], 'Israel has come back to life' [GW], 'surely that will bring them life after death' [NCV], 'it will be life for those who were dead' [NLT], 'life for the dead' [TEV].

QUESTION—Who is the implied agent of the event 'acceptance'?
1. Just as in the previous clause, God is the agent; he will accept the Jews [BECNT, ICC2, Mor, Mu, NICNT, NTC, SSA, WBC; CEV, NCV]. God takes the initiative and acts to restore Israel to his saving favor [BECNT].
2. The Jews are the agent of the action; Paul expects that they will accept the gospel [AB].

QUESTION—In what way will Israel's acceptance be life from the dead?
1. When the people of Israel finally believe in Christ it will be time for the end, culminating in the resurrection of the dead [BECNT, HNTC, ICC1, ICC2, NICNT, WBC]. This will be the climax of history, in keeping with the Jewish tradition that the end will come when the full number of the elect are saved [BECNT]. It refers not to the resurrection itself but to the new life that comes after the resurrection [NICNT].
2. When the people of Israel believe in Christ it will bring unprecedented blessing to the world in general [Gdt, Ho, Mor, Mu, St, TH]. Gentile Christendom will a great spiritual benefit when the Jews experience spiritual renovation [Gdt]. There will be a time of unprecedented blessing and prosperity, including religious prosperity [Ho].
3. When the people of Israel believe in Christ it will be as though they were made alive again [AB, NAC, NTC, SSA].

DISCOURSE UNIT—11:16–24 [NICNT]. The topic is a warning to Gentile believers.

11:16 And[a] if the firstfruit[b] (is) holy,[c] (so) also the lump;[d]

LEXICON—a. δέ (LN 89.94): 'and' [BECNT, ICC2, LN, NTC; NASB, NLT], 'now' [NICNT], not explicit [AB, HNTC, WBC; CEV, GW, KJV, NCV, NET, NIV, NRSV, REB, TEV]. This conjunction marks an additive relation, but with the possible implication of some contrast [LN].
b. ἀπαρχή (LN 53.23) (BAGD 1.a. p. 81): 'firstfruits' [AB, BAGD, BECNT, HNTC, NICNT; KJV], 'first portion, first offering' [LN], 'first-fruit cake' [ICC2], 'initial offering' [WBC], 'the first loaf' [REB]. This word is translated by a phrase: 'the cake that is offered as firstfruits' [NTC], 'part of a batch of dough…being offered to God' [CEV], 'the first handful of dough' [GW], 'the first piece of dough' [NASB], 'the first piece of bread' [NCV], 'the first portion of the dough' [NET], 'the part of

the dough offered as first fruits' [NIV, NRSV], 'the first piece of bread' [TEV], 'the portion given as an offering' [NLT]. This entire clause is translated 'And since Abraham and the other patriarchs were holy, their descendants will also be holy—just as the entire batch of dough is holy because the portion given as an offering is holy' [NLT]. This noun denotes the first portion of something which has been set aside and offered to God before the rest can be used [LN].
- c. ἅγιος (LN 53.46) (BAGD 1.a.β. p. 9): 'holy' [AB, BECNT, HNTC, ICC2, NICNT, NTC, WBC; all versions except NCV, TEV], 'dedicated' [LN], 'worthy of God' [BAGD]. This word is translated as a phrase: 'offered to God' [NCV], 'given to God' [TEV]. This adjective describes being dedicated or consecrated to the service of God [LN].
- d. φύραμα (LN 63.12, 79.92) (BAGD p. 869): 'lump' [BAGD, BECNT, HNTC, LN (79.92), NICNT; KJV, NASB], 'batch of dough' [AB, BAGD, LN (63.12); GW], 'the whole batch' [NET, NIV, NRSV, REB], 'the whole mixture' [ICC2], 'the entire batch' [NTC; NLT], 'the mixture as a whole' [WBC], 'all of the dough (is holy)' [CEV], 'the whole loaf' [NCV]. This noun denotes that which is mixed or kneaded [LN (63.12)], or a three-dimensional object with irregular rounding contours [LN (79.92)].

QUESTION—What relationship is indicated by δέ 'and'?

It indicates a loose transition and can be translated 'now' [NICNT]. This sentence introduces a new idea [TH], and some versions begin a new paragraph here [NICNT; GW, NCV, TEV]. However, many leave it in the same paragraph with the preceding verse [CEV, NASB, NET, NIV, NRSV, REB]. This verse is giving the grounds for Paul's confidence shown in 11:11–15 that unbelieving Israel also has a spiritual future [ICC1, ICC2, NICNT].

QUESTION—In the metaphor of the firstfruit, what is the relation between the portion that is offered and the lump of dough from which it is taken?

Paul is drawing on various passages in the Torah in which a portion of the first part of the grain harvest must be offered to God, and after which the rest is made acceptable to be used legitimately for ordinary purposes [AB, BECNT, ICC2, Mor, NICNT, TH, TNTC, WBC]. The argument is that the holiness of the portion of the dough extends to the whole lump of dough [ICC1, ICC2, NICNT, SSA]. If a portion is consecrated to God, all the rest belongs to him [St], and they may then use it as a gift from his own hand [NTC].

QUESTION—In this metaphor, what do the firstfruit and the lump represent?

1. The firstfruit represents the Jewish patriarchs and the lump represents all of Israel, their descendants [BECNT, Gdt, Ho, ICC1, Mor, Mu, NICNT, NTC, SSA, TH]. It does not mean all the people of Israel are set apart for salvation, just that they have been set aside for a special role in salvation history [NICNT].

2. The firstfruit represents the first Jewish Christians, the believing remnant of Israel, and the lump would be all the rest of Israel [AB, HNTC, ICC2, NAC, St, TNTC]. Paul is saying that Jewish Christians 'sanctify' the unbelieving majority of their nation in a way similar to how a believing spouse 'sanctifies' the other partner and the children [ICC2].
3. The firstfruit represents the early Christian converts, both Jews and Gentiles, and the lump represents all those who will eventually believe in Christ, the 'fullness' that will come to experience the same sanctification that the firstfruit has [WBC].

QUESTION—What does the term 'holy' mean here?

'Holy' means that something or someone is given to God [TH]. The people of Israel were set apart by God for a particular role in salvation history [NICNT]. They had been set apart from the rest of the world for the service of God [Ho], set apart for sacred use or duty, and to live for God [NTC]. They were consecrated to God [ICC1], and to the awesome service of God [AB]. It refers to the sanctification of all the saints, that is, believers [WBC]. They are not cast off corporately, that is, as a nation [BECNT]. Paul uses the term in a way similar to how he uses it in 1 Cor. 7:14, where he says that a believing spouse 'sanctifies' the other partner and the children; here he is not saying that unbelieving Jews are saved because of their relation to Abraham, just that God will be faithful to his promises to them [ICC2].

and if the root^a (is) holy, (so) also the branches.^b

LEXICON—a. ῥίζα (LN 3.47) (BAGD 1.b. p. 736): 'root' [AB, BAGD, BECNT, HNTC, ICC2, LN, NICNT, NTC, WBC; all versions]. This noun denotes the underground part of a plant [LN].
  b. κλάδος (LN 3.49) (BAGD p. 433): 'branch' [AB, BECNT, HNTC, ICC2, LN, NICNT, NTC, WBC; all versions except CEV], 'rest of the tree' [CEV].

QUESTION—In this metaphor, what do the root and branches represent?
1. The root represents the patriarchs [AB, BECNT, Gdt, Ho, ICC1, ICC2, Mor, Mu, NAC, NICNT, NTC, St, TNTC, WBC], especially Abraham [NAC], possibly only Abraham [Mor], and the branches are their Jewish descendants [AB, Gdt, Ho, ICC1, ICC2, Mor, Mu, NAC, NICNT, St, TNTC, WBC], Israel as a whole [BECNT]. The existing branches and the newly grafted-in branches become eschatological Israel, the people of God, in its final full expression, composed of both believing Jews and believing Gentiles [WBC].
2. The root represents Jewish Christians, and possibly even Christ himself, who are the pledge of the salvation of the branches, that is, the rest of Israel [HNTC].

QUESTION—What is the relation between this verse and the context?
1. It ends a section and bridges to the next section which begins with 11:17 [BECNT, HNTC, Ho, ICC2, NTC, SSA, WBC]. It ends the section beginning with 11:11 [BECNT, HNTC, Ho, ICC2, NTC, WBC]. It ends

the section beginning with 11:13 and has a tail-head link with the idea of root and branches in the section that follows [SSA].
2. It is the beginning of a new section [Gdt, ICC1, NICNT; TEV], introducing the metaphor of root and branches that follows [NICNT].

11:17 But[a] if some of-the branches were-broken-off,[b] you(sg)[c] being a wild-olive-tree[d] having-been-grafted[e] among[f] them,

LEXICON—a. δέ (LN 89.124): 'but' [HNTC, ICC2, LN, WBC; GW, NASB, NLT, NRSV, REB], 'now' [BECNT, NICNT; NET], 'moreover' [NTC], 'and' [KJV], not explicit [AB; CEV, NCV, NIV, TEV]. This conjunction marks contrast [LN].
  b. aorist pass. indic. of ἐκκλάω (LN **19.36**) (BAGD p. 240): 'to be broken off' [BAGD, BECNT, HNTC, ICC2, LN, WBC; GW, KJV, NASB, NCV, NET, NIV, NLT, NRSV, TEV], 'to be lopped off' [AB, NTC; REB], 'to be cut off' [NICNT], 'to be cut away from' [CEV]. This verb means to break off a part [LN].
  c. σύ: 'you'. This word is emphatic here [Gdt, ICC2, Mor, NTC, SSA].
  d. ἀγριέλαιος (LN **3.11**) (BAGD p. 13): 'wild olive tree' [BAGD, LN]. The phrase σὺ ἀγριέλαιος ὤν 'you being a wild olive tree' [KJV] is also translated 'you being a wild olive' [**LN**; NASB], 'you, a wild olive' [HNTC, ICC2, WBC; REB], 'you, a wild olive shoot' [NET, NIV, NRSV], 'you, being a wild olive shoot' [NTC], 'you, a wild olive branch' [NICNT; GW], 'even though you are a wild olive branch' [BECNT], 'you, though a branch from a wild olive tree' [AB], 'you Gentiles, who were branches from a wild olive tree' [NLT], 'you Gentiles are like branches of a wild olive tree' [CEV], 'you non-Jewish people are like the branch of a wild olive tree' [NCV], 'a branch of a wild olive tree has been joined to it. You Gentiles are like that wild olive tree' [TEV]. This word is an adjective ('wild olive') that is used as a substantive: 'wild olive tree' [BAGD, NICNT, WBC]. Here the word ἀγριέλαιος refers not to the whole tree but to a branch or shoot of a wild olive tree [SSA]. It is not neglect which makes the tree wild, it is just essentially different from the cultivated one [LN]. This word occurs only here and in 11:24 in the NT.
  e. aorist pass. indic. of ἐγκεντρίζω (LN **43.10**) (BAGD p. 216): 'to be grafted' [AB, BAGD, BECNT, HNTC, ICC2, LN, NICNT, NTC, WBC; GW, KJV, NASB, NET, NIV, NLT, NRSV, REB], 'to be joined to' [NCV, TEV]. This verb is translated as a phrase: 'You have taken the place of' [CEV]. This verb means to insert a shoot or bud into a growing plant [LN]. It occurs only in this passage in the NT.
  f. ἐν (LN 83.9): 'among' [BECNT, HNTC, ICC2, LN, NICNT, NTC, WBC; KJV, NASB, NET, NIV, REB], 'in their place' [GW, NRSV], 'into their place' [AB], 'in' [NLT], not explicit [CEV, NCV, TEV]. This preposition marks a position within an area determined by other objects and distributed among such objects [LN].

QUESTION—What relationship is indicated by δέ 'but'?

The phrase εἰ δέ provides a structural unity to the paragraph, linking this verse with 11:12, 11:16, and 11:18 [WBC].
1. It is contrastive [HNTC, ICC2, LN, WBC; GW, NASB, NLT, NRSV, REB].
2. It is continuative, moving his argument forward [BECNT, Gdt, NICNT, NTC; KJV, NET].

QUESTION—What relationship is indicated by εἰ 'if'?

It states a condition that is assumed to be true [Mor, NICNT, SSA, TH; TEV]: if, as is true, branches were broken off, etc. It introduces the protasis of a conditional sentence that is completed in the next verse: do not boast over the branches [NICNT, SSA]. It introduces the first of three concessive statements in 11:17 which are countered by the contraexpectation in the form of an exhortation in 11:18; that is, although God rejected many of the Jews, you must not despise them [SSA].

QUESTION—Who are the branches that were broken off?

These branches represent ethnic Jews who do not believe in Christ [AB, BECNT, Ho, ICC2, Mor, Mu, NICNT, NTC, SSA, St, WBC].

QUESTION—Why does he use the word τινες 'some' to describe Jews who did not believe, who are actually in the majority?

It is meiosis, a polite understatement [AB, BECNT, ICC1, ICC2, WBC]. He wants to stress to Gentile readers that not all of the branches have been cut away [NICNT], not all Jews were faithless [Mor]. He is focusing only on the fact of Gentiles being adding in and people of Israel being cut out, and not on the extent to which the cutting out took place [Mu]. 'Some' can refer to any amount, large or small [Gdt].

QUESTION—Who is the agent of the passive verb 'were broken off'?

God is the agent of the passive verb [ICC2, Mor, NICNT, TH, WBC]. The breaking off is God's punitive act against Israel [WBC].

QUESTION—What relationship is indicated by ἐν αὐτοῖς 'among them'?

The antecedent of αὐτοῖς 'them' is the branches that remain on the tree; that is, the believing Jews [AB, BECNT, ICC1, ICC2, Mor, Mu, NICNT, SSA, WBC]. They were grafted in the place of those who were cut out [Gdt].

QUESTION—Was grafting a branch from a wild olive into a cultivated olive tree an actual horticultural practice, or is it just an analogy that Paul has created to show something unusual that God has done?

Paul is free to use a metaphor however he likes to make his theological point, and it is irrelevant whether it was an actual horticultural practice [BECNT, Gdt, Ho, ICC2, Mu, NAC, NICNT, NTC].
1. It is an actual horticultural practice to invigorate a cultivated olive tree that has ceased to produce fruit by grafting in branches from a wild olive [AB, BECNT, Gdt, Mor, St, TNTC, WBC]. Paul describes this practice as 'contrary to nature', meaning that it was not the norm in any event [Mor].
2. This practice was not one that was actually done, which Paul underscores by saying that it is contrary to nature [ICC1].

and a partaker[a] of-the root of-the richness[b] of-the olive-tree,[c]
TEXT—Some manuscripts include καί 'and' after τῆς ῥίζης 'the root'. It is omitted by GNT with a B rating, indicating that the text is almost certain. It is included only by KJV.
LEXICON—a. συγκοινωνός (LN 34.6, 57.10) (BAGD p. 774): 'partaker' [HNTC, NICNT; NASB], 'sharer' [LN (57.10), WBC], 'partner' [BAGD, LN], 'associate, one who joins in with' [LN (34.6)], 'participant' [BAGD, BECNT]. The phrase συγκοινωνὸς...ἐγένου 'became partakers' is translated 'have come to share' [AB, NTC; REB], 'made to share (the root)' [ICC2], '(were grafted) to share' [NRSV], 'being part of' [CEV], '(you) get your nourishment from' [GW], 'with them partakest' [KJV], 'share the strength' [NCV], 'participated in' [NET], 'share in' [NIV], '(you also) receive (the blessing)' [NLT], 'to share (the strong spiritual life)' [TEV], 'jointly share in it' [BAGD]. This noun denotes one who participates with another in some enterprise or matter of joint concern [LN (34.6)], or one who shares jointly with someone else in a possession or relationship, with emphasis upon that which is in common [LN (57.10)].
b. πιότης (LN **3.59, 65.7**) (BAGD p. 659): 'richness' [BAGD, LN (65.7), WBC; NET], 'fatness' [BAGD, ICC2, LN (3.59); KJV], 'rich quality' [LN (3.59)], 'nourishment' [GW], 'strength and life' [NCV]. The genitive phrase τῆς ῥίζης τῆς πιότητος 'the root of the richness' is translated 'the fatness of the root' [**LN** (3.59)], 'the valuable root' [**LN** (65.7)], 'the rich sap' [AB], 'the fatness' [BECNT], 'rich root' [BAGD, HNTC, NICNT; NASB, NRSV], 'the nourishing sap from the root' [NTC; NIV], 'the rich nourishment from the root' [NLT], 'the same root and sap (as the olive)' [REB]. The phrase 'the root of the richness of the olive tree' is also translated without the metaphor: 'the rich tradition of Judaism' [**LN** (65.7)], 'the strong spiritual life of the Jews' [TEV]. This clause is translated 'you enjoy the blessings that come from being part of that cultivated tree' [CEV]. This adjective describes a nutritionally rich, fatty quality [LN (3.59)], or a rich, valuable substance [LN (65.7)]. It is found only here in the NT.
c. ἐλαία (LN 3.9) (BAGD 1. p. 247): 'olive tree' [BAGD, BECNT, HNTC, ICC2, LN, NICNT; GW, KJV, NASB, NLT, NRSV], 'olive root' [AB, NTC; NIV], 'olive tree's root' [WBC], 'that cultivated tree' [CEV], 'that first tree' [NCV], 'the olive' [REB], 'olive root' [NET], not explicit [TEV].
QUESTION—How are the nouns related in the genitive phrase τῆς ῥίζης τῆς πιότητος 'of the root of the richness'?
 1. The sap flowing from the root is rich [AB, ICC1, Mu, WBC] and nourishing [NTC, WBC]. The root of the tree is rich [NICNT, TH].
 2. τῆς πιότητος 'of the richness' is in apposition to τῆς ῥίζης 'the root'; the root, that is, the fatness [BECNT, ICC2]. It refers to God's electing grace, the elective promises given to the patriarchs, in which believing Gentiles

had been invited to share [BECNT]. They share in the root, that is, the fatness of the root [ICC2].

QUESTION—What does the root of richness of the olive tree represent?

It is the spiritual Israel, from which now Gentiles are sharing in its vitality and richness [AB]. It represents the rich Jewish heritage which is the basis of the Gentile Christians' spiritual standing, and which brings about a united people of God that transcends history as well as ethnicity [NICNT]. It represents the rich Jewish spiritual heritage that has benefited the Gentiles [WBC]. The gospel was based on and the church was built on Jewish roots [NTC]. The root is the patriarchs, and God's gracious election of them [BECNT]. It represents the privileges and benefits of the supernatural life of God's people in the previous age [HNTC]. It represents the patriarchs, who were holy by virtue of having been consecrated to the Lord [ICC1].

11:18 don't boast-over[a] the branches; and[b] if you(sg) boast, you(sg)[c] do-not support[d] the root but the root (supports) you(sg).

LEXICON—a. pres. mid. or pass. (deponent = act.) impera. of κατακαυχάομαι (LN **33.370, 88.194**) (BAGD 1. p. 411): 'to boast over' [AB, BECNT, HNTC, NICNT; NET, NIV, NRSV], 'to boast against' [BAGD, LN (33.370); KJV], 'boast and in so doing degrade' [**LN** (33.370)], 'to despise' [**LN** (88.194); TEV], 'to triumph over' [ICC2], 'to gloat over' [NTC, WBC], 'to think you are better than' [CEV], 'to brag about' [GW, NCV, NLT], 'to be arrogant toward' [NASB], 'to make yourself superior to' [REB]. This verb means to boast about something by downgrading something else, and here it would mean that they must not say that they are so much better than the broken-off branches [LN (33.370)], or it means to despise someone because of feeling superior to that person [LN (88.194)].

b. δέ (LN 89.94): 'and' [BECNT, HNTC, LN], 'but' [NICNT, NTC; KJV, NASB, NET], not explicit [AB, ICC2, WBC; CEV, GW, NCV, NIV, NLT, NRSV, REB, TEV]. This conjunction marks an additive relation, but with the possible implication of some contrast [LN].

c. σύ: 'you'. This word is emphatic here [AB, ICC2, Mor, WBC].

d. pres. act. indic. of βαστάζω (LN **35.32**) (BAGD 2.a. p. 137): 'to support' [AB, BAGD, BECNT, **LN**, NICNT, NTC; CEV, GW, NASB, NCV, NET, NIV, NRSV, TEV], 'to bear' [HNTC, ICC2; KJV], 'to sustain' [WBC; REB], not explicit [NLT]. This verb means to provide continuous and possibly prolonged assistance and help by supplying the needs of someone [LN].

QUESTION—Are the branches referred to here only those who were 'cut off' for unbelief, or all Jews?

1. It refers to Jews in general, both Christian and non-Christian [Gdt, ICC1, ICC2, NICNT]. Since the reference to 'some of the branches' in the previous verse regards the word 'branches' in an inclusive sense, that sense probably carries through here [ICC1]. The comparison has been

made between Gentile Christians and the unbelieving Jews who have been cut off, but here Paul's concern is to reconcile Jews and Gentiles within the church since Gentile Christians seemed to think that they were the new people of God who had now replaced Israel [NICNT]. Anti-Semitism was not uncommon in the Roman world [ICC2, Mor]. Pride tends to be indiscriminate [Mor], so they may have looked down on both groups [Mor, NTC].
2. It refers specifically to those who were broken off, the Jews who were rejected [SSA, TH; CEV, NCV, NLT, TEV].

QUESTION—What is implied by the word εἰ 'if'?

The condition 'if you boast' does not imply that they were actually engaged in this boasting, but has the sense of 'if any of you are inclined to boast' [SSA]. For the sake of argument, Paul assumes that the Gentile Christians will boast over Jews [NICNT]. 'If you boast' has an implied proposition in the consequence, such as such as 'remember this' [AB, NICNT], 'remember that' [SSA; GW, NASB, NCV, NET, NRSV, REB], 'just remember' [CEV], 'consider this' [Ho; NIV], 'the fact remains that' [Gdt]. Some present the consequence as a statement: 'you are just a branch, not the root' [NLT], 'you are just a branch; you don't support the roots—the roots support you' [TEV].

QUESTION—What is meant by the word βαστάζω 'support'?

It refers to nourishment [NICNT, SSA, TH]. The root sustains them [BECNT]. Israel carries life and salvation to the world [AB]. It implies both structural support as well as fruit-bearing [WBC]. It refers to the source of the spiritual nourishment that believers require [NICNT].

11:19 You(sg)-will-say then, branches were-broken-off[a] so-that I might-be-grafted-in.[b]

LEXICON—a. aorist pass. indic. of ἐκκλάω (LN 19.36) (BAGD p. 240): 'to be broken off' [BAGD, BECNT, HNTC, ICC2, LN, NICNT, WBC; KJV, NASB, NCV, NET, NIV, NLT, NRSV, TEV], 'to be lopped off' [AB, NTC; REB], 'to be cut away' [CEV], 'to be cut off' [GW]. See above at 11:17.
b. ἐγώ: I. This word is emphatic here [Gdt, Mor, Mu, NICNT, NTC].
c. aorist pass. subj. of ἐγκεντρίζω (LN 43.10) (BAGD p. 216): 'to be grafted' [AB, BAGD, BECNT, HNTC, ICC2, LN, NICNT, NTC, WBC; GW, KJV, NASB, NET, NIV, NRSV, REB], 'to be joined to' [NCV], 'to make room for' [NLT, TEV], 'to be put in (their place)' [CEV]. See above at 11:17. This verb means to insert a shoot or bud into a growing plant [LN].

QUESTION—What relationship is indicated by οὖν 'then'?

It introduces a challenge that Paul anticipates will be given based on what he has said in the previous verse [Gdt, NICNT, SSA, TH, WBC]. This is the logic behind Gentile boasting [ICC1, ICC2].

QUESTION—What is the problem Paul is addressing?
A person who boasts in such a way believes that he has been chosen by God to replace Israel [Mor]. This boasting expresses egotism [ICC2, Mor, Mu, NICNT] and vainglory [Mor, Mu]. Such a person considers himself or herself more important because of what has befallen the Jews [AB]. The contrast between the singular 'I' and the plural 'branches' heightens the presumption involved in this statement [WBC]. Such a person thinks that God's manifold plan focuses only on his or her own salvation, and they have a sense of pride in having a place among the people of God [NICNT]. Believing Gentiles should not think of themselves as better than the Jews who had been rejected [Ho]. The Gentile believers were tempted to be arrogant, presumptuously confident, and self-righteous [Mu].

11:20 Very-well;ᵃ they-were-broken-off by-unbelief,ᵇ andᶜ you(sg) standᵈ by-faith.ᵉ

LEXICON—a. καλῶς (LN 72.12) (BAGD 4.c. p. 401): 'very well' [REB], 'well' [KJV], 'correctly, right' [LN], 'true' [AB, ICC2, NICNT, NTC; NCV, NRSV, TEV], 'true enough' [HNTC], 'quite so' [WBC], 'that's true enough' [CEV], 'that is true' [BAGD], 'that's right' [GW], 'quite right' [NASB], 'quite rightly' [BAGD], 'granted' [NET, NIV], 'yes' [NLT], 'you are correct' [BECNT]. This adverb pertains to being accurate and right, with a possible implication of being commendable [LN].
b. ἀπιστία (LN **31.97**, 31.105) (BAGD 2.b. p. 85): 'unbelief' [BAGD, BECNT, HNTC, ICC2, WBC; KJV, NASB, NET, NIV, NRSV], 'refusing to believe' [LN (31.97)], 'not believing' [LN], 'lack of faith' [AB, NICNT, NTC; REB]. This noun is translated as a verb phrase: 'they did not believe' [GW, NCV, TEV], 'they did not believe in Christ' [NLT], 'they did not have faith' [CEV]. The relationship indicated by the dative case of the noun τῇ ἀπιστίᾳ is translated 'by' [ICC2], 'because of' [AB, BECNT, NICNT; KJV, NIV, NRSV], 'because (they)' [LN; CEV, GW, NCV, NLT, TEV], 'it was for (unbelief)' [HNTC, NTC], 'on the ground of' [WBC], 'for' [NASB, REB]. This noun denotes a refusal to put one's trust or reliance in something or someone [LN (31.97)], or not believing in the good news about Jesus Christ [LN (31.105)].
c. δέ (LN 89.94, 89.124): 'and' [BECNT, HNTC, ICC2, LN (89.94), NICNT, NTC; CEV, KJV, NCV, NIV, NLT, REB], 'but' [LN (89.124), WBC; GW, NASB, NET, NRSV], 'whereas' [AB], 'while' [TEV]. This conjunction marks contrast [LN (89.124)], or an additive relation, but with the possible implication of some contrast [LN (89.94)].
d. perf. act. indic. of ἵστημι (LN 85.40) (BAGD II.2.c.α. p. 382): 'to stand' [BECNT, HNTC, ICC2, NICNT, NTC, WBC; KJV, NASB, NET, NIV, NRSV], 'to make stand' [LN], 'to stand firm' [BAGD], 'to be there' [AB, LN; NLT], 'to be where you are' [CEV], 'to remain' [GW, TEV], 'to be part of' [NCV], 'to hold (one's place)' [REB]. This verb means to cause

to be in a place [LN]. In the perfect tense, this verb has the sense of 'stand firm' [SSA, WBC].

e. The dative noun τῇ πίστει is translated 'by faith' [HNTC, ICC2, NTC; KJV, NASB, NET, NIV, REB], 'by means of faith' [BECNT], 'through faith' [WBC; NRSV], 'because you do have faith' [CEV], 'because of faith' [AB, NICNT], 'because you do believe' [GW, NLT, TEV], '(only) because you believe' [NCV].

QUESTION—What is implied in the use of καλῶς 'very well'?

Paul is expressing some agreement, but it is qualified by what follows [BECNT, Gdt, ICC2, NICNT, NTC, WBC]. The statement just expressed is a dangerous half-truth since 'so that I might be grafted in' was not the whole purpose for breaking off the branches [ICC2]. Paul grants the fact, but denies what might easily be inferred from it [Gdt].

QUESTION—What relationship is indicated by the use of the dative case in the phrase τῇ ἀπιστίᾳ 'by unbelief'?

It is causal: [AB, BECNT, Ho, ICC2, Mor, NAC, NICNT, TH, WBC; CEV, GW, NCV, NLT, TEV]: because of unbelief.

QUESTION—What relationship is indicated by the use of the dative case in the phrase τῇ πίστει 'by faith'?

The position in the sentence of the phrase τῇ πίστει 'by faith' shows that the statement is emphatic [TNTC]. It is only by faith that they stand [NCV, NRSV].

1. It is instrumental [BECNT, NICNT, WBC; KJV, NASB, NET, NIV, REB]: through or by faith. Although it could indicate the cause, the fact that it concerns a continuing relationship to God probably indicates that it is instrumental [NICNT].
2. It is causal [AB, ICC2, SSA, TH; CEV, GW, NCV, NLT, TEV]: because of faith.

Don't think[a] proudly[b] but[c] fear;[d]

LEXICON—a. pres. act. impera. of φρονέω (LN 26.16) (BAGD 1. p. 866): 'to think' [BECNT, NICNT; NLT], 'to have an attitude, to think in a particular manner' [LN], 'to become' [AB; NRSV], 'to grow (boastful) about' [HNTC], 'to be' [ICC2, NTC; KJV, NASB, NCV, NET, NIV, TEV], 'to cherish (proud thoughts)' [WBC], 'to feel (arrogant)' [GW]. This verb means to employ one's faculty for thoughtful planning, with emphasis upon the underlying disposition or attitude [LN].

b. ὑψηλός (LN 88.208, **88.209**) (BAGD 2. p. 850): 'arrogant' [LN], 'proud' [BAGD, LN], 'haughty, exalted' [BAGD]. The phrase μὴ ὑψηλὰ φρόνει 'don't think proudly' is translated 'don't be proud' [**LN** (88.209)], 'do not become haughty' [AB], 'do not think in a haughty way' [BECNT], 'there is nothing for you to grow boastful about' [HNTC], 'do not be haughty' [ICC2], 'do not think highly of yourself' [NICNT; NLT], 'do not be arrogant' [NTC; NET, NIV], 'don't feel arrogant' [GW], 'be not high-minded' [KJV], 'do not be conceited' [NASB], 'do not be proud' [BAGD;

NCV, TEV], 'do not be arrogant' [NET, NIV], 'do not become proud' [NRSV], 'put away your pride' [REB], 'do not cherish proud thoughts' [WBC]. This adjective describes an arrogant, haughty attitude [LN (88.209)], or being arrogant or proud [LN (88.208)].

c. ἀλλά (LN 89.125): 'but' [BECNT, ICC2, LN, NICNT, NTC, WBC; GW, KJV, NASB, NCV, NET, NIV, NLT, NRSV], 'instead, on the contrary' [LN], 'rather' [HNTC], 'and' [REB], 'instead' [TEV], not explicit [AB]. This conjunction marks emphatic contrast [LN].

d. pres. mid. or pass. (deponent = act.) impera. of φοβέομαι (LN 25.252): 'to fear' [BECNT, ICC2, LN, NICNT, NTC, WBC; KJV, NASB, NLT], 'to be afraid' [LN; GW, NCV, NIV, TEV], 'to be fearful' [AB], 'to show fear' [HNTC], 'to stand in awe' [NRSV], 'to be on your guard' [REB]. This verb means to be in a state of fearing [LN].

QUESTION—What does he mean by the command to 'fear'?

It is an awe of God [Mor], reverence for God [AB, Mor], the fear of God in the full biblical sense, meaning fear of his judgments [ICC2]. It is the fear of God that is the beginning of wisdom, and which will prevent a person's faith from becoming presumption [WBC]. This kind of fear is wholesome, and involves trusting completely on sovereign grace, not personal merit [NTC]. It is respect for the God of majesty and glory combined with a genuine desire to live and express his grace in daily living [NICNT]. They should beware of something that may happen [TH], they should beware lest they fall [BECNT].

11:21 For[a] if God did- not -spare[b] the according-to nature[c] branches, perhaps[d] he-will- not -spare you(sg).

TEXT—The words μή πως 'perhaps' do not occur in some manuscripts. It is included by GNT with a C rating, indicating difficulty in deciding whether or not to place it in the text. It is omitted or not translated by BECNT, HNTC, ICC2, NICNT, NTC, SSA; GW, NASB, NCV, NIV, NLT.

LEXICON—a. γάρ (89.23): 'for' [AB, BECNT, HNTC, ICC2, LN, NICNT, NTC, WBC; all versions except CEV, GW, NCV, TEV], not explicit [CEV, GW, NCV, TEV]. This conjunction marks cause or reason between events [LN].

b. aorist mid. (deponent = act.) indic. of φείδομαι (LN 22.28) (BAGD 1. p. 854): 'to spare' [AB, BAGD, BECNT, HNTC, ICC2, LN, NICNT, NTC, WBC; all versions except CEV, NCV], 'to let stay' [NCV]. The phrase 'God did not spare' is translated 'God cut away' [CEV]. This verb means to cause someone not to be troubled [LN].

c. φύσις (LN 58.8) (BAGD 1. p. 869): 'nature' [BAGD, LN], 'natural endowment or condition' [BAGD]. The prepositional phrase κατὰ φύσιν 'according to nature' is translated 'natural' [AB, BAGD, BECNT, ICC2, NICNT, NTC, WBC; all versions except NLT], '(branches) by nature' [HNTC], 'original' [NLT]. This noun denotes the nature of something as the result of its natural development or condition [LN].

d. μή πως (LN 89.62) (BAGD 1.b. p. 519): 'perhaps...not' [AB, BAGD; NET, NRSV]. This expression is used to indicate apprehension [BAGD, LN], or negative purpose [LN]. The clause μή πως οὐδὲ σοῦ φείσεται 'perhaps he will not spare you' [NET, NRSV] is also translated '(it is to be feared) that perhaps he will not spare you, either' [BAGD], 'take heed lest he also spare not thee' [KJV], 'do you think he will spare you?' [TEV], 'couldn't he do the same for you' [CEV]. Some leave out the softening of the statement that μή πως 'perhaps' implies (possibly because they do not include that phase in the Greek text): 'he will not spare you either' [NASB, NIV, NLT; similarly GW], 'neither will he spare you' [WBC], 'no more will he spare you' [REB]. One translation includes the implied condition: 'then he will not let you stay if you don't believe' [NCV].

QUESTION—What relationship is indicated by γάρ 'for'
It introduces grounds for why the non-Jewish believer should fear [BECNT, ICC2, Mor, NICNT].

QUESTION—What is the implied condition behind this warning?
He won't spare you if you become proud and presumptuous [Mu, WBC], or presume on his mercy [Mor]. He won't spare you if you fall away from him [SSA], or if you don't continue in faith [BECNT, NICNT], and in the fear of God [NICNT].

11:22 Consider[a] then[b] (the) kindness[c] and severity[d] of-God;

LEXICON—a. aorist act. impera. of εἶδον (the aorist form of ὁράω) (LN 30.45) (BAGD 3. p. 221): 'to consider' [AB, BECNT, ICC2, LN, NTC, WBC; NIV], 'to see' [HNTC, NICNT; CEV, NCV, TEV], 'behold' [KJV, NASB], 'to notice' [BAGD; NET, NLT], 'to note' [BAGD; NRSV], 'to observe' [REB], not explicit [GW]. This verb means to take special notice of something, with the implication of concerning oneself [LN].

b. οὖν (LN 89.50): 'then' [AB, HNTC, ICC2, LN, NTC, WBC; NASB, NRSV], 'so, accordingly, so then' [LN], 'therefore' [BECNT, NICNT; KJV, NET, NIV], 'now' [CEV], not explicit [GW, NCV, NLT, REB, TEV]. This conjunction marks result, often implying the conclusion of a process of reasoning [LN].

c. χρηστότης (LN 88.67) (BAGD 2.b. p. 886): 'kindness' [AB, BAGD, BECNT, HNTC, ICC2, LN, NICNT, NTC; NASB, NET, NIV, NRSV, REB], 'goodness' [BAGD, WBC; KJV]. This noun is translated as an adjective: 'kind' [CEV, GW, NCV, NLT, TEV]. This noun denotes something beneficial for someone done as an act of kindness [LN].

d. ἀποτομία (LN 88.73) (BAGD p. 101): 'severity' [AB, BAGD, BECNT, HNTC, ICC2, NICNT, NTC, WBC; KJV, NASB, NRSV, REB], 'harshness' [LN; NET], 'sternness' [NIV]. This word is translated as an adjective: 'severe' [GW, NLT, TEV], 'hard' [CEV], 'strict' [NCV], 'harsh' [**LN**]. This word refers to God's inflexible moral purpose, and his unyielding opposition to evil [Mor]. This noun denotes a harsh act toward someone [LN]. It occurs only in this verse in the NT.

QUESTION—What relationship is indicated by οὖν 'then'?

It draws a conclusion from what he has been arguing [BECNT, ICC1, Mor]. It introduces an implication of several things he has said in 11:17–21 [NICNT]. It introduces 11:22 as a restatement of what he has said in 11:20 [BECNT].

on[a] those having-fallen[b] severity, but on you(sg) (the) kindness of-God,

LEXICON—a. ἐπί with accusative object (LN 90.57) (BAGD III.1.b.ε. p. 289): 'on' [BAGD, LN; CEV, KJV], 'to' [AB, ICC2, LN, WBC; GW, NASB, NIV, REB], 'upon' [BECNT], 'for' [BAGD, HNTC, NICNT], 'toward' [BAGD, NTC; NET, NLT, NRSV, TEV], not explicit [NCV]. This preposition marks the experiencer, often with the implication of an action by a superior force or agency [LN].

b. aorist act. participle of πίπτω (LN 13.59) (BAGD 2.a.β. p. 660): 'to fall' [AB, BAGD, BECNT, HNTC, ICC2, LN, NICNT, NTC, WBC; CEV, GW, KJV, NASB, NET, NIV, NRSV, TEV], 'to disobey' [NLT], 'to fall away' [REB]. The phrase 'on those having fallen severity' is translated 'He punishes those who stop following him' [NCV]. This verb means to change for the worse, with emphasis upon extent and suddenness [LN].

QUESTION—What point is he making about God's kindness and severity?

In speaking of God's mercy and justice, he says that God's election is entirely by grace, but Christians must responsibly fulfill their obligations to him [AB]. Perseverance in faith is not an unconditional promise, it is the responsibility of the Christian [WBC]. In the NT continuing in faith is always the proof of whether or not that faith is real [TNTC, WBC]. Perseverance in faith is the distinguishing mark of God's true children [St]. While there is kindness for the unbeliever, those who remain in unbelief have nothing to look forward to but severity [Mor]. God's goodness is not an automatic benefit upon which someone can presume, but must involve an ongoing relationship [NICNT]. Both his kindness and his severity are aspects of his holy and faithful love [ICC2].

QUESTION—How does this statement compare with what he has said in 11:11 where he uses the same verb?

1. Those who have fallen are the Jews spoken of in 11:11 [AB].
2. Here he is speaking of the fate of individual branches who were cut off because of unbelief, whereas in 11:11 he says that the fate of Israel will not ultimately be disaster [Mor].

if you-remain-in[a] (his) kindness, otherwise[b] you(sg)[c] also will-be-cut-off. [d]

LEXICON—a. pres. act. subj. of ἐπιμένω (LN 68.11) (BAGD 2. p. 296): 'to remain in' [AB, BECNT, ICC2, LN, NICNT, NTC], 'to continue in' [BAGD, HNTC, WBC; KJV, NASB, NET, NIV, NRSV, TEV], 'to continue to hold on to' [GW], 'to continue following in' [NCV], 'to continue to trust in' [NLT], 'to keep on' [LN], 'to keep on trusting in'

[CEV], 'to remain within its scope' [REB]. This verb means to continue in an activity or state [LN].
- b. ἐπεί (BAGD 2. p. 284): 'otherwise' [HNTC, NICNT, NTC, WBC; CEV, GW, KJV, NASB, NET, NIV, NRSV, REB], 'for otherwise' [BECNT, ICC2]. The clause 'otherwise you also will be cut off' is translated 'if you do not, you will be cut off from the tree' [NCV], 'but if you stop trusting, you also will be cut off' [NLT], 'but if you do not, you too will be broken off' [TEV], 'for you too may be cut off' [AB].
- c. σύ: 'you'. This word is emphatic here [Gdt, ICC1, Mor]. It means 'you too as well as the Jews' [ICC1].
- d. fut. pass. indic. of ἐκκόπτω (LN 19.18) (BAGD 1. p. 241): 'to be cut off' [AB, BAGD, BECNT, ICC2, LN, NICNT, NTC, WBC; all versions except CEV, TEV], 'to be cut away' [HNTC; CEV], 'to be broken off' [TEV]. This verb means to cut in such a way as to cause separation [LN].

QUESTION—What does it mean to remain in his kindness?

It is relying humbly on God's kindness, as opposed to a proud self-sufficiency [Mor]. They persist in their faith as they recognize that it is the goodness of God that has given them their salvation [AB]. It means to stand in faith, as in 11:20, trusting in God and depending solely on his kindness in humble thanksgiving, as opposed to assuming God's grace to be a personal right [WBC]. There must be an ongoing relationship and continuing faith [NICNT]. Living in God's kindness and grace is living by faith [ICC2]. They must trust in God's goodness, not their own merits or favored position [ICC1]. They must not do anything that would cause them to forfeit God's favor [Ho]. They must continue to believe so that God will continue to be kind to them [TH]. Believers must continue in their enjoyment of the goodness God has granted them, with lowliness and especially perseverance in faith, apart from which there is no security [Mu]. They must continue in humble faith [Gdt].

QUESTION—What does he mean when he says 'you will be cut off'?

The verb continues the metaphor [SSA], and the passive form implies that God is the one who will cut them off [TH]. It means to be severed from God's people and eternally condemned [NICNT]. It means to face God's final judgment [BECNT], ultimate rejection [NTC].

11:23 And/but[a] those-also[b] if they- do-not -remain in unbelief, shall-be-grafted;[c] for God is able[d] to graft them again.[e]

LEXICON—a. δέ (LN 89.94, 89.124): 'and' [LN (89.94); KJV, NASB, NCV, NET, NIV, NLT, NRSV, TEV], 'whereas' [WBC; REB], 'but' [LN (89.124), NTC], 'on the other hand' [LN (89.124)], not explicit [CEV, GW]. This conjunction can mark contrast (89.124), or it can mark an additive relation, but with the possible implication of some contrast (LN 89.94).
- b. κἀκεῖνος (BAGD 1.b. p. 396): 'those also' [BAGD], 'those others' [AB], 'those other branches' [CEV], 'those' [BECNT, NICNT], 'they' [HNTC,

ICC2, NTC, WBC; NIV, REB], 'they also' [KJV, NASB], 'even they' [NET], 'Jewish people' [GW], 'the Jews' [NCV, TEV], 'even those of Israel' [NRSV], 'the people of Israel' [NLT]. This word marks an emphatic change of subject [NICNT].
- c. fut. pass. indic. of ἐγκεντρίζω (LN 43.10) (BAGD p. 216): 'to be grafted' [AB, BAGD, BECNT, HNTC, ICC2, LN, NICNT, NTC, WBC; GW, KJV, NASB, NET, NIV, NLT, NRSV, REB], 'to accept (them back)' [NCV], 'to be put back' [CEV, TEV]. This verb means to insert a shoot or bud into a growing plant [LN].
- d. δυνατός (LN 74.2) (BAGD 1.a.β. p. 208): 'able' [BAGD, BECNT, HNTC, ICC2, LN, NICNT, WBC; GW, KJV, NASB, NCV, NET, NIV, TEV], 'to have the power' [AB, NTC; CEV, NLT, NRSV]. The word 'able' is translated 'it is in God's power' [REB]. This adjective describes having the ability to perform some function [LN].
- e. πάλιν (LN 67.55) (BAGD 1.b. p. 606): 'again' [AB, BAGD, BECNT, HNTC, ICC2, LN, NICNT, NTC, WBC; GW, KJV, NASB, NET, NIV, NRSV, REB], 'back into the tree' [NLT], not explicit [CEV, NCV, TEV]. This adverb marks a subsequent point of time involving repetition [LN].

11:24 **For if you(sg) were-cut-off from a wild-olive-tree[a] according-to nature[b]**

LEXICON—a. ἀγριέλαιος (LN 3.11) (BAGD p. 13): 'wild olive tree' [BAGD, BECNT, ICC2, LN, NICNT, WBC; CEV, GW, NASB, NCV, NET, NLT, NRSV, TEV], 'olive tree (that is wild)' [AB, NTC; KJV, NIV], 'wild olive' [HNTC; REB]. This noun denotes a tree that is essentially different from the cultivated one [LN].
- b. φύσις (LN 58.8) (BAGD 1. p. 869): 'nature' [AB, BAGD, HNTC, LN, NICNT, NTC]. The prepositional phrase κατὰ φύσιν is translated 'natural' [BAGD, BECNT, WBC; CEV, NCV], 'native' [ICC2; REB], 'by nature' [NICNT, NTC; KJV, NASB, NET, NIV, NLT, NRSV], not specific [GW, TEV]. This noun denotes the nature of something as the result of its natural development or condition [LN].

QUESTION—What relationship is indicated by γάρ 'for'?
It introduces grounds for his statement that God is able to restore Jews who turn away from their unbelief [NICNT]. It introduces grounds for his statement that God actually will graft the Jews in again [Ho].

QUESTION—What relationship is indicated by εἰ 'if'?
It introduces a conditional sentence that is assumed to be true [Mor]: if, as is the case. It introduces grounds for the statement he will now make about the Jews being grafted back in again [SSA].

QUESTION—What does κατὰ φύσιν 'according to nature' describe?
1. 'According to nature' describes the wild olive tree to which you, the branch belong [AB, BECNT, HNTC, Mor, NTC, SSA, TH, WBC; KJV, NASB, NET, NIV, NRSV; probably GW, TEV which omit the phrase 'according to nature']: you, who were a branch of what is by nature a wild

olive tree. Since it is unnatural in English to speak of a tree being some kind of a tree by nature, it can be translated simply 'a wild olive tree' [TH].
2. 'According to nature' describes the way 'you', the cut-off branch, belong to the wild olive tree [ICC2, NICNT, NTC; NLT, REB]: you who are by nature branches of a wild olive. There is no point in saying that a wild olive tree is by nature a wild olive tree, since it can't be anything else. Rather, 'according to nature' describes the branch and means that the Gentile Christian is a branch that has been cut off from a tree he belongs to by nature (the wild olive tree) and has been grafted into a cultivated olive tree to which by nature he does not belong [ICC2]. The Gentile Christians, who belong to a wild olive tree by nature, have been cut off and grafted into the cultivated olive tree [NICNT].

and against[a] nature you-were-grafted into a cultivated-olive-tree,[b]
LEXICON—a. παρά with accusative object (LN 89.137) (BAGD II.2.b. p. 610): 'contrary to' [AB, BECNT, HNTC, LN, NTC; KJV, NASB, NET, NIV, NLT, NRSV, TEV], 'not in accordance' [LN]. The prepositional phrase παρὰ φύσιν is translated 'against nature' [NICNT; REB], 'unnaturally' [WBC], '(to which thou) by nature didst not belong' [ICC2], not specific [CEV, GW, NCV]. The position of this phrase in the sentence shows emphasis [Mor]. This preposition marks that which is contrary to what should be or to what is expected [LN].
  b. καλλιέλαιος (LN **3.10**) (BAGD p. 400): 'cultivated olive tree' [BECNT, ICC2, LN, NICNT, NTC, WBC; CEV, NASB, NET, NIV, NRSV, TEV], 'cultivated olive' [HNTC; REB], 'cultivated one' [AB; GW], 'good olive tree' [KJV, NCV], 'cultivated tree' [NLT]. This word is found only here in the NT.
QUESTION—What does παρὰ φύσιν 'against nature' describe?
  1. It describes Gentile Christians who, by their nature, don't naturally belong to the cultivated olive tree [Gdt, ICC2, NICNT, NTC, TH]. Grafting a branch onto a different kind of tree of any kind is contrary to the nature of the branch [ICC2, NAC]. Paul's point is that the restoration of the Jews will be easier than the call of the Gentiles to faith [AB].
  2. It describes the act of grafting such a branch into a cultivated olive tree [ICC1, Mor, Mu, TNTC, WBC], that it is contrary to nature [ICC1, Mor], or at least surprising [WBC]. By παρὰ φύσιν 'against nature' he means that grafting a wild olive branch into a cultivated olive tree was not normally done [ICC1]. Any form of grafting is contrary to nature [TNTC].

how-much more[a] these the according-to nature shall-be-grafted to their-own[b] olive-tree.
LEXICON—a. The phrase πόσῳ μᾶλλον 'how much more' [BECNT, ICC2, NICNT, NTC, WBC; KJV, NASB, NET, NRSV], is translated 'how much more readily' [AB; NIV, REB], 'so much more' [HNTC], '(so it is) much more (likely)' [CEV], 'so wouldn't it be much easier' [GW], '(it

will be) much easier' [TEV], 'far more (eager)' [NLT], not specific [NCV].

b. ἴδιος (LN 57.4) (BAGD 1.a.β. p. 369): 'one's own' [AB, BECNT, HNTC, ICC2, LN, NICNT, NTC, WBC; KJV, NASB, NCV, NET, NIV, NRSV, TEV], 'the (cultivated olive tree)' [CEV], '(the olive tree) they belong to' [GW], 'where they belong' [NLT], 'their native stock' [REB]. This adjective describes being the exclusive property of someone [LN].

QUESTION—What is being expressed by the phrase πόσῳ μᾶλλον 'how much more'?

It introduces a rhetorical question that expresses an emphatic statement [SSA]. It is a 'lesser to greater' argument [NICNT, WBC]; if God has made Gentiles to be the 'seed' of Abraham and heirs of the promise, how much easier would it be to do so with those who are naturally his descendants [WBC]. The re-grafting of Jews would be more probable than was his having called the Gentiles [Ho]. If God is able to graft Gentiles in contrary to their nature, he is much more able to do that for those who by nature belong to the tree [NICNT]. Restoring Israel to faith will be an easier thing than calling the Gentiles to faith [ICC1, NAC, St]. It is not so much a matter of something being easier, since God is omnipotent, as of it being more fitting [Mor]. His point is not that God is able to graft them in again, but that he is willing to do so [BECNT, Mu]. God is both able and willing to do this [ICC2]. God will much more readily graft them in [NTC]. The engrafting of Israel back in the tree is wholly consistent with God's purpose of grace [Mu]. The restoration of the Jews is not only possible, it is morally necessary [Gdt].

DISCOURSE UNIT—11:25–36 [ICC1, NAC; CEV, NIV, NLT, NRSV]. The topic is mercy to all the ultimate purpose of God [ICC1], the salvation of all Israel [NAC], the people of Israel will be brought back [CEV], all Israel will be saved [NIV, NRSV], God's mercy is for everyone [NLT].

DISCOURSE UNIT—11:25–32 [AB, HNTC, Ho, Mor, Mu, NICNT, NTC, WBC; TEV]. The topic is the mystery of Israel: they will all be saved [AB], God's plan complete [HNTC], restoration of Israel is the plan of God [Ho], the conversion of Israel [Mor], the fullness of the Gentiles and the restoration of Israel [Mu], the salvation of all Israel [NICNT], God's mercy on the fullness of the Gentiles and on all Israel [NTC], the final mystery revealed [WBC], God's mercy on all [TEV].

DISCOURSE UNIT—11:25–29 [TNTC]. The topic is the restoration of Israel.

11:25 For[a] I-want you(pl) not to-be-unaware,[b] brothers,[c] (of) this mystery[d], that you not be wise[e] to yourselves,[f]

LEXICON—a. γάρ (LN 89.23): 'for' [BECNT, HNTC, ICC2, LN, NICNT, NTC, WBC; KJV, NASB, NET], 'because' [LN], not explicit [AB; CEV, GW, NCV, NIV, NLT, NRSV, REB, TEV]. This conjunction marks cause or reason between events [LN].

b. pres. act. infin. of ἀγνοέω (LN 28.13, 32.7) (BAGD 1. p. 11): 'to be unaware' [AB, NTC, WBC], 'to not know' [BAGD, HNTC, LN (28.13)], 'to be ignorant of/about' [BAGD, BECNT, LN, NICNT; KJV, NET, NIV], 'to not understand, to fail to understand' [LN (32.7)], 'to be uninformed' [NASB], not explicit [CEV]. The phrase Οὐ θέλω ὑμᾶς ἀγνοεῖν 'I want you not to be unaware' is a litotes, which is the negating of an opposition (a kind of double negative). This litotes is expressed positively as 'I want you to know' [ICC2; TEV], 'I want you to understand' [GW, NCV, NLT, NRSV], 'I want to share (with you)' [REB]. This verb means to not have information about something [LN (28.13)], or to not understand something [LN (32.7)].

c. ἀδελφός (LN 11.23): 'fellow believer, Christian brother' [LN]. This plural noun is translated 'brothers' [AB, NTC, WBC; NIV, TEV], 'brothers and sisters' [BECNT, NICNT; GW, NCV, NET, NRSV], 'brethren' [HNTC, ICC2; KJV, NASB], 'my friends' [CEV, REB], 'dear friends' [NLT]. This noun denotes a close associate of a group of persons having a well-defined membership [LN].

d. μυστήριον (LN 28.77) (BAGD 2. p. 530): 'mystery' [AB, BAGD, BECNT, ICC2, LN, NICNT, NTC, WBC; CEV, GW, KJV, NASB, NET, NIV, NLT, NRSV], 'secret' [BAGD, HNTC, LN; NCV], 'divine secret' [REB], 'secret truth' [TEV]. This noun denotes the content of that which has not been known before but which has been revealed to an in-group or restricted constituency [LN].

e. φρόνιμος (LN 32.31) (BAGD p. 866): 'wise' [AB, BAGD, BECNT, HNTC, ICC2, LN, NICNT, WBC; KJV, NASB, REB, TEV], 'proud' [CEV, NLT], 'wiser (than you are)' [NRSV], not explicit [NCV]. The phrase 'wise to yourselves' is translated 'conceited' [NTC; NET, NIV], 'arrogant' [GW]. This adjective describes understanding resulting from insight and wisdom [LN].

f. The phrase παρ' ἑαυτοῖς 'to yourselves' is translated 'in yourselves' [BECNT], 'in your own estimation' [AB, NICNT, WBC; NASB], 'in your own conceit' [HNTC; KJV], 'in your own eyes' [ICC2]. The clause ἵνα μὴ ἦτε [παρ'] ἑαυτοῖς φρόνιμοι 'that you not be wise to yourselves' is translated 'so that you may not be conceited' [NTC; NET, NIV], 'I don't want you to be too proud of yourselves' [CEV], 'so you won't become arrogant' [GW], 'so you will understand that you do not know everything' [NCV], 'so that you will not feel proud about yourselves' [NLT], 'so that you may not claim to be wiser than you are' [NRSV], 'to keep you from thinking yourselves wise' [REB], '(it will keep you) from thinking how wise you are' [TEV].

QUESTION—What relationship is indicated by γάρ 'for'?

It indicates grounds, elaborated in 11:25–32, for his expectation expressed in 11:24 that the branches will be grafted in again [NICNT]. It connects what he will say in 11:25–32 with all of 11:11–24 [ICC2, NICNT, WBC]. It indicates grounds for what has said in 11:24 and previously, which is that all he has told them is not just conjecture, because he has been given revelation concerning this issue [Mor]. It indicates grounds for what he said in 11:24 about Israel being regrafted into the olive tree, and in 11:11 where he said that Israel had not stumbled permanently [BECNT]. It indicates grounds for what he has just said in the previous paragraph about the olive tree analogy [HNTC]: I gave you this analogy because I want you to know this divine secret so that you won't be wise in your own conceit.

QUESTION—What is the function of his statement 'I want you not to be unaware, brothers'?

It introduces something important to which he wants to draw attention [AB, BECNT, Gdt, Ho, ICC1, Mor, Mu, NAC, NICNT]. It gives extra weight to what follows [WBC], showing that he wants them to take this to heart [NTC]. It marks a new phase in his discussion, especially so with the use of the word 'brothers' [TH]. 'Brothers' makes it more familiar [NTC, WBC], and shows that he is not taking a position of superiority [Mor].

QUESTION—Whom is he primarily addressing here?

Paul now resumes his use of the plural 'you' in place of the singular [NTC, WBC].

1. He is primarily addressing the Gentile believers in Rome [AB, HNTC, ICC2, Mor, Mu, NICNT, NTC, SSA, WBC], although he is including Jewish readers as well [NTC, WBC].
2. He is addressing both Jewish and Gentile believers in Rome [St].

QUESTION—What is the meaning of the word 'mystery' in this context?

It is truth that cannot be known unless God reveals it [Gdt, HNTC, Ho, ICC2, Mor, Mu, NAC, NTC, TH, WBC]. It is a truth that God has not revealed previously [AB, BECNT, NAC, SSA, TH, TNTC]. It is something that has been openly revealed and should be made known publicly [NAC]. It is something that is now revealed in Christ and should be proclaimed to anyone willing to listen [ICC2]. Paul uses it here in the sense in which it is used in Jewish apocalyptic literature, where it describes something that God has pre-determined about the end of history and revealed to a prophet for the encouragement of his people [NICNT]. Paul uses the term here primarily to describe eschatological mystery about salvation history, how God will bring about salvation for his people in the end time [WBC]. It is a decision God made long ago and that he has now revealed concerning the salvation of all humanity [AB]. It is revealed so that all may understand [NAC].

QUESTION—What is the content of the mystery?

1. It is that all Israel will be saved [NAC, SSA].
2. It is that Israel has experienced a partial hardening [Gdt, Mor].
3. It is that although Israel has experienced a partial hardening, it will be saved [TNTC].
4. It is that all Israel will be saved *after* the Gentiles are brought in [BECNT, NICNT, WBC].
5. It is that Israel has experienced a partial hardening, which will last until the fullness of the Gentiles comes in [Mu].

6. The mystery involves three elements; that part of Israel is hardened, that they will be saved, but especially that it will happen after the Gentiles are brought in [BECNT]. The mystery involves three elements; that Israel has experienced a partial hardening, that it will end when all the Gentiles who will enter have come in, and that all Israel will be saved [HNTC, ICC2, St], which is the most important of the three [ICC2].
7. It is that Israel has experienced a partial insensibility, that Israel will be saved after the full number of Gentiles comes in, and that all humanity will be saved through the grace given through Christ [AB].
8. It is the whole plan of redemption whereby both Jews and Gentiles will be brought into God's kingdom, and toward which all things are now moving [ICC1].

QUESTION—What does he mean by being 'wise to yourselves'?

The phrase 'wise to yourselves' means 'wise in your own estimation', and here he is challenging them not to have an attitude of exclusiveness or ethnic pride relative to the Jews [NICNT]. They might either think they know God's plans for the Jews, or that they are more favored than the Jews [Mor, SSA]. It would be expressed in giving glory to themselves instead of God, who is infinitely glorious and wise [BECNT]. He is warning them against pride and presumption [WBC]. He did not want them to think that their part in salvation history was a result of their own merits [AB, ICC2], nor to think that their view of human history was the only valid one [AB]. He does not want them to think they have superior wisdom [ICC2], that they were wiser than the Jews because they accepted the gospel [HNTC]. He does not want the Gentile Christians in Rome to speculate or form strange ideas about Israel's place in salvation history [Gdt], or to vainly imagine that they know what the destiny of the Jews will be [Ho]. The antidote to pride is truth [NAC].

that a hardening[a] has-happened[b] in part[c] to Israel until[d] the fullness[e] of-the Gentiles comes-in,[f]

LEXICON—a. πώρωσις (LN 27.52) (BAGD p. 732): 'hardening' [AB, BAGD, BECNT, HNTC, ICC2, NICNT, NTC, WBC; NASB, NET, NIV, NRSV, REB], 'stubbornness' [**LN**; TEV], 'unwillingness to learn, mental stubbornness, closed mind' [LN], 'blindness' [KJV]. This noun is translated as a verb: 'to become stubborn' [CEV], 'to become closed' [GW], 'to be made stubborn' [NCV], 'to have hard hearts' [NLT].

b. perf. act. indic. of γίνομαι (LN 13.107): 'to happen' [LN; KJV, NASB, NET], 'to occur' [LN], 'to come upon' [AB, NTC; NRSV], 'to come on' [BECNT, NICNT; REB], 'to fall upon' [HNTC], 'to affect' [ICC2], 'to come over' [WBC], 'to experience' [NIV], 'been made (stubborn)' [NCV], 'to have (hard hearts)' [NLT], not explicit [CEV, TEV]. The phrase 'a hardening has happened in part' is translated 'the minds of some Israelites have become closed' [GW]. This verb means to happen, with the implication that what happens is different from a previous state [LN].

c. ἀπὸ μέρους (LN 63.15) (BAGD 1.c. p. 506): 'in part' [BAGD, LN, WBC; KJV, NIV]. This prepositional phrase is also translated as an adverb: '(has come) partially' [LN, NICNT]; as an adjective: 'partial (hardening)' [AB, BECNT, HNTC; NASB, NET, REB], '(the minds of) some (Israelites)' [GW], '(the stubbornness is) not permanent' [TEV]; as a noun or pronoun: 'part (of Israel)' [ICC2, NTC; NCV, NRSV], 'some (of them)' [CEV], 'some (of the people of Israel)' [NLT].

d. ἄχρις (LN 67.119) (BAGD 2.a. p. 129): 'until' [AB, BAGD, BECNT, HNTC, ICC2, LN, NICNT, NTC, WBC; all versions except NCV]. This word is translated by a clause: 'that will change when' [NCV]. This preposition marks the continuous extent of time up to a point [LN].

e. πλήρωμα (LN 59.32) (BAGD 3.a. p. 672): 'fullness' [BECNT, ICC2, LN, NICNT, NTC; KJV, NASB], 'complete number' [LN; CEV], 'full number' [AB, BAGD, HNTC, LN, WBC; NET, NIV, NLT, NRSV], 'all of' [GW], '(when) many' [NCV], 'in full strength' [REB], 'full measure' [LN]. This noun denotes a total quantity, with emphasis upon completeness [LN].

f. aorist act. subj. of εἰσέρχομαι (LN 15.93) (BAGD 2.a. p. 233): 'to come in/into' [AB, BAGD, BECNT, HNTC, ICC2, LN, NICNT, NTC, WBC; CEV, KJV, NASB, NET, NIV, NRSV], 'to enter' [LN], 'to be included' [GW], 'to come to God' [NCV, TEV], 'to come to Christ' [NLT], 'to be admitted' [REB]. This verb means to move into a space [LN].

QUESTION—What aspect of hardening does the phrase ἀπὸ μέρους 'in part' limit?

1. Part of Israel has been hardened [AB, BECNT, Gdt, HNTC, Ho, ICC2, Mor, Mu, NAC, NICNT, NTC, St, TNTC, WBC; CEV, GW, NCV, NLT, NRSV]. It is also limited in time in that it won't last indefinitely [BECNT, Ho, NAC, St].
2. Israel has been hardened for a limited period of time [TEV].

QUESTION—What is meant by 'the fullness of the Gentiles'?

1. It is a numerical completion, the full number of all those Gentiles that God has elected to save [AB, ICC1, ICC2, NICNT, NTC, SSA, TH; NIV, NRSV, TEV]. All those Gentiles who will come to faith in Christ [BECNT].
2. It is the fullness of blessing for the Gentiles, which is parallel to and corresponds to the idea of the fullness of blessing for Israel spoken of in 11:12 and 11:15 [Mu].

QUESTION—What is it that the Gentiles come into?

They come into the kingdom of God [ICC2, Mor, NICNT, TH], into the kingdom of Christ [ICC1], into the messianic salvation [NICNT], into life [ICC2], into the church [Gdt], into God's fold [NTC]. They come to God in the sense that they come to have faith in God [SSA, TH]. They enter into the people of God and thus experience salvation [BECNT]. Paul probably was repeating Jesus' use of this term to describe coming into the kingdom or into life, which in traditional Jewish belief was conceived of as Gentiles coming on pilgrimage to Jerusalem [WBC]. They will come into the community of salvation [AB].

11:26 and thus[a] all[b] Israel will-be-saved;[c]

LEXICON—a. οὕτως (LN 61.9) (BAGD 2. p. 598): 'thus' [LN; NASB], 'so' [AB, BECNT, LN, NTC, WBC; KJV, NET, NIV, NLT, NRSV], 'when this is done' [HNTC], 'then' [ICC2], 'in this way' [BAGD, NICNT; CEV, GW], 'that is how' [NCV], 'once that has happened' [REB], 'this is how' [TEV]. This adverb marks reference to that which precedes [LN]. Or, in the combination οὕτως...καθώς 'in this way...as (it is written)', οὕτως refers to the written words that follow [BAGD].

b. πᾶς (LN **59.23**) (BAGD 1.a.ε. p. 631): 'all' [AB, BAGD, BECNT, HNTC, ICC2, LN, NICNT, NTC, WBC; all versions except GW, REB], '(Israel) as a whole' [GW], 'the whole of' [REB]. This adjective describes the totality of any object, mass, collective, or extension [LN].

c. fut. pass. indic. of σῴζω (LN 21.27) (BAGD 2.b. p. 798): 'to be saved' [AB, BAGD, BECNT, HNTC, ICC2, LN, NICNT, NTC, WBC; all versions]. This verb means to cause someone to experience divine salvation [LN].

QUESTION—Should this clause be seen as the ending of 11:25 or the beginning of 11:26?

1. It begins the thought of 11:26 [BECNT, ICC1, NICNT, NTC, SSA; CEV, GW, KJV, NCV, NET, NIV, NLT, NRSV, TEV]. However, the οὕτως 'thus' indicates a close connection with 11:25b [NICNT].
2. It completes the thought of 11:25b [AB, GNT, HNTC, ICC2, WBC; NASB, REB].

QUESTION—What relationship is indicated by οὕτως 'thus'?

1. It indicates a similarity of manner [BECNT, ICC2, NAC, NICNT, NTC, TNTC, WBC], which is consistent with the process he has been describing in 11:11–24, a process that unfolds in stages [NICNT]. The manner in which ethnic Israel is to be saved is that they experience salvation after the fullness of the Gentiles has come in [BECNT, ICC2, TNTC].
2. It indicates the consequence of a process [AB, Gdt, ICC1, Mor, TH]. Israel's salvation is the end result of a process he has been describing [Mor]. It will happen not only *when* the Gentiles come in, but also *because* they come in [AB]. Israel will be saved by the coming of the Gentile world into the kingdom, which rouses the Jews to jealousy [ICC1]. When the Gentile nations turn to God, the Jewish people will be prompted to turn to God also [TH]. Israel will be saved by means of the Gentiles coming into the church [Gdt].
3. It has a temporal meaning [HNTC, SSA]: after this happens, Israel will be saved.
4. It indicates that Israel will be saved just as it is written [BAGD].

QUESTION—To whom does the term 'all Israel' refer?
1. It refers to ethnic Israel in a collective sense, though that does not necessarily mean *every* Jewish person [AB, BECNT, Ho, ICC1, ICC2, Mor, Mu, NAC, NICNT, SSA, St, TNTC, WBC]. The Jewish nation as a whole will turn to God [TH]. 'All' is used hyperbolically [SSA].
   1.1 There will be a great ingathering or restoration at the end of history [BECNT, ICC1, ICC2, NAC]. At some point in the future Israel and the kingdoms of the Gentiles will all be united in the church of God [ICC1].
   1.2 It refers to *all* Israel throughout all time, though not necessarily including every single Israelite [AB].
2. It refers to all the collective elect of Israel throughout all time [NTC].

QUESTION—When will this event occur?
1. It will occur at the end of history [BECNT, ICC2, NAC, NICNT, TNTC, WBC].
2. Paul does not say when it will occur, but he is not necessarily speaking of the second coming of Christ [AB].

just-as it-is-written, The delivering-one[a] will come out-of[b] Zion,[c] he-will-remove[d] ungodliness[e] from Jacob;

LEXICON—a. pres. mid. or pass. (deponent = act.) participle of ῥύομαι (LN 21.23) (BAGD p. 737): 'to deliver' [BAGD, LN]. This participle is translated as a noun: 'the deliverer' [AB, BAGD, BECNT, HNTC, ICC2, NICNT, NTC, WBC; KJV, NASB, NET, NIV, NRSV, REB], 'the Savior' [GW, NCV, TEV], 'the one who rescues' [NLT]. It is translated as a phrase: 'someone will come to rescue us' [CEV]. This verb means to rescue from danger, with the implication that the danger in question is severe and acute [LN].

b. ἐκ (LN 89.3): 'out of' [HNTC, ICC2, NTC, WBC; KJV, NET, NRSV], 'from' [AB, BECNT, LN, NICNT; CEV, GW, NASB, NCV, NIV, NLT, REB, TEV]. This preposition marks the source from which someone or something is physically or psychologically derived [LN].

c. Σιών (LN 93.582) (BAGD 2.b. p. 752): 'Zion' [AB, BAGD, BECNT, HNTC, ICC2, LN, NICNT, NTC, WBC; all versions except NCV, NLT], 'Jerusalem' [NCV, NLT]. This noun denotes Mount Zion, a hill within the city of Jerusalem [LN]. In poetic usage, Zion stands for the city of Jerusalem, and, more generally, for the people of Israel [BAGD].

d. fut. act. indic. of ἀποστρέφω (LN **13.63**) (BAGD 1.a.β. p. 100): 'to remove' [BAGD, HNTC, LN; GW, NASB, NET, REB, TEV], 'to turn away' [AB, ICC2, NICNT, NTC, WBC; KJV, NIV, NLT], 'to turn back' [BECNT], 'to take away' [NCV], 'to banish' [NRSV], not explicit [CEV]. The phrase 'he will remove ungodliness from Jacob' is translated 'he will turn Israel away from ungodliness' [NLT], 'then Jacob's descendants will stop being evil' [CEV]. This verb means to cause something to turn into or to become something else [LN].

e. ἀσέβεια (LN 53.10) (BAGD p. 114): 'ungodliness' [BAGD, BECNT, NICNT, WBC; KJV, NASB, NET, NLT, NRSV], 'godlessness' [AB, BAGD, LN, NTC; GW, NIV], 'impiety' [BAGD, HNTC], 'iniquity' [ICC2], 'all evil' [NCV], 'wickedness' [REB, TEV], not explicit [CEV]. This plural noun is translated as plural: 'iniquities' [ICC2], 'impieties' [HNTC]. This noun denotes living in a manner contrary to proper religious beliefs and practice [LN].

QUESTION—What does it mean that the deliverer 'will come out of Zion'?
1. 'Zion' refers to heaven, from whence Christ will come at his second coming [BECNT, ICC2, NICNT, WBC].
2. It means that he originates from the Jewish people [AB, Mu, NTC, SSA].

QUESTION—Does this mean he will remove guilt or change how they live?
1. He will change how they live [AB, BECNT, ICC2, Mor, Mu, NTC, WBC]. He will remove their sins, [Mor, WBC], their unbelief [BECNT], their impiety [WBC], their godlessness [AB, NTC], their ungodliness [Ho, ICC2, Mu].
2. He will remove their guilt [SSA], granting forgiveness of sins [NICNT, TH].

QUESTION—What is meant by the name 'Jacob'?
The name Jacob is used figuratively for Jacob's descendants, and this came to signify the nation of Israel [BAGD (1. p. 367)], all of the Jewish people [SSA]. Some translate 'Jacob' as 'the descendants of Jacob' [TEV], 'Jacob's descendants' [CEV], 'the family of Jacob' [NCV], 'Israel' [NLT].

11:27 **and this (will be)[a] the covenant[b] with me to-them, when[c] I-take-away[d] their sins.[e]**

LEXICON—a. There is no lexical entry for the words 'will be' in the Greek text, since the verb 'to be' is often left out and is implied. This is represented in translation as 'will be' [BECNT, WBC], 'is' [AB, HNTC, ICC2, NICNT, NTC; CEV, KJV, NASB, NET, NIV, NLT, NRSV, REB], 'will be (fulfilled)' [GW]. The phrase 'this (will be) the covenant' is translated 'I will make this agreement/covenant' [NCV, TEV].

b. διαθήκη (LN **34.43**) (BAGD 2. p. 183): 'covenant' [AB, BAGD, BECNT, HNTC, ICC2, **LN**, NICNT, NTC, WBC; KJV, NASB, NET, NIV, NLT, NRSV, REB, TEV], 'promise' [GW], 'agreement' [NCV], 'the making of a covenant' [LN]. The phrase αὐτοῖς ἡ παρ' ἐμοῦ διαθήκη 'the covenant with me to them' is translated 'my covenant with them' [AB, BECNT, NICNT, NTC, WBC; KJV, NASB, NET, NIV, NLT, NRSV], 'the covenant I will make with them' [HNTC, ICC2], 'my promise to them' [GW]. The first clause in this verse is translated 'this is what the Lord has promised to do' [CEV], 'this is the covenant I will grant them' [REB], 'I will make this agreement with those people' [NCV], 'I will make this covenant with them' [TEV]. This noun denotes a solemn agreement involving reciprocal benefits and responsibilities [LN].

c. ὅταν (LN 67.31): 'when' [AB, HNTC, ICC2, LN, NICNT, WBC; all versions except NLT], 'whenever' [BECNT, LN, NTC], 'that' [NLT]. This conjunction marks an indefinite point or points of time, which may be roughly simultaneous to or overlap with another point of time [LN].

d. aorist mid. subj. of ἀφαιρέω (LN 68.47) (BAGD 3. p. 124): 'to take away' [AB, BAGD, BECNT, HNTC, ICC2, LN, NTC, WBC; all versions except CEV], 'to remove' [NICNT], 'to forgive' [CEV]. This verb means to cause to cease [LN].

e. ἁμαρτία (LN 88.310): 'sin' [AB, BECNT, HNTC, ICC2, LN, NICNT, NTC, WBC; all versions], 'guilt' [LN]. This noun denotes the moral consequence of having sinned [LN].

QUESTION—What is the referent of the demonstrative pronoun αὕτη 'this'?
1. It refers to what follows, which is the forgiving or removal of their sins [HNTC, Ho, ICC2, SSA; NLT].
2. It refers to what he has just said; when God removes their sins from them it will be a sign of his fulfilling his part of the new covenant, as expressed in the scripture cited in the first half of the verse [ICC1, NAC; probably AB].
3. It refers to what he has just said as well as to what follows; God's covenant with them consists of his rescuing them from their impieties and removing their sins once and for all [Gdt, Mu, NTC, WBC; probably St]. When Israel's sin is pardoned, God will renew with them his broken covenant [Gdt]. The deliverer will bring Israel to repentance and so to forgiveness, according to God's covenant promise [St].

QUESTION—What covenant does this refer to?
1. It is a fulfilling of the prophecy of the new covenant in Jer. 31:31–34 [AB, HNTC, ICC2, NAC, NTC, St, TNTC]. It is the aspect of the new covenant in Jer. 31:34 that focuses on the removing of sin [HNTC, Mor].
2. It is a fulfilling of his covenant promises to Abraham [NICNT].
3. It is the covenant given at Sinai being renewed at a deeper and more effective level [WBC].

QUESTION—What relationship is indicated by ὅταν 'when'?
1. It introduces the content of the covenant, which is that God will forgive their sins [Ho, ICC2, SSA; NLT].
2. It is temporal, referring to a time when this covenant will be put into effect [AB, Mor, NAC, NICNT, NTC; all versions except NLT], or renewed in its effect [WBC].

11:28 With-regard-to[a] the gospel[b] (they are) enemies[c] for-the-sake-of[d] you(pl),

LEXICON—a. κατά with accusative object (LN 89.4) (BAGD II.6. p. 407): 'with regard to' [LN, WBC], 'in regard to' [NET], 'in relation to' [BAGD, LN], 'as regards' [ICC2; NRSV], 'as far as (the gospel) is concerned', [AB, NTC; NIV], 'according to' [BECNT, NICNT], 'as far as (the immediate results of the preaching of)' [HNTC], 'as concerning' [KJV],

'from the standpoint of' [NASB], 'judged by their response to' [REB], 'because (they reject)' [TEV], not explicit [CEV, GW, NCV, NLT]. This preposition marks a specific element bearing a relation to something else [LN].
  b. εὐαγγέλιον (LN 33.217) (BAGD 1.a. p. 318): 'the gospel' [AB, BECNT, HNTC, ICC2, LN, NICNT, NTC, WBC; KJV, NASB, NET, NIV, NRSV, REB], 'the good news' [BAGD, LN; CEV, GW, NCV, NLT, TEV]. This noun denotes the content of good news, referring in the NT to the gospel about Jesus [LN].
  c. ἐχθρός (LN 39.11) (BAGD 1. p. 331): 'enemy' [AB, BECNT, HNTC, ICC2, LN, NICNT, NTC, WBC; all versions], 'being in opposition to' [LN], 'hated' [BAGD]. This noun denotes one who is at enmity with someone [LN].
  d. διά with accusative object (LN 90.44): 'for the sake of' [AB, BECNT, ICC2, LN (90.38), NTC; KJV, NASB, NET, NRSV, REB, TEV], 'for, on behalf of, for the benefit of' [LN (90.38), NICNT], 'because of' [LN, WBC; GW], 'on account of' [LN], 'on your account' [NIV], 'for the advantage' [HNTC], not explicit [CEV, NCV]. The prepositional phrase δι' ὑμᾶς 'for the sake of you' is translated as a clause: 'and this benefits you Gentiles' [NLT]. This preposition marks a participant constituting the cause or reason for an event or state [LN].

QUESTION—To what does the word εὐαγγέλιον 'gospel' refer?
  1. It refers to the advance of the message, the growth of the Christian faith [Ho, ICC2].
  2. It includes both the advance of the message, as well as its content [BECNT].
  3. It refers to the current phase of salvation history in which God reaches out to include the Gentiles in the present moment, and which corresponds to his election of the Jews in times past [WBC].
  4. It refers to the immediate result of the preaching of the gospel, which is that the Jews rejected it [HNTC].
  5. It refers to the gospel order, the principles by which God has brought the gospel into the world [ICC1].

QUESTION—Is the word 'enemies' used in an active sense, describing someone who is opposing or hating, or in a passive sense, describing those who are opposed or hated?
  1. It is passive; they are those whom God opposes or treats as enemies [BECNT, Gdt, HNTC, Ho, ICC1, ICC2, Mor, Mu, NAC, SSA, St; CEV, NCV, NRSV, REB, TEV]. They are objects of God's wrath [Gdt]. They have put themselves under the wrath of God by having rejected the gospel [HNTC, ICC2]. They are under judgment [St]. Now they are aliens from their own covenants of promise [Ho]. The word 'enemies' is parallel to 'beloved' so that both refer to how God is related to them [BECNT, Ho, Mor, Mu]. They also oppose God, but that sense is secondary here [BECNT].

2. It is active; they have put themselves in a position of enmity with God and opposition to him [AB].
3. It is active; they are enemies of the good news [NLT].
4. It has both the active and passive sense [NICNT, WBC]. Paul has used words such as 'hated', 'hardened', and 'rejected' to describe God's actions toward them, and words such as 'disobedient', 'unbelieving', and 'stubborn' to describe their attitude toward God [NICNT]. With regard to the parallelism with 'beloved', we must recognize that Paul may use a parallelism of form without necessarily implying an exact parallelism in meaning [NICNT, WBC].

QUESTION—What relationship is indicated by διά 'for the sake of'?

It indicates that the Gentiles gain benefit from the enmity between Israel and God [AB, BECNT, ICC1, ICC2, NICNT, SSA, TH, TNTC, WBC]. The Gentiles benefited when the Jews rejected the gospel [BECNT, Mor, WBC]. The Gentiles needed to have the gospel offered as free grace so they could see it as a gift of forgiveness offered to an enemy, and not as the gospel of the Jews defined in terms of ethnicity; the Jews on the other hand needed to experience what it means to stand outside the gospel for a time so they could discover its character of free grace for all people [WBC].

but with-regard-to[a] election[b] (they are) beloved[c] for-the-sake-of[d] the fathers;[e]

LEXICON—a. κατά with accusative object (LN 89.4) (BAGD II.6. p. 407): 'with regard to' [LN, WBC], 'in regard to' [NET], 'as regards' [ICC2; NRSV], 'in relation to' [BAGD, LN], 'as far as (election) is concerned' [AB, NTC; NIV], 'according to' [BECNT, NICNT], 'when you bear in mind' [HNTC], 'as touching' [KJV], 'from the standpoint of' [NASB], 'judged by' [REB], 'because of' [TEV], not explicit [CEV, GW, NCV, NLT]. This preposition marks a specific element bearing a relation to something else [LN].

b. ἐκλογή (LN **30.92**) (BAGD 1. p. 243): 'election' [AB, BAGD, BECNT, HNTC, ICC2, NICNT, NTC, WBC; KJV, NET, NIV, NRSV], 'the chosen ones' [CEV], 'God's choice' [LN; GW, NASB, TEV], 'God's chosen people' [NCV], 'his choice' [REB]. This noun is also translated with the actor or recipient of the election specified: 'God's/his choice' [LN; GW, NASB, REB, TEV], 'the chosen ones' [CEV], 'God's chosen people' [NCV], 'he chose their ancestors' [NLT]. The phrase 'with regard to election' is translated 'because he chose their ancestors' [NLT]. This noun denotes a special choice based upon significant preference, often implying a strongly favorable attitude toward what is chosen [LN].

c. ἀγαπητός (LN 25.45) (BAGD 2. p. 6): 'beloved' [AB, BAGD, BECNT, HNTC, ICC2, LN, NICNT, NTC, WBC; KJV, NASB, NRSV], 'dear' [LN; REB], not explicit [NLT]. The word 'beloved' is translated 'God loves them' [CEV], 'he loves them' [NCV], 'they are his friends' [TEV],

'they are loved' [GW, NIV], 'they are dearly loved' [NET], 'they are still the people he loves' [NLT]. This noun denotes one who is loved [LN].
- d. διά with accusative object (LN 90.38, 90.44): 'for the sake of' [ICC2, LN (90.38), NTC, WBC; KJV, NASB, NET, NRSV, REB], 'for, on behalf of, for the benefit of' [LN (90.38)], 'because of' [AB, BECNT, NICNT; CEV, GW, TEV], 'on account of' [HNTC, LN (90.44); NIV]. The phrase διὰ τοὺς πατέρας 'for the sake of the fathers' is translated 'because of the promises he made to their ancestors' [NCV], 'because he chose their ancestors Abraham, Isaac, and Jacob' [NLT]. This preposition marks a participant who is benefited by an event or for whom an event occurs [LN (90.38)], or a participant constituting the cause or reason for an event or state [LN (90.44)].
- e. πατήρ (LN 10.20): 'ancestor' [LN; CEV, GW, NRSV, TEV], 'forefather' [LN]. This plural noun is translated 'the fathers' [BECNT, HNTC, ICC2, NICNT, NTC, WBC; KJV, NASB, NCV, NET], 'the patriarchs' [AB; NIV, REB], 'their ancestors' [GW, NRSV, TEV], 'their famous ancestors' [CEV], 'Abraham, Isaac, and Jacob' [NLT]. This noun denotes a person several preceding generations removed from the reference person [LN].

QUESTION—What relationship is indicated by διά 'for the sake of'?

It has a causal sense [AB, ICC2, NICNT]: they are loved because of the patriarchs. They are loved because of the promises God made to the patriarchs [BECNT, SSA, TH, WBC], not because of any merits on the part of the patriarchs [BECNT, WBC]. They are loved for the sake of the fathers [ICC1].

QUESTION—What is the election of which Paul speaks here?

It is the election of the nation of Israel [AB, Gdt, HNTC, Ho, ICC1, ICC2, Mor, Mu, NICNT, SSA, WBC], to which he refers in 11:1–2 [NICNT], and which refers not to salvation for each one, but blessing for the nation as a whole [Mor, NICNT, SSA].

11:29 for[a] irrevocable[b] (are) the gifts[c] and the calling[d] of-God.

LEXICON—a. γάρ (LN 89.23): 'for' [AB, BECNT, HNTC, ICC2, LN, NICNT, NTC, WBC; KJV, NASB, NET, NIV, NLT, NRSV, REB, TEV], 'because' [LN], not explicit [CEV, GW, NCV]. This conjunction marks cause or reason between events [LN].
- b. ἀμεταμέλητος (LN 25.271) (BAGD 1. p. 45): 'irrevocable' [AB, BECNT, ICC2, NICNT, NTC, WBC; NASB, NET, NIV, NRSV, REB], 'without repentance' [KJV], 'without regret' [BAGD]. This adjective is translated as a verb: '(God does not) go back on' [HNTC], '(God doesn't) take back' [CEV], '(God never) changes His mind' [GW, NCV], '(God does not) change his mind' [TEV], '(God's gifts and his call) can never be withdrawn' [NLT]. This word comes first in the sentence for emphasis [ICC2, NAC, WBC]. This adjective describes not feeling regret as the result of what one has done [LN].

c. χάρισμα (LN 57.103) (BAGD 1. p. 878): 'gift' [AB, BAGD, BECNT, ICC2, LN, NICNT, WBC; CEV, GW, KJV, NASB, NET, NIV, NLT, NRSV], 'gracious gift' [LN, NTC; REB], 'act of grace' [HNTC]. This noun is translated as a phrase: 'the things he gives (them)' [NCV], '(whom he) blesses' [TEV]. This noun denotes that which is given freely and generously [LN].
   d. κλῆσις (LN 33.313) (BAGD 1. p. 435): 'calling' [BAGD, BECNT, HNTC, LN, NTC; KJV, NASB, NRSV, REB], 'call' [AB, BAGD, ICC2, NICNT, WBC; NET, NIV, NLT]. This noun is translated as a phrase: 'the people he calls' [NCV], '(the people he has) chosen' [CEV], '(when he) calls someone' [GW], '(whom he) chooses' [TEV]. This noun denotes the state of having been called to a particular task and/or relation [LN].

QUESTION—What relationship is indicated by γάρ 'for'?

It indicates the grounds for what has just been said [BECNT, ICC1, Mor, NICNT], which is that God does not change his mind after he has issued a call or given a gift [Mor]. It indicates grounds for what was said in the last part of 11:28, which is that the Jews are still loved by God because his gifts and call are irrevocable [NICNT]. It indicates justification for what has just been said in the last part of 11:28, which is that God's having chosen them is still valid [SSA].

QUESTION—What are the gifts and calling that are irrevocable?

1. The gifts are all the privileges of Israel summarized in 9:4–5 [BECNT, ICC1, ICC2, Mor, Mu, NICNT, SSA, St, WBC]. The calling is their election by God [Ho, NICNT], by which they became the beloved [NICNT], by which they became his special people and to fulfill his purposes in history [ICC2]. It is the calling to the kingdom [ICC1]. God calls both people and nations, and he commissions them to function in certain tasks [Mor]. The call is God's summons of Abraham, which eventually came to be God's election of Israel to be his chosen people [AB]. The calling is God's effectual calling of Abraham and Israel to salvation [BECNT].
2. The Jews are gifted with regard to understanding divine truth, and the calling is his call to them to use those gifts to show the world the way of salvation [Gdt].
3. The call is the effectual call to believe in Christ, and the gifts are such products of God's grace as faith, hope, love, peace, and everlasting life, things which are experienced only by God's elect [NTC].

DISCOURSE UNIT—11:30–36 [TNTC]. The topic is God's purpose for the world.

11:30 **For^a just-as^b you(pl) once^c were-disobedient^d to-God,**

LEXICON—a. γάρ (LN 89.23): 'for' [AB, BECNT, HNTC, ICC2, LN, NICNT, NTC, WBC; KJV, NASB], not explicit [CEV, GW, NCV, NET, NIV, NLT, NRSV, REB, TEV]. This conjunction marks cause or reason between events [LN].

b. ὥσπερ (LN 64.13): 'just as' [BECNT, LN, NICNT, NTC, WBC; NASB, NET, NIV, NRSV, REB], 'as' [AB, HNTC, ICC2, LN; KJV, TEV], not explicit [CEV, GW, NCV, NLT]. This conjunction marks similarity between events and states [LN].
c. ποτέ (BAGD 1. p. 695): 'once' [AB, BAGD, ICC2, WBC; NASB, NLT, NRSV], 'formerly' [BAGD, BECNT, HNTC; NET, REB], 'at one time' [NICNT, NTC; CEV, NCV, NIV], 'in the past' [GW, TEV], 'in times past' [KJV].
d. aorist act. indic. of ἀπειθέω (LN 36.23) (BAGD 1. p. 82): 'to disobey' [AB, BAGD, BECNT, HNTC, ICC2, LN, NICNT, NTC, WBC; GW, NASB, NET, NIV, NRSV, REB, TEV], 'to reject God' [CEV], 'to refuse to obey' [NCV], 'to be rebels (against)' [NLT], 'to not believe' [KJV]. This verb means to refuse to comply with the demands of some authority [LN].

QUESTION—What relationship is indicated by γάρ 'for'?
1. It is explanatory [BECNT, ICC2]. It indicates an explanation and summary restatement of what he has said in 11:11–29 [BECNT]. It indicates an explanation of what he has said in 11:28–29 [ICC2].
2. It indicates grounds for his statement in 11:29 [ICC1].
3. It indicates a repeating and confirmation of his statement in 11:29 [Ho].

QUESTION—What relationship is indicated by ὥσπερ 'just as'?
It introduces the first element of a formal parallelism in which he describes the similarity of God's merciful treatment of the Gentiles and the Jews, the second element of which is introduced by οὕτως καί 'thus also' in 11:31 [ICC2, NICNT, WBC].

but[a] now[b] you(pl)-received-mercy[c] (by)[d] the disobedience[e] of-those,

LEXICON—a. δέ (LN 89.124, 89.94): 'but' [AB, BECNT, HNTC, ICC2, LN (89.124), NTC, WBC; CEV, GW, NASB, NCV, NET, NLT, NRSV, REB, TEV], 'and' [LN (89.94), NICNT], 'yet' [KJV], not explicit [NIV]. This conjunction can mark contrast [LN (89.124)], or an additive relation, with the possible implication of some contrast [LN (89.94)].
b. νῦν (LN 67.38) (BAGD 1.c. p. 545): 'now' [AB, BAGD, BECNT, HNTC, ICC2, LN, NICNT, NTC, WBC; all versions except NLT], 'when' [NLT]. This adverb marks a point of time simultaneous with the event of the discourse itself [LN].
c. aorist pass. indic. of ἐλεέω (LN 88.76) (BAGD p. 249): 'to have received mercy' [BAGD, HNTC, ICC2, NICNT, NTC, WBC; NCV, NET, NIV, NRSV, REB, TEV], 'to have been shown mercy' [AB, BAGD, BECNT, LN; CEV, NASB], 'to have obtained mercy' [KJV], 'to be merciful' [GW, NLT]. This verb means to show kindness or concern for someone in serious need [LN].
d. There is no lexical entry for this word in the Greek text, the grammatical relation being indicated in Greek by the dative case of the noun ἀπείθεια 'disobedience'. The phrase τῇ τούτων ἀπειθείᾳ '(by) the disobedience of

those' is translated 'by their disobedience' [ICC2, WBC], 'through their unbelief' [KJV], 'due to their disobedience' [NET], 'because of their disobedience' [NICNT; NASB, NRSV, REB], 'because of the disobedience of these' [BECNT], 'because of the disobedience of the Jewish people' [GW], 'because the Jews were disobedient' [TEV], 'because those people refused to obey' [NCV], 'as a result of their disobedience' [AB, NTC; NIV], 'corresponding to their disobedience' [HNTC], 'Israel has rejected God, (and you have been shown mercy)' [CEV], 'when the people of Israel rebelled against him, (God was merciful to you instead)' [NLT].

e. ἀπείθεια (LN 36.23, 31.107) (BAGD p. 82): 'disobedience' [AB, BAGD, BECNT, HNTC, ICC2, LN (36.23), NICNT, NTC, WBC; GW, NASB, NET, NIV, NRSV, REB], 'unbelief' [KJV], 'rejection of the Christian message' [LN]. This noun is translated as a verb: 'to be disobedient' [TEV], 'to reject God' [CEV], 'to refuse to obey' [NCV], 'to rebel against' [NLT]. This noun denotes unwillingness or refusal to comply with the demands of some authority [LN (36.23)], or refusal to believe the Christian message [LN (31.107)].

QUESTION—What is implied in his use of the temporal adverb νῦν 'now'?

It signals a shift from the old era of salvation history to the new era [NICNT, WBC], one in which salvation is now open to all who believe, whether Jew or Gentile [NICNT]. It sets up a contrast with the pre-Christian state of the Roman believers [Mor].

QUESTION—What relationship is indicated by the dative case of ἀπείθεια 'disobedience'?

1. It is causal, indicating the reason why God was merciful to them [BECNT, Ho, Mor, NICNT, SSA, St, TH; GW, NASB, NCV, NET, NIV, NRSV, REB, TEV]. The disobedience of the Jews prompted the spread of the gospel to the Gentiles [BECNT, Mor]. Israel's disobedience was the occasion of God's mercy that came to the Gentiles as a result [AB, Ho].
2. It is instrumental, indicating the means by which the gospel was spread to the Gentiles [Gdt, WBC; KJV]. It indicates a temporal element as well as instrumentality, but behind all that is also the sovereign activity of God [HNTC].

QUESTION—How is it that the disobedience of the Jews caused the Gentiles to receive mercy?

When the Jews rejected the gospel, as they usually did when Paul preached, he turned to the Gentiles, who were much more receptive [NICNT]. When Jews rejected the gospel it was preached to Gentiles [Mor].

11:31 thus[a] also these now disobeyed,[b] (for/by)[c] the mercy[d] for-you, so-that also they-themselves now might-receive-mercy.[e]

TEXT—The second occurrence of the word νῦν 'now' in this verse does not occur in some manuscripts. It is included by GNT with a C rating, indicating difficulty in deciding whether or not to place it in the text. It is omitted or not translated by WBC; CEV, GW, KJV, NCV, NET, NLT.

LEXICON—a. οὕτως (LN 61.9): 'thus' [BECNT, LN], 'so' [AB, HNTC, ICC2, LN, NICNT, NTC, WBC; KJV, NASB, NET, NIV, NRSV, REB], 'in the same way' [GW, TEV], not explicit [CEV, NCV, NLT]. This adverb marks a reference to that which precedes [LN].

b. aorist act. indic. of ἀπειθέω (LN 36.23) (BAGD 2. p. 82): 'to disobey' [LN (36.23); GW, TEV], 'to reject the Christian message, to refuse to believe' [LN (31.107)], 'to refuse to obey' [NCV], 'to be the rebels' [NLT], not explicit [CEV]. This aorist tense is translated as a perfect tense: 'have become disobedient' [AB, BECNT, HNTC, ICC2, NTC; NIV], 'have disobeyed' [NICNT], 'have (now) been disobedient' [WBC; NASB, NET, NRSV], 'they have proved disobedient' [REB], 'have (these also now) not believed' [KJV]. This verb means to refuse to comply with the demands of some authority [LN].

c. There is no lexical entry for this word in the Greek text, the grammatical relation being indicated in Greek by the dative case of the noun ἔλεος 'mercy'. For an explanation of the meaning of this dative case relation see the question below.

d. ἔλεος (LN 88.76) (BAGD 2. b. p. 250): 'mercy' [AB, BECNT, HNTC, ICC2, LN, NICNT, NTC, WBC; all versions except GW], '(he was) merciful' [GW]. This noun denotes compassion and concern for someone in difficulty, despite that person's having committed a moral offense [LN].

e. aorist pass. subj. of ἐλεέω (LN 88.76) (BAGD p. 249): 'to receive mercy' [HNTC, ICC2, NICNT, NTC, WBC; NCV, NET, NIV, NRSV, REB, TEV], 'to be shown mercy' [AB, BECNT, LN; CEV, NASB], 'to obtain mercy' [KJV], 'to share in (God's) mercy' [NLT], 'to be merciful' [GW]. This verb means to show kindness or concern for someone in serious need [LN].

QUESTION—What relationship is indicated by the phrase οὕτως καὶ 'thus also'?

It introduces the second element of a formal parallelism in which he describes the similarity of God's merciful treatment of the Gentiles and the Jews, the first element of which is introduced by ὥσπερ 'just as' in 11:30 [ICC2, NICNT, WBC]. In a tight and clever way of treating the disobedience of Jews and Gentiles and the grace shown to each in the two verses in a somewhat artificial formulation of rhythm of clause and phrase, a degree of ambiguity is obtained [ICC2].

QUESTION—What is meant by the phrase τῷ ὑμετέρῳ ἐλέει 'the mercy for you' and how is it connected to the rest of the sentence?

1. It goes with the following verb, ἐλεηθῶσιν 'might receive mercy', and expresses cause or instrument [AB, Gdt, Ho, ICC1, ICC2, Mor, Mu, NTC, SSA; GW, KJV, NASB, NET, NIV, NLT, NRSV]: so that because of the mercy shown to you Gentiles, the Jews now may receive mercy. The

phrase belongs to the purpose clause following but precedes the ἵνα 'so that' for emphasis [Gdt, Ho, ICC2]. A parallelism of elements exists between 11:30 and 11:31, as well as between the two clauses of each verse [ICC1, ICC2]: you once disobeyed, and have now received mercy through their disobedience; they now disobey so they might receive mercy through your receiving mercy. This verse is translated 'even so have these also now not believed, that through your mercy they may obtain mercy' [KJV], 'in the same way, the Jewish people have also disobeyed so that God may be merciful to them as he was to you' [GW], 'so these also now have been disobedient, that because of the mercy shown to you they also may now be shown mercy' [NASB], '(now Israel has rejected God)…and because of the mercy shown to you, they will also be shown mercy' [CEV], 'so that they too have now been disobedient in order that, by the mercy shown to you, they too may now receive mercy' [NET], 'so they too have now become disobedient in order that they too may now receive mercy as a result of God's mercy to you' [NIV], 'so they have now been disobedient in order that, by the mercy shown to you, they too may now receive mercy' [NRSV], 'now they are the rebels, and God's mercy has come to you so that they, too, will share in God's mercy' [NLT].

2. It goes with the preceding verb ἠπείθησαν 'they disobeyed' [BECNT, HNTC, NICNT, WBC; NCV, REB, TEV]. A chiasm exists between the end of 11:30, which focuses on the Gentiles, and the beginning of 11:31, which focuses on the Jews [BECNT, NICNT]: when you were disobedient you received mercy by their disobedience; when they disobeyed you received mercy so they might receive mercy. The ἵνα 'so that' following this phrase marks the beginning of a new clause [BECNT, HNTC, NICNT, WBC].

2.1 it shows purpose [BECNT, NICNT], or advantage [WBC]: the Jews were disobedient so that mercy could be shown to you Gentiles. This verse is translated 'So also they have now been disobedient for your mercy, in order that they also might receive mercy.' [WBC].

2.2 It is causal [REB, TEV]. This verse is translated 'so now, because of the mercy shown to you, they have proved disobedient, but only in order that they too may receive mercy' [REB], 'In the same way, because of the mercy that you have received, the Jews now disobey God, in order that they also may now receive God's mercy' [TEV], 'And now the Jews refuse to obey, because God showed mercy to you. But this happened so that they also can receive mercy from him' [NCV].

2.3 It shows a correspondence [HNTC]: the Jews' disobedience corresponds to the mercy received by the Gentile believers.

QUESTION—How is the disobedience of the Jews related to mercy for the Gentiles?

The Gentiles received mercy through Paul's preaching of the gospel after the Jews rejected it [NICNT].

QUESTION—What relationship is indicated by ἵνα 'so that'?
1. It indicates purpose [HNTC, ICC2, NICNT, WBC]. It is translated as indicating purpose ('in order that') by BECNT, NTC; NASB, NET, NIV, NRSV, REB, TEV. The majority of the Jews disobeyed, but behind this was God's merciful purpose [ICC2].
2. It indicates result [BAGD, SSA], a result which follows according to the purpose of God [BAGD].

QUESTION—What does 'now' in the last clause mean?
1. It expresses imminence; that is, it could happen at any time [BECNT, NICNT]. It puts it in the present age, though possibly at the end of the age [Mor]. It refers to an event that is still in the future, but is used by Paul for rhetorical balance with other temporal words in this passage [SSA]. It speaks of the present age, the eschatological 'now', which began at the coming of Christ and which will end at Christ's parousia [ICC2]. The Jews' return to faith will happen now, in this present age [HNTC].
2. The final eschatological age has been inaugurated by Christ, and the eschatological 'now' has already begun, in which some Jews are believing in Christ [WBC].

QUESTION—How is mercy for the Jews logically related to their previous disobedience and mercy for the Gentiles?
Just as Paul expressed in 11:11, the mercy the Gentiles have received will stimulate the Jews to jealousy, to want the same thing [ICC2].

11:32 for[a] God imprisoned[b] all-people[c] into[d] disobedience,[e] so-that[f] he-might-show-mercy[g] to all.

LEXICON—a. γάρ (LN 89.23): 'for' [AB, BECNT, HNTC, ICC2, LN, NICNT, NTC, WBC; KJV, NASB, NET, NIV, NLT, NRSV, REB, TEV], not explicit [CEV, GW, NCV]. This conjunction marks cause or reason between events [LN].
b. aorist act. indic. of συγκλείω (LN **13.125**) (BAGD 2. p. 774): 'to imprison' [AB, BAGD, ICC2; NLT, NRSV], 'to shut up' [BECNT, HNTC, NICNT; NASB], 'to lock up' [NTC], 'to confine' [BAGD, WBC], 'to place into prison' [GW], 'to conclude' [KJV], 'to give over' [NCV], 'to consign' [NET], 'to bind over' [NIV], 'to make (people) prisoners' [TEV], 'to shut up' [REB], 'to cause to occur, to restrict' [LN]. The phrase συνέκλεισεν γὰρ ὁ θεὸς τοὺς πάντας εἰς ἀπείθειαν 'for God imprisoned all people into disobedience' is translated 'all people have disobeyed God and that's why he treats them as prisoners' [CEV], 'God has locked up all in the prison of disobedience' [NTC], 'in shutting all mankind in the prison of their disobedience, God's (purpose was)' [REB], 'God made all people prisoners of disobedience' [TEV]. This aorist verb is translated as a perfect tense verb [AB, BECNT, HNTC, ICC2, NICNT, NTC, WBC; all versions except CEV, REB]. This verb means to cause to happen, with the implication of significant restrictions [LN].

c. The phrase τοὺς πάντας 'all people' [AB; CEV, GW, NCV, NET, TEV] is also translated 'all' [BECNT, NICNT, NTC, WBC; NASB, NRSV], 'them all' [KJV], 'all men' [HNTC, ICC2; NIV], 'all mankind' [REB], 'everyone' [NLT].

d. εἰς (LN 84.22, 83.13, 84.16): 'into' [GW], 'in' [AB, ICC2, LN (83.13), NTC, WBC; KJV, NASB, NLT, NRSV, REB], 'to' [BECNT, HNTC, LN (84.16), NICNT; NCV, NET, NIV], 'inside, within' [LN (83.13)], 'toward, in the direction of' [LN (84.16)], not explicit [CEV, TEV]. This preposition marks extension toward a goal which is inside an area [LN (84.22)], or a position defined as being within certain limits [LN (83.13)], or extension toward a special goal [LN (84.16)].

e. ἀπείθεια (LN 36.23) (BAGD p. 82): 'disobedience' [AB, BAGD, BECNT, HNTC, ICC2, LN, NICNT, NTC, WBC; GW, NASB, NET, NIV, NLT, NRSV, REB, TEV], 'unbelief' [KJV], '(their) stubborn ways' [NCV]. This noun is translated as a verb: '(all people) have disobeyed' [CEV]. This noun denotes refusal to comply with the demands of some authority [LN].

f. ἵνα (LN 89.59): 'so that' [LN; CEV, GW, NCV, NET, NIV, NRSV, TEV], 'that' [AB; KJV, NASB], 'in order that' [BECNT, HNTC, ICC2, NICNT, NTC, WBC], 'so' [NLT], 'in order to, for the purpose of' [LN], 'God's purpose was' [REB]. This conjunction marks purpose for events and states [LN].

g. aorist act. subj. of ἐλεέω (LN 88.76) (BAGD p. 249): 'to show mercy' [AB, BAGD, LN; NASB, NCV, NET, REB, TEV], 'to have mercy on' [BAGD, BECNT, ICC2, LN, NICNT, NTC, WBC; CEV, KJV, NIV, NLT], 'to be merciful toward' [LN; GW, NRSV]. This verb is translated by the phrase 'in order that he may deal with all men in mercy' [HNTC]. This verb means to show kindness or concern for someone in serious need [LN].

QUESTION—What relationship is indicated by γάρ 'for'?
It indicates a conclusion to what Paul has been saying in 11:30–31 [Gdt, Mor].

QUESTION—What is implied in his use of the verb συνέκλεισεν 'imprisoned'?
God hands people over to the consequence of their sin, thus confining them in the state they have chosen for themselves [NICNT]. All people are sinners, and he allows this sinfulness to be shown [Mor, SSA, WBC]. It is only to the disobedient that God can show mercy, and people need to realize that they cannot trust in anything else [WBC]. God has providentially determined that people will be imprisoned in their own disobedience so that they can realize that they can escape only if God releases them [ICC2, Mu, St]. God has ordained that Gentiles as well as Jews should show their real character as sinners, and recognize their history of unbelief [Ho]. People must be brought into the position where they know they merit only wrath, so that his dealing with them will be experienced as mercy, since only the disobedient can understand mercy [HNTC].

QUESTION—Who are the 'all' who will be shown mercy?
1. He is referring to Jews as well as Gentiles [BECNT, Ho, ICC1, ICC2, Mor, Mu, NAC, NICNT, SSA, St, TNTC, WBC]. This does not mean that all the individuals from these groups will be saved [BECNT, NICNT], but that there is no distinction between Jews and Gentiles with regard to God's saving grace [BECNT]. It means all without distinction of ethnicity, not all without exception [St, TNTC]. It may or may not mean that all people without exception will be saved [ICC2]. It refers to all people of all nations, whether Jew or Gentile, who are granted the offer of salvation if they will choose it as a free act of faith [Gdt]. God treats all people in the same way, as his mercy comes as a free gift for all who believe, regardless of ethnicity or anything they have done [NAC].
2. He is referring to all the elect, who will be shown mercy in being saved [NTC].

DISCOURSE UNIT—11:33–36 [AB, BECNT, HNTC, Ho, Mor, Mu, NICNT, NTC, WBC; NCV, TEV]. The topic is a hymn of praise to God's wisdom and mercy [AB], concluding doxology [BECNT], the praise of God [HNTC], the wisdom of God is unsearchable [Ho], the mercy of God [Mor], the doxology [Mu], conclusion: praise to God in light of his awesome plan [NICNT], doxology [NTC], the concluding hymn of adoration [WBC], praise to God [NCV, TEV].

11:33 O (the) depth[a] of-(the)-riches[b] and[c] of-(the)-wisdom[d] and of-(the)-knowledge[e] of-God;
LEXICON—a. βάθος (LN **78.22**) (BAGD 2. p. 130): 'depth' [AB, BAGD, BECNT, HNTC, ICC2, NICNT, NTC, WBC; KJV, NASB, NET, NIV, NRSV], 'exceedingly great' [**LN**], 'extremely' [LN]. The phrase ῏Ω βάθος πλούτου 'O the depth of the riches' is translated 'who can measure the wealth' [CEV], 'yes, God's riches are very great' [NCV], 'God's riches...are so deep' [GW], 'how great are God's riches' [NLT, TEV], 'how deep are the wealth...' [REB]. This noun denotes an extreme point on a scale of extent [LN].
b. πλοῦτος (LN 57.30) (BAGD 2. p. 674): 'riches' [AB, BECNT, ICC2, LN, NICNT, NTC, WBC; GW, KJV, NASB, NCV, NET, NIV, NLT, NRSV, TEV], 'wealth' [BAGD, HNTC, LN; CEV, REB]. This noun denotes an abundance of possessions exceeding the norm of a particular society [LN].
c. καί (LN 89.102, 89.92) (BAGD I.6. p. 393): 'and' [HNTC, ICC2, LN (89.92), NICNT, WBC; CEV, NCV, NET, NLT, NRSV, REB], 'both...(and)' [BECNT, LN (89.102), NTC; KJV, NASB]. This conjunction is omitted before 'wisdom' but included before 'knowledge' by AB; GW, NIV, TEV. This conjunction marks a totality of two closely related elements [LN (89.102)], or coordinate relations [LN (89.92)].

d. σοφία (LN 33.32) (BAGD 3.b. p. 760): 'wisdom' [AB, BAGD, BECNT, HNTC, ICC2, LN, NICNT, NTC, WBC; all versions]. This noun denotes the capacity to understand and, as a result, to act wisely [LN].

e. γνῶσις (LN 28.17) (BAGD 1. p. 163): 'knowledge' [AB, BAGD, BECNT, HNTC, ICC2, LN, NICNT, NTC, WBC; all versions]. This noun denotes the content of what is known [LN].

QUESTION—What is the function of ῏Ω 'O' here?

It introduces an exclamation [Mor, NICNT], an emotional expression of awe [NICNT]. It expresses strong emotion [BAGD, SSA, WBC].

QUESTION—Which of the following nouns does the noun βάθος 'depth' describe?

1. 'Depth' describes all three nouns [AB, HNTC, Ho, ICC1, ICC2, NICNT, St, TH; CEV, GW, NCV, NET, NLT, NRSV, REB, TEV]: God's deep riches, deep wisdom, and deep knowledge. In this hymn there are three strophes, three words related to 'depth', three questions, and three prepositional phrases in 11:36a [NICNT, WBC].
2. 'Depth' describes only 'riches' [BECNT, Gdt, NTC, SSA, TNTC; KJV, NASB, NIV]: the deep riches of God's wisdom and knowledge. Although the three nouns are connected by 'and', semantically 'riches' is an attribute that modifies 'wisdom and knowledge' [SSA]. 'Depth of the riches' emphatically describes the immeasurable extent and the greatness of God's wisdom and knowledge [BECNT].
3. The noun 'depth' grammatically describes all three nouns, but 'the riches' are the riches of God's wisdom and knowledge [WBC].

QUESTION—What are the riches?

The words 'riches' and 'depth' communicate profundity and immensity [ICC2, WBC].

1. They are the riches of God's mercy [Ho, ICC2], kindness [ICC2, NICNT], goodness [Ho], and grace [ICC1, TH]. They are the riches of God's kindness, shown in how he blesses sinners who don't deserve it [NICNT]. They are the riches of salvation, which he generously bestows on those who call upon him [St].
2. They are the riches of God's wisdom and knowledge [BECNT, Gdt, HNTC, Mu, SSA, WBC].

QUESTION—Are 'wisdom' and 'knowledge' to be distinguished, or are they a couplet?

1. They are different [AB, Gdt, Ho, ICC1, ICC2, Mu, NICNT, WBC].
2. There is significant overlap between the terms 'wisdom' and 'knowledge', and they should not be differentiated [BECNT]. They are nearly identical in meaning here [SSA].

QUESTION—What wisdom is he referring to here?

Paul is still thinking about God's saving purpose for all; the wisdom is the way God works to bring about salvation [WBC]. This is the wisdom that informs God's purposes and how he carries them out, as well as the love and care that is involved [ICC2]. It is that capacity by which he arranges and adapts everything to accomplish his will [Mu]. It primarily has to do with what God has done to bring both Jews and non-Jews to himself [SSA]. God's wisdom and knowledge primarily focus on his saving plan, as outlined in chapters 9–11 [BECNT]. It is God's comprehension of how everything in the world relates [AB]. It is a comprehensive grasp of the relationships of how things fit together [ICC1]. It speaks of the skill by which God takes the free actions of human beings, transforms them, and weaves them together into means to accomplish his eternal plan [Gdt]. By his infinite wisdom God chooses the means to accomplish his purposes for his glory and the good of his creatures [Ho].

QUESTION—What knowledge is he referring to here?

It is God's foreknowledge of his own people [WBC], his special relational knowing of those whom he chooses for salvation [NICNT]. It is his electing love, and his loving concern and care for his people [ICC2]. It focuses primarily on his saving plan, not only in the fact of his foreknowledge of all that happens, but the in the fact that he ordains it [BECNT]. It is a penetrating grasp of particular truths [ICC1]. God intuitively knows the details of all things [AB]. The omniscient God knows the very essence of all things, people, and ideas [NTC]. In his foreknowledge he knows completely all the free choices of men and nations [Gdt]. God knows all that will be required to accomplish his purposes [Ho]. God fully and exhaustively knows and understands all things [Mu].

how unfathomable[a] his judgments[b] and untraceable[c] his ways.[d]

LEXICON—a. ἀνεξεραύνητος (LN 32.23) (BAGD p. 65): 'unfathomable' [BAGD, LN, WBC], 'unsearchable' [BAGD, BECNT, HNTC, ICC2, NICNT, NTC; KJV, NASB, NET, NIV, NRSV], 'inscrutable' [AB; REB], 'impossible to understand, impossible to comprehend' [LN]. This clause is translated 'who can understand his decisions or explain what he does' [CEV], 'it is impossible to explain his decisions or to understand his ways' [GW], 'no one can explain the things God decides or understand his ways' [NCV], 'how impossible it is for us to understand his decisions and his ways' [NLT], 'Who can explain his decisions? Who can understand his ways?' [TEV]. This adjective describes being impossible to understand on the basis of careful examination or investigation [LN]. This word is found only here in the NT.

b. κρίμα (LN **30.110**) (BAGD 2. p. 450): 'judgment' [AB, BECNT, HNTC, ICC2, LN, NICNT, NTC, WBC; KJV, NASB, NET, NIV, NRSV, REB], 'decision' [BAGD, LN; CEV, GW, NLT, TEV], 'decree' [BAGD]. This noun is translated as a verb phrase: '(the things God) decides' [NCV]. This noun denotes the content of the process of judging [LN].

c. ἀνεξιχνίαστος (LN 32.23) (BAGD p. 65): 'untraceable' [AB, BECNT, NTC], 'unsearchable' [REB], 'unfathomable' [LN; NASB], 'impossible to comprehend' [LN], 'incomprehensible' [BAGD, ICC2, WBC], 'inscrutable' [BAGD, NICNT; NRSV], 'fathomless' [NET], 'impossible to understand' [LN]. The phrase 'untraceable his ways' is translated 'how his ways baffle our attempts to track them down' [HNTC], 'his ways past finding out' [KJV], 'his paths beyond tracing out' [NIV]. See a. above for CEV, GW, NCV, NLT, TEV. This adjective describes being impossible to understand on the basis of careful examination or investigation [LN].

d. ὁδός (LN 41.16) (BAGD 2.b. p. 554): 'way' [AB, BAGD, BECNT, HNTC, ICC2, NICNT, NTC, WBC; GW, KJV, NASB, NCV, NET, NLT, NRSV, REB, TEV], 'what he does' [CEV], 'paths' [NIV], 'way of life, way to live' [LN]. This noun denotes a customary manner of life or behavior, with probably some implication of goal or purpose [LN].

QUESTION—What are the 'judgments' he refers to?

1. It is used in parallel with 'ways', with similar meaning [BECNT, Mor, NICNT]. It is not judicial decisions [AB, ICC1, NICNT], but judgments about the world and everything in it [AB], about the ways and plans of life [ICC1]. It is not necessarily negative or punitive judgments [Mor], but God's decisions in general [SSA]. It includes not only God's judicial decisions, but of all the decisions he executes in the world [BECNT]. It refers to God's executive decisions concerning salvation history, and how he directs it [NICNT]. It is God's sovereign decisions and decrees, especially those that are expressed in his plan of salvation and in how he implements that plan [NTC].

2. It refers to judicial judgments [Gdt, ICC2, Mu]. This word refers to the execution or carrying out of God's judgments [ICC2]. It is primarily judicial decisions, although it can refer to other decisions and determinations as well [Mu]. It is God's judicial decrees by which he chastises people [Gdt].

QUESTION—What are the 'ways' he refers to?

It is the ways God takes to carries out his purposes [ICC2]. It is God's actions in the world, which would include both his saving actions as well as his judging actions [BECNT]. It is God's dealings with men [Mu, SSA], including divine providences by which his divine decrees are carried out [Mu]. It is God's characteristic ways of acting [WBC]. This word is used in a way that is essentially synonymous with 'judgments' [NICNT]. In meaning it overlaps with 'judgments' [BECNT]. God's judgments become the ways his wisdom employs to carry out his plan [Gdt]. It is God's various providences by which he executes his decrees in his dealings with men [Mu].

11:34 For[a] who has-known[b] (the) mind[c] of-(the) Lord? Or who became his counselor?[d]

LEXICON—a. γάρ (LN 89.23): 'for' [BECNT, HNTC, ICC2, LN, NICNT, NTC, WBC; KJV, NASB, NET, NLT, NRSV], 'because' [LN], not explicit [AB; CEV, GW, NLT, REB]. This word is translated as introducing the content of a citation from the OT: 'as the Scripture says' [NCV, TEV]. This conjunction marks cause or reason between events [LN].

b. aorist act. indic. of γινώσκω (LN 28.1): 'to know' [AB, BECNT, HNTC, ICC2, LN, NICNT, NTC, WBC; all versions]. This aorist verb is translated as a perfect tense verb: 'has known' [AB, BECNT, HNTC, ICC2, NICNT, NTC, WBC; CEV, KJV, NASB, NCV, NET, NIV, NRSV]; as a present tense verb: 'knows' [GW, REB, TEV], 'can know' [NLT]. This verb means to possess information about something or someone [LN].
c. νοῦς (LN 26.14) (BAGD 4. p. 545): 'mind' [AB, BAGD, BECNT, HNTC, ICC2, LN, NICNT, NTC, WBC; KJV, NASB, NCV, NET, NIV, NRSV, REB, TEV], 'thoughts' [BAGD; CEV, NLT]. This noun is translated as a verb: '(how the Lord) thinks' [GW]. This noun denotes the psychological faculty of understanding, reasoning, thinking, and deciding [LN].
d. σύμβουλος (LN 33.297) (BAGD p. 778): 'counselor' [AB, BAGD, BECNT, HNTC, ICC2, NICNT, NTC, WBC; KJV, NASB, NET, NIV, NRSV, REB], 'adviser' [BAGD, LN; GW]. The phrase 'became his counselor' is translated 'given him advice' [CEV], 'able to give him advice' [NCV, TEV], 'knows enough to give him advice' [NLT]. This noun denotes one who gives advice [LN]. This word is found only here in the NT.

QUESTION—What relationship is indicated by γάρ 'for'?
1. It indicates a transition of thought but also introduces a citation from the OT [WBC].
2. It introduces 11:34–35 as grounds for what has been said in 11:33 [BECNT, SSA].

QUESTION—Who is 'the Lord' spoken of here?
The subject of the entire hymn is God the Father [BECNT, NICNT, WBC], not Christ [BECNT, WBC]. There is no basis for a Trinitarian interpretation of this hymn [ICC1, ICC2, Mu, NICNT, WBC].

11:35 Or who first-gave[a] to-him, and[b] will-be-repaid[c] by-him?

LEXICON—a. aorist act. indic. of προδίδωμι (LN 57.74) (BAGD 1. p. 704): 'to give first' [HNTC, LN; KJV], 'to give something' [GW], 'to give' [NLT], 'to give in advance' [BAGD]. This aorist verb is translated as a perfect tense verb in most of the commentaries and versions. The question 'who first gave to him' is translated '(who) has first given' [NASB, NET], 'who has (ever) given him a gift?' [AB; NRSV], 'who has ever given (something/anything) to God' [NTC; NIV, TEV], 'who has given to him beforehand?' [BECNT], 'who has anticipated him in giving' [ICC2], 'who has given to him in advance' [NICNT], 'who has given in advance to him' [WBC], 'has anyone loaned something to the Lord' [CEV], 'no one has ever given God anything (that he must pay back)' [NCV], 'who has made a gift to him first' [REB]. This verb means to give in advance of some other event [LN]. This word is found only here in the NT.

b. καί (LN 89.87): 'and' [LN, WBC; KJV, REB], 'and then' [LN]. This conjunction is translated as indicating result: 'that' [HNTC, NTC; CEV, NASB, NCV, NET, NIV, NLT], 'to (receive)' [AB; NRSV], 'so that' [BECNT; TEV], 'so as to (receive)' [ICC2, NICNT], 'which (the Lord must pay back)' [GW]. This conjunction marks a sequence of closely related events [LN].

c. fut. pass. indic. of ἀνταποδίδωμι (LN **57.154**) (BAGD 1. p. 73): 'to be repaid' [BAGD, BECNT, LN; WBC; CEV], 'to be paid back' [BAGD, LN; NASB], 'to receive in return' [AB; NRSV], 'to receive (from him) a payment' [ICC2], 'to give back' [NICNT], 'to repay' [NTC; NET, NIV], 'to pay back' [GW, NCV, NLT, TEV], 'to be recompensed' [KJV], 'to earn a gift in return' [REB]. The clause 'will be repaid by him' is translated 'recompense might be made him' [HNTC]. This verb means to pay something back to someone as the result of an incurred obligation [LN].

QUESTION—What idea is Paul addressing here?

He is refuting the idea that Israel somehow had a claim on God's mercy, that it was their national right [WBC]. God's bounty is not based on anything that anyone has done [AB, NICNT]. No one can build a store of merit with God such that they might claim a reward [Gdt, HNTC]. No creature can place God under obligation [Ho, Mor, SSA, TH], as the creature has neither merit nor power [Ho], and God is debtor to no one [NAC].

11:36 For[a] from[b] him and through[c] him and to/for[d] him (are) all-things;[e]

LEXICON—a. ὅτι (LN 89.33): 'for' [AB, HNTC, ICC2, LN, NICNT, NTC; KJV, NASB, NET, NIV, NLT, NRSV, TEV], 'because' [BECNT, LN, WBC; CEV], not explicit [GW, NCV, REB]. This conjunction marks cause or reason, based on an evident fact [LN].

b. ἐκ (LN 89.3) (BAGD 3.c. p. 235): 'from' [AB, BAGD, BECNT, ICC2, LN, NICNT, NTC, WBC; GW, NASB, NET, NIV, NLT, NRSV, REB], 'of' [HNTC; KJV], not explicit [CEV, NCV, TEV]. The phrase ἐξ αὐτοῦ...τὰ πάντα 'from him...are all things' is translated 'everything comes from him' [NLT], 'everything comes from the Lord' [CEV], 'God made all things' [NCV], 'all things were created by him' [TEV]. This preposition marks the source from which someone or something is physically or psychologically derived [LN].

c. διά with genitive object (LN 90.4) (BAGD A.III.2.b.β. p. 180): 'through' [AB, BAGD, BECNT, HNTC, ICC2, LN, NICNT, NTC, WBC; KJV, NASB, NCV, NET, NIV, NRSV, REB, TEV], 'because of' [CEV], 'by' [GW], not explicit [NLT]. The phrase δι' αὐτοῦ...τὰ πάντα 'through him are all things' is translated 'all things exist through him' [TEV], 'everything exists by his power' [NLT], 'all things were made because of him' [CEV], 'everything continues through him' [NCV]. This preposition marks an intermediate agent, with implicit or explicit causative agent [LN].

d. εἰς (LN 90.41): 'to' [BECNT, NTC, WBC; KJV, NASB, NET, NIV], 'unto' [HNTC, ICC2], 'for' [AB, LN, NICNT; GW, NCV]. The phrase εἰς αὐτὸν τὰ πάντα 'to/for him are all things' is translated 'all things will return to him' [CEV], 'everything is intended for his glory' [NLT], 'everything continues for him' [NCV], 'all things exist for him' [TEV]. This preposition marks persons benefited by an event, with the implication of something directed to them [LN].

e. πᾶς (LN 59.23) (BAGD 2.b.β. p. 633): 'all things' [AB, BAGD, BECNT, HNTC, ICC2, NICNT, NTC, WBC; CEV, KJV, NASB, NCV, NET, NIV], 'all' [LN], 'everything' [GW, NLT], 'the universe' [BAGD]. This noun denotes the totality of any object, mass, collective, or extension [LN].

QUESTION—What relationship is indicated by ὅτι 'for'?
1. It reflects back on all of 11:33–35 [NICNT]. It indicates support and explanation for 11:33–35 [ICC2].
2. It indicates grounds [BECNT, SSA]. It introduces 11:36 as grounds for 11:34–35 [BECNT], or possibly for 11:33 only [SSA].

QUESTION—What does it mean that all things are from him?
He is the source of all things [BECNT, Ho, ICC1, NAC, NICNT, St, TNTC, WBC], the creator [AB, Gdt, ICC2, Mu, SSA, St, TH], the originator [HNTC, Mor]. He is the source of our salvation [HNTC, NTC].

QUESTION—What does it mean that all things are through him?
He is the sustainer [AB, ICC2, Mor, NAC, NICNT, SSA], ruler [Gdt, ICC2], means [BECNT, Ho, St], agent [ICC1, NAC], inspirer [ICC1], or medium [WBC] of all things. He keeps the created order in existence [TH]. He is the accomplisher of our salvation [NTC], he puts it into effect [HNTC]. He is the agent through whom everything subsists and is directed to its fitting goal and purpose [Mu]. All things exist through him [TNTC].

QUESTION—What does it mean that all things are to/for him?
He is the goal of all things [AB, BECNT, Gdt, HNTC, Ho, ICC1, ICC2, Mor, NAC, NICNT, St, WBC], he is the director of all things [NAC]. He is the goal of our salvation [NTC]. He is the final end, to whom all glory will come [Mu]. All things exist for his glory [NAC], that they might praise God [SSA]. Everything is moving in the direction that God intends it to [TH].

QUESTION—Is this intended to be a Trinitarian statement?
It is not Trinitarian [AB, Gdt, Ho, ICC1, ICC2, Mor, Mu, NICNT, NTC, SSA, WBC]. It is about the relation of the triune God to all things [Gdt, Ho, ICC1, Mu, NTC].

to-him (be)[a] the glory[b] to-the ages,[c] amen.[d]

LEXICON—a. There is no lexical entry for this word in the Greek text, it is implied. It is represented in translation as 'be' [AB, BECNT, HNTC, ICC2, NICNT, NTC, WBC; all versions except CEV, GW, NLT], 'belongs' [GW], not explicit [CEV, NLT].

b. δόξα (LN 33.357) (BAGD 3. p. 204): 'glory' [AB, BAGD, BECNT, HNTC, ICC2, NICNT, NTC, WBC; all versions except CEV], 'praise' [BAGD, LN], 'honor' [BAGD]. The phrase αὐτῷ ἡ δόξα 'to him be the glory' is translated 'praise the Lord' [CEV]. This noun denotes speaking of something as being unusually fine and deserving honor [LN].

c. εἰς τοὺς αἰῶνας (LN 67.95): 'forever' [AB, BECNT, HNTC, ICC2, LN, NICNT, NTC, WBC; all versions], 'forever and ever' [LN]. This phrase means an unlimited duration of time, with particular focus upon the future [LN].

d. ἀμήν (LN 72.6) (BAGD 1. p. 45): 'amen' [AB, BAGD, BECNT, HNTC, ICC2, NICNT, NTC, WBC; all versions], 'so let it be' [BAGD], 'truly' [BAGD, LN], 'indeed' [LN]. This word is a strong affirmation of what is declared [LN].

QUESTION—What is the function of the doxology in these last four verses?

This expresses the assumptions underlying his arguments, not the conclusion of them [ICC1]. It stands in stark contrast to the great sorrow he expressed in 9:1 [NTC]. Doxology and theology should always go together, they should never be separated [St].

1. It brings to a close what he has been discussing in chapters 9–11 [Gdt, ICC2, Mor, Mu, NICNT], and especially 11:32 [BECNT].
2. It sums up chapters 9–11, but also brings to a close the doctrinal section that began at 1:16 [AB].
3. It brings to a close the arguments begun in 1:18–25 [WBC].
4. It concludes chapters 9–11, but also the entire first part of the epistle [SSA].
5. It is a fitting conclusion to all of chapters 1–11 [TNTC].

QUESTION—What does 'amen' signify here?

It is a typical Jewish conclusion to a prayer or doxology [AB]. It expresses solemn affirmation and enthusiastic personal approval [NTC]. It indicates that these things are certainly true [TH]. It expresses Paul's deep wish that God's purpose to receive glory and praise will actually come about [BECNT]. It closes this part of the epistle [Gdt].

DISCOURSE UNIT—12:1–15:33 [REB]. The topic is Christian service and the community.

DISCOURSE UNIT—12:1–15:13 [AB, BECNT, Gdt, ICC2, Mor, Mu, NAC, NICNT, St, TNTC, WBC]. The topic is hortatory section: the demands of upright life in Christ [AB], God's righteousness in everyday life [BECNT], the life of the justified believer [Gdt], the obedience to which those who are righteous by faith are called [ICC2], Christian living [Mor], the Christian way of life [Mu], how righteousness manifests itself [NAC], the transforming power of the gospel: Christian conduct [NICNT], the will of God for changed relationships [St], the Christian way of life [TNTC], the outworking of the gospel for the redefined people of God in everyday terms [WBC].

DISCOURSE UNIT—12:1–13:14 [AB, Gdt]. The topic is the Spirit-guided Christian life must be worship paid to God [AB], exposition of Christian holiness [Gdt].

DISCOURSE UNIT—12:1–21 [Mu, NAC; GW, NCV, NLT, TEV]. The topic is manifold practical duties [Mu], how righteousness manifests itself among believers [NAC], dedicate your lives to God [GW], give your lives to God [NCV], a living sacrifice to God [NLT], life in God's service [TEV].

DISCOURSE UNIT—12:1–8 [CEV, NIV, NRSV]. The topic is Christ brings new life [CEV], living sacrifices [NIV], the new life in Christ [NRSV].

DISCOURSE UNIT—12:1–2 [AB, BECNT, HNTC, Ho, ICC1, ICC2, NICNT, St, TNTC, WBC]. The topic is life in the world as worship of God [AB], paradigm for exhortations: total dedication to God [BECNT], the ground of Christian ethics [HNTC], devotion to God [Ho], the new life [ICC1], the theme of this main division of the epistle is set forth [ICC2], the heart of the matter: total transformation [NICNT], the Christian attitude toward God [Mor], our relationship to God: consecrated bodies and renewed minds [St], the living sacrifice [TNTC], the basis for responsible living—the Christian's worship [WBC].

12:1 I-exhort[a] you therefore,[b] brothers,[c] through[d] the mercies[e] of God

LEXICON—a. pres. act. indic. of παρακαλέω (LN 25.150) (BAGD 2. p. 617): 'to exhort' [BAGD, BECNT, HNTC, ICC2, NICNT, NTC; NET], 'to beseech' [KJV], 'to urge' [AB; NASB, NIV], 'to encourage' [BAGD, LN (25.150); GW], 'to appeal to' [BAGD, LN (33.168), WBC; NRSV, TEV], 'to implore' [REB], 'to beg' [CEV, NCV], 'to plead' [NLT]. This word expresses a note of authority; in the name of the gospel he summons them to obedience [ICC2]. It combines authority with appeal [St]. This verb means to cause someone to be encouraged or consoled, either by verbal or non-verbal means [LN].
  b. οὖν (LN 89.50): 'therefore' [AB, HNTC, ICC2, LN, NICNT, NTC, WBC; KJV, NASB, NET, NIV, NRSV, REB], 'consequently, accordingly' [LN], 'so' [LN; CEV, NCV], 'and so' [NLT], 'so then' [LN; TEV], 'then' [AB, LN], not explicit [GW]. This conjunction indicates result, often implying the conclusion of a process of reasoning [LN].
  c. ἀδελφός (LN 11.23): 'fellow believer, Christian brother' [LN]. This plural noun is translated 'brothers' [AB, NTC, WBC; NIV], 'brethren' [HNTC, ICC2; KJV, NASB], 'my brothers' [TEV], 'brothers and sisters' [BECNT, NICNT; GW, NCV, NET, NRSV], 'dear friends' [CEV], 'dear Christian friends' [NLT], 'my friends' [REB]. This noun denotes a close associate of a group of persons having a well-defined membership [LN].
  d. διά with genitive object (LN 89.26) (BAGD A.III.1.f. p. 180): 'through' [BAGD, NICNT, WBC], 'by' [AB, BAGD, HNTC, ICC2; KJV, NASB, NET, NRSV, REB], 'because of' [BECNT, LN; GW, NLT, TEV], 'on account of, by reason of' [LN], 'in view of' [NTC; NIV], not explicit

[CEV]. The phrase 'through the mercies of God' is translated 'since God has shown us great mercy' [NCV]. This preposition marks cause or reason, with focus upon instrumentality, either of objects or events [LN].

e. οἰκτιρμός (LN 88.80) (BAGD p. 561): 'mercy' [AB, BAGD, BECNT, HNTC, ICC2, LN, NICNT, WBC; KJV, NASB, NET, NIV, REB, TEV], 'great mercy' [BECNT, NTC; NCV, TEV], 'compassion' [BAGD; GW], 'tender compassion' [LN]. This plural noun is translated as singular [AB, NTC; GW, NCV, NIV, REB, TEV]; as plural [BECNT, HNTC, ICC2, NICNT, WBC; KJV, NASB, NET, NRSV]. The phrase 'through the mercies of God' is translated 'God is good. So (I beg you)' [CEV], 'because of all he has done for you' [NLT]. This noun denotes mercy and concern, with the implication of sensitivity and compassion [LN].

QUESTION—What relationship is indicated by οὖν 'therefore'?

It draws a logical conclusion to all he has said so far [AB, BECNT, Gdt, HNTC, Ho, ICC1, ICC2, Mor, NAC, NICNT, NTC, St, TH]. It shows the connection between Paul's ethical exhortations, in this and subsequent chapters, and his dogmatic statements in the first eleven chapters [HNTC]. It indicates a transition from Paul's arguments up to this point, and how they are to be applied in living [TH]. It introduces Paul's appeal, which is a reasonable conclusion to be drawn from all he has said previously [NTC]. It refers to all he has said so far, and transitions from that theology of redemption to the practical exhortation that follows [NAC]. It draws a conclusion from all he has said so far in chapters 1–11 [AB, Gdt, HNTC, ICC1, Mor, NAC, NICNT, St], or from 1:16 through 11:36 [BECNT], or from 1:18 through 11:36 [ICC2], or from chapters 5–11 [WBC], but especially from chapters 9–11 [BECNT, HNTC, ICC2, St, WBC], or just from chapter 11 [ICC1].

QUESTION—What relationship is indicated by διά 'through'?

1. It indicates the basis of his appeal to them [BECNT, Gdt, ICC2, Mor, NICNT, SSA; NCV, TEV]. God's mercies are the power that will move the believer's will [Gdt]. It is not the means, but the basis of his appeal and it is better translated 'because' [NICNT]. Paul bases his exhortation on God's compassion which is revealed in his dealing with men through Christ [ICC2]. He appeals to their sense of gratitude for all that God has done to spur them to devotion to God [Ho].
2. It is instrumental; his authority to urge them to action is based on his own role and experience as an agent of God's mercy [WBC].

QUESTION—Why is 'mercies' a plural noun?

It reflects the Hebrew noun *rach^{a}mim*, which is also plural [AB, ICC1, ICC2, Mor, NICNT, NTC, St, TH, WBC]. Even the singular form, 'mercy', speaks of the depth and variety of God's mercy and love [BECNT].

1. The plural form speaks of the greatness or tenderness of God's mercy, as spelled out in the first eleven chapters, and specifically his kindness, patience, love, and grace [NTC]. It refers to the greatness of God's mercy [NCV, TEV]. 'Mercies' summarizes all of what has been said in the first

ROMANS 12:1 193

eleven chapters, and especially in chapters 9–11 [HNTC, Mor, St]. The plural speaks of the many times God has shown mercy [TH], of all that God has done for them [NLT], or the many ways that God has acted in mercy [SSA, St], probably referring back to all that he has said since 3:21 [SSA]. It recalls the great mercy of God which he discussed in chapter 11 [ICC1].

2. It has a singular meaning [ICC2, NICNT]. Paul picked up the plural form from the Septuagint which uses the plural form 'mercies' to translate the Hebrew word which has a singular meaning, so in English it is best to translate with the singular form [NICNT]. It is translated as singular by GW, NCV, NIV, REB, TEV.

to-offer[a] your bodies[b] (as a) sacrifice[c]

LEXICON—a. aorist act. infin. of παρίστημι (LN 57.81) (BAGD 1.d. p. 628): 'to offer' [AB, BAGD, HNTC, LN, NTC; CEV, GW, NCV, NIV, REB, TEV], 'to present' [BAGD, BECNT, ICC2, LN, NICNT, WBC; KJV, NASB, NET, NRSV], 'to give' [NLT]. This is a term deriving from Jewish worship practice [BECNT, ICC1, ICC2, WBC]. This verb means to make something available to someone without necessarily involving actual change of ownership [LN].

b. σῶμα (LN 9.8, 8.1) (BAGD 1.b. p. 799): 'body' [AB, BAGD, BECNT, HNTC, LN (8.1), NICNT, WBC; CEV, GW, KJV, NASB, NET, NIV, NLT, NRSV], 'self, physical being' [LN (9.8)]. The phrase 'your bodies' is translated 'your lives' [NCV], 'yourselves' [ICC2, NTC; TEV], 'your very selves' [REB]. This noun denotes a person as a physical being, including natural desires [LN (9.8)], or the physical body of persons, animals, or plants [LN (8.1)].

c. θυσία (LN 53.20) (BAGD 2.b. p. 366): 'sacrifice' [AB, BAGD, BECNT, HNTC, ICC2, LN, NICNT, NTC, WBC; all versions]. This noun denotes that which is offered as a sacrifice [LN].

QUESTION—Why does he urge them to offer their bodies to God?

1. The body represents the whole person [AB, BECNT, HNTC, ICC2, NICNT, SSA, TH, WBC; NCV, REB, TEV], the entire personality [NTC]. It represents the person in his corporeal and concrete living in this world [WBC]. It is a synecdoche [SSA]. Since Paul is using sacrificial language in this metaphor, the presenting of a 'body' is an appropriate choice of words even though he intends the body to refer to the whole person [NICNT].

2. He is saying that the body must be consecrated to God, and sanctification must include the body [Mu]. The entire person, body as well as soul, must be dedicated to God [Ho]. Paul is saying that they must be holy and pure in body as well as spirit, living as temples of the Holy Spirit and unstained by passion [ICC1]. He is saying that worship must not be only inward, but must be expressed in acts of service done by our bodies, and that there also must be a putting to death of the sin that so often expresses itself

through bodily acts [St]. In Christian teaching even the body should be yielded to God as an implement of righteousness, and is a temple of the Holy Spirit [Mor]. Paul assumes that the will of the believers has already been consecrated, and now urges them to offer their bodies as well, as the instruments for consecrated living [Gdt].

QUESTION—Does the aorist form of the imperative 'offer' imply that the action of offering is to be done only once?

The use of the aorist imperative does not imply anything about once-for-all action [BECNT].

living,[a] holy,[b] well-pleasing[c] to-God, (which is) your spiritual/reasonable/true[d] worship/service;[e]

LEXICON—a. pres. act. participle of ζάω (LN 23.88) (BAGD 4.b. p. 337): 'to live' [BAGD, LN]. This participle is translated 'living' [AB, BAGD, BECNT, HNTC, ICC2, NICNT, NTC, WBC; all versions except NET], 'alive' [NET].

b. ἅγιος (LN 88.24, 53.46) (BAGD 1.a.β. p. 9): 'holy' [AB, BAGD, BECNT, HNTC, ICC2, LN (88.24), NICNT, NTC, WBC; KJV, NASB, NET, NIV, NLT, NRSV], 'pure' [CEV], 'dedicated' [LN (53.46); REB], 'dedicated to God' [BAGD; GW], 'dedicated to his service' [TEV]. This word is translated by a phrase: 'your offering must be only for God' [NCV]. This adjective describes superior moral qualities and certain essentially divine qualities in contrast with what is human [LN (88.24)], or being dedicated or consecrated to the service of God [LN (53.46)].

c. εὐάρεστος (LN **25.94**) (BAGD 1. p. 318): 'well pleasing' [BECNT, HNTC, ICC2, NICNT, NTC], 'pleasing' [BAGD, **LN**; CEV, GW, NCV, NET, NIV, TEV], 'acceptable' [AB, BAGD, WBC; KJV, NASB, NRSV]. The phrase 'a sacrifice living, holy, well pleasing to God' is translated 'let them be a living and holy sacrifice—the kind he will find acceptable' [NLT], 'a living sacrifice, dedicated and fit for his acceptance' [REB]. This adjective describes that which causes someone to be pleased [LN].

d. λογικός (LN **73.5**) (BAGD p. 476): 'spiritual' [BAGD, HNTC, NTC, WBC; NASB, NRSV], 'spiritual way' [NCV], 'reasonable' [KJV, NET], 'rational' [BAGD, BECNT, LN], 'rational nature' [AB], 'understanding' [ICC2], 'genuine' [LN], 'true' [**LN**, NICNT; TEV]. The phrase 'which is your spiritual/reasonable worship' is translated 'that's the most sensible way to serve God' [CEV], 'this kind of worship is appropriate for you' [GW], 'the worship offered by mind and heart' [REB], 'This is truly the way to worship him' [NLT]. This adjective describes being genuine, in the sense of being true to the real and essential nature of something [LN].

e. λατρεία (LN 53.14) (BAGD p. 467): 'worship' [BAGD, HNTC, ICC2, LN, NICNT, NTC, WBC; GW, NCV, NRSV, REB, TEV], 'service' [BAGD, BECNT; KJV, NET], 'service of worship' [NASB], 'act of worship' [NIV], 'a cult' [AB]. This word is translated as an infinitive: 'to worship' [NLT], 'to serve God' [CEV]. This noun denotes religious rites as a part of worship [LN].

QUESTION—What is a living sacrifice?

A sacrifice is something that is put to death, so a living sacrifice is a contradiction in terms [TH]. This contrasts a sacrifice that consists in killing an animal with a sacrifice that consists in the quality of daily living [WBC]. 'Living' modifies 'sacrifice', and it refers to the nature of the sacrifice that does not die but goes on living so that the sacrifice continues in its efficacy until the person who offered dies [NICNT]. The Christian is to offer himself or herself to God continually [SSA]. The person so offered must be a living agent of God's will at every moment [Gdt]. Sanctification involves deliberative acts of the will that continue throughout life [NAC]. The sacrifice proceeds from the new life that is in the believer [NTC]. They are to offer is themselves and their conduct to God as worship, which recalls the offering of themselves mentioned in 6:13 [AB]. It is living in the sense that it is perpetual, and is never neglected or recalled [Ho]. It is a continual dedication of oneself [Mu, WBC]. The offering of self that a Christian makes is to be positive and dynamic, demanding the full energy of life, not the destruction of life [Mor]. 'Living' describes the spiritual condition of people who believe in Christ, who, through Christ, are now alive to God as Paul has already said in 6:11, 13, and 8:13 [BECNT]. Although the believer belongs to God both by creation and by redemption, he must also belong to God by self-surrender, an act that must continually be repeated [ICC2]. The Christian also is 'living' in a deeper, theological sense, which is the spiritual newness of life that Paul spoke of in 6:4 [ICC1, ICC2]. They are to present their bodies as alive from the dead, as temples of the Holy Spirit, as members of Christ and as instruments of righteousness [Mu].

QUESTION—How are the three modifiers 'living', 'holy', and 'well-pleasing' used in this sentence?

1. The sacrifice is to be living, and that living sacrifice is to be holy and well-pleasing to God [AB, HNTC, ICC1, NAC; all versions except NET].
2. The modifiers are coordinate: the sacrifice is to be living, holy, and well-pleasing to God [BECNT, Ho, ICC2, Mor, NICNT, NTC, SSA, TH, WBC; NET].

QUESTION—What area of meaning is intended by the word 'holy'?

It is a term drawn from the temple worship [HNTC, TH, WBC], and means that the sacrifice is dedicated wholly to God [HNTC, Mor, NICNT, WBC]. The sacrifice is set apart from the ordinary [NICNT]. It has the connotation both of dedication to God as well as of ethical quality, which is likeness to God's character [ICC2]. It means to be morally pure, free from the stains of passion [ICC1]. It speaks of the sanctifying work of the Holy Spirit [NTC]. 'Holy' and 'well-pleasing' are the moral equivalents of a sacrifice being unblemished or without defect [St]. The body is not to be defiled by sexual lust [Mu]. This is in contrast to how their bodies were used when they were under the domination of sin [Gdt].

QUESTION—To what does the phrase τὴν λογικὴν λατρείαν ὑμῶν 'your spiritual/reasonable worship/service' relate?
1. It is in apposition to and describes the entire previous sentence that speaks of dedicating oneself to God [BECNT, Ho, ICC1, ICC2, NICNT, WBC].
2. It is in apposition to and describes the sacrifice [HNTC].

QUESTION—What area of meaning is intended by the adjective λογικός 'spiritual/reasonable'?
1. It describes worship that is *spiritual* [Ho, ICC1, TNTC; NASB, NCV, NIV, NRSV, REB]. It is spiritual in nature, as opposed to the external nature of the temple worship [TNTC]. It is inner worship involving the mind and spirit as opposed to ceremonial and external worship [Ho]. It is the offering of one's whole self, one's thoughts, feelings, aspirations, words, and deeds [ICC1].
2. It describes worship that is *reasonable* to expect, the most sensible or appropriate way to respond to God [AB, BECNT, Gdt, HNTC, ICC2, NAC, NTC, SSA; CEV, GW, KJV, NET]. It is eminently reasonable to offer oneself entirely to God, and not to do so would be foolish and irrational [BECNT]. It is what is to be expected of those who have a proper understanding of truth as revealed in Christ [NAC]. It relates to the mind, reason, and intellect, and stands in contrast to worship that is mechanical or automatic [Mu]. It is the most sensible way to serve God [SSA; CEV], and therefore the most appropriate [SSA]. It is worship and service that is fitting for rational beings, but that also is spiritual [Mor]. It is worship that is intelligent and understanding, meaning that it is consistent with the truth of the gospel, and requires the offering of oneself in the course of everyday living, not only in thoughts and feelings but also in words and deeds [ICC2].
3. It describes worship as being *true* worship [LN, NICNT, TH; NLT, TEV], worship that is in keeping with someone's true nature as human beings, that which is fitting and proper [TH]. The usual translations of either spiritual or reasonable miss an important part of the meaning, and it is best to translate it as 'true worship' so as to describe the involvement of a renewed mind that can understand God aright, thus making this the only finally appropriate and true worship [NICNT].

QUESTION—What area of meaning is intended by λατρεία 'worship/service'?
(Note that there is considerable overlap between the concepts of 'worship' and 'service', and any distinction should not be pressed too far.)
1. It refers to worshipping God [AB, BECNT, HNTC, Ho, ICC2, NAC, NICNT, NTC, TH, TNTC, WBC; GW, NCV, NIV, NLT, REB, TEV]. It is a worship that includes deeds as well as thoughts and words [NTC]. It is the service of worship [NASB]. This is a cultic term, referring to actions in the temple worship [BECNT]. It is worship that embraces the entirety of the Christian's everyday life [ICC2].
2. It refers to serving God [CEV, KJV, NET].
3. It refers to worshipping as well as serving God [Mor, SSA; NASB].

12:2 And do- not -be-conformed[a] to this age,[b] but be-transformed[c] by[d] the renewing[e] of-the mind[f]

LEXICON—a. pres. mid. or pass. impera. of συσχηματίζω (LN **41.29**) (BAGD p. 795): 'to be conformed' [BAGD, BECNT, HNTC, ICC2, WBC; KJV, NASB, NET, NRSV], 'to conform' [NICNT], 'to conform yourselves' [AB; TEV], 'to shape one's behavior' [**LN**], 'to conform one's life' [LN], 'to conform to the pattern of' [NIV, REB], 'allow yourselves to be fashioned after the pattern of' [NTC], 'to change yourselves to be like' [NCV], 'to be like' [CEV], 'to become like' [GW], 'to copy' [NLT], 'to be guided by' [BAGD]. This verb is translated as passive ('do not be conformed') by BECNT, HNTC, ICC2, NTC, WBC; KJV, NASB, NCV, NET, and NRSV. It is translated as middle ('do not conform yourselves') by AB; TEV. It is translated as simple intransitive active ('do not conform') by NICNT; CEV, GW, NIV, NLT, REB. This verb means to form or mold one's behavior in accordance with a particular pattern or set of standards [LN].

b. αἰών (LN 41.38) (BAGD 2.a. p. 27): 'age' [BAGD, BECNT, HNTC, ICC2, NICNT, WBC], 'present age' [BAGD], 'evil age' [NTC], 'world' [BAGD, LN; KJV, NASB, NIV, NRSV], 'present world' [AB; NET, REB], 'the people of this world' [CEV, GW, NCV], 'world system' [LN], 'the behavior and customs of this world' [NLT], 'the standards of this world' [TEV]. This noun denotes the system of practices and standards associated with secular society as existing apart from and without reference to any demands or requirements of God [LN].

c. pres. pass. impera. of μεταμορφόομαι (LN **13.53**) (BAGD 2. p. 511): 'to be transformed' [AB, BAGD, BECNT, HNTC, **LN**, NICNT, WBC; KJV, NASB, NET, NIV, NRSV, REB], 'to be changed' [LN; NCV], 'to be changed into the same form (as)' [BAGD]. The imperative verb μεταμορφοῦσθε 'be transformed' is translated 'continue to let yourselves be transformed' [ICC2, NTC], 'let God transform you' [NLT, TEV]. The phrase 'be transformed by the renewing of your mind' is translated 'change the way you think' [GW], 'let God change the way you think' [CEV]. This verb means to change the essential form or nature of something [LN]. The present imperative indicates a continual or ongoing action of transformation [SSA].

d. There is no lexical entry for the word 'by' in the Greek text, but it is used here to represent the relationship indicated by ἀνακαινώσει, the dative case of the noun ἀνακαίνωσις 'renewing'. This relationship is represented in translation as 'by' [AB, BECNT, HNTC, ICC2, NTC, WBC; all versions except CEV, GW], 'through' [NICNT], not explicit [CEV, GW].

e. ἀνακαίνωσις (LN **58.72**) (BAGD p. 55): 'renewing' [HNTC, ICC2, NICNT, NTC; KJV, NASB, NET, NIV, NRSV], 'renewal' [AB, BAGD, BECNT, LN, WBC; REB], not explicit [CEV, GW, NCV]. The phrase 'be transformed by the renewing of the mind' is translated 'let God transform you into a new person by changing the way you think' [NLT], 'let God transform you inwardly by a complete change of your mind' [TEV]. This noun denotes something new and different, with the implication of being superior [LN].

f. νοῦς (LN 26.14, 30.5) (BAGD 3.a. p. 544): 'mind' [BAGD, BECNT, HNTC, ICC2, LN (26.14), NICNT, NTC, WBC; KJV, NASB, NET, NIV], 'your minds' [NRSV, REB], 'way of thinking' [BAGD, LN (30.5)], 'whole way of thinking' [AB], 'the way you think' [CEV, GW, NLT], 'attitude' [BAGD]. The phrase 'be transformed by the renewing of the mind' is translated 'be changed within by a new way of thinking' [NCV], 'let God transform you inwardly by a complete change of your mind' [TEV]. This noun denotes the psychological faculty of understanding, reasoning, thinking, and deciding [LN (26.14)], or a particular manner or way of thinking [LN (30.5)].

QUESTION—How is this verse related to the one preceding it?

12:2 indicates the means by which the exhortations of 12:1 are to be carried out [NICNT]. 12:1 describes the somatic aspects of Christian living, those having to do with the body, and 12:2 describes the noetic aspects, those having to do with the mind [AB]. It partly describes how the command of the previous verse is to be carried out practically [BECNT, Gdt].

QUESTION—What difference is there between συσχηματίζω 'be conformed' and μεταμορφόομαι 'be transformed'?

1. There is no significant difference [BECNT, HNTC, ICC2, NICNT, St]. Conforming to this age is not just an outward matter and Paul uses them more or less interchangeably in other contexts [HNTC, ICC2, NICNT]. Conformity to this age is not just a matter of external behavior [BECNT, HNTC, ICC2], because being transformed requires a renewal of the thinking [BECNT].
2. There is a contrast intended; the difference is that one is conformity to a pattern that is external, whereas the other is transformation that proceeds from within [Gdt, ICC1, Mor, Mu, NAC, NTC, TH, WBC]. Inner transformation happens at the deepest level, which is infinitely more significant than outward conformity to the world's pattern that is typical of so many people [Mor].

QUESTION—What area of meaning is intended with the noun αἰών 'age'?

It is the present age and order, which is passing away [ICC2]. It is the non-Christian world, which leaves God out of consideration [SSA]. It is the current society, both in human and demonic terms, which regulates life for those within it [HNTC]. It is temporary and imperfect, and is contrasted with the age to come [AB]. It is the realm of this world during the present age, a realm and period dominated by sin and Satan, and to which all people belong by nature because of the effects of Adam's fall; those belonging to Christ have been transferred to his new realm of righteousness and life [NICNT]. It is this world in this age, with a temporal aspect to it, which is that it is perishing [Mor]. Typical of Jewish thinking, Paul conceived of the present age as evil, as opposed to the coming age, which is blessed [BECNT, WBC]. It is the present evil age, set in contrast to the age of renewal and resurrection that is to come [TNTC]. The present age is imperfect and temporary, but the age to come will be perfect and eternal [ICC1]. The term αἰών 'world/age' stands in contrast to 'the will of God' mentioned in the next clause; the two are incompatible [St]. This age is temporal, transient, and evil, and stands in contrast with the age to come [Mu]. It speaks of the mass of unsaved humanity, representing the present age, as opposed to those who are in the kingdom of God, representing the age to come [Ho].

QUESTION—Who or what is the agent of the verb μεταμορφοῦσθε 'be transformed'?

Transformation happens as believers meditate on the Lord, and on his splendor and beauty [BECNT].

1. God is the agent [NAC, SSA, TH, WBC; CEV, NLT, TEV]. The Holy Spirit does that work [ICC2, Mor, NTC]. We must put ourselves at God's disposal for that transformation to happen [NAC]. The believer must respond to the leading of God's sprit in this process of transformation [ICC2]. This transformation is done with the help of God's grace and the Holy Spirit [AB]. God is the source and power of the transformation [WBC]. This is an ongoing process [Mor].
2. Believers are to change the way they think [GW].

QUESTION—What is the relationship between the transforming and the renewing?

The renewing of the mind is the means for the transformation of the life [BECNT, ICC2, NICNT]. The transformation is begun at conversion and baptism, but the ongoing renewal occurs with every decision that is made which glorifies God and which is nurtured by Christian instruction [HNTC]. They are basically expressing the same idea [NTC].

QUESTION—What human faculty is described by the noun νοῦς 'mind'?

Changing the thinking results in changing every aspect of life [SSA]. It is human nature, which undergoes a radical renewal in conversion and baptism [HNTC]. It is the seat of moral and intellectual judgment [AB, NAC], of thought and understanding, the center of consciousness [Mu]. The thinking, willing, and acting aspects of personality are to be transformed [AB]. The νοῦς speaks of human rationality, that which distinguishes people from the rest of creation, and which consists of attitude, understanding, and ways of thinking [WBC]. It is practical reasoning as well as the capacity to reason morally [NICNT]. It is the aspect of a person that embraces moral concerns as well as the intellectual; Paul envisions the Christian response as a deeply intelligent approach to life [Mor]. It is the moral disposition, sensitivity, and perception [ICC2]. It is the intellectual and rational principle [ICC1], the moral faculty by which a person perceives what is good and true [Gdt]. It is approximately equivalent to the word 'heart', and represents the entire soul [Ho].

so-that[a] you(pl) prove[b] what (is) the will[c] of-God, the good[d] and well-pleasing[e] and perfect[f].

LEXICON—a. The phrase εἰς τό is translated 'so that (you may/might)' [AB, BECNT, ICC2, NICNT, NTC, WBC; NET, NRSV], 'so that (you can)' [NICNT], 'that (you may)' [HNTC; KJV, NASB], 'then (you will)' [CEV, GW, NCV, NIV, NLT, REB, TEV].

 b. pres. act. infin. of δοκιμάζω (LN 30.114, 27.45) (BAGD 1., 2.b. p. 202): 'to prove' [ICC2, NTC; KJV, NASB], 'to test' [LN (27.45)], 'to put to the test, to examine' [BAGD (1)], 'to test and approve' [NET, NIV], 'to try and approve' [HNTC], 'to approve' [BAGD (2.b.), BECNT, LN (30.114), NICNT], 'to accept as approved' [BAGD (2.b.)], 'to discern' [AB; NRSV], 'to be able to discern' [REB], 'to decide' [NCV], 'to ascertain' [WBC], 'to be able to determine' [GW], 'to learn to know' [NLT], 'to be able to know' [TEV], 'to know how to do' [CEV]. This verb means to regard something as genuine or worthy on the basis of testing [LN (30.114)], or to try to learn the genuineness of something by examination and testing, often through actual use [LN (27.45)].

 c. θέλημα (LN 30.59) (BAGD 1.c.γ. 354): 'will' [AB, BAGD, BECNT, HNTC, ICC2, LN, NICNT, NTC, WBC; KJV, NASB, NET, NIV, NLT, NRSV, REB, TEV], 'intent, purpose, plan' [LN]. The phrase 'the will of God' is translated 'everything that is good and pleasing to him' [CEV], 'what God really wants' [GW], 'what God wants for you' [NCV]. This noun denotes that which is purposed, intended, or willed [LN].

 d. ἀγαθός (LN 88.1): 'good' [AB, BECNT, ICC2, LN, NICNT, NTC, WBC; all versions], 'holy' [HNTC]. This adjective describes positive moral qualities of the most general nature [LN].

 e. εὐάρεστος (LN **25.94**) (BAGD 1. p. 318): 'well pleasing' [BECNT, NICNT, NTC; NET], 'pleasing' [BAGD, LN; CEV, GW, NCV, NIV, NLT, TEV], 'acceptable' [AB, ICC2, LN, WBC; KJV, NASB, NRSV, REB]. This adjective describes that which causes someone to be pleased [LN].

 f. τέλειος (LN 88.36) (BAGD 1.a.β. p. 809): 'perfect' [AB, BAGD, BECNT, HNTC, ICC2, LN, NICNT, NTC, WBC; all versions except CEV], not explicit [CEV]. This adjective describes being perfect in the sense of not lacking any moral quality [LN].

QUESTION—What relationship is indicated by the preposition εἰς in the phrase εἰς τὸ δοκιμάζειν 'so that (you) prove'?

 1. It indicates purpose [ICC2, NICNT, SSA, WBC; KJV, NASB, NET].
 2. It indicates result [ICC1, St; CEV, GW, NCV, NIV, NLT, REB, TEV].
 3. It indicates both purpose and result [Ho].

QUESTION—In what sense are they to 'prove' the will of God?

 By their experience they come to discern and know what is good [AB, Gdt, SSA]. They are to come to know from experience that the will of God is good [Mu]. They come to understand and agree with what God wants people to do [NICNT]. They come to know and to delight in the will of God [Ho].

They come to approve of it as a result of testing; having found that it is good, they put it into practice [Mor]. They approve it as a result of the process of testing and examining [BECNT]. The renewed mind, led by the Spirit and taught by the gospel, is able to exercise a responsible freedom in discerning, embracing, and obeying the will of God [ICC2]. The intellect comes to the point of being able to judge rightly in spiritual and moral issues [ICC1], to form proper Christian ethical judgment [WBC]. It means to come to discern the will of God and decide to obey it [St].

QUESTION—What relation is there between τὸ θέλημα τοῦ θεοῦ 'the will of God' and the three adjectives that follow?

'The will of God' refers to how God wants people to live, to moral direction [NICNT].

1. They are in apposition; the will of God is that which is good, which is pleasing to God, and which is perfect [AB, BECNT, HNTC, Ho, ICC1, ICC2, Mor, Mu, NICNT, NTC, SSA, TH, WBC; GW, NASB, NCV, NET, NIV, NLT, NRSV, REB, TEV].
2. They are adjectival: the good, well-pleasing, and perfect will of God [Gdt; KJV].

QUESTION—To whom would it be 'well-pleasing'?

1. It would be well-pleasing to God [AB, BECNT, ICC2, Mor, NAC, NICNT, NTC, SSA, TH, WBC; CEV, GW, NCV, TEV].
2. It would be acceptable to people who observe the effects of God's will being realized in the life of the Christian [Gdt].

QUESTION—What is the relationship of 12:1–2 to what follows?

It introduces and describes the theme of 12:1–15:13 [BECNT, ICC2, SSA], and linking that appeal with 1:16–11:36, which is the basis for the appeals of 12:1–15:13 [SSA]. It introduces and summarizes the exhortations of 12:1–15:13 [BECNT]. The renewed mind needs instruction, which is what now follows [HNTC]. It requires a renewed mind to properly evaluate oneself and one's identity and gifts, and only the renewed mind can be humble, as Christ was [St]. The humility and unity he calls for in the following verses is one way the transformation spoken of in 12:1–2 is to be manifested [NICNT]. The 'good' that the person with the renewed mind approves of is further spelled out in 12:9–21 [NICNT]. He now describes how the consecration spoken of in 12:1–2 is to be expressed in living [Gdt].

DISCOURSE UNIT—12:3–13:14 [BECNT]. The topic is marks of the Christian community.

DISCOURSE UNIT—12:3–21 [HNTC]. The topic is the Christian offering.

DISCOURSE UNIT—12:3–16 [Mor]. The topic is the Christian attitude to other Christians.

DISCOURSE UNIT—12:3–8 [AB, Ho, ICC1, ICC2, NICNT, St, TNTC, WBC]. The topic is sober existence using God's gifts for all [AB], the proper use of gifts [Ho], the right use of spiritual gifts [ICC1], the believer as a member of the congregation in his relations with his fellow members [ICC2], humility and mutual service [NICNT], our relationship to ourselves: thinking soberly about our gifts [St], the common life of Christians [TNTC], the body of Christ as the social context of faith [WBC].

DISCOURSE UNIT—12:3 [Mor]. The topic is humility.

12:3 For[a] through[b] the grace[c] having-been-given[d] to-me I-say to everyone being among[e] you

LEXICON—a. γάρ (LN 89.23) (BAGD 4. p. 152): 'for' [BECNT, HNTC, ICC2, LN, NICNT, NTC, WBC; KJV, NASB, NET, NIV, NRSV], 'and' [TEV], not explicit [AB; CEV, GW, NCV, NLT, REB]. This particle may be used here to express continuity [BAGD; TEV]. This conjunction marks cause or reason between events, though in some contexts the relation is often remote or tenuous [LN].

b. διά with genitive object (LN 89.26, 89.76) (BAGD A.III.1.e. p. 180): 'through' [BAGD, LN (89.76), NICNT, NTC, WBC; KJV, NASB], 'by' [LN (89.76); NET, NIV, NRSV], 'by means of' [BAGD], 'by authority of' [REB], 'because of' [BECNT, LN; GW, NLT, TEV], 'because' [NCV], 'on account of, by reason of' [LN (89.26)], 'in virtue of' [AB], 'by virtue of' [ICC2]. The phrase 'through the grace having been given to me' is translated 'I realize how kind God has been to me, and so...' [CEV]. This preposition can mark cause or reason, with focus upon instrumentality, either of objects or events [LN (89.26)], or can mark the means by which one event makes another event possible [LN (89.76)].

c. χάρις (LN 88.66) (BAGD 4. p. 878): 'grace' [AB, BAGD, BECNT, HNTC, ICC2, LN, NICNT, NTC, WBC; KJV, NASB, NET, NIV, NRSV, REB], 'gracious gift' [TEV], 'special gift' [NCV]. This may be used here to refer to the special effects produced by divine grace [BAGD]. The phrase 'the grace having been given to me' is translated 'how kind God has been to me' [CEV], 'the kindness God has shown me' [GW], 'the privilege and authority' [NLT]. This noun denotes kindness to someone, with the implication of graciousness on the part of the one showing such kindness [LN].

d. aorist pass. participle of δίδωμι (LN 57.71): 'to be given' [AB, BECNT, ICC2, LN, NICNT, NTC, WBC; KJV, NASB, NET, NIV, NRSV, REB], 'to give' [HNTC; NCV, NLT]. The phrase 'the grace having been given to me' is translated 'how kind God has been to me' [CEV], 'the kindness God has shown me' [GW], 'God's gracious gift to me' [TEV]. This verb means to give something, usually implying that it is valuable [LN].

e. The phrase παντὶ τῷ ὄντι ἐν ὑμῖν 'everyone being among you' is translated 'every person among you' [NICNT], 'every man that is among you' [KJV], 'every man among you' [NASB], 'everyone among you' [NTC; NCV, NRSV, REB], 'all who are among you' [WBC], 'to every one of you' [AB, BECNT; NET, NIV, TEV], 'every single one of you'

[ICC2], 'you, everyone' [HNTC], 'each of you' [CEV, NLT], 'you' [GW].

QUESTION—What relationship is indicated by γάρ 'for'?

It introduces the first, more specific, step by which the general appeals of 12:1–2 can be put into practice [NICNT, SSA]. It indicates the ground of his authority to give the following exhortations as an explanation of the principles he has just stated in the previous two verses [HNTC]. It introduces various instructions that explain the implications of what he has just told them [BECNT, Gdt, ICC2, Mor].

QUESTION—What relationship is indicated by διά 'through'?

It is causal; Paul can say these things because God has graciously given him this apostolic ministry [SSA]. He says these things by virtue of the office he has [AB, BECNT, ICC2, Mor, NAC, NICNT]. He says these things on account of all the ways God has been gracious to him, including the apostolic authority God gave him [Ho].

QUESTION—What is the grace given to him?

It is his authority as an apostle [BECNT, Gdt, Ho, ICC1, ICC2, Mor, Mu, NICNT, NTC, St, TNTC], but would include other gifts that Paul has as well [Ho, Mor]. His being made an apostle was an act of God's favor [ICC2, NAC]. It is the apostolic ministry that God graciously gave Paul [SSA]. He is called and graced by God himself [AB]. Paul was specially gifted for edifying the churches [HNTC].

QUESTION—What is conveyed by his use of the verb λέγω 'I say'?

It expresses a note of authority [Gdt, ICC2, Mor, NICNT, WBC]. It introduces a command [NTC], even a solemn command [ICC2]. It is parallel to 'I exhort' in 12:1 [NICNT], or expresses even more authority than 'I exhort' in 12:1 [Gdt].

not to-think-too-highly[a] (of-yourself) beyond[b] what (you) ought[c] to-think[d]

LEXICON—a. pres. act. infin. of ὑπερφρονέω (LN 88.210) (BAGD p. 842): 'to think too highly of oneself' [BAGD, BECNT, WBC; REB], 'to think more highly of oneself' [AB, HNTC, ICC2, NTC; GW, KJV, NASB, NET, NIV, NRSV, TEV], 'to be conceited, to be arrogant, to be proud' [LN], 'to think highly of oneself' [**LN**], 'to think beyond what is necessary to think' [NICNT], 'to think you are better than' [CEV, NCV, NLT], 'to be haughty' [BAGD]. This verb means to have an unwarranted pride in oneself or in one's accomplishments [LN]. This word occurs only here in the NT.

b. παρά with accusative object (LN 78.29) (BAGD III.3. p. 611): 'beyond' [BAGD, LN, NICNT, WBC], 'more than' [BAGD, LN], 'more (highly) than' [AB, HNTC, ICC2, NTC; GW, KJV, NASB, NET, NIV, NRSV, TEV], 'to a greater degree than' [LN], 'better than' [CEV, NCV], not explicit [BECNT; NLT, REB]. This preposition marks a degree which is beyond that of a compared scale of extent [LN].

c. pres. act. indic. of the impersonal verb δεῖ (LN 71.21): 'ought' [AB, HNTC, ICC2, LN, NTC, WBC; KJV, NASB, NET, NIV, NRSV], 'should' [LN; GW, TEV], '(what is) necessary' [NICNT], not explicit [BECNT; CEV, NCV, NLT, REB]. This verb refers to something which should be done as the result of compulsion, whether internal (as a matter of duty) or external (law, custom, and circumstances) [LN].

d. pres. act. infin. of φρονέω (LN 26.16) (BAGD 1. p. 866): 'to think' [BAGD, HNTC, ICC2, NICNT, NTC, WBC; KJV, NASB, NET, NRSV], 'to have an attitude, to think in a particular manner' [LN], not explicit [AB, BECNT; GW, NIV, REB, TEV]. The phrase 'not to think too highly of yourselves beyond what you ought to think' is translated 'not to think you are better than you really are' [CEV], 'don't think you are better than you really are' [NCV, NLT]. This verb means to employ one's faculty for thoughtful planning, with emphasis upon the underlying disposition or attitude [LN].

but to-think so-as[a] to-think-sensibly,[b] as[c] to-each God distributed[d] a measure[e] of-faith.

LEXICON—a. The phrase εἰς τό is translated 'so as' [ICC2, NTC; NASB], not explicit [AB, BECNT, HNTC, NICNT, WBC; all versions except NASB].

b. pres. act. infin. of σωφρονέω (LN **32.34**) (BAGD 2. p. 802): 'to think sensibly' [BECNT], 'to be sensible' [BAGD, LN], 'to have sound judgment' [NASB], 'to use good sense' [LN; CEV], 'to be sober-minded' [HNTC], 'to think soberly' [ICC2, NTC; KJV], 'to be reasonable or serious' [BAGD], 'to be modest in your thinking' [TEV], 'to observe proper moderation' [WBC]. The phrase 'to think so as to think sensibly' is translated 'think of yourself with sober judgment' [AB; NIV], 'think with sober judgment' [NRSV], 'think with sober discernment' [NET], 'think with sober thinking' [NICNT], 'form a sober estimate' [REB], 'be honest in your evaluation of yourselves' [NLT], 'your thoughts should lead you to use good judgment' [GW], 'you must decide what you really are' [NCV]. This verb means to have understanding about practical matters and thus be able to act sensibly [LN].

c. ὡς (LN 89.37) (BAGD I.2.c. p. 897): 'as' [BAGD, BECNT, HNTC, NICNT, WBC; NASB, NET], 'according as' [KJV], 'according to' [AB, ICC2, NTC; NRSV, TEV], 'in accordance with' [NIV], 'because' [LN], 'based on' [GW, REB], 'by' [NCV, NLT], not explicit [CEV]. This conjunction marks cause or reason, implying the special nature of the circumstances [LN].

d. aorist act. indic. of μερίζω (LN 57.89) (BAGD 2.b. p. 504): 'to distribute' [LN; NET], 'to give to each in turn' [LN], 'to give' [HNTC; CEV, GW, NCV, NIV, NLT, TEV], 'to apportion' [AB, BAGD, BECNT, NTC], 'to measure' [NICNT, WBC], 'to deal out' [BAGD], 'to deal' [KJV, REB], 'to assign' [BAGD; NRSV], 'to allot' [NASB], 'to impart' [ICC2]. This verb means to distribute objects to a series of persons [LN].

e. μέτρον (LN 81.1) (BAGD 2.b. p. 515): 'measure' [AB, BAGD, BECNT, HNTC, ICC2, LN, NICNT, NTC, WBC; KJV, NASB, NET, NIV, NRSV, REB], 'amount' [CEV, NCV, TEV]. The phrase 'to each God distributed a measure of faith' is translated 'what God has given each of you as believers' [GW], 'measuring yourselves by the faith God has given us' [NLT]. This noun denotes a unit of measurement, either of length or volume [LN].

QUESTION—What is meant by 'a measure of faith'?

1. 'Faith' is used as a metonymy [SSA]; it refers to all the effects that are caused or brought about by faith, that is, spiritual gifts [Gdt, Ho, ICC1, Mu, SSA]. People are exercising faith when they exercise their spiritual gift [Mu]. People have various abilities granted to them by the Holy Spirit [SSA]. This is a gift of faith to do certain things that is granted by the Holy Spirit, not unlike that in 1 Corinthians 13 [HNTC]. This faith is a trust in God by which a person lays hold of God's promises, but he specifically has in mind their use of those gifts God has given them in association with their faith [NTC]. It is spiritual power enabling a believer to fulfill his or her special responsibility [TNTC]. Faith, which itself is a gift from God, is the evidence as well as the measuring standard of the Christian life [ICC1].
2. He refers here to the quantity of faith that each person has and can exercise [BECNT, WBC]. They are to evaluate themselves based on how much faith they have [CEV, NCV]. The faith a person has is a gift from God, so no one should be proud [BECNT]. Faith is a confident trust in God that recognizes that all grace and faith come from him [WBC].
3. 'Faith' is in apposition to μέτρον, which would mean 'standard' here, the standard by which things are to be measured [AB, ICC2, Mor, NICNT, St; CEV, NLT]. God has given the basic Christian faith equally to all Christians, and this common faith is the means of measurement, or the 'standard' against which each Christian is to estimate himself [NICNT]. Here the standard is the object of faith, Jesus Christ [AB, ICC2], or the gospel of Jesus Christ, and Christ himself [ICC2, St]. The believer is to evaluate himself according to his relationship to Christ, which is a gift of God, by faith, and it must be remembered that the most important and governing element in that faith is not the subject (the one who believes), but the object, Jesus Christ [ICC2].

DISCOURSE UNIT—12:4–8 [Mor]. The topic is difference of function.

12:4 For[a] just-as[b] in one body[c] we-have many[d] members,[e] and/but[f] all the members do- not -have the same function,[g]

LEXICON—a. γάρ (LN 89.23): 'for' [AB, BECNT, HNTC, ICC2, LN, NICNT, NTC, WBC; KJV, NASB, NET, NRSV, REB], not explicit [CEV, GW, NCV, NIV, NLT, TEV]. This conjunction marks cause or reason [LN].

b. καθάπερ (LN 64.15) (BAGD p. 387): 'just as' [AB, BAGD, BECNT, LN, NTC, WBC; NASB, NET, NIV, NLT, REB], 'even as' [ICC2, NICNT], 'as' [HNTC; KJV, NRSV], not explicit [CEV, GW, NCV, TEV]. This emphatic conjunction marks comparison between events or states [LN].

c. σῶμα (LN 8.1) (BAGD 1.b. p. 799): 'body' [AB, BAGD, BECNT, HNTC, ICC2, LN, NICNT, NTC, WBC; CEV, KJV, NASB, NCV, NET, NIV, NRSV, TEV], 'single human body' [REB], 'our bodies' [GW, NLT]. This noun denotes the physical body of persons, animals, or plants [LN].

d. πολύς (LN 59.1) (BAGD I.1.a.α. p. 687): 'many' [AB, BAGD, BECNT, HNTC, ICC2, LN, NICNT, NTC, WBC; all versions]. This adjective describes a relatively large quantity of objects or events [LN].

e. μέλος (LN **8.9**) (BAGD 1. p. 501): 'member' [AB, BAGD, BECNT, HNTC, ICC2, LN, NICNT, NTC, WBC; KJV, NASB, NET, NIV, NRSV], 'parts' [BAGD; CEV, GW, NCV, NLT, TEV], 'body part' [LN], 'limb' [BAGD], 'limbs and organs' [REB]. This noun denotes a part of the body [LN].

f. δέ (LN 89.94, 89.124): 'and' [AB, BECNT, HNTC, LN (89.94), NICNT, NTC, WBC; all versions except GW, REB], 'but' [ICC2, LN (89.124); GW], not explicit [REB]. This conjunction marks an additive relation [LN (89.94)], or contrast [LN (89.124)].

g. πρᾶξις (LN **42.5**) (BAGD 1. p. 697): 'function' [AB, BAGD, BECNT, HNTC, ICC2, **LN**, NICNT, NTC, WBC; NASB, NET, NIV, NRSV], 'special function' [NLT], 'task' [LN], 'office' [KJV], 'use' [CEV]. The phrase 'all the members do not have the same function' is translated 'these parts don't all do the same thing' [GW], 'these parts all have different uses' [NCV], 'all these parts have different functions' [TEV], 'all with different functions' [REB]. This noun denotes a function, implying sustained activity and/or responsibility [LN].

QUESTION—What relationship is indicated by γάρ 'for'?

It indicates the basis, stated in 12:4–5, for the appeal in 12:3 [BECNT, ICC2, NICNT, SSA]; that is, think reasonably about yourselves, since believers are all members of the same body.

QUESTION—What relationship is indicated by καθάπερ 'just as'?

It indicates that what follows is an analogy [AB, HNTC]. It introduces the basis for the comparison he will make in 12:4 [NICNT].

12:5 so[a] we- many[b] -are one body in[c] Christ, and each[d] one members of-one-another.

LEXICON—a. οὕτως (LN 61.9): 'so' [AB, HNTC, ICC2, LN, NTC, WBC; KJV, NASB, NET, NIV, NRSV, REB], 'so also' [NICNT], 'thus' [LN], 'thus also' [BECNT], 'in the same way' [GW, NCV, TEV]. This word is translated 'that's how it is with us' [CEV], 'so it is with Christ's body' [NLT]. This conjunction marks reference to that which precedes [LN].

b. πολύς. See above.

c. ἐν with dative object (LN 89.119): 'in' [AB, BECNT, HNTC, ICC2, LN, NICNT, NTC, WBC; KJV, NASB, NCV, NET, NIV, NRSV], 'in union

with' [LN; TEV], 'to be united with' [REB]. The phrase 'we many are one body in Christ' is translated 'there are many of us, but we each are part of the body of Christ' [CEV], 'we are many parts of one body' [NLT], 'even though we are many individuals, Christ makes us one body' [GW]. This preposition marks close personal association [LN].
   d. κατά (LN 89.90). The phrase καθ' εἷς is translated 'each' [NIV], 'we each' [CEV], 'every one' [KJV], 'individually' [AB, BECNT, NICNT, WBC; NASB, NET, NRSV], 'severally' [HNTC, ICC2, NTC], 'individuals who' [GW], not explicit [REB]. The phrase 'each one members of one another' is translated 'each one is part of that body, and each part belongs to all the other parts' [NCV], 'we are all joined to each other as different parts to one body' [TEV], 'we all belong to each other' [NLT]. This preposition marks distributive relations, whether of place, time, or number [LN].

QUESTION—What relationship is indicated by οὕτως 'so'?
   It indicates a similarity of process; that is, Christians are intended to fit and function together in the same way that a human body does [SSA]. It introduces the second half of the analogy [HNTC].

QUESTION—How does he use the metaphor of 'one body' in this passage?
   He is stressing the idea of unity [BECNT]. Christians form a single group [SSA]. They are to function in unity, as parts of a body do [HNTC]. It speaks of an organic unity with diversity [NAC, NTC], a moral unity based on each one being in Christ, all interrelated, and no one in isolation [AB]. Because of their incorporation into Christ, they have an organic unity with one another [Mor]. He uses this metaphor to describe the vital bond that links the life of believers to the life of the risen Christ [TNTC]. Because they belong to a greater whole, all of them are under obligation to serve the others [ICC2]. They are mutually interdependent [St]. He does not specifically say here that they are the body of Christ, but that should be understood [Mu].

QUESTION—What does he mean by the phrase ἐν Χριστῷ 'in Christ'?
   It means that they trust in Christ and are united with him [SSA]. It speaks of their common union with him [St]. They are part of the body of Christ and united with each other through faith in Christ [NAC]. They draw life from Christ [AB]. They are incorporated into Christ [BECNT, Mor] as the second Adam [BECNT, WBC]. The unity they have is a result of the grace of God [ICC2]. They are a living, organic unit because of their common union with Christ [Ho].

12:6 And[a] having[b] differing[c] gifts[d] according-to the grace[e] given to us,
LEXICON—a. δέ (LN 89.94): 'and' [BECNT, LN, NICNT; NET], 'also' [CEV], 'moreover' [NTC], 'but' [ICC2], not explicit [AB, HNTC, WBC; GW, KJV, NASB, NCV, NIV, NLT, NRSV, REB, TEV]. This conjunction marks an additive relation, but with the possible implication of some contrast [LN].

b. pres. act. participle of ἔχω (LN 57.1): 'to have' [AB, BECNT, HNTC, ICC2, LN, NICNT, NTC, WBC; KJV, NASB, NCV, NET, NIV, NRSV], 'to possess' [LN], 'to be allotted' [REB]. The phrase 'and having differing gifts according to the grace given to us' is translated 'God has also given each of us different gifts to use' [CEV], 'God in his kindness gave each of us different gifts' [GW], 'God has given us different gifts for doing certain things well' [NLT], 'so we are to use our different gifts in accordance with the grace that God has given us' [TEV]. This verb means to have or possess objects or property (in the technical sense of having control over the use of such objects) [LN].

c. διάφορος (LN **58.40**) (BAGD 1. p. 190): 'differing' [HNTC, ICC2, **LN**; KJV], 'to differ' [AB, NICNT, WBC; NASB, NRSV], 'different' [BAGD, BECNT, LN, NTC; CEV, GW, NCV, NET, NIV, NLT, REB, TEV], 'varied' [LN]. This adjective describes that which is different [LN].

d. χάρισμα (LN 57.103) (BAGD 2. p. 879): 'gift' [AB, BAGD, BECNT, ICC2, LN, NICNT, NTC; all versions], 'gracious gift' [LN], 'gift of grace' [HNTC], 'charisma' [WBC]. This noun denotes that which is given freely and generously [LN].

e. χάρις (LN 88.66) (BAGD 4. p. 878): 'grace' [AB, BAGD, BECNT, HNTC, ICC2, LN, NICNT, NTC, WBC; KJV, NASB, NCV, NET, NIV, NRSV, TEV], 'God's grace' [REB], 'in his grace' [NLT], not explicit [CEV]. This may be used here to refer to the special effects produced by divine grace [BAGD]. This noun denotes kindness to someone, with the implication of graciousness on the part of the one showing such kindness [LN].

QUESTION—Should this be seen as the beginning of a new sentence, or as a continuation of the thought of the previous two verses?

1. It begins a new sentence and a new thought [AB, BECNT, Gdt, HNTC, Ho, ICC1, ICC2, Mor, Mu, NICNT, NTC, SSA].
2. It is a continuation of the thought of the previous two verses [WBC].

QUESTION—What relationship is indicated by the use of the participle ἔχοντες 'having'?

1. It indicates grounds for the implied exhortation that they should do the things God has given them the ability to do [HNTC, NICNT, SSA; NASB]: because we have differing gifts, let us use them.
2. It continues the description of the body imagery [WBC]: we are one body, having differing gifts.

QUESTION—What is the relation between χαρίσματα 'gifts' and χάρις 'grace'?

The χαρίσματα 'gifts' are products of God's χάρις 'grace' [BECNT, ICC1, ICC2, NICNT, NTC]. They are the visible expression and embodiment of grace [WBC]. The χάρις 'grace' bestows the χαρίσματα 'gifts' [St]. The χαρίσματα 'gifts' are special abilities in Christian service, and χάρις 'grace' is an attribute of the event by which God enabled them to perform the service [SSA]. Although the gifts are diverse, the grace is experienced in common by all believers [NICNT]. In his grace God has poured out these gifts on the church [NAC]. The χαρίσματα 'gifts' are the specific participation of the believers in χάρις 'grace' [AB]. The various χαρίσματα 'gifts' are grounded in the one χάρις 'grace' of God, which is shown to everyone [ICC2].

QUESTION—What is the implied predicate in this sentence?
1. Paul is saying that they should do the things God has given them special enabling to do [BECNT, HNTC, ICC1, ICC2, Mor, Mu, NICNT, SSA].
2. There is no implied predicate, it further describes the members of the body already mentioned [WBC].

if[a] prophecy[b] (then) according-to[c] the proportion[d] of-faith,[e]

LEXICON—a. εἴτε (LN 89.69) (BAGD VI.13.b. p. 220): 'if' [AB, BAGD, BECNT, HNTC, ICC2, LN, NICNT, NTC; CEV, GW, NASB, NET, NIV, NLT, TEV], 'whether' [BAGD, LN, WBC; KJV], not explicit [NCV, NRSV, REB]. This conjunction marks condition [LN].
  b. προφητεία (LN 33.461) (BAGD 2. p. 722): 'prophecy' [AB, HNTC, NICNT, WBC; KJV, NASB, NET, NRSV], 'the gift of prophecy' [BAGD, BECNT, ICC2; NCV], 'prophesying' [BAGD, NTC; NIV], 'to prophesy' [CEV], 'the ability to prophesy' [LN; NLT], 'the gift of inspired utterance' [REB], 'to speak God's word' [GW], 'to speak God's message' [TEV]. This noun denotes the capacity or ability to utter inspired messages [LN].
  c. κατά with accusative object (LN 89.8): 'according to' [AB, BECNT, HNTC, ICC2, NICNT; CEV, KJV, NASB, TEV], 'in accordance with' [ICC2, LN, NTC], 'in relation to' [LN], not explicit [AB, WBC; GW, NCV, NET, NIV, NLT, NRSV, REB]. This preposition marks a relation involving similarity of process [LN].
  d. ἀναλογία (LN **89.10**) (BAGD p. 57): 'proportion' [AB, BECNT, HNTC; KJV, NASB, NET, NIV, REB], 'standard' [ICC2, NTC], 'amount' [CEV], 'analogy' [NICNT], 'in relation to' [LN]. The phrase 'then according to the proportion of faith' is translated 'let it be used in proportion to one's faith' [AB], 'let us use in proportion to our faith' [REB], 'let him use it in proportion to his faith' [NIV], 'exercise it according to the proportion of your faith' [BECNT], 'let us exercise it according to the proportion of faith' [HNTC], 'let him exercise it in accordance with the standard of faith' [NTC], 'let us prophesy according to the proportion of faith' [KJV], 'we should do it according to the amount of faith we have' [CEV], 'we should do it according to the faith that we have' [TEV], 'make sure what you say agrees with the Christian faith' [GW], '(the person who has the gift of prophecy) should use that gift in agreement with the faith' [NCV], 'that individual must use it in proportion to his faith' [NET], 'speak out with as much faith as God has given you' [NLT]. This noun denotes a relation of proportion [LN]. This word occurs only here in the NT.

e. πίστις (LN 31.85) (BAGD 2.d.α. p. 663, or 3. p. 664): 'faith' [BAGD (2.d.α.), HNTC, ICC2, LN, NICNT, NTC, WBC; CEV, KJV, NLT, NRSV], 'the faith' [NCV, TEV], 'our faith' [REB], 'your faith' [BECNT], 'one's faith' [AB], 'his faith' [NASB, NET, NIV], 'the Christian faith' [GW], 'trust' [LN], 'body of faith, belief, doctrine' [BAGD (3.)]. This noun denotes belief to the extent of complete trust and reliance [LN].

QUESTION—What is the gift of prophecy?

It is the ability to speak words that come directly from God [Mor, SSA]. It is speech inspired by the Holy Spirit and not primarily formulated consciously by the mind [WBC]. It is not primarily a matter of predicting the future [AB, Ho, NICNT, SSA, TH]. It was a direct communication from God to his own people, and which may or may not involve prediction of future events [HNTC]. The prophet received special revelation directly from the Holy Spirit [NTC]. The prophet is like the eye of the church in the sense of receiving new revelations [Gdt]. It is inspired Christian preaching that speaks in behalf of God and exposes the secrets of the heart [AB]. It is a message inspired by God, revelatory in nature, given for the edification of the church, but which had less authority than the message of an apostle [NICNT]. It is a proclaiming of God's message [TH]. The prophet was God's channel for revelation [Mu]. It is spontaneous revelation, given for the congregation, and often involving practical matters relevant to their circumstances; it is not to be equated with preaching [BECNT]. It was often given with reference to a particular specific situation, may have involved predicting the future, and fulfilled a pastoral function [ICC2]. Prophecy addressed a current local situation [St].

QUESTION—Is τῆς πίστεως 'of faith' to be understood as the objective Christian faith, or as subjective, personal faith?

1. It is subjective, referring to the faith of the person prophesying [HNTC, ICC1, Mor, Mu, NTC, SSA, TH, WBC; NASB, NET, NIV]. It refers to the person's belief that that what he is saying is a message from God [SSA]. He has faith for the function he must perform [HNTC, Mu].
2. It is subjective, referring to the faith of the whole church [Gdt].
3. It is objective, referring to the Christian faith as a body of belief [AB, Ho, St].
4. It is both subjective and objective, in that it is the basic Christian faith, which the person prophesying holds [ICC2, NICNT].

QUESTION—What is meant by κατὰ τῆς ἀναλογίαν τῆς πίστεως 'according to the proportion of faith'?

1. Prophets should speak in accordance with their own faith in God or Christ, that is, the *fides qua creditor*, the personal faith by which someone believes [BECNT, WBC]. The prophet should speak in accordance with the special faith-gift that God has granted him [ICC1]. They are equipped with faith, granted by God, for what they do, but it is 'a measure', meaning that they must be realistic about their own importance, and also

not go beyond the faith that they personally have when one of them speaks a prophetic message [HNTC, ICC1]. Prophets must speak according to what they believe God has said [Mu, NTC, SSA].
2. The prophet speaks in a way that agrees with the objective standard of Christian doctrine [Ho; GW, NCV], the Christian faith [AB], the *fides quae creditor*, the faith or creed which someone believes. The Christian faith is a norm or standard by which such things are to be evaluated [AB].
3. Prophets should speak in accordance with basic, objective Christian faith, which they themselves hold [ICC2, NICNT, St].
4. Prophets should speak in a way that corresponds to the stage of faith and maturity of the church; they are to develop God's work of faith among believers beginning at the point where they currently stand, the present state being a reference point for any new instruction that would be given [Gdt].

12:7 if service[a] in service, if the-one teaching[b] in teaching,[c]

LEXICON—a. διακονία (LN 35.19) (BAGD 5. p. 184): 'service' [LN, NICNT, WBC; NASB, NET], 'ministry' [AB, HNTC; KJV, NRSV], 'gift of serving' [BECNT; NCV], 'gift of administration' [REB], 'gift of practical service' [ICC2], 'to render practical service' [NTC], 'to serve' [CEV, GW, NIV, TEV], 'to serve others' [NLT], 'office of a deacon' [BAGD]. This noun denotes assistance or help by performing certain duties, often of a humble or menial nature [LN].
  b. pres. act. participle of διδάσκω (LN 33.224): 'teaching' [LN; GW, NET, NIV], 'gift of teaching' [NCV, REB], 'to teach' [BECNT, WBC; CEV, KJV, NASB, TEV]. The phrase 'the one teaching' is translated 'one is a teacher' [AB, HNTC, ICC2, NICNT, NTC], 'you are a teacher' [NLT], 'the teacher' [NRSV]. This verb means to provide instruction in a formal or informal setting [LN].
  c. διδασκαλία (LN 33.224) (BAGD 1. p. 191): 'teaching' [BECNT, HNTC, ICC2, LN, NICNT, NTC, WBC; GW, KJV, NASB, NRSV], 'the act of teaching' [BAGD], 'instruction' [AB, BAGD]. This noun is translated as a verb: 'to teach' [CEV, NCV, NET, NIV, NLT, REB, TEV]. This noun denotes instruction in a formal or informal setting [LN].

QUESTION—How is the term διακονία 'service' to be understood?
1. It is used in a general sense to describe the activity of serving [BECNT, Mor, SSA, TH]. It is giving financial and material help [BECNT]. It is serving the needy [HNTC]. It is meeting practical needs [NAC]. It is helping generally [TH].
2. It is the function of the deacon, by which the church would assist the needy [Gdt, Ho, Mu, NTC]. It is a specific gifting that enabled a person to fulfill the office of deacon, which helped organize the work of providing for the material needs of Christian people [NICNT]. It involves the kind of practical service that eventually came to be the special role of the deacon [ICC2]. It is the administration of alms and of the meeting of

physical needs [ICC1]. It is service given *ad hoc* for the meeting of various needs, regularly done by the same persons, but not yet formalized into the office of deacon [WBC].

QUESTION—Is it significant that Paul changes in the middle of the list from abstract nouns for the gift itself (prophecy and service) to personal designations of the one who exercises the gift (the one teaching, etc.) in the last four gifts?

The reason for the change is not clear [NICNT]. Perhaps the change is stylistic to avoid too much repetition, but it may be because the last four gifts are for regular ministry; however the focus throughout is on the functions of the gifts themselves [WBC]. In this clause, the change in form makes it clear that the person is imparting instructions, not receiving them [ICC1].

QUESTION—What is the function of διδασκαλία 'teaching' in the early church?

Most people had little education and very few people had books, so they were very dependent on teachers for their understanding of the Christian faith [Mor]. In those days it was primarily moral teaching, guiding people about what they ought to do [NAC]. People needed to be taught about the faith, about interpretation of Scripture, and about God's will [AB]. The function of teaching was to transmit the truth of the gospel as the church had preserved it [NICNT]. It was explaining written tradition, whether the OT Scriptures, catechetical material, or traditions about Jesus' ministry [BECNT, ICC2], and which required study and effort on the part of the teacher [BECNT]. The teacher had to depend on the Holy Spirit for inspired insight into the traditional formulations that he was teaching and passing on [WBC]. The teacher's task was to nurture new believers in their faith [St]. The job of the teacher was not to give revelation, but to expound the meaning of what had already been revealed and to explain it so that people could understand [Mu]. Where the prophet gives new revelation, the teacher sets forth in an orderly way revelation already given, explaining the relation of one concept to another [Gdt]. Whereas the prophet had immediate inspiration from God, the teacher taught what he had learned from Scripture or from other inspired persons [Ho].

12:8 if the-one exhorting[a] in exhortation;[b] the one-giving[c] in generosity,[d]

LEXICON—a. pres. act. participle of παρακαλέω (LN 25.150) (BAGD 2., 4. p. 617): 'to exhort' [BAGD (2.), BECNT; KJV, NASB], 'to encourage' [BAGD (2., 4.), LN, WBC; CEV, GW, NIV], 'to encourage others' [NLT, TEV], 'to console' [LN], 'to urge, to appeal to' [BAGD (2.)], 'to have the gift of encouraging others' [NCV], 'gift of counseling' [REB], 'exhortation' [NET]. This participle is translated as a noun: 'exhorter' [AB, HNTC, ICC2, NICNT, NTC; NRSV]. This verb means to cause someone to be encouraged or consoled, either by verbal or non-verbal means [LN].

b. παράκλησις (LN 25.150) (BAGD 1. p. 618): 'exhortation' [BAGD, HNTC; KJV, NASB, NRSV], 'encouragement' [AB, BAGD, LN], 'to exhort' [BECNT, ICC2, NICNT, NTC; NET], 'to encourage' [WBC; CEV, NCV, NIV], 'to give encouragement' [GW], 'to counsel' [REB]. The phrase 'if the one exhorting in exhortation' is translated 'if your gift is to encourage others, be encouraging' [NLT], 'if it is to encourage others, we should do so' [TEV]. This noun denotes encouragement or consolation, either by verbal or non-verbal means [LN].

c. pres. act. participle of μεταδίδωμι (LN 57.96) (BAGD p. 511): 'to give' [BAGD, BECNT, LN; CEV, KJV, NASB, NLT], 'to share' [BAGD, LN, WBC; GW], 'to share with others' [NICNT; TEV], 'to contribute' [NET], 'to contribute to the needs of others' [NTC; NIV], 'to distribute' [ICC2], 'to give to charity' [REB], 'to practice charity' [HNTC], 'to have the gift of giving to others' [NCV]. The phrase 'the one giving in generosity' is translated 'the giver, in generosity' [NRSV], '(if) one is a contributor to charity, let him use it with simple generosity' [AB]. This verb means to share with someone else what one has [LN].

d. ἁπλότης (LN **57.106**) (BAGD 2. p. 86): 'generosity' [BAGD, LN; NRSV], 'simple generosity' [AB], 'simplicity' [NICNT; KJV], 'liberality' [BAGD; NASB], 'sincerity' [NET], 'sincere concern' [WBC]. The phrase ἐν ἁπλότητι 'in generosity' is translated 'generously' [BECNT, **LN**; NIV, NLT, TEV], 'be generous' [CEV, GW], 'freely' [NCV], 'wholeheartedly' [HNTC], 'without ulterior motive' [ICC2], 'without grudging' [REB]. This noun denotes an act of generosity [LN].

QUESTION—What is the nature of παράκλησις 'exhortation'?

It was primarily encouragement, since life in the first century was generally fairly grim [Mor]. It could be to encourage or to exhort [SSA]. Teaching was guiding people about how they should live, and encouragement was what helped people to do it [NAC]. Teaching was directed to the understanding, but exhortation was directed to the heart and will [Gdt, Mu], to the conscience and feelings [Ho]. It is urging people to live in a way that is consistent with the truth of the gospel message [NICNT]. It is the giving of consolation, admonition, counsel, and teaching of ethical conduct by the spiritual fathers of the community [AB]. It is an appeal to take action, applying the implication of the gospel message to everyday living [BECNT]. It is the pastoral application of principles derived from the gospel message, and intended to help Christians to live out their obedience in practical ways [ICC2]. There is overlap with the gift of prophecy; 'exhort' describes a polite way of exercising authority [WBC]. It may be exercised as stirring public speech, but more often it will be counseling others and encouraging the disheartened [St].

QUESTION—Does the use of the verb μεταδίδωμι 'give' here describe the giving of one's own goods, or the distribution of the alms of the church?
It is the distribution of one's own goods [Gdt, ICC1, ICC2, Mu, St, WBC]. The qualification 'with generosity' best describes a situation where one shares his personal goods [NICNT].

QUESTION—What is the nature of ἁπλότης 'generosity'?
1. It is giving characterized by a singleness of purpose that has no ulterior motives [AB, Gdt, Ho, ICC1, ICC2, Mor, Mu, NICNT, NTC, SSA]. They are to do it whole-heartedly [HNTC], without self-exaltation [AB].
2. It means that they should give with generosity [BECNT, NAC, WBC]. They are to give sacrificially [BECNT]. Their generosity is borne of simplicity or singleness of purpose [WBC].

the one-leading[a] in diligence,[b] the one-showing-mercy[c] in cheerfulness.[d]

LEXICON—a. pres. mid. participle of προΐσταμαι (LN 36.1) (BAGD 1., 2. p. 707): 'to lead' [LN], 'to rule' [BAGD (1.)]. The phrase 'the one leading' is translated 'the one who leads' [BECNT], 'he who leads' [NASB], 'the leader' [NRSV], 'him who exercises leadership' [NTC], 'the gift of being a leader' [NCV], 'the president' [HNTC], 'him who presides' [ICC2], 'one who presides' [NICNT], 'he that ruleth' [KJV], 'he who cares' [WBC], 'whoever has authority' [TEV], 'if one is a leader' [AB], 'if you are a leader' [REB], 'if we are leaders' [CEV], 'if it is leadership' [GW, NET, NIV], 'if God has given you leadership ability' [NLT]. This verb means to so influence others as to cause them to follow a recommended course of action [LN].

b. σπουδή (LN **68.63**) (BAGD 2. p. 763): 'diligence' [AB, BAGD, ICC2, NICNT, NTC; KJV, NASB, NET], 'eagerness, earnestness' [BAGD], 'cheerfulness' [WBC], 'zeal' [HNTC], 'enthusiasm' [REB]. The phrase ἐν σπουδῇ 'in diligence' is translated 'diligently' [BECNT; NIV], 'enthusiastically' [GW]. The clause ὁ προϊστάμενος ἐν σπουδῇ 'the one leading in diligence' is translated 'whoever has authority must work hard' [LN], 'whoever has authority should work hard' [TEV], 'anyone who has the gift of being a leader should try hard when he leads' [NCV], '(if) we are leaders, we should do our best' [CEV], '(if) God has given you leadership ability, take the responsibility seriously' [NLT]. This noun denotes doing something with intense effort and motivation [LN].

c. pres. act. participle of ἐλεέω (LN 88.76) (BAGD p. 249): 'to show mercy' [BECNT, ICC2, LN, NICNT, NTC; KJV, NASB, NET, NIV], 'to have the gift of showing mercy' [NCV], 'to do works of mercy' [AB], 'to do acts of mercy' [HNTC, WBC], 'to be merciful toward' [LN], 'to have mercy on' [BAGD, LN], 'to be good to others' [CEV], 'to help others in distress' [REB], 'to help people in need' [GW], 'to show kindness to others' [TEV], 'to have a gift for showing kindness to others' [NLT]. The phrase 'the one showing mercy' is translated 'the compassionate'

[NRSV]. This verb means to show kindness or concern for someone in serious need [LN].

d. ἱλαρότης (LN **25.116**): 'cheerfulness' [AB, HNTC, ICC2, LN, NTC, WBC; KJV, NASB, NET, NRSV], 'gladness' [NICNT], 'joy' [NCV]. The phrase 'in cheerfulness' is translated 'cheerfully' [BECNT; CEV, GW, NIV, REB, TEV], 'gladly' [NLT]. This noun denotes a state of happiness characterized by being cheerful [LN].

QUESTION—What area of meaning is intended for the participle προϊστάμενος 'leading'?

1. It means to govern [Mu, SSA], lead [BECNT, Mor, TH], or preside [AB, ICC1, NICNT]. It means to preside over some function, though it is not clear what function would be meant [HNTC]. It is anyone who exercises authority in the church [Ho]. These are the presbyters [Mu, NTC]. It is leadership that serves in order to benefit others [NAC].
2. It means to preside in some way over the church's charitable work [Gdt, ICC2, WBC].

QUESTION—What area of meaning is intended for the noun σπουδή 'diligence'?

The leading was to be done with diligence [BECNT, Mor, NICNT, SSA, TH, WBC], with eagerness and earnestness [WBC], with conscientiousness [TH]. It means putting one's whole self into the effort [SSA], working with zeal and energy [ICC1]. Because the responsibility was a heavy one, he warns them against the temptation to shirk their duty [NTC]. They must work with zeal and dispatch [AB], even eagerness [Mor]. They must not be careless or lazy [Ho]. They must be responsible and resist the temptation to be lazy just because no one is supervising them [BECNT].

QUESTION—What did showing mercy primarily involve?

It is helping those in need [HNTC, NAC, SSA, St], particularly the sick [AB, BECNT, Gdt, Ho, ICC2, Mor, NAC, NICNT, NTC], the hungry [NAC], the poor [ICC2, Mor, NICNT], the disabled [ICC2, NICNT], the elderly [ICC2, NAC, NICNT], the suffering [Mor], those in emotional distress or financial need [BECNT, St], the alien, orphans, and widows [St], those who were dying or who had lost a loved one [NTC], burying the dead, or helping those in prison [AB]. It is expressed especially in almsgiving [WBC]. It involved bringing comfort and cheer to such people [NTC]. It is any act of mercy to others in need [NICNT]. Although all people are to show mercy, these people are specially appointed by the church to minister to those in distress [ICC2]. It is a ministry to people in need that is direct and personal [Mu].

DISCOURSE UNIT—12:9–21 [AB, Ho, ICC1, ICC2, NICNT, TNTC, WBC; CEV, NET, NIV, NRSV]. The topic is counsels for Christians living in the community [AB], exercising Christian virtues—love [Ho], maxims to guide the Christian life [ICC1], a series of loosely connected items of exhortation [ICC2], love and its manifestations [NICNT], the law of Christ [TNTC], love as the norm for social relationships [WBC], rules for Christian living [CEV], conduct in love [NET], love [NIV], marks of the true Christian [NRSV].

DISCOURSE UNIT—12:9–10 [Mor, St]. The topic is love of the brothers [Mor], our relationship to one another: love in the family of God [St].

12:9 (Let)- love[a] -(be) without-hypocrisy.[b] Abhorring[c] the evil,[d] clinging[e] to- the -good,[f]

LEXICON—a. ἀγάπη (LN 25.43) (BAGD I.1.a. p. 5): 'love' [AB, BAGD, BECNT, HNTC, ICC2, LN, NICNT, NTC, WBC; all versions], 'loving concern' [LN]. This noun denotes love for someone or something, based on sincere appreciation and high regard [LN].

b. ἀνυπόκριτος (LN 73.8) (BAGD p. 76): 'without hypocrisy' [BAGD; NASB, NET], 'without pretense' [WBC], 'free from dissimulation' [HNTC], 'without dissimulation' [KJV], 'genuine' [BAGD, BECNT, ICC2, LN, NTC; NRSV], 'real' [NCV], 'sincere' [BAGD, LN, NICNT; NIV], 'completely sincere' [TEV], 'to be sincere' [CEV], 'to be unfeigned' [AB]. The phrase 'let love be without hypocrisy' is translated 'love sincerely' [GW], 'love in all sincerity' [REB], 'don't just pretend to love others' [NLT]. This adjective describes that which is genuine and sincere, and hence lacking in pretense or show [LN].

c. pres. act. participle of ἀποστυγέω (LN **88.203**) (BAGD p. 100): 'to abhor' [BAGD, HNTC, ICC2, NICNT, NTC; KJV, NASB, NET], 'to hate' [BAGD, BECNT, **LN**, WBC; CEV, GW, NCV, NIV, NLT, NRSV, TEV], 'to detest' [AB], 'to loathe' [REB]. This is a strong term [BECNT, Ho, ICC1, ICC2, Mor, St, WBC], and expresses an utter abhorrence of evil [ICC1, Mor, St]. This verb means to have a strong dislike for someone or something, implying repulsion and desire for avoidance [LN]. This word occurs only here in the NT.

d. πονηρός (LN 88.110) (BAGD 2.c. p. 691): 'evil' [BAGD, LN]. The phrase τὸ πονηρόν 'the evil' is translated 'what is evil' [ICC2, NICNT; NASB, NCV, NET, NIV, NRSV, TEV], 'that which is evil' [KJV], 'everything that is evil' [CEV], 'what is wrong' [NLT], 'evil' [GW, REB]. This adjective describes being morally corrupt and evil [LN].

e. pres. pass. participle of κολλάομαι (LN 18.21) (BAGD 2.c. p. 441): 'to cling to' [AB, BAGD, LN, NICNT, NTC; NASB, NET, NIV], 'to cleave to' [BECNT, HNTC, ICC2; KJV], 'to hold tightly to' [CEV, NLT], 'to hold on to' [GW, NCV, TEV], 'to hold fast to' [NRSV, REB], 'to be devoted to' [BAGD, WBC]. This is a strong term also [Ho, St, WBC]. This verb means to stick or cling to something [LN].

f. ἀγαθός (LN 88.1) (BAGD 2.a.α. p. 3): 'good' [BAGD, LN]. The phrase 'the good' is translated 'what is good' [ICC2, NICNT; GW, NASB, NCV, NET, NIV, NLT, NRSV, TEV], 'that which is good' [KJV], 'the good' [REB], 'everything that is good' [CEV]. This adjective describes positive moral qualities of the most general nature [LN].

QUESTION—What is the relationship between the concept of genuine love and what follows?

What follows explains what genuine love is [Mor, NICNT, SSA, St, WBC]. Love is an underlying motif through the section 12:9–21, though not specifically in every verse [NICNT]. Real love leads a person to do the 'good' referred to in 12:2, which is the fruit of the transformed mind [NICNT]. This chapter and the three that follow it (chapters 12–15) are an exhortation to allow love to govern all they do [St].

12:10 in-brotherly-love[a] to-one-another (being) affectionate[b], excelling[c] in-honor[d] to-one-another,

LEXICON—a. φιλαδελφία (LN 25.34) (BAGD p. 858): 'brotherly love' [AB, BAGD, NICNT, NTC; KJV, NASB, NIV], 'brotherly and sisterly love' [BECNT], 'love that befits a brotherhood' [HNTC], 'love for one's fellow believer, affection for a fellow believer' [LN], 'love for the brethren' [ICC2], 'mutual love' [NET]. This noun denotes affection for one's fellow believer in Christ [LN].

b. φιλόστοργος (LN **25.41**) (BAGD p. 861): 'affectionate' [HNTC], 'kindly affectioned' [KJV], 'devoted' [AB, BAGD, NTC; GW, NASB, NET, NIV], 'very loving, warmly devoted to, very affectionate' [LN], 'loving dearly' [BAGD]. This adjective is translated as a noun or noun phrase: 'affectionate kindness' [ICC2], 'family affection' [WBC], 'tender family affection' [BECNT], 'heartfelt (in your) love' [NICNT]. The phrase 'in brotherly love to one another being affectionate' is translated 'have tender family affection for one another in brotherly and sisterly love' [BECNT], 'show family affection to one another in brotherly love' [WBC], 'love each other as brothers and sisters' [CEV], 'love each other like brothers and sisters' [NCV], 'love each other with genuine affection' [NLT], 'love one another with mutual affection' [NRSV], 'let love of the Christian community show itself in mutual affection' [REB], 'love one another warmly as Christian brothers' [TEV], 'be devoted to each other like a loving family' [GW]. This adjective describes love or affection for those closely related to one, particularly members of one's immediate family or in-group [LN]. This word occurs only here in the NT.

c. pres. mid. or pass. (deponent = act.) participle of προηγέομαι (LN **68.70, 78.35**) (BAGD p. 706): 'to excel' [LN (78.35); GW], 'to outdo' [AB, BAGD; NRSV], 'to do exceedingly' [LN (78.35)], 'to be eager' [TEV], 'to show eagerness in' [**LN** (68.70); NET], 'to do with eagerness' [LN (68.70)], 'to take delight in' [NLT], 'to consider, to esteem' [BAGD], 'to prefer' [BECNT, ICC2, NTC; KJV], 'to give preference' [NASB], 'to give the higher rank' [HNTC], 'to go ahead of' [NICNT], 'to show the way' [WBC]. The clause τῇ τιμῇ ἀλλήλους προηγούμενοι 'excelling in honor to one another' is translated 'honor one another to an exceptional degree' [**LN** (78.35)], 'honor others more than you do yourself' [CEV], 'give each other more honor than you want for yourselves' [NCV], 'honor one another above yourselves' [NIV], 'esteem others more highly than yourself' [REB], 'showing eagerness in honoring one another' [LN (68.70)]. This verb means to exhibit a type of behavior far above the norm [LN (78.35)]. This word is found only here in the NT.

    d. τιμή (LN 87.4) (BAGD 2.a. p. 817): 'honor' [BAGD, BECNT, HNTC, ICC2, LN, NICNT, NTC; KJV, NASB, NCV], 'to honor' [CEV, NET, NIV, NLT], 'to show honor' [AB; NRSV], 'respect' [BAGD, LN, WBC], 'to show respect' [GW, TEV], 'reverence' [BAGD]. This noun denotes honor as an element in the assignment of status to a person [LN].

QUESTION—Is there any difference in meaning between φιλαδελφία 'brotherly love' and ἀγάπη 'love' in the previous verse?

    The noun ἀγάπη 'love' is more wide-embracing and inclusive, and φιλαδελφία 'brotherly love' is more narrow and specific, referring to love for other believers [AB, Ho, ICC1, ICC2, NTC]. The noun ἀγάπη 'love' expresses a general sense, and φιλαδελφία 'brotherly love' and φιλόστοργοι 'full of tenderness' are more immediate manifestations of that love [Gdt]. Although other groups had ties of loyalty within the group, φιλαδελφία seems to have been a uniquely Christian virtue, and was based on their seeing God as their father and themselves as brothers and sisters [Mor]. The noun φιλαδελφία 'brotherly love' appears not to have been used in a metaphorical sense prior to its use in the NT [HNTC]. Both φιλαδελφία 'brotherly love' and φιλόστοργος 'affectionate' are terms that speak of affection within the family [BECNT, NICNT, St, WBC], indicating that the church functions as an extended family [NICNT].

QUESTION—What relationship is indicated by the use of the dative case of φιλαδελφία 'brotherly love' and the eight other dative nouns that follow?

    They are datives of respect, meaning 'as regards, regarding, with respect to' [Gdt, Mor, NICNT]. The dative nouns come first in their clauses to show emphasis [Mor].

QUESTION—What area of meaning is intended by the word φιλόστοργος 'affectionate'?

    It is the special affection and love experienced within a family [BECNT, Gdt, Ho, ICC1, ICC2, Mor, Mu, NAC, NICNT]. It is particularly the love of a parent for a child [St, WBC].

QUESTION—What is the meaning of προηγέομαι 'excelling'?

    This rare expression is unclear and very difficult to translate [Mor]. The difference between the interpretations should not be exaggerated [BECNT].

1. They are to give higher honor to others or give preference to others in honor [BECNT, Gdt, HNTC, ICC1, ICC2, NTC, TNTC; CEV, KJV, NASB, NCV, NIV, REB]. Since Christ lives in other believers, we honor Christ himself when we show honor and preference to them [ICC2].
2. They are to 'go before' one another in the sense of outdoing one another in showing honor [AB, NAC, NICNT, SSA, WBC; NRSV], or of setting an example of showing honor to one another [Ho].

3. They are to be eager to honor one another [NET, NLT, TEV], or are to excel in showing one another honor [GW].

DISCOURSE UNIT—12:11-16 [Mor]. The topic is some practical advice.

12:11 not lazy[a] in-zeal,[b] being-fervent[c] in-spirit,[d] serving[e] the Lord,

LEXICON—a. ὀκνηρός (LN **88.250**) (BAGD 1. p. 563): '(to be) lazy' [BAGD, BECNT, LN, NICNT; GW, NCV, NLT, TEV], '(to be) slothful' [KJV], 'idle' [BAGD], 'lacking in ambition' [LN], '(to be) slack' [ICC2], 'to allow to slacken' [HNTC], 'to lag' [NET, NRSV], 'to lag behind' [NASB], 'to come on behind' [NTC], 'to be negligent' [WBC], '(to be) lacking (in zeal)' [**LN**; NIV], not explicit [CEV]. The phrase 'not lazy in zeal' is translated 'unflagging in diligence' [AB], 'with unflagging zeal' [REB], 'do not be/never be lazy but work hard' [NCV, NLT], 'work hard and do not be lazy' [TEV], 'never give up' [CEV]. This noun denotes shrinking from or hesitating to engage in something worthwhile, possibly implying lack of ambition [LN].
  b. σπουδή (LN 25.74) (BAGD 2. p. 763): 'zeal' [ICC2, NICNT; NET, NIV, NRSV, REB], 'Christian zeal' [HNTC], 'eagerness' [BAGD, LN, WBC], 'earnestness' [BAGD], 'enthusiasm' [NTC], 'diligence' [AB, BAGD, BECNT; NASB], 'business' [KJV], 'devotion' [LN], 'in showing your devotion' [GW], not explicit [NLT]. This noun denotes eagerness to do something, with the implication of readiness to expend energy and effort [LN].
  c. pres. act. participle of ζέω (LN 25.73) (BAGD p. 337): 'to be fervent' [AB, HNTC; KJV, NASB], 'to keep your spiritual fervor' [NIV], 'to be ardent' [NRSV], 'to show enthusiasm' [LN], 'to be enthusiastic' [NET], 'to boil, to seethe' [BAGD], 'to burn' [BECNT], 'to be aglow' [ICC2, NTC, WBC; REB], 'to be set on fire' [NICNT]. The phrase 'being fervent in spirit' is translated 'eagerly follow the Holy Spirit' [CEV]. The phrase 'being fervent in spirit, serving the Lord' is translated 'use your energy to serve the Lord' [GW], 'serving the Lord with all your heart' [NCV], 'work hard and serve the Lord enthusiastically' [NLT], 'serve the Lord with a heart full of devotion' [TEV]. This verb means to show great eagerness toward something [LN].
  d. πνεῦμα (LN 26.9, 12.18) (BAGD 5.d.α. p. 677): 'spirit' [AB, BECNT, LN; KJV, NASB, NET, NRSV], 'spiritual nature, inner being' [LN], 'the Spirit' [HNTC, ICC2, NICNT, NTC, WBC; REB], 'the Holy Spirit' [LN (12.18); CEV], not explicit [GW, NLT]. The phrase 'being fervent in spirit' is translated 'keep your spiritual fervor' [NIV]. This noun denotes the non-material, psychological faculty which is potentially sensitive and responsive to God [LN (26.9)], or denotes the Holy Spirit [LN (12.18)].
  e. pres. act. participle of δουλεύω (LN 35.27) (BAGD 2.b. p. 205): 'to serve' [AB, BECNT, HNTC, ICC2, LN, NICNT, NTC, WBC; all versions]. This verb means to serve, normally in a humble manner and in response to the demands or commands of others [LN].

QUESTION—How is σπουδή used here, as opposed to its use in 11:8?

It speaks of diligence in one's commitment [Mor]. It is Christian zeal [AB, HNTC]. They are not to be passive, but instead have enthusiasm [NTC]. They are not to be weary in well-doing [Mu]. They are not to be lazy [NAC, TH]. It is zeal in the rational worship that Christians are called to offer [ICC2, NICNT], not being slack or slothful or avoiding the dust, heat, and exertion that Christian service may require [ICC2]. Such zeal comes as a result of Christian love [ICC1].

QUESTION—Does πνεῦμα 'spirit' refer to the human spirit or to the Spirit of God?

1. It refers to the Spirit of God [BAGD, HNTC, ICC2, NAC, NICNT, NTC, St, WBC; CEV, REB]. The Christian is to be set on fire by the Holy Spirit [ICC2]. It refers primarily to the Holy Spirit, though it includes the human spirit as well; Christians are to burn in their spirits by the power of God's spirit [BECNT].
2. It refers to the human spirit [AB, Ho, Mu; GW, KJV, NASB, NCV, NET, NIV, NRSV, TEV].
3. It refers to the human spirit as filled with and indwelt by the Spirit of God [ICC1, Mor]. It relates to the human spirit, but what is accomplished occurs by the working of the Spirit of God [Gdt, ICC1, SSA].

12:12 rejoicing[a] in-hope,[b] enduring[c] in-tribulation,[d] being-devoted[e] to-prayer,[f]

LEXICON—a. pres. act. participle of χαίρω (LN 25.125) (BAGD 1. p. 873): 'to rejoice' [AB, BAGD, BECNT, HNTC, ICC2, LN, NICNT, WBC; KJV, NASB, NET, NLT, NRSV], 'to be glad' [BAGD, LN], 'to be joyful' [NTC; NCV, NIV], 'to be happy' [GW]. The phrase 'rejoicing in hope' is translated 'let your hope make you glad' [CEV], 'let hope keep you joyful' [REB], 'let your hope keep you joyful' [TEV]. This verb means to enjoy a state of happiness and well-being [LN].

b. ἐλπίς (LN 25.59) (BAGD 2.b. p. 253): 'hope' [AB, BAGD, BECNT, HNTC, ICC2, LN, NICNT, NTC, WBC; KJV, NASB, NCV, NET, NIV, NRSV, REB, TEV], 'your hope' [CEV], 'confident hope' [NLT], 'your confidence' [GW]. This noun denotes looking forward with confidence to that which is good and beneficial [LN].

c. pres. act. participle of ὑπομένω (LN 25.175) (BAGD 2. p. 846): 'to endure' [BAGD, BECNT, ICC2, LN, NTC; NET], 'to show endurance' [HNTC], 'to bear up' [LN, NICNT], 'to persevere' [NASB], 'to be patient' [AB; CEV, GW, KJV, NCV, NIV, NLT, NRSV, TEV], 'to be steadfast' [WBC], 'to stand firm' [REB]. This verb means to continue to bear up despite difficulty and suffering [LN].

d. θλῖψις (LN 22.2) (BAGD 1. p. 362): 'tribulation' [BAGD, NICNT; KJV, NASB], 'affliction' [AB, BAGD, BECNT, HNTC, ICC2, NTC, WBC; NIV], 'suffering' [LN; NET, NRSV], 'trouble and suffering, persecution' [LN], 'trouble' [GW, NLT, REB], 'in your troubles' [TEV], 'time of trouble' [CEV], 'when trouble comes' [NCV]. This noun denotes trouble involving direct suffering [LN].

e. pres. act. participle of προσκαρτερέω (LN **68.68**) (BAGD 2.a. p. 715): 'to be devoted to' [BAGD, BECNT, NICNT; NASB], 'to devote oneself to' [**LN**], 'to be faithful in' [NIV], 'to persist in' [LN; NET, REB], 'to be persistent' [AB, NTC, WBC], 'to persevere' [HNTC, ICC2; NRSV], 'to keep on' [NLT]. The phrase 'being devoted to prayer' is translated 'never stop praying' [CEV], 'pray continually' [GW], 'pray at all times' [NCV, TEV], 'continuing instant in prayer' [KJV]. This verb means to continue to do something with intense effort, with the possible implication of doing it despite difficulty [LN].

f. προσευχή (LN 33.178) (BAGD 1. p. 713): 'prayer' [AB, BAGD, BECNT, HNTC, ICC2, LN, NICNT, NTC, WBC; KJV, NASB, NET, NIV, NRSV, REB], 'to pray' [CEV, GW, NCV, NLT, TEV]. This noun denotes speaking to God, or making requests of God [LN].

QUESTION—What relationship is indicated by the use of the dative case of the noun ἐλπίς 'hope'?

1. It is causal [AB, Gdt, Ho, ICC1, ICC2, Mor, Mu, NAC, NTC, SSA, TH; CEV, NCV, REB, TEV]. They rejoice because they have hope of future salvation [NTC], because they are confidently awaiting what they know God will do for them [SSA]. Their confident hope brings them joy [ICC2, NAC, St].
2. Hope is the object in which we rejoice [NICNT]: rejoice about your hope.
3. The distinctions between causal, instrumental, and local should not be pressed [BECNT, WBC], since Paul was probably not thinking about such distinctions [BECNT].

QUESTION—What is the nature of the θλῖψις 'tribulation' which they must endure?

It is persecution [ICC1, ICC2, Mu]. It is the suffering of the final age, coming primarily because of their faith in Christ [HNTC, ICC2]. The world will always oppose true Christianity [ICC2]. It is opposition from the world [NTC]. It is serious trouble [Mor]. Life itself can be an obstacle course [NAC].

QUESTION—What does it mean to be devoted to prayer?

It is perseverance in prayer [HNTC, Ho]. It speaks of persistence [Mor, NICNT, NTC], of constancy, and of effort in prayer [Mor], of fervor [Ho], of being regular and effective in prayer [NAC]. They must learn to be in continual communion with God [AB]. Prayer is not something that automatically happens, and we must consciously decide to do it [BECNT]. They must resist the laziness, discouragement, and self-confidence that would tempt a Christian to give up praying [ICC2]. Keeping a constant communication with God in prayer is the only way the difficulty and tension typical of this eschatological age can become a positive and helpful experience [WBC].

12:13 sharing-with[a] the needs[b] of-the saints,[c] pursuing[d] hospitality.[e]

LEXICON—a. pres. act. participle of κοινωνέω (LN 57.98) (BAGD 1.b.γ. p. 438): 'to share' [BAGD, LN, WBC; NCV], 'to contribute' [AB; NASB, NET, NIV, NRSV, REB], 'to distribute' [KJV], 'to help with' [BECNT], 'to help' [NLT], 'to help to relieve' [ICC2, NTC], 'to minister to' [HNTC], 'to participate in meeting' [NICNT]. The phrase 'sharing with the needs of the saints' is translated 'take care of God's needy people' [CEV], 'share what you have with God's people who are in need' [GW], 'share your belongings with your needy fellow Christians' [TEV]. This verb means to share one's possessions, with the implication of some kind of joint participation and mutual interest [LN].

b. χρεία (LN **57.40**) (BAGD 2. p. 885): 'need' [AB, BAGD, BECNT, HNTC, **LN**, NICNT, NTC, WBC; NASB, NET, NRSV, REB], 'lack' [BAGD, LN], 'what is needed' [LN], 'necessity' [ICC2; KJV]. The phrase 'the needs of the saints' is translated 'God's needy people' [CEV], 'your needy fellow Christians' [TEV], 'God's people who are in need' [GW, NIV], 'when God's people are in need' [NLT], 'God's people who need help' [NCV]. This noun denotes that which is lacking and particularly needed [LN].

c. ἅγιος (LN 11.27) (BAGD 2.d.β. p. 10). This plural noun is translated 'saints' [BAGD, BECNT, HNTC, ICC2, NICNT, NTC, WBC; KJV, NASB, NET, NRSV], 'fellow Christians' [TEV], 'God's people' [LN; GW, NCV, NIV, NLT, REB], 'God's dedicated people' [AB], 'God's (needy) people' [CEV]. This noun denotes persons who belong to God, and as such constitute a religious entity [LN].

d. pres. act. participle of διώκω (LN **68.66**) (BAGD 4.b. p. 201): 'to pursue' [BAGD, BECNT, NICNT; NET], 'to aspire to' [WBC], 'to be given to' [KJV], 'to practice' [AB; NASB, NIV, REB], 'to practice with enthusiasm' [HNTC], 'to be eager' [NLT], 'to eagerly practice' [NTC], 'to strive toward' [LN], 'to run after' [BAGD]. This verb means to do something with intense effort and with a definite purpose or goal [LN]. This is a rather strong term, indicating that some effort must be expended [Mor].

e. φιλοξενία (LN **34.57**) (BAGD p. 860): 'hospitality' [AB, BAGD, BECNT, HNTC, LN, NICNT, NTC, WBC; KJV, NASB, NET, NIV, NRSV, REB], 'to be hospitable' [GW]. The phrase 'strive for hospitality' is translated 'pursue the opportunities you get to be hospitable' [ICC2], 'welcome strangers into your home' [CEV], 'bring strangers in need into your homes' [NCV], 'open your homes to strangers' [TEV], 'always be eager to practice hospitality' [NLT]. This noun denotes receiving and showing hospitality to a stranger, that is, someone who is not regarded as a member of the extended family or a close friend [LN].

QUESTION—In what way were they to share with the needs of the saints?

Paul wanted them to give assistance to the needy [BECNT, ICC2, Mor, NAC, NICNT, NTC, SSA, WBC]. They were to minister to the needs of other Christians [HNTC, TH]. They were to pool their resources and provide for material needs such as food, shelter, and clothing [NICNT]. They were to identify with and even participate in the needs of the needy, making them their own [Mu].

QUESTION—What was the hospitality they were to practice?

Paul is speaking of the needs of Christian travelers [AB, BECNT, ICC1, ICC2, Mor, Mu, NAC, NICNT, NTC, SSA, St, TH, WBC], especially those traveling in Christian ministry [BECNT, Mor, Mu, NICNT, WBC]. This might also refer to helping those who have been displaced by persecution [Mu]. Some churches also needed to have a place provided for their meetings [ICC2].

12:14 Bless[a] the-ones persecuting[b] you(pl), bless and do-not curse.[c]

LEXICON—a. pres. act. impera. of εὐλογέω (LN 33.470) (BAGD 2.a. p. 322): 'to bless' [AB, BAGD, BECNT, HNTC, ICC2, LN, NICNT, NTC, WBC; GW, KJV, NASB, NET, NIV, NLT, NRSV], 'to wish good for' [NCV], 'to call down blessings on' [REB]. The phrase 'bless the ones persecuting you' is translated 'ask God to bless everyone who mistreats you' [CEV], 'ask God to bless those who persecute you' [TEV]. This verb means to ask God to bestow divine favor on, with the implication that the verbal act itself constitutes a significant benefit [LN].
   b. pres. act. participle of διώκω (LN 39.45) (BAGD 2. p. 201): 'to persecute' [AB, BAGD, BECNT, HNTC, ICC2, LN, NICNT, NTC, WBC; GW, KJV, NASB, NET, NIV, NLT, NRSV, TEV], 'to harass' [LN], 'to mistreat' [CEV], 'to harm' [NCV]. The phrase 'the ones persecuting you' is translated 'your persecutors' [REB]. This verb means to systematically organize a program to oppress and harass people [LN].
   c. pres. mid. or pass. (deponent = act.) impera. of καταράομαι (LN 33.471) (BAGD p. 417): 'to curse' [AB, BAGD, BECNT, HNTC, ICC2, LN, NICNT, NTC, WBC; CEV, GW, KJV, NASB, NCV, NET, NIV, NLT, NRSV, TEV], 'to call down curses' [REB]. This verb means to cause injury or harm by means of a statement regarded as having some supernatural power, often because a deity or supernatural force has been invoked [LN].

QUESTION—What area of meaning is intended with the word εὐλογέω 'bless'?

He is telling them to pray for God's blessing on such people [AB, BECNT, Ho, ICC2, Mor, Mu, NAC, NICNT, NTC, SSA, TH; CEV, NLT, TEV]. It is asking God to grant favor to them [NICNT, WBC]. They are to wish good for them [NCV], and do good to them [Ho]. It is to wish our enemies well, and to show that by prayer and action [St].

12:15 Rejoice[a] with those-rejoicing, weep[b] with those-weeping.

LEXICON—a. pres. act. infin. of χαίρω (LN 25.125) (BAGD 1. p. 873): 'to rejoice' [AB, BAGD, BECNT, HNTC, ICC2, LN, NICNT, NTC, WBC; KJV, NASB, NET, NIV, NRSV, REB], 'to be happy' [CEV, GW, NCV,

NLT, TEV], 'to be glad' [BAGD, LN]. This verb means to enjoy a state of happiness and well-being [LN].
   b. pres. act. infin. of κλαίω (LN 25.138) (BAGD 1. p. 433): 'to weep' [BAGD, BECNT, HNTC, ICC2, LN, NICNT, NTC, WBC; KJV, NASB, NET, NLT, NRSV, REB, TEV], 'to cry' [BAGD], 'to mourn' [AB; NIV], 'to lament' [LN], 'to be sad' [CEV, GW, NCV]. This verb means to weep or wail, with emphasis upon the noise accompanying the weeping [LN].

QUESTION—Is he primarily speaking about how they are to relate within the Christian community, or outside of it?
   1. He is primarily referring to how Christians should relate to one another [AB, BECNT, Gdt, Ho, Mor, Mu, NAC, NICNT, St, WBC]. The style and topic now change as Paul shifts from relationships with those outside the church in 12:14 to mutual and intimate relations with fellow Christians in 12:15–16 [NICNT]. He is primarily talking about relationships between believers, but they could also apply this to their relationships with non-Christians [Ho, WBC].
   2. Since this follows the command to bless a Christian's persecutors, Paul is still probably thinking particularly of those who are outside the church [ICC2].
   3. He is referring to how believers should relate to all people, both believers and unbelievers [NTC].

12:16 Having- the same[a] -concern[b] toward one-another, not setting-the-mind-on[c] the high-things,[d] but associating-with[e] the humble.

LEXICON—a. αὐτός (LN 58.31): 'same' [LN, NICNT; KJV, NASB, TEV], not explicit [AB, BECNT, HNTC, ICC2, NTC, WBC; all versions]. This adjective describes that which is identical to something [LN].
   b. pres. act. participle of φρονέω (LN 26.16) (BAGD 1. p. 866): 'to have concern' [TEV], 'to have an attitude, to think in a particular manner' [LN]. The phrase τὸ αὐτὸ φρονοῦντες 'having the same concern' is translated 'be of the same mind' [KJV, NASB], 'have a common mind' [HNTC], 'be in agreement' [BAGD], 'agree together' [ICC2], 'think the same thing' [BAGD, NICNT], 'think in harmony' [AB], 'to live in agreement' [REB], 'live in harmony' [BAGD, BECNT, NTC, WBC; GW, NET, NIV, NLT, NRSV], 'live in peace' [NCV], 'be friendly' [CEV]. See this word also at 12:3. This verb means to employ one's faculty for thoughtful planning, with emphasis upon the underlying disposition or attitude [LN].
   c. pres. act. participle of φρονέω (LN 30.20) (BAGD 2. p. 866): 'to set one's mind on' [BAGD], 'to ponder, to let one's mind dwell on, to keep thinking about, to fix one's attention on' [LN]. See the following item d. for translations of this word. This verb means to keep on giving serious consideration to something [LN]. See this word also at 12:3.
   d. ὑψηλός (LN 88.209) (BAGD 2. p. 850): 'proud, haughty' [BAGD]. The phrase 'not setting the mind on the high things' is translated 'mind not

high things' [KJV], 'do not set your mind on exalted things' [HNTC], 'put aside haughty thoughts' [AB], 'do not cherish proud thoughts' [WBC], 'do not be haughty' [BECNT, ICC2; NET, NRSV], 'do not be haughty in mind' [NASB], 'do not think highly of yourself' [NICNT], 'do not be snobbish' [NTC], 'do not be proud' [CEV, NCV, NIV, REB, TEV], 'don't be too proud' [NLT], 'don't be arrogant' [GW]. This adjective describes an arrogant, haughty attitude [LN].

e. pres. pass. participle of συναπάγομαι (LN **34.1, 41.22**) (BAGD p. 784): 'to associate with' [AB, BECNT, NICNT, WBC; NASB, NET, NRSV], 'to readily associate with' [ICC2, NTC], 'to be willing to associate with' [NIV], 'to be ready to mix with' [REB], 'to keep company with' [HNTC], 'to enjoy the company of' [NLT], 'to condescend to' [KJV]. The clause τοῖς ταπεινοῖς συναπαγόμενοι 'associating with the humble' is translated 'associate with humble people' [**LN** (34.1)], 'make friends with ordinary people' [CEV], 'make friends with those who seem unimportant' [NCV], 'be friendly to humble people' [GW], 'share in doing what is humble' [**LN** (41.22)], 'accept humble duties' [TEV]. This verb means to associate with one another, normally involving spatial proximity and/or joint activity, and usually implying some kind of reciprocal relation or involvement [LN (34.1)], or it means to share in engaging continuously in some activity [LN (41.22)].

QUESTION— What does the command 'having the same concern toward one another' describe?

They are to seek for others what they would seek for themselves [Gdt, SSA]. They are to agree with each other so they can live in harmony [NTC]. They are to have harmonious relationships with each other [ICC1]. Their unity is based on their common understanding of God's way of seeing things [NAC]. It is mutual esteem [AB]. He is telling them to have a common attitude and purpose [WBC]. Their attitudes toward one another must spring from their renewed minds [NICNT]. He is telling them to be of the same mind, that is, to have true unity and concern for one another [Mor]. He is telling them to have the oneness that is agreement in faith in Jesus Christ and in loyal obedience to Christ [ICC2]. Paul is concerned about possible tensions between Jews and Gentiles [BECNT]. They should share the same basic convictions and concerns [St]. It speaks of the thoughts and sentiments Christians have toward other Christians [Mu]. There should be a general agreement in feelings, interests, and objectives [Ho].

QUESTION—What does the command 'not setting the mind on the high things' describe?

They are not to think too highly of themselves [Mor, NICNT]. They are not to be ambitious to achieve things that could cause them to be proud [ICC1, SSA]. Pride is destructive to community living [AB]. It is a warning against haughtiness [ICC2]. They are not to be proud in their thinking [WBC]. They are not to grasp for high positions or for honor [Gdt, Mu].

QUESTION—To what or whom does τοῖς ταπεινοῖς 'the humble' refer?
1. It refers to people of low position [AB, BECNT, Gdt, ICC2, NICNT, NTC, St; CEV, GW, KJV, NASB, NCV, NET, NIV, NLT, NRSV, REB].
2. It refers to things of low estate, humble tasks or menial work [ICC1, Mu, SSA; TEV].
3. Lowly people as well as lowly things or work are included [Mor, Mu]. Paul may not have intended to exclude either meaning [HNTC, WBC]. There should be no aristocracy or cliques in the church [Mu].

Do-not be wise[a] to yourselves.[b]
LEXICON—a. φρόνιμος (LN 32.31) (BAGD p. 866): 'wise' [AB, BAGD, BECNT, HNTC, ICC2, LN, WBC; KJV, NASB, REB, TEV], 'smart' [NCV], 'smarter' [CEV, GW], 'wiser' [NRSV], 'prudent, thoughtful, sensible' [BAGD], 'proud' [NICNT], 'conceited' [NTC; NET, NIV], not explicit [NLT]. This adjective describes understanding resulting from insight and wisdom [LN].
b. The phrase παρ' ἑαυτοῖς 'to yourselves' is translated 'in your own estimation' [AB, BECNT, HNTC, NICNT, WBC; NASB], 'in your own conceits' [KJV], not explicit [NTC; NET, NIV]. The phrase 'do not be wise to yourselves' is translated 'do not esteem yourselves wise' [ICC2], 'do not think of yourselves as wise' [TEV], 'do not keep thinking how wise you are' [REB], 'do not claim to be wiser than you are' [NRSV], 'don't…feel that you are smarter than others' [CEV], 'do not think how smart you are' [NCV], 'don't think that you are smarter than you really are' [GW], 'and don't think you know it all!' [NLT], 'do not be conceited' [NET]. The person who views himself as wise is usually not viewed as wise by other people [Mor]. See this expression also at 11:25.

DISCOURSE UNIT—12:17–21 [Mor, St]. The topic is the Christian attitude to non-Christians [Mor], our relationship to our enemies: not retaliation, but service [St].

12:17 Repaying[a] no-one[b] evil[c] for[d] evil,
LEXICON—a. pres. act. participle of ἀποδίδωμι (LN 38.16) (BAGD 3. p. 90): 'to repay' [AB, NICNT, WBC; NET, NIV, NRSV, TEV], 'to pay back' [BECNT; GW, NASB, NCV, NLT, REB], 'to return' [HNTC, ICC2, NTC], 'to recompense' [BAGD, LN; KJV], 'to render' [BAGD], not explicit [CEV]. This verb means to recompense someone, whether positively or negatively, depending upon what the individual deserves [LN].
b. μηδείς (LN 92.23) (BAGD 2.a. p. 518): 'no one' [AB, BECNT, HNTC, ICC2, LN, WBC], 'no man' [KJV], 'nobody' [BAGD], '(not)…anyone' [NTC; NET, NIV, NRSV], '(never)…anyone' [NASB], 'someone' [CEV, NCV, TEV], 'people' [GW], not explicit [NICNT; NLT, REB]. This adjective is a negative reference to an entity, event, or state [LN].

c. κακός (LN 88.106) (BAGD 3. p. 398): 'evil' [AB, BAGD, BECNT, HNTC, ICC2, LN, NICNT, NTC, WBC; GW, KJV, NASB, NET, NIV, NLT, NRSV, REB], 'harm' [BAGD], 'wrong' [BAGD; NCV, TEV]. The phrase 'repaying no one evil for evil' is translated 'don't mistreat someone who has mistreated you' [CEV]. This adjective describes being bad, with the implication of being harmful and damaging [LN].

d. ἀντί with genitive object (LN 57.145) (BAGD 2. p. 73): 'for' [AB, BAGD, BECNT, HNTC, ICC2, LN, NICNT, NTC, WBC; GW, KJV, NASB, NET, NIV, NRSV, REB], 'with' [TEV], 'with more' [NLT], 'in place of' [BAGD], 'by doing' [NCV]. The phrase 'repaying no one evil for evil' is translated 'don't mistreat someone who has mistreated you' [CEV], 'if someone does wrong to you, do not pay him back by doing wrong to him' [NCV], 'if someone has done you wrong, do not repay him with a wrong' [TEV]. This preposition marks an exchange relation [LN].

giving-attention-to^a (what is) good^b in-the sight-of^c all people;^{d}

LEXICON—a. pres. mid. participle of προνοέω (LN **30.47**) (BAGD 2. p. 708): 'to give attention to doing' [**LN**], 'to give attention beforehand, to have in mind to do' [LN], 'to think beforehand' [BECNT], 'to take thought for' [AB, BAGD, ICC2, NICNT; NRSV], 'to take into consideration' [WBC], 'to consider' [NET], 'to focus your thoughts on' [GW], 'to let your aims be' [REB], 'to have regard for' [BAGD], 'to respect' [NASB], 'to do' [NLT], 'to try to do' [NCV, TEV], 'try to (earn the respect)' [CEV], 'to be careful to do' [NIV], 'to provide' [KJV], 'to plan' [HNTC], 'to always see to it' [NTC]. This verb means to think about something ahead of time, with the implication that one can then respond appropriately [LN].

b. καλός (LN 88.4) (BAGD 2.b. p. 400): 'good' [BECNT, ICC2, LN, NICNT; NET, TEV], 'noble' [AB, BAGD, WBC; GW, NRSV], 'fine' [LN], 'right' [NTC; NASB, NCV, NIV], 'honest' [KJV], 'honest life' [HNTC], 'honorable' [NLT, REB], 'praiseworthy' [BAGD, LN], not explicit [CEV]. This adjective describes a positive moral quality, with the implication of being favorably valued [LN].

c. ἐνώπιον (LN 90.20): 'in the sight of' [AB, BECNT, ICC2, LN, NICNT, NTC, WBC; KJV, NASB, NRSV], 'in the eyes of' [NIV], 'before' [HNTC; NET], 'in the opinion of, in the judgment of' [LN]. The phrase 'giving attention to what is good in the sight of all people' is translated 'do things in such a way that everyone can see you are honorable' [NLT], 'but try to earn the respect of others' [CEV], 'try to do what everyone thinks is right' [NCV], 'try to do what everyone considers to be good' [TEV], 'let your aims be such as all count honorable' [REB], 'focus your thoughts on those things that are considered noble' [GW]. This preposition marks a participant whose viewpoint is relevant to an event [LN].

d. ἄνθρωπος (LN 9.1): 'person, human being, individual' [LN]. The phrase πάντων ἀνθρώπων 'all people' [BECNT, NICNT; NET] is also translated 'all men' [HNTC, ICC2; KJV, NASB], 'all' [WBC; NRSV, REB], 'everybody' [NTC; NIV], 'everyone' [GW, NCV, NLT, TEV], 'others' [CEV], 'human beings' [AB].

QUESTION—To what does ἐνώπιον πάντων ἀνθρώπων 'in the sight of all people' refer?

1. It modifies καλά 'what is good'; they are to do what all people consider to be good [AB, BECNT, Ho, Mu, NICNT, NTC, TNTC, WBC; NCV, REB, TEV], which is based on the general knowledge of right and wrong that all people have as described in 2:15 [NTC]. This is similar to what he has said in 2 Cor. 8:21 [NICNT].
2. It modifies the action of doing; their doing good is to be observed by all people [Gdt, ICC2, Mor, NAC; NLT]. They are to live such good lives that even the heathen would recognize the goodness [Mor, SSA]. The standard of what is good is the gospel itself, not some commonly held moral consensus, so this tells them to do in the sight of all men what is good according to the gospel, whether others recognize it as good or not [ICC2]. Their lifestyle should be consistent with the moral and ethical implications of the gospel [NAC].

12:18 **if possible[a] from[b] you, with all people[c] living-at-peace;[d]**

LEXICON—a. δυνατός (LN 71.2) (BAGD 2.a. p. 208): 'possible' [BAGD, BECNT, HNTC, ICC2, LN, NICNT, NTC, WBC; all versions except CEV, NCV, NLT]. The phrase 'if possible from you' is translated 'if it possibly lies in your power' [AB], 'do your best' [CEV, NCV], 'do all that you can' [NLT]. This adjective describes that which is possible, with the implication of power or ability to alter or control circumstances [LN].

b. ἐκ (LN 90.16) (BAGD 3.f. p. 235): 'from' [LN], 'by' [LN], 'by reason of' [BAGD], 'it depends on' [BAGD], 'as far as it depends on' [NTC; NIV], 'so far as it depends on' [BECNT, WBC; NASB, NET, NRSV], 'in so far as it depends on' [ICC2], 'to the extent that it depends on' [NICNT], 'as far as it rests with' [HNTC], 'so far as it lies with' [REB], 'as much as lieth in' [KJV]. The phrase εἰ δυνατὸν τὸ ἐξ ὑμῶν 'if possible from you' is translated 'if it possibly lies in your power' [AB], 'as much as it is possible' [GW], 'do all that you can' [NLT], 'do everything possible on your part' [TEV], 'do your best' [CEV, NCV]. This preposition marks the source of an activity or state, with the implication of something proceeding from or out of the source [LN].

c. The phrase μετὰ πάντων ἀνθρώπων is translated 'with all people' [BECNT, NICNT; NET], 'with all men' [HNTC, ICC2; KJV, NASB], 'with all' [NRSV, REB], 'with everyone' [AB, NTC, WBC; CEV, GW, NCV, NIV, NLT], 'with everybody' [TEV].

d. pres. act. participle of εἰρηνεύω (LN 88.102) (BAGD 2.b. p. 227): 'to live at peace' [AB, HNTC, NTC, WBC; CEV, NIV, REB], 'to live in peace' [LN; GW, NCV, NLT, TEV], 'to live peaceably' [KJV, NET, NRSV], 'to be at peace' [BECNT, ICC2, NICNT; NASB], 'to behave peacefully'

[LN], 'to keep the peace (with someone)' [BAGD]. This verb means to live in peace with others [LN].

QUESTION—What is meant by εἰ δυνατόν τὸ ἐξ ὑμῶν 'if possible from you'?

It is not always possible to live at peace with others, but at least it should not be the Christian who is disrupting the peace [HNTC, Ho, Mor, NTC]. They are to live at peace with others if the others will allow that [SSA]. They are not to sacrifice holiness or truth just to maintain peace [NTC]. Conflict with the world is inevitable, but Christians should still attempt to maintain a positive witness and certainly should not needlessly make matters worse by their behavior [NICNT]. The Christian should be friendly and should delight in peace and harmony, but it is not always possible to have peace with all people, and believers should not compromise the truth of the gospel to keep peace with people who resist truth [BECNT]. Christians are not to engage in moral compromise for the sake of peace [St], nor sacrifice truth or principle for peace [Ho]. Harmony with neighbors may or may not be possible, as hostility and persecution are ever present, and Paul does not expect them to compromise their faith for the sake of peace [WBC]. Peace must be sacrificed when it requires compromise with sin and error [Mu].

12:19 do-not avenge[a] yourselves, beloved, but[b] give[c] room[d] to-the wrath[e] for it-is-written, Vengeance[f] (is) mine, I-myself will-repay,[g] says (the) Lord.

LEXICON—a. pres. act. participle of ἐκδικέω (LN 39.33) (BAGD 1. p. 238): 'to avenge' [BAGD], 'to take revenge' [LN]. The phrase 'do not avenge yourselves' [BECNT, HNTC, ICC2, NICNT; NET], is also translated 'never avenge yourselves' [NRSV], 'avenge not yourselves' [KJV], 'never take your own revenge' [NASB], 'never take revenge' [NLT, TEV], 'don't/do not take revenge' [NTC; GW, NIV], 'do not take your own revenge' [WBC], 'take no revenge' [AB], 'do not seek revenge' [REB], 'do not try to punish others when they wrong you' [NCV], 'don't try to get even' [CEV]. This verb means to repay harm with harm, on the assumption that the initial harm was unjustified and that retribution is therefore called for [LN].

b. ἀλλά (LN 89.125): 'but' [AB, BECNT, HNTC, ICC2, LN, NICNT, NTC, WBC; NASB, NCV, NET, NIV, NRSV, REB], 'but rather' [KJV], 'but instead' [TEV], 'instead' [LN; GW], 'on the contrary' [LN], not explicit [CEV, NLT]. This conjunction marks emphatic contrast [LN].

c. aorist act. impera. of δίδωμι (LN 13.142): 'to give' [BECNT, ICC2, NICNT, WBC; KJV, NET], 'to allow' [LN], 'to leave' [AB, HNTC, NTC; NASB, NIV, NRSV, REB]. The phrase 'give room to wrath' is translated 'leave that to the righteous anger of God' [NLT], 'let God take revenge' [CEV], 'let God's anger take care of it' [GW], 'but instead let God's anger do it' [TEV], 'but wait for God to punish them with his anger' [NCV]. This verb means to grant someone the opportunity or occasion to do something [LN].

d. τόπος (LN 80.1) (BAGD 2.c. p. 823): 'room' [AB, HNTC, NTC; NASB, NIV, NRSV], 'place' [BECNT, ICC2, LN, NICNT; KJV, NET, REB], 'space' [LN], 'opportunity' [BAGD, WBC], 'possibility, chance' [BAGD], not explicit [CEV, GW, NCV, NLT, TEV]. This noun denotes an area of any size [LN].

e. ὀργή (LN 38.10, 88.173) (BAGD 2.a., 2.b. p. 579): 'wrath' [BAGD, BECNT, NICNT], 'God's wrath' [AB, HNTC, WBC; NET, NIV], 'wrath of God' [ICC2, NTC; NASB], 'anger' [BAGD, LN (88.173)], 'God's anger' [GW, TEV], 'punishment' [LN (38.10)], 'divine retribution' [REB]. The phrase 'give room to wrath' is translated 'leave that to the righteous anger of God' [NLT], 'let God take revenge' [CEV], 'wait for God to punish them with his anger' [NCV]. This noun denotes divine punishment based on God's angry judgment against someone [LN (38.10)], or denotes a relative state of anger [LN (88.173)].

f. ἐκδίκησις (LN **39.33**) (BAGD p. 238): 'vengeance' [AB, BAGD, BECNT, HNTC, ICC2, NTC, WBC; KJV, NASB, NET, NRSV, REB], 'seeking retribution' [LN], 'the responsibility for seeking retribution' [**LN**], 'punishment' [BAGD]. The phrase 'vengeance is mine' is translated 'I will avenge' [NICNT], 'it is mine to avenge' [NIV], 'I will take revenge' [NLT, TEV], 'I will punish those who do wrong' [NCV], 'I am the one to take revenge' [CEV], 'I alone have the right to take revenge' [GW]. This noun denotes repaying harm with harm, on the assumption that the initial harm was unjustified and that retribution is therefore called for [LN].

g. fut. act. indic. of ἀνταποδίδωμι (LN **38.19**) (BAGD 2. p. 73): 'to repay' [AB, BAGD, BECNT, ICC2, LN, NTC, WBC; KJV, NASB, NCV, NET, NIV, NRSV, REB], 'to pay back' [LN, NICNT; CEV, GW, NLT, TEV], 'to pay in return, to cause retribution' [LN], 'to recompense' [HNTC]. This verb means to cause someone to suffer in turn because of actions which merit such retribution [LN].

QUESTION—What is the function of the vocative ἀγαπητοί 'beloved' here?

As he gives them this command that will not be easy to fulfill, Paul wants to make especially clear how much he loves them [Gdt, ICC1, ICC2, Mor], or how much they have experienced the unmerited love of God [NICNT]. It is a tender appeal [Mu, NTC]. As he calls them to live in love, he assures them of his love for them [St]. It functions to encourage those who might experience extreme provocation from Rome, as well as to remind them that God is on their side [WBC].

QUESTION—What does it mean to 'give room to wrath'?

They are to allow God to punish [BECNT, Ho, ICC1, Mu, SSA, St, WBC], they are not to punish [SSA]. They are not to usurp God's prerogative of taking vengeance [NTC]. They are to give God's avenging actions room to work [Gdt, Ho, NICNT]. They should leave vengeance to God, knowing that he is the one who strikes in order that he may heal [ICC2].

QUESTION—What does it mean that vengeance belongs to the Lord?
It is God's responsibility to avenge wrong [Ho, Mor, Mu, NTC, SSA, St, TNTC]. The Christian should leave all avenging of wrong to God, and pursue only what is good [AB].

12:20 But^a if your enemy^b should-hunger,^c feed^d him; if he-should-thirst,^e give- him -drink;^f

LEXICON—a. ἀλλά (LN 89.125): 'but' [AB, BECNT, ICC2, LN, NICNT, WBC; GW, NASB], 'instead' [LN; NLT], 'on the contrary' [LN, NTC; NIV], 'rather' [HNTC; NET], 'therefore' [KJV], 'no' [NRSV]. The word 'but' is translated as a clause: 'but there is another text' [REB], 'the Scriptures also say' [CEV], 'instead, as the scripture says' [TEV], 'but you should do this' [NCV]. This conjunction marks emphatic contrast [LN].
  b. ἐχθρός (LN 39.11) (BAGD 2.b.β. p. 331): 'enemy' [AB, BAGD, BECNT, HNTC, ICC2, NICNT, NTC, WBC; all versions]. This noun denotes being at enmity with someone [LN].
  c. pres. act. subj. of πεινάω (LN 23.29) (BAGD 1. p. 640): 'to hunger' [BAGD, BECNT; KJV], 'to be hungry' [AB, BAGD, HNTC, ICC2, LN, NICNT, NTC, WBC; all versions except KJV]. This verb means to be in a state of hunger, without any implications of particular contributing circumstances [LN].
  d. pres. act. impera. of ψωμίζω (LN **23.5**) (BAGD 1. p. 894): 'to feed' [AB, BAGD, BECNT, HNTC, ICC2, LN, NICNT, NTC, WBC; all versions except CEV], 'to give (something) to eat' [**LN**; CEV]. This verb means to give (something) to eat [LN].
  f. pres. act. subj. of διψάω (LN 23.39) (BAGD 1. p. 200): 'to thirst' [BECNT, HNTC, ICC2, LN, NICNT; KJV], 'to be thirsty' [AB, BAGD, LN, NTC, WBC; all versions except KJV], 'to suffer from thirst' [BAGD].
  g. pres. act. impera. of ποτίζω (LN 23.35) (BAGD 1. p. 695): 'to give to drink' [AB, BAGD, BECNT, HNTC, ICC2, LN, NICNT, NTC, WBC; all versions]. This verb means to cause to drink [LN].

QUESTION—What relationship is indicated by ἀλλά 'but'?
It contrasts with what was just said in 12:19 about retaliating [SSA, WBC]. Instead of retaliating, Paul is calling for acts of kindness as a positive response to hostility [WBC].

QUESTION—What does giving food and drink represent here?
It represents doing good of every kind [BECNT, Ho, ICC2]. It represents hospitality [WBC].

for (by) doing^a this you(sg)-will-heap^b coals^c of-fire^d on his head.^e

LEXICON—a. pres. act. participle of ποιέω (LN 90.45): 'to do' [LN]. The phrase τοῦτο...ποιῶν 'by doing this' is translated 'by doing this' [BECNT, HNTC, NICNT, NTC; NRSV, REB, TEV], 'in doing this' [NET, NIV, NLT], 'by doing so' [ICC2], 'in doing so' [AB], 'in so doing'

[WBC; KJV, NASB], 'if you do this' [GW], 'doing this will be like' [NCV], 'this will be the same as' [CEV].
b. fut. act. indic. of σωρεύω (LN **25.199**) (BAGD 1. p. 800): 'to heap' [AB, BAGD, BECNT, ICC2, NICNT, NTC, WBC; KJV, NASB, NET, NIV, NLT, NRSV, REB], 'to heap up' [HNTC], 'to pile up' [BAGD], 'to pile' [CEV], 'to pour' [NCV]. When used with 'heap coals of fire on someone's head' it carries the meaning 'to make ashamed' [**LN**], 'to cause to be ashamed' [LN]. The phrase 'you will heap coals of fire on his head' is translated 'you will make him burn with shame' [TEV], 'you will make him feel guilty and ashamed' [GW]. This verb means to treat someone in such a positive manner as to cause that person to be ashamed or embarrassed [LN].
c. ἄνθραξ (LN **3.67**) (BAGD p. 67): 'coals' [AB, BECNT, HNTC, ICC2, **LN**, NICNT, NTC, WBC; CEV, KJV, NASB, NCV, NET, NIV, NLT, NRSV, REB], 'charcoal' [LN], not explicit [GW, TEV]. This word is found only here in the NT.
d. πῦρ (LN 2.3) (BAGD 1.a. p. 729): 'fire' [AB, BAGD, BECNT, ICC2, LN, NICNT, NTC, WBC; KJV], not explicit [GW, TEV]. The phrase 'coals of fire' is translated 'burning coals' [HNTC; CEV, NASB, NCV, NET, NIV, NRSV], 'burning coals of shame' [NLT], 'live coals' [REB].
e. κεφαλή (LN 8.10) (BAGD 1.a. p. 430): 'head' [AB, BAGD, BECNT, HNTC, ICC2, LN, NICNT, NTC, WBC; CEV, KJV, NASB, NCV, NET, NIV, NLT, NRSV, REB], '(their) heads' [CEV, NLT, NRSV], not explicit [GW, TEV].

QUESTION—What does the metaphor about coals of fire mean?
1. Paul is saying that the offending person will feel ashamed of what he or she has done, and perhaps change his or her attitude [Gdt, ICC1, ICC2, LN, Mor, Mu, SSA, St, TH, TNTC; GW, TEV]. They are to subdue enemies with kindness, which can be very hard to withstand [Ho]. Paul is citing a passage in Proverbs that probably reflects an Egyptian custom in which a person might show repentance by carrying a dish with burning coals on the head [ICC2, WBC]; whether or not Paul knew of this custom is not known and is unimportant [WBC]. The coals represent remorse on the part of the guilty person [HNTC, NTC]. The unexpected kindness will cause the offender to feel shame and contrition [ICC2, NAC, NICNT, NTC, WBC]. The meaning is not obvious, but it does involve acts of love bringing about a change in the offending person [Mor]. This is a dead metaphor and means that you will cause him to feel ashamed and change his attitude toward you [SSA].
2. Consistent with its use in the OT, the metaphor of coals of fire represents the judgment of God that will come on the ungodly [BECNT].

12:21 Don't be-conquered[a] by evil[b] but conquer[c] evil with good.[d]

LEXICON—a. pres. pass. impera. of νικάω (LN 39.57) (BAGD 2.b. p. 539): 'to be conquered' [BAGD, LN], 'to be overcome' [AB, BAGD, BECNT,

HNTC, ICC2, NICNT, NTC, WBC; KJV, NASB, NET, NIV, NRSV]. The passive verb phrase 'don't be conquered by evil' is translated as active: 'don't let evil conquer you' [GW, NLT, REB], 'don't let evil defeat you' [CEV, NCV, TEV]. This verb means to win a victory over [LN].
  b. κακός (LN 88.106) (BAGD 3. p. 398): 'evil' [AB, BAGD, BECNT, HNTC, ICC2, LN, NICNT, NTC; all versions], 'bad' [WBC]. This adjective describes being bad, with the implication of harmful and damaging [LN].
  c. pres. act. impera. of νικάω (LN 39.57) (BAGD 2.b. p. 539): 'to conquer' [BAGD, LN; GW, NLT, REB, TEV], 'to defeat' [CEV, NCV], 'to overcome' [AB, BAGD, BECNT, HNTC, ICC2, NICNT, NTC, WBC; KJV, NASB, NET, NIV, NRSV], 'to be victorious over' [LN].
  d. ἀγαθός (LN 88.1): 'good' [AB, BECNT, HNTC, ICC2, LN, NICNT, NTC, WBC; all versions]. This adjective describes positive moral qualities of the most general nature [LN].

QUESTION—In what way might they be conquered by evil?
  They would be overcome by evil if they were to return evil for evil; such retaliation would then be a defeat [Gdt, Ho, ICC1, Mor, NTC, SSA, St]. If they retaliate they would be overcome by the evil of the enemy as well as by the evil of their own hearts [ICC2]. God's mercy triumphs over rebellion and disobedience [HNTC]. They are to get rid of enemies by turning them into friends [NAC, TNTC]. Returning evil for evil causes a person to become like the one who offended, and promotes more evil [AB]. Returning malevolence for evil done against them would only cause evil to feed on itself and cause even more evil [WBC]. They would be overcome if the pressures put on them by the world's hostility would cause them to corrupt their moral integrity and act in a way that is inconsistent with the transformed character appropriate to the new realm, the character of Christ [NICNT]. This statement summarizes the content of 12:17–20 [TH].

QUESTION—How would they overcome evil with good?
  They would overcome the evil that others would do to them [NICNT]. They would overcome that evil in their enemies that would prompt them to bring misery on others [BECNT]. They would be succeeding in the sense of not furthering evil, as well as by living as people who are being transformed by the renewing of the mind [ICC2]. They are to do what would benefit their enemy [ICC1]. Motivated by the same love that characterizes their relationships with other Christians, they should live out their lives in their relations with the people of this world with sympathy and hospitality, and so respond to evil done against them with positive acts of good [WBC]. It means to serve an enemy so as to win him over [St], to transform a hostile relationship to one of love [Gdt]. Instead of inciting resentment, they become the instruments of quenching the ill-will of those who mistreat them [Mu]. They were to subdue their enemies by kindness [Ho].

DISCOURSE UNIT—13:1–14 [Ho, NAC]. The topic is duties to authorities [Ho], how righteousness manifests itself in the word [NAC].

DISCOURSE UNIT—13:1–7 [AB, HNTC, Ho, ICC1, ICC2, Mor, Mu, NICNT, St, TNTC, WBC; CEV, GW, NCV, NET, NIV, NLT, NRSV, TEV]. The topic is the relation of Christians to civil authorities [AB], civil authority [Ho], authorities [HNTC], maxims on obedience to rulers [ICC1], the believer's obligation to the state [ICC2], the Christian attitude to civil rulers [Mor], the civil magistrate [Mu], the Christian and secular rulers [NICNT], our relationship to the state: conscientious citizenship [St], the Christian and the state [TNTC], live as good citizens [WBC], obey the government [GW], Christians should obey the law [NCV], obey rulers [CEV], submission to civil government [NET], submission to authorities [NIV], respect for authority [NLT], duties toward state authorities [TEV], being subject to authorities [NRSV].

13:1 Let- every soul[a] -be-subject[b] to-(the)-governing[c] authorities.[d]

LEXICON—a. ψυχή (LN 9.20) (BAGD 2. p. 894): 'soul' [NICNT; KJV], 'person' [AB, BECNT, ICC2, LN, NTC, WBC; GW, NASB, NET, NRSV, REB]. This noun is translated as a pronoun: 'you' [CEV, NCV]. The phrase πᾶσα ψυχή 'every soul' [NICNT], is translated 'everyone' [BAGD HNTC; NIV, NLT, TEV]. This noun denotes a person as a living being [LN].

  b. pres. pass. impera. of ὑποτάσσω (LN 37.31) (BAGD 1.b.β. p. 848): 'to be subject to' [AB, BAGD, BECNT, ICC2, LN, WBC; KJV, NET, NRSV], 'to be in subjection to' [HNTC, NTC], 'to be submissive to' [NICNT], 'to be subordinated to' [BAGD]. This passive verb is translated as an active verb: 'to obey' [BAGD; CEV, GW, TEV], 'to yield to' [NCV], 'to submit to' [NIV, NLT, REB]. This verb means to bring something under the firm control of someone [LN].

  c. pres. act. participle of ὑπερέχω (LN 37.17) (BAGD 2.a. p. 841): 'to govern' [AB, BAGD, ICC2, NICNT, NTC, WBC; NASB, NET, NIV, NLT, NRSV], 'to control' [LN], 'to rule' [BECNT], not explicit [CEV]. This participle is translated as an adjective: 'supreme' [HNTC], 'higher' [KJV]. It is translated as a noun: 'government' [NCV], 'power' [GW, REB], 'state' [TEV]. This verb means to exercise continuous control over someone or something [LN].

  d. ἐξουσία (LN 37.38) (BAGD 4.c.α. p. 278): 'authority' [AB, BAGD, BECNT, HNTC, ICC2, LN, NICNT, NTC, WBC; NASB, NET, NIV, NLT, NRSV, REB, TEV], 'ruler' [LN; CEV, NCV], 'power' [GW, KJV]. This noun denotes one who has the authority to rule or govern [LN].

QUESTION—To whom does πᾶσα ψυχή 'every soul' refer?

  This phrase is typically Semitic [AB, HNTC, ICC2, Mor, NICNT, NTC, TH, WBC]. 'Soul' designates the entire person [NICNT, NTC, WBC]. Its use here is emphatic [Ho].

1. It applies to all people, not just Christians [AB, BECNT, Gdt, Mor, Mu, NICNT, WBC], but given that the recipients of the letter were Christians, it was primarily addressed to them [BECNT, Mu, WBC].
2. Paul is referring to Christians in Rome [ICC1, ICC2, SSA]. His use of 'every soul' emphasizes the responsibility of each individual [ICC1].

QUESTION—What is meant by the verb ὑποτάσσω 'be subject'?

It is to acknowledge one's subordinate place with regard to government authority [Mu, NICNT], but does not mean unquestioning obedience in everything [NICNT, St]. This is not a matter of being servile, but of recognizing that the ruler is in one sense Christ's representative [Mor]. It primarily means respecting them [AB, ICC2, NAC], which expresses the Christian's relation to God and his order [AB], and involves obedience to the degree that it would not conflict with God's laws [ICC2]. It is to be a willing subjection [NAC, NTC], humbly recognizing the claim that the authority has over oneself [NAC]. It means to obey [ICC1; CEV, GW, TEV]. It means to subject oneself, which includes obedience [Mu].

QUESTION—Who or what are these authorities?

Paul is referring to government officials, not to angelic beings [AB, BECNT, Gdt, HNTC, ICC2, Mor, Mu, NAC, NICNT, NTC, SSA, St, TH, TNTC, WBC].

For there-is no authority except by[a] God, and the-ones existing[b] are (those) having-been-appointed[c] by[d] God;

LEXICON—a. ὑπό with genitive object (LN 90.1): 'by' [BECNT, HNTC, ICC2, LN, NICNT, WBC; GW, NET], 'from' [AB, NTC; NASB, NLT, NRSV, REB], 'without (God's permission)' [TEV], 'of' [KJV], not explicit [CEV, NCV, NIV]. This preposition marks an agent or force, whether person or event [LN].

b. pres. act. participle of εἰμί (LN 13.69) (BAGD V. p. 226): 'to exist' [AB, BAGD, BECNT, HNTC, LN, NICNT, NTC; GW, NASB, NET, NIV, NRSV, REB, TEV], 'to be' [ICC2, LN, WBC; KJV], not explicit [CEV, NCV, NLT]. This verb means to exist in an absolute sense [LN].

c. pres. pass. participle of τάσσω (LN 37.96) (BAGD 1.a. p. 805): 'to be appointed' [BAGD, HNTC, LN; NICNT], 'to be designated' [LN], 'to be set up' [AB], 'to be ordained' [BECNT, ICC2, NTC; KJV], 'to be established' [BAGD, WBC; NASB, NIV], 'to be put' [CEV, GW, TEV], 'to be instituted' [NET, NRSV, REB], 'to be placed' [NLT], not explicit [NCV]. This verb means to assign someone to a particular task, function, or role [LN].

d. ὑπό with genitive object (LN 90.1): 'by' [AB, BECNT, HNTC, ICC2, LN, NICNT, NTC, WBC; GW, NASB, NET, NIV, NLT, NRSV, REB, TEV], 'of' [KJV]. The phrase 'having been appointed by God' is translated 'he puts (these rulers) in their places of power' [CEV], 'no one rules now without that power from God' [NCV]. This preposition marks an agent or force, whether person or event [LN].

QUESTION—What relationship is indicated by γάρ 'for'?
It indicates the grounds for his command that they must submit to government authority, which is that God has established it [ICC1, ICC2, Mor, Mu, NICNT, SSA]. God is the one who sets up and overthrows rulers, so no one is able to exercise rule unless God has set him up, at least for the present [ICC2].

QUESTION— Does ἐξουσία 'authority' refer to the concept of authority in an abstract way or to the person who exercises authority?
It refers to the individuals who are in office [Ho, ICC1, ICC2, Mu, NICNT], namely the emperor and his representatives [ICC2]. Here the abstract noun 'authority' is used to represent the concrete, those in authority [ICC1, NICNT, WBC]. Each office holder has received his appointment and his right to govern from God [NTC].

13:2 therefore^a the-one resisting^b the authority has-opposed^c the ordinance^d of-God,

LEXICON—a. ὥστε (LN 89.52) (BAGD 1.a. p. 899): 'therefore' [BAGD, LN; GW, KJV, NASB, NRSV], 'for this reason' [BAGD], 'accordingly' [LN], 'as a result, so that, and so' [LN], 'so then' [BECNT, LN, WBC], 'so' [ICC2; NET, NLT], 'so that' [LN, NICNT], 'consequently' [AB, NTC; NIV], 'it follows that' [HNTC; REB], not explicit [CEV, TEV]. This conjunction indicates result [LN].
  b. pres. mid. participle of ἀντιτάσσω (LN 39.1) (BAGD p. 76): 'to resist' [AB, BAGD, BECNT, NICNT; GW, KJV, NASB, NET, NRSV], 'to oppose' [BAGD, LN, NTC, WBC; CEV, TEV], 'to set oneself against' [BAGD, HNTC], 'to refuse to be subject to' [ICC2], 'to be against' [NCV], 'to rebel' [NIV, NLT, REB]. This verb is the opposite of ὑποτάσσω 'be subject' in the previous verse [Mor]. This verb means to oppose someone, involving not only a psychological attitude but also a corresponding behavior [LN].
  c. pres. act. indic. of ἀνθίστημι (LN 39.1, 39.18) (BAGD 2. p. 67): 'to oppose' [AB, BAGD, ICC2, LN (39.1); CEV, GW, NASB, TEV], 'to resist' [BAGD, BECNT, HNTC, LN (39.18), NICNT, NTC, WBC; KJV, NET, NRSV, REB], 'to be against' [NCV], 'to rebel' [NIV, NLT]. This verb means to oppose someone, involving not only a psychological attitude but also a corresponding behavior [LN (39.1)], or to resist by actively opposing pressure or power [LN (39.18)].
  d. διαταγή (LN **33.326**) (BAGD p. 189): 'ordinance' [BAGD, BECNT, HNTC, LN, NICNT, NTC, WBC; KJV, NASB, NET], 'command' [LN], 'decree' [LN], 'a divine institution' [REB], not explicit [NLT]. This noun is translated as a phrase: 'what God had ordered' [**LN**; TEV], 'what God has instituted' [AB; NIV, NLT], 'God's ordering' [ICC2], 'what God has done' [CEV], 'what God has established' [GW], 'what God has commanded' [NCV], 'what God has appointed' [NRSV]. This noun denotes that which has been specifically ordered or commanded [LN].

QUESTION—What relationship is indicated by ὥστε 'therefore'?
It indicates the logical conclusions in 13:2 that are to be drawn from the fact that God has established the existing authorities [BECNT, HNTC, Ho, ICC1, ICC2, Mor, NICNT, SSA, TH].

and those having-opposed will-receive[a] judgment[b] to-themselves.
LEXICON—a. future mid. (deponent = act.) indic. of λαμβάνω (LN 57.125) (BAGD 2. p. 465): 'to receive' [BAGD, BECNT, LN, WBC; KJV, NASB, REB], 'to bring (judgment/punishment) on' [AB, ICC2, NICNT, NTC; GW, NCV, NIV, TEV], 'to be responsible for (their own condemnation)' [HNTC], 'to incur' [NET, NRSV]. The phrase 'will receive judgment' is translated as 'will be punished' [CEV, NLT]. This verb means to receive or accept something for which the initiative rests with the giver, but the focus of attention in the transfer is upon the receiver [LN].
b. κρίμα (LN 56.30) (BAGD 4.b. p. 450): 'judgment' [AB, BECNT, ICC2, NICNT, NTC, WBC; NET, NIV, NRSV, TEV], 'condemnation' [BAGD, HNTC, LN; NASB], 'sentence of condemnation' [BAGD], 'punishment' [GW, NCV, REB], 'damnation' [KJV], not explicit [CEV, NLT]. This noun denotes judging a person to be guilty and liable to punishment [LN].
QUESTION—What is the judgment that will happen to those who resist authority?
1. It is punishment from the secular ruler [BECNT, HNTC, ICC1, Mu, SSA, TH], in whose actions God's own judgment is present [HNTC, ICC1, Mu, SSA].
2. It is judgment from God [Gdt, Ho, ICC2, NAC, NICNT].
   2.1 It is judgment from God at the last day [AB, NICNT, WBC], but which also may be expressed through secular rulers [AB, WBC]. It is primarily but not exclusively judgment from God at the last day [NAC].
   2.2 It is a punishment that comes from God in some fashion in this life, but it is not eternal condemnation at the day of judgment [Gdt, Ho].

13:3 For[a] the rulers[b] are not a fear[c] to the good deed[d] but to the evil[e] (deed).
LEXICON—a. γάρ (LN 89.23): 'for' [AB, BECNT, HNTC, ICC2, LN, NICNT, NTC, WBC; KJV, NASB, NET, NIV, NLT, NRSV, TEV], 'because' [LN], not explicit [CEV, GW, NCV, REB]. This conjunction indicates cause or reason between events [LN].
b. ἄρχων (LN 37.56) (BAGD 2. p. 113): 'ruler' [AB, BECNT, HNTC, LN, NICNT, NTC, WBC; CEV, KJV, NASB, NCV, NET, NIV, NLT, NRSV, TEV], 'governor' [LN], 'government' [GW, REB], 'authority' [BAGD]. This noun is translated as a phrase: 'those engaged in government' [ICC2]. This noun denotes one who rules or governs [LN].
c. φόβος (LN **25.254**) (BAGD 1. p. 863): 'fear' [NET], 'cause for fear' [BECNT, ICC2, NICNT; NASB], 'something to be feared' [LN], 'that which arouses fear' [BAGD], 'terror' [AB, BAGD, HNTC, NTC, WBC;

KJV, NIV, NRSV, REB], 'threat' [CEV]. This noun is also translated as a verb with the rulers as the subject: 'to be feared' [TEV], '(do not) strike fear in' [NLT]; with the rulers as the object: 'to fear' [NCV], 'to be afraid of' [GW]. This noun denotes the occasion or source of fear [LN].

d. ἔργον (LN 42.11) (BAGD 1.c.β. p. 308): 'deed' [BAGD, LN], 'act' [LN], 'conduct' [AB, NTC; NET, NRSV], 'work' [BECNT, HNTC, ICC2, NICNT; KJV], 'behavior' [NASB], not explicit [WBC]. The phrase 'to the good deed' is translated 'for those who do right' [NIV], 'to people who do what is right' [GW; similarly NCV, NLT], 'by those who do good' [TEV], 'to good people' [CEV], 'for the law-abiding' [REB]. This noun denotes that which is done, with possible focus on the energy or effort involved [LN].

e. κακός (LN 88.106) (BAGD 1.b. p. 397): 'evil' [BAGD, LN], 'bad' [BAGD, LN]. The phrase ἀλλὰ τῷ κακῷ 'but to the evil (deed)' is translated 'but to the evil' [ICC2; KJV], 'only to evil' [AB], 'but for the evil one' [BECNT], 'but only to the man who does evil' [HNTC], 'but to the bad' [NICNT], 'but to bad' [NTC, WBC; NRSV], 'but for bad' [NET], 'but for evil' [NASB], '(Rulers are a threat to) evil people' [CEV], 'only those who do wrong' [NCV], 'people who do wrong' [GW], 'but for those who do wrong' [NIV], 'those who are doing wrong' [NLT], 'but by those who do evil' [TEV], 'but only for the criminal' [REB]. This adjective describes being bad, with the implication of harmful and damaging [LN].

QUESTION—What relationship is indicated by γάρ 'for'?

1. It indicates the grounds for the command in 13:1 to submit to the governing authorities [Ho, ICC2, NICNT, SSA]. All of 13:3–4 constitutes the basis for the appeal to submit to rulers [SSA]. Since the judgment in 13:2 refers to God's judgment and here the judgment is by human authorities [NICNT], it is a second reason that Christians should submit to the authorities, which is that God has ordained their role for establishing and maintaining order in society [Ho, ICC2, NICNT].
2. It indicates an explanation of the preceding verse [Mu, WBC]. Verses 13:3–4 give a further explanation of the right that rulers have to exercise judgment [Mu]. 13:3–4 is an elaboration of what it means that God has ordained order within society [WBC].
3. It indicates the grounds for what he says in 13:2b about the secular ruler imposing judgment on those who resist [BECNT].

QUESTION—What does he mean when he says that rulers are not a fear to the good deed?

He is saying that rulers should not be a cause of fear for those whose deeds are good [AB, BECNT, HNTC, ICC2, Mu, NICNT, TH, WBC; NASB]. 'The good deed' is a personification [Mu, NICNT, NTC], and speaks of good deeds in the collective sense [ICC1].

Do-you-want[a] to- not -fear[b] the authority? Do the good, and you-will-have praise[c] from it;[d]

LEXICON—a. pres. act. indic. of θέλω (LN 25.1): 'to want' [LN; NICNT, NTC, WBC; NASB, NCV, NIV], 'to desire' [LN; NET], 'to wish' [BECNT, HNTC, ICC2, LN; NRSV, REB], 'to like' [GW, NLT, TEV]. The phrase 'do you want' is translated 'wilt thou then' [KJV], 'there is no need (to be afraid)' [CEV]. This verb means to desire to have or experience something [LN].

b. pres. mid. or pass. (deponent = act.) infin. of φοβέομαι (LN 25.252) (BAGD 1.b.α. p. 863): 'to fear' [BAGD, BECNT, ICC2, LN; NET], 'to be afraid' [HNTC, LN; CEV, GW, KJV]. The phrase 'to not fear' is translated 'to live without being afraid' [GW], 'to live without fear' [NLT], 'to be free from fear' [AB, NTC; NIV], 'to avoid fear' [NICNT], 'to be without fear' [WBC], 'to have no fear' [NASB, REB], 'to be unafraid' [NCV, TEV]. This verb means to be in a state of fearing [LN].

c. ἔπαινος (LN 33.354) (BAGD 1.a.α. p. 281): 'praise' [BAGD, BECNT, HNTC, ICC2, LN, NICNT; KJV, NASB], 'approval' [AB, BAGD, NTC; NRSV, REB], 'commendation' [WBC; NET], 'recognition' [BAGD]. This noun is translated as a verb: 'to praise' [CEV, GW, NCV, TEV]; 'to commend' [NIV], 'to honor' [NLT]. This noun denotes speaking of the excellence of a person, object, or event [LN].

d. This pronoun is feminine, in grammatical agreement with the noun ἐξουσία 'authority' which it modifies. It is translated impersonally as though referring impersonally to authority as authority: 'it' [HNTC, ICC2; CEV, GW, NET]. It is translated personally: 'him' [NICNT], 'his' [AB, NTC, WBC], 'the same' [BECNT; KJV, NASB], 'they' [NCV, NLT], 'he' [NIV].

QUESTION—Is the first clause a question or a statement?

The meaning is more or less the same whether it is viewed as a question or as a statement [Mor, Mu, NICNT], but the question expresses it somewhat more forcefully [ICC1, Mu].

1. It is a question [Gdt, Mu, SSA, WBC]. It is a rhetorical question, but semantically it expresses a conditional relationship [SSA]. It is translated as a question by AB, BECNT, ICC2, NICNT, NTC, WBC; GW, KJV, NASB, NCV, NET, NIV, NLT, NRSV, REB, TEV.
2. It is a statement, the protasis of a conditional sentence [HNTC]; that is, if you wish to be free of fear, do what is good. It is translated as a statement by CEV.

QUESTION—What is meant by 'you will have praise from it'?

It means that you will have the approval of the person in authority [AB, BAGD, NTC, TH; NRSV, REB]. You will be honored by him [NLT]. Although some early interpreters thought that this meant that the praise would come from God, this contrasts with the parallel clause 'Do you want to not fear the authority', so it clearly refers to the praise of the secular ruler [NICNT].

13:4 for[a] he-is[b] a servant[c] of-God to-you for the good.[d]

LEXICON—a. γάρ (LN 89.23): 'for' [AB, BECNT, HNTC, ICC2, LN, NICNT, NTC, WBC; KJV, NASB, NET, NIV, NRSV, REB], 'because' [LN; TEV], 'after all' [CEV], not explicit [GW, NCV, NLT]. This conjunction marks cause or reason between events [LN].
  b. The third person singular subject implied in the verb is expressed personally: 'he' [AB, HNTC, NICNT, NTC, WBC; KJV, NIV]; 'they' [CEV, REB, TEV]; impersonally: 'it' [BECNT, ICC2; NASB, NET, NRSV]. It is translated as a noun: 'the government' [GW], 'the ruler' [NCV], 'the authorities' [NLT].
  c. διάκονος (LN 35.20) (BAGD 2.a. p. 184): 'servant' [AB, HNTC, LN, NICNT, NTC, WBC; CEV, GW, NCV, NET, NIV, NLT, NRSV, TEV], 'minister' [BECNT, ICC2; KJV, NASB], 'agent' [BAGD; REB]. This noun denotes a person who renders service [LN].
  d. ἀγαθός (LN 88.1) (BAGD 2.a.β. p. 3): 'good' [AB, BAGD, BECNT, HNTC, ICC2, LN, NICNT, NTC, WBC; all versions except CEV, NCV]. The phrase 'to you for the good' is translated 'it is their duty to help you' [CEV], 'to help you' [NCV]. This adjective describes positive moral qualities of the most general nature [LN].

QUESTION—To what does the phrase εἰς τὸ ἀγαθόν 'for the good' refer?
  1. 'The good' refers to the benefit brought to the believer by the government authorities as they fulfill their duty [AB, Ho, ICC2, Mu, NAC, NTC]. It is the official's duty to help citizens [CEV, NCV], to work for their good [GW, REB, TEV].
    1.1 'The good' is the general peace and civil order to be brought about by government [AB, Ho, Mu, NAC, NTC, WBC]. As the magistrate promotes civil order he also helps promote the interests of piety as well [Mu].
    1.2 'The good' is ultimate good, or good of a spiritual nature; by encouraging what is right and discouraging evildoing the authority helps the believer along on the way toward ultimate salvation [ICC2].
  2. 'The good' is the good that the civil government encourages believers to do [Mor, NICNT].

but if you-would-do[a] the evil,[b] fear;[c] for he-does- not -bear[d] the sword[e] without-reason;[f]

LEXICON—a. pres. act. subj. of ποιέω (LN 90.45) (BAGD I.1.b.ε. p. 681): 'to do' [AB, BAGD, BECNT, HNTC, ICC2, LN, NICNT, NTC, WBC; all versions], 'to practice' [LN]. This verb form is subjunctive due to the particle ἐάν 'if', which usually takes a subjunctive verb. This verb marks an agent relation with a numerable event [LN].
  b. κακός (LN 88.106) (BAGD 1.c. p. 398): 'evil' [BAGD, BECNT, HNTC, ICC2, LN; KJV, NASB, TEV], 'bad' [LN, NICNT], 'wrong' [AB, NTC, WBC; CEV, GW, NCV, NET, NIV, NLT, NRSV, REB]. This adjective describes being bad, with the implication of harmful and damaging [LN].

c. pres. mid. impera. of φοβέομαι (LN 25.252): 'to fear' [BECNT, HNTC, ICC2, LN, NICNT], 'to be afraid' [AB, LN, NTC, WBC; all versions except NET, REB], 'to be in fear' [NET], 'to have cause to fear' [REB]. This verb means to be in a state of fearing [LN].

d. pres. act. indic. of φορέω (LN **38.3**) (BAGD 1. p. 865): 'to bear' [AB, BECNT, HNTC, NICNT, NTC, WBC; KJV, NASB, NET, NIV, NRSV], 'to be armed with' [ICC2]. The phrase 'to bear the sword' is translated 'to have the power to punish' [**LN**]. The phrase 'he does not bear the sword without reason' is translated 'he has the power to punish' [NCV], 'they have the power to punish you' [NLT], 'their power to punish is real' [TEV], 'these rulers have the right to punish you' [CEV], 'the government has the right to carry out the death sentence' [GW]. The idiom 'to bear the sword' means to have the capacity or authority to punish [LN].

e. μάχαιρα (LN 6.33) (BAGD 2. p. 496): 'sword' [AB, BAGD, BECNT, HNTC, ICC2, LN, NICNT, NTC, WBC; KJV, NASB, NET, NIV, NRSV, REB], not explicit [CEV, GW, NCV, NLT, TEV]. This noun denotes a relatively short sword (or even dagger) used for cutting and stabbing [LN].

f. εἰκῇ (LN **89.63**) (BAGD 3. p. 222): 'for no purpose' [LN], 'to no purpose' [BAGD, ICC2, WBC], 'for nothing' [AB, HNTC; NASB, NIV, REB], 'in vain' [BECNT, NICNT, NTC; KJV, NET, NRSV], not explicit [CEV, GW, NCV, NLT, TEV]. This adverb describes an action as being without purpose [LN].

QUESTION—What relationship is indicated by γάρ 'for'?

It indicates the reason that evildoers should fear, which is that the government has the right to punish [BECNT, Mu].

QUESTION—To what does the phrase 'bear the sword' refer?

It refers generally to the government's right to punish lawbreakers [AB, BECNT, Gdt, Ho, ICC1, Mor, Mu, NAC, NICNT, NTC, SSA], to government's coercive power to maintain order and promote the common good [AB]. It means that the government's capacity to punish is great [Mor]. It does not necessarily refer specifically or exclusively to capital punishment [BECNT, ICC2, Mor, Mu, NICNT], although that would be included among other punishments the state could impose [BECNT, HNTC, Mu, NICNT]. The sword is a metonymy representing the government's power to punish [SSA]. The sword is a symbol of capital punishment [Gdt, Ho, NTC, WBC].

for[a] he-is a servant[b] of-God, an avenger[c] for[d] wrath[e] to-the-one practicing[f] the evil.

LEXICON—a. γάρ (LN 89.23): 'for' [BECNT, HNTC, ICC2, LN, NICNT, WBC; KJV, NASB, REB], 'because' [LN], not explicit [AB, NTC; CEV, GW, NCV, NET, NIV, NLT, NRSV, TEV]. This conjunction marks cause or reason between events [LN].

b. διάκονος (LN 35.20) (BAGD 2.a. p. 184): 'servant' [AB, HNTC, LN, NICNT, NTC, WBC; CEV, GW, NCV, NET, NIV, NLT, NRSV, TEV],

'minister' [BECNT, ICC2; KJV, NASB], 'agent' [BAGD; REB]. This noun denotes a person who renders service [LN].
   c. ἔκδικος (LN 38.9) (BAGD p. 238): 'avenger' [AB, BAGD, BECNT, NICNT, NTC, WBC; GW, NASB], 'punisher' [LN], 'an instrument of vengeance' [HNTC], 'agent' [ICC2; NIV, REB], 'revenger' [KJV], 'one who punishes' [BAGD], not explicit [CEV, NCV, NET, NLT, NRSV, TEV]. This noun denotes a person who punishes [LN].
   d. εἰς with accusative object (LN 89.57) (BAGD 4.e. p. 229): 'for' [BECNT, ICC2, WBC], 'for the very purpose' [NLT], 'for the purpose of' [LN], not explicit [AB, HNTC, NICNT; CEV, NASB, REB, TEV]. The phrase 'for wrath' is translated 'bringing wrath' [AB], 'who brings wrath' [NICNT; NASB], 'to bring God's wrath' [NTC], 'to carry out God's wrath' [HNTC], 'to execute God's anger' [GW], 'to execute wrath' [KJV, NRSV], 'to punish' [NCV], 'to administer retribution' [NET], 'to bring punishment' [NIV]. This preposition marks intent, often with the implication of expected result [LN].
   e. ὀργή (LN 38.10) (BAGD 2.a. p. 579): 'wrath' [AB, BAGD, BECNT, HNTC, ICC2, NICNT, NTC, WBC; KJV, NASB, NIV, NRSV], 'God's anger' [GW], 'retribution' [NET], 'punishment' [LN; REB, TEV], 'punishing' [NLT], not explicit [NCV]. This clause is translated 'They are God's servants who punish criminals to show how angry God is' [CEV]. This noun denotes divine punishment based on God's angry judgment against someone [LN].
   f. pres. act. participle of πράσσω (LN 42.8) (BAGD 1.a. p. 698): 'to practice' [BECNT, HNTC, NICNT, NTC; NASB], 'to do' [BAGD, ICC2, LN]. The phrase 'the one practicing the evil' is translated 'the wrongdoer' [AB; NET, NIV, NRSV], 'evildoer' [WBC], 'criminals' [CEV], 'the offender' [REB], 'who does what is wrong' [GW], 'those who do wrong' [NCV], 'those who do what is wrong' [NLT], 'him that doeth evil' [KJV], 'those who do evil' [TEV]. This verb means to carry out some activity (with possible focus upon the procedures involved) [LN].

QUESTION—Whose wrath is in view here?
   1. It is the wrath of God [AB, Gdt, HNTC, ICC1, ICC2, Mor, Mu, NICNT, NTC, SSA, TH, WBC]. The magistrate is the agent of God's wrath [HNTC, Mu, WBC]. God's wrath of the day of judgment is brought forward into the present by authorities who punish evil [HNTC].
   2. It is the wrath of the magistrate imposed upon evildoers, but it should not be separated from the wrath of God coming at the day of judgment [BECNT].

13:5 Therefore[a] (it is) a necessity[b] to-be-subject,[c]
LEXICON—a. διό (LN 89.47) (BAGD p. 198): 'therefore' [AB, BAGD, BECNT, HNTC, LN, NICNT; GW, NET, NIV, NRSV], 'for this reason' [BAGD, LN; TEV], 'wherefore' [ICC2, WBC; KJV, NASB], 'so' [NCV, NLT], not explicit [CEV]. This word is translated by a phrase 'That is

why' [NTC; REB]. This conjunction marks result, usually denoting the fact that the inference is self-evident [LN].
b. ἀνάγκη (LN 71.30) (BAGD 1. p. 52): 'necessity' [BAGD], 'necessary obligation' [LN]. This word is translated by a phrase: 'one must' [AB; NRSV], 'you must' [NCV, NLT, TEV], 'you should' [CEV], 'ye must needs be' [KJV], 'you are obliged' [REB], 'it is necessary' [BAGD, BECNT, HNTC, NICNT, NTC, WBC; GW, NASB, NET, NIV], 'there is a necessity' [ICC2]. This noun denotes an obligation of a compelling nature [LN].
c. pres. pass. infin. of ὑποτάσσω (LN 37.31) (BAGD 1.b.β. p. 848): 'to be subject' [AB, ICC2, WBC; KJV, NRSV], 'to be subjected to' [BAGD, LN], 'to submit' [BECNT; NIV, NLT, REB], 'to be in subjection' [HNTC, NTC; NASB, NET], 'to subject oneself' [BAGD], 'to be submissive' [NICNT], 'to obey' [BAGD; CEV, GW, TEV], 'to yield' [NCV]. This verb means to bring something under the firm control of someone [LN].

QUESTION—What relationship is indicated by διό 'therefore'?
It indicates a conclusion [AB, BECNT, ICC2, Mor, Mu, NICNT, WBC]. It draws a conclusion for what has been said in 13:4 [Mor, TH], or in 13:1–4 [BECNT, ICC2, Mu, NICNT, WBC].

not only because-of[a] wrath[b] but also because-of conscience/knowledge.[c]
LEXICON—a. διά with accusative object (LN 89.26): 'because of' [AB, BECNT, LN, NICNT; NASB, NET, NIV, NRSV, TEV], 'through' [HNTC], 'by reason of' [ICC2], 'on account of' [WBC], 'because' [CEV, GW, NCV], 'for' [KJV], 'not merely by' [REB], not explicit [NLT]. The preposition translated 'because of' is translated as a verb: 'to avoid' [NTC; NLT]. This preposition marks cause or reason, with focus upon instrumentality, either of objects or events [LN].
b. ὀργή (LN 38.10): 'wrath' [AB, BECNT, HNTC, ICC2, NICNT, NTC, WBC; KJV, NASB, NET, NRSV], 'punishment' [LN; NIV, NLT, TEV], 'God's anger' [CEV, GW], '(fear of) retribution' [REB]. The word 'wrath' is translated as a verb: 'to be punished' [NCV]. This noun denotes divine punishment based on God's angry judgment against someone [LN].
c. συνείδησις (LN 26.13, 28.4) (BAGD 2. p. 786): 'conscience' [AB, BAGD, BECNT, HNTC, ICC2, LN (26.13), NICNT, NTC, WBC; all versions except CEV, NCV]. The word 'conscience' is translated as a phrase: 'you know it is the right thing to do' [CEV], 'you know it is right' [NCV]. This noun denotes the psychological faculty which can distinguish between right and wrong [LN (26.13)], or the awareness of information about something [LN (28.4)].

QUESTION—What is meant by συνείδησις 'conscience/knowledge'?
1. It means 'conscience', an inner feeling or voice that acts as a moral guide to the rightness or wrongness of one's behavior [AB, BECNT, Ho, ICC1, Mor, NAC, SSA, TH, TNTC, WBC; CEV, NCV]. It is a sense of moral

responsibility [BECNT, WBC], and of obligation to do what one should [BECNT, Mu].
2. It means being guided by the knowledge of the true facts of the matter [ICC2, NICNT]. Here, this word has the sense of 'knowledge' and refers to the Christian being subject to rulers because he knows that a ruler is God's minister [ICC2]. A Christian submits to the government not just to avoid punishment, but especially because he knows that rulers are appointed by God and therefore function as his servants [NICNT].

QUESTION—What is meant by the phrase διὰ τὴν συνείδησιν 'because of conscience/knowledge'?

They are to obey not just because of possible consequences, but because it is the right thing to do [AB, Ho, ICC1, Mor, NAC, SSA, TH], because they know it to be God's will [Mu, NTC, TNTC], because they know God has established the state to serve his purposes [HNTC]. They obey because they know in their conscience that God established the state to mediate his rule [BECNT]. Paul is saying that because the Christians know that God has providentially ordered human history and has himself appointed secular rulers to their position, they must obey those rulers, and failing to do so would violate what they know to be right [ICC2, NICNT]. It is a matter of obedience, not just fear of punishment [WBC].

13:6 For because-of^a this also you-pay^b taxes;^c

LEXICON—a. διά with accusative object (LN 89.26): 'for, because' [LN]. The phrase γὰρ διὰ τοῦτο 'for because of this' is translated 'for this reason' [AB, BECNT], 'for this cause...also' [KJV], 'for because of this...also' [NASB], 'for also, because of this' [NICNT], 'moreover, this is why' [HNTC], 'this is why' [NTC], 'this is also why' [NIV], 'for that is why' [WBC], 'that is also why' [GW, NCV, REB, TEV], 'for this reason...also' [NET], 'for these same reasons' [NLT], 'for the same reason...also' [NRSV], not explicit [CEV]. This preposition marks cause or reason, with focus upon instrumentality, either of objects or events [LN].

b. pres. act. indic. of τελέω (LN **57.178**) (BAGD 3. p. 811): 'to pay' [AB, BAGD, BECNT, HNTC, ICC2, LN, NICNT, NTC, WBC; all versions]. This verb means to pay tax or tribute [LN].

c. φόρος (LN 57.182) (BAGD p. 865): 'tax' [AB, BECNT, HNTC, NICNT, NTC; all versions except KJV], 'tribute' [ICC2, WBC; KJV]. This noun denotes a payment made by the people of one nation to another, with the implication that this is a symbol of submission and dependence [LN].

QUESTION—What relationship is indicated by γάρ 'for'?

It indicates what follows as the grounds or further explanation for his statement in 13:5 that they are subject to government authority [Gdt, ICC2, NICNT]. It strengthens the idea of the causal relationship indicated by διὰ τοῦτο 'because of this' [Mor].

QUESTION—What relationship is indicated by διὰ τοῦτο 'because of this'?
1. The conjunction διά indicates reason and τοῦτο 'this' refers to what was just said in 13:5 about conscience [ICC1, ICC2, Mor, Mu, NICNT, NTC, TH]; that is, you pay taxes because of conscience, because you know it to be the right thing to do. It refers back to what has been said in 13:1–5, but also looks forward to what will be said in 13:6b [BECNT].
2. It indicates reason, and refers to what was said in 13:4; that is, you pay taxes because the government is ordained by God to promote what is good and punish what is evil [Ho].
3. It indicates reason, and refers to all of what has been said in 13:1–5 [Gdt].
3. It indicates reason, and refers to what he is saying in the next clause; that is, you pay taxes because rulers are servants of God [NAC].

for they-are servants[a] of-God devoting-themselves[b] to[c] this very (thing).[d]
LEXICON—a. λειτουργός (LN **35.23**) (BAGD 1. p. 471): 'servant' [BAGD, HNTC, ICC2, LN, NICNT; CEV, GW, NASB, NET, NIV, NRSV], 'minister' [AB, BECNT, NTC, WBC; KJV]. The phrase 'they are servants of God' is translated 'the authorities/rulers are working for God' [NCV, TEV], '(they) are in God's service' [REB], 'government workers...are serving God' [NLT]. This noun denotes a person who renders special service [LN].
b. pres. act. participle of προσκαρτερέω (LN 68.68) (BAGD 2.a. p. 715): 'to devote oneself to' [AB, LN, NICNT, NTC; NASB, NET], 'to busy oneself with, to be busily engaged in, to be devoted to' [BAGD], 'to adhere' [BECNT], 'to attend' [HNTC], 'to busy oneself (earnestly)' [ICC2], 'to engage in' [WBC]. The phrase 'devoting themselves' is translated 'it is their duty' [CEV], '(they) do the work (he has given them)' [GW], 'attending continually' [KJV], 'give their time' [NCV], 'who give their full time' [NIV], 'in what they do' [NLT], 'busy with' [NRSV], 'they devote their energies' [REB], 'when they fulfill (their duties)' [TEV]. This verb means to continue to do something with intense effort, sometimes implying that this is done in spite of difficulties [LN].
c. εἰς with accusative object (LN 90.23, 89.57): 'to' [AB, BECNT, NICNT, NTC; CEV, NASB, NCV, NET, NIV, REB], 'concerning, with respect to' [LN (90.23)], 'in' [LN (90.23), WBC], 'for the purpose of' [LN (89.57)], 'upon' [HNTC; KJV], 'with' [ICC2; NRSV], 'while' [GW], not explicit [NLT]. The phrase 'to this very thing' is translated '(when they fulfill) their duties' [TEV]. This preposition marks content as a means of specifying a particular referent [LN (90.23)], or intent, often with the implication of expected result [LN (89.57)].
d. There is no lexical entry in the Greek text for this word, it is supplied for considerations of English style. In the phrase αὐτὸ τοῦτο 'this very' the word 'this' refers to a supplied word 'thing'. This phrase is translated 'this very thing' [BECNT, NICNT; KJV, NASB, NRSV], 'this very task' [AB, WBC], 'this very matter' [ICC2], 'these matters' [CEV], 'the purpose I

have described' [HNTC], 'this end' [NTC], 'this' [REB], 'the work (God) has given them' [GW], 'their work' [NCV], 'their duties' [TEV], 'in what they do' [NLT], 'governing' [NET, NIV].

QUESTION—What relationship is indicated by γάρ 'for'?

It indicates grounds for the statement made in 13:6a [BECNT, Ho, Mor, Mu, NICNT]. The reason you pay taxes is that you know that government officials are God's servants [BECNT, Mu], and that they have legitimate authority over you [NICNT]. Responsible government cannot continue apart from the paying of taxes [Mor]. It introduces an application of the principle of being subject to the authorities, which is the paying of taxes [SSA].

QUESTION—What difference, if any, is there between λειτουργός 'servant' in this verse and διάκονος 'servant' in 13:4?

1. The two nouns are basically synonymous [BECNT, NICNT]. Although the noun λειτουργός and its related verb and adjective often have connotations of religious service, it also is used widely in secular Greek to describe public servants in general [AB, Ho, ICC2, NICNT, WBC], so no particular religious significance is implied [NICNT]. The term λειτουργός suggests a bit more solemnity and dignity than διάκονος [ICC2]. The term is used generally of public servants and is not a particularly theological term, but it gains theological meaning from the genitive phrase 'of God', meaning that they served God whether they knew it or not [HNTC].

2. Paul is implying that secular rulers are performing a religious or spiritual function, whether they know it or not [Gdt]. In the NT the term λειτουργός almost always refers to the service of God [Mor, Mu, NTC], and is service of a serious nature [Mor]. Both terms speak of a dignified office [Mu].

QUESTION—What is the referent for the pronominal phrase εἰς αὐτὸ τοῦτο 'this very thing'?

1. The phrase εἰς αὐτὸ τοῦτο goes with προσκαρτεροῦντες 'devoting themselves' [AB, HNTC, Ho, ICC2, Mu, NAC, NICNT, NTC, SSA, TH, WBC; NET, NIV]: they devote themselves to this very thing.

   1.1 They devote themselves to collecting taxes [AB, Ho, ICC2, Mu, NTC, WBC].

   1.2 They devote themselves to promoting good and restraining evil [HNTC, TH].

   1.3 They devote themselves to their administrative service [BECNT, Mor, NAC, NICNT, SSA, St; NET, NIV, TEV], which is governing [NAC; NET, NIV]. They devote themselves to fulfilling their duties [TEV]. They devote themselves to serving God in what they do [REB].

2. The phrase εἰς αὐτὸ τοῦτο goes with λειτουργοὶ θεοῦ 'servants of God' [Gdt, ICC1]: they are servants of God for this very thing. They function as agents of God's will by checking evil and promoting what is good [Gdt].

13:7 Pay[a] to-everyone what-is-due,[b] to-the-one (due) the tax,[c] the tax,
LEXICON—a. aorist act. impera. of ἀποδίδωμι (LN 57.153) (BAGD 1. p. 90):
'to pay' [AB, BECNT, LN, NTC; CEV, GW, NCV, NET, NRSV, TEV],
'to render' [HNTC, ICC2, LN; WBC; KJV, NASB], 'to pay back'
[NICNT], 'give' [NIV, NLT], 'discharge' [REB], 'to fulfill one's duty to'
[BAGD]. This verb means to make a payment, with the implication of
such a payment being in response to an incurred obligation [LN].
- b. ὀφειλή (LN **57.221**) (BAGD 2.a. p. 598): 'what is due' [HNTC; NASB, NRSV], 'their due' [AB, BAGD, WBC; KJV], 'what you owe' [NICNT; NCV, NIV, NLT, TEV], 'whatever you owe' [NTC; GW], 'what is owed' [BECNT; NET], 'the amount that you owe' [**LN**], 'all that you owe' [CEV], 'obligation' [BAGD; REB], 'that which it is your obligation to render to them' [ICC2], 'debt' [LN]. This noun denotes that which is owed [LN].
- c. φόρος (LN 57.182) (BAGD p. 865): 'tax' [AB, BAGD, BECNT, HNTC, NICNT, NTC; CEV, GW, NASB, NET, NIV, NLT, REB], 'tribute' [BAGD, ICC2, WBC; KJV], 'personal taxes' [TEV], 'revenue' [NRSV]. The phrase 'the tax...the tribute' is translated 'any kind of tax' [NCV]. This noun denotes a payment made by the people of one nation to another, with the implication that this is a symbol of submission and dependence [LN].

QUESTION—To whom does 'everyone' refer?
1. It refers to civil authorities [AB, Mor, Mu, NAC, SSA; TEV], to secular officials [NICNT, NTC, St], and rulers [NICNT], to all persons in office [Gdt]. It primarily, though not exclusively, refers to those in authority [Ho].
2. It refers to all people [REB].

to-the-one (due) the government fees,[a] the government fees, to-the-one (due) the respect,[b] the respect, to the one (due) the honor,[c] the honor.
LEXICON—a. τέλος (LN 57.179) (BAGD 3. p. 812): 'government fees' [NLT], 'tax' [BAGD, LN, WBC; KJV, NASB], 'indirect tax' [ICC2], 'revenue' [AB, LN; NET, NIV, NRSV], 'levy' [HNTC; REB], 'custom' [BAGD, BECNT, NTC; KJV, NASB], 'custom duties' [NICNT], 'fees' [CEV], 'tolls' [GW], 'duties' [BAGD]. The phrase 'the tax...the government fees' is translated 'any kind of tax' [NCV], 'personal and property taxes' [TEV]. This noun denotes payments customarily due a governmental authority [LN].
- b. φόβος (LN 53.59) (BAGD 2.b.β. p. 864): 'respect' [AB, BAGD, NICNT; CEV, GW, NCV, NET, NIV, NLT, NRSV, TEV], 'reverence' [HNTC, LN; REB], 'custom' [BECNT, NTC], 'fear' [ICC2, WBC; KJV, NASB]. This noun denotes profound respect and awe [LN].
- c. τιμή (LN 87.4) (BAGD 2.b. p. 817): 'honor' [AB, BAGD, HNTC, ICC2, LN, NTC; all versions except CEV, REB], 'respect' [BAGD, LN, NICNT, WBC; CEV, REB], 'fear' [BECNT, ICC2, WBC], 'reverence'

[HNTC]. This noun denotes honor as an element in the assignment of status to a person [LN].

QUESTION—What is the difference between φόρος 'tax' and τέλος 'tribute'?

Φόρος is direct taxation, whereas τέλος is indirect taxation in the form of customs duties, fees for services, tolls, etc. [AB, HNTC, Mor, NICNT]. 'Tax' is levied on persons and property, and 'custom' is levied on goods [Gdt, Ho, Mu, NAC, NTC]. Paul is probably not making any sharp distinction between the two, but is telling them to pay whatever kind of taxes they owe [Mor, TH].

QUESTION—Do the persons referred to by the terms 'the one due the respect' and 'the one due the honor' speak of two different ranks of people?

1. The two phrases concern all authorities in general who might deserve respect or honor [BECNT, NTC, TH; NLT, TEV; probably Mor, Mu, NAC, St; NCV]. In the Greek the two terms are given as a means of emphasis without intending to make distinctions [TH]. 'Give respect and honor to those who are in authority' [NLT], 'and show respect and honor for them all' [TEV].
2. Two ranks of people are implied [AB, Gdt, Ho]. 'Respect' (or 'fear') is directed toward the highest officials, those with the power of life and death, and 'honor' is directed toward all officials generally [Gdt]. The adjectives differ only in degree, 'fear' being appropriate with regard to superiors and 'honor' with regard to equals [Ho].
3. This concerns everybody who might deserve respect or honor [probably CEV, GW]. 'Pay all that you owe, whether taxes and fees, or respect and honor' [CEV].

QUESTION—What is meant by φόβος 'respect'?

φόβος is respectful awe [ICC1], veneration and respect [Mu]. They are to show respect and honor to the officials [BECNT]. They are to show respect [AB, NTC, SSA], which is a higher form of reverence than 'honor', which he mentions next [AB, WBC]. Not just respect, but fear was appropriate to the political realities of Paul's day [WBC]. φόβος 'fear' and τιμή 'honor' differ only in degree, 'fear' being appropriate with regard to superiors and 'honor' with regard to equals [Ho]. 'Fear' is the feeling directed toward the highest officials, those with the power of life and death [Gdt].

QUESTION—What is meant by τιμή 'honor'?

This word overlaps in meaning with φόβος 'respect' [BECNT, Mu, TH]. Honor is the attitude that is to be directed toward all officials generally [Gdt]. While they were to respect officials for their office, they were to honor them for the work they do [NTC]. Honor is the attitude that is to be shown toward equals [Ho]. Christians are called on to recognize differences of rank in the social and political order [AB].

QUESTION—Does Paul envision the possibility of any limitations or qualifications to the Christian's submission to governmental authority?

Paul is not calling for absolute obedience to government, as there may be times that its demands conflict with moral principle as known and understood in the light of the gospel [NICNT]. He is not calling for blind obedience, because God is the ultimate authority [ICC2]. This command is not absolute, and Christians are not obligated to follow uncritically in whatever the state demands [BECNT]. Paul is not giving an exhaustive treatment of a believer's relationship to the state [AB, BECNT, WBC]. Paul is referring to a Christian's relation to government functioning in its normal capacity, not to that which is outrageous or mistaken [NTC]. There are God-ordained limits to submission to the state [WBC]. The gospel is opposed both to tyranny as well as anarchy [Ho, St]. Civil disobedience becomes the Christian's duty when the government demands something that would violate the laws of God [NAC, St]. The state must be resisted when it demands the allegiance due only to God [TNTC].

DISCOURSE UNIT—13:8–14 [GW, NCV, NIV, NLT, TEV]. The topic is love one another [GW], loving others [NCV], love, for the day is near [NIV], love fulfills God's requirements [NLT], duties toward one another [TEV].

DISCOURSE UNIT—13:8–10 [AB, HNTC, Ho, ICC1, ICC2, Mor, Mu, NICNT, St, TNTC, WBC; CEV, NET, NRSV]. The topic is the debt of love that fulfills the law [AB], the law of love [HNTC], love the fulfillment of all law [ICC1], the debt of love [ICC2], general obligations [Ho], the Christian attitude to people in general [Mor], the primacy of love [Mu], love and the law [NICNT], our relationship to the law: neighbor-love as its fulfillment [St], love and duty [TNTC], love of neighbor as fulfillment of the law [WBC], love [CEV], exhortation to love neighbors [NET], love for one another [NRSV].

13:8 To-no-one[a] nothing[b] be-owing[c] except[d] to-love[e] one-another;
LEXICON—a. μηδείς (LN 92.23) (BAGD 2.a. p. 518): 'no one' [AB, LN; NET, NRSV, TEV], 'nobody' [BAGD], '(nothing to) anyone' [BECNT, ICC2, NICNT, NTC, WBC; NASB, NLT], 'no man' [HNTC; KJV], 'people' [NCV], not explicit [CEV, GW, NIV, REB]. This adjective describes a negative reference to an entity, event, or state [LN].
b. μηδέν (LN 92.23) (BAGD 2.b.α. p. 518): 'nothing' [AB, BAGD, BECNT, LN, NICNT, WBC; NASB, NLT], 'no debt' [ICC2; CEV, GW, NIV, REB], '(owe no man/one) anything' [HNTC; KJV, NET, NRSV], 'not (owing/owe) anything' [NTC; NCV], not explicit [TEV]. The double negative μηδενὶ μηδέν 'to no one nothing' makes Paul's command very emphatic [TH, WBC]. This adjective describes a negative reference to an entity, event, or state [LN].
c. pres. act. impera. of ὀφείλω (LN **71.25**) (BAGD 2.a.α. p. 598): 'to owe' [AB, BAGD, BECNT, HNTC, NICNT, NTC, WBC; KJV, NASB, NCV, NET, NRSV], 'to be under obligation' [LN; TEV], 'to be indebted' [BAGD]. The clause 'to no one nothing be owing' is translated 'Pay your debts as they come due' [GW], 'let no debt remain outstanding' [NIV], 'leave no debt outstanding' [ICC2; REB], 'do not owe people anything' [NCV]. This entire clause is translated 'Let love be your only debt'

[CEV]. This verb means to be obligatory in view of some moral or legal requirement [LN].

d. εἰ μή (LN 89.131): 'except' [BECNT, ICC2, NICNT, NTC, WBC; NASB, NCV, NET, NIV, NLT, NRSV], 'save (that of)' [AB], 'but' [HNTC, LN; KJV, REB], 'however' [LN; GW], not explicit [CEV, TEV]. This conjunction marks contrast by designating an exception [LN].

e. pres. act. infin. of ἀγαπάω (LN 25.43) (BAGD 1.a.α. p. 4): 'to love' [LN]. The articular infinitive phrase τὸ...ἀγαπᾶν is translated as a simple infinitive: 'to love' [BAGD, BECNT, NICNT, NTC, WBC; KJV, NASB, NET, NIV, NRSV, TEV]. It is translated with the article indicating a noun modified by the infinitive phrase: 'the debt to love' [HNTC], 'the debt of (mutual) love' [ICC2; GW, REB], 'the obligation to love' [NLT]. The phrase 'except to love' is translated 'save that of loving' [AB], 'except always owe love' [NCV]. The whole clause is translated 'Let love be your only debt' [CEV]. This verb means to have love for someone or something, based on sincere appreciation and high regard [LN].

QUESTION—What is the intent of Paul's prohibition about owing?

He is not telling them that they should never borrow, but that they should pay their debts promptly [BECNT, Ho, Mor, Mu, NICNT, NTC, SSA, St]. They are not to leave their obligations unfulfilled [HNTC, ICC1, ICC2]. They also should not incur debt unless they know they can repay the debt [Ho, St].

QUESTION—Whom is Paul telling them they should love?

The reflexive pronoun ἀλλήλους 'one another' refers to other Christians, but the words 'no one' in this clause and 'the other' in the following clause indicate that their love is not to be limited just to other Christians [BECNT, NICNT]. Normally 'one another' would refer to other Christians, but 'the other' in the next clause shows he is talking about all other people [AB, Mor, Mu, NTC, WBC], meaning anyone with whom the Christian would come in contact with in daily living [Mor, NTC, WBC]. Genuine love must also include those who differ from us in every way [HNTC]. He is telling Christians to love one another, but that does not mean that they should only love Christians [HNTC]. He is telling them to love everyone without exception [ICC2].

QUESTION—What is the function of the neuter singular definite article τό in the phrase τὸ ἀλλήλους ἀγαπᾶν 'to love one another' (the definite article not being translated here)?

In Greek the neuter singular definite article can function to introduce a quotation, which in this sentence would be the well-known command of Jesus to love one another [NICNT, WBC]. The definite article turns the following phrase into a substantive, that is, 'the *command* to love one another' [NICNT].

QUESTION—What relationship is indicated by εἰ μή 'except'?

1. It indicates an exception to the command just given [AB, BECNT, Gdt, ICC2, NAC, NICNT, NTC, St, WBC; KJV, NASB, NCV, NET, NIV,

NLT, NRSV]: don't have any ongoing debts *except* the debt of loving one another. Although KJV translates 'but', it is used to show exception, not an adversative relation.
  2. It is adversative [HNTC, Mu, SSA; REB]: don't have any ongoing debts, but do love one another.

QUESTION—What does he mean when he says owe nothing *except* to love one another?

He uses the image of debt to indicate an obligation, which in this case is a permanent obligation that is never completely discharged [Mor, NICNT, St, TNTC]. The obligation to love one another never comes to an end [BECNT]. The obligation to love others is a response to their having been loved and accepted by God in Christ [WBC]. The more one loves, the more one sees the need for loving [Gdt]. There is no limit to the obligation to love others [NAC].

for the-one loving[a] the other has-fulfilled[b] (the) law.[c]

LEXICON—a. pres. act. participle of ἀγαπάω (LN 25.43) (BAGD 1.a.α. p. 4). 'to love' [AB, BAGD, BECNT, HNTC, ICC2, NICNT, NTC, WBC; all versions except TEV]. The phrase 'for the one loving' is translated 'whoever does this' [TEV]. This verb means to have love for someone or something, based on sincere appreciation and high regard [LN].
  b. perf. act. indic. of πληρόω (LN 33.144) (BAGD 4.b. p. 671): 'to fulfill' [AB, BAGD, BECNT, HNTC, ICC2, NICNT, NTC, WBC; GW, KJV, NASB, NET, NIV, NRSV], 'to fulfill the requirements' [NLT], 'to do (all)' [CEV], 'to obey' [NCV, TEV], 'to meet (every requirement)' [REB], 'to give the true meaning to, to provide the real significance of' [LN]. This verb means to give the true or complete meaning to something [LN].
  c. νόμος (LN 33.55, 33.333) (BAGD 3. p. 542): 'the Law' [LN (33.55)], 'law' [LN (33.333)]. This noun, which lacks the article, is translated as having the article: 'the law' [AB, BECNT, HNTC, ICC2, NICNT, NTC, WBC; KJV, NASB, NCV, NET, NIV, NRSV, REB], 'the Law' [CEV, TEV], 'Moses' Teachings' [GW], 'God's law' [NLT]. This noun denotes the first five books of the OT called the Torah [LN (33.55)], or a formalized rule (or set of rules) prescribing what people must do [LN (33.333)].

QUESTION—What relationship is indicated by γάρ 'for'?
  1. It indicates the reason why a Christian has an obligation to love others [ICC1, NICNT, SSA, WBC; probably all versions]. Love is important because when a Christian truly loves another person he has fulfilled the whole law in respect to that person [ICC1]. The alternative interpretation is overly subtle and also ignores the fact that Paul has said in 8:4 that Christians in fact do fulfill the law [NICNT]. After having said that we must love one another, it would be illogical for Paul to then support his statement by explaining that it was impossible to completely do so [SSA].

2. It indicates the reason why the obligation to love others always remains outstanding. The obligation can never be fully discharged because there are no people who can really love another in the fullest sense [ICC2].

QUESTION—In what sense is the law fulfilled by loving others?

Fulfilling the law does not refer to attaining sinless perfection, but to doing what the law really asks for [WBC]. It speaks of doing all that God's law requires [SSA], or properly performing what the law requires [BECNT, WBC], of treating others as the law requires [HNTC]. It is completely conforming to or giving the full measure of what the law requires [Mu]. A new age of eschatological fulfillment has begun in which a complete and final doing of the law is possible, and in which those Christians who love others have satisfied all that the law demands; however, this has only just begun to be fulfilled in the Christian, and won't be perfected during this life [NICNT]. Love guarantees that a person will fulfill the duties of justice toward others, as he will not offend those whom he loves [Gdt].

QUESTION—Who is 'the other'?

It refers to whatever specific individuals the believers would encounter in daily living [Mor, NICNT, WBC]. 'Other' has a generalizing effect, and means anyone they may encounter [ICC2, SSA], for everyone the believer encounters has been brought his way by God himself [ICC2]. It refers to any other person [AB, Mu], one's fellowman [NAC]. It includes all people [NAC, TH]. It is anyone other than oneself [HNTC]. It is synonymous with 'neighbor' in the following verse [AB, BECNT].

QUESTION—What law is he referring to?

1. He is speaking of the law of Moses [AB, BECNT, HNTC, ICC2, Mor, NICNT, TH, WBC]. It is the law of God [Mu, SSA], specifically as it pertains to mutual relationships among people [Mu]. It is the ten commandments, as summarized in Lev 19:18 [NTC].
2. He is speaking of law as principle, even though the specific examples he cites are from the law of Moses [ICC1].

13:9 For the You-shall- not -commit-adultery,a You-shall- not -murder,b You-shall- not -steal,c You-shall- not -covet,d

LEXICON—a. fut. act. indic. of μοιχεύω (LN 88.276) (BAGD 1. p. 526): 'to commit adultery' [AB, BAGD, BECNT, HNTC, ICC2, LN, NICNT, NTC, WBC; all versions except CEV, NCV], 'be faithful in marriage' [CEV], 'to be guilty of adultery' [NCV]. This verb means sexual intercourse of a man with a married woman other than his own spouse [LN].

b. fut. act. indic. of φονεύω (LN 20.82) (BAGD p. 864): 'to murder' [BAGD, BECNT, LN, NICNT, NTC; CEV, GW, NASB, NCV, NET, NIV, NLT, NRSV], 'to commit murder' [BAGD, LN; REB, TEV], 'to do murder' [HNTC], 'to kill' [AB, ICC2, WBC; KJV]. This verb means to deprive a person of life by illegal, intentional killing [LN].

c. fut. act. indic. of κλέπτω (LN 57.232) (BAGD p. 434): 'to steal' [AB, BAGD, BECNT, HNTC, ICC2, LN, NICNT, NTC, WBC; all versions]. This verb means to take the property of someone else secretly and without permission [LN].

d. fut. act. indic. of ἐπιθυμέω (LN 25.20) (BAGD p. 293): 'to covet' [AB, BECNT, HNTC, ICC2, LN, NICNT, NTC, WBC; KJV, NASB, NET, NIV, NLT, NRSV, REB], 'to lust' [LN], 'to want what belongs to others' [CEV], 'to have wrong desires' [GW], 'to want to take (your neighbor's things)' [NCV], 'to desire (what belongs to someone else)' [TEV], 'to desire, to long for' [BAGD]. This verb means to strongly desire to have what belongs to someone else [LN].

QUESTION—What relationship is indicated by γάρ 'for'?

It indicates the logical connection between what was said in 13:8 with what follows, which is that if a person loves, he has fulfilled the commandments, and he cites these four commandments as examples to prove his point [Mor]. It indicates 13:9 as a confirmation of what he meant in 13:8b [ICC2]. It indicates the grounds for his statement that loving others fulfills the law, which is that the commandments are summed up in this one command taken from Leviticus 19:18 [NICNT]. It indicates that what follows corroborates and expands what was just said in 13:8 [Mu].

QUESTION—What is signified by the article το 'the' accompanying γάρ 'for' at the beginning of the verse?

The article 'the' is used as a substantive that introduces the commands that are then quoted [NET]. It is used to refer to he series that follows, the list of commandments [TH]. It signifies 'the well-known commandments' which are then quoted [WBC]. It is translated 'the commandments' [GW, NET, NIV, NRSV, REB, TEV], 'the commandment' [WBC], 'the series of commandments' [NICNT], 'the commandments say' [NLT], 'the Law says' [NCV], 'in the Law there are many commands, such as' [CEV], 'this' [KJV, NASB].

(and) if (there-is)[a] any other commandment,[b]

LEXICON—a. There is no lexical entry in the Greek text for the conjunction 'and', or for the implied verb 'there is', but they are supplied for considerations of English style. The phrase εἴ τις ἑτέρα 'and if there is any other' [BECNT, NICNT; NASB, NET], is translated 'or any other' [AB], 'and any other' [HNTC, WBC; NRSV, REB], 'whatever other' [ICC2, NTC], 'and every other' [GW], 'and other such' [NLT], 'and if there be any other' [KJV], '(all these commands) and all others' [NCV], 'and whatever' [NIV], '(all these), and any others besides' [TEV].

b. ἐντολή (LN 33.330) (BAGD 2.a.γ. p. 269): 'commandment' [AB, BAGD, BECNT, HNTC, ICC2, LN, NICNT, NTC, WBC; all versions except CEV, NCV, TEV], 'command' [CEV, NCV, TEV]. This noun denotes that which is authoritatively commanded [LN].

QUESTION—What 'other commandment' might he be referring to?

He is referring to any other of the ten commandments [AB, Mor, WBC]; he is not giving a complete list of them here [Mor]. It refers to any other of the ten commandments [AB, WBC], but can also be extended more generally to the rest of the commandments pertaining to the covenant [WBC], or even further, to any legal system [AB]. He is referring to any of the many other commandments in the law of Moses that govern human relations [NICNT]. Loving is compatible with any of the other norms of the Mosaic law [BECNT].

in this word[a] it-is-summed-up[b] You-shall-love your neighbor[c] as[d] yourself.

LEXICON—a. λόγος (LN 33.98) (BAGD 1.b.α. p. 478): 'word' [BECNT, ICC2, LN, WBC; NRSV], 'saying' [HNTC, LN, NTC; KJV, NASB], 'statement' [LN; GW], 'one' [AB], 'commandment' [NICNT; NET, NLT], 'command' [CEV, TEV], 'rule' [NCV, NIV, REB]. This noun denotes that which has been stated or said, with primary focus upon the content of the communication [LN].

b. pres. pass. indic. of ἀνακεφαλαιόω (LN 63.8) (BAGD p. 56): 'to be summed up' [AB, BAGD, HNTC, ICC2, NICNT, NTC, WBC; all versions except KJV, NCV], 'to be fulfilled' [BECNT], 'to be briefly comprehended' [KJV], 'to be brought together' [LN]. The phrase 'and if there is any other commandment in this word it is summed up' is translated 'all these commands and all others are really only one rule' [NCV]. This verb means to bring everything together in terms of some unifying principle or person [LN].

c. πλησίον (LN 11.89) (BAGD 1.b. p. 672): 'neighbor' [AB, BAGD, BECNT, HNTC, ICC2, LN, NICNT, NTC, WBC; all versions except CEV], 'others' [CEV]. This word can be used to describe any person other than oneself, and refers to anyone whom Paul's readers would actually encounter from day to day [Mor]. This adjective describes a person who lives close beside others and who thus by implication is a part of the group with which an individual identifies both ethnically and culturally [LN].

d. ὡς (LN 64.12): 'as' [AB, BECNT, HNTC, ICC2, LN, NICNT, NTC, WBC; all versions]. This conjunction marks a relationship of similarity between events or states [LN].

QUESTION—Who is the neighbor in this command?

They are to love whomever they come into contact with in their daily living [AB, Mor, NICNT, SSA]. It refers to all fellow human beings [AB, TH]. The neighbor is anyone whom God brings our way, and whose need may lay claim to our resources [WBC]. It is anyone, not just other Christians [ICC2]. It is anyone who may need our help [NAC].

QUESTION—What is assumed in the phrase 'as yourself'?

It recognizes that people do, in fact, love themselves [BECNT, ICC2, Mor, NAC, NICNT, NTC, St], and naturally act to preserve their own self-interest

[BECNT]. There is nothing here to justify self-love [ICC2, Mor], nor does it contain an implicit command to love oneself [BECNT], nor does it give an excuse for egotism or selfishness [NICNT]. Self-love is not the basis for love of others, as it tends to be self-engrossed and exclusive; yet love for others does require a proper self-respect or self-esteem [WBC]. We do in fact love ourselves, but such self-love is the essence of sin; agape is selfless love, which cannot be turned inward on the self [NAC, St].

QUESTION—In what way is the law 'summed up' in the command to love?

In loving others all the commandments are fulfilled [Mu]. Love includes all social duties [Ho]. It is the indispensable auxiliary of justice [Gdt]. Love is the summation of all the obligations of the law; one who lives in love does not need all the prohibitions and prescriptions of the law [AB]. Love is the heart and soul of the law, and the center of Paul's ethics [BECNT]. This command to love could stand in the place of much of the law, and is the passage from the Pentateuch most quoted by NT writers [WBC]. The essence of the Mosaic law has been summarized in this one command, and in a sense replaces that law for the believer in Christ, who as a member of the new covenant people is no longer under that law; so he is not saying that the love commandment is the only one that is relevant to the Christian, only that the Mosaic law is no longer of central importance in the life of the Christian [NICNT].

13:10 Love[a] for-the neighbor does- not -work[b] evil;

LEXICON—a. ἀγάπη (LN **25.43**) (BAGD I.1.a. p. 5): 'love' [AB, BAGD, BECNT, HNTC, ICC2, LN, NICNT, NTC, WBC; all versions except CEV]. This noun is translated as a verb: 'to love' [CEV]. The abstract noun 'love' refers concretely to the person who loves [TH]. This noun denotes love for someone or something, based on sincere appreciation and high regard [LN].

b. pres. mid. or pass. indic. (deponent = act.) of ἐργάζομαι (LN 90.47, 13.9) (BAGD 2.a. p. 307): 'to do' [AB, BAGD, BECNT, ICC2, LN (90.47), NICNT, NTC, WBC; GW, NASB, NET, NIV, NLT, NRSV], 'to cause to be, to bring about' [LN (13.9)], 'to work' [HNTC; KJV], 'to hurt' [NCV], 'to wrong (a neighbor)' [REB], 'to do wrong' [TEV]. The phrase 'work evil' is translated 'will harm them' [CEV]. This verb means to cause a state or condition [LN (13.9)], or marks an agent relation with numerable events, with the probable implication of comprehensiveness [LN (90.47)].

therefore[a] love (is) (the) fulfillment[b] of-(the) law.[c]

LEXICON—a. οὖν (LN 89.50) (BAGD 1.a. p. 593): 'therefore' [BAGD, BECNT, ICC2, LN, NICNT, NTC, WBC; GW, KJV, NASB, NET, NIV, NRSV, REB], 'consequently' [BAGD, LN], 'accordingly' [BAGD, LN], 'then' [BAGD], 'so' [LN; CEV, NCV, NLT], 'for' [AB], 'that is why' [HNTC]. The phrase 'therefore love is' is translated 'to love, then, is' [TEV]. This conjunction marks result, often implying the conclusion of a process of reasoning [LN].

b. πλήρωμα (LN 59.32) (BAGD 4. p. 672): 'fulfillment' [AB, BAGD, BECNT, HNTC, NICNT, NTC, WBC; NASB, NET, NIV, REB], 'the fulfilling' [BAGD, ICC2; KJV, NRSV], 'fullness, completeness' [LN]. The noun 'fulfillment' is translated 'all that (the Law) demands' [CEV]. It is also translated as a verb: 'to fulfill' [GW, NLT], 'to obey' [NCV, TEV]. This noun denotes a total quantity, with emphasis upon completeness [LN].

c. νόμος (LN 33.55, 33.333) (BAGD 3. p. 542): 'the Law' [BAGD, LN (33.55)], 'law' [LN (33.333)], 'Moses' Teachings' [GW], 'the requirements of God's law' [NLT]. This noun without the article is translated as having the article: 'the law' [AB, BECNT, HNTC, ICC2, NICNT, NTC, WBC; KJV, NASB, NCV, NET, NIV, NRSV, REB], 'the Law' [CEV]; 'the whole Law' [TEV]. This noun denotes the first five books of the OT called the Torah [LN (33.55)], or a formalized rule (or set of rules) prescribing what people must do [LN (33.333)].

QUESTION—What relationship is indicated by οὖν 'therefore'?

It indicates a conclusion to what has just been said [Gdt, ICC2]. It indicates the consequence of this kind of love, which is that it fulfills the law [Mor]. It indicates the reason that love fulfills the law, which is that love does no harm to others [NICNT, St, TNTC].

QUESTION—How does love fulfill the law?

Love fully satisfies all that the law requires [NAC]. The Christian who loves does what the law requires, and has brought the law to its eschatological fulfillment and culmination [NICNT]. If love dominates human life, the requirements and prohibitions of the law are upheld and sustained, and all the obligations of Christian living are summed up [AB]. A realistic, active love seeks the good of others, and meets the requirements of God's law [WBC]. The one who loves is putting the law into practice [BECNT], and is therefore doing what the law requires [HNTC, ICC2]. Anyone who loves another will not do him any harm [ICC1, NTC], but will act to benefit him instead [NTC]. Love is the full measure of what the law demands [Mu]. It is the pledge of fulfilling what justice requires [Gdt].

DISCOURSE UNIT—13:11–14 [AB, HNTC, Ho, ICC1, ICC2, Mor, Mu, NICNT, St, TNTC, WBC; CEV, NET, NRSV]. The topic is an eschatological exhortation: Christian life as vigilant conduct [AB], the urgency of the time [HNTC], exhortation to a holy life [Ho], the day is at hand [ICC1], the eschatological motivation of Christian obedience [ICC2], the approaching consummation [Mu], living in the light [Mor], living in light of the day [NICNT], our relationship to the day: living in the 'already' and the 'not yet' [St], Christian life in days of crisis [TNTC], the imminence of the end as spur [WBC], the day when Christ returns [CEV], motivation to Godly conduct [NET], an urgent appeal [NRSV].

13:11 And this (do)[a] knowing[b] the time,[c]

LEXICON—a. There is no lexical entry in the Greek text for this word, it is implied. The phrase καὶ τοῦτο is translated as indicating an implied imperative: 'and this do' [NASB], 'and do this' [NICNT, NTC; NET, NIV], 'do this' [AB; NCV], 'you must do this' [TEV]. 'all these things you must do' [HNTC]. It is translated as indicating an additive relation: 'besides this' [NRSV], 'and this' [BECNT, ICC2, WBC], 'and that' [KJV]; not explicit [CEV, GW, REB]. It is also translated as a clause: 'this is all the more urgent' [NLT].
  b. perf. act. participle of οἶδα (LN 28.1, 32.4): 'to know' [LN (28.1)], 'to understand' [LN (32.4)]. This participle is translated as a participle: 'knowing' [BECNT, ICC2, NICNT, WBC; KJV, NASB], 'understanding' [NIV], 'realizing' [AB]; as a finite verb: 'you know' [HNTC, NTC; CEV, GW, NLT, NRSV, TEV], 'we know' [NET]; as an imperative: 'remember' [REB]; not explicit [NCV]. This verb means to possess information about something [LN (28.1)], or to comprehend the meaning of something, with focus upon the resulting knowledge [LN (32.4)]. This verb uses a perfect tense form to express a present tense meaning.
  c. καιρός (LN 67.145) (BAGD 1. p. 394, 3. p. 395): 'time' [BAGD, BECNT, HNTC, ICC2, NICNT, NTC, WBC; all versions except NLT, REB], 'age, era' [LN], 'moment' [AB], 'hour of crisis' [REB], 'time of crisis, the last times' [BAGD (4.)]. The phrase 'knowing the time' is translated 'for you know how late it is' [NLT]. This word is used here with an eschatological sense [BECNT, HNTC, ICC2, Mor, Mu, NAC, NICNT]. This noun denotes an indefinite period of time, but probably with the implication of the relation of a period to a particular state of affairs [LN].

QUESTION—What relationship is indicated by καὶ τοῦτο 'and this'?
  1. There is an implied imperative verb, 'do' [AB, HNTC, NICNT, NTC, St; NASB, NCV, NET, NIV, TEV]: 'do this, knowing…'
  2. It is transitional and indicates an added comment [Ho, ICC1, ICC2, Mor, Mu, WBC; KJV, NLT, NRSV]: 'and this, knowing…' It gathers up what has just been said and resumes the discussion with new comments [BECNT, Gdt, Mor, WBC]. It intensifies what has been said, with the sense 'indeed, all the more so' [Ho, Mu]. It introduces a new circumstance to intensify what has just been said [ICC2; NLT].

QUESTION—To what action does τοῦτο 'this' refer?
  1. It refers to all of what he has said in 12:1-13:10 [BECNT, Gdt, HNTC, ICC2, NICNT, NTC], especially the command to love others immediately preceding this statement [NTC].
  2. It refers to the command to love others [AB, Mu, St], and possibly to his exhortations about submission to government and the payment of taxes [St].

QUESTION—How is the participle used in this sentence?
It is causal [BECNT, HNTC, Ho, ICC2, Mu, NICNT, NTC; NCV, NET, NLT, TEV]: because you know the time. Their recognition of the significance of the present time should give them incentive to moral earnestness [ICC2]. The imminence of the end should give them a sense of urgency [BECNT].

QUESTION—What is the 'time' he is speaking of?
It is the current period of Christian existence in which believers are called on to show their faith in their actions [AB]. It is the time in which final salvation is drawing nearer [NICNT]. It is the age in which Christ has already come and made all things new, and which is looking forward to the final consummation of everything [Mor]. It is a time of opportunity and decision [St], of the opportunity for obedience and faith, but one which was passing by [ICC2], of opportunity to preach the gospel that may soon be cut short by the forces of darkness and disorder [TNTC]. It is the final period of the present age [NAC], the last epoch in the world's history [Mu].

that (it is) already[a] (the) hour[b] (for) you to-rise[c] from[d] sleep,[e]

TEXT—Instead of ὑμᾶς '(for) you', some manuscripts have ἡμᾶς '(for) us'. GNT selects the reading ὑμᾶς 'you' with a B rating, indicating that the text is almost certain. The reading ἡμᾶς 'us' is taken only by NET. The word ὑμᾶς 'you' does not occur in some manuscripts. It is omitted by KJV only.

LEXICON—a. ἤδη (LN 67.20): 'already' [AB, BECNT, HNTC, LN, NICNT, WBC; NASB, NET], 'now' [NCV, NRSV]. The phrase 'already the hour' is translated 'high time' [ICC2; KJV, REB], 'how critical the time' [NTC], 'the hour has come' [NIV], 'time is running out' [NLT], 'the time has come' [TEV], not explicit [CEV, GW]. This word increases the sense of urgency in the passage [WBC]. This adverb describes a point of time preceding another point of time and implying completion [LN].

b. ὥρα (LN 67.1) (BAGD 3. p. 896): 'hour' [BECNT, HNTC, NICNT, NTC, WBC; NASB, NET, NIV], 'time' [AB, BAGD, ICC2, LN; CEV, GW, KJV, NCV, NLT, REB], 'occasion' [LN], 'moment' [NRSV, TEV]. This word is used here with an eschatological sense [BECNT, HNTC, ICC2, WBC]. This noun denotes points of time consisting of occasions for particular events [LN].

c. aorist pass. infin. of ἐγείρω (LN **23.74**) (BAGD 2.a. p. 215): 'to rise up' [NICNT], 'to awaken' [BAGD, LN; NASB], 'to wake up' [BAGD, LN, NTC, WBC; CEV, GW, NCV, NIV, NLT, TEV], 'to awake' [HNTC, ICC2; KJV, NET], 'to wake' [NRSV, REB], 'to be roused' [AB], 'to be aroused' [BECNT]. This verb means to become awake after sleeping [LN].

d. ἐκ with genitive object (LN 68.54) (BAGD 1.c. p. 234): 'from' [AB, BAGD, BECNT, LN, NICNT, NTC, WBC; NASB, NCV, NET, NIV, NRSV, TEV], 'out of' [HNTC, ICC2; KJV, REB], not explicit [CEV, GW, NLT]. This preposition marks the aspect of cessation [LN].

e. ὕπνος (LN 23.66) (BAGD p. 843): 'sleep' [AB, BAGD, BECNT, HNTC, ICC2, LN, NICNT, WBC; KJV, NASB, NCV, NET, NRSV, REB, TEV], 'slumber' [NTC; NIV], not explicit [CEV, GW, NLT]. This noun denotes the state of being asleep [LN].

QUESTION—What relationship is indicated by ὅτι 'that'?
1. It indicates the content of what they know [AB, ICC2, NICNT, WBC; KJV, NASB, NET, TEV]: you know *that* it is the hour to rise.
2. It indicates grounds for his eschatological use of the word καιρός 'time' [BECNT]; you know you are in the last times *because* it is the hour to rise.

QUESTION—What does the metaphor of sleep represent?
It is a state characterized by a lack of concern for one's conduct and existence [AB]. It is a metaphor for spiritual insensitivity, for absorption in and conformity to the present age of darkness and evil [NICNT]. It is being lethargic in the Christian life, forgetful of God [Mor]. It means to be unprepared for the imminent crisis [ICC2]. It is a moral drowsiness that inclines people to do the works of darkness, the vices that people practice in secret [BECNT]. It is a state of spiritual torpor or sleepiness [Mu]. The 'waking' is the renewal mentioned in 12:2 [WBC]. It is a term used with eschatological connotation; here it refers to a relaxing of vigilance [HNTC]. It is the state of being estranged from God and forgetful of God, as well as all the carnal activity of a worldly person [Gdt].

for now[a] (is) nearer[b] to-us/our salvation[b] than when we-believed.[d]

LEXICON—a. νῦν (LN 67.38) (BAGD 1.c. p. 545): 'now' [AB, BAGD, HNTC, ICC2, LN, NICNT NTC, WBC; all versions], not explicit [BECNT]. This adverb describes a point of time simultaneous with the event of the discourse itself [LN].
b. ἐγγύτερον (LN 67.61) (BAGD 2.a. p. 214): 'nearer' [BAGD, BECNT, HNTC, ICC2, LN, NICNT, NTC, WBC; all versions except TEV], 'closer' [AB; TEV]. This adverb describes a point of time subsequent to another point of time, but relatively close [LN].
c. σωτηρία (LN 21.18) (BAGD 2. p. 801): 'salvation' [AB, BAGD, BECNT, HNTC, ICC2, NICNT, NTC, WBC; all versions except CEV, REB, TEV], 'deliverance' [LN; REB]. This noun is translated by a verb 'to be saved' [CEV, TEV]. This noun denotes rescue from danger and restoration to a former state of safety and well being [LN].
d. aorist act. indic. of πιστεύω (LN 31.102) (BAGD 2.b. p. 661): 'to believe' [AB, BAGD, BECNT, HNTC, NICNT, NTC, WBC; KJV, NASB, NCV, NIV, NLT, REB, TEV], 'to become a believer' [ICC2; GW, NET, NRSV], 'to be a believer, to be a Christian' [LN], 'to put one's faith in (the lord)' [CEV]. The adverb 'first' is used with this verb to indicate that Paul is referring to the time when they initially became believers [AB, HNTC, NTC, TH; CEV, GW, NCV, NIV, NLT, REB, TEV]. This is an ingressive aorist, describing the beginning of an ongoing

action or state [BECNT, ICC2, Mor, NICNT], the act of commitment that began their Christian experience [WBC]. This verb means to believe in the good news about Jesus Christ and to become a follower [LN].

QUESTION—What relationship is indicated by γάρ 'for'?

It indicates the grounds for the previous exhortation; that is, you should wake from sleep because salvation is near [BECNT, ICC2, Mor].

QUESTION—With what word in the sentence should the pronoun ἡμῶν 'to us/our' be connected?

1. It is connected to 'salvation' and shows possession [AB, NICNT, NTC, WBC; GW, KJV, NCV, NET, NIV, NLT; probably CEV, TEV]: *our salvation is nearer*.
2. It is connected to 'nearer' and is its object [BECNT, HNTC, ICC2, Mor, NAC; NASB, NRSV, REB]: *salvation is nearer to us*.

QUESTION—What is the salvation that is 'nearer'?

He is referring to the time of Christ's return [BECNT, ICC2, Mor, NAC, NICNT, TNTC], when God's work on the church's behalf will be complete [NICNT]. It is the final consummation at the time of Christ's parousia, that is, his return [AB]. It is the complete wholeness that God's grace will one day effect in them [WBC]. Salvation is viewed here as a universal eschatological event, the consummation of God's redemptive acts at the parousia of Christ on the last day [HNTC]. It is the culmination of their salvation which will be experienced when the Lord returns [NAC, NTC]. This salvation is the future realization of their final adoption as God's children, of the freedom of glory, and of the redemption of the body [St]. It is the future completion of their adoption as sons and the redemption of their bodies when Christ returns [TNTC].

13:12 The night[a] drew-to-a-close,[b] the day[c] has-drawn-near.[d]

LEXICON—a. νύξ (LN 14.59) (BAGD 2. p. 546): 'night' [AB, BAGD, BECNT, HNTC, ICC2, LN, NICNT, NTC, WBC; all versions]. This noun denotes darkness of the night in contrast with daylight [LN].

b. aorist act. indic. of προκόπτω (LN **67.118**) (BAGD 1. p. 708): 'to draw to a close' [LN], 'to be advanced, to be far gone' [BAGD]. The phrase ἡ νὺξ προέκοψεν is translated 'the night is nearly over' [LN; NIV, TEV]. 'the night is far spent' [AB; KJV], 'the night has advanced' [BECNT; NET], 'the night is advanced' [HNTC], 'the night has far advanced' [ICC2], 'the night is far advanced' [NTC, WBC], 'the night is far along' [NICNT], 'the night is almost over' [CEV, GW], 'the night is almost gone' [NASB, NLT], 'the night is far gone' [NRSV], 'the "night" is almost finished' [NCV], 'it is far on in the night' [REB]. This verb means to extend in time, with focus upon the end point [LN].

c. ἡμέρα (LN 14.40) (BAGD 1.b. p. 346): 'day' [AB, BAGD, BECNT, HNTC, ICC2, NICNT, NTC, WBC; all versions except NLT], 'the day of salvation' [NLT], 'daylight' [LN]. This noun denotes the light of the day in contrast with the darkness of night [LN].

d. perf. act. indic. of ἐγγίζω (LN 67.21) (BAGD 5.b. p. 213): 'to draw near' [AB, BECNT, NICNT, NTC], 'to be near' [HNTC; GW, NET, NRSV, REB], 'to come near' [BAGD, LN], 'to be close at hand' [ICC2], 'to be at hand' [WBC; KJV, NASB], 'to soon appear' [CEV], 'to be almost here' [NCV, NIV, TEV], 'to soon be here' [NLT]. This verb refers to the occurrence of a point of time close to a subsequent point of time [LN].

QUESTION—What is the 'day' that has drawn near?

1. It is the day of Christ's return [Gdt, NICNT, St], when believers will experience the completion of their redemption [Gdt, NICNT]. It is the day of the Lord [BECNT]. This statement does not necessarily mean that Paul thought Christ's parousia or return was imminent [BECNT, Gdt, Ho, ICC2, Mor, Mu, NAC, NTC, St], but simply that Christ's coming brought about a decisiveness and finality to this era of history such that what now remains is to await his return [ICC2, Mor, NAC, St].
2. It is the age to come [HNTC]. It is the never-ending era of light, holiness, and gladness [NTC]. It is the coming age of God's new order [ICC2]. It is the eschatological destiny of Christians [AB].
3. It is the consummation of Christ's work in them personally in terms of their eternal destiny, which would mean being delivered from the present evil world, with all its sins and sorrows, and being brought into the purity and blessedness of heaven [Ho].

Therefore[a] let-us-put-off[b] the works[c] of-the darkness,[d]

LEXICON—a. οὖν (LN 89.50): 'therefore' [BECNT, HNTC, LN, NICNT, WBC; KJV, NASB, REB], 'so' [LN, NTC; GW, NCV, NIV, NLT], 'so then' [LN; NET], 'then' [AB, ICC2; NRSV], 'consequently' [LN], 'accordingly' [LN], not explicit [CEV, TEV]. This conjunction marks result, often implying the conclusion of a process of reasoning [LN].

b. aorist mid. subj. of ἀποτίθημι (LN 85.44) (BAGD 1.b. p. 101): 'to put off' [HNTC, NICNT, WBC], 'to put aside' [BECNT, NTC; NIV], 'to lay aside' [BAGD, ICC2; NASB, NET, NRSV], 'to throw off' [REB], 'to cast off' [AB; KJV], 'to remove' [LN; NLT], 'to get rid of' [GW], 'to rid oneself' [BAGD], 'to put away, to put out of the way' [LN]. This clause is translated 'we must stop behaving as people do in the dark' [CEV], 'we should stop doing things that belong to darkness' [NCV], 'let us stop doing the things that belong to the dark' [TEV]. This verb means to put or take something away from its normal location [LN].

c. ἔργον (LN 42.11) (BAGD 1.c.β. p. 308): 'act' [LN], 'deed' [BAGD, LN]. This plural noun is translated 'works' [BECNT, HNTC, ICC2, NICNT, WBC; KJV, NET, NRSV], 'deeds' [AB, BAGD, NTC; NASB, NIV, NLT, REB], 'things' [GW, NCV, TEV], not explicit [CEV]. This noun denotes that which is done, with possible focus on the energy or effort involved [LN].

d. σκότος (LN 88.125) (BAGD 2.b. p. 758): 'darkness' [AB, BAGD, BECNT, HNTC, ICC2, LN, NICNT, NTC, WBC; KJV, NASB, NCV,

NET, NIV, NRSV, REB], 'dark' [CEV, GW, NLT, TEV], 'evil world, realm of evil' [LN]. The phrase 'works of the darkness' is translated 'evil deeds' [NLT]. This noun denotes the realm of sin and evil [LN].

QUESTION—What relationship is indicated by οὖν 'therefore'?

It indicates the basis for his appeal to them to turn from the works of darkness [Mor]. It indicates a transition from his statements about the time to his exhortation based on the fact of what time it is [St].

QUESTION—What is meant by the metaphor of putting off the works of the darkness?

He uses the imagery of changing clothes to describe the change of values the Christian conversion involves, with darkness symbolizing the present evil age and light symbolizing the new age of salvation [NICNT]. They are to turn decisively away from wicked works [Mor]. They are to turn away from those vices that people do in secret [BECNT]. Night and darkness represent sin and sorrow, the opposite of the knowledge, purity, and happiness that daytime symbolizes [Ho].

QUESTION—What relationship is indicated by the genitive phrase τοῦ σκότους 'of the darkness'?

It describes behaviors that are typical of the realm of evil [NICNT], of the habitat of evil [Mor]. The sinful acts that are characteristic of the metaphorical 'night' of this present age are often those things that are done during the actual nighttime, and which people would be ashamed to do during daylight hours [ICC2]. These actions are often done in the dark [Ho, NTC, St, TH], under the cover of darkness [AB, St], and are always encouraged by the prince of darkness [NTC]. These things flourish in darkness because people who do them do not want to be seen doing them [NAC]. They don't dare do these things in the daylight [Gdt].

and let-us-put-on[a] the weapons/armor[b] of-the light.[c]

LEXICON—a. aorist mid. subj. of ἐνδύω (LN 49.1) (BAGD 2.a. p. 264): 'to put on' [BAGD, BECNT, HNTC, ICC2, LN, NICNT, NTC, WBC; KJV, NASB, NET, NIV, NLT, NRSV, REB], 'to don' [AB], 'to take up' [GW, NCV, TEV], 'to clothe' [BAGD]. This clause is translated 'be ready to live in the light' [CEV], 'clothe yourselves with the armor of right living, as those who live in the light' [NLT]. This verb means to put on clothes, without implying any particular article of clothing [LN].

b. ὅπλον (LN 6.29) (BAGD 2.b. p. 575): 'weapon' [BAGD, BECNT, LN, NICNT, WBC; GW, NCV, NET, TEV], 'armor' [AB, HNTC, ICC2, NTC; KJV, NASB, NIV, NLT, NRSV, REB], not explicit [CEV]. This noun denotes an instrument used in fighting, whether offensive or defensive [LN].

c. φῶς (LN 14.36) (BAGD 3.a. p. 872): 'light' [AB, BAGD, BECNT, HNTC, ICC2, LN, NICNT, NTC, WBC; all versions except NLT]. The phrase 'of the light' is translated 'shining' [NLT]. This noun denotes light, in contrast with darkness [LN].

QUESTION—What does ὅπλα 'weapons/armor' signify?
Note that those commentaries and versions cited in options 1 and 2 below may or may not intend to exclude the other option by their choice of wording, in which case they would fit into option 3.
1. It is weaponry [BAGD, BECNT, LN, Mor, NICNT, TH; GW, NCV, NET, TEV].
2. It is armor [AB, St; KJV, NASB, NIV, NLT, NRSV, REB].
3. It is both offensive weaponry and defensive armor [HNTC, Ho, ICC2, LN, NAC, NTC, WBC].
4. It is the clothing of a workman [Gdt]

QUESTION—What relationship is indicated by the genitive construction τοῦ φωτός 'of the light'?
It describes weaponry appropriate for people who have been rescued from the kingdom of darkness and brought into the kingdom of light [NICNT]. It is those virtues and actions that are suited to the light, meaning those that people have no need to be ashamed of [Ho].

13:13 Let-us-walk[a] decently[b] as[c] in (the) day,[d]

LEXICON—a. aorist act. subj. of περιπατέω (LN 41.11) (BAGD 2.a.α.,β. p. 649): 'to walk' [BAGD, BECNT, HNTC, ICC2, NICNT, NTC; KJV], 'to live' [BAGD, LN; GW, NCV, NET, NLT, NRSV], 'to behave' [LN; CEV, NASB, NIV, REB], 'to conduct oneself' [AB, BAGD, WBC; TEV]. This verb means to live or behave in a customary manner, with possible focus upon continuity of action [LN].

b. εὐσχημόνως (LN 88.50) (BAGD p. 327): 'decently' [BAGD, BECNT, LN, NICNT, WBC; GW, NET, NIV], 'with decency' [AB; REB], 'decent' [NLT], 'with propriety' [LN], 'in a becoming manner' [LN], 'becomingly' [BAGD], 'honorably' [HNTC, ICC2, NTC; NRSV], 'properly' [CEV, NASB, TEV], 'honestly' [KJV], 'in a right way' [NCV]. This adverb describes a fitting or becoming manner of behavior [LN].

c. ὡς (LN 64.12) (BAGD I.2.a. p. 897): 'as' [AB, BAGD, BECNT, HNTC, ICC2, LN, NICNT, NTC, WBC; all versions except NCV, NLT], 'like' [BAGD, LN; NCV], not explicit [NLT]. This conjunction marks a relationship of similarity between events or states [LN].

d. ἡμέρα (LN 14.40): 'daylight' [AB, LN], 'day' [BECNT, HNTC, ICC2, NICNT, WBC; all versions except NET, NIV], 'daytime' [NTC; NET, NIV]. This noun denotes the light of the day in contrast with the darkness of night [LN].

QUESTION—What is meant by the metaphor of 'walking'?
It represents one's daily conduct [AB, NICNT, WBC], one's manner of living [NICNT, TH]. It is the steady progress of the believer [Mor]. It is moral conduct [ICC2].

QUESTION—What is implied by his statement 'as in the day'?
1. He is referring to the current era, in which Christians are now living in the light [BECNT, NICNT].

2. They are now living as in the light of day, but 'day' also has connotations of the coming 'day of the Lord', the parousia of Christ; the light that now shines within the soul of the believer will break upon the whole world on the day when Christ returns [Gdt]. The coming day of Christ's return in great splendor is already casting its light into their lives, and they are to live in that light [Mu].
3. He is referring to the 'day' of the coming age, which, in a sense, believers are already living in [HNTC, ICC2]. It is equivalent to 'kingdom', referring to the coming of the kingdom of God [WBC].

not in[a]-carousings[b] and in-drunkenesses,[c]

LEXICON—a. There is no lexical entry for the preposition 'in' in the Greek text, the dative case being used to describe the abstract noun as an event or series of events in process of being carried out. In conjunction with the negating particle μή this relation is translated 'not in' [AB, BECNT, HNTC, ICC2, NICNT, NTC, WBC; KJV, NASB, NET, NIV, NRSV], 'no' [REB, TEV], 'don't go to' [CEV], 'we should not have' [NCV], '(wild parties) cannot be part of our lives' [GW], 'don't participate in' [NLT].
   b. κῶμος (LN **88.287**) (BAGD p. 461): 'carousing' [BAGD, HNTC, LN, NICNT; NASB, NET], 'orgy' [AB, LN, NTC; NIV, TEV], 'drinking parties' [BECNT], 'revels' [ICC2], 'revelry' [BAGD, WBC], 'wild parties' [CEV, GW, NCV, NLT], 'rioting' [KJV], 'reveling' [NRSV]. This entire phrase is translated 'no drunken orgies' [REB]. This noun denotes drinking parties involving unrestrained indulgence in alcoholic beverages and accompanying immoral behavior [LN].
   c. μέθη (LN **88.283**) (BAGD p. 498): 'drunkenness' [AB, BAGD, BECNT, HNTC, ICC2, LN, WBC; GW, KJV, NASB, NET, NIV, NLT, NRSV, TEV], 'drinking bouts' [BAGD, NICNT, NTC]. This plural noun 'drunkennesses' is translated as a verb phrase: 'to get drunk' [CEV, NCV]. These two nouns are difficult to distinguish [BECNT, HNTC, TH], and reinforce each other [HNTC]. Used together here they suggest the composite idea of drunken revelries [BECNT, ICC2, NAC, WBC], or all kinds of drunkenness [TH]. There is a close association between drunkenness and sexual sins, which he mentions next [BECNT, ICC2]. This noun denotes becoming drunk on alcoholic beverages [LN].
QUESTION—What is signified by his use of the plural of these two nouns and the two that follow?
   The plural of these nouns signifies multiple acts of such things [BECNT, HNTC, ICC2, Mor, NAC, WBC].

not in-acts-of-immorality[a] and in-indecencies,[b] not in-strife[c] and in-envy,[d]

LEXICON—a. κοίτη (LN **88.273**) (BAGD 2.a. p. 440): 'immorality' [TEV], 'sexual immorality' [LN; GW, NET, NIV], 'sexual sin' [BECNT; NCV], 'sexual excess' [BAGD, NICNT, NTC], 'lasciviousness' [HNTC, LN], 'debauchery' [AB, WBC; NRSV, REB], 'sexual promiscuity' [NASB,

NLT], '(repeated) promiscuity' [ICC2], 'chambering' [KJV], not explicit [NCV]. The phrase μὴ κοίταις καὶ ἀσελγείαις 'not in acts of immorality and in indecencies' is translated 'don't...be vulgar or indecent' [CEV], 'there should be no sexual sins of any kind' [NCV]. This noun denotes engaging in immoral sexual excess [LN].

b. ἀσέλγεια (LN 88.272) (BAGD p. 114): 'indecency' [TEV], 'licentious behavior, extreme immorality' [LN], 'immoral living' [NLT], 'sexual excess' [AB, WBC], 'sensuality' [BECNT; NASB, NET], 'uncleanness' [HNTC], 'debauchery' [ICC2, NTC; NIV], 'licentiousness' [NICNT; NRSV], 'promiscuity' [GW], 'wantonness' [KJV], 'immoral living' [NLT], 'vice' [REB], not explicit [NCV]. This noun is translated as an adjective: 'indecent' [CEV]. This word describes being enslaved to shameful immorality [NAC]. This noun denotes behavior completely lacking in moral restraint, usually with the implication of sexual licentiousness [LN].

c. ἔρις (LN 39.22) (BAGD p. 309): 'strife' [BAGD, BECNT, HNTC, ICC2, LN, NICNT; KJV, NASB], 'discord' [BAGD, LN; NET], 'dissension' [NTC; NIV], 'quarrel' [CEV, REB], 'quarreling' [AB, WBC; NLT, NRSV], 'rivalry' [GW], 'fighting' [NCV, TEV], 'contention' [BAGD]. This noun coupled with the one following indicate self-will and a readiness to quarrel, a determination to have things one's own way [Mor]. This noun denotes conflict resulting from rivalry and discord [LN].

d. ζῆλος (LN 88.162) (BAGD 2. p. 337): 'envy' [HNTC, LN, WBC], 'envying' [KJV], 'jealousy' [AB, BECNT, ICC2, LN, NICNT, NTC; all versions except CEV, KJV], 'resentment' [LN]. This noun is translated by the verb phrase 'to be jealous' [CEV]. This noun denotes a particularly strong feeling of resentment and jealousy against someone [LN].

QUESTION—What difference, if any, is there between κοίταις 'acts of immorality' and ἀσελγείαις 'indecencies'?

Whereas κοίταις is specifically sexual misdeeds, ἀσελγείαις refers more generally to any kind of unseemly or licentious behavior, which would include acts of sexual immorality [NICNT]. The second noun, ἀσελγείαις, speaks more generally to unrestrained lust [Mor], debauchery or licentiousness [WBC]. It is difficult to distinguish between these two concepts [BECNT, TH]. These two nouns together could be understood as one composite idea [ICC2, NAC], and treated as a hendiadys meaning 'debauched sexual excess' [WBC], or all kinds of immorality [TH].

13:14 but[a] put-on[b] the Lord Jesus Christ and do- not -make provision[c] for[d] the flesh[e] for lusts.[f]

LEXICON—a. ἀλλά (LN 89.125): 'but' [ICC2, LN, NICNT; KJV, NASB, NCV, TEV], 'instead' [LN; GW, NET, NLT, NRSV], 'on the contrary' [LN], 'rather' [AB, HNTC, NTC, WBC; NIV], not explicit [BECNT; CEV, REB]. This conjunction marks emphatic contrast [LN].

b. aorist mid. impera. of ἐνδύω (LN 49.1) (BAGD 2.b. p. 264): 'to put on' [AB, BAGD, BECNT, HNTC, ICC2, LN, NICNT, WBC; KJV, NASB, NET, NRSV], 'to clothe (oneself)' [BAGD, NTC; NCV, NIV]. The clause 'put on the Lord Jesus Christ' is translated 'let the Lord Jesus Christ be as near to you as the clothes you wear' [CEV], 'live like the Lord Jesus Christ did' [GW], 'let the Lord Jesus himself be the armor that you wear' [REB], 'clothe yourself with the presence of the Lord Jesus Christ' [NLT], 'take up the weapons of the Lord Jesus Christ' [TEV]. This verb means to put on clothes, without implying any particular article of clothing [LN].

c. πρόνοια (LN 30.47) (BAGD 2. p. 709): 'provision' [BAGD, BECNT, ICC2, NICNT, NTC, WBC; KJV, NASB, NET, NRSV]. The phrase καὶ τῆς σαρκὸς πρόνοιαν μὴ ποιεῖσθε εἰς ἐπιθυμίας 'and do not make provision for the flesh for lusts' is translated 'and make no provision for the flesh in regard to its lusts' [NASB], 'and make not provision for the flesh, to fulfill the lusts thereof' [KJV], 'stop planning ahead so as to satisfy the desires of your sinful nature' [LN], 'and give no more thought to the desires of the flesh' [AB], 'and do not make provision for the flesh and its desires' [BECNT], 'and take no thought in advance for the flesh, with a view to fulfilling its desires' [HNTC], 'and cease to make provision for the flesh for the satisfaction of its lusts' [ICC2], 'and make no provision for the flesh, to carry out its desires' [NICNT], 'and make no provision for (the fulfillment of) the lusts of the flesh' [NTC], 'and make no provision for the flesh to satisfy its desires' [WBC], 'then you won't try to satisfy your selfish desires' [CEV], 'and forget about satisfying the desires of your sinful nature' [GW], 'and forget about satisfying your sinful self' [NCV], 'and make no provision for the flesh to arouse its desires' [NET], 'and do not think about how to gratify the desires of the sinful nature' [NIV], 'and don't let yourself think about ways to indulge your evil desires' [NLT], 'and make no provision for the flesh, to gratify its desires' [NRSV], 'give your unspiritual nature no opportunity to satisfy its desires' [REB], 'and stop paying attention to your sinful nature and satisfying its desires' [TEV]. This noun denotes to think about something ahead of time, with the implication that one can then respond appropriately [LN].

d. There is no lexical entry for the preposition 'for' in the Greek text, the genitive case being used to express the relation between 'provision' and 'flesh'. This relation is translated 'for' [BECNT, HNTC, ICC2, NICNT, NTC, WBC; KJV, NASB, NET, NRSV], 'to' [AB; REB, TEV], 'about' [GW, NCV, NIV], not explicit [CEV, NLT].

e. σάρξ (LN 26.7) (BAGD 7. p. 744): 'flesh' [AB, BAGD, BECNT, HNTC, ICC2, NICNT, NTC, WBC; KJV, NASB, NET, NRSV], 'unspiritual nature' [REB], 'sinful nature' [GW, NIV, TEV], 'sinful self' [NCV]. This noun is also translated as an adjective: 'selfish (desires)' [CEV], 'evil (desires)' [NLT]. This noun represents the fallen human nature in

rebellion against God [ICC2, NAC]. It is the ugly, self-centered nature [St]. This noun denotes that aspect of human nature which is characterized by or reflects typical human reasoning and desires in contrast with those aspects of human thought and behavior which relate to God and the spiritual life [LN].
   f. ἐπιθυμία (LN 25.20) (BAGD 3. p. 293): 'lust' [ICC2, LN, NTC; KJV, NASB], 'desires' [AB, BAGD, BECNT, HNTC, NICNT; WBC; CEV, GW, NET, NIV, NRSV, REB, TEV], 'evil desires' [LN; NLT], not explicit [NCV]. This noun denotes a strong desire to have what belongs to someone else [LN].
QUESTION—In what sense do they 'put on' the Lord Jesus Christ?
The use of the full phrase 'the Lord Jesus Christ' shows how totally this is to be done and how it is to influence all of life [Mu, NICNT]. They are to embrace Christ in such a way that his character is shown in all they say or do [NICNT]. It means not only putting on his character, but also letting Christ himself be their armor [Mor, St]. Jesus himself is the armor that they wear [Mor; REB]. 'Putting on' the Lord Jesus interprets 'putting on' the armor of light [ICC2]. The Christian has already 'put on' Christ through baptism [AB, HNTC, ICC2]. That identification with Christ that occurs in baptism must bear fruit in the conscious life, and the Christian must live in Christ [AB]. What began sacramentally through baptism must be renewed by living in conformity with his mind [HNTC]. It means to be united with him in his death and his resurrection life [Mu]. It means continually embracing him in faith and devoted obedience, striving to allow our lives to be conformed to the pattern of his earthly life, and depending so totally on his righteousness that we cannot help but live to please him [ICC2]. They are to appropriate Christ's sentiments and manners of acting by continual communion with him [Gdt]. They are to be so united to him that Christ himself and his own virtues are seen in their conduct [Ho]. To put on Christ means to exhibit Christian virtues in all aspects of Christian character [TNTC]. This was the passage that was instrumental in the conversion of St. Augustine [AB, Gdt, Mor, NAC, NTC, TNTC, WBC].

DISCOURSE UNIT—14:1–15:13 [AB, BECNT, Gdt, ICC1, ICC2, Mor, NAC, NICNT, St; NIV]. The topic is the duty of love owed by the strong in the community to the weak [AB], a call for mutual acceptance between the strong and the weak [BECNT], divergence among Christians [Gdt], on forbearance towards those who are scrupulous [ICC1], the strong and the weak [ICC2], love and liberty [Mor], how righteousness manifests itself among the weak and the strong [NAC], a plea for unity [NICNT], our relationship to the weak: welcoming, and not despising [St], the weak and the strong [NIV].

DISCOURSE UNIT—14:1–15:3 [GW]. The topic is how to treat Christians who are weak in faith.

DISCOURSE UNIT—14:1–15:6 [TNTC, WBC]. The topic is Christian liberty and Christian charity [TNTC], the particular problem of food laws and holy days [WBC].

DISCOURSE UNIT—14:1–23 [Mu; NLT]. The topic is the weak and the strong [Mu], the danger of criticism [NLT].

DISCOURSE UNIT—14:1–12 [AB, HNTC, Ho, Mor, NICNT, TNTC, WBC; CEV, NCV, NET, NRSV, TEV]. The topic is Christian solidarity: its extent and its limits [AB], the strong and the weak [HNTC], relationships with those who have scruples [Ho], Christian liberty [Mor, TNTC], do not condemn one another [NICNT], the problem posed: the challenge to the weak [WBC], do not criticize other people [NCV], don't criticize others [CEV], exhortation to mutual forbearance [NET], do not judge another [NRSV], do not judge others [TEV].

14:1 Accept[a] the-one being-weak[b] in-the faith,[c] not for quarrels[d] of-opinions.[e]

LEXICON—a. pres. mid. impera. of προσλαμβάνω (LN **34.53**) (BAGD 2.b. p. 717): 'to accept' [BAGD, NTC; NASB, NCV, NIV, NLT, REB], 'to receive' [BAGD, BECNT, ICC2, NICNT; KJV, NET], 'to welcome' [AB, HNTC, LN, WBC; CEV, GW, NRSV, TEV]. This verb means to accept the presence of a person with friendliness [LN], to welcome into fellowship and into one's heart [St].

b. pres. act. participle of ἀσθενέω (LN **74.26**) (BAGD 2. p. 115): 'to be weak' [AB, BAGD, BECNT, HNTC, ICC2, LN, NICNT, NTC, WBC; all versions]. This verb means to be in a state of incapacity or weakness [LN], or to be over-scrupulous [BAGD].

c. πίστις (LN **31.85**, 31.104) (BAGD 2.d.α.. p. 663): 'faith' [BAGD, BECNT, HNTC, ICC2, LN, NICNT, NTC, WBC; all versions], 'convictions' [AB]. This noun denotes belief to the extent of complete trust and reliance [LN (31.85)], or the content of what Christians believe [LN (31.104)].

d. διακρίσις (LN **33.444**) (BAGD 2. p. 185): 'quarrel' [BAGD], 'contention, dispute' [LN]. The phrase 'not for quarrels of opinions' is translated 'and not for the purpose of quarrels over disputed matters' [NICNT], 'not to quarrel about disputable matters' [AB], 'though not with a view to settling disputes' [WBC], 'and do not have disputes over differing opinions' [NASB], 'but not to doubtful disputations' [KJV], 'without passing judgment on disputable matters' [NIV], 'not for the purpose of passing judgment on his opinions' [BECNT], 'but not for the purpose of getting into quarrels about opinions' [BAGD], 'but not for the purpose of quarreling over opinions' [NRSV], 'but not for the purpose of passing judgment on his opinions' [NASB], 'not with the idea of passing judgments on his opinions' [NTC], 'but do not argue with them about their personal opinions' [TEV], 'and do not argue about opinions' [NCV], 'do not argue about his personal opinions' [**LN**], 'without debate about his misgivings' [REB], 'but don't get into an argument over differences of opinions' [GW], 'not...simply for discussions of his scruples' [HNTC], 'not in order to pass judgments on his scruples' [ICC2], 'don't criticize them for having beliefs that are different from yours' [CEV], 'and don't argue with them about what they think is right or wrong' [NLT]. This noun denotes a dispute with someone on the basis of different judgments [LN].

e. διαλογισμός (LN 30 16) (BAGD 1. p. 186): 'opinion' [BAGD, BECNT, NTC; GW, NASB, NCV, NET, NRSV, TEV], 'thought' [BAGD], 'reasoning' [BAGD, LN], 'dispute' [WBC], 'disputed matter' [AB, NICNT; NIV], 'scruple' [HNTC, ICC2]; 'misgiving' [REB], 'what they think is right or wrong' [NLT], 'beliefs that are different from yours' [CEV]. This noun is translated as an adjective: 'doubtful' [KJV]. It denotes the content or result of one's thorough reasoning [LN].

QUESTION—What does 'weak in faith' mean?

It is a lack of confidence that one is free to do certain things [ICC2, SSA, St]. Those who were 'weak in faith' did not fully understand that salvation is by faith alone, and were adding other regulations they thought were necessary in order to be acceptable before God [HNTC, ICC1]. There was a deficiency in their understanding, and their faith was defective because they did not trust God completely and without qualification, leaning instead on the crutches of their customs and practices [WBC]. Those who were 'weak in faith' believed that observing certain practices made one a stronger or better Christian, so there was a deficiency in their faith, even though they didn't think that such observances were necessary for salvation [BECNT]. Their faith in Christ was strong, but their understanding of what that faith allowed them to do in daily living was weak [Mor]. The 'weak' were unable to grasp the meaning of Christ's death in terms of what it meant for matters of daily living such as eating and drinking [NTC]. While they were persuaded of certain truths, they were weak in regard to others [Ho]. They were uncertain about what faith in Christ meant with regard to the ritual law of the OT [NAC]. They were immature and untaught [St, TNTC], and mistaken in their understandings [St].

QUESTION—Who were the 'weak in faith' and who were the others?

The weak in faith were mostly Jewish believers who felt compelled to maintain ritual requirements of the Mosaic law, and those who were not 'weak' were mostly Gentile believers along with some Jewish believers who did not feel obligated to observe those requirements [AB, BECNT, ICC2, NAC, NICNT, NTC, SSA, St, WBC]. That the issue had to do with Jewish dietary concerns is shown by such words as κοινός 'impure' in 14:14 and καθαρός 'pure' in 14:20, which were Jewish terms [AB, NICNT, WBC]. Since Rome was a large cosmopolitan area, with people of diverse backgrounds, there could be a variety of reasons why different people had the scruples they did [Mu]. They were ascetic Jewish believers [Ho].

QUESTION—What is the 'faith' he is discussing here?
1. Here it has to do with confidence or convictions about what practices would be legitimate for a believer to follow [AB, BECNT, ICC2, Mor, NICNT, SSA, St]. It does not primarily refer to belief in Christ, although the words 'faith' and 'believe' do have some general reference to that basic response to God he describes in the rest of this epistle; this conviction is related to a more basic faith in Christ [NICNT]. He is not referring to saving faith here [AB].
2. It is recognizing one's dependence on God [HNTC]. It is their faith in God, as opposed to trusting in ritual observances [WBC]. It has to do with conviction about the spiritual nature of the gospel and the gracious and free nature of justification [Ho]. 'Faith' means having a grasp of the principle of salvation by faith in Christ [ICC1].

14:2 One^a believes^b (it-is-permissible)^c to-eat^d all^e (foods),

LEXICON—a. ὅς (LN 92.27) (BAGD II.2. p. 585): 'one' [AB, BECNT; KJV], 'one man' [HNTC, ICC2; NIV], 'one person' [NICNT, NTC; NASB, NCV, NET, NLT, REB], 'the one who' [LN], 'the one, this one' [BAGD], 'someone' [WBC], 'some' [CEV, NRSV], 'some people' [GW, TEV]. This adjective describes a relative reference to any entity, event, or state, either occurring overtly in the immediate context or clearly implied in the discourse or setting [LN].
b. pres. act. indic. of πιστεύω (LN 31.35) (BAGD 4. p. 662): 'to believe' [BAGD, BECNT, LN, NICNT, NTC; GW, KJV, NCV, NET, NLT, NRSV], 'to have faith' [HNTC, ICC2, WBC; NASB, REB], 'to think, to consider, to trust himself' [BAGD], 'to think to be true' [LN], 'to think it is all right' [CEV], 'to be convinced' [AB]. This verb is translated as a noun: 'faith' [NIV, TEV]. It means to believe something to be true [LN].
c. There is no lexical entry for 'it is permissible' in the Greek text, but it is added to show the implied meaning of the text. It is represented in translation as 'that one may' [AB], 'he may' [NTC; KJV, NASB], 'he can' [BECNT, NICNT], 'they can' [GW], 'he can and does' [HNTC], 'it is all right' [CEV, NLT], 'it is right' [NCV], '(faith) allows' [NIV, TEV], not explicit [ICC2, WBC; NET, NRSV, REB].
d. aorist act. infin. of ἐσθίω (LN 23.1) (BAGD 1.a. p. 312): 'to eat' [AB, BAGD, BECNT, HNTC, ICC2, LN, NICNT, NTC, WBC; all versions]. This verb means to consume food, usually solids, but also liquids [LN].
e. πᾶς (LN 58.28): 'anything' [AB, LN, NTC; CEV, NLT, NRSV, TEV], 'everything' [BECNT, WBC; NET, NIV], 'all things' [HNTC, NICNT; KJV, NASB], 'any food' [ICC2, LN], 'all kinds of food' [LN; GW, NCV, REB]. This noun denotes a totality of kinds or sorts [LN (58.28)], or any one of a totality [LN (59.24)].

QUESTION—What is the nature of 'believe' and what is the object of 'believe'?
1. Here the believing is a confidence to do something [AB, BECNT, Ho, ICC2, Mor, NICNT, NTC, SSA]. The confidence is based on a deeper faith in Christ and the freedom that comes from faith in him [NICNT]. 'Conviction' and 'faith' are related [BECNT], though here 'faith' is not the faith that brings salvation [AB].
2. It is essentially a trust in God with no reservation or qualification [WBC]. This person's faith in God and what God has done is so strong that he does not think he has to add anything to it [HNTC]. It is a grasp of what it means to be Christian, and to have perspective on all lesser things as being indifferent [ICC1]. It is a faith that is firm enough to allow eating without scruple [TH].

but the-one being-weak[a] eats vegetables[b] (only).[c]

LEXICON—a. pres. act. participle of ἀσθενέω (LN 74.26) (BAGD 2. p. 115): 'weak' [BAGD, BECNT, LN; NRSV], 'one who is weak' [AB], 'he who is weak' [ICC2; NASB], 'weak man' [HNTC], 'weak person' [WBC; NET], 'person who is weak' [TEV], 'another, who is weak' [KJV, NCV], 'another, being weak' [NTC], 'another who is weaker' [REB], 'another man whose faith is weak' [NIV], 'another' [NICNT], 'another believer with a sensitive conscience' [NLT], 'other people with weak faith' [GW], 'those whose faith is weak' [CEV]. This verb refers to religious and moral weakness [BAGD]. This verb means to be in a state of incapacity or weakness [LN].
b. λάχανον (LN 3.29) (BAGD p. 467): 'vegetable' [AB, BAGD, BECNT, HNTC, ICC2, LN, NICNT, NTC, WBC; all versions except KJV], 'herbs' [KJV]. This noun denotes any one of the smaller plants cultivated in a garden, for example, herbs and vegetables [LN].
c. There is no lexical entry for 'only' in the Greek text, it is implied. It is represented in translation as 'only' [AB, HNTC, ICC2, NTC, WBC; CEV, GW, NASB, NCV, NET, NIV, NLT, NRSV, REB, TEV], not explicit [BECNT, NICNT; KJV].

QUESTION—Why did these people not eat any meat?
They may have been concerned about whether the meat had been sacrificed and offered to idols or whether it was ritually unclean in some way [AB, ICC2, NTC, TNTC, WBC]. They were concerned that the meat available in the market would not have been slaughtered in the way prescribed by Jewish ritual law, so they avoided it altogether [NICNT, NTC, St, WBC]. They may have feared that meat found in the meat market may have been offered in sacrifice to idols or that it had been made ritually unclean in some way [Ho].

14:3 The-one eating[a] let-(him)- not -look-down-on[b] the-one not -eating, and the-one not eating let-(him)- not -judge[c] the-one eating, for God accepted[d] him.

LEXICON—a. pres. act. participle ἐσθίω (LN 23.1): 'to eat, to drink, to consume food, to use food' [LN]. This participial phrase is translated 'the one who eats' [AB, BECNT, LN, NICNT, WBC; NASB], 'one who eats everything' [NET], 'him who eats' [ICC2, NTC; KJV], 'the man who eats' [HNTC], 'the man who eats everything' [NIV], 'those who eat' [NRSV], 'people who eat all foods' [GW], 'those who eat meat' [REB], 'those who feel free to eat anything' [NLT], 'the person who will eat anything' [TEV], 'one who knows that it is right to eat any kind of food' [NCV]. The first two clauses of this verse are translated, 'But you should not criticize others for eating or for not eating' [CEV]. This verb means to consume food, usually solids, but also liquids [LN].

   b. pres. act. impera. of ἐξουθενέω (LN **88.195**) (BAGD 1. p. 277): 'to look down on' [NTC; NIV, REB], 'to despise' [AB, BAGD, BECNT, HNTC, ICC2, **LN**, NICNT, WBC; GW, KJV, NET, NRSV, TEV], 'to disdain' [BAGD], 'to reject' [NCV], 'to regard with contempt' [NASB], 'to criticize' [CEV]. This verb means to despise someone or something on the basis that it is worthless or of no value [LN], to judge someone in a way that is disdainful and condescending [NICNT]. It conveys a strong note of contempt [WBC].

   c. pres. act. impera. of κρίνω (LN 56.30) (BAGD 6.b. p. 452): 'to judge' [BAGD, HNTC, NICNT, NTC; KJV, NASB, NET], 'to judge as guilty' [LN], 'to pass judgment' [AB, BAGD, ICC2, WBC; NRSV, REB, TEV], 'to condemn' [BAGD, LN; NIV, NLT], 'to criticize' [BAGD; CEV, GW], 'to find fault with' [BAGD], 'to think that the one who eats all food is wrong' [NCV]. This verb means to judge a person to be guilty and liable to punishment [LN].

   d. aorist mid. indic. of προσλαμβάνω (LN 34.53) (BAGD 2.b. p. 717): 'to accept' [BAGD, BECNT, LN, NTC; GW, NASB, NCV, NET, NIV, REB, TEV], 'to welcome' [AB, HNTC, LN, WBC; CEV, NRSV], 'to receive' [BAGD, ICC2, LN, NICNT; KJV]. This verb means to accept the presence of a person with friendliness [LN]. This verb in the aorist tense is translated as a perfect tense by AB, BECNT, HNTC, ICC2, NICNT, NTC, WBC; GW, KJV, NASB, NCV, NET, NIV, NLT, NRSV, REB, TEV; as a present tense by CEV.

QUESTION—According to what Paul is saying here, whom has God accepted?
   1. God has accepted both the weak and the strong [AB, Ho, Mor, St; CEV].
   2. God has accepted both, but here he is referring specifically to the person who eats meat [BECNT, Gdt, HNTC, ICC1, Mu, NICNT, NTC, TH, WBC; GW, NCV, NLT, NRSV, REB, TEV].

14:4 **Who are you**[a] **the-one judging (the) servant**[b] **of-another?**[c]

LEXICON—a. σὺ τίς εἶ 'who are you' is translated 'who are you' [AB, BECNT, HNTC, ICC2, LN, NICNT, NTC, WBC; GW, KJV, NASB, NET, NIV, NLT, NRSV, REB, TEV], 'what right do you have' [CEV], 'you cannot' [NCV].
- b. οἰκέτης (LN 46.5) (BAGD p. 557): 'servant' [AB, BECNT, HNTC, NTC, WBC; all versions], 'household servant' [LN, NICNT], 'house slave' [BAGD, ICC2], 'personal servant' [LN]. This noun denotes a servant in a household [LN].
- c. ἀλλότριος (LN 92.20) (BAGD 1.a. p. 40): 'of another' [AB, NICNT; NASB, NRSV], 'another's' [BECNT, ICC2], 'another man's' [BAGD, HNTC; KJV], 'another person's' [NCV], 'of someone else' [WBC; TEV], 'someone else's' [NTC; CEV, GW, NIV, NLT, REB], 'belonging to another' [LN]. This adjective describes what belongs to someone else [LN].

QUESTION—Whom is Paul addressing in this admonition?

He is addressing the 'weak' believers who abstain from eating meat [AB, BECNT, Gdt, HNTC, ICC1, ICC2, NICNT, SSA, TH, WBC], most of whom would have been Jewish, and who would judge others who did not follow the ritual law, most of whom would be Gentiles [NICNT, WBC].

QUESTION—What is the significance of Paul's use of σύ 'you' and why did he put it first in the sentence?

It is emphatic [BECNT, Mor, NICNT, SSA], showing the depth of Paul's concern [NICNT], and even setting such a person as over against God, who is the one whose verdict really matters [Mor]. They are not to usurp God's role as judge [BECNT].

To- his-own -master[a] **he-stands**[b] **or he-falls;**[c]

LEXICON—a. κύριος (LN 57.12) (BAGD 1.a.β. p. 459): 'master' [AB, HNTC, NTC, WBC; KJV, NASB, NCV, NET, NIV, REB, TEV], 'Lord' [BAGD, BECNT, ICC2, NICNT; CEV, GW, NLT, NRSV]. This noun denotes one who owns and controls property, including especially servants and slaves, with important supplementary semantic components of high status and respect [LN].
- b. pres. act. indic. of στήκω (LN **13.30, 87.56**) (BAGD 2. p. 768): 'to stand' [AB, BAGD, BECNT, HNTC, ICC2,**LN** (13.30, 87.56), NICNT, NTC, WBC; KJV, NASB, NET, NIV, NRSV, REB], 'to stand firm, to be steadfast' [BAGD], 'to succeed' [LN (87.56); TEV], 'to be honored' [**LN** (87.56)], 'to do right' [CEV], 'to be successful' [GW], 'to do well' [NCV], 'to be right' [NLT]. The clause 'to his own master he stands or falls' was probably a familiar saying that meant whether one maintains one's status or relationship to a master depends on the master's judgment or evaluation [LN (87.56)]. This verb means to continue in a state, with a possible implication of acceptability [LN (13.30)].

c. pres. act. indic. of πίπτω (LN 15.118, **87.56**) (BAGD 2.a.β. p. 660): 'fall' [AB, BAGD, BECNT, HNTC, ICC2, LN (15.118, **87.56**), NICNT, NTC, WBC; KJV, NASB, NET, NIV, NRSV, REB], 'to be completely ruined' [BAGD], 'to fail' [**LN** (87.56); TEV], 'to be disgraced' [**LN** (87.56)], 'to be wrong' [NLT]. The clause 'To his own master he stands or he falls' is translated 'Only their Lord can decide if they are doing right' [CEV], 'The Lord will determine whether his servant has been successful' [GW], 'The master decides if the servant is doing well or not' [NCV]. This verb means to fall from one level to another [LN (15.118)].

QUESTION—What relationship is indicated by the dative noun κυρίῳ 'to (his own) master'?

1. It indicates reference, focusing on his relationship with the master, meaning that he stands or falls with reference to his own master [BECNT, HNTC, ICC1, Mu, NICNT, NTC, WBC]. He will stand or fall with reference to his own master's judgment [Ho, Mu], or by virtue of the decision of his own master, not anyone else [BECNT]. His own master will determine whether or not his service is acceptable [HNTC].
2. It indicates advantage, meaning that he stands or falls with regard to his own master's interest [Gdt, ICC2, Mor].
3. The two verbs 'stand' and 'fall' are metonymies, where the result of standing or falling indicate the cause, which is that the master either vindicates the servant or condemns him [SSA].

QUESTION—To whom does 'his own master' refer?

Here the word κύριος is translated 'master' [AB, HNTC, NTC, WBC; KJV, NASB, NCV, NET, NIV], 'Master' [REB, TEV], 'lord' [NICNT; NRSV], 'Lord' [BECNT, ICC2; CEV, GW, NLT], and in the following clause it is translated 'Lord' [CEV, GW, NASB, NCV, NET, NIV, NLT, NRSV, TEV], 'Master' [REB], 'master' [WBC].

1. It refers to the master or lord of the slave in the metaphor [ICC1, NICNT, SSA, TH, WBC; probably NASB, NCV, NET, NIV, NRSV, which translate κύριος 'master' or 'lord' here and 'Lord' in the last clause]. In the case of a personal house slave, the maser's approval counts for everything [WBC]. The slave owner determines whether his slave's service is satisfactory or not [TH, WBC]. This slave metaphor clearly uses κύριος with its normal secular meaning of 'master' here, although Paul expects his readers to see an allusion to their heavenly Lord [NICNT].
2. It refers to the Lord (either Christ or God) [ICC2; probably CEV, GW, NASB, NCV, NET, NIV, NLT, NRSV, TEV which capitalize 'Lord' or 'Master']. Throughout this section Paul vacillates between references to Christ and references to God [ICC2]. It refers to Christ [Gdt, ICC2, Mu, NTC]. It refers to God [AB, HNTC, Mor, NAC].

QUESTION—To what do 'stand' and 'fall' refer?

1. It refers to whether or not the slave pleases the master [Gdt, HNTC, Mu, NICNT, SSA, WBC]. It is success or failure in responsible conduct [AB], in devotion to Christ [Mu]. It is moral stability or failure [ICC1].

2. 'Standing' would mean persevering in this life in faith and obedience, and 'falling' would be failing to do so [ICC2].
3. It refers to acquittal or condemnation at the final judgment [BECNT, Ho].

and he-will-stand,[a] for the Lord is-able[b] to-make- him -stand.
TEXT—Instead of ὁ κύριος 'Lord', some manuscripts have ὁ θεός 'God'. GNT selects the reading 'Lord' with an A rating, indicating that the text is certain. The reading 'God' is taken by KJV only.
LEXICON—a. fut. pass. indic. of ἵστημι (LN 13.29) (BAGD II.1.d. p. 382): 'to stand' [AB, BAGD, BECNT, HNTC, ICC2, NICNT, NTC, WBC; NASB, NET, NIV, REB], 'to stand firm, to hold one's ground' [BAGD], 'to firmly remain, to continue steadfastly' [LN], 'to be upheld' [NRSV], 'to be held up' [KJV], 'to do right' [CEV], 'to do what is right' [NLT], 'to do well' [NCV], 'to succeed' [TEV], 'to be successful' [GW]. This verb means to continue firmly or to be well-established in a particular state [LN].
  b. pres. act. indic. of δυνατέω (LN **74.5**) (BAGD 2. p. 208): 'to be able' [AB, BAGD, BECNT, HNTC, **LN**, NICNT, NTC, WBC; KJV, NET, NIV, NRSV, TEV], 'to have the power' [ICC2; REB], 'to be strong' [BAGD], 'to help' [NCV]. This verb means to be able to do or to experience something [LN].
QUESTION—Who is 'the Lord' in this clause?
1. It refers to the Lord (either Christ or God) [AB, BECNT, Gdt, HNTC, Mor, Mu, NICNT; probably all versions since they capitalize the word]. It refers to Christ [NICNT]. It refers to God [AB, HNTC, Mor]. The question is academic; it refers to Christ, and therefore refers to God also [NTC].
2. This is still part of the metaphor and it refers to the master of the slave [WBC].

14:5 **For one regards[a] (one) day more-than (another) day, but one regards each day (the-same);[b]**
TEXT—The word γάρ 'for' does not occur in some manuscripts. It is included by GNT with a C rating, indicating difficulty in deciding whether or not to place it in the text. It is included by NICNT only.
LEXICON—a. pres. act. indic. of κρίνω (LN **30.99**) (BAGD 1. p. 451): 'to prefer' [BAGD, LN], 'to distinguish' [BAGD], 'to judge as superior, to regard as more valuable' [LN]. The clause 'one regards one day more than another day' is translated 'the one prefers one day to another' [BAGD], 'one person thinks a certain day is better than other days' [**LN**], 'one regards one day as more important than another' [AB], 'one person judges one day above another' [BECNT], 'one man distinguishes day from day' [HNTC], 'one man esteems one day more than another' [ICC2], 'one man esteemeth one day above another' [KJV], 'one person judges one day to be more important than another day' [NICNT], 'one person regards one day as being better than another' [NTC], 'someone judges one day to be

more important than another' [WBC], 'some of the Lord's followers think one day is more important than another' [CEV], 'one person decides that one day is holier than another' [GW], 'one person regards one day above another' [NASB], 'some think that one day is more important than another' [NCV], 'one person regards one day holier than other days' [NET], 'one man considers one day more sacred than another' [NIV], 'some think one day is more holy than another day' [NLT], 'some judge one day to be better than another' [NRSV], 'some make a distinction between this day and that' [REB], 'some people think that a certain day is more important than other days' [TEV]. This verb means to judge something to be better than something else, and hence, to prefer [LN].
b. There is no lexical entry for this word in the Greek text, the meaning being implied. It is represented in translation as 'the same' [AB, BECNT, NICNT; CEV, GW, NCV, TEV], 'alike' [HNTC, ICC2, WBC; KJV, NASB, NET, NIV, NLT, NRSV, REB]. The phrase κρίνει πᾶσαν ἡμέραν 'regards each day (the same)' is translated 'regards every day as being good' [NTC].

QUESTION—What was involved in this question about observing days?

It probably had to do with observing the Jewish Sabbath [AB, BECNT, HNTC, NAC, NICNT, NTC, WBC], and possibly to other Jewish festival days [AB, BECNT, ICC2, NAC, NICNT, NTC, WBC]. He is probably referring to observances related to the new moon, feasts, jubilee years, and Sabbaths [AB], to Jewish festival days [Gdt, Ho, Mu].

let- each -be-fully-convinced[a] in his-own mind.[b]

LEXICON—a. pres. pass. impera. of πληροφορέω (BAGD 2. p. 670): 'to be fully convinced' [AB, BAGD, BECNT, HNTC, NTC, WBC; NASB, NET, NLT, NRSV], 'to be thoroughly convinced' [NICNT], 'to be sure' [NCV], 'to be fully persuaded' [KJV], 'to be settled' [ICC2], 'to act on (his own) convictions' [REB], 'to make (his own) decision' [GW], 'to firmly make up' [TEV].
b. νοῦς (LN 26.14, 30.5) (BAGD 4. p. 545): 'mind' [AB, BAGD, BECNT, HNTC, ICC2, LN, NICNT, NTC, WBC; all versions except GW, NLT, REB], 'decision' [GW], 'convictions' [REB], 'way of thinking' [LN], 'thought, opinion' [BAGD]. The phrase 'in his own mind' is translated 'that whichever day you choose is acceptable' [NLT]. This noun denotes the psychological faculty of understanding, reasoning, thinking, and deciding [LN].

14:6 The-one observing the day observes[a] to-[b] (the) -Lord; and the-one eating eats to-[c] (the) -Lord for he-gives-thanks to-God;[d] and the one- not - eating, to- the -Lord he-does- not -eat, and gives-thanks to-God.

LEXICON—a. pres. act. participle of φρονέω (LN 87.12, 31.1) (BAGD 2. p. 866): 'to observe' [AB, ICC2, NICNT; GW, NASB, NET, NRSV], 'to think' [BAGD, BECNT], 'to regard' [LN, NTC; KJV, NIV], 'to honor' [**LN**; REB], 'to count' [CEV], 'to hold an opinion' [LN, WBC]. The phrase ὁ φρονῶν τὴν ἡμέραν 'the one observing the day' is translated 'the one who observes a set day' [AB], 'the one who thinks a day is special' [BECNT], 'he who regards one day as special' [NIV], 'he who regards one day as being special' [NTC], 'he that regardeth the day' [KJV], 'the one who holds an opinion on the day' [WBC], 'he who is concerned about the day' [HNTC], 'when people observe a special day' [GW], 'those who think highly of a certain day' [TEV]. The clause ὁ φρονῶν τὴν ἡμέραν κυρίῳ φρονεῖ 'the one observing the day observes to the Lord' is translated 'any followers who count one day more important than another day do it to honor their Lord' [CEV], 'those who think one day is more important than other days are doing that for the Lord' [NCV], 'those who worship the Lord on a special day do it to honor him' [NLT]. This verb means to acknowledge the high status of a person or event [LN (87.12)], or to hold a view or have an opinion with regard to something [LN (31.1)].

b. There is no lexical entry for this word in the Greek text, the grammatical relation being indicated in Greek by the dative case of the noun κύριος 'Lord'. This relation is translated 'to' [BECNT, HNTC, ICC2, NICNT, WBC; NIV], 'for' [AB; NASB, NCV, NET], 'unto' [KJV], 'to honor' [CEV, GW, NLT, REB], 'in honor of' [NTC; NRSV, TEV].

c. There is no lexical entry for this word in the Greek text, the grammatical relation being indicated in Greek by the dative case of the noun κύριος 'Lord'. This relation is translated 'to' [BECNT, HNTC, ICC2, NICNT, WBC; KJV, NIV], 'for' [AB; NASB, NET], 'in honor of' [NTC; NRSV], not explicit [CEV]. The phrase 'eats to the Lord' is translated 'they honor the Lord as they eat' [GW], 'are doing that for the Lord' [NCV], 'do so to honor the Lord' [NLT], 'do so in honor of the Lord' [TEV], 'honor the Lord' [REB]

d. pres. act. indic. of εὐχαριστέω (LN 33.349) (BAGD 2. p. 328): 'to give thanks' [AB, BAGD, BECNT, HNTC, ICC2, LN, NICNT, NTC, WBC; all versions]. This verb means to express gratitude for benefits or blessings [LN].

QUESTION—Who are the various persons he describes here?

The one who observes the day and also does not eat (meat) is the 'weak' believer, and the one who eats (meat) is the one who does not feel compelled to follow Jewish ritual law [BECNT, HNTC, Ho, ICC2, NICNT].

QUESTION—What does he imply by saying 'and (he) gives thanks to God'?

This describes the thanks given at their mealtimes [ICC1, NICNT, WBC], and they thank God for the food they do eat [ICC2, SSA]. It shows that those on both sides of this issue want to serve and honor the Lord [AB, Ho, ICC2, NICNT, NTC, WBC]. They want to please the Lord [BECNT], and they recognize his Lordship [HNTC]. They both have a sense of indebtedness to God and devotion to Christ [Mu].

QUESTION—What relationship is indicated by the use of the dative κυρίῳ 'to the Lord'?

It shows advantage [ICC2, NICNT, NTC]; they do it for the Lord, for his benefit. They do it in relation to the Lord; it is a responsibly held opinion and practice, one which is maintained in grateful dependence on God [WBC]. They do what they do to honor and thank God [AB], to serve the Lord [Gdt, ICC1, ICC2, Mor], to honor the Lord [NAC, NTC, SSA, St, TH], to show devotion to the Lord [Mu], out of regard for him [Ho], to please him [St]. He keeps the Sabbath commandment with reference to the one who commanded it, and when he eats he gives thanks to show that the meal is not a secular function [HNTC].

QUESTION—Who is 'the Lord' in this and the following three verses?
1. It is Christ [BECNT, Ho, Mu, NICNT].
2. It is God [AB, HNTC, WBC].
3. In this verse it is God, and in 14:8 it is Christ [ICC1].

14:7 For[a] no-one[b] of-us to-himself[c] lives[d] and no-one to-himself dies;[e]

LEXICON—a. γάρ (LN 89.23): 'for' [BECNT, HNTC, ICC2, LN, NICNT, NTC, WBC; KJV, NASB, NET, NIV, NLT, REB], 'yet' [AB], 'whether' [CEV], 'it's clear that' [GW], not explicit [NCV, NRSV, TEV]. This conjunction marks the cause or reason between events [LN].

b. οὐδείς (LN 92.23) (BAGD 2.a. p. 592): 'no one' [BAGD, LN, NICNT, WBC], 'nobody' [BAGD], 'none' [AB, BECNT, HNTC, ICC2, LN, NTC; KJV, NET, NIV, REB], 'not one' [NASB]. The phrase οὐδεὶς ἡμῶν 'no one of us' is translated 'we' [CEV, GW, NCV, NLT, NRSV, TEV]. This adjective describes a negative reference to an entity, event, or state [LN].

c. ἑαυτοῦ (LN 92.25): 'himself' [LN]. This dative case pronoun is translated 'to himself' [BECNT, HNTC, ICC2, LN, NICNT, NTC; KJV], 'for himself' [AB, WBC; NASB, NET], 'to himself alone' [NIV], 'for himself alone' [REB], 'to ourselves' [NRSV], 'for ourselves' [NCV, NLT], 'for ourselves only' [TEV], 'to honor ourselves' [GW]. CEV adds a phrase and translates: '(it must be for God, rather than) for ourselves'. This noun denotes a reflexive reference to a person or thing spoken or written about [LN].

d. pres. act. indic. of ζάω (LN 23.88) (BAGD 3.b. p. 337): 'to live' [AB, BAGD, BECNT, HNTC, ICC2, LN, NICNT, NTC, WBC; all versions].

e. pres. act. indic. of ἀποθνῄσκω (LN 23.99) (BAGD 1.a.α. p. 91): 'to die' [AB, BAGD, BECNT, HNTC, ICC2, LN, NICNT, NTC, WBC; all versions].

QUESTION—What relationship is indicated by γάρ 'for'?

It indicates 14:7–8 as the grounds for his statement in 14:6 that both the strong in faith and the weak in faith do what they do for the Lord [Ho, Mor, NICNT, NTC]. It indicates 14:7–9 as the grounds for his statement in 14:6 [ICC2]. It indicates 14:7–8 as the grounds for the conclusion implied by 14:6

that neither eating meat nor abstaining from eating it is intrinsically wrong [SSA]. It also amplifies what he said in 14:6 [Ho].

QUESTION—What relationship is indicated by the dative ἑαυτῷ 'to himself'?

He is saying that no believer lives or dies with reference to himself only or only for his own benefit [NICNT], only for his own gratification [ICC2], only to please himself [SSA]. To live for oneself would be to live selfishly [WBC], to live a self-centered life [NTC]. Self-preservation is not to be the primary concern of our lives [AB]. No believer lives in dependence on himself and for his own will or glory or ends [Ho]. We are not responsible only to ourselves [ICC1].

QUESTION—What conclusion is to be drawn from what Paul asserts in this verse?
 1. We should live for God [NICNT], live in relation to God [HNTC, TH]. We should live in devotion to Christ [Mu]. It is God, not self who is ultimately important, for all that we do and are, we do and are before God [Mor]. We are accountable to God [NAC].
 2. No one is an island; we need to live in an interdependent network of relationships with other people [WBC].

14:8 For[a] if we-live, to- the -Lord we live, and if we-die, to- the -Lord we die. So[b] whether[c] we live or whether we die we-are[d] the Lord's.

LEXICON—a. γάρ (LN 89.23): 'for' [BECNT, HNTC, ICC2, NICNT, WBC; KJV, NASB], 'because' [LN], not explicit [AB, NTC; CEV, GW, NCV, NET, NIV, NLT, NRSV, REB, TEV]. This conjunction marks cause or reason between events [LN].
 b. οὖν (LN 89.50) (BAGD 5. p. 593): 'so' [AB, LN, WBC; GW, NCV, NIV, NLT, REB, TEV], 'so then' [NTC; NRSV], 'therefore' [BAGD, LN, NICNT; KJV, NASB, NET], 'then' [BAGD, HNTC, ICC2, LN], 'consequently, accordingly' [BAGD], not explicit [BECNT; CEV]. This conjunction marks result, often implying the conclusion of a process of reasoning [LN].
 c. ἐάν τέ (LN **89.103**) (BAGD I.3.d. p. 211): 'whether' [AB, BAGD, BECNT, HNTC, ICC2, NICNT, NTC, WBC; all versions except CEV, NCV], 'if' [LN]. The phrase 'whether we live or whether we die' is translated 'alive or dead' [CEV], 'living or dying' [NCV]. This conjunction marks a closely related coordinate set [LN].
 d. pres. act. indic. of εἰμί (LN 58.67): 'to be' [HNTC, LN, NICNT, NTC, WBC; KJV, NASB, NET, NRSV], 'to belong to' [AB, BECNT, ICC2, LN; CEV, GW, NCV, NIV, NLT, REB, TEV]. This verb means to belong to a particular class [LN].

QUESTION—What relationship is indicated by γάρ 'for'?

It indicates that the positive statement in 14:8 is an explanation of the negative statement in 14:7 [BECNT, Ho, ICC2, NICNT]. That is, the statement that believers do not live or die with reference to themselves means that they consciously live to please the Lord [BECNT, Mu]. It indicates 14:8 as the grounds for what is said in 14:7 [Gdt].

QUESTION—What relationship is indicated by οὖν 'so'?

It indicates the relation of 13:7–8a to what follows in 13:8b [BECNT].

QUESTION—What does it mean to live or die to the Lord?

The dative case of 'the Lord' means that we live 'to the Lord' [ICC1, NICNT; KJV, NIV, NRSV]. 'for the Lord' [WBC; CEV, NASB, NCV, NET, REB, TEV], 'to please the Lord' [SSA], 'to honor the Lord' [GW, NLT]. To 'live to the Lord' means that the believer directs all of his thoughts, actions, ambitions, and decisions to please and glorify the Lord. However, 'to die to the Lord' means that the time and circumstances of the believer's death are completely in the hands of the Lord [NICNT]. Christians live to please Christ in his service, and when it comes to dying, they glorify him by committing themselves to his care [ICC2]. For the Christian the true basis of life is to serve God in everything [AB]. Whether we are alive or dead, we are his; even our death is in God's hands, and for his purpose [Mor]. In the first century Stoics sought to choose the time and manner of their own death [Mor, SSA], and Paul is saying here that it should not be this way [SSA]. God must be allowed to direct both our death and life according to his will and glory [Ho, SSA]. To live to the Lord means that for believers the goal and purpose of life is to do his will, and even at the time of death believers try to please him in how they die [BECNT]. Even at the time of death the believer is fully conscious of devotion to the Lord [Mu]. the Christian lives in faith and obedience, and even in death belongs to God [HNTC]. We are not our own, we are his, owing him all devotion and obedience because he has bought us with a price [Ho]. Death does not free us from our obligations to the Lord [ICC1]. Life and death are far more important differences than the issues of diet and observing special days, and even they don't disrupt the relationship between believers and the Lord [WBC].

14:9 For[a] to this (purpose)[b] Christ died and lived,[c]

TEXT—Some manuscripts include καὶ ἀνέστη 'and rose' after ἀπέθανεν 'died' and before καὶ ἔζησεν 'and lived'. It is omitted by GNT with an A rating, indicating that the text is certain. It is included only by KJV.

LEXICON—a. γάρ (LN 89.23): 'for' [BECNT, HNTC, ICC2, LN, NICNT, NTC, WBC; KJV, NASB, NIV, NRSV, TEV], not explicit [AB; CEV, GW, NCV, NET, NLT, REB]. This conjunction marks cause or reason between events [LN].

  b. There is no lexical entry for 'purpose' in the Greek text, the meaning being implied in the phrase εἰς τοῦτο γάρ 'for to this'. The phrase has been translated: 'for this (very) purpose' [HNTC, ICC2, WBC; NLT], 'for this reason' [AB, NICNT; GW, NCV, NET, NIV], 'on account of this' [BECNT], 'to this end' [NTC; KJV, NASB, NRSV], 'this is why' [REB], 'this is because' [CEV], not explicit [TEV].

c. aorist act. indic. of ζάω (LN **23.93**, 23.88) (BAGD 1.a.β. p. 336): 'to live' [LN, NTC], 'to live again' [ICC2, **LN**, WBC; NASB, NRSV, REB], 'to come to life' [AB, HNTC, NICNT], 'to come back to life' [**LN**; GW], 'to return to life' [NET, NIV], 'to rise' [NCV, NLT, TEV], 'to arise' [BECNT], 'to rise to life' [CEV], 'to become alive again' [BAGD], 'to revive' [KJV]. In this context this verb means to come back to life after having once died [LN].

QUESTION—To what does εἰς τοῦτο 'to this purpose' refer?

It refers to the purpose clause that follows [AB, Gdt, ICC1, ICC2, Mor, NAC, NICNT, SSA, WBC]: Christ died and rose so he would become Lord of the dead and the living. The purpose of his atoning work was to establish his lordship [Mor]. The word order shows a parallel with what has already been said about the dead and the living [Mor, NTC, WBC], and emphasizes Christ's power over the world of death [WBC].

QUESTION—What is the purpose that was accomplished in Christ's death and resurrection?

Paul is creating the closest possible link between Christ's redemptive acts, death and returning to life, with the two most basic aspects of a Christian's experience, which are living and dying [NICNT, WBC]. Christ's death and resurrection establish his lordship over his people [Ho, ICC1]. Christ's death and resurrection establish his lordship over all people, regardless of whether they are living or dead [NICNT]. Christ has become the Lord of history [AB]. There is no need to speculate or differentiate about *whose* purpose it was, whether God's or Christ's [ICC2, Mor]. Jesus brought about the lordship of redemptive relationship [Mor, Mu].

QUESTION—What is indicated by the use of the aorist ἔζησεν 'lived'?

It is an ingressive aorist [ICC2, Mor, NAC, SSA], and indicates that Christ lived after having died, meaning that he lived again or rose from the dead [Gdt, ICC2, Mu, NTC, SSA, TNTC, WBC; CEV, NCV, NLT, TEV]. He came to life again [AB, HNTC, ICC1, ICC2, LN, Mor, NAC, WBC; GW, KJV, NASB, NRSV, REB].

so-that[a] he-might-be-Lord[b] of-dead-ones[c] and of-those-living.[d]

LEXICON—a. ἵνα (LN 89.59, 91.15, 89.49) (BAGD I.5. p. 377): 'so that' [LN; CEV, GW, NET, NIV, NRSV], 'in order that' [AB, BAGD, BECNT, NICNT, WBC], 'that' [HNTC, ICC2, NTC; KJV, NASB], 'so' [NCV], 'in order to' [LN; TEV], 'to' [NLT, REB], 'for this purpose, for this reason' [BAGD]. This conjunction indicates the purpose for events and states [LN (89.59)], or it indicates the result, and implies an underlying purpose [LN (89.49)].

b. aorist act. subj. of κυριεύω (LN 37.50) (BAGD 1. p. 458): 'to be Lord' [BAGD, BECNT, NICNT, NTC, WBC; CEV, GW, KJV, NASB, NCV, NET, NIV, NLT, NRSV, TEV], 'to become Lord' [ICC2], 'to reign as Lord' [HNTC], 'to exercise lordship' [AB], 'to establish (his) lordship' [REB], 'to rule' [BAGD, LN], 'to govern, to reign over' [LN]. This verb

means to rule or reign over [LN]. It aorist is ingressive, meaning 'so that he might become Lord' [ICC2, Mor].
   c. νεκρός (LN 23.121) (BAGD 2.a. p. 535): 'dead' [AB, BAGD, BECNT, HNTC, ICC2, LN, NICNT, NTC, WBC; all versions]. The phrase 'of the dead and of the living' means 'all mankind past and present' [BAGD].
   d. pres. act. participle of ζάω (LN 23.88) (BAGD 1.a.α. p. 336). This participle is translated 'living' [AB, BAGD, BECNT, HNTC, ICC2, LN, NICNT, NTC, WBC; all versions].

QUESTION—What meant by κυριεύσῃ 'he might be Lord'?

He was always Lord, but there is a unique way in which the resurrection established his kingdom power and rule, and make the benefits of those available to those who believe [NICNT]. This focuses on the completeness of his lordship, that nothing can possibly escape his rule, which also means that no one has the right to judge Christ's other servants [WBC]. By virtue of his death and resurrection he now has the right to exercise mediatorial lordship over believers, mediating to his children all the benefit merited by his substitutionary death [NTC]. He has secured and is exercising his Lordship over all people [ICC2]. His death and resurrection led to his being exalted and reigning now in heaven [HNTC]. Although he has always been lord by virtue of being son of God and creator, the lordship he refers to here is that which is achieved by virtue of what he accomplished in his humiliation and as mediator [Mu], and is the lordship of redemptive relationship [Mor, Mu].

QUESTION—Who are 'the dead ones and those living'?

He is talking about Christians [Gdt, HNTC, Ho, Mor, Mu, NTC, St, TH, TNTC, WBC]. What he says is true for all people, but here he is primarily talking about Christians, whether living or dead [NICNT].

14:10 But[a] you—why do-you-judge[b] your brother?[c] Or also you—why do-you-look-down-on[d] your brother?

LEXICON—a. δέ (LN 89.124): 'but' [ICC2, LN, NTC; KJV, NASB, NET], 'then' [AB; NIV, REB, TEV], 'now then' [BECNT], 'well then' [HNTC], 'so' [WBC; NCV, NLT], 'now' [NICNT], not explicit [CEV, GW, NRSV]. This conjunction marks contrast [LN].
   b. pres. act. indic. of κρίνω (LN 56.30, 30.108) (BAGD 6.b. p. 452): 'to judge' [BAGD, BECNT, HNTC, LN (30.108), NICNT, WBC; KJV, NASB, NCV, NET, NIV], 'to pass judgment on' [ICC2, NTC; NRSV, REB, TEV], 'to sit in judgment over' [AB], 'to criticize' [BAGD; CEV, GW], 'to condemn' [BAGD, LN (56.30); NLT]. This verb means to make a judgment based upon the correctness or value of something [LN (30.108)], or to judge a person to be guilty and liable to punishment [LN (56.30)].
   c. ἀδελφός (LN 11.23): 'brother' [AB, HNTC, ICC2, LN, NICNT, NTC, WBC; KJV, NASB, NIV], 'brother or sister' [BECNT; NET, NRSV], 'brothers or sisters in Christ' [NCV], 'another believer' [NLT], 'fellow

believer' [LN], 'fellow-Christian' [REB], 'other Christians' [GW], 'other followers of the Lord' [CEV], 'others' [TEV]. This noun denotes a close associate of a group of persons having a well-defined membership [LN].
  d. pres. act. indic. of ἐξουθενέω (LN 88.195) (BAGD 1. p. 277): 'to look down on' [NTC; CEV, NIV, REB], 'to despise' [AB, BAGD, BECNT, HNTC, ICC2, LN, NICNT, WBC; GW, NET, NRSV, TEV], 'to disdain' [BAGD], 'to regard with contempt' [NASB], 'to set at nought' [KJV], 'to think you are better' [NCV]. This verb means to despise someone or something on the basis that it is worthless or of no value [LN].
QUESTION—Who is judging others, and who is looking down on others?
  The believers who had 'weak' faith were judging those who did not, and those of stronger faith who felt free to eat all foods were looking down on those who did not [Gdt, HNTC, Ho, ICC2, Mor, Mu, NAC, NICNT, NTC, SSA, WBC; NET, TEV]. The pronoun 'you' is emphatic in its position in both clauses [Mor].Here the singular pronoun συ 'you', occurring twice, is used in diatribe style, the first to rebuke the representative of the weak Christians in the same terms used in 14:4, and the second to rebuke the representative of the strong Christians in the terms used to describe their attitude in 14:3 [NICNT]. Since the two emphatic pronouns 'you' are not addressed to the same person, this could be shown in translation as 'why do some of you pass judgment on your fellow Christians, and why do others of you despise your fellow Christians?' [TH], or more specifically, 'But you who eat vegetables only—why do you judge your brother or sister? And you who eat everything—why do you despise your brother or sister?' [NET; similarly TEV]. Other translations appear to address the congregation as a whole: 'Why do you criticize other followers of the Lord? Why do you look down on them?' [CEV], or even 'Why do you criticize or despise other Christians' [GW].

For we- all -shall-stand-before[a] the judgment-seat[b] of-God,
TEXT—Instead of θεοῦ 'God', some manuscripts have Χριστοῦ 'Christ'. GNT selects the reading 'God' with a B rating, indicating that the text is almost certain. The reading 'Christ' is taken only by KJV.
LEXICON—a. fut. mid. indic. of παρίστημι (LN 85.14) (BAGD 2.a.α. p. 628): 'to stand before' [BECNT, HNTC, ICC2, NTC, WBC; KJV, NASB, NCV, NET, NIV, NLT, NRSV, REB, TEV], 'to stand in front of' [GW], 'to appear before' [AB, NICNT], 'to approach, to come (to someone)' [BAGD], 'to present (oneself)' [LN]. The clause 'For we all shall stand before the judgment seat of God' is translated 'The day is coming when God will judge all of us' [CEV]. This verb means to cause to be in a place [LN]. The verb is used as a legal technical term for standing before a judge [BAGD, NICNT].
  b. βῆμα (LN **7.63**) (BAGD 2. p. 140): 'judgment seat' [BECNT, HNTC, ICC2, LN, NICNT, NTC, WBC; KJV, NASB, NET, NIV, NLT, NRSV], 'tribunal' [AB, BAGD; REB]. The noun 'judgment seat' is translated as a

verb: 'to be judged' [GW, NCV, TEV]. This clause is translated 'God will judge all of us' [CEV]. This noun denotes a raised platform mounted by steps and usually furnished with a seat, used by officials in addressing an assembly, often on judicial matters [LN].

QUESTION—To whom does 'we' in this verse and 'each of us' in the next verse refer?

He is primarily talking about believers [AB, Ho, ICC2, Mu, NAC, NICNT, WBC]. Paul is addressing the Roman Christians here to remind them that that it is God to whom each believer is answerable, but this does not imply that non-Christians will not have to stand before God's judgment seat also [NICNT].

QUESTION—What is his purpose in reminding them of the fact of eventual judgment?

He is warning them that if they judge another, they are usurping a role that rightly belongs only to God [BECNT, HNTC, Ho, Mu, NICNT, St]. Any judgments they might make are irrelevant in view of the judgment of God that they all must face [ICC2, Mor, Mu]. Since all Christians must be judged by God, there is no point in judging one another in matters that are indifferent [AB]. At the judgment people will also be judged by how they treated other believers [WBC]. No one should be so presumptuous as to condemn someone whom God has accepted [Ho].

14:11 For it-is-written,ᵃ (As) I liveᵇ says (the) Lord, that to-me will-bendᶜ every kneeᵈ and every tongueᵉ will-confess/will-give-praiseᶠ to-God.

LEXICON—a. perf. pass. indic. of γραφω (LN 33.61) (BAGD 2.c. p. 166): 'to be written' [AB, BAGD, BECNT, HNTC, ICC2, LN, NICNT, NTC, WBC; KJV, NASB, NCV, NET, NIV, NRSV]. This verb is translated as a phrase: 'Scripture says' [GW, NLT, TEV], 'in the Scriptures God says' [CEV], 'we read in Scripture' [REB]. The word translated 'it is written' is a formula used to introduce OT quotations [BAGD].

b. pres. act. indic. of ζάω (LN 23.88) (BAGD 1.a.ε. p. 336): 'to live' [BAGD, LN]. The phrase ζῶ ἐγώ 'as I live' [AB, BECNT, HNTC, ICC2, NICNT, WBC; KJV, NASB, NET, NRSV, REB] is also translated 'as surely as I live' [NTC; NCV, NIV, NLT], 'as surely as I am the living God' [TEV], 'as certainly as I live' [GW], 'I swear by my very life' [CEV].

c. fut. act. indic. of κάμπτω (LN **53.61**) (BAGD 2. p. 402): 'to bend' [AB, BAGD, ICC2, WBC; NLT], 'to bow' [BECNT, HNTC, NICNT, NTC; KJV, NASB, NCV, NET, NIV, NRSV, REB], 'to bow before' [**LN**], 'to kneel' [CEV, TEV]. The phrase 'to bend the knee' is translated 'to worship' [LN; GW]. This verb means to bend or bow the knee as a symbol of religious devotion [LN].

d. γόνυ (LN 8.47) (BAGD p. 165): 'knee' [AB, BECNT, HNTC, ICC2, LN, NICNT, NTC, WBC; all versions except CEV, GW, NCV, TEV]. The phrase 'to me will bend every knee' is translated 'everyone

will kneel before me' [TEV], 'everyone will bow before me' [NCV], 'everyone will worship me' [GW], 'everyone will kneel down (and praise my name)' [CEV].
- e. γλῶσσα (LN 8.21) (BAGD 2. p. 162): 'tongue' [AB, BECNT, HNTC, ICC2, LN, NICNT, NTC, WBC; KJV, NASB, NET, NIV, NLT, NRSV, REB]. The phrase 'every tongue' is translated 'everyone' [CEV, GW, NCV, TEV].
- f. fut. mid. indic. of ἐξομολογέω (LN 33.359, 33.275) (BAGD 2.c. p. 277): 'to confess' [LN (33.275)], 'to praise' [BAGD, LN (33.359)]. The phrase 'will confess/will give praise to God' is translated 'shall confess to God' [BECNT; KJV], 'will confess that I am God' [TEV], 'shall acknowledge God' [REB], 'will say that I am God' [NCV], 'will/shall give praise to God' [AB, WBC; NASB, NET, NLT, NRSV], 'will praise God' [NICNT; GW], 'will praise my name' [CEV, NIV], 'shall/will acclaim God' [ICC2, NTC], 'shall render praise to God' [HNTC]. This verb means to express praise or honor, with a possible implication of acknowledging the nature of someone or something [LN (33.359)], or to acknowledge a fact publicly [LN (33.275)].

QUESTION—What is meant by the oath formula 'as I live'?

It means that something is a sure as the fact that God lives [Gdt, Mor, NTC, SSA, TH; GW, NCV, NIV, NLT, TEV].

QUESTION—Who is 'the Lord' in this passage?

It refers to God [AB, BECNT, HNTC, ICC2, NAC, NICNT, WBC]. Several times in these verses he refers to 'God', and he is quoting from the OT here, so no doubt it refers to God the Father [NICNT].

QUESTION—What does it mean to 'confess to God'?

The Greek word ἐξομολογέω usually means 'to confess'. However in the Greek Septuagint translation of the OT this word has the meaning 'to praise' when followed by the one being praised in the dative case as here [BAGD, NICNT].

1. It means to confess or to acknowledge God [Ho, NAC, SSA, TH; KJV, NCV, REB, TEV]. It means to acknowledge that he is God [NAC, SSA, TH]. It means to recognize God's authority as supreme ruler and judge [Ho], and to give account of one's own life [BECNT], to admit before God what one has done [AB].
2. It means to give praise to God [BAGD, Gdt, HNTC, ICC1, ICC2, Mor, NICNT, St, WBC; CEV, GW, NASB, NET, NIV, NLT, NRSV]. It means to worship and do homage to God [Gdt, ICC2, Mor, St], to praise him [HNTC, ICC1, NICNT, WBC].

14:12 So then,[a] each of-us will-give[b] account[c] about[d] himself to-God.

TEXT—The phrase τῷ θεῷ 'to God' does not occur in some manuscripts. This is included by GNT with a C rating, indicating difficulty in deciding whether or not to place it in the text. It is included by all commentaries and versions.

LEXICON—a. οὖν (LN 89.50): 'so then, accordingly, so, therefore, consequently, then' [LN]. The phrase ἄρα οὖν 'so then' [ICC2, NTC, WBC; KJV, NASB, NIV, NRSV] is also translated 'then' [AB; TEV], 'therefore' [BECNT, HNTC, NICNT; NET], 'so' [NCV], 'and so' [CEV], 'so, you see' [REB], 'yes' [NLT], not explicit [GW].
   b. fut. act. indic. of δίδωμι (LN 57.71) (BAGD 4. p. 193): 'to give' [AB, BECNT, HNTC, ICC2, LN, NICNT, NTC, WBC; all versions except NCV, NRSV, REB], 'to render, to yield, to give back' [BAGD], not explicit [NCV, NRSV, REB]. This verb means to give an object, usually implying value [LN].
   c. λόγος (LN 57.228) (BAGD 2.a. p. 478): 'account' [AB, BAGD, BECNT, HNTC, ICC2, LN, NICNT, NTC, WBC; all versions except NCV, NLT, NRSV, REB], 'personal account' [NLT]. The phrase λόγον δώσει 'will give account' is translated 'will be accountable' [NRSV], 'will be answerable' [REB], 'will have to answer' [NCV]. This noun denotes a record of assets and liabilities [LN].
   d. περί (LN 90.24, 89.6): 'about' [LN], 'of' [AB, HNTC, ICC2, LN, NICNT, NTC, WBC; GW, KJV, NASB, NET, NIV], 'concerning' [BECNT, LN], not explicit [NCV, NLT, NRSV, REB, TEV]. The phrase 'about himself' is translated 'for what we do' [CEV]. This preposition marks general content, whether of a discourse or mental activity [LN].
QUESTION—What relationship is indicated by ἄρα οὖν 'so then'?
Indicates a logical conclusion to be drawn from what has been said [ICC1, Mor]. It indicates a summary of what has been said in 14:10c-14:11 [NICNT, NTC]. It gives a second evidential grounds for the statement in 14:10, which is that no one should judge or despise others because all will be judged by God [SSA]. It is an exhortation based on the OT quote in 14:11 [ICC2, TH]. The words 'each', 'give account', and 'of himself' are all emphatic in this sentence [ICC2]. Every word in this sentence is emphatic [ICC2, Mor, NAC].

DISCOURSE UNIT—14:13–15:13 [NCV]. The topic is do not cause others to sin.

DISCOURSE UNIT—14:13–23 [AB, HNTC, Ho, Mor, NICNT, TNTC, WBC; CEV, NET, NRSV, TEV]. The topic is the mark of Christ's rule in the community [AB], walking in love [HNTC], exercise of Christian liberty by the strong in faith [Ho], the way of peace and love [Mor], do not cause your brother to stumble [NICNT], Christian charity [TNTC], the responsibility of the strong [WBC], don't cause problems for others [CEV], exhortation for the strong not to destroy the weak [NET], do not make another stumble [NRSV], do not make others fall [TEV].

14:13 Therefore[a] let-us-judge[b] one-another no-longer;[c] but rather[d] decide[e] this,

LEXICON—a. οὖν (LN 89.50): 'therefore' [BECNT, HNTC, ICC2, LN, NICNT, NTC, WBC; KJV, NASB, NET, NIV, NRSV, REB], 'so' [AB, LN; GW, NLT], 'so then' [LN; TEV], 'for that reason' [NCV], 'consequently, accordingly' [LN], not explicit [CEV]. This conjunction marks result, often implying the conclusion of a process of reasoning [LN].

b. pres. act. subj. of κρίνω (LN 56.30) (BAGD 6.b. p. 452): 'to judge' [BECNT, HNTC, LN; CEV, KJV, NASB, NCV, REB, TEV], 'to pass judgment' [AB, BAGD, ICC2, NTC, WBC; NET, NIV, NRSV], 'to be judging' [NICNT], 'to criticize' [BAGD; GW], 'to condemn' [BAGD, LN; NLT], 'to find fault with' [BAGD]. This verb means to judge a person to be guilty and liable to punishment [LN].

c. μηκέτι (LN 67.130) (BAGD 6.c. p. 518): 'no longer' [AB, BAGD, BECNT, HNTC, LN, NICNT, WBC; NRSV], 'no more' [ICC2], 'not...anymore' [KJV, NASB], not explicit [NET]. This adverb is translated as an imperative verb: 'to stop' [NTC; CEV, GW, NCV, NIV, NLT, TEV], 'to cease' [REB]. It marks the extension of time up to a point but not beyond [LN].

d. μᾶλλον (LN 89.126) (BAGD 3.a.α. p. 489): 'rather' [AB, BAGD], 'instead' [BAGD, LN], 'but rather, on the contrary' [LN]. The phrase ἀλλὰ...μᾶλλον 'but rather' [HNTC, ICC2, NICNT, NTC, WBC; KJV, NASB, NET, REB], is translated 'rather' [AB], 'instead' [BECNT; GW, NIV, NLT, TEV], 'but instead' [NRSV], not explicit [CEV, NCV]. This adverb marks contrast indicating an alternative [LN].

e. aorist act. impera. of κρίνω (LN 30.75) (BAGD 3. p. 451): 'to decide' [BAGD, BECNT, ICC2, LN, WBC; GW, NLT, TEV], 'to determine' [NASB, NET], 'to resolve' [NRSV], 'to judge' [NICNT; KJV], 'to make up (our) minds' [LN; CEV, NCV, NIV, REB]. This verb is translated as a phrase: 'make this decision' [AB], 'come to this decision' [HNTC], 'let this be your judgment' [NTC]. This verb means to come to a conclusion in the process of thinking and thus be in a position to make a decision [LN]. In the Greek text there is a play on the word κρίνω here: let us *judge* (condemn) one another no longer; but rather *judge* (decide) this [NICNT].

QUESTION—What relationship is indicated by οὖν 'therefore'?

It indicates a conclusion to be drawn from what he has just said about judgment [ICC2, Mor]. It indicates a conclusion to be drawn from 14:10–12 [ICC2, SSA, WBC]. It indicates 14:13 as a summary of 14:1–12 and a transition to 14:13–23 [Gdt, NICNT].

not to-put[a] a cause-for-stumbling[b] for-the brother or a cause-for-sin.[c]

LEXICON—a. pres. act. infin. of τίθημι (LN 85.32) (BAGD I.1.a.α. p. 816): 'to put' [AB, BAGD, BECNT, HNTC, ICC2, LN, NTC, WBC; KJV, NASB,

NIV, NRSV], 'to place' [BAGD, LN, NICNT; NET, REB], 'to lay' [BAGD], 'to do' [GW, NCV, TEV], not explicit [CEV, NLT]. This verb means to put or place in a particular location [LN].

b. πρόσκομμα (LN **25.183**, 15.229, 88.307) (BAGD 2.b. p. 716): 'stumbling block' [AB, BECNT, HNTC, ICC2, NICNT, NTC; KJV, NASB, NIV, NRSV, REB], 'stumbling stone' [LN (15.229)], 'occasion for offense' [BAGD, WBC], 'obstacle' [BAGD; NET], 'offense, something to cause offense, what causes someone to be offended' [**LN** (25.183)]. See c. below for CEV, GW, NCV, NLT. In non-metaphorical uses this noun denotes that which causes someone to stumble physically [LN (15.229)]. In other uses it denotes an occasion or reason for taking offense [LN (25.183)], or that which provides an opportunity or occasion for causing someone to sin [LN (88.307)].

c. σκάνδαλον (LN 6.25, 88.306) (BAGD 2. p. 753): 'temptation to sin, enticement' [BAGD], 'occasion of falling' [ICC2; KJV], 'hindrance' [NICNT; NRSV], 'occasion for ... downfall' [WBC], 'trap' [BAGD, LN (6.25); NET], 'obstacle' [AB, BECNT, NTC; NASB, NIV, REB], 'offense' [HNTC]. The phrase 'not to put a cause for stumbling for the brother or a cause for sin' is translated 'not to do anything that will make another Christian sin' [NCV], 'not to cause another believer to stumble and fall' [NLT], 'not to upset anyone's faith' [CEV], 'never to do anything that would make other Christians have doubts or lose their faith' [GW]. This noun is a figurative extension of 'trap' (6.25), and denotes someone or something that causes someone to sin [LN (88.306)].

QUESTION—Whom is he addressing in this verse?
1. The first clause addresses both groups, but the second clause addresses only the strong [BECNT, Gdt, HNTC, ICC2, Mor, NICNT, WBC].
2. He addresses only the strong [Mu].
3. Both clauses address both groups [NTC].

QUESTION—What does it mean to cause 'stumbling' or 'sin'?
It means to cause someone else to sin by compromising his own principles or do what he thinks is wrong [BECNT, Gdt, Mu, NAC, NICNT, SSA, TNTC, WBC]. It would be to induce someone to do what his conscience tells him is wrong, such that he falls into sin and possible spiritual ruin as a consequence [NICNT, WBC]. It would be to cause someone to fall from their own faith and practice as a believer [HNTC]. It would be to hurt another believer's feelings or hinder that person from being a more effective witness for Christ [NTC].

14:14 I-know[a] and I-have-become-convinced[b] in[c] (the) Lord Jesus that nothing (is) impure[d] in[e] itself,

LEXICON—a. perf. act. indic. of οἶδα (LN 28.1): 'to know' [AB, BECNT, HNTC, ICC2, LN, NICNT, NTC, WBC; all versions except CEV, GW, NIV, TEV]. The clause 'I know and I have become convinced in the Lord Jesus' is translated 'as one who is in the Lord Jesus, I am fully convinced'

[NIV], 'all that I know of the Lord Jesus convinces me' [REB], 'the Lord Jesus has made it clear to me' [CEV], 'my union with the Lord Jesus makes me certain' [TEV], 'the Lord Jesus has given me the knowledge and conviction' [GW]. This verb means to possess information about something [LN].
   b. perf. pass. indic. of πείθω (LN 33.301, 31.82) (BAGD 4. p. 640): 'to be convinced' [AB, BAGD, LN, NTC, WBC; NASB, NET, NIV, NLT], 'to be persuaded' [BECNT, ICC2, LN, NICNT; KJV, NRSV], 'to be confident' [HNTC], 'to rely on, to trust in, to have confidence in' [LN (31.82)], 'to be certain' [BAGD], not explicit [NCV]. See lexical item a. for [CEV, GW, REB, TEV]. This passive form of this verb means to be convinced to believe something and to act on the basis of what is recommended [LN (33.301)], or to believe in something or someone to the extent of placing reliance or trust in or on [LN (31.82)].
   c. ἐν (LN 13.8, 89.119) (BAGD I.5.d. p. 259): 'in' [BAGD, LN (13.8)]. The phrase ἐν κυρίῳ Ἰησοῦ is translated: 'in the Lord Jesus' [AB, BECNT, HNTC, ICC2, NICNT, NTC, WBC; NASB, NCV, NET, NIV, NRSV], 'by the Lord Jesus' [KJV], 'on the authority of the Lord Jesus' [NLT], 'my union with the Lord Jesus (makes me certain)' [TEV], 'the Lord has made it clear to me' [CEV], not explicit [GW, REB]. This preposition marks a close personal relation [BAGD, LN (89.119)], or a state or condition [LN (13.8)].
   d. κοινός (LN 53.39) (BAGD 2. p. 438): 'impure' [REB], 'unclean' [AB, HNTC, NICNT, NTC; KJV, NASB, NET, NIV, NRSV], 'ritually unclean' [ICC2, LN; TEV], 'common' [BAGD, BECNT], 'ordinary' [BAGD], 'defiled' [LN], 'profane' [BAGD, WBC], 'unacceptable' [GW], 'wrong to eat' [NCV, NLT]. The phrase 'nothing is impure in itself' is translated 'God considers all foods fit to eat' [CEV]. This adjective describes being ritually unacceptable, either as the result of defilement or because of the very nature of the object itself [LN]. In terms of ritual purity as defined by the OT law it denotes the opposite of 'clean' in 14:20 [ICC2, NICNT, WBC].
   e. διά (LN 90.56): 'in relation to' [LN]. The phrase δι' ἑαυτοῦ 'in itself' [AB, BECNT, HNTC, NICNT, NTC, WBC; NASB, NET, NIV, NRSV, REB] is also translated 'in and of itself' [GW, NLT], 'of itself' [KJV, TEV], 'objectively' [ICC2], not explicit [CEV, NCV].
QUESTION—What does it mean that he is convinced ἐν κυρίῳ Ἰησοῦ 'in the Lord Jesus'?
   It is possible, though not certain, that Paul is referring to statements made by Jesus on this topic [ICC2, Mu, NICNT, TNTC, WBC]. It is Jesus who put an end to the ceremonial law, and those who have faith in him find liberty not only through his teaching, but also through the redemption he provided [Gdt]. This sentence is very emphatic [ICC2, Mor, Mu, NTC, WBC]. The phrase 'in the Lord Jesus' intensifies the other two [WBC].

1. It refers to his union with the Lord Jesus [AB, ICC2, Mor, Mu, NICNT, NTC, SSA, TH, TNTC; NCV, NIV, TEV]. His relationship with Christ is the basis for this conviction [AB, Mor, NICNT, TNTC]. It is something he has naturally deduced based on his faith and life in Christ [ICC1].
2. It is a conclusion based on what he knows and understands of the truth that is revealed in Jesus Christ [BECNT, Ho, ICC2, NICNT, St; NLT, REB]. It is a deduction based on theological principles [HNTC]. It had come as a divine revelation [Ho]. His certainty about this comes from Christ himself; that is, his conviction did not originate in himself nor is it self-authenticating [BECNT]. It comes in part from Christ's own teaching [Gdt, NTC, St].
3. The Lord Jesus revealed this to him [Gdt, Ho, NTC, St; CEV, GW, KJV]. It had come as a divine revelation [Ho]. It comes in part from Christ's own teaching [Gdt, NTC, St].

QUESTION—What does he mean by the assertion that *nothing* is unclean in itself?

He is talking about things such as food [ICC2, NTC, SSA, WBC], not about impure thoughts or actions [ICC2]. He is not talking about things that are inherently evil, such as stealing, murder, etc. [TH].

however[a] to-the-one considering[b] it to-be impure, to-that-one (it is) impure.

LEXICON—a. εἰ μή (LN 89.131): 'however' [LN], 'but' [AB, BECNT, ICC2, LN, NICNT, NTC; CEV, GW, KJV, NASB, NCV, NIV, NLT, NRSV, TEV], 'still' [NET], 'except that' [LN, WBC], 'instead, but only' [LN], 'only' [HNTC; REB]. This conjunction marks contrast by designating an exception [LN].

b. pres. mid. or pass. (deponent = act.) participle of λογίζομαι (LN 31.1) (BAGD 3. p. 476): 'to consider' [AB, LN, NTC; CEV, NET, REB], 'to think' [BAGD, BECNT; GW, NASB, NRSV], 'to hold a view, to have an opinion' [LN], 'to reckon' [HNTC, ICC2, NICNT, WBC], 'to believe' [BAGD; NCV, NLT, TEV], 'to regard' [LN; NIV], 'to esteem' [KJV]. This verb means to hold a view or have an opinion with regard to something [LN].

QUESTION—What relationship is indicated by εἰ μή 'however'?

It is adversative [AB, BECNT, Ho, ICC2, Mor, Mu, NICNT, NTC, SSA; CEV, GW, KJV, NASB, NCV, NIV, NLT, NRSV, TEV, WBC]: nothing is impure, *but* if someone thinks it is, it is impure for him. It can also be seen as expressing an exception [Gdt, Ho, ICC1]: nothing is impure, except to the person who thinks it is impure.

14:15 **For if because-of[a] food[b] your brother is-grieved,[c] no-longer are-you-walking[d] according-to[e] love.[f]**

LEXICON—a. διά (LN 90.44): 'because of' [AB, BECNT, LN, NTC; NASB, NET, NIV, TEV], 'on account of' [HNTC, ICC2, LN, WBC], 'by' [CEV, NLT, NRSV, REB], 'through' [NICNT], 'with' [KJV], not explicit [GW].

This preposition marks something constituting the cause or reason for an event or state [LN].
b. βρῶμα (LN **5.7**) (BAGD 1. p. 148): 'food' [BAGD, BECNT, LN, NICNT, WBC; NASB], 'food which you eat' [HNTC], 'thy food' [ICC2], 'foods you eat' [CEV], 'what you eat' [AB, NTC; GW, NET, NIV, NLT, NRSV, REB], 'something you eat' [NCV, TEV], 'thy meat' [LN; KJV]. This noun denotes any type of solid food, particularly meat [LN].
c. pres. pass. indic. of λυπέω (LN 25.275) (BAGD 2.b. p. 481): 'to be grieved' [BAGD, BECNT, HNTC, ICC2; KJV], 'to be sad' [BAGD], 'to be made sad' [LN], 'to be distressed' [AB, BAGD; NET, NIV, NLT], 'to be upset' [NTC, WBC], 'to be caused pain' [NICNT], 'to be hurt' [NASB], 'to be injured' [NRSV], 'to be outraged' [REB]. The passive verb is translated as an active verb: 'if you hurt' [CEV, NCV, TEV], 'so if what you eat hurts (another Christian)' [GW]. This verb means to cause someone to be sad, sorrowful, or distressed [LN].
d. pres. act. indic. of περιπατέω (LN 41.11) (BAGD 2.a.δ. p. 649): 'to walk' [BAGD, BECNT, HNTC, ICC2, NICNT, NTC; KJV, NASB, NET, NRSV], 'to live' [BAGD, LN; GW], 'to act' [NIV, NLT, TEV], 'to be guided' [CEV, REB], 'to follow (the way)' [NCV], 'to conduct yourself' [AB, WBC], 'to behave, to go about doing' [LN]. This verb means to live or behave in a customary manner [LN].
e. κατά (LN 89.8): 'according to' [BECNT; NASB], 'in accordance with' [ICC2, LN], 'in' [AB, HNTC, NICNT, NTC; NET, NIV, NLT, NRSV], 'in terms of' [WBC], 'in relation to' [LN], 'by' [CEV, GW, REB], 'from' [TEV], 'of' [NCV], not explicit [KJV]. This preposition marks a relation involving similarity of process [LN].
f. ἀγάπη (LN 25.43) (BAGD I.1.a. p. 5): 'love' [AB, BAGD, BECNT, HNTC, ICC2, LN, NICNT, NTC, WBC; all versions except KJV]. This noun is translated as an adverb: 'charitably' [KJV].

QUESTION—What relationship is indicated by γάρ 'for'?
1. It relates to 14:13, with 14:14 being a parenthetical statement [BECNT, ICC2, Mor, NICNT, NTC, WBC]. It indicates grounds for the proposition in 14:13b [BECNT, ICC2, NTC, WBC]. That is, don't cause your brother to stumble because if you do, you have forsaken love [BECNT]. It indicates 14:15 as an explanation for 14:13 [NICNT].
2. It relates to 14:13–14 [Mu].
3. It relates to an unexpressed thought, which would be that although you don't share his scruples, you must respect them [ICC1].
4. It indicates an additional grounds for the exhortation in the exhortation in the last clause in this verse about not destroying another believer [SSA].

QUESTION—What is meant by 'grieved'?
1. It is to damage someone else spiritually by tempting him to violate his conscience [ICC2, Mor, St, TH, WBC], or his religious scruples [Mu]. It means to be have his faith seriously compromised and brought to ruin by violating norms which he has accepted, but is unable to defend logically

and thus is vulnerable to falling into compromise of those norms [ICC2]. It is to violate his own conscience so badly that his faith is jeopardized [ICC1, WBC]. One sense has to do with the affront to the weak believer when he sees others doing what he thinks is wrong, and the other sense has to do with him even being made bold to do something he believes is wrong [HNTC, Mor]. It is to damage his soul or conscience [SSA].
2. It means to cause emotional pain to the conscience of the weak believer when he knows that he has done what he believed to be wrong [NICNT].
3. It means to be made angry [REB], to be seriously upset or to have one's feelings hurt [Gdt, NTC], to be deeply offended at seeing others do what the 'weak' believer thinks is wrong, which damages relationships among Christian brothers [Gdt].

Do- not by-food of-you -destroy^a that-one^b for^c whom Christ died.
LEXICON—a. pres. act. impera. of ἀπόλλυμι (LN 20.31) (BAGD 1.a.α. p. 95): 'to destroy' [BECNT, HNTC, ICC2, LN, NICNT, NTC, WBC; CEV, GW, KJV, NASB, NCV, NET, NIV], 'to ruin' [BAGD, LN; NLT, TEV], 'to be the ruin of' [REB], 'to cause the ruin of' [NRSV], 'to bring to ruin' [AB]. This verb means to destroy or to cause the destruction of persons, objects, or institutions [LN].
   b. ἐκεῖνος (LN 92.30) (BAGD 1.d. p. 239): 'that one' [LN, WBC], 'the one' [BECNT], 'one' [NICNT; NRSV, REB], 'that' [BAGD, LN], 'such a one' [AB], 'him' [HNTC, ICC2; KJV, NASB], 'your brother' [NTC; NIV], 'someone' [CEV, NET, NLT], 'anyone' [GW], 'the person' [TEV]. The phrase 'that one for whom Christ died' is translated 'someone's faith…because Christ died for him' [NCV].
   c. ὑπέρ (LN 90.36) (BAGD 1.a.ε. p. 838): 'for' [AB, BAGD, BECNT, HNTC, ICC2, LN, NICNT, NTC, WBC; all versions], 'in behalf of' [BAGD, LN], 'for the sake of' [BAGD]. This preposition marks a participant who is benefited by an event or on whose behalf an event takes place [LN].
QUESTION—How is 14:15b related to 14:15a?
   14:15b draws a conclusion from 14:15a: if you truly love your brother, then don't destroy him [BECNT]. 14:15b intensifies 14:15a [NICNT].
QUESTION—What does he mean by 'destroy'?
1. It is to come to spiritual ruin and forfeit final salvation [ICC2, NICNT]. Paul warns the strong Christians that their scorn for the weak might cause the weak to turn away from their faith and be spiritually ruined [NICNT]. It would be to induce a weak believer to violate his beliefs in such a way that he concludes he has violated the covenant with God and is now outside of that covenant, possibly causing him even to lose faith in Christ altogether [WBC]. He could be in danger of perishing [ICC1]. It is eternal spiritual destruction [SSA]. It may refer to eternal destruction [TH]. It is condemnation at the final judgment, as opposed to acquittal [WBC].

2. It is to do serious religious damage to the weak brother through inducing him to violate his conscience, though this would not be to the point of apostasy from the Christian faith [Mu, St]. He could be destroyed if it were not for God's irresistible grace [NTC]. Although believers are warned of the danger of apostasy and that they must endure to the end to be saved, if they are truly elect they will be kept from apostasy [Ho]. It would be to seriously damage their Christian discipleship, although a true believer will ultimately persevere in faith [St].

QUESTION—What relationship is indicated by ὑπέρ 'for'?

He is saying that Christ died for their sake or for their benefit [WBC]. Christ died to provide salvation for them [NICNT].

14:16 Therefore[a] do- not -let-be-spoken-evil-of[b] your good (thing).[c]

LEXICON—a. οὖν (LN 89.50): 'therefore' [BECNT, LN, NICNT, NTC, WBC; NASB, NET], 'so' [ICC2, LN; NRSV], 'then' [LN; KJV, NLT], 'consequently, accordingly' [LN], 'and' [HNTC], not explicit [AB; CEV, GW, NCV, NIV, REB, TEV]. This conjunction marks result, often implying the conclusion of a process of reasoning [LN].

b. pres. pass. impera. of βλασφημέω (LN 33.400) (BAGD 2.b.ε. p. 142): 'to be spoken of as evil' [KJV, NASB, NET, NIV, NRSV], 'to say ... is evil' [GW], 'to become what others say is evil' [NCV], 'to be reviled' [BECNT, ICC2, LN], 'to be reviled as evil' [AB], 'to be criticized' [NLT], 'to be brought into disrepute' [REB], 'to blaspheme' [BAGD, LN, NICNT], 'to become a source of reproach' [HNTC], 'to be brought into contempt' [WBC], 'to become an occasion for slanderous talk' [NTC], 'to bring shame to Christ' [CEV], 'to let get a bad name' [TEV]. This verb means to speak against someone in such a way as to harm or injure his or her reputation [LN].

c. ἀγαθός (LN 88.1) (BAGD 2.a.γ. p. 3): 'good' [BAGD, LN]. The phrase ὑμῶν τὸ ἀγαθόν 'your good thing' [BECNT, ICC2] is translated 'your good' [NICNT, WBC; KJV, NRSV], 'this good thing of yours' [HNTC], 'what is good for you' [AB], 'what is for you a good thing' [NASB], 'that which for you is a good thing' [NTC], 'what you think is good' [NCV, REB], 'what you consider good' [GW, NET, NIV], 'what you regard as good' [TEV], '(doing) something you believe is good' [NLT], 'your right to eat' [CEV]. This adjective describes positive moral qualities of the most general nature [LN].

QUESTION—What relationship is indicated by οὖν 'therefore'?

It indicates a conclusion that Paul is drawing [Mor, NICNT, SSA], based on what he has said in 14:14–15 [NICNT], or what he has said in the first clause of 14:15 concerning loving other Christians [SSA].

QUESTION—Who would possibly speak 'evil'?

1. It would be non-believers [HNTC, ICC2, Mor, Mu, NAC, NTC, SSA, TH, WBC].
2. It would be other believers [ICC1].

3. It would be the 'weak' Christians [Gdt, NICNT].

QUESTION—What is the 'good thing'?
1. It is their Christian liberty [Gdt, HNTC, ICC1, Mu, NICNT, SSA, St, TH; probably Ho; CEV].
2. It is the gospel [ICC2, Mor, NTC].
3. It is both the community of believers, as well as the God they claim to serve [WBC].

14:17 For the kingdom[a] of-God is not food and drink[b]

LEXICON—a. βασιλεία (LN 37.64, 1.82) (BAGD 3.b, 3.g. p. 135): 'kingdom' [AB, BAGD, BECNT, HNTC, ICC2, LN (1.82), NICNT, NTC, WBC; all versions], 'rule, reign' [LN (37.64)]. In the phrase 'the kingdom of God' this expression refers to the fact of ruling, not a particular place or special time [LN (37.64)]. This noun denotes an area or district ruled by a king [LN (1.82)].
b. The phrase βρῶσις καὶ πόσις 'food and drink' [NET, NRSV], is also translated 'meat and drink' [KJV], 'eating and drinking' [AB, BECNT, HNTC, ICC2, NICNT, NTC; CEV, NASB, NCV, REB], 'a matter of eating and drinking' [WBC; NIV, TEV], 'what a person eats or drinks' [GW], 'a matter of what we eat or drink' [NLT].

QUESTION—What relationship is indicated by γάρ 'for'?

It indicates grounds for what he has just said, and carries the argument forward [Mor]. It indicates grounds for what he has said in 14:13–16 as well as what he will say in 14:20–23 [NICNT]. It indicates grounds for 14:15b–16 [ICC2].

QUESTION—What is meant by 'the kingdom of God'?

It is Paul's summary way of describing the essence of the Christian faith, what Christianity is all about [WBC]. Whereas the gospels speak often of the kingdom of God, Paul's theology focuses on righteousness and the Spirit [BECNT, WBC]. It is a present reality [HNTC, ICC2], experienced in the presence and activity of Jesus Christ among them [ICC2]. It is the rule of God, which governs those who have faith [HNTC]. Paul's description here means that 'kingdom' is more or less equivalent to 'salvation', expressed as God's royal reign among his people [NTC]. He is describing God's sovereignty, his supreme will, and his rule, which believers recognize and in which they live [Mu]. It is the inward spiritual theocracy that consists of all Christian people, and particularly in their religious practice [Ho]. Paul usually conceives of the kingdom of God as the future messianic kingdom that was to be the reward and goal of Christian living, but here he is speaking of the basic foundational principles and ideas of that kingdom, which are already being seen in the world [ICC1]. It is God's rule in the lives of Christians [SSA, St, TH]. It is the future inheritance of God's children, the blessings of which can be enjoyed even now through the Holy Spirit [TNTC].

ROMANS 14:17

QUESTION—Whom is he addressing here?
He is addressing the 'strong' [ICC1, ICC2, Mu, NICNT, St; probably HNTC]. He is primarily addressing the ones who felt free to eat and drink [WBC].

QUESTION—Does his mention of πόσις 'drink' indicate that drinking wine was a controversial issue as well?
He may be introducing this as a hypothetical matter [ICC2]. It may be hypothetical since drinking is a natural complement to eating, but it may also be that the 'weak' were concerned that wine had been involved in a pagan religious practice, and therefore contaminated by that [NICNT].

but righteousness[a] and peace[b] and joy[c] in[d] (the) Holy Spirit;

LEXICON—a. δικαιοσύνη (LN 88.13) (BAGD 2.b. p. 196): 'righteousness' [BAGD, BECNT, HNTC, ICC2, LN, NICNT, NTC, WBC; KJV, NASB, NET, NIV, NRSV, TEV], 'uprightness' [AB, BAGD], 'doing what God requires, doing what is right' [LN], 'living right with God' [NCV], 'living a life of goodness' [NLT], 'pleasing God' [CEV], 'God's approval' [GW], 'justice' [REB]. This noun denotes the act of doing what God requires [LN].

b. εἰρήνη (LN 25.248) (BAGD 3. p. 227): 'peace' [AB, BAGD, BECNT, HNTC, ICC2, LN, NICNT, NTC, WBC; all versions except CEV], 'living in peace' [CEV]. This noun denotes a state of freedom from anxiety and inner turmoil [LN].

c. χαρά (LN 25.123) (BAGD 1. p. 875): 'joy' [AB, BAGD, BECNT, HNTC, ICC2, LN, NICNT, NTC, WBC; all versions except CEV], 'true happiness' [CEV], 'gladness, great happiness' [LN]. This noun denotes a state of joy and gladness [LN].

d. ἐν (LN 90.6, 89.119): 'in' [AB, BAGD, BECNT, HNTC, ICC2, LN (89.119), NICNT, NTC, WBC; KJV, NASB, NCV, NET, NIV, NLT, NRSV], 'in union with' [LN (89.119)], 'by, from' [LN (90.6)], 'inspired by' [REB], 'all this comes from' [CEV], 'that the Holy Spirit gives' [GW], 'which the Holy Spirit gives' [TEV]. This preposition marks an agent [LN (90.6)], or close personal association [LN (89.119)].

QUESTION—What are the righteousness, peace, and joy he is referring to?
1. They are pure gifts of God, caused by the Holy Spirit [Ho, ICC2, WBC]. 'Righteousness' is a status before God, and which is given by God; 'peace' is that state that results from having been reconciled to God, and 'joy in the Holy Spirit' is that joy that the Spirit produces in the believer [ICC2, NTC]. Righteousness is God's power at work sustaining and enabling the believer in daily living; joy is a confidence in God that sustains believers even in persecution, and is both corporate as well as individual [WBC]. These are objective states of justification through Christ, peace with God, and the joy in expectation of experiencing God's glory [St].

2. They are ethical qualities, which are expressed in believers' relationships with one another [Gdt, ICC1, Mu, NICNT, SSA]. They are righteous living [NAC]. 'Peace' refers to harmonious relations within the community of believers [Gdt, NAC, NICNT], and when the relationships within the believing community are harmonious, all will experience joy [NICNT]. They are subjective, reflecting that which the believer experiences [HNTC, Mu].
3. 'Righteousness' is an ethical quality, and 'peace' is being in a state of reconciliation and peace with God [TH].
4. He is not differentiating between gifts of God and ethical qualities in believers [BECNT, Mor].

QUESTION—What is meant by ἐν πνεύματι ἁγίῳ 'in the Holy Spirit'?

It speaks of the believer's experience of the Holy Spirit as the cause of the righteousness, peace, and joy [HNTC, NICNT, TH]. It is causal, and describes a joy that is brought by the Holy Spirit [ICC2, Mu, NTC]. It indicates that the Holy Spirit is the source [Gdt, SSA]. The power of the Holy Spirit produces righteousness, peace, and joy [BECNT]. It implies instrumentality as well as location, and means 'in the power of' the Holy Spirit [WBC].

QUESTION—What element(s) in the sentence does ἐν πνεύματι ἁγίῳ 'in the Holy Spirit' describe?
1. It describes the quality of joy [Ho, ICC1, ICC2, Mu, NAC, NTC].
2. It describes all three qualities [BECNT, Gdt, HNTC, Mor, NICNT, TH].

14:18 for[a] the-one serving[b] Christ in this (way)[c] (is) well-pleasing[d] to-God and acceptable[e] to people.[f]

LEXICON—a. γάρ (LN 89.23): 'for' [BECNT, HNTC, ICC2, LN, NICNT, NTC, WBC; KJV, NASB, NET], 'because' [LN; NIV], 'and when' [TEV], not explicit [AB; CEV, GW, NCV, NLT, NRSV, REB]. This conjunction marks cause or reason between events [LN].
b. pres. act. participle of δουλεύω (LN 35.27) (BAGD 2.b. p. 205): 'to serve' [AB, BAGD, BECNT, HNTC, ICC2, LN, NICNT, NTC, WBC; all versions except REB], 'to show (himself) a servant' [REB], 'to obey' [BAGD]. This verb means to serve, normally in a humble manner and in response to the demands or commands of others [LN].
c. The phrase ἐν τούτῳ 'in this (way)' is translated 'in this way' [HNTC, NTC; CEV, NASB, NET, NIV, REB, TEV], 'this way' [AB], 'in this' [BECNT, NICNT, WBC], 'in these things' [KJV], 'with this in mind' [GW], 'by living this way' [NCV], 'with this attitude' [NLT], 'thus' [NRSV], 'therein' [ICC2].
d. εὐάρεστος (LN 25.94) (BAGD 1. p. 318): 'pleasing' [AB, BAGD, BECNT, HNTC, ICC2, LN, NICNT, NTC, WBC; GW, NCV, NET, NIV], 'acceptable' [BAGD; KJV, NASB, NRSV, REB]. This adjective is translated as a verb: 'to please (God)' [CEV, NLT, TEV]. This adjective describes that which causes someone to be pleased [LN].

e. δόκιμος (LN **87.7**) (BAGD 2. p. 203): 'accepted' [NCV], 'respected' [BAGD, **LN**, NTC; CEV, GW], 'esteemed' [AB, BAGD, NICNT], 'approved' [BECNT, WBC; KJV, NASB, NET, NIV, REB, TEV], 'honored' [**LN**], 'irreproachable' [HNTC], 'deserves approval' [ICC2], 'has approval' [NRSV]. This adjective is translated as a verb: 'to approve' [NLT]. This adjective describes being respected on the basis of proven worth [LN].
f. ἄνθρωπος (LN 9.1): This plural noun is translated 'people' [BECNT, LN, NICNT; CEV, GW, NET], 'other people' [NCV], 'people in general' [WBC], 'men' [HNTC, ICC2 NTC; KJV, NASB, NIV, REB], 'others' [NLT, TEV], 'human beings' [AB, LN]. This noun is translated as an adjective: 'human (approval)' [NRSV]. This noun denotes a human being [LN].

QUESTION—What relationship is indicated by γάρ 'for'?

It indicates 14:18 as accenting or emphasizing what he has just said in 14:17 [ICC2, NICNT]. It carries the argument further forward [Mor].

QUESTION—To what does ἐν τούτῳ 'in this (way)' refer?

The singular word τούτῳ 'this' refers collectively to the righteousness peace and joy just mentioned [AB, Ho, ICC1, ICC2, Mor, Mu, NTC, SSA, TNTC]. The word τούτῳ 'this' refers to the principle implied by the three virtues mentioned [ICC1]. The one who knows he or she has been justified by God and reconciled to God, and that he has received from the Holy Spirit the gift of joy, and is able to serve Christ in a way that is rooted in these realities and shaped by them, is pleasing to God [ICC2]. It means in the way or manner generally described in 14:17 [BECNT, HNTC, NICNT, NTC]. They must recognize that food and drink are matters of secondary importance [BECNT, HNTC, St], and that they should focus on those matters that are central to the kingdom [BECNT, NICNT, St]. It refers generally to what he has been discussing in the section beginning at 14:13 [TH], or even in the entire chapter [WBC].

QUESTION—Who are the people to whom such a person will be acceptable?
1. They will be acceptable to all people, whether Christian or non-Christian [Ho, ICC2, Mor, Mu, NTC; probably HNTC, ICC1]. They will be acceptable to anyone of good will [WBC].
2. They will be acceptable to the 'weak' believers [NICNT].

14:19 So then^a let-us-pursue^b the (things) of-peace^c and the (things) of-edification^d to each-other.^{e}

TEXT—Instead of διώκωμεν 'let us pursue', some manuscripts have διώκομεν 'we pursue'. GNT selects the reading διώκωμεν 'let us pursue' with a D rating, indicating great difficulty in deciding which variant to place in the text. The reading 'we pursue' is taken by WBC; NASB.

LEXICON—a. The phrase ἄρα οὖν is translated 'so then' [ICC2, WBC; NLT, TEV], 'then' [AB, NTC; NASB, NET, NRSV, REB], 'so' [GW, NCV], 'therefore' [BECNT, HNTC, NICNT; KJV, NIV], not explicit [CEV].

b. pres. act. subj. of διώκω (LN 68.66) (BAGD 4.b. p. 201): 'to pursue' [AB, BAGD, BECNT, HNTC, ICC2, NICNT, NTC, WBC; GW, NASB, NET, NRSV, REB], 'to follow after' [KJV], 'to run after, to chase after' [BAGD], 'to try to do' [NCV], 'to try to live' [CEV], 'to make every effort to do' [NIV], 'to do with effort, to strive toward' [BAGD, LN], 'to aim for' [NLT], 'to aim at' [TEV]. This verb means to do something with intense effort and with definite purpose or goal [LN].

c. The phrase τὰ τῆς εἰρήνης 'the (things) of peace' is translated 'the things that make for peace' [BECNT, HNTC; KJV, NASB, REB], 'those things that make for peace' [NICNT], 'those things which bring peace' [GW, TEV], 'the things that lead to peace' [NTC], 'what leads to peace' [NIV], 'what makes for peace' [AB, ICC2, WBC; NET, NRSV], 'what makes peace' [NCV], 'harmony in the church' [NLT]. The clause 'let us pursue the things of peace' is translated 'we should try to live at peace' [CEV].

d. οἰκοδομή (LN 74.15, 42.34) (BAGD 1.b.α. p. 559): 'edification' [AB, BECNT, ICC2, NICNT, NTC; NIV], 'building up' [HNTC, LN (42.34, 74.15), WBC; NASB, NET], 'upbuilding' [NRSV], 'good' [GW], '(the process of) building, construction' [BAGD]. This noun is translated as a verb: 'to edify' [KJV], 'to build up' [LN; NLT, REB], 'to help' [NCV], 'to help strengthen' [TEV]. The phrase 'the things of edification to each other' is translated 'help each other have a strong faith' [CEV]. This noun denotes the increase of the potential of someone or something, with the focus upon the process involved [LN (74.15)], or the construction of something, with the focus on the event of building up or on the result of such an event [LN (42.34)].

e. The phrase εἰς ἀλλήλους 'to each other' is translated 'mutual' [AB, HNTC, ICC2, NTC; NIV, NRSV], 'of one another' [BECNT, NICNT, WBC; NASB], 'one another' [NCV, NET, TEV], 'each other' [CEV, GW, NLT], 'another' [KJV], 'the common life' [REB]. This phrase modifies only the noun 'edification', not the other noun 'peace' [AB, BECNT, HNTC, ICC2, NICNT, NTC, WBC; all versions].

QUESTION—Does he use the word 'peace' in the same sense, or in a different sense than he uses it in 14:17?

'Peace' refers to peaceful and harmonious relationships between members of the church [HNTC, ICC2, Mor, Mu, NICNT, NTC, SSA, TH, WBC]. The decision that here it refers to peace with other Christians is clearer than at 4:17, since the following verse makes it clear that Paul is telling the 'strong' to maintain the kind of attitude and behavior that will foster harmony between the strong and the weak in regard to their matters of dispute [NICNT]. Such harmonious relations are based on peace with himself that God established in Christ [ICC2]. Those who have peace with God are obligated to seek peace with other people [Mor].

QUESTION—What is meant by 'edification'?

It is causing the congregation to develop in harmony and grow in number [WBC]. It is to build one another up by helping one another instead of criticizing one another [Mor]. It is the building up of the church [HNTC, ICC1]. It refers to what leads to peace in the church, the building up of the church as a whole, as opposed to what builds up individuals [NICNT]. It is to build the church as well as to promote growth of the individual members in faith and obedience [ICC2]. It is to help other Christians grow spiritually in their faith [SSA], to help their faith become stronger [SSA, TH].

14:20 Do-not for-the-sake-of[a] food destroy[b] the work[c] of-God.

LEXICON—a. ἕνεκα (LN 89.31) (BAGD p. 264): 'for the sake of' [AB, BAGD, BECNT, HNTC, ICC2, LN, NTC, WBC; NASB, NET, NIV, NRSV, REB], 'on account of' [BAGD, LN, NICNT], 'because of' [BAGD, LN; GW, TEV], 'for' [KJV], 'over' [NLT], not explicit [CEV, NCV]. This preposition marks cause or reason, often with the implication of purpose in the sense of 'for the sake of' [LN]. The position in the sentence of the phrase 'not for the sake of food' shows that it is emphatic [Mor].

b. pres. act. impera. of καταλύω (LN **20.55**) (BAGD 1.b.β. p. 414): 'to destroy' [BAGD, BECNT, HNTC, ICC2, **LN**, WBC; CEV, KJV, NCV, NET, NIV, NRSV, REB, TEV], 'to tear down' [BAGD, NICNT, NTC; NASB], 'to tear apart' [NLT], 'to demolish' [AB, BAGD], 'to ruin' [GW], 'to ruin utterly' [LN]. This verb means to destroy completely the efforts or work of someone else [LN].

c. ἔργον (LN 42.12) (BAGD 3. p. 308): 'work' [AB, BAGD, BECNT, HNTC, ICC2, LN, NICNT, NTC, WBC; GW, KJV, NASB, NCV, NET, NIV, NLT, NRSV, REB], 'what God has done' [CEV, REB]. This noun denotes the result of someone's activity or work [LN].

QUESTION—What is meant by 'the work of God'?

1. It is God's work in the weak believer [AB, Gdt, ICC2, Mor, Mu, NAC, NTC], especially his making a new person out of the weak believer [ICC2]. It is what God has done in the life of any believer [SSA, TNTC], his developing the inner spiritual life of a believer by his grace [TNTC].
2. It is the community of believers [HNTC, ICC1, NICNT, St, WBC], what God has done in establishing the church [WBC]. They must not destroy the unity of the church and impair its strength through their attitudes and actions toward the 'weak' [NICNT].

All-things[a] (are) clean,[b] but wrong[c] to-the man eating with offense.[d]

LEXICON—a. πᾶς (LN 59.23, 58.28): 'all things' [AB, BECNT, HNTC, ICC2, NICNT; KJV, NASB, NET], 'everything' [NTC, WBC; NRSV, REB], 'all foods' [CEV, NCV, NLT, TEV], 'all food' [GW, NIV], 'all, every, each' [LN (59.23)], 'every kind of, all sorts of' [LN (58.28)]. This adjective describes the totality of any object, mass, collective, or extension [LN (59.23)], or a totality of kinds or sorts [LN (58.28)].

b. καθαρός (LN 53.29) (BAGD 2. p. 388): 'clean' [AB, BECNT, HNTC, ICC2, LN, NICNT, NTC, WBC; NASB, NET, NIV, NRSV], 'pure' [LN; KJV], 'pure in itself' [REB], 'ceremonially pure' [BAGD], 'acceptable'

[GW, NLT], 'all right to eat' [NCV], 'may be eaten' [TEV], 'fit to eat' [CEV]. This adjective describes being ritually clean or pure [LN].
   c. κακός (LN 88.106) (BAGD 1.c. p. 397): 'wrong' [AB, NICNT, NTC, WBC; CEV, GW, NCV, NET, NIV, NLT, NRSV, REB, TEV], 'evil' [BAGD, BECNT, ICC2, LN; KJV, NASB], '(they) work harm' [HNTC]. This adjective describes being bad, with the implication of being harmful and damaging [LN].
   d. πρόσκομμα (LN 88.307, 25.183,) (BAGD 1.b. p. 716): 'offense' [HNTC, LN (25.183), WBC; KJV, NASB], 'stumbling block' [AB, ICC2], 'stumbling' [BAGD], 'problems' [CEV]. The phrase διὰ προσκόμματος 'with offense' [WBC; KJV], is also translated 'and gives offense' [NASB], 'that causes someone else to stumble' [NTC; NIV], '(you) cause another to stumble' [REB], 'to cause anyone to stumble' [NET], 'if it makes another person stumble' [NLT], 'that creates a stumbling block for another' [AB], '(who eats) and stumbles' [BECNT], 'in such a way as results in the presence of a stumbling block' [ICC2], 'while causing another to stumble' [NICNT], 'that will cause someone else to fall into sin' [TEV], 'that causes someone else to sin' [NCV], 'to make others fall' [NRSV], 'it causes someone else to have doubts' [GW], 'that causes problems for others' [CEV], 'so as to cause offense' [HNTC]. This noun denotes that which provides an opportunity or occasion for causing someone to sin [LN (88.307)], or an occasion or reason for taking offense [LN (25.183)].

QUESTION—What relationship is indicated by ἀλλά 'but'?
   The statement 'all things are clean' is probably a slogan used by those who eat without restrictions, but ἀλλά 'but' introduces Paul's qualification of that statement [ICC2, NICNT].

QUESTION—What relationship is indicated by διά 'with'?
   It indicates an attendant circumstance [HNTC, ICC2, Mu, NICNT, NTC].

QUESTION—What does it mean to eat with offense?
   1. It would be the 'strong' believer inducing a 'weak' believer to violate his conscience in the matter by eating something he believes he should not eat [Ho, ICC1, ICC2, NICNT, NTC, SSA, TH].
   2. It would be the weak believer violating his own conscience by eating what he does not believe he should eat [Gdt, Mu].
   3. It is ambiguous, and his admonition could be applied to either group [HNTC, Mor, WBC].

14:21 (It is) good[a] not to-eat[b] meat nor to-drink wine[c] nor (to-do anything)[d] in which your brother stumbles.[e]

TEXT—Some manuscripts include ἢ σκανδαλίζεται ἢ ἀσθενεῖ 'or is offended, or is made weak' after προσκόπτει 'stumbles'. It is omitted by GNT with a B rating, indicating that the text is almost certain. It is included by AB and KJV only.

LEXICON—a. καλός (LN 65.43, 88.4) (BAGD 3.c. p. 400): 'good' [BAGD, BECNT, LN, NICNT; KJV, NASB, NET, NRSV], 'right' [REB], 'a good thing' [ICC2], 'fine, praiseworthy' [LN], 'a fine thing' [WBC], 'the right thing' [GW, TEV], 'advantageous' [LN (65.43)], 'better' [AB, LN (65.43), NTC; NCV, NIV, NLT], 'best' [CEV], 'well' [HNTC]. This adjective describes providing some special or superior benefit [LN (65.43)], or describes a positive moral quality [LN (88.4)].
  b. aorist act. infin. of ἐσθίω (LN 23.1) (BAGD 1.a. p. 312): 'to eat' [AB, BAGD, BECNT, HNTC, ICC2, LN, NICNT, NTC, WBC; all versions].
  c. οἶνος (LN 6.197) (BAGD 1. p. 562): 'wine' [AB, BAGD, BECNT, HNTC, ICC2, LN, NICNT, NTC, WBC; all versions]. This noun denotes a fermented beverage made from the juice of grapes [LN].
  d. There is no lexical entry for 'to do anything' in the Greek text, it is implied by the contrastive μηδέ 'nor'. This implied verb phrase is represented in translation as 'to do anything' [AB, BECNT, WBC; CEV, KJV, NASB, NCV, NET, NRSV], 'to do anything else' [ICC2, NICNT, NTC; GW, NIV, NLT, TEV], 'to do any other thing' [HNTC], 'to abstain from anything else' [REB].
  e. pres. act. indic. of προσκόπτω (LN **25.182**) (BAGD 2.a. p. 716): 'to stumble' [AB, BECNT, HNTC, ICC2, NICNT, NTC, WBC; KJV, NASB, NET, NLT, NRSV, REB], 'to fall' [NIV, TEV], 'to take offense' [BAGD, **LN**], 'to cause to be offended' [**LN**], 'to have doubts' [GW], 'to sin' [NCV], 'to cause problems' [CEV]. This verb means to take offense, with the implication of a feeling of repugnance or rejection [LN].

QUESTION—What relationship is indicated by ἐν ᾧ 'in which'?
  It is causal, meaning anything that causes or makes someone else to stumble [AB, HNTC, ICC2, NAC, NICNT, NTC, SSA, TH; CEV, GW, NCV, NET, NIV, NLT, NRSV, REB, TEV].

QUESTION—Is Paul talking about a more general and permanent abstention from eating meat, or about not eating meat in a particular situation or occasion?
  He is speaking about abstention on particular occasions [HNTC, Mor, NAC, NICNT, SSA, WBC]. The use of aorist infinitives probably indicates abstention only on specific occasions [HNTC, Mor, NAC, SSA, WBC]. The aorist infinitives may indicate specific occasions, but that is not certain [ICC2], and the use of the aorist infinitive is not relevant to the argument [NICNT]. Those who think that this applies to specific occasions contend that since these things are not wrong in themselves, they may be participated in at occasions where there is no danger of causing someone else to fall [TH].

QUESTION—Does his reference to wine indicate that drinking wine was also an issue that divided people?
  1. More than likely it is used as a hypothetical example, and Paul was not addressing a specific controversy [ICC1, ICC2]. Paul uses it as an example of a more general principle, but it probably was also a point of tension [NICNT]. Paul was using the extremes as examples [ICC1].

2. It was probably a real concern in Rome due to the possibility that the wine may have been offered to pagan gods at some point [Ho, NTC, WBC]. The 'weak' also abstained from drinking wine [HNTC, Mu].

14:22 **(The) faith[a] which you have,[b] have to yourself before[c] God.**
TEXT—Instead of πίστιν ἣν ἔχεις '(the) faith which you have', some manuscripts have only πίστιν ἔχεις which might be translated as 'do you have faith?' or as '(the) faith you have'. GNT selects the reading 'the faith which you have' with a C rating, indicating difficulty in deciding which variant to place in the text. The reading 'do you have faith?' is taken by KJV only.
LEXICON—a. πίστις (LN 31.104) (BAGD 2.d.ε. p. 664): 'faith' [BAGD, BECNT, HNTC, ICC2, LN, NICNT, WBC; KJV, NASB, NET, NRSV], 'beliefs' [LN; NCV], 'conviction' [AB, BAGD], 'firm conviction' [REB], 'what you believe' [CEV, TEV], 'whatever you believe' [NTC; GW, NIV]. The phrase 'the faith which you have' is translated 'you may believe there's nothing wrong with what you are doing' [NLT]. This noun denotes the content of what Christians believe [LN].
  b. pres. act. indic. of ἔχω (LN 31.1, 90.65) (BAGD I.2.e.β. p. 332): 'to have' [AB, BAGD, HNTC, ICC2, LN, NICNT, WBC; KJV, NASB, NET, NRSV, REB], 'to possess' [BECNT], not explicit [NTC; CEV, GW, NCV, NIV, NLT, TEV]. This verb means to hold a view or have an opinion with regard to something [LN].
  c. ἐνώπιον (LN 90.20) (BAGD 2.b. p. 270): 'before' [AB, BAGD, BECNT, HNTC, ICC2, NICNT, WBC; KJV, NASB, NET, NRSV], 'between (yourself and God)' [NTC; CEV, GW, NCV, NIV, NLT, REB, TEV], 'in the sight of' [BAGD, LN], 'in the presence of' [BAGD]. This preposition marks a participant whose viewpoint is relevant to an event [LN].
QUESTION—What is the faith he is discussing here?
  1. It is a conviction or belief about such things as food, drink, and calendar observance [AB, BECNT, Gdt, Ho, ICC2, Mu, NAC, NICNT, NTC, SSA, St, TH, TNTC]. Such conviction may be kept to oneself out of concern for the well-being of another person, whereas basic saving faith should not be kept to oneself [ICC2]. It is not saving faith, but faith that enables someone to take a course of action without doubting [Mor]. He is telling the 'strong' not to boast before the 'weak' about the confidence they have in these issues [NICNT].
  2. It is more generally a trust in and reliance on God [WBC], a confidence in God [HNTC].

Blessed[a] (is) the-one not condemning[b] himself in what he-approves.[c]
LEXICON—a. μακάριος (LN 25.119) (BAGD 1.b. p. 486): 'blessed' [AB, BAGD, BECNT, HNTC, ICC2, NICNT, NTC; GW, NET, NIV, NLT, NRSV], 'happy' [BAGD, LN, WBC; KJV, NASB, NCV, TEV], 'fortunate' [BAGD; CEV, REB]. This adjective describes being happy, with the implication of enjoying favorable circumstances [LN].

b. pres. act. participle of κρίνω (LN 56.30) (BAGD 6.b. p. 452): 'to condemn' [BAGD LN], 'to judge, to criticize, to find fault with' [BAGD], 'to judge as guilty' [LN]. The phrase 'the one not condemning himself in what he approves' is translated 'the man/he who does not condemn himself in/by what he approves' [WBC; NASB, NIV; similarly ICC2], 'the one who does not condemn himself for what he approves' [AB], 'those who do not condemn themselves in that which they approve' [BECNT], 'the person who does not need to condemn himself over what he approves' [NTC], 'who does not judge himself in what he approves' [NICNT], 'he that condemneth not himself in that thing which he alloweth' [KJV], 'the one who does not judge himself by what he approves' [NET], 'the man who doesn't cause himself to be condemned by what he judges to be good' [LN (30.114)], 'the person who does what he knows is right shouldn't feel guilty' [GW], 'those who do not feel guilty when they do something they judge is right' [TEV], 'those who don't feel guilty for doing something they have decided is right' [NLT], 'he who does not waver in respect of what his conscience affirms' [HNTC], 'those who have no reason to condemn themselves because of what they approve' [NRSV], 'anyone who can make his decisions without misgivings' [REB], 'if they can do what they think is right without feeling guilty' [NCV], 'if your actions don't make you have doubts' [CEV].
c. pres. act. indic. of δοκιμάζω (LN **30.114**) (BAGD 2.b. p. 202): 'to approve' [BAGD, LN], 'to accept as proved' [BAGD], 'to judge as good' [LN]. See the preceding lexical item for translations of this word. This verb means to regard something as genuine or worthy on the basis of testing [LN].

QUESTION—What is the intent of Paul's admonition here?
1. He is describing the freedom of the person whose conscience is not troubled by doubts and scruples [ICC1, Mor, Mu, St; TEV]. This saying is the first element of a principle that is continued in the following verse; that is, the strong person who is free from unnecessary scruples is blessed if he eats, but the weak person who violates his scruples by eating brings judgment on himself [ICC2, NICNT].
2. He is describing the person who does not violate his own scruples [HNTC, Ho, SSA, TH].
3. He is describing the 'strong' person who is blessed for not causing harm to his fellow-believer through the exercise of his liberty [NTC].
4. He is describing the 'strong' person who does not cause harm to other believers by his actions, as well as to the 'weak' person who does not violate his own scruples [NAC].

14:23 But[a] the-one doubting[b] when he-eats has-been-judged[c] (already),[d]

LEXICON—a. δέ (LN 89.124): 'but' [AB, BECNT, HNTC, ICC2, LN, NICNT, NTC, WBC; all versions except KJV], 'and' [KJV]. This conjunction marks contrast [LN].

b. pres. mid. participle of διακρίνω (BAGD 2.b. p. 185): 'to doubt' [BAGD, BECNT, NICNT, WBC; KJV, NASB, NET], 'to have doubts' [AB; CEV, GW, NIV, NLT, NRSV, TEV], 'to be troubled by doubts' [ICC2], 'to have misgivings' [NTC; REB], 'to waver' [BAGD, HNTC], 'to not be sure' [NCV], 'to be at odds with oneself' [BAGD].

c. perf. pass. indic. of κατακρίνω (LN 56.31) (BAGD p. 412): 'to be condemned' [AB, BAGD, BECNT, HNTC, ICC2, LN, NICNT, NTC, WBC; GW, NASB, NET, NIV, NRSV], 'to be damned' [KJV], 'to be wrong' [NCV], 'to sin' [NLT], 'to be guilty' [REB], 'to render a verdict as guilty' [LN], 'to go against your beliefs' [CEV]. This passive verb is translated as an active verb: 'God condemns them when they eat it' [TEV]. This verb means to judge someone as definitely guilty and thus subject to punishment [LN].

d. There is no lexical entry for 'already' in the Greek text, it is implied by the perfect passive form of the verb κατακρίνω. It is represented in translation as: 'already' [AB], 'when they eat it' [TEV], as a perfect passive [AB, BECNT, HNTC, ICC2, NICNT, NTC, WBC; GW, KJV, NASB, NET, NIV, NRSV], not represented [CEV, NCV, NLT, REB].

QUESTION—Who is the agent of the passive verb κατακέκριται 'has been judged'?

1. God is the one judging [Mu, NICNT, NTC, TH, WBC]. They are judged by God as well as by their own consciences [SSA]. Some commentators simply say that such a person stands condemned, without specifying whether this is an action of God or merely a general condition [AB, Ho, ICC2, Mor, NTC].
2. It is the sense of guilt from his own conscience [St, TNTC]. It is probably not God but his own conscience that judges him [St].

because not from[a] faith; and all[b] that (is) not from[c] faith is sin.[d]

LEXICON—a. ἐκ (LN 90.16) (BAGD 3.g.γ. p. 235): 'from' [AB, BAGD, ICC2, LN, NTC; NASB, NET, NIV, NRSV, REB], 'by' [BAGD, LN], 'of' [BAGD, BECNT, HNTC, WBC; KJV], 'out of' [NICNT], 'based on' [TEV], 'in' [GW], not explicit [CEV, NCV, NLT]. The phrase οὐκ ἐκ πίστεως 'not from faith' [NASB, NET], is translated 'not of faith' [BECNT, HNTC, WBC; KJV], 'not out of faith' [NICNT], 'not in faith' [GW], 'not based on faith' [TEV], 'does not spring from faith' [NTC], 'does not come from faith' [NIV], 'does not proceed from faith' [NRSV], 'does not do so from faith' [NTC], 'does not proceed from conviction' [AB], 'does not arise from conviction' [REB], 'anything you do against your beliefs' [CEV], 'without believing it is right' [NCV], 'anything you believe is not right' [NLT]. This preposition marks the source of an activity or state, with the implication of something proceeding from or out of the source [LN].

b. πᾶς (LN 59.24, 59.23) (BAGD 1.c.γ. p. 632): 'whatever' [AB, BAGD, BECNT, ICC2; NASB, NET, NRSV], 'whatsoever' [KJV], 'everything'

[HNTC, NICNT, NTC, WBC; NIV], 'anything' [LN; CEV, GW, NCV, NLT, REB, TEV], 'all, every, each' [LN]. This adjective describes any one of a totality [LN].

c. ἐκ (LN 90.16) (BAGD 3.g.γ. p. 235): 'from' [AB, BAGD, ICC2, LN, NTC; NASB, NET, NIV, NRSV, REB], 'by' [BAGD, LN], 'of' [BAGD, BECNT, HNTC, WBC; KJV], 'out of' [NICNT], 'based on' [TEV], 'in' [GW], not explicit [CEV, NCV, NLT]. The phrase 'not from faith' is translated 'against your beliefs' [CEV], 'without believing (it is right)' [NCV], 'you believe is not right' [NLT]. This preposition marks the source of an activity or state, with the implication of something proceeding from or out of the source [LN].

d. ἁμαρτία (LN 88.289): 'sin' [AB, BECNT, HNTC, ICC2, LN, NICNT, NTC, WBC; all versions]. This noun denotes an act contrary to the will and law of God [LN].

QUESTION—What is 'faith' here?

1. It is the convictions of conscience [AB, Ho, ICC1, ICC2, NICNT, NTC, SSA, TH]. As it does elsewhere in this chapter, it means conviction that is an outgrowth of a more basic faith in Christ [NICNT, NTC]. The conviction springs from faith [Mor]. It is also conviction of the principles of salvation [ICC1].

2. It is a creaturely dependence on God the creator [WBC]. It is humble reliance on God [HNTC, Mor], the faith by which one receives salvation [Gdt, Mor], and also lives the Christian life [Mor].

QUESTION—What is the scope of his definition of things not done 'from faith'?

He is talking only about the subject at hand, which concern things a believer does that do not spring from a right faith, and not about whatever was done before entering the life of faith [ICC2, Mor, Mu]. Anything that springs from selfish motives, greed, or fear, does not spring from faith, and as such is sinful [Mor]. 'All' refers to indifferent matters [AB]. It is any act that is inconsistent with our deeply held convictions about what our Christian faith would allow us to do, that is, violating our conscience [NICNT]. It is any act that does not arise from the inner conviction that what one does is consistent with Christian faith [NAC, NTC]. It is any act that the person believes to be wrong [Ho, ICC1], or is not sure if it is right to do [SSA, TH]. The person whose highest priority is his own pleasure or fails to recognize God's lordship and give him thanks falls into an idolatry of the worst kind, in which the idol is self; all such living outside of the basic relation to God, which is faith, is sin [HNTC]. The principle Paul espouses is broader than eating, drinking, and closely related issues [NAC, WBC], and is saying that any action that does not spring from dependence on God and trust in him will by nature be marked by human presumption and self-indulgence, and is therefore sin [WBC]. Anything done that is contrary to the witness of one's own conscience is wrong [TNTC]. The conscience should not be violated, although it should be educated [St].

QUESTION—How does he use the term 'sin' here?
He is using it, not in the sense of sinful human nature, but of a particular act that should not be done [AB, ICC2, Mu, WBC]. To act against one's own convictions [Ho, Mu, WBC], or to do anything that is inconsistent with one's faith in God is to disrupt the relationship with God [WBC]. It is anything that is not in accord with the relation to Christ [Mor]. It is living in the false and negative relation to God which fails to acknowledge his lordship [HNTC].

DISCOURSE UNIT—15:1–13 [HNTC, Ho, Mor; NLT]. The topic is unity in love [HNTC], the example of Christ [Ho], Christian unity [Mor], living to please others [NLT].

DISCOURSE UNIT—15:1–6 [AB, Mu, NICNT, TNTC, WBC; CEV, NET, NRSV, TEV]. The topic is Christ is our model in all conduct [AB], Christ's example [Mu], put other people first [NICNT], the example of Christ [TNTC], Christ as exemplar [WBC], please others and not yourself [CEV, TEV], please others, not yourselves [NRSV], exhortation for the strong to help the weak [NET].

15:1 Now[a], we the strong[b] ought[c] to-bear-with[d] the weaknesses[e] of-those-not-strong[f]

LEXICON—a. δέ (LN 89.87, 89.93, 89.124) (BAGD 1, 2, 3. p. 171): This conjunction can mark a sequence of closely related events: 'and, and then' [LN (89.87)], or an additive relation that is not coordinate: 'and, and also, also, in addition, even' [LN (89.93)], or a contrast: 'but, on the other hand' [LN (89.124)]. It can emphasize a contrast: 'but', or mark a simple transition: 'now, then', or mark a resumption of an interrupted discourse: 'and also, but also' [BAGD]. Here it is translated 'now' [BECNT; NASB], 'so' [GW], 'then' [KJV], 'but' [ICC2, LN, NICNT; NET], not explicit [AB, HNTC, NTC, WBC; CEV, NCV, NIV, NLT, NRSV, REB, TEV].

b. δυνατός (LN 74.2) (BAGD 1.a.β. p. 208): 'strong' [AB, BAGD, BECNT, HNTC, ICC2, NICNT, NTC, WBC; all versions], 'able, capable' [LN]. The phrase 'now, we the strong' is translated 'if our faith is strong' [CEV], 'so those of us who have a strong faith' [GW], 'we who are strong in the faith' [TEV]. This noun denotes having the ability to perform some function [LN]. Paul includes himself in this category [ICC2].

c. pres. act. indic. of ὀφείλω (LN 71.25) (BAGD 2.a.β. p. 599): 'ought' [AB, BAGD, BECNT, HNTC, LN, NICNT, NTC, WBC; KJV, NASB, NET, NIV, NRSV, TEV], 'should' [CEV, NCV], 'must' [BAGD; GW, NLT, REB], 'to be under obligation' [LN], 'to be obligated' [BAGD], 'to have an obligation' [ICC2]. This verb indicates that something is obligatory in view of some moral or legal requirement [LN].

d. pres. act. infin. of βαστάζω (LN 25.177) (BAGD 2.b.β. p. 137): 'to bear with' [AB; NET, NIV], 'to bear' [BECNT, HNTC, NICNT, NTC; KJV,

NASB], 'to carry' [ICC2], 'to help...to carry' [TEV], 'to support' [WBC], 'to endure' [BAGD, LN], 'to put up with' [NRSV]. The phrase 'ought to bear' is translated 'should be patient with' [CEV], 'must be patient with' [GW], 'should help...with (their weaknesses)' [NCV], 'must be considerate of' [NLT], 'must accept as our own burden' [REB]. This verb means to continue to bear up under unusually trying circumstances and difficulties [LN].

e. ἀσθένημα (LN **74.24**) (BAGD p. 115): 'weakness' [BAGD, BECNT, HNTC, LN, NICNT, WBC; GW, NASB, NCV], 'tender scruple' [REB], 'failing' [AB, NTC; NET, NIV, NRSV], 'infirmity' [ICC2; KJV], 'burden' [TEV], not explicit [CEV, NLT]. This noun denotes an instance of weakness or limited capacity [LN]. This word occurs only here in the NT.

f. ἀδύνατος (LN **74.22**) (BAGD 1.b. p. 19): 'weak' [BAGD], 'not capable' [LN]. The phrase 'those not strong' is translated 'those who are not strong' [HNTC], 'those whose faith is not so strong' [GW], 'those without strength' [BECNT, NICNT, WBC; NASB], 'those who are not capable' [**LN**], 'the weak' [AB, ICC2, NTC; KJV, NCV, NET, NIV, NRSV, REB, TEV], 'the Lord's followers whose faith is weak' [CEV], 'those who are sensitive about things like this' [NLT]. This adjective describes not being able to do or experience something [LN].

QUESTION—What is the relationship between this section and what precedes?

The chapter division does not represent a genuine break in Paul's thought [BECNT, Ho, ICC1, Mor, WBC]. 15:1–3 sum up what Paul has been saying to the strong about the weak in the previous chapter [ICC2, NTC]. This section continues the same theme as in the previous chapter [Mu]. The conjunction δέ shows a link to the previous section, as though continuing a subject he has been discussing previously [Mor], and enlarging upon it [Gdt]. Paul continues the theme of unity, but a shift in vocabulary and argument indicates a slight shift in his discussion [NICNT].

QUESTION—What is Paul communicating by the use of the first person plural pronoun ἡμεῖς 'we'?

Paul is including himself among those whom he considers strong [AB, BECNT, Gdt, HNTC, ICC2, Mor, NAC, NICNT, NTC, St, TH, WBC]. The ἡμεῖς 'we' is emphatic [Mor].

QUESTION—In what sense are the strong 'to bear with' the weak?

He is calling for more than mere toleration [BECNT, ICC2, Mor, Mu, NAC, NICNT, NTC, SSA, TH, WBC]. They are to help bear the burdens of the weak [BECNT, Gdt, NAC, SSA, WBC]. They are to help them in their need [Mu, NTC], in their weakness [NTC], and in their difficulties [HNTC]. They are to support them and help compensate for their weakness [St]. They are to help or assist the weak with the encumbrances that they have due to their lack of inner freedom [ICC2]. They are to tolerate the weak rather than criticize them, but also they are to support and sustain them [Mor]. It does not mean that they must adopt the scruples of the weak, but they are to be sympathetic to the attitudes of the weak and instead of criticizing them, act in love toward them [NICNT]. They are to tolerate their weaknesses [HNTC, Ho], tolerate their scruples [ICC1]. They are to be willing to limit their own freedom to help the weak with their problems [TH].

and not (merely)[a] please[b] ourselves.
LEXICON—a. There is no lexical entry for 'merely' in the Greek text, it is implied. It is represented in translation as 'merely' [AB, BECNT], 'just' [NET, NLT, REB], 'only' [GW, NCV], not explicit [HNTC, ICC2, NICNT, NTC, WBC; KJV, NASB, NIV, NRSV, TEV].
   b. pres. act. infin. of ἀρέσκω (LN **25.90**) (BAGD 1. p. 105): 'to please' [BECNT, HNTC, ICC2, LN, NICNT, NTC, WBC; all versions except GW], 'to suit our own pleasure' [AB], 'to accommodate' [BAGD], 'to think of (ourselves)' [GW]. The phrase 'not merely please ourselves' is translated 'we should try to please them instead of ourselves' [CEV]. This verb means to cause someone to be pleased with someone or something [LN].
QUESTION—What is implied in this statement?
   They are to do more than just please themselves [AB, BECNT, Ho, NTC, TH; GW, NCV, NET, NLT, REB]. Paul is not telling them to abstain from any and every pleasure, but is telling them not to please themselves without regard to how doing so might affect others [ICC2, Mor, NTC, SSA], which in this case would be openly exercising their freedom to the extent that another person's faith would be hurt [ICC2]. Concern for those who are weaker is more important than personal preferences [Mor]. They are not to use their Christian liberty in a selfish way [NICNT]. Selfish concern should not be their motive [AB].

15:2 Let- each of-us -please (our) neighbor[a] for[b] good[c] for[d] edification.[e]
LEXICON—a. πλησίον (LN 11.89) (BAGD 1.b. p. 672): 'neighbor' [AB, BAGD, BECNT, HNTC, ICC2, LN, NICNT, NTC, WBC; GW, KJV, NASB, NCV, NET, NIV, NRSV, REB], 'other believers' [TEV], 'others' [NLT], not explicit [CEV].
   b. εἰς (LN 89.57): 'for' [AB, BECNT, ICC2, NICNT, NTC; KJV, NASB, NCV, NET, NIV, NRSV, REB, TEV], 'for the purpose of, in order to' [LN], 'with a view to' [WBC], not explicit [CEV, GW, NLT]. The phrase 'for good' is translated 'with some good purpose' [HNTC].
   c. ἀγαθός (BAGD 2.a.β. p. 3): 'good' [AB, BAGD, BECNT, ICC2, NICNT, NTC; CEV, KJV, NASB, NCV, NET, NIV, REB, TEV], 'good purpose' [HNTC; NRSV], 'good things' [GW], 'what is good' [WBC]. The clause 'Let each of us please our neighbor for good' is translated 'we should think of their good' [CEV], 'we should help others do what is right' [NLT]. This sentence is translated 'we should all be concerned about our neighbor and the good things that will build his faith' [GW].
   d. πρός with the accusative (LN 89.60) (BAGD III.3.a. p. 710): 'for' [BAGD, BECNT, NICNT], 'for the purpose of' [BAGD, LN], 'for the

sake of, in order to' [LN], 'so as to effect' [HNTC], 'with a view to' [ICC2, NTC, WBC], 'in order to' [TEV], 'to' [KJV, NASB, NCV, NET, NIV], 'and' [CEV, NLT, REB], 'that' [GW], not explicit [AB; NRSV]. This preposition marks purpose [LN].
  e. οἰκοδομή (LN 74.15) (BAGD 1.b.α. p. 559): 'edification' [BECNT, ICC2, NICNT, NTC; KJV, NASB], 'upbuilding' [WBC], 'building up' [HNTC; NRSV], 'building' [BAGD]. This noun is translated as a verb or verb phrase: 'to build up' [AB, LN; NET, NIV], 'to build them up in the Lord' [NLT], 'to try to help' [CEV], 'to build…faith' [GW], 'to help them be stronger in faith' [NCV], 'to build them up in the faith' [TEV], 'to build up the common life' [REB], 'to strengthen' [LN]. This noun denotes increasing the potential of someone or something, with focus upon the process involved [LN].

QUESTION—Does 'each of us' refer to only the strong or to both the strong and the weak?
  1. It refers to all Christians, the strong as well as the weak [Gdt, Mor]. Paul includes himself in this [Mor].
  2. It refers to strong Christians [BECNT, ICC2, NICNT, WBC].

QUESTION—What does Paul mean by 'please'?
  The following phrase 'for good for edification' qualifies what the 'pleasing' is: a person is to be concerned with the true good of the neighbor relative to the neighbor's salvation [ICC2]. It means to live in love, and so fulfill the command to love [NICNT]. It means to strengthen others in their faith [BECNT], to help them develop and mature as Christians [NAC]. It means to exercise benevolence in behalf of another to promote his spiritual welfare [Ho]. They are to try to help the weak maintain peace of conscience [Mu].

QUESTION—Who is the 'neighbor'?
  This is a reference to Lev 19:18 [AB, BECNT, NICNT, St, WBC], which was alluded to in 13:8–9 [BECNT, NICNT, St, WBC].
  1. It would be fellow Christians [BECNT, NAC, SSA, TH], or weak fellow Christians [NICNT].
  2. It would be anyone, whether Christian or not [Mor].

QUESTION—How does the phrase 'the good' relate to 'edification'?
  1. 'Edification' states more specifically what the 'good' is [Gdt, NICNT; NRSV]. It further clarifies [ICC2], and explains 'good' [HNTC, Ho, ICC1, Mor, NICNT]. They mutually explain one another [BECNT].
  2. They are represented in translation as two coordinate ideas mentioned in sequence [CEV, NLT, REB].

QUESTION—What is οἰκοδομή 'edification'?
  It relates to the neighbor's salvation [ICC2], his spiritual profit, [Mor, NICNT], his spiritual advantage [NTC], his spiritual maturity [SSA], his spiritual welfare [Ho]. This spiritual profit includes salvation [ICC2, NICNT], but its scope is broader than that [NICNT, WBC]. It stands in contrast to doing spiritual harm to the other person through insensitive behavior [NICNT]. It is growth toward Christian maturity [NAC, WBC]. It

is to help others grow in goodness, faith, and godliness [BECNT]. It is helping another become stronger in faith [TH]. It will include helping to educate and strengthen his conscience [St].

15:3 For[a] even[b] Christ did- not -please himself, but[c] as it-has-been-written, The reproaches[d] of-those reproaching[e] you fell[f] on me.

LEXICON—a. γάρ (LN 89.23) (BAGD 1.b. p. 151): 'for' [AB, BAGD, BECNT, HNTC, ICC2, LN, NICNT, NTC, WBC; KJV, NASB, NET, NIV, NLT, NRSV, TEV], not explicit [CEV, GW, NCV, REB].
  b. καί (LN 89.93): 'even' [AB, BECNT, HNTC, ICC2, LN, NICNT, NTC; CEV, KJV, NASB, NCV, NET, NIV, NLT], 'too' [WBC; REB], not explicit [GW, NRSV, TEV].
  c. ἀλλά (LN 89.126): 'but' [AB, BECNT, ICC2, LN, NICNT, NTC, WBC; CEV, KJV, NASB, NET, NIV, NRSV], 'rather' [GW], 'on the contrary' [HNTC, LN], 'instead' [TEV, LN], not explicit [NCV, NLT, REB].
  d. ὀνειδισμός (LN 33.389) (BAGD p. 570): 'reproach' [BAGD, BECNT, HNTC, ICC2, NICNT, NTC, WBC; KJV, NASB, REB], 'insult' [AB, BAGD, LN; GW, NET, NIV, NLT, NRSV, TEV]. This noun is translated as a verb: 'to insult' [CEV, NCV]. This noun connotes speaking disparagingly of a person in a manner which is not justified [LN].
  e. pres. act. participle of ὀνειδίζω (LN 33.389) (BAGD 1. p. 570): 'to reproach' [BAGD, BECNT, HNTC, ICC2, NICNT, NTC, WBC; KJV, NASB, REB], 'to revile, heap insults upon' [BAGD], 'to insult' [AB, LN; CEV, GW, NCV, NET, NIV, NLT, NRSV]. The clause 'the reproaches of those reproaching you fell on me' is translated 'the people who insulted you also insulted me' [CEV], 'when people insult you, it hurts me' [NCV], 'the insults which are hurled at you have fallen on me' [TEV]. This verb means to speak disparagingly of a person in a manner which is not justified [LN].
  f. aorist act. indic. of ἐπιπίπτω (LN 13.122) (BAGD 2. p. 297): 'to fall on' [HNTC, NICNT, NTC, WBC; GW, KJV, NASB, NET, NIV, NLT, NRSV, REB, TEV], 'to fall upon' [AB, BAGD, BECNT, ICC2, LN], not explicit [CEV, NCV]. This verb means to happen suddenly to, with the connotation of something bad and adverse [LN].

QUESTION—What relationship is indicated by γάρ 'for'?
  It indicates that what follows about Christ's example is the basis for the appeal in 15:1–2 [Gdt, ICC1, SSA]. We should please our fellow Christians since Christ set us an example by not doing things to please himself [SSA]. The strong should not think that giving in to others is incompatible with being strong, since even the Messiah did not please himself [NICNT].

QUESTION—Is there any significance in the use of the definite article ὁ with Χριστός 'Christ'?
  The words ὁ Χριστός are translated 'Christ' [AB, BECNT, HNTC, ICC2, NTC; all versions]; 'the Christ' [WBC], 'the Messiah' [SSA].

1. The article gives significance to 'Christ' as a title [ICC2, NICNT, SSA, WBC]. It calls attention to his messianic status [BECNT]. Even when Paul uses 'Christ' as a proper name, he is aware of its significance as a title [ICC2]. Paul is saying that even the Messiah did not just please himself [NICNT].
2. Paul does not seem to be using it as a title here [Mor]. (Note that the majority of commentaries do not comment one way or the other on this issue, meaning that they probably assume that 'Christ' is being used as a name.)

QUESTION—Who are the 'you' and the 'me' in this statement as Paul uses it?
1. Christ is addressing God [AB, BECNT, ICC2, Mor, NAC, NICNT, NTC, St]. However, Paul is applying it to how Christians should relate to one another [AB]. Paul is not saying that the pre-existent Christ actually said these words, but is using the passage typologically, that the suffering of the righteous person quoted in Psalm 69 is a type of the suffering Jesus [Gdt, WBC]. Paul has put the words of the Psalm on the lips of Jesus, so that Jesus is saying that the reproaches or insults people directed at God fell on himself instead [ICC2, NICNT].
2. Paul applies these words as though Christ is addressing human beings, whose sufferings and reproaches he bore [ICC1].

QUESTION—In what way did Christ not please himself?
It refers to his passion and crucifixion [AB, BECNT, Mu, NICNT]. This probably refers to the time when people reproached and taunted Christ at his crucifixion [NICNT]. It refers to all his suffering and to his self-sacrifice [NTC]. It refers to his incarnation [ICC2], and the character of his entire earthly life [HNTC, ICC2, NAC]. It refers primarily to the passion, but also to Jesus' entire earthly ministry [WBC].

QUESTION—What is meant by this statement?
Rather than focusing on God's wrath under which Christ suffered, Paul focuses here on the humiliation involved in Christ's suffering such reproach from people, since there is no good reason for the wrath that men have toward God, as it is irrational and absurd [ICC2, Mor]. He focuses on reproach from people because it was obvious and visible, whereas the wrath of God that Christ suffered was unseen [NTC]. Christ suffered from the anger of traditionalist Jews who were angered at the thought that God would equally be the God of the Gentiles as well as of the Jews [WBC].

QUESTION—How does Paul apply this passage and its implied application to Christ?
Paul is saying that since Christ was willing to suffer scorn for God's honor, the strong should be willing to limit their freedom for the sake of others [BECNT, Mu, WBC]. Jesus' self-sacrifice in serving others is a model to be imitated [NICNT]. Christ's example is both a model and a motive [Ho, Mor].

DISCOURSE UNIT—15:4–13 [GW]. The topic is God gives us unity.

15:4 For[a] whatever[b] was-written-beforehand,[c] was-written for[d] our instruction,[e]

LEXICON—a. γάρ (LN 89.23): 'for' [BECNT, HNTC, ICC2, LN, NICNT, NTC, WBC; KJV, NASB, NET, NIV, NRSV], 'and' [AB; CEV], not explicit [GW, NCV, NLT, REB, TEV].

b. ὅσος (LN 59.7): 'whatever' [BECNT, NICNT, NTC; NASB, NRSV], 'whatsoever' [ICC2; KJV], 'what' [AB], 'all the things' [HNTC], 'everything' [GW, NCV, NET, NIV, TEV], 'such things' [NLT], 'as much as' [LN, WBC], 'the Scriptures' [CEV, REB]. This adjective describes a comparative quantity of objects or events [LN].

c. aorist pass. indic. of προγράφω (LN **33.66**) (BAGD 1.b. p. 704): 'to be written beforehand' [BAGD, LN]. This aorist verb is translated 'written beforehand' [HNTC, NICNT, WBC], 'written in advance' [BECNT], 'written in former times' [NTC; NET], 'written in former days' [NRSV], 'written in earlier times' [BAGD; NASB], 'written long ago' [GW], 'written in the past' [NCV, NIV], 'written aforetime' [KJV], 'written formerly' [**LN**], 'written of old' [AB, ICC2], 'written in the Scriptures long ago' [NLT], 'the scriptures written long ago' [REB], 'written in the scriptures' [TEV], 'the Scriptures were written' [CEV]. This verb means to write in advance or in anticipation of [LN].

d. εἰς (LN 89.57) (BAGD 4.d. p. 229): 'for' [AB, BAGD, BECNT, HNTC, ICC2, NICNT, NTC, WBC; KJV, NASB, NET, NRSV, REB], 'for the purpose of' [LN], not explicit [CEV, GW, NCV, NIV, NLT, TEV]. This preposition marks intent, often with the implication of expected result [LN].

e. διδασκαλία (LN 33.224) (BAGD 1 p. 191): 'instruction' [AB, BECNT, HNTC, ICC2, NICNT, NTC, WBC; NASB, NET, NRSV, REB], 'teaching' [BAGD, LN], 'learning' [KJV]. This noun is translated as a verb: 'to teach' [CEV, GW, NCV, NIV, NLT, TEV]. It is instruction in a formal or informal setting [LN].

QUESTION—What relationship is indicated by γάρ 'for'?

It indicates 15:4 as providing the justification for how he uses the Scripture passage cited in the previous verse [Gdt, HNTC, ICC2, Mor, Mu, NICNT, WBC]. Or, instead of specifically being a reason for just the previous verse, it is better treated as a parenthetical comment giving a justification of Paul's use of Scripture both here and elsewhere in his letter [SSA].

in-order-that[a] through[b] endurance[c] and through the encouragement[d] of-the scriptures, we-might-have hope.[e]

LEXICON—a. ἵνα (LN 89.59): 'in order that' [ICC2, NICNT, NTC, WBC; REB, TEV], 'so that' [BECNT, LN; GW, NASB, NET, NIV, NRSV], 'that' [AB, HNTC; KJV], 'and' [NLT], not explicit [CEV, NCV].

b. διά with genitive (LN 89.76): 'through' [AB, BECNT, HNTC, LN, NICNT, NTC, WBC; GW, KJV, NASB, NET, NIV, REB, TEV], 'by' [LN; NRSV], 'with' [ICC2], not explicit [CEV, NCV, NLT]. This

preposition marks the means by which one event makes another event possible [LN].
c. ὑπομονή (LN 25.174) (BAGD 1. p. 846): 'endurance' [AB, BECNT, HNTC, NICNT; GW, NET, NIV], 'patient endurance' [ICC2, NTC], 'patience' [BAGD, WBC; KJV, NCV, TEV], 'perseverance' [NASB, REB], 'steadfastness' [NRSV], not explicit [CEV]. The phrase 'through endurance' is translated 'as we wait patiently for God's promises to be fulfilled' [NLT]. This noun denotes the capacity to continue to bear up under difficult circumstances [LN].
d. παράκλησις (LN 25.150) (BAGD 3. p. 618): 'encouragement' [AB, LN, NTC; GW, NASB, NCV, NET, NIV, NLT, NRSV, REB, TEV], 'comfort' [BAGD, ICC2, NICNT, WBC; KJV], 'consolation' [BAGD, BECNT], 'exhortation' [HNTC]. This noun is translated as a verb: 'to encourage (us)' [CEV]. It denotes the action of causing someone to be encouraged or consoled, either by verbal or non-verbal means [LN].
e. ἐλπίς (LN 25.59) (BAGD 2.b. p. 253): 'hope' [AB, BAGD, BECNT, HNTC, ICC2, LN, NICNT, NTC, WBC; all versions except GW], 'confidence' [GW]. The phrase 'we might have hope' is translated 'we might hold hope fast' [ICC2], 'we might hold fast hope' [WBC]. This entire clause is translated 'in order that through the encouragement they give us we may maintain our hope with perseverance' [REB]. This entire verse is translated 'and the Scriptures were written to teach and encourage us by giving us hope' [CEV]. This noun denotes looking forward with confidence to that which is good and beneficial [LN].

QUESTION—What relationship is indicated by the two uses of διά 'through'?
1. The first occurrence of the preposition indicates an attendant circumstance and the second occurrence indicates means or cause [ICC2, Mor, NICNT, WBC; REB]: in order that we might have hope *along with* endurance *by means of* the encouragement that comes from the Scriptures.
2. Both prepositions indicate means or cause [BECNT, Gdt, Ho, NAC, TH; NRSV; probably GW, KJV, NASB, NCV, NIV, TEV which use the preposition only once]: in order that we might have hope *by means of* the endurance *and* the encouragement that come from the Scriptures.

QUESTION—What area of meaning is intended by παράκλησις 'encouragement'?
1. It means encouragement [AB, Mor, NAC, NTC, SSA, St; GW, NASB, NCV, NET, NIV, NLT, NRSV, REB, TEV].
2. It means consolation or comfort [BAGD, BECNT, Gdt, Ho, ICC2, Mu, NICNT].

QUESTION—With what should τῶν γραφῶν 'of the Scriptures' be associated?
1. It is associated with 'encouragement' [AB, BECNT, HNTC, ICC2, Mor, NICNT, NTC, TNTC, WBC].
2. It is associated with both 'endurance' and 'encouragement' [Gdt, Ho, Mu, NAC, St, TH; CEV, GW, NCV]. Paul is speaking of the endurance that the Scripture teaches and the encouragement that it brings [NAC].

QUESTION—What is implied by his use of the present tense subjunctive verb ἔχωμεν in the phrase ἐλπίδα ἔχωμεν '(that) we might have hope'?

It indicates that an existing hope is to be strengthened and maintained [ICC2, NICNT, WBC].

15:5 Now^a may the God of-endurance and encouragement grant^b to-you

LEXICON—a. δέ (LN 89.94): 'now' [BECNT, NICNT; KJV, NASB, NET], 'and' [HNTC, LN; REB, TEV], not explicit [AB, ICC2, NTC, WBC; CEV, GW, NCV, NIV, NLT, NRSV]. This conjunction marks an additive relation, with some implication of contrast [LN]. It indicates that this prayer and wish is the conclusion of the paragraph [ICC2].

b. aorist act. optative of δίδωμι (LN 57.71) (BAGD p. 192): 'to grant' [AB, BECNT, HNTC, ICC2, NTC; KJV, NASB, NRSV, REB], 'to give' [BAGD, LN, NICNT, WBC; NET, NIV], 'to enable' [TEV], 'to help' [CEV, NLT], 'to allow' [GW, NCV]. This verb means to give an object, usually implying value [LN].

QUESTION—What is meant by the two genitives 'of endurance' and 'of encouragement'?

It indicates that God is the source or giver of endurance and encouragement [AB, BECNT, Gdt, HNTC, Ho, ICC2, Mor, Mu, NICNT, NTC, SSA, TH; GW, NASB, NCV, NIV, NLT, REB, TEV]. God enables us to be patient and cheerful [CEV].

QUESTION—What is the function of this sentence?

It expresses a wish that is also a prayer [BECNT, NTC, SSA, WBC]. Formally, this is a wish and not a prayer, since it is not addressed to God, yet it is more like prayer than exhortation, and here it may be called a prayer-wish [ICC2]. By expressing his prayer-wish, Paul indirectly uses it as a means of exhortation [Mu, NICNT]. Or, this prayer is not intended to be an exhortation at all [AB, Mor].

to-think^a the same among one-another according-to^b Christ Jesus.

LEXICON—a. pres. act. infin. of φρονέω (LN 26.16) (BAGD 1. p. 866): 'to think' [BAGD], 'to have an attitude, to think in a particular manner' [LN]. The phrase τὸ αὐτὸ φρονεῖν ἐν ἀλλήλοις 'to think the same among one another' [NICNT], is translated 'a spirit of mutual harmony' [AB], 'to be in harmony with one another' [BECNT], 'that you may have a common mind' [HNTC], 'to agree together among yourselves' [ICC2], 'to live in harmony with one another' [NTC; NRSV], 'to live in harmony among yourselves' [WBC], 'to live at peace with each other' [CEV], 'to live in harmony with each other' [GW, NCV], 'to be likeminded one toward another' [KJV], 'to be of the same mind with one another' [NASB], 'unity with one another' [NET], 'a spirit of unity among yourselves' [NIV], 'to live in complete harmony with each other' [NLT], 'to agree with one another' [REB], 'to have the same point of view among yourselves' [TEV]. This verb means to employ one's faculty for thoughtful planning, with emphasis upon the underlying disposition or attitude [LN].

b. κατά with accusative (LN 89.8) (BAGD II.5.a.α. p. 407): 'according to' [BAGD, BECNT, HNTC, ICC2, NICNT; KJV, NASB], 'in accord with' [AB, NTC], 'in accordance with' [LN, WBC; NET, NRSV], 'after the manner of' [REB], 'by following the example of' [GW, TEV], 'as you follow' [CEV, NIV], 'as is fitting for followers of' [NLT]. The phrase 'according to Christ Jesus' is translated 'the way Christ Jesus wants' [NCV]. This preposition marks a relation involving similarity of process [LN].

QUESTION—What is the agreement of thinking that Paul hopes they will experience?

He is not expecting them to hold the same opinions about the debated issues [BECNT, Mor, NAC, NICNT, NTC, St], but to have harmony among themselves [Mor], to have a common outlook and purpose [NICNT], to love one another and do Christ's will [NTC], to love and accept one another in their differences [BECNT]. He wants them to have the values and priorities of Christ [NAC]. He no doubt wishes they would agree on these issues he has been dealing with, but here he is looking beyond that to a more basic determination to obey the Lord Jesus and have mutual respect and sympathy toward each other as brothers should [ICC2]. He wants them to have unity in essentials [NAC]. He wants them to have mutual esteem for one another [Mu]. They are to have communion of heart and pursue the same supreme good [Gdt].

QUESTION—What relationship is indicated by the phrase 'according to Christ Jesus' modify?

The unity would be in accord with the example of Christ [Ho, ICC1, SSA, TH] and with his character [ICC1], as well as with the command of Christ [Ho]. The unity could be in accord with the example of Christ, or perhaps with the will or spirit of Christ [NICNT]. It is a unity that is in accord both with the will as well as the example of Christ [BECNT, Mu, NTC, WBC]. Paul himself is not going to presume to say what the content of that should be, only that it should be in accord with the will of Christ Jesus [ICC2]. He wants them to have a unity that is in accord with Christ Jesus, which only God can give [Mor]. Christ himself is the model of Christian unity [AB] and Christian conduct [NAC]. The person of Jesus Christ is the focus of Christian unity, and the more Christians agree with him and about him, the more likely they will be to agree with each other [NAC].

15:6 **so-that[a] with-one-mind[b] with one mouth[c] you-may-glorify[d] the God and father of-our Lord Jesus Christ.**

LEXICON—a. ἵνα (LN 89.59): 'so that' [AB, BECNT, LN, NTC; NASB, NET, NIV, NRSV, TEV], 'in order that' [ICC2, NICNT, WBC], 'that' [HNTC; KJV], 'then' [CEV, GW, NCV, NLT], 'and so' [REB]. This conjunction marks purpose for events and states (sometimes occurring in highly elliptical contexts) [LN].

b. ὁμοθυμαδόν (LN 31.23) (BAGD p. 566): 'with one mind' [AB, BAGD, BECNT, LN, WBC; KJV, REB], 'with one accord' [HNTC, NICNT; NASB], 'with one heart' [ICC2, NTC; NIV], 'together' [CEV, NET, NRSV, TEV], 'having the same goal' [GW]. The phrase ἵνα ὁμοθυμαδόν 'so that with one mind' is translated 'you will all be joined together' [NCV], 'then all of you can join together' [NLT]. This adverb describes something as involving mutual consent or agreement [LN].

c. στόμα (LN 33.74) (BAGD 1.a. p. 770): 'mouth' [BAGD, BECNT, HNTC, ICC2, NICNT, NTC; KJV, NIV], 'voice' [AB, WBC; NASB, NET, NLT, NRSV, REB, TEV], 'speech' [LN], not explicit [CEV, GW, NCV].

d. pres. act. subj. of δοξάζω (LN 33.357) (BAGD 1. p. 204): 'to glorify' [AB, BECNT, HNTC, ICC2, LN, NICNT, NTC, WBC; KJV, NASB, NET, NIV, NRSV], 'to give glory' [NCV], 'to praise' [BAGD, LN; CEV, GW, TEV], 'to honor, to magnify' [BAGD], 'to give praise and glory' [NLT]. This verb means to speak of something as being unusually fine and deserving honor [LN].

QUESTION—In the phrase τὸν θεὸν καὶ πατέρα τοῦ κυρίου ἡμῶν Ἰησοῦ Χριστοῦ 'the God and father of our Lord Jesus Christ' how are we to understand the relation of 'God' to what follows?

1. He is both the God as well as the father of the Lord Jesus Christ [AB, BECNT, Gdt, HNTC, ICC1, ICC2, Mor, Mu, NICNT, NTC, WBC; GW, NASB, NET, NIV, NRSV, REB, TEV]. He is 'God' to Jesus with respect to Jesus' humanity, that is, his existence as a human being [Mor, NTC], and 'father' with respect to his divine nature [NTC].
2. God is the father of the Lord Jesus Christ [SSA; CEV, KJV, NCV, NLT]. Here καί would mean 'even' [KJV]: God, even the father of our Lord Jesus Christ.

QUESTION—What is meant by 'with one mouth'?

It means 'with one voice' [AB, ICC2, NICNT, WBC; NASB, NET, NLT, NRSV, REB, TEV], that is, as being united [NICNT], in one accord [ICC2], joined together [CEV, NCV], praising God together in unity [BECNT, TH], worshipping God together [St, TNTC], singing the hymn of redeemed humanity [Gdt]. Harmony in Christian living glorifies God, which is the goal of all Christian existence [AB]. Faith and worship are expressed in speech [WBC].

DISCOURSE UNIT—15:7–13 [AB, Mu, NICNT, TNTC, WBC; CEV, NET, NRSV, TEV]. The topic is welcome all who turn to Christ as Lord, Jew and Gentile [AB], Jews and Gentiles (are) one [Mu], receive one another [NICNT], Christ and the Gentiles [TNTC], concluding summary: God's mercy and faithfulness—Jew first, but also Gentile [WBC], the good news is for Jews and Gentiles [CEV], exhortation to mutual acceptance [NET], the gospel for Jews and Gentiles alike [NRSV], the gospel to the Gentiles [TEV].

15:7 Therefore[a] accept[b] one-another just-as[c] Christ also has-accepted you, to[d] the glory of-God.

TEXT—Instead of ὑμᾶς 'you' some manuscripts have ἡμᾶς 'us'. GNT selects the reading 'you' with an A rating, indicating that the text is certain. The reading 'us' is taken by KJV, NASB, REB.

LEXICON—a. διό (LN 89.47): 'therefore' [BECNT, LN, NICNT, WBC; GW, NASB, NLT, NRSV], 'so' [HNTC; NCV], 'then' [AB, NTC; NET, NIV, TEV], 'so then' [LN], 'wherefore' [ICC2; KJV], 'in a word' [REB], not explicit [CEV]. This conjunction is a relatively emphatic marker of result, usually denoting the fact that the inference is self-evident [LN].

   b. pres. mid. impera. of προσλαμβάνω (LN 34.53) (BAGD 2.b. p. 717): 'to accept' [BAGD, BECNT, LN, NTC; CEV, GW, NASB, NCV, NIV, NLT, REB, TEV], 'to receive' [BAGD, ICC2, LN, NICNT; KJV, NET], 'to welcome' [AB, HNTC, LN, WBC; NRSV], 'to take' [BAGD]. This verb means to accept the presence of a person with friendliness [LN]. It is an acceptance that is genuine and heartfelt [NAC].

   c. καθώς (LN 64.14) (BAGD 1. p. 391): 'just as' [BAGD, BECNT, LN, NICNT, NTC; NASB, NET, NIV, NLT, NRSV], 'as' [AB, BAGD, HNTC, WBC; CEV, KJV, REB, TEV], 'in the same way' [GW], 'because' [ICC2]. The clause 'receive one another as Christ has also received you' is translated 'Christ accepted you, so you should accept each other' [NCV]. This conjunction describes similarity in events and states, with the possible implication of something being in accordance with something else [LN].

   d. εἰς (LN 89.48): 'to' [HNTC, ICC2, NICNT, NTC, WBC; KJV, NASB, NET, REB], 'for' [AB, BECNT; NRSV, TEV], 'with the result that, so that as a result, to cause' [LN]. The phrase 'to the glory of God' is translated 'in order to bring praise to God' [NIV], 'which will bring glory to God' [NCV], 'so that God will be given glory' [NLT], 'he did this to bring glory to God' [GW], 'honor God by accepting...' [CEV]. This preposition marks result, with the probable implication of a preceding process [LN].

QUESTION—What relationship is indicated by διό 'therefore'?

It indicates the paragraph that follows as the conclusion to be drawn from all that he has said since 14:1 [BECNT, HNTC, ICC1, ICC2, NICNT, SSA, WBC]. It draws a conclusion from what was just said in the previous verse about glorifying God together [Ho].

QUESTION—What relationship is indicated by καθώς 'just as'?

   1. It indicates similarity of manner [SSA, WBC; GW]: in the same way as Christ has accepted you.

   2. It indicates a causal relation [BECNT, ICC2, NICNT]: because Christ has accepted you.

QUESTION—What action does 'to the glory of God' modify?
1. It modifies 'accept one another' [AB, Gdt, Ho, ICC2, NICNT, SSA, TH, TNTC; CEV, NCV, TEV; probably NIV, NRSV]: Glorify God by accepting one another.
2. It modifies 'Christ accepted you' [ICC1, Mu; GW, KJV, NASB]: Christ glorified God by accepting you.
3. It modifies both clauses [BECNT, HNTC, NAC, WBC], but primarily modifies 'Christ accepted you' [HNTC, WBC].

15:8 For,ᵃ I-say,ᵇ Christ has-becomeᶜ a servantᵈ of- (the) -circumcisionᵉ

LEXICON—a. γάρ (LN 89.23): 'for' [AB, BECNT, HNTC, ICC2, LN, NICNT, NTC, WBC; NASB, NET, NIV, NRSV, TEV], 'now' [KJV], not explicit [CEV, GW, NCV, NLT, REB]. This conjunction marks cause or reason between events, though in some contexts the relation is often remote or tenuous [LN].
b. pres. act. indic. of λέγω (LN 33.69) (BAGD II.1.e. p. 469): 'to say' [BECNT, LN, NICNT; KJV, NASB], 'to declare' [BAGD, ICC2, NTC, WBC], 'to tell' [AB, HNTC, LN; CEV, NCV, NET, NIV, TEV]. The phrase λέγω γάρ 'for I say' is translated 'let me explain' [GW], 'remember that' [NLT, REB]. This verb means to speak or talk, with apparent focus upon the content of what is said [LN].
c. perf. pass. infin. of γίνομαι (LN 13.48): 'to become' [LN]. This perfect tense infinitive is translated as a perfect tense finite verb: 'has become' [BECNT, HNTC, ICC2, NICNT, NTC, WBC; NASB, NET, NIV, NRSV]; as an aorist tense finite verb: 'became' [AB; GW, NCV, REB], 'came (as)' [CEV, NLT], 'was' [KJV], 'was on behalf of' [TEV]. This verb means to come to acquire or experience a state [LN].
d. διάκονος (LN 35.20) (BAGD 1.b. p. 184): 'servant' [AB, HNTC, LN, NICNT, NTC, WBC; CEV, GW, NASB, NCV, NET, NIV, NLT, NRSV, REB], 'minister' [BECNT, ICC2; KJV]. The clause 'Christ has become a servant of' is translated 'Christ's life of service was on behalf of' [TEV]. This noun denotes a person who renders service [LN].
e. περιτομή (BAGD 4.a. p. 653): 'circumcision' [BAGD, BECNT, HNTC, ICC2, NICNT; KJV, NASB], 'circumcised' [AB, NTC, WBC; NET, NRSV], 'Jews' [CEV, NCV, NIV, NLT, TEV], 'Jewish people' [GW, REB]. In this sentence the noun 'circumcision' is used as a metonymy to represent the Jews, whose males were to be circumcised [NICNT, SSA].

QUESTION—What relationship is indicated by γάρ 'for'?
It indicates that what follows is the grounds for the exhortation just given [Mor]. It relates 15:8–12 to the main clause of 15:7, which is 'accept one another...to the glory of God' [ICC2]. It indicates that what follows is further grounds for the exhortation to accept one another in 15:7 [HNTC, Mu]. It indicates that what follows is a further explication of what he just said about Christ accepting Jews and Gentiles for the glory of God [BECNT].

QUESTION—What is the function of λέγω 'I say'?

It functions rhetorically to indicate that what follows is an especially solemn doctrinal statement [ICC2, NICNT, WBC]. It gives additional emphasis [Mor, SSA]. It introduces a clarification or explanation of what he meant that Christ accepted them [Ho].

QUESTION—What significance, if any, is there in the use of the perfect tense of the verb γίνομαι 'has become'?

Christ's ministry to the Jews continues even to the present [Gdt, HNTC, ICC2, Mor, NICNT, SSA, WBC], and is not confined to his earthly life [NICNT]. Christ's being a servant is a permanent state [Mor].

QUESTION—How does he use the term περιτομή 'the circumcision'?

1. He is referring to the Jews as those whom Christ served [BECNT, HNTC, Ho, ICC2, Mu, NICNT, SSA, TH, TNTC, WBC], but circumcision also is significant as a sign of the covenant [Mor, Mu]. Christ fulfilled his mission as a minister of that covenant of which circumcision was the sign, and brings that covenant to fruition [Mu]. This is a metonymy [SSA].
2. The use of the genitive case of this noun means that Christ's origin was from among the Jews; that is, he was Jewish [Gdt].
3. He is a minister of circumcision in the sense that he carries out the promises of the Mosaic covenant, of which the seal was circumcision [ICC1].

on-behalf-of[a] (the) truth[b] of-God in-order-to[c] confirm[d] the promises[e] (to) the patriarchs,[f]

LEXICON—a. ὑπέρ with genitive (LN 90.36) (BAGD 1.b. p. 838): 'on behalf of' [LN; NASB, NET, NIV, NRSV, TEV], 'in behalf of' [BAGD], 'for' [KJV], 'for the sake of' [BECNT, ICC2, LN, NICNT, NTC, WBC], 'for the vindication of' [HNTC], 'to show' [AB; CEV, NCV, NLT], 'to reveal' [GW], 'to maintain' [REB]. This preposition marks a participant who is benefited by an event or on whose behalf an event takes place [LN].

b. ἀλήθεια (LN 72.2) (BAGD 1 p. 35): 'truth' [BECNT, HNTC, NICNT, NTC, WBC; GW, KJV, NASB, NET, NIV, NRSV], 'truthfulness, dependability, uprightness' [BAGD], 'fidelity' [AB], 'faithfulness' [ICC2; REB]. The phrase 'on behalf of the truth of God in order to confirm the promises' is translated 'to show that God has kept the promises he made' [CEV], 'to show that God is true to the promises he made' [NLT], 'to show that God is faithful, to make his promises...come true' [TEV], 'to show that God's promises...are true' [NCV]. This noun denotes the content of that which is true and thus in accordance with what actually happened [LN].

c. εἰς (LN 89.57): 'in order to' [BECNT, ICC2, LN], 'in order that' [NRSV], 'so as to' [HNTC], 'to' [AB, NICNT, NTC, WBC; KJV, NASB, NET, NIV, TEV], 'by' [REB], 'as a result' [GW], not explicit [CEV, NCV, NLT]. This preposition marks intent, often with the implication of expected result [LN].

d. aorist act. infin. of βεβαιόω (LN 24.88) (BAGD 1. p. 138): 'to confirm' [AB, BAGD, BECNT, HNTC, LN, NICNT, NTC, WBC; KJV, NASB, NET, NIV, NRSV], 'to establish' [BAGD, ICC2], 'to fulfill' [GW], 'to verify, to prove to be true and certain' [LN]. This verb means to cause something to be known as certain [LN].

e. ἐπαγγελία (LN 33.288) (BAGD 2.a. p. 280): 'promise' [AB, BAGD, BECNT, HNTC, ICC2, NICNT, NTC, WBC; all versions]. This noun denotes the content of what is promised [LN].

f. πατήρ (LN 10.20): 'patriarch' [AB; NIV, NRSV, REB], 'father' [BECNT, HNTC, ICC2, NICNT, NTC, WBC; KJV, NASB, NET], 'ancestor' [LN; NLT, TEV], 'Jewish ancestor' [NCV], 'ancestor of the Jewish people' [GW], 'famous ancestor' [CEV], 'forefather' [LN]. The genitive construction τῶν πατέρων '(to) the patriarchs' indicates that the promises were made to the patriarchs [AB, BECNT, HNTC, ICC2, Mor, NICNT, NTC, WBC; all versions]. This noun denotes a person several preceding generations removed from the reference person [LN].

QUESTION—What relationship is indicated by ὑπέρ in the phrase 'on behalf of God's truth'?

It indicates the purpose of Christ's being a servant, which was to show that God is faithful [AB, BECNT, ICC2, NICNT], that his promises are true [BAGD].

QUESTION—What promises is Paul referring to?

They are the promises made to the Jewish people [HNTC, NICNT]. They are the messianic promises [Gdt, HNTC, SSA], the promises made to the patriarchs [Ho, ICC2]. They are the promises of salvation God made to the Jews [BECNT]. One of those promises was the one in Gen 22:18 that God would bless all the nations of the world through Abraham [NAC].

QUESTION—In what way did Christ confirm the promises?

He did this by fulfilling the promises [Gdt, ICC2, NAC, NICNT, SSA, TH], thus proving that they were reliable [ICC2, NICNT]. He showed his fidelity to those promises [Gdt], his faithfulness to the covenant [WBC]. He vindicated God's truthfulness by fulfilling the promises [Ho, Mu]. He describes how Christ fulfilled those promises in Rom 9–11 [BECNT].

15:9 and (so that) the Gentiles[a] might-glorify[b] God for[c] (his) mercy,[d]

LEXICON—a. ἔθνη (LN 11.37): 'Gentiles' [AB, BECNT, HNTC, ICC2, NICNT, NTC, WBC; CEV, KJV, NASB, NET, NIV, NLT, NRSV, REB, TEV], 'people who are not Jewish' [GW], 'those who are not Jews' [NCV], 'heathen, pagan' [LN]. This plural noun usually denotes those who do not belong to the Jewish or Christian faith [LN].

b. aorist act. infin. of δοξάζω (LN 33.357) (BAGD 1. p. 204): 'to glorify' [AB, BECNT, HNTC, ICC2, NICNT, NTC; KJV, NASB, NET, NIV, NRSV, REB], 'to give glory' [NCV, NLT], 'to praise' [BAGD, LN, WBC; CEV, GW, TEV], 'to honor, to magnify' [BAGD]. This verb

means to speak of something as being unusually fine and deserving honor [LN].
c. ὑπέρ with genitive (LN 89.28) (BAGD 1.d. p. 839): 'for' [AB, HNTC, ICC2, NICNT, NTC, WBC; all versions], 'for the sake of' [BECNT], 'because of, in view of' [LN]. This preposition marks cause or reason, often with the implication of something which has been beneficial [LN].
d. ἔλεος (LN 88.76) (BAGD 2.b. p. 250): 'mercy' [AB, BAGD, BECNT, HNTC, ICC2, NICNT, NTC, WBC; all versions]. This noun denotes kindness or concern that is shown for someone in serious need [LN].

QUESTION—What is the relation of this clause to what precedes?
1. Paul's assertions in 15:8b and 15:9 are purpose clauses dependent on 'Christ has become a servant' in 15:8a. That is, Christ became a servant in order to confirm the promises and in order that the Gentiles would glorify God [BECNT, HNTC, ICC1, Mor, Mu, NAC, NICNT, SSA, TNTC; CEV, KJV, NASB, NCV, NIV, NLT, NRSV, TEV]. Christ became a servant for the purposes of showing God's truth or fidelity and for confirming the promises, and with the result, which was also purposed, that the Gentiles would glorify God [AB].
2. Paul's assertions in 15:8 and 15:9a are dependent on 'I say' in 15:8. That is, I say that Christ has become a servant...and/but that the Gentiles are glorifying God [Gdt, Ho, ICC2; NET].
3. Paul's statement in 15:8 that Christ became a servant, etc., is supported by two clauses indicating the means. That is, Christ became a servant to maintain the faithfulness of God by fulfilling his promises to the patriarchs and by causing the Gentiles to glorify God [REB].

as it-is-written, Because[a] of-this I-will-give-praise[b] to-you among (the) Gentiles and I-will-sing-praise[c] to- your -name.[d]
LEXICON—a. διά (LN 89.26): 'because of, on account of, by reason of' [LN]. The phrase διὰ τοῦτο 'because of this' [NICNT; NET] is also translated 'for this reason' [BECNT, WBC], 'for this cause' [HNTC; KJV], 'for this' [NLT], 'that is why' [GW], 'therefore' [AB, NTC; NASB, NIV, NRSV, REB], 'wherefore' [ICC2], 'so' [NCV], 'and so' [TEV], not explicit [CEV]. This conjunction marks cause or reason, with focus upon instrumentality, either of objects or events [LN].
b. fut. mid. indic. of ἐξομολογέω (LN 33.359) (BAGD 2.c. p. 277): 'to give praise' [NASB], 'to praise' [BAGD, BECNT, HNTC, ICC2, LN, NICNT, NTC; NCV, NIV, NLT, REB, TEV], 'to give thanks' [GW], 'to proclaim' [AB], 'to tell' [CEV], 'to confess' [BAGD, WBC; KJV, NET, NRSV]. This verb means to express praise or honor, with a possible implication of acknowledging the nature of someone or something, and occurs in the NT only in quotations from the Septuagint [LN].
c. fut. act. indic. of ψάλλω (LN 33.111) (BAGD p. 891): 'to sing praise' [AB, BAGD, HNTC, WBC], 'to sing praises' [LN, NICNT; CEV, GW, NCV, NET, NLT, NRSV, TEV], 'to sing hymns' [ICC2, NTC; NIV,

REB], 'to sing' [BAGD, BECNT, LN; KJV, NASB]. This verb means to sing songs of praise, with the possible implication of instrumental accompaniment [LN].

d. ὄνομα (LN 33.126) (BAGD I.4.b. p. 572): 'name' [AB, BAGD, BECNT, HNTC, ICC2, LN, NICNT, NTC, WBC; all versions except TEV], 'you' [TEV]. The phrase 'your name' is used as a metonymy for the pronoun 'you' [SSA].

QUESTION—Who is the speaker in this statement of praise?
1. It is a messianic passage, as though Christ were speaking [Gdt, ICC1, ICC2]. It is David, but as representing Christ [Gdt, NICNT].
2. It is David, and Israel whom he represents [BECNT, WBC].

15:10 And again he-says, Rejoice,[a] Gentiles, with his people.[b]

LEXICON—a. aorist pass. impera. of εὐφραίνω (LN 25.131) (BAGD 2. p. 327): 'to rejoice' [AB, BAGD, BECNT, HNTC, ICC2, NICNT, NTC, WBC; KJV, NASB, NIV, NLT, NRSV, TEV], 'to be made glad' [BAGD], 'to be happy' [GW, NCV], 'to join in celebration' [REB], 'to come and celebrate' [CEV]. This verb means to be caused to be or become happy or glad [LN].

b. λαός (LN 11.12) (BAGD 3.a. p. 466): 'people' [AB, BAGD, BECNT, HNTC, ICC2, NICNT, NTC, WBC; all versions]. This noun is a collective term for people who belong to God [LN].

15:11 And again, Praise[a] the Lord, all the Gentiles, and let- all the peoples[b] -praise[c] him.

LEXICON—a. aorist pass. impera. of αἰνέω (LN 33.354) (BAGD p. 23): 'to praise' [AB, BAGD, BECNT, HNTC, ICC2, LN, NICNT, NTC, WBC; all versions]. This verb means to speak of the excellence of a person, object, or event [LN].

b. λαός (LN 11.55) (BAGD 3.a. p. 466): 'nation, people' [LN]. This plural noun is translated 'peoples' [AB, BAGD, BECNT, HNTC, ICC2, NICNT, NTC, WBC; NASB, NET, NIV, NRSV, REB, TEV], 'people' [KJV, NCV], 'people of the earth' [NLT], 'people of the world' [GW], 'nations' [CEV]. This noun represents the largest unit into which the people of the world are divided on the basis of their constituting a socio-political community [LN].

c. aorist act. impera. of ἐπαινέω (LN 33.354) (BAGD p. 281): 'to praise' [BAGD, HNTC, ICC2, LN, NICNT, NTC, WBC; GW, NASB, NET, NLT, NRSV, REB, TEV], 'to give praise' [BECNT], 'to sound praise' [AB], 'to sing praises' [NCV, NIV], 'to laud' [KJV], 'to worship' [CEV]. This verb means to speak of the excellence of a person, object, or event [LN].

15:12 and again Isaiah says, The shoot[a] of-Jesse will-come,[b] even[c] the-one rising-up[d] to rule[e] the Gentiles, on[f] him the Gentiles will-hope.[g]

LEXICON—a. ῥίζα (LN **10.33**) (BAGD 2. p. 736): 'shoot' [BAGD, BECNT, WBC], 'root' [AB, HNTC, LN, NICNT, NTC; GW, KJV, NASB, NET, NIV, NRSV], 'descendant' [**LN**], 'offspring' [LN], 'scion' [BAGD, ICC2; REB]. The phrase 'the shoot of Jesse' is translated 'someone from David's family' [CEV], 'a new king...from the family of Jesse' [NCV], 'the heir to David's throne' [NLT]. The noun ῥίζα 'root' refers to a shoot springing from the root, which is Christ [AB, BAGD, BECNT, ICC2, Mor, NAC, NICNT, NTC, WBC]. This figurative extension of 'root' denotes a descendant, with probable connotations of continuing relation [BAGD, LN].

b. fut. mid. (deponent = act.) indic. of εἰμί (LN 13.69): 'to come' [BECNT, NICNT; NASB, NCV, NET, NLT, NRSV, REB], 'to come forth' [WBC], 'to appear' [AB; TEV], 'to spring up' [NTC; NIV], 'to be' [HNTC, ICC2, LN; GW, KJV]. The phrase Ἔσται...καὶ ὁ ἀνιστάμενος 'will come, even the one rising up' is translated 'will come to power' [CEV].

c. καί (LN 89.93): 'even' [BECNT, LN, NICNT, WBC], 'and' [HNTC, ICC2, LN; KJV, NASB, NET, NLT], not explicit [AB, NTC; CEV, GW, NCV, NIV, NRSV, REB, TEV]. This conjunction marks an additive relation which is not coordinate [LN].

d. pres. mid. participle of ἀνίστημι (BAGD 2.a. p. 70): 'to rise up' [BECNT, HNTC], 'to rise' [AB, BAGD, ICC2; GW, KJV, NET, NRSV, REB], 'to arise' [LN, NICNT, NTC, WBC; NASB, NIV], 'to come' [TEV], 'to come into existence, to appear' [LN], not explicit [CEV, NLT]. The phrase ὁ ἀνιστάμενος ἄρχειν 'the one rising up to rule' is translated 'he will come to rule' [NCV]. The verb ἀνίστημι 'rise' is frequently used with reference to the resurrection, and Paul probably is intending a double reference [NAC, WBC]. This verb means to come into existence, and it implies assuming a place or position [LN].

e. pres. act. infin. of ἄρχω (LN **37.54**) (BAGD 1. p. 113): 'to rule' [AB, BAGD, BECNT, HNTC, ICC2, **LN**, NICNT, WBC; CEV, GW, NRSV, TEV], 'to rule over' [NTC; NASB, NCV, NET, NIV, NLT], 'to reign over' [KJV], 'to govern' [LN; REB]. This verb means to rule or govern, with the implication of preeminent position and status [LN].

f. ἐπί with dative (LN 90.57) (BAGD II.1.b.γ. p. 287): 'on' [BAGD, ICC2, LN, NICNT; NLT, REB], 'in' [AB, BECNT, HNTC, NTC, WBC; CEV, KJV, NASB, NET, NIV, NRSV, TEV], not explicit [GW, NCV]. This preposition marks an experiencer [LN].

g. fut. act. indic. of ἐλπίζω (LN 25.59) (BAGD 3. p. 252): 'to hope' [BAGD, BECNT, HNTC, ICC2, LN, NICNT, NTC, WBC; NASB, NET, NIV, NRSV], 'to have hope' [NCV], 'to find hope' [AB], 'to put (their) hope' [CEV, TEV], 'to place (their) hope' [NLT], 'to set (their) hope' [REB], 'to trust' [KJV]. The clause 'on him the Gentiles will hope' is translated 'he will give the nations hope' [GW], 'they will have hope

324 ROMANS 15:12

because of him' [NCV]. This verb means to look forward with confidence to that which is good and beneficial [LN].

15:13 Now,[a] may- the God of-hope[b] -fill[c] you with[d] all joy and peace[e] in[f] believing[g]

LEXICON—a. δέ (LN 89.94): 'now' [BECNT, NICNT; KJV, NASB, NET], 'and' [LN; REB], 'so' [AB], not explicit [HNTC, ICC2, NTC, WBC; CEV, GW, NCV, NIV, NLT, NRSV, TEV]. This conjunction marks an additive relation, but has the possible implications of some contrast [LN]. Here it indicates a transition to something new [Mor].

b. ἐλπίς (LN 25.59) (BAGD 2.b. p. 253): 'hope' [AB, BAGD, BECNT, HNTC, ICC2, LN, NICNT, NTC, WBC]. The genitive phrase ὁ θεὸς τῆς ἐλπίδος 'the God of hope' is translated 'God who gives hope' [CEV], 'God who is thus the ground of hope' [HNTC]. This noun denotes looking forward with confidence to that which is good and beneficial [LN].

c. aorist act. optative of πληρόω (LN 59.37) (BAGD 1.b. p. 671): 'to fill' [AB, BAGD, BECNT, HNTC, ICC2, LN, NICNT, NTC, WBC]. The phrase πληρῶσαι ὑμᾶς πάσης χαρᾶς 'fill you with all joy' is translated 'bless you with complete happiness' [CEV], 'fill you completely' [NLT]. This verb means to cause something to become full [LN].

d. There is no lexical entry for the word 'with' in the Greek text, it is supplied to express the relationship indicated by the genitive case of the noun phrase πάσης χαρᾶς 'all joy'. It is represented in translation as 'with' [AB, BECNT, HNTC, ICC2, NICNT, NTC, WBC; all versions].

e. εἰρήνη (LN **25.248**) (BAGD 3. p. 227): 'peace' [AB, BAGD, BECNT, HNTC, ICC2, LN, NICNT, NTC, WBC; all versions]. This noun denotes a state of freedom from anxiety and inner turmoil [LN].

f. ἐν (LN 67.33, 89.76, 89.26): 'in' [AB, BECNT, HNTC, ICC2, WBC; KJV, NASB, NRSV], 'as (you believe/trust)' [NICNT; NET, NIV], 'as (you lead the life of faith)' [REB], 'in the exercise of (your faith)' [NTC], 'when' [LN (67.33)], 'while' [NCV], 'through' [LN (89.76); GW], 'by means of' [LN (89.76); TEV], 'because' [NLT], 'because of' [LN (89.26)].

g. pres. act. infin. of πιστεύω (LN 31.85) (BAGD 2.b.): 'to believe' [BAGD], 'to believe in, to trust, to have faith in' [LN]. This infinitive is translated as a participle: 'believing' [AB, BECNT, ICC2, WBC; KJV, NASB, NRSV]; as a noun phrase: 'your faith' [HNTC, NTC; CEV, GW, TEV]; as a finite verb: 'you believe' [NICNT], 'you believe in him' [NET], 'you trust in him' [NCV, NIV, NLT], 'you lead the life of faith' [REB]. This verb means to believe to the extent of complete trust and reliance [LN].

QUESTION—How are the nouns related in the genitive phrase ὁ θεὸς τῆς ἐλπίδος 'the God of hope'?

1. God is the source of hope, or gives hope [BECNT, HNTC, Ho, ICC2, NICNT, SSA, TH, TNTC; CEV, GW, NCV, NLT, TEV]. He is the

ground of hope [HNTC; REB]. He gives people confidence that he will do what he promised [SSA].
2. God is both the source of hope as well as the object of hope [Mor, Mu, WBC].

QUESTION—What is the nature of this peace?
1. It is social in nature, referring to relationships among believers [NICNT].
2. It is personal in nature [Mor, Mu]. It refers to the believer's peace of mind, which in this case is a fruit of peace with God [Mor]. It is peace with God [ICC1].
3. It is personal as well as social [Ho, WBC]. It is concord with each other, peace of conscience, and peace with God [Ho].

QUESTION—What relationship is indicated by ἐν 'in'?
1. It indicates instrumentality; they experience these by believing [Gdt, Ho, ICC2, TH].
2. It marks attendant circumstance [LN, Mor, SSA].

so-that^a you may-abound^b in^c hope by^d (the) power^e of-(the) Holy Spirit.

LEXICON—a. εἰς (LN 89.57): 'so that' [AB, BECNT, ICC2, NTC; NASB, NET, NIV, NRSV], 'that' [HNTC, WBC; KJV], 'in order that' [NICNT], 'with the result that, so that as a result' [LN], 'then (you will)' [GW, NLT], 'then (your hope will)' [NCV, TEV], 'until (you)' [REB], not explicit [CEV]. This preposition marks intent, often with the implication of expected result [LN].
b. pres. act. infin. of περισσεύω (LN 59.52) (BAGD 1.b.α. p. 651): 'to abound' [AB, BAGD, BECNT, HNTC, ICC2, LN, NICNT; KJV, NASB, NET, NRSV, REB], 'to be in abundance' [LN], 'to overflow' [NTC, WBC; GW, NCV, NIV, NLT], 'to continue to grow' [TEV]. This clause is translated 'and may the power of the Holy Spirit fill you with hope' [CEV]. This verb means to be or exist in abundance, with the implication of being considerably more than what would be expected [LN]. Paul wants them to have nothing less than a full measure of hope [Mor].
c. ἐν (LN 89.5): 'in' [AB, BECNT, HNTC, ICC2, LN, NICNT, WBC; KJV, NASB, NET, NRSV], 'with' [NTC; CEV, GW, NIV, NLT, REB], 'with regard to' [LN], not explicit [NCV, TEV]. This preposition marks an area of activity which bears some relation to something else [LN].
d. ἐν (LN 90.10): 'by' [AB, BECNT, ICC2, LN, NICNT, NTC; GW, NASB, NCV, NET, NIV, NRSV, REB, TEV], 'through' [KJV, NLT], 'in' [HNTC, WBC], 'with' [LN], not explicit [CEV]. This preposition marks an immediate instrument [LN].
e. δύναμις (LN 76.1) (BAGD 1. p. 207): 'power' [AB, BAGD, BECNT, HNTC, ICC2, LN, NICNT, NTC, WBC; all versions]. This noun denotes the potentiality to exert force in performing some function [LN].

QUESTION—What relationship is indicated by ἐν 'by'?
1. It is instrumental [BECNT, Ho, ICC2, NICNT, SSA, TNTC]. It indicates the agency of the Holy Spirit [Mu, TH].

2. It indicates location ('in') as well as instrument ('by') [WBC].

DISCOURSE UNIT—15:14–16:27 [Gdt, ICC2, Mor, NAC, NICNT, St, TNTC, WBC]. The topic is epistolary conclusions [Gdt], conclusion [Mor, NAC, WBC], conclusion to the epistle [ICC2], the letter closing [NICNT], epilogue [TNTC], the providence of God in the ministry of Paul [St].

DISCOURSE UNIT—15:14–16:23 [BECNT]. The topic is the extension of God's righteousness through the Pauline mission.

DISCOURSE UNIT—15:14–33 [AB, BECNT, HNTC, Ho, Mu, NICNT, TNTC, WBC; GW]. The topic is Paul's plans, coming task, and request for prayers [AB], the establishment of churches among the Gentiles [BECNT], Paul's plans and God's purpose [HNTC], Paul's confidence in the Romans and his plans to visit [Ho], Paul's Gentile ministry, policy, and plans [Mu], Paul and his plans [NAC], Paul's ministry and travel plans [NICNT], Paul's mission and travel plans [WBC], personal narrative [TNTC], Paul's desire to tell the good news to the world [GW].

DISCOURSE UNIT—15:14–24 [AB]. The topic is Paul's missionary principle in his work so far; his desire to visit the Romans in route to Spain.

DISCOURSE UNIT—15:14–22 [Mor, NAC, St]. The topic is the minister of the Gentiles [Mor], Paul's ministry to the Gentiles [NAC], his apostolic service [St].

DISCOURSE UNIT—15:14–21 [ICC1, NICNT, WBC; CEV, NCV, NET, NIV, NLT, NRSV, TEV]. The topic is an apology for admonitions [ICC1], looking back: Paul's ministry in the east [NICNT], Paul's mission [WBC], Paul talks about his work [NCV], Paul's work as a missionary [CEV], Paul the minister to the Gentiles [NIV], Paul's motivation for writing the letter [NET], Paul's reason for writing [NLT], Paul's reason for writing so boldly [NRSV, TEV].

15:14 Now[a] my brothers,[b] I also myself have-been-convinced[c] concerning[d] you

LEXICON—a. δέ (LN 89.94): 'now' [BECNT], 'but' [HNTC, ICC2, NICNT; NET], 'and' [LN; KJV, NASB], not explicit [AB, NTC, WBC; CEV, GW, NCV, NIV, NLT, NRSV, REB, TEV].

 b. ἀδελφός (LN 11.23). This plural noun is translated 'brothers' [AB, ICC2, NTC, WBC; NIV], 'brothers and sisters' [BECNT, NICNT; CEV, NCV, NET, NRSV], 'dear brothers and sisters' [NLT], 'brethren' [HNTC; KJV, NASB], 'friends' [CEV, REB, TEV]. This noun denotes a close associate of a group of persons having a well-defined membership, which in the NT refers specifically to fellow believers in Christ [LN]. The addition of μου 'my', gives special warmth to this vocative noun [ICC2, WBC].

 c. perf. pass. indic. of πείθω (LN 33.301) (BAGD 4. p. 640): 'to be convinced' [AB, BAGD, LN, NTC, WBC; GW, NASB], 'to be fully

convinced' [NET, NLT], 'to be persuaded' [BECNT, ICC2, LN; KJV], 'to be confident' [HNTC, NICNT], 'to feel confident' [NRSV], 'to be sure' [CEV, NCV], 'to feel sure' [TEV]. The phrase 'I also myself have been convinced' is translated 'I have no doubt in my mind' [REB].
d. περί with genitive (LN 90.24): 'concerning' [BECNT, ICC2, LN, NICNT, WBC; NASB], 'about' [AB, HNTC, LN; NET], 'of' [LN; KJV], not explicit [NTC; CEV, GW, NCV, NIV, NLT, REB, TEV]. This preposition marks general content, whether of a discourse or mental activity [LN].

QUESTION—What relationship is indicated by δέ 'now'?
1. It expresses some degree of contrast [HNTC, ICC1, ICC2, NICNT; NET].
2. It is transitional, indicating no sense of contrast with what has preceded it [Mor].

QUESTION—What is the function of his use of the phrase καὶ αὐτὸς ἐγώ 'I also myself'?

The phrase 'I also myself' is emphatic [AB, BECNT, ICC1, ICC2, Mor, Mu, NAC, TH, WBC]. It expresses his personal confidence about their maturity in Christian living [AB]. Paul is saying that, despite some of the things he has said earlier, he does not find their faith deficient [Mor], or that he lacks confidence in their Christian growth [Gdt]. It emphasizes his conviction about what he is saying [ICC2, NAC, SSA, WBC], as well as his feeling for the believers in Rome, whom he did not know personally [SSA, WBC]. It implies that others held this opinion as well [Mu]. It implies that he held this opinion apart from the testimony of others [Ho]. The phrase καὶ αὐτοί 'you yourselves also', which follows, emphasizes the fact that Paul acknowledges that the Roman Christians are mature believers [ICC2, WBC], and capable of dealing appropriately with one another in their grasp of gospel truth [ICC2], and that they had grown spiritually without his help [NAC].

that[a] also[b] you-yourselves are full-of[c] goodness,[d]

LEXICON—a. ὅτι (LN 90.21): 'that' [AB, BECNT, HNTC, ICC2, LN, NICNT, NTC, WBC; all versions], 'the fact that' [LN]. This conjunction marks discourse content, whether direct or indirect

b. καί (LN 89.93): 'also' [LN; KJV], 'too' [GW], not explicit [AB, BECNT, HNTC, ICC2, NICNT, NTC, WBC; all versions except GW, KJV]. This conjunction marks an additive relation that is not coordinate [LN].

c. μεστός (LN 68.77) (BAGD 2.a. p. 508): 'full of' [AB, BAGD, BECNT, ICC2, LN, NICNT, WBC; all versions except CEV, GW], 'rich in' [NTC], 'filled with' [GW], 'to be constantly engaged in' [LN], 'very' [CEV]. This adjective describes being extensively engaged in some activity or attitude [LN].

d. ἀγαθωσύνη (LN 88.1) (BAGD p. 3): 'goodness' [AB, BAGD, BECNT, HNTC, LN, NICNT, NTC, WBC; all versions except CEV], 'honesty' [ICC2]. This noun is translated as an adjective: 'good' [LN; CEV]. It denotes positive moral qualities of the most general nature [LN].

QUESTION—What is the 'goodness' that they are full of?
It is honesty and frankness in their dealings with one another [ICC2]. It is kindness [St]. It includes uprightness, kindness, and general benevolence, and is opposed to whatever would be evil or mean [Mu]. They are inclined to do good and act kindly toward others [SSA]. 'Goodness' here is love, as the rule of Christian conduct [TH]. The descriptions in this verse generally describe them as spiritually mature [BECNT, Gdt]. Paul's language here may be polite hyperbole [NAC, St], but it is not insincere [Gdt, St].

having-been-filled[a] (with)-all[b] knowledge[c] and being-able[d] to-admonish[e] one-another.

LEXICON—a. perf. pass. participle of πληρόω (LN 59.37) (BAGD 1.b. p. 671): 'to be filled' [BAGD, LN]. This participle is translated 'filled with' [BECNT, ICC2, NICNT, NTC, WBC; KJV, NASB, NET, NRSV], 'equipped with' [AB; REB], 'replete with' [HNTC], 'you have' [TEV]. The phrase πεπληρωμένοι πάσης [τῆς] γνώσεως 'having been filled with all knowledge' is translated 'complete in knowledge' [NIV], 'you have all the knowledge you need' [CEV, GW, NCV], 'you know these things so well' [NLT]. He is speaking here of a deep and comprehensive understanding of the principles of Christian faith [ICC1]. This verb means to cause something to become full [LN].

b. πᾶς (LN 59.23, 58.28): 'all' [AB, BECNT, HNTC, ICC2, LN (59.23), NICNT, NTC, WBC; CEV, GW, KJV, NASB, NCV, NET, NRSV, TEV], 'of every kind' [LN (58.28); REB], not explicit [NIV]. This adjective describes the totality of any object, mass, collective, or extension [LN (59.23)], or a totality of kinds or sorts [LN (58.28)].

c. γνῶσις (LN 28.17): 'knowledge' [AB, BECNT, HNTC, ICC2, LN, NICNT, NTC, WBC; all versions except NLT], 'to know' [NLT]. This noun denotes the content of what is known [LN].

d. pres. middle or passive (deponent = act.) participle of δύναμαι (LN 74.5): 'to be able to' [BECNT, HNTC, ICC2, LN, NICNT, WBC; GW, KJV, NASB, NCV, NET, NRSV, TEV], 'to be well able to' [REB], 'can' [LN; NLT], not explicit [CEV]. This participle is translated as an adjective: 'capable' [AB], 'competent' [NTC; NIV]. This verb means to be able to do or to experience something [LN].

e. pres. act. infin. of νουθετέω (LN 33.418, 33.231, 33.424) (BAGD p. 544): 'to admonish' [AB, BAGD, HNTC, ICC2, LN (33.418), NICNT, NTC, WBC; KJV, NASB], 'to rebuke' [LN (33.418)], 'to warn' [BAGD, LN (33.424)], 'to instruct' [BAGD, BECNT, LN (33.231); GW, NET, NRSV], 'to teach' [LN (33.231); CEV, NCV, NLT, TEV], 'to give advice' [REB]. This verb means to admonish someone for having done something wrong [LN (33.418)], or to provide instruction as to correct behavior and belief [LN (33.231)], or to advise someone concerning the dangerous consequences of some happening or action [LN (33.424)].

QUESTION—What area of meaning is intended with the verb νουθετέω 'to admonish'?

It refers to admonishing [AB], of correcting what is amiss in someone [ICC2, Mor], and urging the person to do what is right [ICC2]. It speaks of the willingness to try to influence the thinking and disposition of others by teaching, warning, and correction [WBC]. It is to appeal to the will for moral change [NAC]. It is teaching and admonishing [St], instructing, warning, and encouraging [TH]. It is to speak the truth at the right time to address the mind and conscience [Ho]. It refers generally to instruction [BECNT, SSA], which would include admonition, correction, and rebuke, but it would not be limited to those [BECNT].

15:15 But[a] I-wrote to-you boldly[b] in part[c] as reminding[d] you,

LEXICON—a. δέ (LN 89.124): 'but' [BECNT, HNTC, ICC2, LN, WBC; CEV, NASB, NCV, NET, TEV], 'yet' [AB], 'now' [NICNT], 'nevertheless' [NTC; KJV, NRSV, REB], 'however' [GW], 'even so' [NLT], not explicit [NIV]. This conjunction marks contrast [LN].
  b. τολμηρός (LN **25.162**) (BAGD p. 822): 'boldly' [LN], 'very boldly' [NASB], 'rather boldly' [BAGD, BECNT, ICC2, NICNT, NTC, WBC; NRSV], 'more boldly' [NET], 'rather bold' [GW], 'quite boldly' [AB; NIV], 'the more boldly' [KJV], 'somewhat boldly' [HNTC; REB], 'very openly' [NCV], 'plainly' [CEV]. The phrase 'I wrote to you boldly' is translated 'I have been bold enough to write' [NLT], 'in this letter I have been quite bold' [TEV]. This comparative adverb describes an activity as involving unusual boldness or daring [LN].
  c. ἀπὸ μέρους (LN 63.15) (BAGD 1.c. p. 506): 'in part' [BAGD, LN]. This idiom is translated 'on some points' [BAGD, BECNT, NICNT, NTC; NASB, NET, NIV, NRSV], 'about some of these points' [NLT], 'about some things' [NCV], 'about certain subjects' [LN (29.10)], '(of/about) some things' [CEV, NCV], 'in some sort' [KJV], 'partly (to remind)' [AB], 'in part (as a way of reminding)' [WBC], 'partly with the intention (of reminding)' [HNTC], 'in part (of my letter)' [ICC2], '(letter)…parts of which' [GW], 'at times' [REB].
  d. pres. act. participle of ἐπαναμιμνῄσκω (LN **29.10**) (BAGD p. 282): 'to remind' [AB, BAGD, BECNT, **LN**, NICNT, WBC; NET, NIV], 'to remind again' [NASB], 'to try to remind' [CEV], 'to put (you) in remembrance' [ICC2], 'to put (you) in mind' [KJV], 'as a reminder' [GW], 'to cause to remember, to cause to think about again' [LN]. The phrase ὡς ἐπαναμιμνῄσκων ὑμᾶς 'as reminding you' is translated 'reminding you of what you already know' [HNTC]. The phrase ἀπὸ μέρους ὡς ἐπαναμιμνῄσκων ὑμᾶς 'in part as reminding you' is translated 'about some things I wanted you to remember' [NCV], 'all you need is this reminder' [NLT]. This verb means to cause to recall and to think about again [LN]. This word occurs only here in the NT.

QUESTION—What does 'in part' modify?
1. It refers to some parts of the letter [BAGD, BECNT, ICC1, ICC2, LN (29.10), NAC, NICNT, NTC, SSA, WBC; GW, NASB, NET, NIV, NLT, NRSV, REB, TEV]: I wrote to you boldly in parts of this letter. These were the parts of the letter in which Paul has written rather boldly [NICNT]. These parts were where he was making some emphatic point [BAGD, BECNT, LN (29.10), NTC; NASB, NET, NIV, NLT, NRSV, TEV]: I wrote to you boldly on some points.
2. Part of his purpose was to remind them [AB, Gdt, HNTC]: I wrote to you partly with the intention of reminding you. Or, Paul is reminding them of things that they already knew and were partly remembering, that is, to a certain degree [Gdt].
3. It moderates 'boldly', meaning that he has written somewhat boldly [Mu]. He has written, perhaps, somewhat too boldly [Ho].

QUESTION—What did Paul write as a reminder?
He is reminding them of the great truths of the gospel and also how they ought to live as Christians [Mor]. He is reminding them of things they already know [AB, ICC1, ICC2, NAC, WBC]. He is recalling to their minds the recognized principles of Christianity [ICC1], the basic tenets of Christian faith [NAC]. He is referring to the exhortations of 12:1–15:13 [SSA]. The apostles reminded the churches of the original message of the gospel, and would continually call them back to it [St].

because-of^a the grace^b given^c to-me by^d God

LEXICON—a. διά with accusative (LN 89.26) (BAGD B.II.1. p. 181): 'because of' [BAGD, BECNT, HNTC, ICC2, LN, NICNT, NTC; KJV, NASB, NET, NIV, NRSV, TEV], 'by virtue of' [AB, WBC], 'in virtue of' [REB], 'on account of' [LN], 'because' [GW, NCV], 'for by' [NLT], not explicit [CEV]. This preposition marks cause or reason, with focus upon instrumentality, either of objects or events [LN].
b. χάρις (LN 57.103) (BAGD 4. p. 878): 'grace' [AB, BAGD, BECNT, HNTC, ICC2, NICNT, WBC; KJV, NASB, NET, NIV, NLT, NRSV], 'gift' [LN; REB], 'gracious gift' [LN], 'privilege' [TEV]. This phrase is translated 'because of the commission God in his grace has granted me' [NTC], 'God was so kind to me!' [CEV], 'I'm doing this because God gave me the gift' [GW], 'I did this because God gave me this special gift' [NCV]. This noun denotes that which is given freely and generously [LN].
c. aorist pass. participle of δίδωμι (LN 57.71): 'to be given' [AB, BECNT, ICC2, LN, NICNT, WBC; KJV, NASB, NET, NRSV], 'to give' [GW, NCV, NIV, TEV], 'to grant' [NTC], not explicit [CEV, NLT]. The phrase 'given to me by God' is translated 'I have from God' [REB]. This verb means to give an object, usually implying value [LN].
d. ὑπό (LN 90.1): 'by' [AB, BECNT, LN, NICNT; NET, NRSV], 'from' [HNTC, ICC2, WBC; NASB, REB], 'of' [KJV], not explicit [NTC; CEV,

GW, NCV, NIV, NLT, TEV]. This preposition marks agent or force, whether person or event [LN].

QUESTION—What relationship is indicated by διά 'because of'?

It indicates the basis of Paul's authority to write to the Romans Christians as he has, which is his commission as an apostle [BECNT, ICC2], and the grace God gave him for his apostolic ministry [BECNT, Mor]. His apostolic ministry, which is an expression of God's grace, is the basis of his speaking so boldly [WBC]. It indicates the reason he dares to write as boldly as he did [Mu]. It indicates the means by which God fulfills his purpose of reaching the Gentiles, which is that he commissioned and empowered Paul to preach to them [SSA]. It is in virtue of the mission and gift he has been given that Paul writes to them in this way [Gdt].

15:16 that[a] I-should-be a minister[b] of-Christ Jesus to the Gentiles, serving-as-a-priest[c] the gospel[d] of-God,

LEXICON—a. εἰς (LN 89.57): 'for the purpose of, in order to' [LN]. The infinitive phrase εἰς τὸ εἶναί 'that I should be' [KJV] is also translated 'so that I should be' [BECNT], 'so that I might be' [WBC], 'that I might be' [HNTC], 'with the purpose that I might be' [NICNT], 'to be' [AB, ICC2, NTC; GW, NASB, NCV, NET, NIV, NRSV], 'he chose me to be' [CEV], '(privilege) of being' [TEV], 'I am' [NLT], '(his grace) has made me' [REB]. This preposition marks intent, often with the expectation of expected result [LN].

b. λειτουργός (LN 35.23) (BAGD 2. p. 471): 'minister' [AB, BECNT, HNTC, ICC2, NICNT, NTC, WBC; KJV, NASB, NCV, NET, NIV, NRSV, REB], 'servant' [BAGD, LN; CEV, GW, TEV], 'special messenger' [NLT]. This noun denotes a person who renders special service [LN].

c. pres. act. participle of ἱερουργέω (LN **53.85**) (BAGD p. 373): 'to serve as a priest' [BECNT, **LN**, NICNT, WBC], 'to act as a priest' [HNTC], 'to be a priest' [LN], 'to minister as a priest' [NASB], 'to serve like a priest' [NET], 'to perform holy service' [BAGD], 'to serve with a holy service' [ICC2], 'to minister' [KJV], 'to be a minister in the priestly service' [NRSV]. The phrase ἱερουργοῦντα τὸ εὐαγγέλιον τοῦ θεοῦ 'serving as a priest the gospel of God' is translated 'with the priestly duty of preaching God's gospel' [AB], 'with the priestly duty of proclaiming the gospel of God' [NTC], 'to do the work of a priest in the service of his good news' [CEV], 'to serve as a priest by spreading his good news' [GW], 'I serve God by teaching his good news' [NCV], 'to be a minister...with the priestly duty of proclaiming the gospel of God' [NIV], 'I am a special messenger...I bring you the good news' [NLT], 'in the service of the gospel of God it is my priestly task' [REB], 'I serve like a priest in preaching the good news from God' [TEV]. This verb means to serve as a priest in the performance of religious rites and duties [LN]. This word occurs only here in the NT.

d. εὐαγγέλιον (LN 33.217) (BAGD 2.b.α., 2.b.β. p. 318): 'gospel' [AB, BAGD, BECNT, HNTC, LN, NICNT, NTC, WBC; KJV, NASB, NET, NIV, REB], 'the good news' [LN; CEV, GW, NCV, NLT, TEV], 'message of good news' [ICC2]. This noun denotes the content of good news, which in the NT refers to the gospel about Jesus [LN].

QUESTION—What relationship is indicated by εἰς τὸ εἶναι 'that I should be'?
  1. It indicates purpose [BECNT, ICC2, Mor, Mu, NICNT, SSA, WBC]: that I should be.
  2. It indicates result [REB]: it has made me.

QUESTION—What is implied by his use of the verb ἱερουργέω 'to serve as a priest'?
  Paul views proclaiming the gospel as a sacred act [ICC2, Mor]. It speaks of the dignity of the gospel ministry [Mu]. Paul's preaching and evangelism were acts of worship [AB]. Paul's function can be compared to the service of the Levites in the temple [AB, ICC2]. This verb, like the noun λειτουργός 'minister' that preceded it and the mention of 'offering' and 'sanctified' in the next verse are clearly cultic terminology, that is, references to the Jewish religious and sacrificial system [WBC]. All these words have associations with priestly and sacrificial system [St], and are the language of religious ceremony [NAC].

QUESTION—What relationship is indicated by the genitive construction τὸ εὐαγγέλιον τοῦ θεοῦ 'the gospel of God'?
  The gospel originates with God [Mor, SSA], showing that it is sacred [Mor]. It is God's gospel [AB, ICC2].

in-order-that[a] the offering[b] of-the Gentiles may-be acceptable,[c] having-been-sanctified[d] by[e] the Holy Spirit.

LEXICON—a. ἵνα (LN 89.59): 'in order that' [HNTC, ICC2, NICNT, NTC, WBC; GW, TEV], 'so that' [AB, BECNT, LN; CEV, NASB, NCV, NET, NIV, NLT, NRSV], 'that' [KJV], 'in order to, for the purpose of that' [LN], not explicit [REB]. This conjunction marks the purpose for events and states, sometimes occurring in highly elliptical contexts [LN].
  b. προσφορά (LN 53.16) (BAGD 2. p. 720): 'offering' [AB, BAGD, BECNT, HNTC, ICC2, LN, NICNT, NTC, WBC; NCV, NET, NIV, NLT, NRSV, TEV], 'my offering' [NASB], 'offering up' [KJV], 'sacrifice' [LN], 'gift' [BAGD], 'that which is brought' [BAGD], 'bring as an offering' [GW], 'to offer...as a sacrifice' [REB]. This noun denotes that which is offered to God in religious activity [LN].
  c. εὐπρόσδεκτος (LN **25.86**) (BAGD 1. p. 324): 'acceptable' [AB, BAGD, BECNT, HNTC, ICC2, NICNT, NTC, WBC; all versions except CEV, NCV], 'very acceptable' [**LN**], 'pleasing' [CEV], 'quite pleasing' [LN], 'that God would accept' [NCV]. This adjective describes that which is particularly acceptable, and hence quite pleasing [LN].
  d. perf. pass. participle of ἁγιάζω (LN 53.44, 88.26) (BAGD 2. p. 8, 4. p. 9): 'to be sanctified' [BAGD (2.), BECNT, HNTC, ICC2, NICNT,

NTC, WBC; KJV, NASB, NET, NIV, NRSV], 'to be consecrated' [AB, BAGD, LN; REB], 'to be dedicated' [BAGD (2.); TEV], 'to be dedicated to God' [LN], 'to be purified' [BAGD (4.)], 'to be made holy' [LN (88.26); GW, NLT]. The phrase 'sanctified by the Holy Spirit' is translated '(so that) the Holy Spirit could make (the Gentiles) holy' [CEV]. This passive verb means to be dedicated to the service of and to loyalty to deity [LN (53.44)], or to be caused to have the quality of holiness [LN (88.26)].
- e. ἐν (LN 90.6): 'by' [AB, BECNT, ICC2, LN, NICNT, NTC, WBC; all versions except CEV], 'in' [HNTC], not explicit [CEV]. This preposition marks agency, often with the implication of an agent being used as an instrument [LN].

QUESTION—What relationship is indicated by the genitive construction ἡ προσφορὰ τῶν ἐθνῶν 'the offering of the Gentiles'?
1. 'Gentiles' is in apposition to 'offering' [AB, BECNT, Gdt, HNTC, Ho, ICC1, ICC2, Mor, Mu, NAC, NICNT, SSA, St, TH, TNTC, WBC; CEV, GW, NCV, NET, NIV, NLT, REB, TEV]: the Gentiles are the offering. The Gentiles who have come to faith are Paul's priestly offering to God [ICC2]. This is a metaphor in which Paul pictures himself as a priest who uses the gospel as the means by which he offers a sacrifice to God, the Gentile converts representing the sacrifice [NICNT]. The acceptable offering is repentant human beings [AB].
2. It refers to Paul's act of offering the Gentiles [KJV, NASB, NRSV].

QUESTION—What is it that Paul wants to be acceptable?
1. Believing Gentiles themselves are acceptable to God and holy [Ho, ICC1, ICC2, Mor, Mu, NAC, NICNT, SSA, St, TH, TNTC].
2. Paul's wants his act of offering the Gentiles to be acceptable to God, and the Gentiles themselves are holy [BECNT].

15:17 Therefore[a] I-have boasting[b] in Christ Jesus concerning[c] the-things pertaining-to God.

LEXICON—a. οὖν (LN 89.50): 'therefore' [AB, BECNT, LN, NICNT, WBC; KJV, NASB, NIV], 'then' [ICC2, LN, NTC; NRSV, TEV], 'so' [GW, NCV, NET, NLT], 'here then (is)' [HNTC], 'indeed' [REB], 'consequently, accordingly, so then' [LN], not explicit [CEV]. This conjunction marks result, often implying the conclusion of a process of reasoning [LN].
- b. καύχησις (LN 33.368) (BAGD 1. p. 426): 'boasting' [BAGD, LN]. The phrase 'I have boasting in Christ Jesus' [BECNT] is also translated 'I have this boasting in Christ Jesus' [NICNT, WBC], 'I have this boast in Christ Jesus' [AB], 'I boast in Christ Jesus' [NET], 'in Christ Jesus…I have reason to boast' [NRSV], 'in Christ Jesus I have found reason for boasting' [NASB], 'this glorying…I have in Christ Jesus' [ICC2], 'here…is the glorying I have in Christ Jesus' [HNTC], 'I glory in Christ Jesus' [NIV], 'I have whereof I may glory through Christ Jesus' [KJV],

'because of Christ Jesus I can take pride' [CEV], 'so Christ Jesus gives me the right to brag' [GW], 'I am proud of what I have done (for God) in Christ Jesus' [NCV], 'I have reason to be enthusiastic about all Christ Jesus has done through me' [NLT], 'in Christ Jesus I have indeed grounds for pride' [REB], 'in union with Christ Jesus...I can be proud' [TEV], 'in Christ Jesus...I have the right to glory' [NTC]. This noun denotes expressing an unusually high degree of confidence in someone or something as being exceptionally noteworthy [LN].

c. There is no lexical entry for 'concerning' in the Greek text, but it is added to show the relation indicated by the neuter accusative plural definite article τά 'the things'. The phrase τὰ πρὸς τὸν θεόν 'concerning the things of God' is translated 'in what pertains to God' [AB], 'in things pertaining to God' [NASB], 'in the things pertaining to God' [BECNT], 'with regard to what pertains to God' [ICC2], 'about the things that pertain to God' [NET], 'in those things which pertain to God' [KJV], 'in reference to what concerns God' [WBC], 'with respect to the things of God' [NICNT], 'with respect to my work for God' [NTC], 'in my service for/to God' [CEV, NIV, NLT], 'in the service of God' [REB], 'of my service for God' [TEV], 'about what I'm doing for God' [GW], 'of what I have done for God' [NCV], 'of my work for God' [NRSV]. The article τά is an adverbial accusative or accusative of reference, and the prepositional phrase that follows is to be taken as a substantive [NICNT].

QUESTION—What relationship is indicated by οὖν 'therefore'?

It indicates a conclusion drawn from what God has done in Paul with regard to the Gentiles [Mor]. It indicates Paul's affirmation that he has reason for boasting about his ministry, as mentioned in the previous verses, which is what God has done in his behalf [BECNT, Gdt, WBC]. It indicates 15:15b–16 as the grounds for his boasting [Mu].

QUESTION—What does 'I have boasting' mean?

1. He boasts [AB, HNTC, ICC2, Mu, NICNT, WBC; NCV, NET, NIV]. The boasting is what he has said in 15:16 [ICC2]. He is proud of his work [SSA, TH], but this is not to be understood in the negative sense that 'boast' has in English [SSA]. He had confidence in joy in the ministry God had worked through him [Ho].
2. He has a basis for boasting [BECNT, Gdt, Mor, NAC, NTC; CEV, GW, KJV, NASB, NLT, NRSV, REB, TEV]: in Christ Jesus I have reason to boast.

QUESTION—What is boasting 'in Christ Jesus'?

Whatever he has done has been done by God working through him and by the strength that Christ has given him [Mor]. It is glorying in what Christ does through him [BECNT, ICC2, NAC; NLT] in the things of God [ICC2]. All Paul had accomplished was to be attributed to Christ [Ho]. He boasts of what he has done for Christ, and for which Christ gave him the grace enabling him to do it [AB]. Christ was acting through Paul, so Paul could take no credit for what was accomplished [WBC]. 'In Christ Jesus' refers to his union with or relationship to Christ [SSA, TH].

QUESTION—What 'things of God' is he referring to?

It is his ministry [BECNT, Mor], done in Christ with reference to the things that concern God [Mor]. It is his mission work, done in obedience to God [ICC2]. It is the service of God [WBC], his work for God [SSA]. It is that which pertains to the gospel and kingdom of God, as expressed in previous verses [Mu]. It is the preaching and success of the gospel [Ho].

15:18 For[a] I-will- not -dare[b] to-speak[c] anything[d]

LEXICON—a. γάρ (LN 89.23): 'for' [AB, BECNT, HNTC, ICC2, LN, NICNT, NTC, WBC; KJV, NASB, NET, NRSV], 'in fact' [CEV], 'yet' [NLT], not explicit [GW, NCV, NIV, REB, TEV]. This conjunction marks cause or reason between events, though in some contexts the relation is often remote or tenuous [LN].

b. fut. act. indic. of τολμάω (LN 25.161) (BAGD 1.b. p. 822): 'to dare' [AB, BAGD, HNTC, ICC2, LN, NICNT, NTC; KJV, NET, NLT], 'to presume' [BECNT, WBC; NASB], 'to be bold' [TEV], 'to be bold enough' [GW], 'to venture' [NIV, NRSV, REB]. The negative statement 'I will not dare to speak anything' is translated positively: 'I will venture to speak only of' [REB], 'I will be bold and speak only about' [TEV], 'I'm bold enough to tell you only about' [GW], 'all I will talk about is' [CEV]. This verb means to be so bold as to challenge or defy possible danger or opposition [LN].

c. pres. act. infin. of λαλέω (LN 33.70): 'to speak' [AB, ICC2, LN, NICNT, NTC; KJV, NASB, NET, NIV, REB, TEV], 'to talk' [LN], 'to talk about' [CEV, NCV], 'to say' [BECNT, HNTC, LN, WBC], 'to tell' [LN; GW], 'to boast' [NLT]. This verb means to speak or talk [LN].

d. τὶς (LN 92.12) (BAGD 1.b.α. p. 820): 'anything' [AB, BAGD, BECNT, HNTC, ICC2, LN, NICNT, NTC, WBC; NASB, NCV, NET, NIV, NLT, NRSV], 'of any of those things' [KJV], not explicit [GW]. This clause is translated 'In fact, all I will talk about' [CEV]. The combination of οὐ 'not' and τι 'anything' is translated 'only' [REB, TEV]. This pronoun refers to someone or something indefinite, spoken or written about [LN].

QUESTION—What relationship is indicated by γάρ 'for'?

It indicates an explanation; although he has spoken boldly, there are some things he won't speak about [Mor]. It indicates 15:18–19a as explaining why the boasting of 15:16 is really a boasting in Christ Jesus, which is that Paul is only going to mention what Christ has done through him [ICC2]. It indicates that Paul is giving more reasons for his boasting about his ministry [BECNT].

of-which[a] Christ did- not -work[b] through[c] me,

LEXICON—a. ὅς (LN 92.27) (BAGD I.4.a. p. 584): 'which' [BAGD, LN], 'that' [BAGD], 'what' [BAGD, LN], 'that which' [LN]. The phrase ὧν οὐ 'of which...not' [HNTC], is translated 'which...not' [ICC2; KJV],

'that...not' [BECNT, NICNT], 'save what' [AB], 'except that which' [NTC], 'except what' [NASB, NCV, NET, NIV, NLT, NRSV], 'except of what' [WBC], not explicit [CEV]. The double negative statement is a litotes [SSA], and is stated positively: 'tell you only what' [GW], 'speak only of/about what' [REB, TEV]. This pronoun is a relative reference to any entity, event, or state, which either occurs overtly in the immediate context or is clearly implied in the discourse or setting [LN].
  b. aorist mid. (deponent = act.) indic. of κατεργάζομαι (LN 42.17) (BAGD 1. p. 421): 'to work' [BECNT, ICC2; KJV], 'to accomplish' [AB, BAGD, LN, NICNT, NTC, WBC; NASB, NET], 'to carry out' [HNTC], 'to achieve' [BAGD], 'to do' [GW, NCV], 'to perform successfully, to do thoroughly' [LN], 'to speak and work' [CEV]. This verb means to do something with success and/or thoroughness [LN].
  c. διά with genitive (LN 90.4): 'through' [AB, BECNT, HNTC, ICC2, LN, NICNT, NTC, WBC; CEV, GW, NASB, NCV, NET], 'by' [LN; KJV], not explicit [CEV]. This preposition marks an intermediate agent, with implicit or explicit causative agent [LN].

by[a] word[b] and deed[c] for[d] (the) obedience[e] of- (the) -Gentiles,
LEXICON—a. There is no lexical entry for 'by' in the Greek text, its meaning is implied by the dative case of the nouns 'word' and 'deed'. This relation is translated 'by' [ICC2, NTC, WBC; GW, KJV, NASB, NET, NIV, NLT, NRSV], 'by means of' [BECNT; CEV], 'in' [AB, HNTC, NICNT; NCV], not explicit [CEV].
  b. λόγος (LN 33.98, 33.99) (BAGD 1.a.α. p. 477): 'word' [AB, BECNT, HNTC, ICC2, LN (33.98), NICNT, WBC; KJV, NASB, NET, NRSV, TEV], 'what I have said' [NTC; GW, NCV, NIV], 'my message' [NLT], 'speaking, speech' [LN (33.99)]. The dative noun λόγῳ 'by word' is translated as a verb phrase: '(Christ let me) speak' [CEV]. This noun denotes that which has been stated or said, with primary focus upon the content of the communication [LN (33.98)], or the act of speaking itself [LN (33.99)].
  c. ἔργον (LN 42.11) (BAGD 1.a. p. 307): 'deed' [AB, BAGD, BECNT, HNTC, ICC2, LN, NICNT, WBC; KJV, NASB, NET, NRSV, TEV], '(what I have) done' [NTC; GW, NCV, NIV], 'act' [LN]. The dative noun ἔργῳ 'by deed' is translated as a verb phrase: '(Christ let me) work' [CEV], 'by the way I worked among them' [NLT]. This noun denotes that which is done, with possible focus on the energy or effort involved [LN].
  d. εἰς (LN 89.48, 89.57): 'for' [AB, BECNT, HNTC, NICNT, WBC], 'resulting in' [NASB], 'to bring about' [ICC2; NET], 'to bring (people to)...' [GW], 'to make (obedient)' [KJV], 'to win (obedience)' [NRSV], 'so that (Gentiles would...)' [CEV], 'to lead (the Gentiles)' [TEV], 'for the purpose of, in order to' [LN (89.57)], 'with the result that, so that as a result, to cause' [LN (89.48)], not explicit [NTC; NIV, NLT]. This preposition can mark intent, often with the implication of expected result

LN (89.57), or it can mark result, with the probable implication of a preceding process [LN (89.48)].
e. ὑπακοή (LN 36.15) (BAGD 1.b. p. 837): 'obedience' [BAGD, BECNT, HNTC, ICC2, LN, NICNT, WBC; GW, NASB, NET], 'commitment' [AB], not explicit [NTC]. The phrase εἰς ὑπακοὴν ἐθνῶν 'for the obedience of the Gentiles' is translated 'bringing the Gentiles to God' [NLT], 'in leading the Gentiles to God' [NTC], 'in leading the Gentiles to obey God' [NIV], 'to lead the Gentiles to obey God' [TEV], 'in leading those who are not Jews to obey God' [NCV], 'to make the Gentiles obedient' [KJV]. This obedience refers to saving faith, as in 1:5 and 16:26 [BECNT]. This noun denotes the action of obeying on the basis of having given attention [LN].

QUESTION—Does 'by word and by deed' refer to Paul's words and deeds to bring about the Gentiles' obedience, or aspects of the Gentiles' obedience?
1. It refers to what Paul has done and said to bring the Gentiles to obedience to God [AB, BECNT, Gdt, HNTC, Ho, ICC2, Mor, Mu, NICNT, NTC, SSA, TH, WBC; CEV, GW, NCV, NET, NIV, NLT, NRSV, REB, TEV]. Some move the phrase 'by word and by deed' to the end of the verse in order to join it with the following list of ways in 15:19 of how Christ worked through Paul [NICNT, WBC; GW, KJV, NCV, NET, NRSV, REB, TEV].
2. It refers to how the Gentiles obeyed [probably NASB which translates it 'resulting in the obedience of the Gentiles by word and deed'].

QUESTION—What relationship is indicated by εἰς 'for'?
1. It indicates result [BECNT, Ho, Mor, NTC; GW, NASB; probably AB].
2. It indicates purpose [NICNT, SSA, St; CEV; probably WBC].

15:19 by[a] (the) power[b] of-signs[c] and wonders,[d] by (the) power of- (the) - Spirit of-God;

TEXT—Instead of πνεύματος θεοῦ 'Spirit of God', some manuscripts have πνεύματος 'Spirit', and others have πνεύματος ἁγίου 'Holy Spirit'. GNT selects the reading 'πνεύματος θεοῦ' 'Spirit of God' with a C rating, indicating difficulty in deciding which variant to place in the text. The reading 'Spirit' is taken by HNTC, ICC2, NICNT, NTC; NASB, NIV. The reading 'Holy Spirit' is taken by CEV, NCV, REB,

LEXICON—a. ἐν (LN 89.76): 'by' [AB, BECNT, LN, NTC, WBC; CEV, NLT, NRSV, REB, TEV], 'in' [HNTC, ICC2, NICNT; GW, NET, NIV], 'through' [LN; KJV], 'by means of' [LN], 'because of' [NCV]. This preposition marks the means by which one event makes another event possible [LN].
b. δύναμις (LN 76.1) (BAGD 1. p. 207): 'power' [AB, BAGD, BECNT, HNTC, ICC2, NICNT, NTC, WBC; all versions except KJV]. This noun is translated as an adjective: 'mighty' [KJV]. This noun denotes the potentiality to exert force in performing some function [LN].
c. σημεῖον (LN 33.477) (BAGD 2.a. p. 748): 'sign' [AB, BAGD, BECNT, HNTC, ICC2, LN, NICNT, NTC, WBC; GW, KJV, NET, NIV, NRSV,

REB], 'miraculous sign' [NLT], 'miracle' [CEV, NCV, TEV]. This noun denotes an event which is regarded as having some special meaning [LN].

d. τέρας (LN 33.480): 'wonder' [AB, BECNT, ICC2, NICNT, NTC, WBC; CEV, KJV, NET, NLT, NRSV, TEV], 'portent' [HNTC, LN; REB], 'miracle' [NIV], 'sign' [LN], 'great things they saw' [NCV]. The phrase 'signs and wonders' is translated 'miraculous and amazing signs' [GW]. This noun denotes an unusual sign, especially one in the heavens, serving to foretell impending events [LN]. In the NT it occurs only in conjunction with the word 'signs', as it does here [Mor].

QUESTION—Is there any distinction intended between 'signs' and 'wonders'?

The phrase 'signs and wonders' was a traditional way of referring to the miracles connected with the Exodus [BECNT, NICNT, SSA, WBC]. In the NT the word 'wonders' is always used in connection with the word 'signs' [ICC2, Mor, NAC].

1. Both of the words 'signs' and 'wonders' refer to miracles [Mor, NTC], but 'sign' points to the purpose or significance of the miraculous event, whereas 'wonder' focuses on its unusual or marvelous nature [Mor, NAC, NICNT]. 'Sign' points to the agency by which it is done, whereas 'wonder' emphasizes the event itself [ICC1, Mu]. 'Signs' signify something [Gdt, St], especially with reference to the coming of the kingdom of God [St], or to the characteristics of God such as his power [Ho, NTC], or his grace and wisdom [NTC]. 'Wonder' describes the effect on people who saw them [Ho, NTC, St].

2. They are a doublet, with little or no distinction in meaning intended [SSA, TH].

QUESTION—What is the relation between the phrases 'by the power of signs and wonders' and 'by the power of the Spirit of God'?

The power of the Spirit was expressed in Paul's words and actions as well as in the miracles he did [AB, Ho, ICC1, ICC2, Mu]. Paul's ministry in word and deed is characterized by the power of the Spirit expressed in signs and wonders [WBC]. The Spirit's power was expressed both in the miracles as well as in the spiritual effectiveness of the preaching of the gospel [Mor, Mu]. The phrase 'by the power of the Spirit' refers both to his words as well as his deeds [BECNT, WBC]. The signs and wonders were performed through the Holy Spirit's power [NAC, NTC]. The Spirit is dynamically at work in what Paul says and does, and in the miracles done through him [BECNT]. 'In the power of the Spirit' relates generally to 'what I have said and done', but the powerful help given by the Spirit is the means by which Paul did those miraculous things [SSA]. 'The power of the Spirit' primarily relates not to the miracles, but to Paul's preaching [St].

so-that[a] from Jerusalem and around[b] as-far-as[c] Illyricum I have-fully[d] (proclaimed) the gospel of-Christ.

LEXICON—a. ὥστε (LN 89.52) (BAGD 2.a.β. p. 900): 'so that' [BAGD, HNTC, ICC2, LN, WBC; KJV, NRSV], 'so' [AB, NTC; NET, NIV], 'and

so' [TEV], 'so then' [BECNT, LN], 'as a result' [LN, NICNT], 'in this way' [NLT], not explicit [CEV, GW, NCV, REB]. This preposition marks result, often in contexts implying an intended or indirect purpose [LN].
b. κύκλῳ (LN 83.19) (BAGD 1.a. p. 457): 'around' [BAGD, LN]. This adjective describes a position completely encircling an area or object [LN]. See entry c.
c. μέχρι (LN 84.19) (BAGD 1.a. p. 515): 'as far as' [BAGD, LN], 'up to' [LN]. The phrase κύκλῳ μέχρι is translated 'round about as far as' [HNTC; NASB], 'even as far as' [NET], 'round even to' [ICC2], 'round about unto' [KJV], 'around to' [NICNT], 'all the way...to' [CEV, NLT], 'in traveling all the way...to' [TEV], 'all the way around to' [AB, NTC; NCV, NIV], 'as far around as' [NRSV, REB], 'in a circle to' [BECNT], 'in a sweep around to' [WBC], 'to' [GW].
d. perf. act. infin. of πληρόω (LN **33.199**) (BAGD 3. p. 671): 'to fully proclaim' [NTC; NIV, NRSV, TEV], 'to fully present' [NLT], 'to fully complete' [BECNT], 'to complete' [HNTC, WBC], 'to complete the preaching' [REB], 'to fully tell' [**LN**], 'to fully preach' [AB; KJV, NET], 'to preach' [CEV], 'to fulfill (the message/gospel)' [ICC2, NICNT], 'to finish spreading (the good news)' [GW], 'to proclaim, to proclaim completely' [LN], 'to bring to completion' [BAGD]. The statement 'I have fully proclaimed the gospel of Christ' is translated 'I have finished that part of my work' [NCV]. This verb means to relate fully the content of a message [LN].

QUESTION—What relationship is indicated by ὥστε 'so that'?

It indicates the result of what Paul had done through the Spirit's power [Gdt, Mor], the result of Paul's ministry among the Gentiles [BECNT]. The progress of the gospel here in 15:19 is the result of the ministry of Christ through Paul described in 15:18–19a [ICC2, WBC]. It indicates the result of Paul's determination to evangelize and win Gentiles to Christ, as described in 15:18–19a [SSA].

QUESTION—What does Paul mean by ἀπὸ Ἰερουσαλὴμ καὶ...μέχρι Ἰλλυρικοῦ 'from Jerusalem and...as far as Illyricum'?

Paul probably is referring to all the territory between those two points, but not including those two places [ICC1, Mor, NAC, SSA]; Jerusalem and Illyricum are the limits [ICC1]. Illyricum marks the furthest boundary up to which he had gone in his preaching [ICC2, Mu, WBC], Illyricum itself not being included [ICC2, WBC]. It is not clear whether he is saying that he had preached in Jerusalem and in Illyricum, or only that Jerusalem was the beginning point from which he went out, and that his preaching extended at least to the region near Illyricum [BECNT, TH]. He is recorded in Acts 9:26–36 as having preached in Jerusalem [Mu].

QUESTION—What does Paul mean when he says that he has fully proclaimed the gospel?

He has spread the gospel in the major urban centers in that region, leaving fellow workers to go to the outlying areas [BECNT, Gdt, St, WBC]. He fulfilled his own calling by founding churches and leaving to others the work of building on that foundation [ICC1, Mu]. He has finished laying the foundation for churches in that region [SSA]. He is saying that he has done what he was commissioned to do, which was to proclaim the gospel and establish churches in the major urban centers [Mor, NICNT]. He has completed his own apostolic mission or pioneering work in that area [ICC2, NAC]. He preached the gospel thoroughly, and with much evidence of God being at work through him, such that there should be no doubt that he was divinely appointed as a minister of the gospel [Ho]. He has fulfilled his commission by preaching in every province from Jerusalem to Illyricum [TNTC].

QUESTION—What relationship is indicated by the genitive construction τὸ εὐαγγέλιον τοῦ Χριστοῦ 'the gospel of Christ'?

The genitive construction means that the gospel is about Christ [AB, ICC2, SSA, TH, WBC].

15:20 And[a] so,[b] aspiring[c] to-preach-the-gospel[d] where Christ has- not been-named[e]

LEXICON—a. δέ (LN 89.94, 89.124): 'and' [BECNT, LN (89.94); NASB, NET], 'but' [ICC2, LN (89.124), NTC; CEV, REB], 'yea' [KJV], not explicit [AB, HNTC, NICNT, WBC; GW, NCV, NIV, NRSV, TEV]. This conjunction marks contrast [LN (89.124)], or an additive relation with the possible implication of some contrast [LN (89.94)].

b. οὕτως (LN 61.9): 'so' [ICC2, LN; KJV], 'thus' [AB, BECNT, LN, WBC; NASB, NRSV], 'in this way' [HNTC, LN, NICNT; NET], not explicit [NTC; CEV, GW, NCV, NIV, REB, TEV]. This adverb describes something by reference to that which precedes [LN].

c. pres. mid. or pass.(deponent = act.) participle of φιλοτιμέομαι (LN 25.78) (BAGD p. 861): 'to aspire' [BAGD, LN], 'to make something one's ambition to' [LN], 'to have as one's ambition' [BAGD]. This present participle is translated as a participial phrase: 'making it my ambition' [BECNT], 'being ambitious' [HNTC], 'making it my intention' [NICNT], 'making it my aim' [WBC]; as a finite verb phrase: 'it has been my ambition' [AB], 'it has always been my ambition' [NTC; NIV], 'my ambition has always been' [TEV], 'I make it my ambition' [NRSV], 'I made it my earnest endeavor' [ICC2], 'my goal was' [GW], 'I have always tried' [CEV], 'I have strived' [KJV], 'I have always made a point of' [REB], 'I aspired' [NASB], 'I always want' [NCV], 'I desire' [NET]. This verb means to earnestly aspire to something, implying strong ambition for some goal [LN].

d. pres. mid. infin. of εὐαγγελίζω (LN 33.215) (BAGD 2.a.δ. p. 317): 'to preach the gospel' [BECNT, HNTC, NICNT, NTC, WBC; KJV, NASB, NIV], 'to preach the good news' [AB, ICC2], 'to spread the Good News' [GW], 'to proclaim the good news' [NRSV, TEV], 'to tell the good news, to announce the gospel' [LN], 'to take the gospel (to places)' [REB], 'to

preach' [BAGD; CEV, NET]. This verb means to communicate good news concerning something, which in the NT refers specifically to the gospel message about Jesus [LN].
e. aorist pass. indic. of ὀνομάζω (LN 28.22) (BAGD 3. p. 574): 'to be named' [AB, BAGD, BECNT, HNTC, NICNT, WBC; KJV, NET, NRSV], 'to be named already' [ICC2; NASB], 'to be known' [BAGD, LN, NTC; NIV], 'to be made known' [LN]. The phrase 'where Christ has not been named' is translated 'where people have never heard about/of Christ' [CEV, NCV], 'where the name of Christ was not known' [GW], 'where the name of Christ has never/not been heard' [NLT, REB], 'where Christ has not been heard of' [TEV]. This verb means to be caused to be made known [LN].

QUESTION—What relationship is indicated by οὕτως δέ 'and so'?
1. It qualifies and explains the statement he just made about preaching the gospel; he had preached it where Christ was not named [Mor]. The word οὕτως 'so' represents the action of proclaiming the gospel mentioned in 15:19b; Paul is saying that, as he preached the gospel, he strived to preach where people had not heard about him [SSA].
2. δέ is adversative [ICC2], and οὕτως 'so' refers to what follows about not preaching where Christ was already acknowledged and worshipped [AB, ICC2].
3. It refers both to what has been said as well as to what he is about to say; that is, he has completed the gospel of Christ by aspiring to preach in unreached territory [WBC].

QUESTION—What does it mean to preach where Christ has not been named?
Paul wants to preach where people have not heard about Christ [Ho, NAC, SSA, TH], and where Christ had not been acknowledged for what his name means [NAC]. He wanted to preach where no one else had yet done so [Gdt, TNTC]. The verb 'has been named' refers to Christ being acknowledged and known or confessed as Lord [AB, BECNT, ICC2, Mor, Mu, WBC], or to Christ being worshipped [ICC1].

so-that[a] I-might- not -build[b] on another's[c] foundation,[d]

LEXICON—a. ἵνα (LN 89.59): 'so that' [LN; NASB, NIV, NRSV], 'in order to' [LN], 'in order that' [BECNT, NICNT], 'that' [ICC2, NTC], 'so as to' [NET, TEV], not explicit [NLT]. The phrase ἵνα μή 'so that...not' is translated 'lest' [AB, HNTC, WBC; KJV]. The phrase ἵνα μή... οἰκοδομῶ 'so that I might not build' is translated 'I am like a builder who doesn't build' [CEV], 'I didn't want to build' [GW], 'I do not want to build' [NCV], 'not wanting to build' [REB].
b. pres. act. subj. of οἰκοδομέω (LN 45.1) (BAGD 2. p. 558): 'to build' [AB, BAGD, BECNT, HNTC, ICC2, NICNT, NTC, WBC; all versions except NLT], not explicit [NLT]. This verb means to make or erect any kind of construction [LN].

c. ἀλλότριος (LN 92.20) (BAGD 1.a. p. 40): 'another's' [BECNT, NICNT, WBC], 'another man's' [BAGD, ICC2; KJV, NASB, REB], 'another person's' [NET], 'belonging to another' [BAGD, LN], 'belonging to someone else' [HNTC, LN], 'of someone else' [AB], 'someone else's' [NTC; NIV, NRSV], 'someone else (has started)' [NCV], '(started by) someone else' [NLT], 'anyone else's' [CEV], 'which others had laid' [GW], 'laid by someone else' [TEV]. This adjective describes what belongs to someone else [LN].

d. θεμέλιος (LN 7.41) (BAGD 2.a. p. 356): 'foundation' [AB, BAGD, BECNT, HNTC, ICC2, LN, NICNT, NTC, WBC; all versions except NCV, NLT]. The phrase ἀλλότριον θεμέλιον 'another's foundation' is translated 'the work someone else has already started' [NCV], 'where a church has already been started by someone else' [NLT]. This noun denotes that on which a structure is built [LN].

QUESTION—What is meant by this metaphor?

Paul did not want to continue the work someone else had already started since he would be like a man who builds a house on a foundation laid by someone else [SSA]. Paul didn't disparage a ministry that builds on what someone else has already started since there is a place for further evangelism and pastoral care. However, Paul knew that Christ had given him the specific task of planting while others would follow with watering the growth (1 Cor. 3:58) [NICNT]. He wanted to achieve the widest possible expansion of the spreading of the gospel with the minimum amount of missionary effort by going where no one else was working [WBC]. He wanted to preach where no one else has planted a church [BECNT]. His main calling was to plant new churches where no one else has worked [Mor]. God had called him to be a trailblazer [NAC] and pioneer [ICC2, NAC].

15:21 but,[a] as it-is-written, Those-to-whom it-was- not -announced[b] concerning[c] him will-see,[d] and those-who have- not -heard[e] will-understand.[f]

LEXICON—a. ἀλλά (LN **91.2**, 89.125): 'but' [AB, BECNT, ICC2, LN (89.125), NICNT, WBC; KJV, NASB, NCV, NET, NRSV], 'rather' [HNTC, NTC; NIV], 'and, yet' [**LN** (91.2)], 'instead' [LN (89.125)], not explicit [CEV, GW, REB, TEV]. The phrase 'but, as it is written' is translated 'I have been following the plan spoken of in the Scriptures' [NLT].

b. aorist pass. indic. of ἀναγγέλλω (LN 33.197) (BAGD 2. p. 51): 'to be announced' [BAGD, ICC2, LN, NICNT], 'to be told' [HNTC, LN, NTC, WBC; CEV, GW, NCV, NIV, NLT, NRSV, TEV], 'to have news' [LN; NASB, REB], 'to be proclaimed' [BAGD, BECNT], 'to be spoken of' [KJV], 'to be informed' [LN]. This verb means to be provided information, with the possible implication of considerable detail [LN].

c. περί with genitive (LN 90.24): 'concerning' [BECNT, ICC2, LN, NICNT], 'about' [HNTC, LN, NTC, WBC; CEV, GW, NCV, NET, NIV,

NLT, TEV], 'of' [AB, LN; KJV, NASB, NRSV, REB]. This preposition marks general content, whether of a discourse or mental activity [LN].
d. fut. mid. (deponent = act) indic. of ὁράω (LN 32.11) (BAGD 1.c.β. p. 578): 'to see' [AB, BAGD, BECNT, HNTC, ICC2, NICNT, NTC, WBC; all versions], 'to notice' [BAGD], 'to understand, to perceive, to recognize' [LN]. This verb means to come to understand as the result of perception [LN].
e. perf. act. indic. of ἀκούω (LN 33.212) (BAGD 3.a. p. 32): 'to hear' [AB, BECNT, HNTC, ICC2, LN, NICNT, NTC, WBC; all versions], 'to receive news' [LN], 'to learn' [BAGD]. This verb means to receive information about something, normally by word of mouth [LN].
f. fut. act. indic. of συνίημι (LN 32.5) (BAGD p. 790): 'to understand' [AB, BAGD, BECNT, HNTC, ICC2, LN, NICNT, NTC, WBC; all versions], 'to comprehend' [BAGD, LN], 'to perceive, to have insight into' [LN]. This verb means to employ one's capacity for understanding and thus to arrive at insight [LN].

QUESTION—What will they hear and see?
Paul is talking about his preaching, and this means that people will hear about Christ and understand Christ's message [SSA]. They will see and understand the message about the Lord's servant, Christ, as described in Isaiah 52:15 [AB, BECNT, Ho, ICC1, ICC2, NAC, NICNT, TNTC].

DISCOURSE UNIT—15:22–33 [ICC1, NAC, St, WBC; CEV, NCV, NET, NIV, NLT, NRSV]. The topic is the apostle's plans [ICC1], Paul's travel plans [St, WBC; NLT], Paul's plans to visit Rome [NAC], Paul's plan to visit Rome [CEV, NCV, NIV, NRSV, TEV], Paul's intention of visiting Rome [NET].

DISCOURSE UNIT—15:22–29 [NICNT]. The topic is looking ahead to Jerusalem, Rome, and Spain.

15:22 Therefore[a] also I-was-being-hindered[d] greatly[c] to-come to you
LEXICON—a. διό (LN 89.47) (BAGD p. 198): 'therefore, wherefore' [BAGD], 'then, consequently, as a result' [LN]. The phrase διὸ καί 'therefore also' [NICNT] is also translated 'wherefore also' [ICC2], 'therefore' [BECNT], 'for which cause also' [KJV], 'for this reason also' [WBC], 'and so' [TEV], 'so' [HNTC], 'for this reason' [NASB], 'this is the reason' [NCV, NET, NRSV], 'this/that is why' [AB, NTC; NIV, REB], 'this is what (has so often kept me from)' [GW], 'in fact...because I have been preaching in these places' [NLT], not explicit [CEV].
b. imperf. pass. indic. of ἐγκόπτω (LN 13.147) (BAGD p. 216): 'to be hindered' [AB, BAGD, BECNT, HNTC, ICC2, LN, NICNT, NTC; KJV, NET, NIV, NRSV], 'to be prevented' [BAGD, LN, WBC; NASB, REB, TEV], 'to be stopped' [NCV], 'to be delayed' [NLT], 'to be thwarted' [BAGD]. This passive verb is translated as active: '(my work) has prevented me' [CEV], '(this)...has prevented me' [GW]. This verb means to use strong measures in causing someone not to do something [LN].

c. πολύς (LN 78.3) (BAGD I.2.b.β. p. 688): 'greatly' [BAGD, LN], 'many times' [BAGD, HNTC, ICC2, NICNT; TEV], 'often' [BAGD, BECNT, NTC; NASB, NET, NIV], 'so often' [AB; GW, NRSV], 'regularly' [WBC], 'always' [CEV], 'many times' [NCV], 'much' [KJV], 'so long' [NLT], 'all this time' [REB]. This adverb marks the upper range of a scale of extent [LN].

QUESTION—What relationship is indicated by διό 'therefore'?

It refers what he said in 15:19 about fulfilling his ministry [BECNT, Gdt, ICC2, Mu, NICNT, WBC]. Paul is saying that he was determined to obey what God had called him to do, and as a result had not been free to go to Rome as he would have liked [Mor].

QUESTION—Who or what hindered Paul from visiting Rome?

1. His evangelistic work had prevented him from visiting Rome [AB, BECNT, Gdt, Ho, ICC1, ICC2, Mor, Mu, NICNT, TH, WBC; CEV, NLT]. It was the needs in those regions that hindered Paul from coming to them [NICNT]. It was Paul's desire to preach the gospel where Christ has not been named (15:20) that kept him from coming to Rome where there already was a church [TH]. This is a divine passive; God hindered Paul because of the work he gave him to do [BECNT].
2. He may have been hindered by Satan as he mentions in 1 Thess. 2:18 [HNTC].

DISCOURSE UNIT—15:23-33 [Mor]. The topic is Paul's plans.

15:23 But now, no-longer having place[a] in these regions,[b] but having a longing[c] for many years to-come to you

LEXICON—a. τόπος (LN 71.6) (BAGD 2.c. p. 823): 'place' [BAGD, NICNT; KJV, NASB, NRSV], 'place for me to work' [NTC; NIV], 'room' [AB, ICC2], 'opportunity' [BAGD, BECNT, LN], 'new opportunities for work' [GW], 'scope' [HNTC, WBC; REB], 'chance' [BAGD, LN]. The phrase μηκέτι τόπον ἔχων 'no longer having place' is translated 'there is nothing left for me to do' [CEV], 'there is nothing more to keep me' [NET], 'I have finished my work' [NCV, NLT, TEV]. This noun denotes the possibility of some occasion or opportunity [LN]. Literally 'place', this word is used metaphorically to mean 'possibility', 'opportunity', or 'chance' [NICNT].

b. κλίμα (LN 1.79) (BAGD p. 436): 'region' [AB, BAGD, BECNT, ICC2, LN, NICNT, NTC, WBC; GW, NASB, NET, NIV, NLT, NRSV, TEV], 'district' [BAGD, LN], 'part' [HNTC; KJV, REB]. The phrase τοῖς κλίμασι τούτοις 'these regions' is translated 'this part of the world' [CEV], 'here' [NCV]. This noun denotes a region or regions of the earth, normally in relation to some ethnic group or geographical center, but not necessarily constituting a unit of governmental administration [LN].

c. ἐπιποθία (LN **25.18**) (BAGD p. 298): 'longing' [BAGD, BECNT, **LN**, WBC; NASB], 'desire' [BAGD, NICNT; KJV]. The phrase ἐπιποθίαν δὲ ἔχων 'having a longing' is translated 'I have been longing' [AB, NTC;

NIV, REB], 'I have had a desire' [HNTC], 'I desire' [NRSV], 'having desired' [ICC2], 'I have desired' [NET], 'I have wanted' [CEV, GW, NCV], 'I have been wanting' [TEV]. The phrase 'having a longing for many years' is translated 'after all these long years of waiting' [NLT]. This noun denotes a strong desire [Mor], or a longing for something with the implication of recognizing a lack [LN]. This word occurs only here in the NT.

QUESTION—What is meant by 'no longer having place'?

His work as a pioneer missionary in that area has been completed [AB, BECNT, ICC2, Mu, NAC, NICNT, St, WBC]. There were no longer places in those regions where people had not heard about Christ [Ho, SSA]. He no longer had opportunity to plant churches [BECNT, Mor], since his work was to plant churches in a region where the gospel had not been preached before [Mor, TH]. Although not everyone had heard the gospel, he had completed his work as a pioneer preacher in laying the foundations for new churches [AB].

QUESTION—What relationship is indicated by the present participle ἔχων 'having' that occurs twice in this sentence?

They are causal [AB, ICC2, NICNT, SSA, WBC]: because I don't have opportunity, because I have the desire, etc. The first occurrence explains why he is now free to visit Rome, and the second explains why he wants to [NICNT].

QUESTION—What is the predicate of the sentence that begins here?

Paul does not finish the sentence so there is no predicate [AB, HNTC, ICC1, ICC2, NICNT, WBC; NASB]. He interrupts his thought and does not resume it until 15:28 [ICC1, NICNT], where he says 'I will go...by way of you' [NICNT]. Most versions make a complete sentence of this by translating the second occurrence of ἔχων 'having' as a finite verb [CEV, NET, NLT, NRSV, REB]. GW divides 15:23 into two sentences. NCV, NIV, TEV add a verb to make a complete sentence. NASB leaves the sentence incomplete.

15:24 whenever[a] I travel[b] to Spain– for[c] I-hope[d] while-traveling-through[e]

TEXT—Some manuscripts include ἐλεύσομαι πρὸς ὑμᾶς 'I will come to you' after Σπανίαν 'Spain'. It is omitted by GNT with an A rating, indicating that the text is certain. It is included by KJV only.

LEXICON—a. ὡς ἄν (BAGD IV.1.c.α. p. 898, 3.d. p. 49): 'whenever' [BECNT, ICC2; NASB], 'whensoever' [KJV], 'when' [BAGD (IV.1.c.α. p. 898), HNTC, NTC, WBC; NET, NIV, NLT, NRSV], 'as soon as' [BAGD (3.d. p. 49)], 'as' [AB, NICNT], not explicit [CEV, NCV, REB, TEV]. The indefiniteness of ὡς ἄν is not due to uncertainty about his desire to go to Rome, but to uncertainty about how his trip to Jerusalem might affect that [NICNT]. The element of uncertainty implied by the use of this conjunction with the following subjunctive verb is expressed 'I am planning to go...and when I do' [NLT], 'I plan...when I go' [NIV].

b. pres. mid. or pass. subj. of πορεύομαι (LN 15.18) (BAGD 1. p. 692): 'to travel' [BAGD, LN, WBC], 'to journey' [LN], 'to take one's journey' [KJV], 'to go' [BECNT, ICC2, NICNT, NTC; NASB, NET, NIV, NLT, NRSV]. The phrase ὡς ἂν πορεύωμαι 'whenever I travel' is translated 'as I proceed on my way' [AB], 'when I am on my way' [HNTC], 'on my way' [CEV, NCV, REB, TEV], 'now I am on my way' [GW]. This verb means to move a considerable distance, either with a single destination or from one destination to another in a series [LN].

c. γάρ (LN 89.23): 'for' [BECNT, ICC2, LN, NICNT, WBC; KJV, NASB, NET, NRSV, REB], 'because' [LN], not explicit [AB, NTC; CEV, GW, NCV, NIV, NLT, TEV]. This conjunction marks cause or reason between events, though in some contexts the relation is often remote or tenuous [LN].

d. pres. act. indic. of ἐλπίζω (LN 25.59, 30.54) (BAGD 2. p. 252): 'to hope' [AB, BAGD, BECNT, HNTC, ICC2, LN (25.59, 30.54), NICNT, NTC, WBC; GW, NASB, NCV, NET, NIV, NRSV, REB], 'to expect' [BAGD, LN (30.54)], 'to plan' [CEV], 'to trust' [KJV], not explicit [NLT]. This entire phrase is translated 'I hope to do so now. (I would like to see you) on my way to (Spain)' [TEV]. This verb means to look forward with confidence to that which is good and beneficial [LN (25.59)], or to expect, with the implication of some benefit [LN (30.54)].

e. pres. mid. or pass. (deponent = act) participle of διαπορεύομαι (LN 15.22) (BAGD p. 187): 'to travel along' [AB], 'to pass through' [LN, NICNT, WBC; NET, NIV], 'to go through' [BAGD], not explicit [CEV]. This participle is translated 'on the way' [BAGD], 'on my way' [HNTC, ICC2; TEV], 'when I come your way' [GW], 'in passing' [BAGD, NTC; NASB, REB], 'in transit' [BECNT], 'in my journey' [KJV], 'on my journey' [NRSV], 'on my trip' [NCV], 'I will stop off (in Rome)' [NLT]. This verb means to go completely through an area [LN].

QUESTION—What is the relation of the phrase 'whenever I travel to Spain' to what precedes?

There is an anacoluthon here, meaning that the sentence is incomplete [BECNT, HNTC, ICC1, ICC2, NICNT]. Possibilities of what Paul is meaning are as follows.

1. For many years I have longed to come to you whenever I travel to Spain [NASB, NET, NRSV, REB].
2. For many years I have longed to come to you, and when I travel to Spain— (Paul breaks off and leaves the sentence incomplete) [ICC1, ICC2, NICNT, WBC].
3. For many years I have longed to come to you. Whenever I will travel to Spain, I hope to see you as I travel through [AB, Ho, Mor, NTC; CEV, GW, KJV, NCV, NIV, NLT, TEV]. Paul's sentence is incomplete, but he seems to be saying that he is eager to visit Rome so he can travel on to Spain [BECNT].

QUESTION—What relationship is indicated by γάρ 'for'?
It indicates an explanation for what he has just said in 15:23–24a [ICC1, ICC2, NICNT].

QUESTION—Did Paul ever actually make it to Spain?
There is not sufficient evidence to determine whether he actually visited Spain [HNTC, ICC1, NAC, NICNT, WBC], although there is at least some evidence to suggest that he may have done so [ICC2, Mu]. It is not impossible that he did, but we just cannot say based on the evidence now available [HNTC].

to-see[a] you and to-be-sent-on[b] there by[c] you
LEXICON—a. aorist mid. (deponent = active) infin. of θεάομαι (LN **34.50**) (BAGD 1.b. p. 353): 'to see' [AB, BECNT, HNTC, ICC2, NICNT, WBC; GW, NRSV, REB, TEV], 'to visit' [BAGD, LN, NICNT; NCV, NET, NIV], 'to come to see' [BAGD], 'to go to see' [LN], not explicit [CEV, NLT]. This verb means to go to see a person on the basis of friendship and with helpful intent [LN].
   b. aorist pass. infin. of προπέμπω (LN **15.72**) (BAGD 2. p. 709): 'to be sent on' [NRSV], 'to be sent on one's way' [BAGD, LN, WBC], 'to be helped' [HNTC], 'to be helped forward' [NTC], 'to be helped on one's journey' [BAGD], 'to be helped on one's way' [**LN**, NICNT], 'to be helped...to go there' [TEV], 'to be sped on my way' [AB], 'to be supported' [BECNT], 'to be set forward' [ICC2]. The phrase ὑφ' ὑμῶν προπεμφθῆναι 'to be sent by you' is translated 'to be sent on my way with your support' [REB], 'you will send me on' [CEV], '(I hope) you will support my trip' [GW], '(I hope) you can help me on my trip' [NCV], '(I hope) that you will help me on my journey' [NET], '(I hope) to have you assist me' [NIV], 'you can provide for my journey' [NLT]. This verb means to send someone on in the direction in which he has already been moving, with the probable implication of providing help [LN].
   c. with genitive ὑπό (LN 90.1): 'by' [AB, BECNT, HNTC, ICC2, LN, NICNT, NTC, WBC; NRSV, TEV], not explicit [CEV, GW, NCV, NET, NIV, NLT]. This preposition marks agent or force, whether person or event [LN].

QUESTION—In what sense was he expecting to be sent there by them?
He was hoping they would assist him in the journey [BECNT, Gdt, Mor, TH]. He was hoping for financial and logistical support [NICNT], and possibly for someone to accompany him and assist him with language and customs of Spain [ICC2, NICNT]. He hoped for their prayers and good wishes, but probably also for financial help and possibly more information about Spain itself [AB, ICC2]. He was hoping for assistance with money, food, letters of introduction [WBC], and possibly someone to travel with him [Gdt, WBC]. He was hoping not only for well-wishes and prayers, but for money, provisions, and possibly a travel companion for at least part of the way [St]. He was hoping for money, guides, information, and provisions

[NTC]. It would not necessarily imply anything more than prayers and good wishes [ICC1]. He expects them to send him on with blessings and commendations [Mu].

when^a first I-have-been-filled^b (visiting) you for a-while.^c

LEXICON—a. ἐάν (LN 67.32): 'when, when and if' [LN]. The phrase ἐὰν πρῶτον 'when first' is translated 'if first' [HNTC, NICNT; KJV], 'when (I have) first (enjoyed)' [NASB], 'even if...first' [BECNT], 'first in some measure' [ICC2], 'once (I have...)' [AB, WBC; NRSV], 'then after' [CEV], 'and after' [NLT], 'after' [NTC; GW, NCV, NET, NIV, REB, TEV]. This adverb marks a point of time which is somewhat conditional and simultaneous with another point of time [LN].

 b. aorist pass. subj. of ἐμπίπλημι (LN **25.114**) (BAGD 3. p. 256): 'to enjoy' [BAGD, LN]. The phrase 'I have been filled visiting you' is translated 'I be filled with your company' [KJV], 'I have my fill of your company' [HNTC], 'having first had my fill' [ICC2], 'I have had the full pleasure of being with you' [WBC], 'I have enjoyed your company' [**LN**, NTC; GW, NASB, NET, NIV, NRSV], '(after) having enjoyed your company' [REB], 'I might enjoy your company' [NICNT], 'I first enjoy your company' [BECNT], 'I have enjoyed your fellowship' [NLT], 'I have enjoyed visiting you' [**LN**; TEV], 'I enjoy being with you' [NCV], 'a (short), but refreshing, visit with you' [CEV], 'I have had the full pleasure of being with you' [WBC]. The expression 'to have one's fill of something' has the sense of enjoying something, and here with the genitive ὑμῶν 'you' it means 'enjoy your company' [BAGD]. This verb means to enjoy something fully and completely, with the implication of satisfying one's desires [LN].

 c. μέρος (LN **67.109**) (BAGD 1.c. p. 506): 'part' [LN]. The phrase ἀπὸ μέρους 'for a while' [BAGD, BECNT, **LN**, NICNT, NTC; GW, NASB, NCV, NET, NIV, REB, TEV] is also translated 'for a little while' [NLT, NRSV], 'a while' [AB, NICNT], 'for a time' [WBC], 'in part' [HNTC], 'in some measure' [ICC2], 'somewhat' [KJV], 'short (visit)' [CEV]. The phrase ἀπὸ μέρους 'from a part' is an idiom pertaining to a relatively short period of time [LN].

QUESTION—How is the expression ἀπὸ μέρους 'in part' used here?

 It is temporal [Gdt, Mor, NICNT, WBC]: he does not plan to stay for very long when he visits them [Mor, Mu, NICNT]. He would never be able to stay long enough to truly satisfy himself with their company [Gdt], or have his fill of fellowship with them [HNTC].

DISCOURSE UNIT—15:25–29 [AB]. The topic is his coming task before that visit: to carry a collection to the poor of Jerusalem.

15:25 But[a] now[b] I-am-going[c] to Jerusalem ministering[d] (to) the saints.[e]

LEXICON—a. δέ (LN 89.124): 'but' [BECNT, HNTC, ICC2, LN, NICNT, WBC; KJV, NASB, NCV, NET, NLT, REB], 'however' [AB, NTC; NIV, NRSV, TEV], not explicit [CEV, GW].

b. νυνί (LN **67.39**): 'now' [BECNT, HNTC, ICC2, NICNT, NTC, WBC; CEV, KJV, NASB, NCV, NET, NIV], 'right now' [GW, TEV], 'just now' [LN], 'at present' [AB; NRSV], 'presently' [**LN**], 'at the moment' [REB], 'before I come' [NLT]. This adverb describes a time shortly before or shortly after the time of the discourse [LN].

c. pres. mid. or pass. (deponent = act) indic. of πορεύομαι (LN 15.18) (BAGD 1. p. 692): 'to go' [BECNT, ICC2, NICNT; GW, KJV, NASB, NCV, NET, NLT, NRSV, TEV], 'to make one's way' [AB], 'to travel' [HNTC, LN, WBC], 'to be on one's way' [LN, NTC; CEV, NIV, REB], 'to journey' [LN]. This verb means to move a considerable distance, either with a single destination or from one destination to another in a series [LN].

d. pres. act. participle of διακονέω (LN 35.19) (BAGD 4. p. 184): 'to minister' [BECNT, ICC2, NICNT; KJV, NET], 'to help' [BAGD, LN; NCV], 'to bring help' [GW], 'to bring aid to' [AB], 'to take a gift to the poor' [NLT], 'to serve' [LN; NASB], 'to render service' [LN], not explicit [CEV]. This participle is translated 'engaged in ministering' [HNTC], 'in the service of' [NTC; NIV, TEV], 'in service to' [WBC], 'in a ministry to' [NRSV], 'on an errand to' [REB]. This verb means to render assistance or help by performing certain duties, often of a humble or menial nature [LN].

e. ἅγιος (LN 11.27) (BAGD 2.b.β. p. 10). This plural noun is translated 'saints' [BAGD, BECNT, HNTC, ICC2, NICNT, NTC, WBC; KJV, NASB, NET, NIV], 'God's people' [NCV, REB, TEV], 'God's dedicated people' [AB], 'God's (needy) people' [CEV], 'believers' [NLT], 'Christians' [GW]. It denotes persons who belong to God, and as such constitute a religious entity [LN].

QUESTION—What is implied by his use of the present tense of πορεύομαι 'I am going'?

He was just about to depart on that journey [AB, ICC2, NAC, NICNT, St, WBC].

QUESTION—What is the function of the present participle διακονῶν 'ministering'?

1. The use of the participial form of this verb indicates purpose [AB, BECNT, ICC2, NICNT; GW, KJV, NCV, NET, NLT]: in order to minister.

2. The present participle indicates that the journey itself was part of the ministry [Gdt, Ho; NIV, NRSV, REB, TEV]. 'I am on my way to Jerusalem in the service of the saints there' [NIV; similarly TEV], 'I am on my way to Jerusalem, on an errand to God's people there' [REB; similarly NRSV].

QUESTION—Why is this trip to Jerusalem so important to Paul that he would delay his plans for ministry in Spain in order to make it?

It signified the unity of all believers, whether Jew or Gentile, and was a way that Gentile Christians could express Christian love to Jewish Christians, who may or may not have fully accepted them [Mor]. He wants to build a bond of solidarity between the Jewish Christians of Jerusalem and Gentile Christians [AB, BECNT]. Paul saw the acceptance of the gift as symbolizing the unity of Jews and Gentiles in the people of God, and he may have hoped that it would stimulate the Jews to jealousy so they might be saved [BECNT]. It would demonstrate the love of Gentile Christians for Jewish Christians, a love which binds them together in unity [NAC]. Paul hoped to foster unity between Jewish and Gentile believers [HNTC]. Paul may have seen the contribution as a fulfillment of the prophecy that the wealth of the nations would flow into Jerusalem in the last days [BECNT, HNTC, WBC]. Such a gift signified the solidarity of God's people in Christ [St]. He was deeply concerned for the poor [Mu, NTC], and he also wanted to break down the barriers between Jews and Gentiles [NTC]. He wants to cement the fellowship that should exist between Christians in Jerusalem and those among the Gentiles [TNTC].

15:26 For[a] Macedonia and Achaia were-pleased[b] to-make some[c] contribution[d] for[e] the poor[f] of-the saints in Jerusalem.

LEXICON—a. γάρ (LN 89.23): 'for' [AB, BECNT, HNTC, ICC2, NICNT, NTC, WBC; KJV, NASB, NET, NIV, NRSV, REB, TEV], 'for you see' [NLT], 'because' [LN; GW], not explicit [CEV, NCV]. This preposition marks cause or reason between events, though in some contexts the relation is often remote or tenuous [LN].

b. aorist act. indic. of εὐδοκέω (LN 25.87) (BAGD 1. p. 319): 'to be pleased' [NTC; NASB, NET, NIV, NRSV], 'to be well pleased' [BAGD, NICNT], 'to be pleased with' [LN], 'to please' [KJV], 'to be happy (to)' [NCV], 'to decide kindly' [AB], 'to decide' [HNTC; GW], 'to freely decide' [TEV], 'to choose' [WBC], 'to be delighted' [BECNT], 'to resolve' [ICC2; REB], 'to be resolved' [BAGD], 'to be determined' [BAGD], not explicit [CEV]. This verb is translated as an adverb: 'eagerly' [NLT]. This verb means to be pleased with something or someone, with the implication of resulting pleasure [LN].

c. τις: 'some' [AB, BECNT, NICNT, WBC; NET], 'a certain' [KJV], not explicit [HNTC, ICC2, NTC; all versions except KJV].

d. κοινωνία (LN **57.101**) (BAGD 3. p. 439): 'contribution' [AB, BAGD, BECNT, HNTC, ICC2, NICNT, NTC, WBC; KJV, NASB, NET, NIV], 'willing contribution' [**LN**], 'gift' [BAGD], 'willing gift, ready contribution' [LN], 'money...collected' [CEV]. The phrase κοινωνίαν τινὰ ποιήσασθαι 'to make some contribution' is translated 'to take up a collection' [GW], 'to take up an offering' [NLT], 'to give an offering' [TEV], 'to give their money' [NCV], 'to share their resources' [NRSV],

'to raise a fund' [REB]. This noun denotes that which is readily shared [LN]. It expresses the fact that all Christians are bound together in deep love in the one body of Christ, the church [Mor].
e. εἰς (LN 90.41) (BAGD 4.g. p. 229): 'for' [AB, BAGD, ICC2, LN, NICNT, NTC, WBC; CEV, GW, KJV, NASB, NET, NIV, NLT], 'to' [HNTC], 'for the benefit of' [REB], 'on behalf of' [LN], 'to share with' [NRSV], 'to help' [NCV, TEV]. This preposition marks persons benefited by an event, with the implication of something directed to them [LN].
f. πτωχός (LN 57.53) (BAGD 1.a. p. 728): 'poor' [AB, BAGD, BECNT, HNTC, ICC2, LN, NICNT, NTC, WBC; all versions except CEV], 'needy' [CEV], 'destitute' [LN]. This adjective describes being poor and destitute, implying a continuous state [LN].

QUESTION—What relationship is indicated by γάρ 'for'?

It indicates 15:26–28a as an explanation for what he meant by 'ministering' in 15:25 [NICNT].

QUESTION—What is the significance of his use of the noun κοινωνία for the collection?

Κοινωνία normally means 'fellowship', and this offering is an expression of Christian fellowship [ICC2]. It was an outward expression of the depth of love that binds believers together [Mor]. The sharing of resources was an expression of their common life in Christ [WBC]. It expresses their solidarity, and their partnership in the gospel [BECNT]. It expresses unity and intimacy among Christian people [NICNT]. They have established a close relation with the poor in Jerusalem [BAGD, NAC]. Such assistance reflects a communion of hearts [Gdt]. The poor of Jerusalem were able to share in the abundance of the Gentile Christians [Ho]. It was the bond of fellowship that prompted their giving [Mu].

QUESTION—What relationship is indicated by the genitive construction τοὺς πτωχοὺς τῶν ἁγίων 'the poor of the saints'?

1. It indicates that some, but not all, among the Christians in Jerusalem were poor [AB, BECNT, HNTC, ICC2, NICNT, TH, WBCGW, NASB, NCV, NET, NIV, NLT, NRSV, REB, TEV]: the poor who are among the saints.
2. The collection was for the entire Jerusalem church, in which Christians in general referred to themselves as 'the poor' [TNTC].

15:27 For/indeed[a] they-were-pleased (to do this)[b] and[c] they-are debtors[d] to-them;

LEXICON—a. γάρ (LN 89.23) (BAGD 3. p. 152): 'for' [AB, LN, WBC; NET], 'because' [LN], 'indeed' [NICNT], 'yes' [NASB], 'so, then' [BAGD], not explicit [AB, HNTC, ICC2, NTC; CEV, GW, KJV, NCV, NIV, NLT, NRSV, REB, TEV]. This conjunction indicates the cause or reason between events, though in some contexts the relation is often remote or tenuous [LN].
b. There is no lexical entry for 'to do this' in the Greek text, but it is added to show the implied meaning of the text as required by the preceding verb

εὐδοκέω. It is represented in translation as 'to do this' [ICC2; NCV, NET, NLT, NRSV], 'to do so' [AB, WBC; NASB, REB], 'to do it' [NTC; NCV], 'something (they really wanted) to do' [CEV], not explicit [BECNT, HNTC, NICNT; GW, KJV, TEV].

c. καί (LN 89.93): 'and indeed' [AB, ICC2, NTC; NET, NIV, NRSV, REB], 'and really' [NCV], 'and also, in addition, even, also' [LN], 'and' [BECNT, HNTC, LN, NICNT; KJV, NASB], 'but' [CEV], 'but, as a matter of fact' [TEV], 'because' [NLT], not explicit [GW]. This conjunction indicates an additive relation that is not coordinate [LN]. Here this conjunction is emphatic [Mor, TH; TEV].

d. ὀφειλέτης (LN 57.222) (BAGD 2.b. p. 598): 'debtor' [BAGD, BECNT, LN, NICNT, WBC; KJV], 'one who is obligated to someone' [BAGD]. This noun is translated as an adjective: 'indebted' [AB; NASB, NET]; as a verb phrase: 'they owe it' [NTC; NCV, NIV, NRSV], 'they owe a real debt' [NLT], 'they have an obligation' [TEV]; as a prepositional phrase: 'under obligation' [HNTC, ICC2; REB]. This noun is conflated with the cognate verb ὀφείλουσιν 'they ought' and translated 'it was like paying back a debt' [CEV], 'they are obligated' [GW]. This noun denotes a person who is in debt [LN].

QUESTION—What relationship is indicated by the conjunction γάρ 'for'?

1. This indicates the reason for the statement in the preceding verse [AB, BECNT, LN, WBC; NET]: because they were pleased to do this. It indicates an explanation for why such a contribution is the right thing to do [BECNT].
2. This indicates an amplification of the statement in the preceding verse [NICNT, SSA; NASB]: indeed, they were pleased to do this. Since 'pleased' is the same verb used in the preceding verse, this is an amplification of the subject of the contribution, not a reason for it [SSA]. The repetition of εὐδόκησαν 'they were pleased' emphasizes the fact that the offering was freely given [Gdt, ICC2].

QUESTION—In what sense are they debtors?

They had a moral obligation to help them, but they did so without compulsion [BECNT, Mor, NICNT, WBC]. It was a voluntary offering, but it was reasonable that they should do so [Ho]. This 'obligation' is not to be understood in the same sense as the temple tax that Diaspora Jews were obligated to send to Jerusalem [AB, BECNT, ICC2, Mor, Mu, NICNT].

for if[a] the Gentiles shared[b] (in) their spiritual-things,[c] they-ought[d] also to minister[e] to-them (in) material-things.[f]

LEXICON—a. εἰ (LN 89.30) (BAGD III. p. 219): 'if' [AB, BAGD, BECNT, HNTC, ICC2, NICNT, NTC, WBC; KJV, NET, NIV, NRSV, REB], 'since' [LN; NLT, TEV], 'because' [LN], not explicit [CEV, NCV]. This conjunction marks cause or reason on the basis that an actual case is regarded formally as a supposition [LN].

b. aorist act. indic. of κοινωνέω (LN 57.98) (BAGD 1.b.α. p. 438): 'to share (in)' [BAGD, BECNT, LN; NASB, NCV, NET, NIV], 'to come to share (in)' [AB, NTC; NRSV], 'to receive a share (in)' [WBC], 'to share' [HNTC; CEV, GW, REB, TEV], 'to partake' [ICC2], 'to participate with' [NICNT], 'to be made partakers' [KJV], 'to receive (spiritual blessings)' [NLT]. This verb means to share one's possessions, with the implication of some kind of joint participation and mutual interest [LN].

c. πνευματικός (LN **15.27**) (BAGD 2.b.α. p. 679): 'spiritual' [BAGD, LN]. This plural adjective, which functions as a substantive, is translated 'spiritual things' [BAGD, HNTC, NICNT; KJV, NASB, NET], 'spiritual good things' [ICC2], 'spiritual benefits' [BECNT, **LN**], 'spiritual blessings' [AB, NTC; CEV, NCV, NIV, NRSV, TEV], 'spiritual treasures' [REB], 'spiritual affairs' [WBC], 'spiritual matters' [BAGD], 'spiritual blessings of the Good News' [NLT]. In this passage this word focuses upon non-material or spiritual aspects of human personality or life in contrast with the physical aspects [LN].

d. pres. act. indic. of ὀφείλω (LN 71.25) (BAGD 2.a.β. p. 599): 'ought' [AB, BAGD, HNTC, LN, WBC; NRSV, TEV], 'should' [BECNT; NCV], 'to be obliged' [NICNT], 'to be obligated' [BAGD; GW, NET], 'one must' [BAGD], 'to owe' [BAGD, NTC; NIV], 'to be indebted' [NASB], 'to have a clear duty' [REB], 'their duty is' [KJV], 'the least they can do is' [NLT], not explicit [CEV]. This verb denotes that which is obligatory in view of some moral or legal requirement [LN].

e. aorist act. infin. of λειτουργέω (LN **35.22**) (BAGD 3. p. 470): 'to minister' [BECNT, HNTC, NICNT, WBC; KJV, NASB, NET], 'to serve' [BAGD, LN], 'to be of service' [AB; NRSV], 'to render service' [ICC2], 'to share (with them)' [NTC; CEV, NIV], 'to help' [NLT], 'to use (earthly wealth/material possessions) to help' [GW, NCV, NRSV], 'to contribute to their material needs' [REB]. This verb means to serve, with the implication of more formal or regular service [LN].

f. σαρκικός (LN **79.1**) (BAGD 1. p. 742): 'material' [BAGD, LN], 'physical' [LN]. This plural adjective, which functions as a substantive, is translated 'material things' [AB, NICNT; NASB, NET, NRSV], 'material benefits' [BECNT], 'material blessings' [**LN**, NTC; NIV, TEV], 'material possessions' [NCV], 'material affairs' [WBC], 'things of flesh and blood' [HNTC], 'things necessary for their bodily welfare' [ICC2], 'their money' [CEV], 'earthly wealth' [GW], 'carnal things' [KJV], '(help them) financially' [NLT], not explicit [REB]. This adjective describes that which pertains to being material or physical, with the possible implication of inferior [LN].

QUESTION—What relationship is indicated by εἰ 'if'?

It assumes that what follows is actually the case [AB, BAGD, Mor, TH; CEV]. The condition is true and can be translated as a statement of fact [TH; CEV, GW, NCV, NLT, TEV].

QUESTION—What are the 'spiritual things' they have shared in?
He is referring most of all to the gospel [Mor], to the news of God's redemptive grace [Mu]. It is the gospel and the blessings associated with it [ICC2, NICNT; NLT], including all the tradition about Jesus' words and works [ICC2]. It is the tradition about Jesus that is the basis of the gospel [HNTC]. It refers to spiritual benefits such as salvation [AB, BECNT, St]. It is everything that Christian people have received from the Spirit [WBC]. It is spiritual blessings [NTC, TH], those that resulted from the gospel [NTC].

15:28 So^a, (after)-having-completed^b this^c and (after)-having-sealed^d this fruit^e to-them, I-will-go to Spain by-way-of^f you.

LEXICON—a. οὖν (LN 89.50): 'so' [AB, HNTC, ICC2, LN; NIV, NRSV, REB], 'therefore' [BECNT, LN, NICNT, WBC; KJV, NASB, NET], 'consequently, accordingly, then, so then' [LN], not explicit [NTC; CEV, GW, NCV, NLT, TEV]. This conjunction marks result, often implying the conclusion of a process of reasoning [LN].

b. aorist act. participle of ἐπιτελέω (LN 68.22) (BAGD 1.p. 302): 'to complete' [AB, BECNT, HNTC, ICC2, LN, NTC, WBC; NET, NIV, NRSV], 'to be completed' [GW], 'to finish' [BAGD, LN, NICNT; NASB, REB, TEV], 'to accomplish' [LN], 'to perform' [KJV], 'to end' [BAGD, LN]. The phrase 'after having completed this' is translated 'when the collection is completed' [GW], 'as soon as I have delivered this money' [NLT], 'after I have (safely) delivered this money' [CEV], 'after (I am sure) the poor in Jerusalem get the money' [NCV]. This verb means to bring an activity to a successful finish [LN].

c. οὗτος (LN 92.29) (BAGD 2.b. p. 597): 'this' [BAGD, BECNT, LN, WBC; KJV, NASB, NET, NRSV], 'this task' [AB, ICC2, LN, NTC; NIV, TEV], 'this matter' [HNTC], 'this business' [REB], 'the collection' [GW], not explicit [NICNT; CEV, NCV, NLT].

d. aorist mid. participle of σφραγίζω (LN **15.189, 57.87**) (BAGD 2.d. p. 796): 'to seal' [BAGD, BECNT, HNTC, ICC2, NTC, WBC; KJV], 'to put a seal on' [NICNT; NASB], 'to deliver safely' [**LN** (15.189); NET, REB], 'to deliver' [NRSV], 'to turn over' [TEV], 'to turn over to in a secure way' [**LN** (57.87)]. The phrase σφραγισάμενος αὐτοῖς τὸν καρπὸν τοῦτον 'after having sealed this fruit to them' is translated 'when I have delivered this contribution under my own seal' [AB], 'I have completed this good deed of theirs' [NLT], 'I have officially turned the money over to the Christians in Jerusalem' [GW], 'I have made sure that they have received this fruit' [NIV]. This verb means to deliver something safely to a destination [LN (15.189)], or to arrange to give something to someone in a secure manner [LN (57.87)]. These two participial phrases are conflated and translated 'after I have safely delivered this money' [CEV], 'after I am sure the poor in Jerusalem get the money that has been given for them' [NCV].

e. καρπός (LN 3.33) (BAGD 2.a. p. 405): 'fruit' [BAGD, BECNT, HNTC, ICC2, LN, NICNT, NTC, WBC; KJV, NASB, NIV], 'contribution' [AB], 'what has been collected' [NRSV], 'money' [CEV, GW, NCV], 'all the money that has been raised for them' [TEV], 'bounty' [NET], 'good deed' [NLT], 'proceeds' [REB].

f. διά with genitive (LN 84.29) (BAGD A.I.1. p. 179): 'through' [BAGD, LN]. The phrase δι' ὑμῶν 'by way of you' [WBC; NASB, NET, NRSV], is translated 'by way of your city' [ICC2], 'through your city' [BAGD], 'passing through your midst' [AB], 'through you' [HNTC, NICNT], 'by you' [KJV], 'via you' [BECNT], '(go) to you on my way' [NTC], '(see) you on my way' [NLT], '(visit) you on my way' [GW, TEV], '(visit) you on the way' [NIV, REB], '(I will visit) you and then go on' [CEV], '(I will leave for Spain) and stop and visit you' [NCV]. This preposition describes extension through an area or object [LN].

QUESTION—What does it mean for Paul to have 'sealed this fruit to them'?

It may come from the practice of sealing sacks of grain prior to delivery [AB, BECNT, NAC, TH, WBC], an action that affirms the genuineness of what is in the sacks [BECNT], or that the full amount is there [TH; TEV]. It would indicate that the money has been delivered safely [AB, BAGD, BECNT, Gdt, Ho, ICC2, St, WBC; CEV, GW, NCV, NET, NIV, REB]. A seal is an official assurance that all was well [Mor], and indicates authenticity, which in this case would mean that Paul would affirm the integrity of the offering and make sure that it is rightly understood [NICNT]. He may also be using the metaphor to imply he was still under suspicion by some in Jerusalem [AB, WBC]. 'Seal' refers to a mark of ownership, and Paul, as a steward might do, will hand over to the Jerusalem church the 'fruit' from their spiritual blessings that had gone to the Gentiles and that, in a sense, is returning to them as their own [ICC1]. These gifts will seal to the churches the fruit that comes from the gospel and will also be the proof of the love that prompted them [Mu]. The handing over of the gift sealed or certified the fact of the genuineness of the faith of the Gentile Christians [NTC].

15:29 And[a] I-know that in-coming[b] to you, I will come in the fullness[c] of-(the)-blessing[d] of-Christ.

TEXT—Instead of Χριστοῦ 'of Christ', some manuscripts have τοῦ εὐαγγελίου τοῦ Χριστοῦ 'of the gospel of Christ'. GNT selects the reading 'of Christ' with an A rating, indicating that the text is certain. The reading 'of the gospel of Christ' is taken by KJV only.

LEXICON—a. δέ (LN 89.94): 'and' [BECNT, HNTC, ICC2, LN, NICNT, WBC; CEV, KJV, NET, NLT, NRSV], not explicit [AB, NTC; GW, NASB, NCV, NIV, REB, TEV]. This conjunction marks an additive relation, but with the possible implication of some contrast [LN].

b. pres. mid. or pass. (deponent = act) participle of ἔρχομαι (LN 15.81) (BAGD I.1.a.β. p. 310): 'to come' [BAGD, BECNT, HNTC, ICC2, LN, NICNT, NTC, WBC; all versions except CEV], 'to arrive' [AB; CEV].

This present participle is translated as a finite verb 'when I come/arrive' [AB, BECNT, HNTC, ICC2, NICNT, NTC, WBC; all versions]. The root of this verb means to move toward or up to the reference point of the viewpoint character or event [LN]. This present participle form is translated as having a temporal meaning: 'when I come' [AB, BECNT, HNTC, ICC2, Mor, NICNT, NTC, WBC; CEV, GW, KJV, NASB, NCV, NET, NIV, NLT, NRSV, REB, TEV].

c. πλήρωμα (LN 59.32) (BAGD 3.b. p. 672): 'fullness' [BAGD, BECNT, ICC2, LN, NICNT, NTC, WBC; KJV, NASB, NET, NRSV], 'full measure' [HNTC, LN; NIV, REB, TEV], 'completeness' [LN]. This noun is translated as an adjective: 'full (blessing)' [AB; CEV, GW, NCV]; as an adverb: 'richly (bless)' [NLT]. This noun denotes a total quantity, with emphasis upon completeness [LN].

d. εὐλογία (LN **88.70**) (BAGD 3.b.α. p. 323): 'blessing' [AB, BAGD, BECNT, HNTC, ICC2, LN, NICNT, NTC, WBC; all versions except CEV, NLT], 'blessings' [CEV]. The phrase πληρώματι εὐλογίας Χριστοῦ 'the fullness of the blessing of Christ' is translated 'Christ will richly bless our time together' [NLT]. This noun denotes the content of the act of blessing [LN].

QUESTION—What is meant by the 'fullness of the blessing'?
Paul expects to bring as well as to find blessing [HNTC]. 'In' indicates that his coming will be accompanied by blessing [NICNT]. He expects that his visit will be pure blessing unmixed with anything else [ICC2]. It will be met with abundant blessing [Ho].

QUESTION—Is the blessing for him or for the Roman believers?
1. It will be a blessing for the Christians in Rome as well as for Paul [BECNT, HNTC, ICC1, Mor, NICNT, NTC].
2. Paul will impart a blessing to the Christians in Rome [AB, Ho, Mu, TH].

DISCOURSE UNIT—15:30–33 [AB, NICNT]. The topic is Paul's request for prayers that his mission to Jerusalem may succeed; his concluding blessing [AB], a request for prayer [NICNT].

15:30 Now[a] I-urge[b] you, brothers, through[c] our Lord Jesus Christ and through the love[d] of-the Spirit

LEXICON—a. δέ (LN 89.94): 'now' [BECNT, NICNT; KJV, NASB, NET], 'and' [LN], not explicit [AB, HNTC, ICC2, NICNT, WBC; CEV, GW, NCV, NIV, NLT, NRSV, REB, TEV].

b. pres. act. indic. of παρακαλέω (LN 33.168) (BAGD 2. p. 617): 'to urge' [AB, BAGD, NICNT; NASB, NET, NIV, NLT, TEV], 'to beg' [HNTC; CEV, NCV], 'to exhort' [BAGD, ICC2, NTC], 'to appeal to' [BAGD, BECNT, LN, WBC; NRSV], 'to beseech' [KJV], 'to encourage' [GW], 'to implore' [REB], 'to ask for earnestly' [LN]. This verb means to ask for something earnestly and with propriety [LN].

c. διά with genitive (LN 90.4) (BAGD A.III.1.f. p. 180): 'through' [BAGD, BECNT, HNTC, LN, NICNT, WBC; GW, NET, TEV], 'by' [AB, BAGD,

ICC2, LN, NTC; CEV, NASB, NIV, NRSV, REB], 'for the sake of' [KJV], 'because of' [NCV], 'in the name of' [NLT]. This preposition marks an intermediate agent, with implicit or explicit causative agent [LN].

d. ἀγάπη (LN 25.43) (BAGD I.1.a. p. 5): 'love' [AB, BAGD, BECNT, HNTC, ICC2, NICNT, NTC, WBC; all versions except NLT], '(your) love (for me)' [NLT], 'affection' [LN]. This noun denotes love for someone or something, based on sincere appreciation and high regard [LN].

QUESTION—What does it mean for Paul to urge them διά 'through' Jesus Christ?

He invokes Christ's authority as his basis for appeal [AB, Gdt, ICC2, Mor, Mu, NICNT, NTC]. Paul urges them with the authority given him by Jesus Christ: 'in the name of our Lord Jesus Christ' [NICNT], 'by the power of our Lord Jesus Christ' [CEV]. Or, the faith in the Lord Jesus that they and Paul share is the basis of his urging them to pray: 'because of our faith in the Lord Jesus Christ' [TH]. Or, their common experience of Christ's lordship is the basis: 'since we belong to our Lord Jesus Christ' or 'because of all that the Lord Jesus Christ means to you and me' [SSA]. Or, Paul invokes their devotion to the Lord: 'whatever regard you have for him, and whatever desire to see his cause prosper, in which I am engaged, let it induce you to pray' [Ho]. The Lord Jesus as well as the Spirit motivate prayer [AB]. Paul is convinced that his ministry is based on the Lord's will and command, and that he and the Romans Christians are bonded together by Christ's lordship [WBC].

QUESTION—What relationship is indicated by the genitive construction 'the love of the Spirit'?

1. The Holy Spirit is the source of the love [AB, BECNT, Gdt, HNTC, Ho, ICC1, ICC2, Mor, NAC, NICNT, NTC, St, TH, TNTC, WBC; CEV, GW, NLT, TEV]. Love is what the Holy Spirit creates [HNTC; GW], gives [NLT, TEV], prompts [WBC], inspires [BECNT, NAC, NICNT], enkindles [Mor], imparts and maintains [TNTC]. The love is a love that believers have for one another, and that comes from the Holy Spirit [BECNT, St].

2. It is the love by which the Holy Spirit loves them [Mu].

QUESTION—What does it mean for Paul to urge them διά 'through' the love of the Spirit?

The preposition διά indicates the grounds for making the request [Ho, ICC1, ICC2, Mu, NICNT, SSA, TH, WBC]. This appeal is based on the Spirit-given love Christians have for each other [ICC2, NICNT, SSA, TH]. It focuses on the Spirit-given love that the Christians have for Paul: 'do this because of your love for me, given to you by the Holy Spirit' [NLT]. Both the Lord and the Spirit motivate Paul's request for their prayers [AB].

to-strive-together[a] with-me in[b] (your) prayers[c] for[d] me to God,
> LEXICON—a. aorist mid. (deponent = act) infin. of συναγωνίζομαι (LN **34.20**) (BAGD p. 783): 'to strive together' [KJV, NASB], 'to strive' [NICNT], 'to contend' [BAGD, BECNT, WBC], 'to join (me) in my struggle' [AB, NTC; GW], 'to join earnestly (with)' [ICC2], 'to join fervently (with)' [**LN;** NET], 'to join in my struggle' [NIV, NLT], 'to be (my) allies in the fight' [REB], 'to help' [BAGD], 'to help (me) in my work' [NCV], 'to fight or contend along with someone' [BAGD], 'to join vigorously in' [LN]. The phrase συναγωνίσασθαί μοι ἐν ταῖς προσευχαῖς 'to strive together with me in your prayers' is translated 'to join me in earnest prayer/prayers' [HNTC; NRSV], 'join me in praying fervently' [TEV], 'to pray sincerely with me' [CEV]. This verb means to join with someone else in some severe effort [LN]. It occurs only here in the NT.
> b. ἐν (LN 89.76): 'in' [BECNT, HNTC, ICC2, NICNT, WBC; KJV, NASB, NET, NRSV, TEV], 'by' [AB, LN, NTC; NCV, NIV, NLT], 'by means of, through' [LN], not explicit [CEV, GW, REB]. This preposition may mark the means by which one event makes another event possible [LN].
> c. προσευχή (LN 33.178) (BAGD 1. p. 713): 'prayer' [BAGD, BECNT, HNTC, ICC2, LN, NICNT, WBC; KJV, NASB, NET, NRSV], 'praying' [AB, NTC; NCV, NIV, NLT, TEV]. This noun is translated as a verb: 'to pray' [CEV, GW, REB]. It denotes the act of speaking to God, or making requests of God [LN].
> d. ὑπέρ with genitive (LN 90.36): 'for' [LN, NTC; CEV, GW, KJV, NASB, NCV, NIV, NLT, REB, TEV], 'on behalf of' [AB, BECNT, HNTC, ICC2, LN, NICNT, WBC; NET, NRSV], 'for the sake of' [LN]. This preposition marks a participant who is benefited by an event or on whose behalf an event takes place [LN].

QUESTION—In what sense is their prayer to be a 'striving'?
> Their prayer ought to be a wholehearted involvement in the struggle of good against evil [Mor]. It is not a matter of struggling with God as Jacob did [ICC2, St, WBC], but of achieving unity between the will of God and man [Mor]. He is inviting the Romans believers to assist him through their prayers in his ministry, which he struggles to fulfill [NICNT]. Using a metaphor taken from wrestling, Paul emphasizes the intensity with which he asks them to pray [SSA]. He is saying that prayer requires energy, discipline, and earnestness [BECNT]. He wants them to pray earnestly and persistently [ICC2, Mu], urgently [ICC1], fervently [TH]. Their prayer should be characterize by intense earnestness and yearning [NTC]. He is aware of great spiritual opposition, and wants the Roman Christians to join him in his struggle through their prayers [ICC1, NAC, WBC]. Such prayer requires earnest striving, diligence, and discipline [WBC]. It requires great exertion and even a struggle with ourselves so as to align ourselves with what God wants [St]. It is a wrestling in prayer against opposing spiritual powers

[ICC1]. He wants them to pray for God's intervention in the struggle he may face in Jerusalem [Gdt].

15:31 that^a I-may-be-rescued^b from^c the-ones disobeying^d in Judea

LEXICON—a. ἵνα (LN 90.22, 89.59): 'that' [AB, BECNT, HNTC, ICC2, LN (90.22), NTC, WBC; all versions], 'in order that' [NICNT], 'in order to, so that' [LN (89.59)]. This word can mark the content of discourse, particularly if and when purpose is implied [LN (90.22)], or it can mark purpose for events and states (sometimes occurring in highly elliptical contexts) [LN (89.59)].
- b. aorist pass. subj. of ῥύομαι (LN 21.23) (BAGD p. 737): 'to be rescued' [BAGD, BECNT, NTC; GW, NASB, NET, NIV, NLT, NRSV], 'to be delivered' [AB, BAGD, HNTC, ICC2, NICNT, WBC; KJV], 'to be protected' [CEV], 'to be saved' [BAGD; NCV, REB], 'to be kept safe' [TEV], 'to be preserved' [BAGD]. This verb means to rescue from danger, with the implication that the danger in question is severe and acute [LN].
- c. ἀπό (LN 89.122): 'from' [AB, BECNT, HNTC, ICC2, LN, NICNT, NTC, WBC; all versions]. This preposition marks dissociation, implying a rupture from a former association [LN].
- d. pres. act. part. of ἀπειθέω (LN 36.23, 31.107) (BAGD 2., 3. p. 82): 'to disobey' [BAGD (2.), LN (36.23)], 'to not believe' [BAGD], 'to refuse to believe, to reject the Christian message' [LN (31.107)]. This participle is translated as an adjective: 'disobedient' [BECNT, HNTC, ICC2, NICNT, NTC, WBC; NASB, NET]; as a noun: 'unbelievers' [AB; CEV, NIV, NRSV, REB, TEV], 'nonbelievers' [NCV]; as a phrase: 'those who refuse to obey God' [NLT], 'those people…who refuse to believe' [GW], 'them that do not believe' [KJV]. This verb means to be unwilling or refuse to comply with the demands of some authority [LN (36.23)], or to refuse to believe the Christian message [LN (31.107)].

QUESTION—What relationship is indicated by ἵνα 'that'?
1. It indicates the content of the prayer [AB, BECNT, Gdt, HNTC, Ho, ICC2, Mor, NTC, SSA; CEV, GW, NCV, NET, NIV, NLT, REB, TEV]: pray that.
2. It indicates the purpose of their praying [NICNT; probably NASB, NRSV]: strive with me in order that.

QUESTION—Does τῶν ἀπειθούντων 'the ones disobeying' primarily refer to unbelief or to disobedience?
1. Here it refers primarily to disobedience [BECNT, Gdt, HNTC, ICC2, Mu, NAC, NICNT, NTC, WBC; GW, NASB, NET, NLT]. They had rejected the faith [NAC].
2. Here it refers primarily to their unbelief [AB, Mor, SSA, TH; CEV, KJV, NCV, NIV, NRSV, REB, TEV], though unbelief is disobedience [Mor].

and (that) my ministry[a] for[b] Jerusalem may-be acceptable[c] to the saints,

LEXICON—a. διακονία (LN 35.19) (BAGD 4. p. 184): 'ministry' [BECNT, HNTC, ICC2, NICNT, NTC; NET, NRSV], 'service' [AB, LN, WBC; KJV, NASB, NIV, TEV], 'errand' [REB], 'contribution (for)' [BAGD], 'donation' [NLT], 'what I am doing' [CEV], 'the help I bring' [GW, NCV].

b. εἰς (LN 90.41): 'for' [BECNT, LN, NICNT, WBC; KJV, NASB], 'to' [HNTC, NTC; NCV, NLT, NRSV, REB], 'on behalf of' [LN], 'in' [AB; NET, NIV, TEV], not explicit [CEV, GW]. This preposition marks persons benefited by an event, with the implication of something directed to them [LN].

c. εὐπρόσδεκτος (LN 25.86) (BAGD 1. p. 324): 'acceptable' [AB, BAGD, BECNT, HNTC, ICC2, NICNT, NTC, WBC; NASB, NET, NIV, NRSV, TEV], 'be accepted' [KJV], 'welcome' [BAGD], 'very acceptable, quite pleasing' [LN]. The phrase εὐπρόσδεκτος τοῖς ἁγίοις γένηται 'may be acceptable to the saints' is translated 'his people...will be pleased' [CEV], 'God's people...will accept' [GW], 'believers will be willing to accept' [NLT], 'will please God's people' [NCV], 'may find acceptance with God's people' [REB]. This adjective describes that which is particularly acceptable, and hence quite pleasing [LN].

QUESTION—Why might Paul be concerned that his ministry for believers in Jerusalem might not be acceptable?

Some of the more conservative Jewish Christians may be hostile to him [Gdt, Ho, ICC1, NICNT], or suspicious of him because they had heard that he taught apostasy from the law of Moses [BECNT]. Some believing Jews were suspicious of him [Mu, TNTC], and prejudiced against him [Mu]. There is the possibility that some of the more conservative Jewish Christians might see accepting an offering from him as condoning what they viewed as his disregard for the Jewish traditions [Mor, St], and as condoning Paul's acceptance of Gentiles into the church without circumcising them [Mor]. Jewish Christians in Jerusalem might be pressured to reject the offering because of Paul's being opposed by other Jews, who were not Christian [WBC]. He was uncertain of his relationship with the church in Jerusalem [HNTC]. Some were still opposed to his gospel of freedom in Christ [NTC]. Paul was sensitive to the potential problems involved in handling any charitable contribution and knows that they may not automatically be well received [ICC2].

15:32 so-that[a] coming to you in[b] joy, by[c] (the) will[d] of-God I-may-enjoy-rest-with[e] you.

LEXICON—a. ἵνα (LN 89.59): 'so that' [BECNT, ICC2, LN, NTC; NASB, NET, NIV, NRSV], 'that' [AB, HNTC; GW, KJV], 'in order that' [NICNT, WBC; REB], 'and so' [TEV], not explicit [CEV, NCV, NLT]. This conjunction marks purpose for events and states, and it sometimes occurring in highly elliptical contexts [LN].

b. ἐν (LN 89.84) (BAGD III.2. p. 261): 'in' [NICNT, WBC; NASB, REB], 'with' [AB, HNTC, LN; GW, KJV, NCV, NET, NIV, NLT, NRSV], not explicit [BECNT, ICC2, NTC; TEV]. The phrase ἐν χαρᾷ 'in joy' is translated 'joyfully' [BAGD, BECNT], 'full of joy' [TEV], 'with a joyful heart' [NLT], 'in a happy frame of mind' [REB], 'may be a matter of joy' [ICC2, NTC], '(have) a pleasant (visit)' [CEV]. This preposition marks the manner in which an event occurs [LN].
c. διά with genitive (LN 89.76) (BAGD A.III.1.d. p. 180): 'by' [AB, HNTC, LN, NTC; GW, KJV, NASB, NET, NIV, NLT, NRSV, REB], 'through' [BAGD, LN, NICNT, WBC]. The phrase διὰ θελήματος θεοῦ 'by the will of God' is translated 'if it be/is God's will' [ICC2; TEV], 'ask God to let me (come)' [CEV], 'if God wants me to' [NCV]. This preposition marks the means by which one event makes another event possible [LN].
d. θέλημα (LN 30.59) (BAGD 2.b. p. 354): 'will' [AB, BAGD, BECNT, HNTC, ICC2, LN, NICNT, NTC, WBC; all versions except CEV, NCV]. The phrase ἐλθὼν πρὸς ὑμᾶς διὰ θελήματος θεοῦ 'coming to you...by the will of God' is translated '(ask God) to let me come to you' [CEV], 'if God wants me to, I will come to you' [NCV]. This noun denotes that which is purposed, intended, or willed [LN].
e. aorist mid. (deponent = act) subj. of συναναπαύομαι (LN 23.86) (BAGD p. 784): 'to rest with' [BAGD, **LN**], 'to find rest with' [BECNT, NICNT], 'to find refreshing rest (in your company)' [NASB], 'to enjoy a time of rest' [REB], 'to rest together with someone else' [LN], 'to be refreshed together with' [AB, NTC; NIV], 'to be refreshed with' [GW, KJV], 'to be refreshed (in your company)' [NET, NRSV], 'to find mutual refreshment' [HNTC], 'to be mutually refreshed (by your company)' [WBC], 'to find full refreshment (in your fellowship)' [ICC2], 'have a refreshing visit' [CEV], 'enjoy a refreshing visit' [TEV], 'you and I will have a time of rest' [NCV], 'we will be an encouragement to each other' [NLT]. This verb means to experience restorative rest together with someone else [LN]. This word occurs only here in the NT.

QUESTION—What relationship is indicated by ἵνα 'so that'?
1. It indicates purpose [BECNT, ICC2, Mor, NICNT, NTC, TH, WBC; NASB, NCV, NET, NIV, NLT, NRSV, REB, TEV]. It is subordinate to the ἵνα in the previous verse, not coordinate with it [Mor]. It expresses the ultimate purpose of the two similar purpose clauses in 15:31 [NICNT].
2. It indicates further content of the prayer he has asked for in 15:31 [AB; CEV, GW]

15:33 Now[a] **(may) the God of-peace[b] (be) with[c] you all. Amen**
LEXICON—a. δέ (LN 89.94): 'now' [KJV, NASB, NET], 'and now' [NLT], 'and' [LN], not explicit [AB, BECNT, HNTC, ICC2, NICNT, NTC, WBC; CEV, GW, NCV, NIV, NRSV, REB, TEV]. This conjunction indicates an additive relationship [LN].

b. εἰρήνη (LN 25.248) (BAGD 3. p. 227): 'peace' [AB, BAGD, BECNT, HNTC, ICC2, LN, NICNT, NTC, WBC; all versions]. The phrase 'the God of peace' is translated 'God, who gives peace' [CEV, NCV], 'God, who gives us his peace' [NLT], 'God, our source of peace' [TEV]. This noun denotes a state of freedom from anxiety and inner turmoil [LN]. It denotes harmonious relationships with God and with other believers, and generally all the blessings of God [NICNT].

c. μετά with the genitive (LN 90.60) (BAGD A.II.1.c.β. p. 509): 'with' [AB, BAGD, BECNT, HNTC, ICC2, LN, NICNT, NTC, WBC; all versions]. This preposition marks the experiencer of an event, with the added implication of association [LN].

QUESTION—What does he mean by 'the God of peace'?

God gives peace [BECNT, ICC2, Mu, NAC, NICNT, NTC, TH, WBC; CEV, NCV, NLT]. He is the source of peace [AB, BECNT, TH; TEV]. Only he can give peace [NAC]. Because real peace is so fully associated with God, Paul can characterize God this way [Mor].

QUESTION—What is the function of 'amen' here?

It indicates that what was just said is a prayer [TH]. This is the normal conclusion to a prayer [AB, Mor]. It is a solemn affirmation of his prayer-wish [NTC]. It expresses his desire that this prayer-wish would be realized in the Roman Christians' experience [BECNT].

DISCOURSE UNIT—16:1–27 [Mu, NAC; GW, NCV, NET, NIV]. The topic is greetings and closing doxology [Mu], some final items [NAC], farewell [GW], greetings to the Christians [NCV], personal greetings [NET, NIV], greetings [REB].

DISCOURSE UNIT—16:1–23 [AB, BECNT, HNTC, NICNT, WBC; CEV]. The topic is conclusion: letter of recommendation for Phoebe and greetings to Roman Christians [AB], coworkers in the gospel [BECNT], personal greetings [HNTC; CEV], greetings [NICNT], final greetings [WBC].

DISCOURSE UNIT—16:1–16 [ICC1, Mu, St; NLT, NRSV, TEV]. The topic is personal greetings [ICC1; NRSV], Paul's own greetings [Mu], commendations and greetings [St], Paul greets his friends [NLT], personal greetings [TEV].

DISCOURSE UNIT—16:1–2 [AB, Ho, NAC, NICNT, TNTC, WBC]. The topic is Paul recommends Phoebe, a minister of Cenchreae [AB], personal matters [Ho], commendation of Phoebe [NAC, NICNT, TNTC, WBC].

16:1 Now[a] I-commend[b] to-you Phoebe our sister, who-is a servant[c] of- the - church in Cenchreae,

LEXICON—a. δέ (LN 89.94): 'and' [LN], 'now' [BECNT, NICNT; NET], not explicit [AB, HNTC, ICC2, NTC, WBC; all versions except NET]. This conjunction marks an additive relation, with the possible implication of some contrast [LN].

b. pres. act. indic. of συνίστημι (LN **33.343**) (BAGD I.1.b. p. 790): 'to commend' [AB, BECNT, HNTC, ICC2, NICNT, NTC; KJV, NASB, NET, NIV, NLT, NRSV, REB], 'to recommend' [**LN**, WBC; NCV], 'to present' [BAGD], 'to introduce' [GW], 'to have good things to say about' [CEV]. This verb means to indicate approval of a person or event, with the implication that others adopt the same attitude [LN].
b. διάκονος ((LN **53.67**) (BAGD 2.b. p. 184): 'servant' [NTC; KJV, NASB, NET, NIV], 'deacon' [BECNT, ICC2, **LN**, NICNT, WBC; GW, NLT, NRSV], 'deaconess' [BAGD, HNTC], 'minister' [AB; REB], 'helper' [NCV], 'leader' [CEV]. This noun denotes one who serves as a deacon, with responsibility to care for the needs of believers [LN].

QUESTION—What relationship is indicated by δέ 'now'?

Some translate this conjunction as 'now', indicating some degree of continuation or transition from what has been said before [AB, BECNT, NICNT; NET]. Most do not translate it, indicating that it is viewed as weakly transitional, but not as contrastive.

QUESTION—Who was Phoebe?

She may have been a freedwoman [Mor], and was probably wealthy [AB, Gdt, Mor, NTC, St, WBC]. She was probably a Gentile [NAC, NICNT]. Her name derives from pagan mythology [Ho, Mor, NAC, NTC], which was not uncommon for Christians and even Jews in the first century [NTC]. Phoebe most likely carried this epistle to Rome when she went [AB, BECNT, Gdt, ICC1, ICC2, Mu, NAC, NTC, SSA, St, TNTC, WBC]. It has been observed that when Phoebe went to Rome with this letter she carried in her clothing the whole future of Christian theology [NAC]. This is the only place in the NT that she is mentioned [TH].

QUESTION—To whom would 'our' refer?

1. It refers to Christians as a whole [BECNT, ICC2, WBC]. She is a fellow believer, a member of the church family [BECNT]. Within the church there is already the understanding of a universal and international brotherhood and sisterhood [WBC].
2. It refers to the Christians of Corinth; she is their Christian sister [AB].

QUESTION—Why did she need to be commended?

Such recommendations were necessary for travelers who would otherwise be unknown to the people whom the traveler hoped would provide hospitality and lodging [BECNT, Mor, NICNT, TNTC]. Phoebe would need their hospitality and help [HNTC, NTC]. Letters of recommendation protected people from becoming the victims of charlatans and imposters [ICC1, St].

QUESTION—Did Phoebe occupy an official position in the church such as deacon or deaconess?

1. She did not occupy any office [Mu, NTC, TH]. She served in the church in mercy ministry to those who were poor, sick, and desolate [Mu], or in hospitality ministry [NTC]. This had probably not yet become a technical term for a church office [TH].

2. She was probably a deacon [BECNT, ICC2, Mor, NICNT, SSA, TNTC, WBC], or a deaconess [Gdt, HNTC, Ho, ICC1]. Female deacons were needed for assisting in the baptism of women or ministry to women [BECNT, ICC1, Mor], and particularly for ministry in women's quarters in homes [ICC1, Mor]. She would have helped the poor, the sick, strangers, and orphans [Gdt]. She would have assisted women who were poor or sick [Ho]. When Paul wrote this letter, offices in the church were still in the process of being established, so this title may not represent the office of deacon as it later came to be known [HNTC, ICC1, NICNT, WBC]. This does not mean that she was a leader of the congregation [BECNT, Mu, NICNT].
3. She may have been a leader in the congregation [AB].

16:2 that you-would-receive^a her in (the) Lord (in a manner) worthy^b of-(the) saints^c

LEXICON—a. aorist mid. (deponent = act.) subj. of προσδέχομαι ((LN 34.53) (BAGD 1.a. p. 712): 'to receive' [AB, BAGD, HNTC, LN, NICNT; KJV, NASB, NIV], 'to welcome' [BECNT, LN, WBC; CEV, NET, NLT, NRSV], 'to give a welcome' [ICC2; GW, REB], 'to extend a welcome' [NTC], 'to accept' [LN; NCV], 'to have as a guest' [LN]. This verb means to accept the presence of a person with friendliness [LN].

b. ἀξίως (LN 66.6) (BAGD p. 78): 'worthy' [AB, BECNT, HNTC, ICC2, LN, NICNT, NTC, WBC; NET, NIV, REB], 'worthily' [BAGD], 'proper' [LN; CEV], 'fitting' [LN; NRSV]. The phrase 'in a manner worthy' [AB, NICNT, WBC] is also translated 'in a way worthy' [BECNT, HNTC; NET, NIV], 'as becometh' [KJV]. The phrase 'in a way worthy of the saints' is translated 'that shows you are God's holy people' [GW], 'in the way that God's people should' [NCV], 'as one who is worthy of honor among God's people' [NLT]. This adverb describes being fitting or proper in corresponding to what should be expected [LN (66.6)].

c. ἅγιος ((LN 11.27). This plural noun is translated 'saints' [BECNT, HNTC, ICC2, NICNT, NTC, WBC; KJV, NASB, NET, NIV, NRSV], 'God's people' [LN; NCV, NLT, REB], 'God's holy people' [GW], 'God's dedicated people' [AB], 'someone who has faith in the Lord and is one of God's own people' [CEV]. This noun denotes persons who belong to God, and as such constitute a religious entity [LN].

QUESTION—What relationship is indicated by ἵνα 'that'?
1. It introduces an implied imperative based on the commendation in 16:1 [BECNT, HNTC]: that. It is translated as though introducing an implied imperative [NTC; CEV, GW, KJV, NASB, NCV, NIV, NLT, REB, TEV]. It introduces the content of Paul's appeal [SSA].
2. It indicates the purpose of the commendation mentioned in 16:1 [Mor, NICNT; NET, NRSV]: so that, in order that.

QUESTION—What does he mean by adding 'in the Lord'?
Receiving someone in the Lord is giving them a Christian welcome [NICNT; GW]. It expresses close relationship in Christian hospitality [AB]. They are to receive her as a Christian [HNTC, SSA, TH, TNTC], in the bond and fellowship of those who are united with Christ [Mu]. He focuses on the life in Christ in this chapter, meaning that everything Christians do, they do in Christ [Mor]. It expresses the unity and community that binds the members of the church into one body [Gdt]. She should be admitted to every spiritual privilege [ICC1].

QUESTION—Does ἀξίως τῶν ἁγίων '(a manner) worthy of the saints' refer to what is fitting for the Roman church to give or to what Phoebe should be given?

1. It refers to the kind of reception saints should give, in this case the Roman church [AB, HNTC, Ho, ICC1, Mu, NTC, SSA, St, TH; GW, NCV, TEV].
2. It refers to the kind of reception by which saints should be received, in this case, Phoebe [CEV, NLT].
3 It refers to the kind of reception saints should give, as well as the kind of reception by which saints should be received [Gdt, NAC, NICNT]. The phrase 'in a manner worthy of the saints' modifies the verb 'receive', and the event of receiving includes both those who receive and those who are received [NICNT].

and assist[a] her in whatever thing of-yours she-might-need[b]

LEXICON—a. aorist act. subj. of παρίστημι ((LN **35.1**) (BAGD 2.a.γ. p. 628): 'to assist' [HNTC, ICC2, NICNT, WBC; KJV], 'to help' [AB, BAGD, BECNT, **LN**; CEV, NASB, NCV, NLT, NRSV], 'to give help' [NTC; NIV], 'to provide' [GW, NET], 'to support' [REB]. This verb means to assist in supplying what may be needed [LN].
b. pres. act. subj. of χρῄζω (LN 57.39) (BAGD p. 885): 'to need' [BAGD, BECNT, HNTC, ICC2, LN, NICNT, NTC, WBC; GW, NCV, NET, NIV, NLT], 'to have need of' [KJV, NASB], 'to need help' [REB], 'to require' [AB; NRSV], 'to lack, to be without' [LN], not explicit [CEV]. This verb means to lack something which is necessary and particularly needed [LN].

for she also has-been a helper[a] of-many and of-me.

LEXICON—a. προστάτις (LN **35.13**) (BAGD p. 718): 'helper' [**LN**, NTC; NASB], 'great help' [NET, NIV], 'benefactor' [NICNT; NRSV], 'protectress' [BAGD, HNTC], 'patroness' [AB, LN], 'patron' [BECNT, WBC], 'source of assistance' [ICC2], 'succourer' [KJV], 'respected leader' [CEV], 'good friend' [REB]. The phrase 'she has also been a helper' is translated 'she has helped' [NCV], 'she has provided help' [GW], 'she has been helpful' [NLT]. This noun denotes one who is active in helping [LN]. It occurs only here in the NT.

QUESTION—In what way was Phoebe a helper?
   She was probably a woman of some status and wealth [AB, BECNT, ICC1, Mor, Mu, NICNT, SSA], and likely assisted others materially [AB, BECNT, ICC1, NICNT, SSA], or with hospitality [AB, BECNT, NTC]. She was a benefactor [Ho]. She may have assisted Paul through hospitality and possibly by helping him during an illness [Gdt].

DISCOURSE UNIT—16:3–16 [AB, NAC, TNTC, WBC]. The topic is Paul's greetings to various persons [AB], salutations [Ho], greetings [NAC, WBC], greetings to Roman Christians [NICNT], greetings to various friends [TNTC].

DISCOURSE UNIT—16:3–13 [Mor]. The topic is greetings.

16:3 Greet[a] **Prisca and Aquila my co-workers**[b] **in Christ Jesus**
LEXICON—a. aorist mid. (deponent = act.) impera. of ἀσπάζομαι (LN 33.20) (BAGD 1.a. p. 116): 'to greet' [BAGD, BECNT, HNTC, ICC2, LN, NICNT, NTC, WBC; CEV, GW, NASB, NET, NIV, NRSV], 'to give greetings' [NCV, NLT, REB], 'to send greetings' [TEV]. This verb is translated as a noun: 'my greetings to' [AB].
   b. συνεργός (LN 42.44) (BAGD p. 787): 'coworker' [BECNT; GW, NLT], 'fellow worker' [AB, HNTC, ICC2, LN, NICNT, NTC, WBC; NASB, NET, NIV, REB, TEV], 'working with' [BAGD]. The phrase 'my co-workers' is translated 'they served...together with me' [CEV], 'who worked together with me' [NCV], 'who worked with me' [NRSV]. This noun denotes one who works together with someone else [LN].
QUESTION—Who were Prisca and Aquila, and in what sense were they co-workers?
   They are mentioned in Acts 18 [Ho, Mu, NTC]. Luke uses the diminutive form 'Priscilla' whereas Paul uses 'Prisca' [Mor, NAC, NICNT, NTC], which is more dignified [NAC]. In order to conform to the translation in Acts her name is given as 'Priscilla' [CEV, KJV, NCV, NIV, NLT, TEV]. They were involved in ministry with Paul [AB, BECNT, Mor, Mu, NICNT, WBC], and were very important to Paul in his missionary work [WBC]. They, like Paul, were missionaries [BECNT], or evangelists [AB]. They were deeply involved in Christian mission [NTC]. Paul had stayed with them in Corinth [NTC, WBC], and they went with him to Ephesus [Gdt, NTC]. They were coworkers in ministry as well as in trade [NTC]. They were probably rather wealthy [WBC]. Although Paul had conflicts with other Christian leaders from time to time (such as Peter, Barnabas, and Mark), his relations with Prisca and Aquila were very harmonious [NTC]. Prisca's name is given first in four of the six times the couple is mentioned by Luke or Paul [Gdt, NICNT, NTC], perhaps because she was superior to Aquila in some way, possibly in Christian activity and work [Gdt, ICC2, NTC], or in abilities [Gdt, WBC], or in personal financial resources [WBC], or because she may have been converted before her husband [ICC2], or for other reasons we just don't know [BECNT, NICNT].

QUESTION—With what is the phrase 'in Christ Jesus' connected?
They are fellow workers in Christ Jesus [AB, HNTC, Ho, Mor, Mu, SSA, TH, WBC; CEV, GW, KJV, NASB, NCV, NET, NIV, NLT, NRSV, REB, TEV]. Paul uses 'in Christ' and 'in the Lord' throughout the list of greetings to describe the love that marked the Christian community [BECNT]. The phrase indicates that they assisted him in ministry [Ho].

16:4 **who risked[a] their necks[b] for my life,[c] to-whom not only I give-thanks[d] but all the churches of-the Gentiles,**

LEXICON—a. aorist act. indic. of ὑποτίθημι (LN **21.8**) (BAGD 1. p. 848): 'to risk' [AB, BAGD, BECNT, HNTC, ICC2, **LN**, NICNT, NTC, WBC; all versions]. The phrase τράχηλον ὑποτίθημι 'to put down one's neck' is an idiom meaning to willingly and purposely expose oneself to extreme danger and risk [LN].

b. τράχηλος (LN **8.25, 21.8**) (BAGD p. 825): 'neck' [AB, BAGD, ICC2, **LN** (8.25), NICNT, NTC, WBC; NASB, NET, NRSV, REB], 'own neck' [BECNT], 'life' [HNTC, **LN** (21.8); CEV, GW, NCV, NIV, NLT, TEV].

c. ψυχή (LN 23.88) (BAGD 1.a.γ. p. 893): 'life' [BAGD, BECNT, LN; NASB, NCV, NET, NRSV, REB], 'soul' [BAGD, NICNT]. The phrase 'for my life' is translated 'for me' [AB; CEV, NIV, NLT, TEV], 'for mine' [HNTC], 'to save my life' [ICC2, NTC], 'to save me' [GW], 'for my sake' [WBC].

d. pres. act. indic. of εὐχαριστῶ (LN **25.100**) (BAGD 1. p. 328): 'to give thanks' [WBC; NASB, NRSV], 'to thank' [NICNT], 'to be thankful' [BAGD, **LN**; GW, NCV, NLT], 'to be grateful' [AB, BECNT, HNTC, ICC2, LN, NTC; CEV, NET, NIV, REB, TEV]. This verb means to be thankful on the basis of some received benefit [LN].

QUESTION—What does it mean to 'risk their necks'?
They intervened in Paul's behalf in some way that endangered them as well [AB, Ho, Mu, NTC, SSA]. They saved his life somehow [NICNT], risking their lives to save his [BECNT]. This may have been connected with the riot in Ephesus [AB, BECNT, ICC1, Mor, NAC, NICNT, NTC]. They were very loyal to Paul [NTC]. They probably used the influence their wealth and social status afforded them in order to help Paul [WBC].

16:5 **and (greet) the church in their house.[a]**

LEXICON—a. οἶκος (LN 7.2) (BAGD 1.a.α. p. 560): 'house' [BAGD, LN]. The phrase 'in their house' [BECNT, ICC2, WBC; NET], is translated 'that is in their house' [KJV, NASB], 'that/which meets in their house' [HNTC;GW, NIV, TEV], 'that meets at their house' [AB, NTC; NCV, REB], 'that meets in their home' [CEV, NLT], 'of their house' [NICNT]. This noun denotes a building consisting of one or more rooms and normally serving as a dwelling place [LN].

QUESTION—What was the nature of house churches?
There were no church buildings in the first century [ICC2, Mor]. Churches met in houses, and Christian people who had large homes allowed them to be

used for such meetings [AB, HNTC, Mor]. The home was central in early Christian life [AB]. Churches regularly met in homes, perhaps weekly, and came together in larger gatherings with other churches less frequently, perhaps once a month [WBC].

Greet Epaenetus my beloved[a] (friend), who is (the) first-fruits[b] of-Asia for Christ.

LEXICON—a. ἀγαπητός (LN 25.45) (BAGD 2. p. 6): 'beloved' [BAGD, BECNT, HNTC, ICC2, LN, NICNT, NTC, WBC; NASB, NRSV], 'dear friend' [AB; CEV, GW, NCV, NET, NIV, NLT, REB, TEV], 'one who is loved, dear' [LN]. This adjective describes one who is loved [LN].

b. ἀπαρχή (LN 61.8) (BAGD 2.a. p. 81): 'first fruits' [BAGD], 'first' [LN]. The phrase ἀπαρχή...εἰς Χριστόν 'firstfruits...for Christ' [ICC2, NICNT, NTC, WBC], is translated 'first convert...for Christ' [NRSV], 'first-fruits...in Christ' [BECNT], 'firstfruits...unto Christ' [HNTC; KJV], 'the first convert...to Christ' [AB; NASB, NET, NIV, REB], 'first person...to have faith in Christ' [CEV], 'first...to believe in Christ' [TEV], 'first person...to become a believer in Christ' [GW], 'first person...to become a follower of Christ' [NLT], 'first person...to follow Christ' [NCV]. This noun denotes the first of a set, often in relation to something being given [LN]. It implies that others would follow [NTC].

16:6 Greet Mary, who worked[a] very-hard[b] for[c] you.

TEXT—Instead of εἰς ὑμᾶς 'for you', some manuscripts have εἰς ἡμᾶς 'for us, on us' or ἐν ἡμῖν 'among us, on us'. GNT does not mention this alternative. Only KJV reads 'on us'.

LEXICON—a. aorist act. indic. of κοπιάω (LN 42.47) (BAGD 2. p. 443): 'to work' [AB, NICNT; all versions], 'to work hard' [LN], 'to labor' [BECNT, ICC2, LN, NTC, WBC], 'to toil' [HNTC, LN], 'to bestow labor' [KJV], 'to become weary' [BAGD]. This verb means to engage in hard work, implying difficulties and trouble [LN]. The context implies that this was Christian work [HNTC].

b. πολύς (LN 59.11, 78.3) (BAGD I.2.b.β. p. 688): 'very hard' [GW, NCV, NET, NIV, NRSV], 'hard' [AB, NICNT; NASB], 'so hard' [CEV, NLT, REB, TEV], 'much' [BECNT, HNTC, ICC2, LN, NTC, WBC; KJV], 'many' [BAGD], 'great, a great deal' [LN]. This adjective describes a relatively large quantity [LN (59.11)], or the upper range of a scale of extent [LN (78.3)].

c. εἰς (LN 90.41): 'for' [AB, BECNT, ICC2, LN, NICNT, NTC, WBC; CEV, GW, NASB, NCV, NET, NIV, NLT, REB, TEV], 'on behalf of' [LN], 'among' [NRSV]. The phrase 'for you' is translated 'for your benefit' [HNTC]. This preposition marks persons benefited by an event, with the implication of something directed to them [LN].

16:7 Greet Andronicus and Junia/Junias,[a] my kinspeople[b] and my fellow-prisoners,[c]

LEXICON—a. Ἰουνιᾶς (LN 93.178). This name is translated as Junia, which would be a woman's name [AB, ICC2, NICNT, WBC; KJV, NCV, NET, NLT, NRSV, REB, TEV], or as Junias, which would be a man's name [HNTC, NTC; CEV, GW, NASB, NIV].
- b. συγγενής (LN **11.57**) (BAGD p. 772): 'kinsmen' [HNTC; KJV, NASB], 'kindred' [BECNT, NICNT], 'kinsfolk' [ICC2, WBC], 'related' [BAGD], 'fellow countrymen' [AB, **LN**, NTC; REB], 'fellow Jews' [NLT, TEV], 'relatives' [CEV, NCV, NIV], 'compatriots' [NET]. The phrase 'my kinspeople' is translated 'who are Jewish by birth, like me' [GW]. This noun denotes a person who is a member of the same nation [LN].
- c. συναιχμάλωτος (LN **37.118**) (BAGD p. 783): 'fellow prisoners' [BAGD, BECNT, HNTC, ICC2, **LN**, NICNT, NTC, WBC; KJV, NASB, NET]. The phrase 'my fellow prisoners' is translated 'comrades in captivity' [REB], 'who were imprisoned/in prison with me' [AB; NCV], 'who have been in prison with me' [NIV], 'who were in prison with me' [NLT, TEV], 'who were in jail with me' [CEV], 'they are prisoners like me' [GW]. This noun denotes one who has been arrested and imprisoned along with someone else [LN].

QUESTION—Is Ἰουνιαν 'Junia/Junias' the name of a woman or a man?

The original unaccented Greek word was Ἰουνιαν. Later it was accented by some as Ἰουνίαν 'Junia', a woman's name, but others accented it as Ἰουνιᾶν 'Junias', a contracted form of 'Junianus', a man's name [NICNT, WBC].
1. It is the name of a woman [AB, BECNT, ICC2, Mor, NAC, NICNT, SSA, St, TNTC, WBC; KJV, NCV, NET, NLT, NRSV, REB, TEV]. Andronicus and Junia were probably husband and wife [BECNT, Mor, NAC, NICNT, WBC]. Until about the thirteenth century, commentary opinion was almost unanimously agreed that Ἰουνιαν was a woman's name, but then it shifted to viewing it as a man's name; now scholarly opinion leans once again to it being the name of a woman [NICNT].
2. It is the name of a man [Gdt, GNT, HNTC, ICC1, LN, NTC; CEV, GW, NASB, NIV].

QUESTION—What does Paul mean by συγγενεῖς μου 'my kinspeople'?
1. They are Jews, not relatives [AB, BECNT, Gdt, HNTC, ICC1, ICC2, Mor, Mu, NAC, NICNT, NTC, SSA, St, TH, WBC].
2. They are his relatives [Ho].

who are outstanding[a] among the apostles, and who were in Christ before me.

LEXICON—a. ἐπίσημος (LN **28.31**) (BAGD 1. p. 298): 'outstanding' [**LN**], 'famous' [LN], 'prominent' [BAGD]. The phrase ἐπίσημοι ἐν τοῖς ἀποστόλοις 'outstanding among the apostles' [AB, BECNT, ICC2, NTC, WBC; NASB, NIV] is also translated 'highly respected by the apostles'

[CEV], 'highly respected among the apostles' [NLT], 'notable in the ranks of the apostles' [HNTC], 'esteemed among the apostles' [NICNT], 'prominent among the apostles' [GW, NRSV], 'eminent among the apostles' [REB], 'of note among the apostles' [KJV], 'well known among the apostles' [TEV], 'well known to the apostles' [NET], 'are very important apostles' [NCV]. This adjective describes being well known or outstanding, either because of positive or negative characteristics [LN].

QUESTION—In what sense does he use the term 'apostles' here?
1. There was a wider group of apostles beyond the twelve, and these two people were in that group [AB, BECNT, Gdt, HNTC, ICC1, ICC2, Mor, NAC, NICNT, NTC, SSA, St, TH, TNTC, WBC]. It is used in a much looser sense than in most of the rest of the NT, not to designate an authoritative leader, but rather an emissary or messenger, a traveling missionary [ICC2, NICNT]. They were missionaries or traveling evangelists [AB, BECNT, Gdt, NAC, NTC, St, WBC]. It appears that they were in some sense senior in standing to Paul himself [HNTC, ICC2]. They were possibly Hellenistic Jews from Palestine who were among the five hundred people that Christ appointed following his resurrection [WBC].
2. He is using 'apostle' in the traditional sense, and saying that in the estimation of the apostles they were considered to be outstanding for their faith and service [Ho, Mu].

16:8 Greet Ampliatus my beloved (friend) in the Lord.
QUESTION—Who was Ampliatus?
Based on his name we can guess that he was probably a slave or a freedman [NICNT]. The name was common among slaves [ICC2, NAC, NTC, St, WBC].
QUESTION—With what element in the sentence is ἐν κυρίῳ 'in the Lord' associated?
It modifies 'beloved' [AB, BECNT, Gdt, Ho, Mu, NICNT, NTC, TH, WBC]: my beloved in the Lord. Their relation to Christ establishes this bond of love [Mu].

16:9 Greet Urbanus our co-worker in Christ and Stachys my beloved (friend).
QUESTION—Who were Urbanus and Stachys?
Urbanus was also probably a slave or freedman [AB, ICC1, ICC2, Mor, NICNT], but Paul may not have actually known him [ICC2, NICNT]. Urbanus may have been a member of the imperial household [WBC]. Nothing is known of Stachys [NICNT]. Stachys may have been a friend of Paul [Mor]. Stachys is not a very common Greek name [AB, ICC2, NTC]. The possessive pronoun 'our' is inclusive [Mu, SSA], meaning that he had not only worked with Paul, but also had worked in Rome [SSA].

16:10 Greet Apelles the (one) approved[a] in Christ. Greet those of-the (household)[b] of-Aristobulus.

LEXICON—a. δόκιμος (LN **73.4**) (BAGD 1. p. 203): 'approved' [AB, BECNT, NICNT, NTC, WBC; KJV, NASB, NET], 'tested and approved' [NIV], 'genuine' [BAGD, HNTC], 'proved' [ICC2], 'sincere' [LN]. The phrase 'the one approved in Christ' is translated 'a faithful servant of Christ' [CEV], 'who was tested and proved he truly loves Christ' [NCV], 'a good man whom Christ approves' [NLT], 'well proved in Christ's service' [REB], 'whose loyalty to Christ has been proved' [TEV], 'whose faith in Christ is genuine' [**LN**]. This adjective describes being genuine on the basis of testing [LN].

   b. There is no lexical entry for the word 'household'; it is supplied to express what is implied. It is represented in translation as 'household' [AB, BECNT, ICC2, NTC, WBC; KJV, NASB, NET, NIV, NLT, REB], 'house' [NICNT], 'family' [CEV, GW, NCV, TEV]. The phrase 'those of the household of Aristobulus' is translated 'the slaves of the household of Aristobulus' [HNTC].

QUESTION—In what way was Apelles approved?

He may have proven himself in some difficult situation or perhaps he was simply well respected [NICNT, WBC]. He demonstrated strength of character under some form of testing [BECNT]. In some specific incident he had proven to be a faithful believer [NAC]. He showed that he is a genuine Christian [AB, HNTC], an approved Christian [ICC1]. He had remained dependable and true to the faith under some difficult circumstance [NTC]. He endured peculiar trials and temptations [Mu]. He was tried and approved [Ho], steadfast under trial [Gdt]. His loyalty to Christ has been proven [TH].

QUESTION—Who was Aristobulus?

This may have been the Aristobulus who was the brother of Herod Agrippa [ICC1, ICC2, NAC, NICNT, TNTC, WBC], grandson of Herod the Great [ICC2, Mor, WBC], and if so, he died about eight or ten years prior to the writing of this letter; Paul is addressing the members of his household, particularly the slaves [NICNT, WBC]. These household members could well have been slaves who passed into the ownership of the emperor Claudius after the death of Aristobulus [ICC1, Mor, NAC, TNTC, WBC]. If this Aristobulus was the brother of Herod Agrippa, and the Christians were slaves in his household, they could have been among the first Christians in Rome, and this could possibly be the way Christianity came to Rome [AB].

16:11 Greet Herodion my kinsman. Greet those of-(the household) of-Narcissus who-are in (the) Lord.

QUESTION—Who was Herodion?

He was a Jewish man who may have been part of the household of Aristobulus [ICC1, ICC2, Mor, TNTC, WBC]. This name was not known in Rome otherwise [NICNT], which suggests that this man was a Jewish freedman in the service of one of the Herods [ICC2, NICNT, WBC].

QUESTION—Who was Narcissus?
Narcissus was the name of a well-known freedman who had served Claudius, the emperor, and who had been forced to commit suicide; Paul is greeting the members of his household [ICC1, ICC2, Mor, NICNT, WBC].

16:12 Greet Tryphena and Tryphosa, the-ones working-hard in (the) Lord. Greet Persis (my) beloved (friend), who worked- very -hard in (the) Lord.
QUESTION—Who were these women?
Their names suggest that they were probably slaves [NICNT], or freedwomen [NICNT, WBC]. Most likely Tryphena and Tryphosa were sisters [AB, Gdt, ICC1, ICC2, NICNT, NTC, SSA, TNTC, WBC]. By saying that Tryphena and Tryphosa 'worked hard', Paul may have intended a humorous or ironic contrast with their names, which mean 'Dainty' and 'Delicate' [Gdt, ICC1, Mor, WBC]. Persis was a name that was often used for a female slave [AB, ICC2, WBC]. She was probably a freedwoman [WBC].

16:13 Greet Rufus the-one chosen[a] in (the) Lord and his mother, (who is) also mine.
LEXICON—a. ἐκλεκτός (LN 30.93) (BAGD 2. p. 242): 'chosen' [AB, BAGD, BECNT, LN, WBC; KJV, NET, NIV, NRSV], 'elect' [ICC2, NICNT, NTC]. The phrase 'the one chosen in the Lord' is translated 'that outstanding Christian' [HNTC; GW], 'an outstanding follower of the Lord' [REB], 'that special servant of the Lord' [CEV], 'special person in the Lord' [NCV], 'a choice man' [NASB], 'whom, the Lord picked out to be his very own' [NLT], 'whose loyalty to Christ has been proved' [TEV]. This adjective describes that which has been chosen [LN].
QUESTION—Who was Rufus?
He may have been the son of Simon of Cyrene, and brother of Alexander, as mentioned in Mark 15:21 [BECNT, Gdt, HNTC, ICC1, ICC2, Mu, NICNT, NTC, St, WBC].
QUESTION—In what sense was Rufus chosen in the Lord?
1. Paul is saying simply that he is a Christian, and chosen in the same sense that all Christians are [BECNT, ICC2, NICNT; NLT]. He is elect, as all Christians are [NTC]. Paul wants to make some kind of positive comment about those he mentions, or at least about the ones he knows personally [BECNT, ICC2].
2. Since all believers are 'chosen' Paul seems to be singling him out, indicating that he is special in some way [AB, HNTC, Ho, ICC1, Mor, Mu, NAC, SSA]. He was outstanding as a believer [AB, HNTC, ICC1, SSA], distinguished in some way [Gdt]. He may have been chosen for some special task [WBC], or for a prominent position in the local church [NAC], or for his service for Christ [TH].
QUESTION—Why does Paul say that Rufus' mother is also his mother?
This woman had been very kind to Paul on some occasion [AB, ICC2, Mor]. She had helped him in some way [BECNT]. There was a close and

supportive relationship, and she had proven to be like a mother to Paul [NAC]. She had helped Paul as though he were her son [ICC1, SSA, TH].

16:14 Greet Asyncritus, Phlegon, Hermes, Patrobas, Hermas, and the brothers with them.

QUESTION—Who were these people?

Their names suggest that they were either slaves or freedmen [ICC2, Mor]. Hermes was a very common slave name [AB, ICC1, NICNT, St, WBC], as was Hermas [NAC]. Phlegon is a slave name [AB, WBC]. These were possibly members of the same house church [AB, ICC1, ICC2, NICNT, NTC, SSA, WBC].

16:15 Greet Philologus, Julia, Nereus and his sister, and Olympas, and all the saints with them.

QUESTION—Who were these people?

Philologus was a commonly used slave name [AB, ICC1, ICC2, NTC, St, WBC], and Julia was a very common female slave name [ICC1, ICC2, Mor, NTC, St, WBC]. Nereus may be the name of a freedman [ICC2, Mor]. Philologus and Julia were probably husband and wife [AB, Gdt, Mu, NICNT, NTC], and Nereus and his sister may have been their children [NICNT]. Julia was either Philologus' wife or sister [ICC2, WBC]. 'All the saints with them' probably refers to the other church members who met in their house [AB, Gdt, Mu, NICNT], or were members of the same house church [NTC, TH].

QUESTION—What can we learn from this list of people whom Paul has mentioned by name?

The majority of the people named are Gentiles, and the majority of the names are recognizable as names of slaves or former slaves [BECNT, NICNT, St]. This would probably reflect the background of the church as a whole [NICNT, St]. Paul's recognition of, and appreciation for his co-workers shows that he depended on many other people for assistance in ministry [NICNT]. Nine of the twenty-six people he greets are women [St], and all whom he credits with hard work (κοπιάω) are women [NAC, St]. The fact that he mentions nine women here shows that women exercised an important role in ministry within the church [NAC, NICNT], and that Paul had a high view of women [ICC2, St]. Of those described as co-workers, there are more women than men, and we can see that women were actively involved in ministry in the early church [BECNT, WBC]. We can also see that the believers in Rome met in house churches [BECNT], and that at least some of them were wealthy [WBC]. The early church was diverse in terms of ethnicity, social rank, and gender, but it was also characterized by unity [St].

QUESTION—Were any of these women considered leaders in the church?
1. It is unlikely that women were leaders in the church [BECNT, Mu, NICNT].
2. Some of these women may have been leaders in the church [WBC].

16:16 Greet one-another with a holy kiss.ᵃ All the churches of-Christ greet you.

LEXICON—a. φίλημα (LN 34.62) (BAGD p. 859): 'kiss' [AB, BAGD, BECNT, HNTC, ICC2, LN, NICNT, NTC, WBC; GW, KJV, NASB, NCV, NET, NIV, NRSV], 'warm greeting' [CEV]. The phrase 'with a holy kiss' is translated 'with the kiss of peace' [REB, TEV], 'in Christian love' [NLT]. This noun denotes a kiss, either as an expression of greeting or as a sign of special affection and appreciation [LN].

QUESTION—What is the 'holy kiss'?

It was a sacred greeting [TH], a way Christians greeted one another [Mor, Mu]. It was part of worship services in the early church [NAC, NICNT], and may have marked the conclusion of the worship gathering [NICNT]. It was a way of symbolizing Christ's love being shared mutually and was a symbol of unity and harmony [NTC]. The kiss was a gesture of social respect and regard throughout the eastern world [WBC]. It expressed equality before God as well as mutual affection [Ho].

1. It was not likely to have been a liturgical gesture [BECNT, Mor].
2. It may have been a liturgical gesture [AB, HNTC, Ho, ICC2], particularly at the Lord's supper [AB, Ho, ICC2].

QUESTION—What churches is he referring to here?

At the time of the writing of this letter there were present with Paul representatives of the churches who were sending the offering to Jerusalem, and they were passing along their greetings [Mor, St, TNTC]. The churches he is referring to were those churches in the east represented by Paul [HNTC, Mu], ones that he had been involved in starting in the eastern Mediterranean area [NICNT], the churches over which he had authority [BECNT], the ones with which he was in contact [ICC2, WBC], the ones in the area where he was [SSA]. They were the various churches that Paul visited [NTC]. This greeting from the churches expresses something of the universality of the gospel, as well as the fact that Paul's gospel has support from churches throughout the eastern Mediterranean area [BECNT]. It is the churches of Greece and Asia that he has been visiting [Gdt].

DISCOURSE UNIT—16:17–27 [St; NLT]. The topic is his warnings, messages and doxology [St], Paul's final instructions [NLT].

DISCOURSE UNIT—16:17–23 [NRSV]. The topic is final instructions.

DISCOURSE UNIT—16:17–20 [AB, Ho, ICC1, Mor, Mu, NAC, NICNT, TNTC, WBC]. The topic is Paul's admonition about false teachers, his concluding blessing [AB], blessings [Ho], warning against false teachers [ICC1, NAC], a doctrinal warning [Mor], warnings against deceivers [Mu], a warning, a promise, and a prayer for grace [NICNT], final exhortation [TNTC], a final personal note [WBC].

16:17 I-urge[a] you, brothers, watch-out-for[b] those causing divisions[c] and obstacles[d]

LEXICON—a. pres. act. indic. of παρακαλέω (LN 33.168) (BAGD 2. p. 617): 'to urge' [AB, BECNT, NICNT; GW, NASB, NET, NIV, NRSV, TEV], 'to appeal' [BAGD, LN, WBC], 'to make an appeal' [NLT], 'to exhort' [ICC2, NTC], 'to beg' [HNTC; CEV], 'beseech' [KJV], 'to ask' [NCV], 'to implore' [REB], 'to earnestly ask for, to request, to plead for, to appeal to' [LN]. This verb means to ask for something earnestly and with propriety [LN].

b. pres. act. infin. of σκοπέω (LN **24.32**, 27.58) (BAGD p. 756): 'to watch out for' [AB, LN, NICNT, NTC; CEV, GW, NET, NIV, NLT, TEV], 'to watch, to notice carefully' [LN (24.32)], 'to take careful notice' [**LN** (24.32)], 'to look out for' [BECNT, WBC; NCV], 'to notice' [BAGD], 'to mark' [ICC2; KJV], 'to give attention to' [HNTC], 'to keep your/an eye on' [NASB, NRSV, REB], 'to beware of, to watch out for, to pay attention to' [LN (27.58)]. This verb means to continue to regard closely [LN (24.32)], or to be ready to learn about future dangers or needs, with the implication of preparedness to respond appropriately [LN (27.58)].

c. διχοστασία (LN **39.13**) (BAGD p. 200): 'division' [HNTC, ICC2, **LN** NTC, WBC; GW, KJV, NIV, NLT, TEV], 'dissension' [AB, BAGD, BECNT, NICNT; NASB, NET, NRSV], 'quarrel' [REB], 'discord' [LN]. The phrase 'those causing divisions' is translated 'anyone who...divides the church' [CEV], 'who cause people to be against each other' [NCV]. This noun denotes a division into opposing groups, generally two [LN].

d. σκάνδαλον (LN 88.306) (BAGD 2. p. 753): 'obstacle' [NTC; NET, NIV], 'stumbling block' [BECNT, NICNT; KJV], 'trap' [BAGD], 'scandal' [AB], 'occasion of stumbling' [ICC2], 'offence' [HNTC; NRSV], 'temptation' [WBC], 'trouble' [CEV], 'hindrance' [NASB]. This noun is translated as a phrase: 'who make others fall away from the Christian faith' [GW], 'who upset people's/other people's faith' [NCV, NLT, TEV], 'who lead others astray' [REB]. It denotes that which provides an opportunity or occasion for causing someone to sin [LN].

QUESTION—Is παρακαλῶ an appeal or a command?

It has been used with various shades of meaning in the previous four chapters [NICNT].

1. It is more of an appeal [Mor, NICNT, TNTC].
2. It is a vigorous admonition [HNTC].

QUESTION—What divisions and obstacles is he warning them about?

He uses the definite article with both these nouns, indicating that these were specific problems that were known about [AB, Mor]. The definite article suggests that these were people Paul knew about, though they may not have come yet to Rome [NICNT]. It may have had to do with dietary laws [Gdt, HNTC, TH]. It is a very broad, non-specific type of warning [WBC]. These people might not have reached Rome yet [Gdt, ICC1, Mu]. These people were various outsiders who traveled from place to place to spread their ideas [NTC].

contrary[a] to the teaching[b] which you learned,[c] and turn-away[d] from them,
LEXICON—a. παρά with accusative (LN **89.137**) (BAGD III.6. p. 611): 'contrary to' [BECNT, HNTC, **LN**, NTC, WBC; KJV, NASB, NET, NIV, NLT, REB], 'in opposition to' [AB, ICC2; NRSV], 'against' [BAGD, NICNT; NCV], 'opposed, not in accordance' [LN], 'not the same as' [GW], 'and go against' [TEV]. The phrase 'contrary to the teaching which you learned' is translated 'refusing to do what all of you were taught' [CEV]. This preposition marks that which is contrary to what should be or to expectation [LN].
b. διδαχή (LN 33.236) (BAGD 2. p. 192): 'teaching' [AB, BAGD, BECNT, HNTC, ICC2, LN, NICNT, NTC, WBC; NASB, NET, NIV, NRSV, REB, TEV], 'true teaching' [NCV], 'doctrine' [LN; GW, KJV], not explicit [CEV, NLT]. The phrase 'contrary to the teaching' is translated 'by teaching doctrine that is not the same' [GW]. This noun denotes or the content of what is taught [LN].
c. aorist act. indic. of μανθάνω (LN **27.12**) (BAGD 1. p. 490): 'to learn' [AB, BAGD, BECNT, HNTC, ICC2, **LN**, NICNT, NTC, WBC; GW, KJV, NASB, NCV, NET, NIV, NRSV, REB], 'to be taught' [CEV, NLT], 'to receive' [TEV]. This verb means to acquire information as the result of instruction [LN].
d. pres. act. impera. of ἐκκλίνω (LN **34.41**) (BAGD p. 241): 'to turn away' [BAGD, NICNT; NASB], 'to keep away' [AB, HNTC, **LN**, WBC; TEV], 'to stay away' [BECNT; CEV, GW, NCV, NIV, NLT], 'to avoid' [ICC2, LN, NTC; KJV, NET, NRSV, REB], 'to shun, to have nothing to do with' [LN]. Paul's use of the present tense indicates that the avoidance must be ongoing [NICNT]. This verb means to purposely avoid association with someone [LN].

QUESTION—What is contrary to the teaching?
1. This describes the obstacles [BECNT, Gdt, Ho, ICC2, Mor, NAC, NICNT, NTC, St, WBC; KJV, NET, NIV]: obstacles that are contrary to the teaching which you learned. This describes the obstacles as being against the teaching they have learned, and thus makes it clear that Paul is thinking of the false doctrines of those people they are to turn away from [BECNT, Gdt, NAC, NICNT, St; KJV, NET, NIV]. Paul stresses unity; dissensions are contrary to what he taught [Mor].
2. This describes the means by which the people cause divisions and obstacles [SSA; CEV, GW, NLT]: 'by refusing to do what all of you were taught' [CEV], 'by teaching doctrine that is not the same as you have learned' [GW], 'by teaching things contrary to what you have been taught' [NLT].
3. This describes the people who cause divisions and obstacles [NCV, TEV]: 'look out for people who cause…They are against the true teaching you

learned' [NCV], 'watch out for those who…go against the teaching which you have received' [TEV].

16:18 **for such (people) serve**[a] **not our Lord Christ but their belly,**[b]
LEXICON—a. pres. act. indic. of δουλεύω (LN **37.25**) (BAGD 2.b., 2.c. p. 205): 'to serve' [AB, BAGD, BECNT, HNTC, ICC2, **LN**, NICNT, NTC, WBC; all versions except NASB, REB], 'to be a slave to' [LN; NASB], 'to be controlled by' [LN]. The phrase 'such people serve' is translated 'such people are servants' [REB]. This verb means to be under the control of some influence and to serve the interests of such [LN].
  b. κοιλία (LN **25.28**) (BAGD 1. p. 437): 'belly' [BAGD, HNTC, NICNT; KJV], 'bellies' [BECNT, ICC2, NTC], 'appetites' [AB, WBC; NET, NIV, NRSV, REB, TEV], 'desires' [GW], 'physical desires' [**LN**], 'desires of the body' [LN], 'personal interests' [NLT]. The phrase 'serve…their belly' is translated 'serve themselves' [CEV], 'doing what pleases themselves' [NCV]. It is possible that this noun refers to Jewish dietary laws and regulations [LN].
QUESTION—What does it mean to serve their belly?
  They are interested in their own pleasure [NICNT]. They are egotistical [ICC2, NTC, St], self-indulgent [St], and self-serving [ICC1, ICC2, NTC, St; CEV]. They serve their own base desires [NAC], their own base appetites [WBC], their sensual appetites [Gdt]. They want to satisfy their own desires [SSA]. It may have been a sarcastic way of referring to preoccupation with dietary laws [AB, HNTC, TH].

and through smooth-talk[a] **and flattery**[b] **deceive**[c] **the hearts**[d] **of-the unsuspecting.**[e]
LEXICON—a. χρηστολογία (LN **33.30**) (BAGD p. 886): 'smooth talk' [AB, NICNT, NTC; GW, NET, NIV, NLT, NRSV], 'smooth speech' [BAGD, BECNT, WBC; NASB], 'gentle speech' [HNTC], 'fancy talk' [CEV, NCV], 'attractive speech, fine language' [LN], 'high sounding plausibility' [ICC2], 'smooth words' [REB], 'good words' [KJV], 'fine words' [**LN**; TEV]. This noun denotes eloquent and attractive speech involving pleasing rhetorical devices [LN]. It is speech that may sound reasonable [TH]. This word occurs only here in the NT.
  b. εὐλογία (LN **33.366**) (BAGD 2. p. 322): 'flattery' [AB, LN, NTC; CEV, NET, NIV, NRSV], 'flattering talk' [LN], 'flattering speech' [**LN**; NASB, TEV], 'flattering words' [GW], 'fine words' [NICNT; NCV], 'fine-sounding words' [WBC], 'glowing words' [NLT], 'specious words' [REB], 'eloquent speech' [BECNT], 'fair speech' [HNTC; KJV], 'praise' [BAGD], 'high sounding plausibility' [ICC2]. This noun denotes excessive praise [LN]. Both 'smooth talk' and 'flattery' make up a near synonymous doublet [SSA, TH] that signifies 'eloquent speech' [SSA].
  c. pres. act. indic. of ἐξαπατάω (LN **31.12**) (BAGD p. 273): 'to deceive' [AB, BAGD, BECNT, HNTC, ICC2, **LN**, NICNT, NTC, WBC; KJV, NASB, NET, NIV, NLT, NRSV, TEV], 'to fool' [CEV, NCV], 'to

seduce' [REB], 'to mislead' [**LN**]. This verb means to cause someone to have misleading or erroneous views concerning the truth [LN].
   d. καρδία (LN **26.3**) (BAGD 1.b.β. p. 403): 'heart' [BAGD, BECNT, HNTC, ICC2, LN, NICNT, NTC, WBC; KJV, NASB, NRSV], 'mind' [AB, LN; NCV, NET, NIV, REB], 'inner self' [LN], 'people' [CEV, GW, NLT, TEV]. This noun denotes the causative source of a person's psychological life in its various aspects, but with special emphasis upon thoughts [LN]. The 'heart' was considered to be the seat of one's intellectual activity [TH].
   e. ἄκακος (LN **31.34**) (BAGD p. 29): 'unsuspecting' [BECNT, LN, WBC; GW, NASB], 'unwary' [NICNT], 'innocent' [BAGD, HNTC; NLT, TEV], 'simple' [AB, ICC2, NTC; KJV], 'simple people' [REB], 'simple minded' [NRSV], 'naïve' [**LN**; NET, NIV], 'who don't know any better' [CEV], 'who do not know about evil' [NCV]. This adjective describes being unsuspecting or naive with regard to possible deception [LN].

16:19 For your obedience[a] has-been-known[b] to all, so I rejoice[c] (in) you,
LEXICON—a. ὑπακοή (LN **36.15**) (BAGD 1.b. p. 837): 'obedience' [BAGD, BECNT, HNTC, ICC2, LN, NICNT, NTC, WBC; GW, KJV, NET, NIV, NRSV, TEV], 'obedience (to the gospel)' [**LN**], 'commitment' [AB], 'the report of your obedience' [HNTC, NTC; NASB], 'loyalty to the gospel' [TEV]. This noun is also translated as a verb phrase: 'you obey' [CEV, NCV], 'you are obedient' [NLT]. This noun denotes obedience on the basis of having paid attention [LN].
   b. aorist mid. (deponent = act.) indic. of ἀφικνέομαι (LN **28.23**) (BAGD p. 126): 'to be known' [AB, ICC2, WBC; NET, NRSV], 'to become known' [**LN**], 'to reach' [BAGD, BECNT, HNTC, NICNT, NTC; NASB], 'to come abroad' [KJV]. The phrase 'has been known to all' is translated 'everyone knows' [CEV, NLT], 'everyone has heard about' [GW, NIV, TEV], 'all the believers have heard' [NCV], 'the fame...has spread everywhere' [REB]. This verb means to become known as the result of information reaching its destination [LN]. This word occurs only here in the NT.
   c. pres. act. indic. of χαίρω (LN 25.125) (BAGD 1. p. 873): 'to rejoice' [BAGD, BECNT, HNTC, ICC2, LN, NICNT, NTC, WBC; NASB, NET, NRSV], 'to be glad' [LN; CEV, KJV], 'to be happy' [AB; TEV], 'to be very happy' [NCV], 'to be full of joy' [NIV]. The phrase 'I rejoice' is translated 'this makes me happy/very happy' [GW, NLT, REB]. This verb means to enjoy a state of happiness and well-being [LN].
QUESTION—What relationship is indicated by γάρ 'for'?
   The connection is not immediately clear [Mor, NICNT]. The γάρ indicates a shift to a different basis of appeal [SSA]. There may be an implied thought, such as 'I have no fears for you *because*...etc.' [Mor]. It indicates 16:19 as support for the exhortation of 16:17-18; that is, he wants them to maintain their reputation [ICC2; probably Mu, NTC]. It refers back to what was just

said in 16:17–18; since Paul knows that the Romans have a reputation for being good, they might become a target for the unscrupulous [Gdt].
QUESTION—To whom or what were they obedient?
1. They were obedient to the gospel message [ICC2, NICNT, SSA, TH, TNTC; TEV], and as a result they are innocent [NICNT]. Their obedience is their commitment to the Christian faith [AB]. Christian faith is obedience [ICC2, WBC].
2. They were obedient to the Lord [CEV].
3. They were obedient to their leaders, those who taught them in the Christian faith [Ho].

But I-want[a] you to-be wise[b] in (what is) good,[c] but innocent[d] in (what is) evil.[e]
LEXICON—a. pres. act. indic. of θέλω (LN 25.1) (BAGD 1. p. 355): 'to want' [AB, BECNT, ICC2, LN, NICNT, NTC, WBC; all versions except KJV], 'to wish' [BAGD, HNTC, LN], 'to desire' [LN]. The phrase 'I want' is translated 'I would have you' [KJV]. This verb means to desire to have or experience something [LN].
  b. σοφός (LN 32.33) (BAGD 3. p. 760): 'wise' [AB, BECNT, HNTC, ICC2, LN, NICNT, NTC, WBC; KJV, NASB, NCV, NET, NIV, NLT, NRSV, TEV], 'expert' [REB], 'learned' [BAGD], 'prudent, understanding' [LN]. The infinitive phrase 'to be wise' is translated 'to understand' [CEV], 'to do' [GW]. This adjective describes understanding resulting in wisdom [LN].
  c. ἀγαθός (LN 88.1) (BAGD 2.a.α. p. 3): 'good' [AB, BAGD, BECNT, HNTC, ICC2, LN, NICNT, NTC, WBC; all versions except NLT, REB], 'goodness' [REB], 'doing right' [NLT]. This adjective describes positive moral qualities of the most general nature [LN].
  d. ἀκέραιος (LN **88.32**) (BAGD p. 30): 'innocent' [AB, BECNT, NICNT, NTC, WBC; NASB, NCV, NET, NIV, NLT, REB, TEV], 'pure' [BAGD, LN], 'kept pure' [ICC2], 'uncontaminated' [HNTC], 'untainted' [**LN**], 'guileless' [NRSV], 'simple' [KJV], 'not have anything to do with' [CEV]. The phrase 'to be…innocent in (what is evil)' is translated 'to avoid (what is evil)' [GW]. This adjective describes being without a mixture of evil and hence being pure [LN].
  e. κακός (LN 88.106) (BAGD 1.c. p. 397): 'evil' [AB, BAGD, BECNT, HNTC, ICC2, LN, NICNT, NTC; all versions except NLT], 'bad' [LN, WBC], 'any wrong' [NLT]. This adjective describes being bad, with the implication of harmful and damaging [LN].
QUESTION—What does it mean to be wise in what is good and innocent in what is evil?
  Morally they should be too good to be deceivers, and too wise to be fooled by deceivers [Ho, Mor]. This recalls Jesus' admonition to be as wise as serpents but as innocent as doves [NICNT, NTC], though Paul may not have been aware of that saying [NTC]. Being wise in what is good means

intending to do good [HNTC]. He wants them to be wise to do good and to avoid evil [NTC, SSA]. It is a play on the meaning of the word ἄκακος 'unsuspecting' in the previous verse, which can also mean 'innocent', and relates to that concern; he knows that these false teachers are capable of deceiving innocent people [NICNT]. He wants them to maintain their integrity in what is morally good, maintaining their obedience [ICC2]. He wants them to recognize, love, and follow whatever is good [St].

16:20 And the God of-peace will-crush[a] Satan under your feet soon.[b] The grace of-our Lord Jesus (be) with you.

TEXT—Some manuscripts include Χριστοῦ 'Christ' after κυρίου ἡμῶν Ἰησοῦ 'our Lord Jesus'. It is omitted by GNT with an A rating, indicating that the text is certain. It is included by KJV only.

LEXICON—a. fut. act. indic. of συντρίβω (LN **39.53**) (BAGD 1.b. p. 793): 'to crush' [AB, BECNT, HNTC, ICC2, **LN**, NICNT, NTC, WBC; all versions except KJV, NCV], 'to shatter' [BAGD], 'to bruise' [KJV], 'to completely overcome' [LN]. The phrase 'will crush Satan under your feet' is translated 'will defeat Satan and give you power over him' [NCV]. This verb means to overcome, resulting in the crushing of the power of the opposition [LN].

b. τάχος (LN 67.56, 67.111) (BAGD p. 807): 'speed' [BAGD]. The phrase ἐν τάχει is translated 'soon' [AB, HNTC, ICC2, LN (67.56), NICNT, NTC; CEV, NASB, NCV, NIV, NLT, REB, TEV], 'very soon' [LN (67.56)], 'quickly' [BECNT, LN; GW, NET], 'speedily' [WBC], 'shortly' [KJV, NRSV], 'a very short while' [LN]. This noun denotes a very brief period of time [LN (67.111)].

QUESTION—What is the relation of this statement within the larger context?
This may be an allusion to what God says to Adam and Eve in Gen 3:15 [AB, BECNT, HNTC, ICC2, Mu, NAC, NICNT, NTC, St, TNTC, WBC].

1. He is saying that God will give them victory over the false teachers, who are under Satan's influence [AB, BECNT, Gdt, Ho, ICC1, Mu, NAC, SSA, St, TNTC]. This verse is a motivational basis for the exhortation to shun the ones who cause divisions [SSA].
2. It is a general statement, and not related to the warning about false teachers [ICC2, WBC].
3. It is a general statement, extending to the final end-time victory over Satan, but also with relevance to the issue of the false teachers [NICNT, NTC].

QUESTION—How are the nouns related in the genitive construction ὁ θεὸς τῆς εἰρήνης 'the God of peace'?
God gives peace [ICC2, WBC; CEV, NCV], and shapes human ways in peace [AB]. God is the author of peace in the full sense that Scripture means by that term [Ho]. God is the source of peace [TH; TEV]. As with the identical phrase in 15:33, it means that God causes them to be peaceful in the sense of having inner peace individually and having concord among

themselves [SSA]. This title contrasts with the divisions mentioned in 16:17 [Mor]. Here the God of peace is depicted in a warlike activity, that of crushing Satan [Mor]. The peace that God gives is the fulfillment of his saving promises given in Gen 3:15 [BECNT]. He is a God of complete salvation [NTC]. Peace only comes when evil is destroyed [St]. Though Satan is the author of discord, God is the giver of peace [TNTC]. God establishes peace by bruising those servants of Satan who would cause divisions [Mu]. The false teachers disturb the peace of the church [ICC1]. God will grant peace when those who would disrupt the church are successfully resisted [Gdt].

DISCOURSE UNIT—16:21–24 [Ho, Mor]. The topic is salutations [Ho], greetings from people with Paul [Mor].

DISCOURSE UNIT—16:21–23 [AB, Ho, ICC1, Mu, NAC, TNTC, WBC]. The topic is greetings from Paul's companions and the scribe Tertius [AB], greetings of St. Paul's companions [ICC1], greetings of friends [Mu], greetings from Paul's companions [NAC, TNTC], additional greetings [WBC].

16:21 **Timothy my co-worker greets you, and (so-do) Lucius and Jason and Sosipater my kinspeople.**
QUESTION—Who were these people?
Timothy was the young man described in Acts, and to whom the two pastoral letters 1 and 2 Timothy are addressed [AB, HNTC, ICC2, Mor, NAC, NICNT, NTC], and who is listed as co-author of six of Paul's epistles [NICNT]. He had traveled with Paul for the previous eight years [St], and was one of Paul's most trusted co-workers [WBC]. Lucius is not the same person as Luke the physician [AB, Gdt, Mor, NICNT, NTC, TNTC], nor the man mentioned in Acts 13:1 [AB, NAC, NICNT, TNTC, WBC]. This Jason could be the man who hosted Paul during his brief stay in Thessalonica [AB, Gdt, HNTC, ICC1, ICC2, NAC, NICNT, NTC, St, WBC]. Sosipater is the Sopater of Berea mentioned in Acts 20:4 [AB, Gdt, HNTC, ICC1, ICC2, NAC, TNTC], and who accompanied Paul when he left Greece [NICNT]. They were probably escorting the collection for the poor to Jerusalem [NICNT].

16:22 **I Tertius the-one having-written[a] the letter[b] greet you in (the) Lord.**
LEXICON—a. aorist act. participle of γράφω (LN 33.61): 'to write' [AB, BECNT, HNTC, ICC2, LN, NICNT, NTC, WBC; CEV, GW, KJV, NASB, NET]. The participial phrase 'the one having written' is translated 'the writer' [NRSV, TEV], 'who wrote down this letter' [NIV], 'who took this letter down' [REB], 'the one writing this letter for Paul' [NLT], 'and I am writing this letter from Paul' [NCV].
b. ἐπιστολή (LN 6.63) (BAGD p. 300): 'letter' [AB, BAGD, BECNT, ICC2, LN, NICNT, NTC, WBC; all versions except KJV, NCV, NLT], 'letter from Paul' [NCV], 'letter for Paul' [NLT], 'epistle' [HNTC; KJV].

This noun denotes an object containing writing addressed to one or more persons [LN].

QUESTION—Who was Tertius?

He was the scribe who wrote the letter at Paul's dictation [AB, BECNT, HNTC, Ho, ICC1, Mor, Mu, NAC, NICNT, NTC, SSA, TH, TNTC, WBC].

QUESTION—What does the phrase ἐν κυρίῳ 'in (the) Lord' modify?

It modifies 'greet' [AB, BECNT, ICC2, NICNT, NTC, SSA, TH, TNTC, WBC; all versions]. He gives them Christian greetings [NICNT, SSA; GW, REB, TEV]. It indicates that he is a Christian [CEV, NLT]. He is part of the mystical fellowship that unites all Christians [NTC]. He is expressing solidarity with the Christians of Rome [ICC2].

16:23 **Gaius my host[a] and-also of-the whole church greets you.**

LEXICON—a. ξένος (LN **34.60**) (BAGD 2.c. p. 548): 'host' [AB, BAGD, BECNT, HNTC, ICC2, **LN**, NICNT, NTC, WBC; GW, KJV, NASB, NLT, NRSV, REB, TEV]. The phrase 'Gaius my host and also of the whole church' is translated 'Gaius welcomes me and the whole church into his home' [CEV], 'Gaius, whose hospitality I and the whole church here enjoy' [NIV]. This noun denotes a person who shows hospitality to guests [LN].

QUESTION—Who is Gaius?

He is probably the one mentioned in 1 Cor 1:14 as having been baptized by Paul [AB, BECNT, Gdt, HNTC, ICC1, ICC2, Mor, Mu, NAC, NICNT, NTC, St, TNTC, WBC]. He may well be the person called Titius Justus in Acts 18:7 [BECNT, ICC2, Mor, Mu, NAC, NICNT, St, TNTC, WBC]. He was fairly wealthy [ICC2, WBC].

QUESTION—What is the relation of καὶ ὅλης τῆς ἐκκλησίας 'and of the whole church' to the sentence?

1. Gaius is a host to Paul as well as to the church that meets in his home [AB, BECNT, ICC1, Mu, SSA, TH, WBC; CEV, GW, KJV, NASB, NCV, NET, NIV, NLT, NRSV, REB].
2. Gaius hosts any Christian who might be traveling through Corinth [Gdt, NICNT, NTC]. He would not be able to host the entire church since the number of Christians in Corinth would be too large to fit into one home, so he was host to any Christian from 'the whole church' who might be passing through [NICNT, NTC].

Erastus, the treasurer[a] of-the city greets you, and also Quartus the brother.

LEXICON—a. οἰκονόμος (LN **57.231**) (BAGD 1.b. p. 560): 'treasurer' [AB, BECNT, HNTC, ICC2, NICNT, NTC, WBC; all versions except KJV, NIV], 'city treasurer' [**LN**], 'chamberlain' [KJV], 'director of public works' [NIV], 'manager' [BAGD]. This noun denotes one who is in charge of the finances of a city [LN].

QUESTION—What was Erastus' office in the city government?

He was the city treasurer [AB, Ho, ICC2, Mor, NAC, NICNT, TH], though at some point he may also have held the office of director of public works

[AB, Mor, NAC, NICNT], which had a one-year term [Mor, NICNT]. He may have been a Roman citizen of wealth and social status [WBC].
1. It is unlikely that this is the Erastus of Acts 19:22 [Gdt, ICC2, Mu, WBC], since it would be difficult for such an official to leave his official responsibilities [ICC2].
2. He may well be the Erastus mentioned in Acts 19:22, whom Paul sent ahead with Timothy to Macedonia [NICNT].

QUESTION—Who was Quartus?
He is otherwise unknown [AB, NICNT, NTC]. 'The brother' means that he is a fellow believer, not Erastus' brother [Mu, WBC].

16:24 (See text note)
TEXT—Some manuscripts include ἡ χάρις τοῦ κυρίου ἡμῶν Ἰησοῦ Χριστοῦ μετὰ πάντων ὑμῶν. ἀμήν 'The grace of our Lord Jesus Christ be with you all. Amen' here. It is omitted by GNT with an A rating, indicating that the text is certain. It is included by KJV only.

DISCOURSE UNIT—16:25–27 [AB, BECNT, HNTC, Ho, ICC1, Mor, Mu, NAC, NICNT, WBC; NRSV]. The topic is the doxology: glory to the God of wisdom through Jesus Christ [AB], a final summary of the gospel of God's righteousness [BECNT], the doxology [HNTC, Ho, Mor, Mu, NAC, TNTC], the concluding doxology [ICC1, NICNT, WBC], final doxology [NRSV].

16:25 Now to-the-one being-able[a] to-establish[b] you according-to my gospel even/and the proclamation[c] of-Jesus Christ,
TEXT—The doxology in 16:25–27 does not occur in some manuscripts, and in other manuscripts is found in different locations in this epistle. It is included here by GNT with a C rating, indicating difficulty in deciding whether or not to place it in the text. It is translated by all versions and commentaries, but considered not to be authentic by AB, HNTC, ICC2, WBC; probably TNTC. It is considered to be authentic by BECNT, Gdt, Ho, ICC1, Mor, Mu, NAC, NICNT, NTC.
LEXICON—a. pres. mid. or pass. (deponent = act.) participle of δύναμαι (LN 74.5): 'to be able' [AB, BECNT, HNTC, ICC2, LN, NICNT, NTC, WBC; NASB, NET, NIV, NLT, NRSV, TEV], 'to be of power' [KJV], 'to have the power' [REB], 'he can' [CEV], 'God can' [GW], 'who can' [NCV]. This verb means to be able to do something [LN].
b. aorist act. infin. of στηρίζω (LN 74.19) (BAGD 2. p. 768): 'to establish' [BAGD, HNTC, NTC; KJV, NASB, NIV], 'to strengthen' [AB, BECNT, LN, NICNT, WBC; GW, NET, NRSV], 'to make strong' [CEV, NLT], 'to make strong in faith' [NCV], 'to make to stand firm' [REB], 'to make to stand firm in faith' [TEV], 'to confirm' [ICC2], 'to make more firm' [LN]. This verb means to cause someone to become stronger in the sense of more firm and unchanging in attitude or belief [LN].
c. κήρυγμα (LN 33.258) (BAGD 2. p. 431): 'proclamation' [BAGD, BECNT, ICC2, NTC; NET, NIV, NRSV, REB], 'preaching' [AB, HNTC,

LN, NICNT, WBC; KJV, NASB], 'good news' [CEV], 'message' [NCV, NLT], not explicit [GW]. The phrase 'my gospel and the proclamation of Jesus Christ' is translated 'the Good News I preach about Jesus Christ' [TEV]. This noun denotes the content of what is preached [LN, Mu].

QUESTION—What relationship is indicated by κατά 'according to'?

1. It refers to the infinitive στηρίξαι 'to establish' [AB, BECNT, ICC2, Mu, NICNT, NTC, SSA, WBC].
    1.1 The gospel is the means by which they are strengthened; they are to be established or strengthened through the gospel revelation [NICNT]. The gospel provides constancy and strength for believers [AB].
    1.2 The gospel is the norm or standard according to which they are strengthened [Gdt, Ho, ICC2, Mu]. God establishes them in a way that is agreeable or in accord with the gospel Paul preaches [Ho]. God confirms them in their belief in the gospel and their obedience to it [ICC2].
    1.3 The gospel is the norm as well as the means of the strengthening; the strengthening is based on the gospel and comes through it [BECNT, WBC].
2. It refers to the participle τῷ...δυναμένῳ 'the one being able' [Gdt]. God is able, just as the gospel says [Gdt].

QUESTION—What relationship is indicated by καί 'even/and'?

It further elaborates what he means by 'my gospel' [Gdt, ICC2, Mu, NICNT, NTC, SSA, St, TH, WBC; CEV, NLT, TEV]: my gospel, which is the proclamation of Jesus Christ. It indicates apposition [TH]. It is explicatory [ICC2], epexegetic [WBC]: that is to say. It is a further definition of 'my gospel' [NICNT]. 'The preaching of Jesus Christ' is the same thing as 'my gospel' described from a different point of view [Mor].

QUESTION—What is τὸ κήρυγμα Ἰησοῦ Χριστοῦ 'the proclamation of Jesus Christ'?

It is the content of the message about Jesus Christ [AB, BECNT, Gdt, ICC1, ICC2, Mor, Mu, NICNT, NTC, SSA, St, TH, TNTC, WBC].

QUESTION—What is the relation of τὸ κήρυγμα Ἰησοῦ Χριστοῦ 'the proclamation of Jesus Christ' to what follows?

The phrase τὸ κήρυγμα Ἰησοῦ Χριστοῦ 'the proclamation of Jesus Christ' in 16:25 is modified by the three participles that follow: σεσιγημένου 'hidden', φανερωθέντος 'manifested', γνωρισθέντος 'made known' (or clarified) [ICC2, WBC]. God strengthens according to the gospel and the revelation of the mystery; the mystery was hidden in ages past, manifested now, and made known; it is made known through the prophetic scriptures, according to God's command, for the obedience of faith, and for all the nations [WBC]. The phrase 'for the obedience of faith' indicates the goal of the last two participles; it is manifested and made known so the nations will believe [ICC2]. The proclamation is about the truth that God has now revealed, but didn't before; God commanded them to proclaim it so the nations can believe; and by proclaiming it they cause them to know the message [SSA].

QUESTION—Why does Paul call it 'my gospel'?

It is the gospel he preaches [ICC2, Mor, SSA], which is no different from what others are preaching [ICC2, Mor]. Paul's gospel is the message about Jesus Christ [NICNT]. 'My gospel' refers to Paul's way of preaching the good news [AB]. It had been revealed to him [Gdt, NAC, NTC], and he had adopted it as his own [NAC], he loved it, proclaimed it, and tried his best to live it [NTC]. God revealed and entrusted it to him [St]. It is the gospel that was entrusted to him to preach [Mu].

QUESTION—What is the predicate of the sentence that begins in this verse?

Verses 16:25–27 consist of one long incomplete sentence with no predicate [AB, Ho, NICNT, SSA]. Some versions move the phrase 'to whom be the glory' in 16:27 to the beginning of this verse: 'Let us give glory to God! He is able' [TEV], 'Praise God! He can' [CEV], 'Now all glory to God, who is able' [NLT], 'Glory to God who can' [NCV].

according-to (the) revelation[a] of-(the) mystery[b] kept-secret[c] (for) eternal ages,[d]

LEXICON—a. ἀποκάλυψις (LN 28.38) (BAGD 1. p. 92): 'revelation' [AB, BAGD, BECNT, HNTC, ICC2, LN, NICNT, NTC; KJV, NASB, NET, NIV, NRSV, REB, TEV], 'disclosure' [**LN**]. This noun is translated 'now at last it has been told' [CEV], 'now is publicly known' [GW], 'is now made known' [NCV], 'has revealed' [NLT]. This noun denotes something made fully known [LN].

b. μυστήριον (LN 28.77) (BAGD 2. p. 530): 'mystery' [AB, BAGD, BECNT, HNTC, ICC2, LN, NICNT, NTC; GW, KJV, NASB, NET, NIV, NRSV], 'secret' [LN], 'secret truth' [TEV], 'divine secret' [REB], not explicit [CEV]. The phrase 'the mystery kept secret' is translated 'a plan kept secret' [NLT], 'the secret that was hidden' [NCV], 'this message was kept secret' [CEV]. This noun denotes the content of that which has not been known before, but which has been revealed to an in-group or restricted constituency [LN].

c. perfect pass. participle of σιγάω (LN 33.121) (BAGD 2. p. 749): 'to be kept secret' [AB, NICNT; CEV, KJV, NASB, NET, NLT, NRSV], 'to be kept silent' [BECNT], 'to be kept in silence' [HNTC; GW, REB], 'to be silent' [BAGD], 'to be kept quiet about, to say nothing about' [LN], 'to be hidden' [ICC2; NCV, TEV]. This verb is translated as an adjective: 'hidden' [NTC; NIV], 'concealed' [WBC]. This verb means to keep quiet, with the implication of preserving something which is secret [LN].

d. χρόνος (LN 67.78) (BAGD p. 888): 'age' [AB, BECNT, HNTC, ICC2, NICNT, NTC, WBC], 'time' [BAGD, LN]. The phrase χρόνοις αἰωνίοις 'eternal ages' [HNTC] is also translated 'past ages' [BECNT], 'long ages' [NICNT, WBC; NET, NRSV, REB], 'long (ages) past' [NTC; NASB, NCV, NIV], 'long ages in the past' [TEV], 'ages and ages'

[CEV], 'a very long time' [GW], 'since the world began' [KJV], 'from ages before creation' [ICC2], 'from the beginning of time' [NLT]. This noun denotes an indefinite unit of time [LN].

QUESTION—What relationship is indicated by κατά 'according to'?

The proclamation is in accord with the revelation [Gdt, Ho, ICC1, ICC2, Mor], in conformity with the revelation [NTC]. The gospel and the mystery are being equated more or less [AB]. The phrase 'according to the revelation' is coordinate with the phrase 'according to my gospel' earlier in the sentence [Ho, SSA]. The gospel is according to or based on the revelation of the mystery [NICNT].

QUESTION—What is the mystery that has been kept secret?

The gospel is a mystery in the same sense that any other doctrine is a mystery, which is that it requires divine revelation for it to be known and understood [Ho]. The gospel is revealed truth, and the mystery that is revealed is Jesus Christ himself, in all his fullness [St]. It is the righteousness of God mentioned in 1:17, and which is the theme of the whole letter; it was kept secret in the sense that it could not be fully understood or experienced, not that it could not be known [NICNT]. In his wisdom God bound the message of salvation up in Christ, who has now been revealed [AB]. Although the truth about Christ was already foretold in the OT, it has now been revealed openly to the world as the gospel has gone forth [Mu]. It is the plan of salvation in Christ, and especially as it relates to the Gentiles [Gdt]. The mystery has to do with Paul's commission as apostle to preach the gospel to the Gentiles, and through which they are able to be incorporated into Christ [TNTC].

16:26 but now having-been-manifested[a] and having-been-made-known[b] through (the) prophetic[c] scriptures according to (the) command[d] of-God

LEXICON—a. aorist pass. participle of φανερόω (LN 28.36) (BAGD 1.b. p. 852): 'to be manifested' [BECNT, HNTC, ICC2, NICNT, NTC; NASB], 'to be made manifest' [WBC; KJV], 'to be made clear' [NCV], 'to be disclosed' [AB, LN; NET, NRSV, REB], 'to be revealed' [BAGD, LN; NIV], 'to be told' [CEV], 'to be foretold' [NLT], 'to be publicly known' [GW], 'to be brought out into the open' [TEV], 'to be made known, to be made plain, to be brought to the light' [LN]. This verb means to cause something to be fully known by revealing clearly and in some detail [LN].

b. aorist pass. participle of γνωρίζω (LN 28.26) (BAGD 1. p. 163): 'to be made known' [AB, BAGD, BECNT, HNTC, LN, NICNT, WBC; all versions except CEV, GW], 'to be clarified' [ICC2, NTC], 'to be shown' [GW]. The phrase 'having been made known through the prophetic scriptures according to the command of God' is translated 'God commanded his prophets to write about the good news' [CEV]. This verb means to cause information to be known by someone [LN].

c. προφητικός (LN **33.462**) (BAGD p. 724): 'prophetic' [AB, BAGD, BECNT, HNTC, ICC2, LN, NTC, WBC; NET, NIV, NRSV, REB], 'prophetical' [NICNT]. The phrase 'the prophetic scriptures' is translated 'the Scriptures of the prophets' [KJV, NASB], 'the writings of the prophets' [**LN**; NCV, TEV], 'what the prophets wrote' [GW], 'as the prophets foretold' [NLT], '(God commanded) his prophets to write about' [CEV]. This adjective describes divinely inspired utterances [LN].
d. ἐπιταγή (LN **33.326**) (BAGD p. 302): 'command' [AB, BAGD, BECNT, ICC2, LN, NICNT, NTC, WBC; NCV, NET, NIV, NRSV, REB, TEV], 'commandment' [KJV, NASB], 'decree' [HNTC, LN], 'order' [**LN**], 'ordinance, instruction' [LN]. This noun is translated as a verb: '(God) commanded' [CEV, NLT], '(God) ordered' [GW]. This noun denotes that which has been specifically ordered or commanded [LN].

QUESTION—What is the relation of the two participles φανερωθέντος 'having been manifested' and γνωρισθέντος 'having been made known' to what follows?

These two participles are very close in meaning [NICNT]. The participle γνωρισθέντος 'having been made known' is modified by the four prepositional phrases that follow it: it is made known through the prophets, according to the command of God, for the obedience of faith, and for all the nations [Gdt, Mu, NICNT, NTC, St, WBC]. These four phrases give, respectively, the cause, means, purpose, and object of the action of making the gospel known: because of the divine command, by means of the prophets' writings, for the purpose of the obedience of faith, and with the Gentiles as the object of this action [Gdt]. These four phrases express the four main ideas of the apostolic message, which are the continuity of the gospel with what God had previously done, the apostles' commission to preach, salvation through faith, and that the message should go to the Gentiles [ICC1]. The words δὲ νῦν 'but now', which precede these participles, expresses a strong contrast [Gdt], and indicates the eschatological significance of the present moment [Mor].

QUESTION—What are the prophetic scriptures he mentions here?

1. It is the OT [NICNT], or the writings of the OT prophets [ICC2, Mor, NAC]. It is the OT and certain Jewish apocalyptic writings that speak of this mystery [AB]. It is especially Gen 12:3 and Gen 22:18 [NTC]. It is the messianic prophecies of the OT [SSA]. Now through the preaching of the gospel people can understand the meaning of the OT in its witness to Christ [St]. In the light of new revelation in Christ they came to understand and explain the OT prophetic scriptures [TNTC].
2. He is referring to the writings of the apostles of the NT era [Gdt].

QUESTION—What command is he referring to?

It is God's decision to make the mystery known when he did [NICNT]. It is his universal commission to preach the gospel [St], his command that all nations should know this truth [TH]. It is his commissioning of Paul to preach the gospel [AB, ICC1, Mu, SSA], as well as his command to others to preach it [ICC1]. It is God's will that the OT Scriptures clarified and attested the gospel message [ICC2].

for (the) obedience[a] of-faith for/to[b] all the nations,[c]

LEXICON—a. ὑπακοή (LN 36.15) (BAGD 1.b. p. 837): 'obedience' [BAGD, BECNT, HNTC, ICC2, LN, NICNT, NTC, WBC; GW, KJV, NASB, NET, NRSV, REB], 'commitment' [AB]. This noun is translated as a verb: 'obey' [CEV, NCV, NIV, TEV]. This noun denotes obedience on the basis of having paid attention [LN].

b. εἰς (LN **90.59**) (BAGD 1.d.β. p. 228): 'for' [HNTC, LN, NICNT, WBC], 'in' [BAGD], 'to' [BECNT, **LN**; KJV, NASB, NCV, NET, NRSV, REB], 'among' [ICC2, NTC], not explicit [CEV, NIV]. The phrase 'for the obedience of faith for all the Gentiles' is translated 'so that all of the Gentiles may come to the commitment of faith' [AB], 'so all nations would obey and have faith' [CEV], 'so that all nations might believe and obey him' [NIV], 'to all nations, so that all may believe and obey' [TEV], 'to all Gentiles everywhere, so that they too might believe and obey him' [NLT], '(to) the people of every nation to bring them to the obedience that is associated with faith' [GW]. This preposition marks an involved experiencer [LN].

c. The phrase πάντα τὰ ἔθνη 'all the nations' [NASB, NET], is translated 'all nations' [CEV, KJV, NCV, NIV, REB, TEV], 'the people of every nation' [GW], 'all the Gentiles' [NRSV], 'all Gentiles' [NLT].

QUESTION—What relationship is indicated by εἰς 'for' in the prepositional phrase εἰς ὑπακοὴν πίστεως 'for the obedience of faith'?

It indicates purpose [AB, Gdt, ICC2, Mor, NICNT, NTC; CEV, GW, NCV, NET, NIV, NLT, NRSV, REB, TEV]: so that they would obey, or to cause them to obey.

QUESTION—How are the nouns related in the genitive phrase ὑπακοὴν πίστεως 'obedience of faith'?

Faith is obedience to God [Gdt]. God wants people to obey and have faith [TH; CEV, NCV, NIV, NLT, REB]. He intends that people should believe and obey the gospel [Ho, NICNT], that they should make the commitment that is faith [AB, ICC2]. Obedience results from faith [SSA]. Obedience is based on faith, on childlike trust in God [NTC]. Obedience is associated with faith [GW]. This is a strong and deliberate repetition of 1:5 [WBC]. Faith should be characterized by obedience as a lifestyle [St].

QUESTION—What relationship is indicated by εἰς 'for' in the prepositional phrase εἰς πάντα τὰ ἔθνη 'for all the nations'?

1. The gospel is made known to all nations [BECNT, Gdt, LN (90.59), Mu; GW, KJV, NASB, NCV, NET, NRSV, REB], or in and among all nations [Ho, ICC2, NTC, SSA], throughout the entire world [NAC].
2. The gospel is for all the nations [HNTC, NICNT, St; probably WBC].

16:27 (the) only^a wise^b God, through^c Jesus Christ, to-whom (be) the glory to the ages,^d amen.^e

LEXICON—a. μόνος (LN 58.50) (BAGD 1.a.δ. p. 527): 'only' [AB, BAGD, BECNT, HNTC, ICC2, NICNT, NTC, WBC; CEV, NASB, NCV, NIV, NLT, NRSV, REB], 'alone' [LN; GW], 'only one' [LN]. The phrase μόνῳ σοφῷ θεῷ 'only wise God' is translated 'only God who alone is all wise' [TEV]. This adjective describes the only entity in a class [LN].
  b. σοφός ((LN 32.33) (BAGD 4. p. 760): 'wise' [AB, BECNT, HNTC, ICC2, LN, NICNT, NTC, WBC; all versions except TEV], 'all wise' [TEV], 'prudent, understanding' [LN]. This adjective describes understanding resulting in wisdom [LN].
  c. διά with genitive (LN 89.76): 'through' [AB, BECNT, HNTC, ICC2, LN, NICNT, NTC, WBC; all versions except CEV], 'because of' [CEV], 'by means of' [LN]. This preposition marks the means or agent by which an event is made possible [LN].
  d. αἰών (LN 67.95) (BAGD 1.b. p. 27). The phrase εἰς τοὺς αἰῶνας 'to the ages' is translated 'forever' [AB, BECNT, LN, NICNT, NTC, WBC; all versions except REB], 'for ever and ever' [HNTC, ICC2, LN], 'for evermore' [BAGD], 'for endless ages' [REB], 'always, eternally' [LN]. This noun denotes unlimited duration of time, with particular focus upon the future [LN].
  e. ἀμήν (LN 72.6) (BAGD 1. p. 45): 'amen' [AB, BAGD, BECNT, HNTC, ICC2, NICNT, NTC, WBC; all versions], 'truly, indeed' [LN]. This adverb marks a strong affirmation of what is declared [LN].

QUESTION—Why does Paul call God the 'only wise God'?
God alone is all wise [Ho, ICC2, NAC, TH; TEV]. He is the only God, and he is wise [AB, Mor]. He is the only God, and he alone is truly wise [SSA; TEV]. God's wisdom is expressed in his wise plan of salvation worked out in history [Mu, NICNT, St]. God's wisdom is shown in his ability to employ the best means for attaining the goal of receiving glory through the genuine worship and praise of redeemed people [NTC].

QUESTION—What is the antecedent of the pronoun ᾧ 'to whom' in the phrase 'to whom be the glory'?
  1. Glory is being ascribed to the only wise God [AB, BECNT, Ho, ICC1, ICC2, Mor, Mu, NAC, NICNT, NTC, SSA, St, TH, TNTC, WBC].
  2. Glory is being ascribed to Jesus Christ [Gdt].
  3. Glory is being ascribed to Jesus Christ as well as to God the Father [HNTC].

QUESTION—What relationship is indicated by διά 'through'?
  1. Glory is given to God through Jesus Christ [AB, Ho, ICC1, ICC2, Mu, NAC, NICNT, NTC], on the basis of what Jesus Christ has done [Mor, TH], or because of Jesus Christ [CEV]. It is through Jesus Christ that God's glory is made known and is extolled [Mu]. Jesus Christ helps us to praise God [SSA]. Paul desires that we forever praise God with the help of Jesus Christ, our mediator and intercessor [SSA].

2. It refers to an implied thought that underlies the entire previous sentence, which is that Paul is trusting in God to do through Jesus Christ all that concerns the Roman Christians [Gdt].